Patricia A. Beste

Miss Alabama

foods AN INTRODUCTORY COLLEGE COURSE SIXTH EDITION

AN INTRODUCTORY
COLLEGE COURSE
SIXTH EDITION

Houghton Mifflin Company · Boston
Atlanta · Dallas · Geneva, Illinois · Hopewell, New Jersey · Palo Alto · London

foods

Gladys E. Vail
Dean Emeritus, Purdue University

Jean A. Phillips
Virginia Polytechnic Institute and State University

Lucile Osborn Rust
Formerly of Kansas State University

Ruth M. Griswold
Late of Indiana University

Margaret M. Justin
Late of Kansas State University

contents

Preface   *vii*

1   Introduction to Nutrition   *2*

The Selection, Preparation, and Use of Foods   **21**

2   Consumer Protection   *22*

3   Fruits   *35*

4   Cereals   *62*

5   Coffee, Tea, and Cocoa   *82*

6   Vegetables   *100*

7   Salads   *132*

8   Milk and Milk Products   *147*

9   Eggs   *169*

10   Meat   *195*

11   Poultry and Fish   *232*

12   Flour and Starch   *257*

13   Introduction to Flour Mixtures   *274*

14   Breads   *298*

15   Cakes and Pies   *322*

16   Sugar, Candy, Frozen Desserts   *350*

17   Seasonings, Nuts, and Gelatin   *369*

The Planning, Preparation, and Service of Meals   **391**

18   Meal Planning   *392*

19   Food Purchasing   *417*

20   Facilities for Meal Preparation   *445*

21   Sanitation in the Kitchen   *463*

22   Management in the Preparation of Meals   *472*

23   Preparation of Meals   *479*

24   Table Appointments   *492*

25   Etiquette—Introductions, Invitations, and Table Manners   *504*

26   Accepted Procedures for Meal Service   *519*

27   Examples of Various Styles of Meal Service in Detail   *538*

The Preservation of Foods   **557**

28   Food Spoilage   *558*

29   Food Preservation   *568*

30   Home Preservation by Canning   *581*

31   Home Preservation by Freezing   *596*

32   Jelly   *608*

33   Preserves, Marmalades, Conserves, Jams, and Butters   *617*

34   Pickles   *624*

Suggested Readings   *633*
Index   *635*

preface

With the publication of this edition, five revisions of *Foods* have been made. While this sixth edition has essentially the same organization as the fifth edition, the subject matter has been substantially updated, references have been added, and some new illustrations have been included. This is the first revision to have an accompanying laboratory manual, organized in line with the text and containing extensive detailed suggestions for foods laboratories.[1] The following statement from the last edition remains valid:

"The combination in one book of the principles of food preparation with marketing, an introduction to nutrition, meal service, and food preservation has proved popular and has been retained. The material on marketing, presented as a separate section in earlier editions, has been reorganized so that most of it is included under the food to which it pertains in the section 'The Preparation, Selection, and Use of Foods.' Some of the more general principles of marketing now appear in Chapter 2, 'Consumer Protection,' and in Chapter 19, 'Food Purchasing.' These two chapters include material on the governmental regulation of food. The first chapter, an 'Introduction to Nutrition,' is intended to furnish a vocabulary for some of the important nutrients considered as individual foods are discussed, and to guide the student in planning meals. This chapter will prove especially valuable for home economics majors who study foods before they study nutrition and for non-majors who elect foods but not nutrition. It is strongly recommended that all students who can do so include a nutrition course in their curriculum.

"An attempt has been made to present material necessary to meet the wide variety of objectives that might be selected for an introductory foods course. Some of the possible objectives of such a course are:
1. To develop an interest in and an understanding and appreciation of the nutritive value of foods.
2. To develop an understanding of the wise expenditure of the food dollar.
3. To promote a working knowledge of principles of food preparation.
4. To foster an understanding of the principles of sanitation as these apply to the work centers and procedures used in food preparation and clean-up.
5. To establish desirable standards for meals prepared and served in the home.
6. To cultivate attractive meal service.
7. To develop managerial skills in planning, preparing, and serving adequate and attractive meals for the day.

[1] Phillips, J.A., and Vail, G.E., *Laboratory Manual to accompany Foods, 6th Edition* (Boston: Houghton Mifflin Co., 1973).

8. To encourage interest in the selection, arrangement, care, and efficient use of the kitchen and its equipment.

9. To develop interest in the selection, care, and use of flatware, glassware, china, and other necessary accessories.

10. To create an understanding and appreciation of the social amenities as a force in our civilization.

"Because it includes material on nutrition, food preparation, marketing, meal service, and food preservation, the book can be used for a one-year course or for one or more shorter courses. Food preparation can be presented as a series of food groups or by the meal-planning method, in which food preparation is combined with meal service. It is hoped that the subject matter included will provide fundamental knowledge and increased understanding of foods by the student who may not carry the study further, and will at the same time give other students an adequate foundation for continued study. To encourage further reading, references to books, bulletins, and periodicals are given at the end of most chapters. A general reference list appears in the appendix."

Activities are suggested at the end of most chapters. Recipes are not included in this book, but a limited number appear in the laboratory manual. The fact that institutions vary widely not only in the number of credits assigned to the beginning foods course but also in the division of those credits between lecture-recitation and laboratory has been taken into account in the preparation of the manual. For additional recipes, *The Basic Cook Book*, by Heseltine and Dow (Houghton Mifflin) and *Practical Cookery*, by the Department of Foods and Nutrition, Kansas State University (Wiley) are excellent sources.

Gladys E. Vail
Jean A. Phillips

foods

AN INTRODUCTORY COLLEGE COURSE

SIXTH EDITION

1

introduction to nutrition

Nutrition may be defined as "the food you eat and how the body uses it" or it may be considered "the science of food and its relation to health."

Food supplies nutrients. Health is dependent on a balanced supply of nutrients; lack of any one essential nutrient, excess of certain nutrients, or imbalance among the nutrients may seriously impair health.

Nutrients are essential for all forms of life. The human body is composed of combinations of elements and requires a variety of substances for growth and for sustaining body activities.

Understanding of the importance of food to health and longevity has been unfolding throughout the centuries of human experience. In comparatively recent years the study of the nutrients in foods and the relationship between these nutrients and the nutritional health of individuals has developed into a science that is continually being expanded by research.

It is recognized that probably not all of the nutrients in foods have been identified and that the relationship of one to another is not entirely understood. Although it is known that each nutrient has a specific function, it has been established that none of them acts alone. Hence it is considered desirable to consume many nutrients at a time—as occurs when a variety of foods is eaten at a meal. A varied diet assures the consumption of all of the nutrients essential for general well-being.

Nutrients

Since 1940, recommended dietary allowances of certain nutrients have been issued periodically by the Food and Nutrition Board of the National Academy of Sciences—National Research Council. These recommendations are referred to as the NRC allowances. From time to time these recommended allowances are modified as research indicates changes are desirable. The allowances are for healthy persons living in the United States where the food supply is adequate. A good state of nutrition means that the body is well supplied with foods containing the essential nutrients and, further,

2

that the body has put those nutrients to work. Except for calories (joules[1]), the NRC allowances provide for amounts of the various nutrients intended to cover individual variations among normal persons living in the United States. These recommendations are safeguards, for it is also recognized that individuals vary in their requirements because of genetic background, size, muscular development, activity, and many other factors.

In spite of efforts on the part of many organizations and individuals to inform consumers of the importance of an adequate diet, nationwide surveys of household food consumption made in 1955 and 1965 showed a downward trend in the nutritional quality of the diets of the nation's families over the ten years.[2]

Carbohydrates, fats, and proteins provide the energy which is necessary for the growth, maintenance, and activity of the body. In other words, they supply the calories. Excess of calories has been reported to be the greatest nutritional problem in the United States. Therefore, consideration should be given to the intake of these energy-providing nutrients in order to prevent obesity.

Nutrients are classified as carbohydrates, fats, proteins, minerals, vitamins, and water. A brief discussion of each group follows.

Carbohydrates

Carbohydrates, long considered chiefly a source of energy, are now recognized as playing a much more complicated and as yet only partly understood role in nutrition.

Among the common carbohydrates are sugars and starches.[3] These are composed of the chemical elements carbon, hydrogen, and oxygen. The term "sugar" to most people means cane or beet sugar, which is sucrose. This is the most common sugar of the several responsible for the characteristically sweet taste of certain foods. Milk, fruit, vegetables, corn syrup, and malt contain sugars other than sucrose. Sucrose contains twelve carbon atoms and is usually referred to as a disaccharide. A disaccharide may be broken down into two six-carbon sugars or monosaccharides. For example sucrose can be hydrolyzed to two six-carbon sugars, glucose and fructose. Maltose, a sugar in malt, breaks down into two molecules of glucose; and lactose, the sugar in milk, yields glucose and galactose. Of the six-carbon

[1] The joule (J), the unit of energy in the metric system, is recommended for energy measurements in all branches of science. Nutritionists in the United States have not made such a conversion at the present time and few references are made to joules as a measure of energy allowances or requirements. Thus calories will be used as a measure of energy throughout this publication but with the realization that conversion to the metric system will no doubt become a reality in the not too distant future.

[2] S. F. Adelson. Changes in Diets of Households. *Journal of Home Economics,* 60: 448–455 (1968).

[3] The chemical formulas of certain carbohydrates follow: $C_6H_{12}O_6$, glucose, fructose, or galactose; $C_{12}H_{22}O_{11}$, cane sugar, beet sugar, or sucrose, maltose, or lactose; $(C_6H_{10}O_5)_x$, starch.

sugars, glucose and fructose are the simple sugars most often found in foods. They are present in many fruits and in honey. Fructose is the sweetest of the sugars commonly found in food. The different sugars vary both in their chemical composition and in their degree of sweetness, but all sugars have a characteristically sweet taste.

Starch, a polysaccharide, is a complex carbohydrate. Like the sugars it is built by the combination of carbon, hydrogen, and oxygen. Starch may be split by acid or enzymes into many molecules of glucose. The production of sugar by the plant is considered to be an intermediate step in the manufacture of starch. The ability of the plant to build starch and of the animal body to utilize it was known long before some of the processes involved in the synthesis and utilization of starch were known. The plant, by means of chlorophyll, takes carbon and oxygen from the air and, combining these with water from the soil, manufactures sugar. The sugar, dissolved in the sap or juice of the plant, is carried to all its parts as food. When the plant produces more sugar than is required for its immediate need, the surplus is stored for future use. Whether the place of storage is seed, root, leaf, or stem depends upon the plant. Usually the plant stores carbohydrate as insoluble starch in the form of tiny grains or granules until need for food causes the starch to be changed back to sugar. In each kind of plant the granules differ in size, shape, and appearance. For example, the starch grains of rice are quite unlike those of corn, potato, or wheat. Such differences are readily observed by means of a microscope. Some foods high in starch are potatoes, sweet potatoes, wheat flour, rice, dried peas, and beans.

Although carbohydrates are considered to be of vegetable origin, sugar is found in the blood streams of animals. Provision is made in the cells of the liver for storage of glycogen, often referred to as animal starch, sufficient to meet the requirements of the body for carbohydrates for a comparatively short time. The animal body, like the plant, synthesizes this more complex substance from sugar and later hydrolyzes it to sugar as needed.

Cellulose is a carbohydrate which, like starch, is made up of many molecules of glucose. However, the glucose molecules in cellulose are joined together in a different way from those in starch. The human body does not contain an enzyme that can release these glucose molecules for use. Cellulose in the diet does not supply energy but gives bulk and provides material for certain regulatory processes such as the elimination of waste from the intestines. Foods high in cellulose are bran, dried fruits and legumes, fruits with skins or seeds, and leafy and coarse-fibered vegetables.

Only a few foods consist of pure carbohydrates. Well-known examples of these are cane and beet sugars and cornstarch. A food is considered high or low in carbohydrate according to the per cent it contains. Foods high in carbohydrates include: sugar, candy, honey, molasses, jams, jellies, cereals and cereal products, and dried fruits.

Fats

Fats are composed of carbon, hydrogen, and oxygen, but in different proportions from those found in carbohydrates. True fats are triglycerides of fatty acids and glycerol. Fats add flavor and variety to foods and make meals palatable and satisfying. They promote efficiency in the utilization of proteins and carbohydrates. They may aid in absorption of fat-soluble vitamins; are, in some cases, important carriers of these vitamins; and are also sources of fatty acids essential for certain body functions.

Fats are of both animal and plant origin and differ in the kinds and proportions of fatty acids contained. In general, fats of plant origin contain more polyunsaturated fatty acids or "poly-enes" than fats of animal origin. A characteristic of all fats is their high caloric value compared to that of carbohydrates and proteins. One gram of fat will supply approximately nine calories whereas a gram of carbohydrate or a gram of protein produces approximately four.

Fats are found throughout the animal body in muscle tissue, as protective tissue around the viscera and other organs, and as subcutaneous tissue. Fats retard the emptying of the stomach which may account in part for the greater satiety value of fats as compared with carbohydrates and proteins. Lipids is a term used to include both fats and fat-like substances characterized by one or more fatty acids. Phospholipids, fat-like substances found in food and in the human body, contain phosphorus and nitrogen as well as carbon, hydrogen, and oxygen. Lecithin, a phospholipid found in seeds, in active tissue of the body, and in egg yolk, is of special interest as an emulsifying agent. Cholesterol, found only in foods of animal origin, is also a fat-like substance and is a normal constituent of blood and tissues. Foods high in fat content include: lard, salad oil, butter, margarine, mayonnaise, pecans, peanuts, egg yolk, and heavy cream.

Proteins

Proteins differ from carbohydrates and fats in that, besides carbon, hydrogen, and oxygen, they also contain nitrogen and in some cases sulfur. Phosphorus and iron are also found in some proteins. Proteins are found in foods of both animal and plant origin. Meat, poultry, fish, eggs, milk, cheese, legumes, nuts, and some cereal foods are good sources of protein.

Proteins are complex in nature, being composed of a number of smaller units called amino acids. The amino acids are linked together and may be linked with other substances. The kind and number of amino acids present may vary. More than 20 amino acids have been isolated.

Proteins provide not only calories, but also the amino acids necessary for building and maintaining tissues and regulating body processes. Genes, which control heredity; hormones, regulators of body processes; and enzymes, which spark the many body processes, are all proteins. Each function has characteristic amino acid requirements. Since the human being is unable to produce all the amino acids which it must have, certain of them must be supplied by the foods eaten. These amino acids are known as the "essential amino acids."

Proteins that contain the amino acids essential for body processes may be referred to as complete or adequate proteins, while others lacking one or more of the essential amino acids may be called incomplete or inadequate proteins. These terms are relative and cannot be taken too literally. It is quite possible that two or more foods containing "inadequate" proteins may, when combined, supplement each other in such a way that the amino acid needs are adequately met.

Most animal foods contain "complete proteins." The proteins of plants are often referred to as incomplete or inadequate, for many are low in one or more essential amino acids, although a few are quite adequate to maintain tissues and regulate body processes.

The protein quality of a diet as varied as that consumed in the United States will most likely be satisfactory if the quantity is adequate. The liberal use of meat, poultry, fish, eggs, milk, and cheese is assurance that the protein requirement is met. However, such foods as cereals and cereal products, dried legumes, and nuts are valuable sources of protein even though they may contain an incomplete assortment of essential amino acids.

Minerals

Minerals are essential constituents of the hard and soft tissues and of the fluids of the body and assist in regulating body processes. They are widely distributed in all foods except the most highly refined, although the kind and quantity may vary widely. The mineral elements needed by the body include calcium, chlorine, cobalt, copper, fluorine, iodine, iron, magnesium, manganese, phosphorus, potassium, sodium, sulfur, zinc, and possibly chromium, molybdenum, and selenium. Many of these are referred to as "trace elements" because of the small quantities needed to carry out their important functions.

The relationship between minerals and certain other nutrients in food is such that it is unnecessary to give consideration to the source of each of the minerals just mentioned. For example, a diet adequate in protein also supplies sufficient sulfur, and one adequate in protein and calcium usually contains sufficient phosphorus. Common use of table salt insures the necessary chlorine and sodium; and the ordinary varied or mixed diet cares for the requirement for manganese and magnesium as well as many other minerals. If the calcium, iron, and iodine needed by the body are provided in adequate amounts, it is not likely that there will be a deficiency of other minerals in the diet.

Calcium is required for all tissues and with phosphorus is largely responsible for the hardness of the bones and teeth. It is essential in the coagulation of blood, the rhythmic beat of the heart, the irritability of nerves, the activity of cells, and the maintenance of the acid-base balance of the body. Foods that are important sources of calcium include: milk, cheese, ice cream, certain leafy green vegetables (as collards, kale, mustard,

and turnip greens), beans (dried), oranges, grapefruit, egg yolk, and bread made with milk. Although beet leaves, chard, rhubarb, and spinach contain calcium, their oxalic acid content makes for low utilization of this mineral by the body.

Phosphorus also is necessary for all tissues and is essential for energy metabolism. It helps in the maintenance of the neutrality of the blood, in the conductivity of nerve impulses, and in the control of cell activity. Important sources of this nutrient include: liver, milk, lean meat, fish, shellfish, legumes, cheese, egg yolk, ice cream, leafy vegetables, and whole grains.

Iron is necessary to form hemoglobin, a substance in the blood which carries oxygen to the cells and plays an essential role in body functions and the activity of cells. Iron is one of the nutrients added to flour, bread, and cereals when they are enriched. Enrichment restores in part the iron lost in the milling process. Valuable food sources of iron include: liver, lean meat, shellfish, legumes, egg yolk, green leafy vegetables, enriched and whole grain bread and cereals, and many fruits.

Copper is widely distributed in foods, and the usual diet is unlikely to be deficient in this nutrient. Its functions in the body are closely related to those of iron and most of the foods that are good sources of iron are also good sources of copper. It apparently has a specific function in the utilization of iron for hemoglobin and red cell production.

Iodine is an important constituent of thyroxin, a hormone which is required for physical and mental growth and development. Iodine is found chiefly in the thyroid gland and in the blood. Thyroxin controls the basal metabolic rate and this influences energy metabolism. Simple goiter develops if iodine is deficient. The use of iodized salt is the best way to provide the necessary amount of this element regularly, although sea foods are excellent sources.

Fluorine has been shown to reduce dental caries. For this reason it is frequently added to the water in communities where the concentration is below a desirable level.

Vitamins

Although it is only in this century that vitamins have been recognized as essential components of the diet, anthropologists and nutrition workers are finding that many primitive people thrived because their food habits were such that vitamins as well as other essential nutrients were consumed. Some of the sources of vitamins may not fall into the present-day classification of foods because included were bark or roots of plants, tea brewed from leaves or needles of trees, and the contents of the stomach of animals killed for food. In some parts of the world even today extracts of pine needles are fed to children as protection against scurvy, which results from a vitamin C deficiency.

Vitamins are essential for optimum nutrition and health and for normal growth and development. They serve the body by promoting growth, by regulating body processes, by protecting against disease, and by contributing to what is sometimes expressed as "the possession of the attributes of youth." Suboptimum quantities may allow continuation of growth and protect against certain diseases connected with inadequate nutrition. In quantities several times the amount required for mere protection they may contribute to a state of nutrition that further safeguards health and enriches living. Furthermore, adequate amounts of vitamins favor the utilization of all other food nutrients. Those vitamins that are generally recognized as essential and others that also may be essential are considered in this chapter. Although many vitamins are available in the form of concentrates or in pure synthetic preparations, foods remain the recommended source of these important substances except when prescribed by a physician for a specific purpose.

Vitamin A was first discovered in butter and egg yolk. Its supply in liberal quantities is essential to good nutrition and vigorous health in the adult as well as in the child. It stimulates growth and normal development. Lack of this vitamin is reflected in diseases of the eye, defective enamel in teeth, low resistance to infection, retarded growth, and loss of reproductive power. Vitamin A occurs, as such, only in foods of animal origin. The bright yellow pigments, carotene in green and yellow fruits and vegetables, and cryptoxanthine in yellow corn, can be changed in the body of animals, including man, to vitamin A. These are called provitamins because they can be transformed into a vitamin. Vitamin A is a fat-soluble substance and thus does not dissolve to any appreciable extent in water. Exposure to air or oxygen, especially in the presence of heat, results in its destruction. Vitamin A may be added to foods. An example is its addition to margarine. In itself this food contains little or no vitamin A, but practically all that is now manufactured is fortified with this vitamin. Foods that are rich in vitamin A or in provitamin A are said to have vitamin A value and include: liver, dark green and deep yellow vegetables (particularly green peppers, spinach and other greens, carrots, sweet potatoes, and yellow squash), yellow fruits, eggs, butter, and fortified margarine.

Vitamin D is the antirachitic vitamin. Sterols or fat-like substances in the skin and food can be transformed into vitamin D. Sunshine itself is an excellent means of providing vitamin D. The skin contains provitamin D, a substance that under direct exposure to the sun or to ultraviolet light for short daily periods is converted into vitamin D within the body. Vitamin D is not easily destroyed and is stable to heat, alkalis, acids, and oxidation. Vitamin D is essential for the development and maintenance of bones and teeth. Growing children require larger amounts of this vitamin than do adults. Vitamin D is rather meagerly distributed in nature, and its sources in our natural foods are few. Sources of vitamin D are: butter, egg yolk, fish liver oils (cod and halibut), oily fish, and foods fortified with vitamin D such as vitamin D milk and irradiated foods.

Vitamin E is apparently related to normal reproduction in animals. Muscular dystrophy and an anemia have been associated with a deficiency of vitamin E in animals. However, the extent to which it is necessary to human beings has not been fully determined. Vitamin E functions as an antioxidant to retard the destruction of other nutrients by oxidation. It is insoluble in water, hence there is little if any loss by extraction in cooking. The vitamin is not easily destroyed by heat but is readily destroyed by oxidation. Although some foods of animal origin contain vitamin E, it is found mainly in plant materials; oils of wheat germ, cottonseed, and other seed germs are the richest sources but leafy green plants, other vegetables, and whole grain cereals are also sources.

Vitamin K is essential for the production of prothrombin, a normal constituent of the blood and one of several components that react together to form a blood clot. Thus vitamin K contributes to normal clotting of the blood and is therefore most important in preventing hemorrhages or excessive bleeding. There appears to be enough vitamin K in the normal diet for ordinary needs. However in special situations or conditions such as childbirth and surgery, therapeutic doses of this vitamin may be administered. Vitamin K is fairly stable to heat and like the other fat-soluble vitamins it is not soluble in water. Good sources of vitamin K are cabbage, cauliflower, green leafy vegetables, liver, and soybeans. In addition to food sources, vitamin K is available through bacterial synthesis in the intestines for all except the newborn infant.

Ascorbic acid, known also as vitamin C, prevents and cures scurvy and hence is often termed the antiscorbutic vitamin. Ascorbic acid has a number of functions. These include production of collagenous or intercellular materials that hold the body cells together, strengthening the walls of blood vessels, promoting the healing of wounds and bones, and helping the body resist infection. Prolonged lack of this vitamin causes bleeding gums, loose teeth, sore joints, loss of appetite and weight, fatigue, and in extreme cases, scurvy. Since the body does not store large amounts of this vitamin, an ample daily supply is essential. Ascorbic acid is the least stable of all the vitamins. It oxidizes readily in the presence of heat, alkali, and oxygen, and considerable amounts may be lost in cooking because it is also water soluble. Important sources of this vitamin include: cantaloupe, citrus fruits, green peppers, strawberries, tomatoes, and green and leafy vegetables, especially those of the cabbage family.

Thiamine, which is sometimes designated as vitamin B_1, belongs to the group of B-complex vitamins. Thiamine is a component of the enzyme system involved in the release of energy from the metabolism of carbohydrates. Thus it is appetite-promoting, aids in the digestion and assimilation of food, and is necessary for growth. Thiamine is important in preserving the general well-being of the body and in protecting against damage to the nervous tissues. Loss of appetite, listlessness, sluggish digestive system, and nervous irritability result from a continued low intake of this vitamin. Beriberi results from a complete lack of it. Thiamine, a water-soluble substance, is not readily destroyed by ordinary cooking processes but is by prolonged heating. Alkalis such as baking soda increase its loss during cooking. Important sources of thiamine are: enriched and whole grain bread and cereals, dried legumes, meat (especially organ meats and pork), milk, and nuts.

Riboflavin is another of the B vitamins and at first was called vitamin B_2 or G. Riboflavin, too, functions as a coenzyme in several enzyme systems of the body and as such is an essential link in the metabolism of amino acids, fatty acids, and carbohydrates. It is essential for growth and important in maintaining health. A deficiency in riboflavin may result in sores on the lips, and reddening and scaling of the skin about the ears, mouth, and nose. The eyes may become sensitive to light and easily fatigued. The sight may become blurred. Riboflavin is little affected by heat but is destroyed by alkalis such as baking soda. It also is readily destroyed by light. Being water-soluble, some of this vitamin is likely to be lost in cooking, especially when cooking water is discarded from vegetables. Foods that are good sources of riboflavin are: enriched and whole grain bread and cereals, milk, eggs, cheese, green leafy vegetables, legumes, lean meat, and liver.

Niacin, another of the B-complex vitamins, is also a component of enzyme systems involved in the utilization of carbohydrates, fats, and proteins. It is essential for growth, and for the normal functioning of the skin and the digestive tract. It also prevents pellagra, early symptoms of which are general weakness and loss of appetite and weight. In the later stages, extreme cases may develop sore mouths, digestive and nervous disturbances, and dermatitis. Tryptophan, one of the essential amino acids, can be changed to niacin in the body. Niacin is stable to air, heat, and light. However, it is readily soluble in water, especially hot water, and therefore is subject to loss in cooking. Foods that furnish generous amounts of niacin or tryptophan are: liver, lean meat, poultry, milk, legumes, peanut butter, and enriched and whole grain bread and cereals.

Vitamin B_6, also a member of the B-complex, is composed of a group of three closely related substances: pyridoxine, pyridoxal, and pyridoxamine. It serves as a coenzyme in a number of enzyme systems and seems to be especially involved in the metabolism of fats and proteins. Many of the symptoms of inadequate vitamin B_6 resemble those seen in deficiencies of some of the other B-vitamins, particularly thiamine, riboflavin, and niacin. Vitamin B_6 is widely distributed in both plants and animals, hence diets that are otherwise adequate are rarely lacking in this vitamin. It is soluble in water and stable to heat, alkalis, and acids. However, it oxidizes readily and is destroyed by light. Good food sources are organ meats (especially kidney, heart, and liver), muscle meats, some vegetables, and whole grain cereals.

Pantothenic acid, also of the vitamin B group, is of great importance in many body processes. It appears to be closely associated with other B-vitamins in utilization of foods by the body. Pantothenic acid is found in many of the commonly eaten foods so deficiencies are not often observed in people. Among the good sources are organ meats, muscle meats, milk, whole grain cereals, eggs, certain vegetables, and legumes.

Folic acid, (folacin) a term which covers a group of closely related substances, has an important place in the list of B vitamins, being necessary for the formation of blood cells in man. It plays an active role in the prevention and treatment of certain types of anemia and accompanying disorders and is associated with the metabolism of certain nitrogenous compounds. It is slightly soluble in water and stable to heat but not to light and acids. Sources of these substances are liver, kidney, green leafy vegetables, legumes, nuts, and whole grain cereals.

Vitamin B₁₂ is essential for normal blood cell formation and has been shown to be effective in the treatment of pernicious anemia. There is evidence that this vitamin has growth-promoting properties and along with certain other nutrients participates in the carrying on of various body processes. Vitamin B₁₂ is soluble in water and the solution, if neutral, is stable at room temperatures. However, in a slightly acid or alkaline solution its stability is lessened. Among the food sources of this vitamin are cheese, eggs, fish, kidney, liver, fresh muscle meats, and milk.

Biotin is another water-soluble vitamin. Its exact function in man is not clearly understood but it is involved in the metabolism of carbohydrates, fats, and proteins. It seems unlikely that a dietary deficiency of this substance will occur in human beings consuming a variety of foods because biotin is present in many foods and is synthesized in the intestinal tract.

Choline, inositol, and *para-aminobenzoic acid* are classified as vitamins by many workers although some question whether or not they should be so classed. A deficiency of any one of these substances has not been reported in man. It seems probable that if other necessary nutrients are present in the diet, these will be adequate also.

Water

Water makes up approximately two-thirds of the body's composition. It is present in every cell and tissue, and is important in regulating body processes. Digestion, assimilation, regulation of heat, and elimination of wastes are all dependent upon the water content of the body. Drinking water frequently contains some of the minerals needed by the body, such as calcium, iron, iodine, fluorine, and sodium.

Water in the body comes from beverages and other fluids consumed, from solid foods in the diet, and from the metabolism of foods within the tissues.

Interrelation-ships of Nutrients

Mention has been made of the importance of certain nutrients in the diet for the best utilization of other nutrients by the body. Proteins, carbohydrates, and fats are all needed for normal metabolic processes. The value of copper in the utilization of iron was noted. Table 1-1 points out that calcium helps regulate the use of other minerals in the body and that vitamin D helps absorb calcium from the digestive tract and build calcium and phosphorus into bones (pages 13–14). Thiamine, riboflavin, niacin, and pantothenic acid are essential for the metabolism of carbohydrates, proteins, and fats. Vitamin B_6 functions in protein and fat metabolism. Many other relationships could be enumerated to emphasize the importance of including all the needed nutrients in the diet. Fortunately many of our foods contribute a number of the nutrients mentioned, as well as many others which are needed. The importance of selecting foods which contain more than one or two nutrients should be recognized.

Meeting Nutrient Needs

The condensed version of the functions and sources of "key nutrients" summarized in Table 1–1 presents the material considered important in evaluating food intake. However, with more and more prepared, imitation, and snack foods being consumed, it becomes increasingly difficult to know which nutrients are contributed by the different foods. Recognizing this

Fig. 1–1. *It is desirable to consume many nutrients at a time as is done when a variety of foods are eaten at one meal.*

Courtesy of the United Fresh Fruit and Vegetable Association

Table 1-1. *The Functions and Sources of Key Nutrients* *

Key Nutrients	Important Functions	Important Sources
Protein	Builds and repairs all tissues Helps build blood and form antibodies to fight infection Supplies energy	Meat, fish, poultry, eggs Milk and all kinds of cheese Dried beans and peas Peanut butter, nuts Bread and cereals
Fat	Supplies large amount of energy in a small amount of food Helps keep infant's skin healthy by supplying essential fatty acids Carries vitamins A, D, E and K	Butter and cream Salad oils and dressings Cooking and table fats Fat in meat
Carbohydrate (Sugars and Starch)	Supplies energy	Bread and cereals Potatoes, lima beans, corn Dried beans and peas Dried fruits, sweetened fruits; smaller amounts in fresh fruits Sugar, sirup, jelly, jam, honey
Minerals Calcium	Helps build bones and teeth Helps blood clot Helps muscles and nerves to work Helps regulate the use of other minerals in the body	Milk Cheese, but less in cottage cheese, ice cream Sardines, other whole canned fish Turnip and mustard greens Collards, kale, broccoli
Iron	Combines with protein to make hemoglobin, the red substance in the blood that carries oxygen to the cells	Liver, other meat and eggs Dried beans and peas Green leafy vegetables Prunes, raisins, dried apricots Enriched or whole grain bread and cereals
Iodine	A constituent of thyroxine, a hormone that controls metabolic rate	Seafoods, iodized salt
Vitamins Vitamin A	Helps keep skin clear and smooth Helps keep mucous membranes firm and resistant to infection Helps prevent night blindness and promote healthy eyes Helps control bone growth	Liver, eggs Dark green and deep yellow vegetables Deep yellow fruits, such as peaches or cantaloupe Butter, whole milk, fortified skim milk, cream Cheddar cheese, ice cream

* From *Nutrition Source Book*. National Dairy Council, Chicago, Illinois, 1971.

Table 1–1 (continued)

Key Nutrients	Important Functions	Important Sources
Thiamin or Vitamin B₁	Helps promote normal appetite and digestion Helps keep nervous system healthy and prevent irritability Helps body release energy from food	Meat, fish, poultry—pork supplies about 3 times as much as other meats Eggs Enriched or whole grain bread and cereals Dried beans and peas Potatoes, broccoli, collards
Riboflavin	Helps cells use oxygen Helps keep eyes, skin, tongue and lips healthy Helps prevent scaly, greasy skin around mouth and nose	Milk All kinds of cheese, ice cream Enriched or whole grain bread and cereals Meat, especially liver Fish, poultry, eggs
Niacin or Its Equivalent	Helps keep nervous system healthy Helps keep skin, mouth, tongue, digestive tract in healthy condition Helps cells use other nutrients	Peanut butter Meat, fish, poultry Milk (high in tryptophan) Enriched or whole grain bread and cereals
Ascorbic Acid or Vitamin C	Helps make cementing materials that hold body cells together Helps make walls of blood vessels firm Helps in healing wounds and broken bones Helps resist infection	Citrus fruits—orange, grapefruit, lemon, lime Strawberries and cantaloupe Tomatoes Green peppers, broccoli Raw or lightly cooked greens, cabbage White potatoes
Vitamin D, The Sunshine Vitamin	Helps absorb calcium from the digestive tract and build calcium and phosphorus into bones.	Vitamin D milk Fish liver oils Sunshine on skin (not a food)

Water is also an essential, although people do not usually think of it as a food. Water helps in carrying nutrients to cells and waste products away, in building tissue, regulating temperature, aiding digestion, replacing daily water loss.

Other B-vitamins are essential human nutrients: vitamin B₆, B₁₂ and folacin. Folacin and vitamin B₁₂ have antianemic properties, while vitamin B₆ helps enzyme and other biochemical systems to function normally. The three vitamins are widely distributed in foods—from meat, fish, poultry, whole grain and enriched bread and cereals, dark green and leafy vegetables. Milk provides vitamin B₁₂ and folacin.

Although the exact biochemical mechanism whereby vitamin E functions in the body is still unknown, it plays an important role as an intracellular antioxidant thus inhibiting the oxidation of unsaturated fatty acids and vitamin A. It is found in a variety of foods such as wheat germ oil, vegetable oil, egg yolk, milk fat, meats, butter, cereal germs and leafy vegetables.

difficulty, the food industry is faced with deciding the most meaningful way of labeling foods so that the information is accurate and complete for all nutrients supplied in significant amounts.[4] Furthermore, such labeling should be meaningful to the average consumer.

Although as many as 40 other nutrients may be essential for a good state of nutrition, observation and research have led to the conclusion that if the food intake furnishes adequate amounts of the key nutrients the supply of other nutrients will also be adequate.

Reference was made earlier to the NRC recommended daily dietary allowances as evidence of the progress made thus far in identifying specific nutrient needs. However, no attempt has been made in this chapter to indicate the amount of each nutrient needed for a family or for individual members of the family but only to point out the major roles and the important sources. An examination of Table 1–1 and a review of the earlier discussion will illustrate the fact that each nutrient has its own specific functions. However, as mentioned earlier, no nutrient acts independently of other nutrients. Just as in building a house one item may not be substituted for another, so one nutrient cannot replace another. In the house two windows are not adequate substitutes for a door and a wall, and likewise a double amount of vitamin D will not compensate for a lack of riboflavin or niacin. Another point to remember is that very large intakes of some nutrients are detrimental to health. However, great excesses, other than calories, are not likely to occur if nutrients are consumed in foods; if they are taken as concentrates, serious imbalances may result.

Food Guides

The nutrient requirements of an individual or a group may be met in many ways. A wide variety of foods and of meal patterns are found among the peoples of the world. Some eat no meat, some no animal products of any kind; some eat only two meals a day, and others may find that five or more meals best fit their way of living. In this country general guides for meeting the nutritional needs of individuals or families have been formulated. These guides have been modified or changed from time to time in an attempt to make them as simple and easy to follow as possible.

Currently the guide most often used is described in the United States Department of Agriculture leaflet *Food for Fitness—A Daily Food Guide*. This food plan is frequently referred to as The Basic Four, or the Guide to Good Eating. The Daily Food Guide is based on the special contributions that the foods in each of four groups make to health and well-being. As illustrated by Figure 1–2, this food plan includes:

[4] R. O. Nesheim. Industry Response to the Nutrition Challenge. *Food Technology,* 25: 605–608 (1971).

Fig. 1–2. *The Basic Four.*
Milk Group: Some milk every day for everyone is recommended in the Daily Food Guide. *Milk is the leading source of calcium, which is needed for bones and teeth, and also provides high quality protein, riboflavin, vitamin A, and many other nutrients.*

Meat Group: Recommended are two or more servings every day of red meat, fish, shellfish, poultry, eggs, or alternates—dry beans, dry peas, lentils, and nuts. These foods are valued for their protein, needed for growth and repair of body tissues, and also provide iron, thiamine, riboflavin, and niacin.

Bread-Cereal Group: *Foods in this group furnish worthwhile amounts of protein, iron, several of the B-vitamins, and food energy. Check labels to be sure all breads and cereals are whole grain, enriched, or restored. Choose four servings or more daily.*

Vegetable-Fruit Group: *The Daily Food Guide recommends four or more servings of vegetables and fruit every day. Include a serving of a good source of vitamin C every day, and a serving of a dark-green or deep-yellow vegetable at least every other day for vitamin A.*

Courtesy of the National Dairy Council

1. Milk group   3. Vegetable and fruit group
2. Meat group   4. Bread and cereal group

An earlier commonly used guide was known as the Basic Seven. In addition to milk, meat, and bread groups, this plan had a butter and fortified margarine group, and three groupings of vegetables and fruits. These were: (1) citrus fruit, tomatoes, cabbage; (2) dark-green and deep-yellow vegetables; and (3) potatoes and other vegetables and fruits.

A third guide—The Family Food Plan—has also been used by the Consumer and Food Economics Research Division of the United States Department of Agriculture. This plan consists of eleven groups:

1. Milk, cheese, ice cream
2. Meat, poultry, fish
3. Eggs
4. Dry beans, peas, nuts
5. Flour, cereals, baked goods
6. Citrus fruit, tomatoes
7. Dark-green and deep-yellow vegetables
8. Potatoes
9. Other vegetables and fruits
10. Fats and oils
11. Sugar, sweets

The Basic Four as currently recommended is considered the simplest of the guides, hence the one easiest to remember and the most readily followed. If foods from the four food groups listed in the Daily Food Guide are included in the quantities suggested, a large share of the needed nutrients will be provided. Additional calories, if needed, may be obtained from fats, sweets, and other foods. The recommended quantities and the contributions of the four food groups are shown in Table 1–2.

Each food varies in its composition. The composition of a given food is affected by genetic characteristics, production practices, and handling and processing procedures. Some of the factors affecting the composition are discussed later in connection with individual foods. The importance of handling foods so that there is maximum retention of nutrients as well as of eating quality is emphasized.

Table 1–2. *Contributions of Four Major Food Groups* *

The Four Food Groups of the Daily Food Guide	*Chief Nutrients Contributed by Each Food Group*
Milk Group	
Some milk for everyone	
Children under 9 . . . . . 2 to 3 cups	High quality proteins
Children 9 to 12 . . . . . 3 or more cups	Calcium
Teenagers. . . . . 4 or more cups	Riboflavin
Adults . . . . 2 or more cups	Vitamin A
	Many other nutrients
Milk, cheese, ice cream	

* Adapted from *Food for Fitness, A Daily Food Guide*. Leaflet 424, Agricultural Research Service, United States Department of Agriculture, Revised 1967.

Table 1–2 *(continued)*

The Four Food Groups of the Daily Food Guide	Chief Nutrients Contributed by Each Food Group
Meat Group	
2 or more servings:	High quality proteins Thiamine
Beef, veal, pork, lamb, poultry, fish, eggs	Niacin Riboflavin
As alternates—dry beans, dry peas, nuts	Iron
Vegetable-Fruit Group	
4 or more servings:	
A citrus fruit or other fruit or vegetable important for vitamin C	Ascorbic Acid
A dark-green or deep-yellow vegetable important for vitamin A, at least every other day	Vitamin A
Other vegetables and fruits including potatoes	Vitamins Minerals
Bread-Cereal Group	
4 or more servings:	Protein Iron
Whole grain, enriched, or restored	Several of the B-vitamins Food energy
Other foods as needed to complete meals and to provide additional food energy and other food values	Vitamin A (butter and fortified margarine) Saturated and unsaturated fatty acids Calories

Activities

1. Keep a 3-day record of all food consumed. How does this compare with recommendations of the Daily Food Guide? Count as a serving:

MILK GROUP

1 cup or 8 ounces of milk
(1-inch cube of cheddar-type cheese = $\frac{1}{2}$ cup milk)
($\frac{1}{2}$ cup of cottage cheese = $\frac{1}{3}$ cup of milk)
(2 tablespoons of cream cheese = 1 tablespoon milk)
($\frac{1}{2}$ cup of ice cream = $\frac{1}{4}$ cup milk)

MEAT GROUP

2 or 3 ounces of lean cooked meat, fish, or poultry
2 eggs
1 cup of cooked dry beans, dry peas, or lentils
4 tablespoons of peanut butter

VEGETABLE–FRUIT GROUP

½ cup of vegetable or fruit or portion as ordinarily served, such as 1 medium apple, banana, orange or potato, or half a grapefruit or cantaloupe

BREAD–CEREAL GROUP

1 slice of bread

1 ounce of ready-to-eat cereal

½ to ¾ cup of cooked cereal, cornmeal, grits, macaroni, noodles, rice, or spaghetti

2. Evaluate the following statements:

a. "What I eat is no one's business but my own."

b. "I eat what I want to, when I want to, and as much as I want to."

c. "If I don't like a food I don't bother to eat it, no matter where I am."

3. Plan meals for 3 days that meet the recommendations of *A Daily Food Guide.*

4. Show how several foods are each a good source of two or more essential food constituents.

References

BOGERT, L. J., G. M. BRIGGS, and D. H. CALLOWAY. *Nutrition and Physical Fitness*, 8th ed. Philadelphia: W. B. Saunders Company. 1966.

CHANEY, M. S. and M. L. ROSS. *Nutrition*, 8th ed. Boston: Houghton Mifflin Company. 1971

Consumers All. The Yearbook of Agriculture, 1965. U.S. Dept. Agr., Washington, D.C.: United States Government Printing Office.

Family Fare, A Guide to Good Nutrition. U.S. Dept. Agr., Home and Garden Bull. No. 1 (1970).

Food. The Yearbook of Agriculture, 1959. U.S. Dept. Agr., Washington, D.C.: United States Government Printing Office.

Food and Nutrition Board, NAS–NRC. *Recommended Dietary Allowances, Revised 1968.* Natl. Acad. Sci.-Natl. Research Council Publ. 1694, Washington, D.C. (1968).

Food for Fitness—A Daily Food Guide. U.S. Dept. Agr., Leaflet 424 (1967).

Food for the Family with Young Children. U.S. Dept. Agr., Home and Garden Bull. No. 5 (1970).

Food for the Young Couple. USDA, Home and Garden Bull. No. 85 (1967).

Food for Us All. The Yearbook of Agriculture, 1969. U.S. Dept. Agr., Washington, D.C.: United States Government Printing Office.

Food Guide for Older Folks. USDA, Home and Garden Bull. No. 17 (1969).

LEVERTON, R. M. *Food Becomes You,* 3rd ed. Ames: Iowa State University Press. 1965.

MARTIN, E. A. *Nutrition in Action,* 3rd ed. New York: Holt, Rinehart & Winston, Inc. 1971.

WILSON, E. D., K. H. FISHER, and M. E. FUQUA. *Principles of Nutrition,* 2nd ed. New York: John Wiley & Sons, Inc., 1965.

the selection, preparation, and use of foods

2

consumer protection

In the United States the strict control of our food supply by government is now recognized as essential to the health and well-being of our people. With today's complex manufacturing methods and the ever-increasing use of prepared and packaged foods, the homemaker can no longer rely solely on her own knowledge and experience to enable her to provide safe and wholesome food for her family. Instead, she must depend in large measure upon the many federal, state, and local agencies that work to protect the safety of the food she buys and upon the conscientious compliance of the majority of the food industry.

The federal government protects all food shipped in interstate commerce. The state governments protect many foods sold locally or solely within the state, although with the passage of the Wholesome Meat Act in 1967, the Wholesome Poultry Products Act in 1968, and the Egg Products Inspection Act in 1970, federal agencies may assume responsibility for these products if the state fails to do so. Some cities and towns have special ordinances controlling the food sold in local markets. Since these vary widely from state to state and from city to city, the consumer needs to acquaint herself with those applicable in her area.

The food laws and the activities of the many agencies provide a framework within which the homemaker can select a safe and economical supply of food for her family. She must, however, be informed and be prepared to play an active role in her own protection. The laws are neither designed to control her selection nor influence her preference. Rather they seek to provide a safe food supply and permit the consumer to have confidence in her own selection.

Federal Protection of the Food Supply

The Constitution of the United States gives the Congress the power to regulate interstate commerce. Under this power the Congress has passed many laws dealing with food and has delegated the authority to make detailed regulations to several federal agencies. All food shipped in interstate commerce, which includes all food imported into this country, must meet the requirements of one or more federal laws and regulations. In this section some of the activities of the Department of Agriculture and of the Food and Drug Administration in protecting our food will be discussed.

Department of Agriculture (USDA)

Although much of the work of the Department of Agriculture concerns food, the Consumer and Marketing Service (C&MS)[1] is of particular importance in the protection of our food supply. The grading and inspection programs of the Consumer and Marketing Service are designed to certify the quality and condition of agricultural commodities and food products. Standards for grades such as U.S. No. 1, U.S. Good, and U.S. Grade A have been developed for most of the important farm commodities.[2] Originally these standards were developed to assist wholesale trading, but more recently they have become increasingly useful to retailers and consumers. The standards of quality developed by the Consumer and Marketing Service are used heavily by other federal agencies as a basis for their purchase specifications.

Meat. The Meat Inspection Act, passed in 1906, required the examination and inspection—before, during, and after slaughter—of all cattle, sheep, swine, and goats to be slaughtered and the meat and meat products used in interstate and foreign commerce. The Consumer and Marketing Service has the responsibility for the enforcement of this Act. The Meat Inspection Division of the C&MS has developed a system of continuous inspection, as a result of which federal inspectors are placed in each plant to supervise the meat handling at every step until it is shipped. When the consumer sees the familiar purple stamp "U.S. Inspected and Passed," she knows that at the time of inspection the meat was found to be sound, wholesome, and fit for human consumption. In the case of packaged and canned meat products, she knows not only that the product is wholesome, but that the label is truthful and that the packaging materials which come into contact with the meat are safe.

[1] Formerly the Agricultural Marketing Service (AMS). On February 8, 1965, the Meat Inspection Division of the Agricultural Research Service was transferred to the Agricultural Marketing Service and the name changed to the Consumer and Marketing Service. *Federal Register*, 30:2160 (1965).

[2] *USDA Standards for Food and Farm Products* and *USDA Grade Names for Food and Farm Products*. Agricultural Handbooks No. 341 and No. 342. United States Department of Agriculture, Washington, D.C. (1967).

Courtesy of the U.S. Department of Agriculture

Fig. 2–1. *The familiar round meat inspection stamp assures the customer that the meat she buys is safe and truthfully labeled.*

The Meat Inspection Division guards against the use of harmful preservatives, residues from pesticides, and from growth-promoting substances and drugs which may be found in the meat or meat products. The Division has also adopted standards of identity for oleomargarine (margarine) containing animal fat, corned beef hash, and chopped ham. In addition, the minimum meat content for such meat products as "Chili Con Carne," hash, meat stew, hamburger, and liver sausage has been set.[3]

The passage of the Meat Inspection Act in 1906 made mandatory the inspection of all meat and meat products intended for interstate and export commerce but left meat destined for intrastate commerce with no requirement for any type of inspection. No doubt this fact influenced the passage of the Wholesome Meat Act by Congress in 1967. This Act, when fully operative, will assure that all meat sold in the United States meets a uniform standard of wholesomeness whether it is federally or state inspected.

The Consumer and Marketing Service is responsible for grading meat. Grading is optional although inspection is required if a product is to be graded. The grading of meat is discussed in Chapter 10.

Poultry. The development of the poultry business into a mass production industry was made possible by the use of medicated feeds to control disease and by high-speed slaughtering processes. Because this necessitated new sanitation controls, in 1957 Congress passed the Poultry Products Inspec-

[3] *Inspection, Labeling, and Care of Meat and Poultry—A Consumer Education Guide,* Agricultural Handbook No. 416. United States Department of Agriculture, Washington, D.C. (1971).

tion Act. The Consumer and Marketing Service is responsible for its enforcement. Under this Act, the C&MS develops standards for quality of poultry and poultry products, standards for facilities, and operating procedures for the processing of poultry and poultry products. It also maintains a compulsory continuous inspection system for products to be shipped in interstate commerce. With the passage of the Poultry Products Inspection Act, inspection was also available to intrastate producers who requested it. However, the Wholesome Poultry Products Act passed by Congress in 1968 is an attempt to assure that all poultry and poultry products reaching the consumer meet a uniform standard of wholesomeness whether or not they have crossed state lines during the marketing process. Each state was given two years (or three if progress was being made) from August, 1968, to develop its own inspection system equal to the federal inspection program.[4] Thus, when the consumer sees that poultry and poultry products have been inspected by either federal or state agencies she is assured of the wholesomeness, sanitation, and truthful labeling of the product. Poultry may also be graded. Inspection is required if the product is to be graded, but grading is optional. The grading of poultry is discussed in Chapter 11.

Food and Drug Administration (FDA)

As the homemaker approaches today's supermarket, she expects a plentiful supply of pure, wholesome food of dependable quality which is attractively packaged with truthful and informative labeling. This was not always true. In the last sixty-five years, the Food and Drug Administration has brought about many reforms. It has adopted regulations to prevent the introduction into interstate commerce of adulterated or misbranded foods. Definitions and standards have been developed in order to promote honesty and fair dealing in the interests of the consumer. It is estimated that in 1970 the personal consumption expenditure of consumers was 610 billion dollars and that for every dollar spent, 38 cents were expended on products regulated by the FDA. Thus the retail sales of products regulated by the FDA was near 230 billion dollars. Not all of these were foods, of course, for the FDA is also concerned with cosmetics, drugs, and other substances.

The Food and Drug Administration is responsible for the enforcement of the federal Food, Drug, and Cosmetic Act, covering the production, manufacture, distribution, and sale of all food in interstate commerce except meat, poultry, and eggs, which are regulated by the Department of Agriculture, and fish for which there is no mandatory inspection program at present. In doing this, the FDA inspects factories for sanitary conditions and examines the raw materials as well as the controls being used in the compounding, processing, packaging, and labeling of products to be shipped in interstate commerce. If adulterated or misbranded food is found, it may be seized and destroyed.

[4] *Poultry Grading Manual.* Agricultural Handbook No. 31. United States Department of Agriculture, Washington, D.C. (1971).

Adulteration. The Food, Drug, and Cosmetic Act prohibits the introduction into interstate commerce of any food that is poisonous, contaminated, unsanitary, or unfit for food. Under this section, much attention has been given in recent years to the use of additives in the preparation of food and the pesticides which may leave a residue in milk, meat, eggs, or on fruits and vegetables. The experts of the Food and Drug Administration seek to permit food producers, farmers, and livestock growers to use additives and pesticides only when they are satisfied that their use will not be harmful to the consumer.

During the past fifty years food technologists have developed many materials useful in food processing and packaging. These include preservatives to prevent spoilage, emulsifiers to improve texture, vitamins to enhance nutritional values, sweeteners, colors, bleaches, and flavors. Before the passage of the Food Additives Amendment in 1958, the Food and Drug Administration could not prevent the use of a chemical simply because it was questionable or had not been adequately tested. In the Food Additives Amendment, Congress recognized the need for additives and adopted the principle of pre-testing, by which the burden of proof was shifted from the Food and Drug Administration to the producer and manufacturer. However, at the time of the passage of the Food Additives Amendment, legislators and scientists concluded that substances which the FDA had previously considered favorably and substances that had an unmarred history of use in food could be safely exempted from pre-marketing clearance. This resulted in the decision that certain substances added to food and generally recognized as safe under the conditions of their intended use would not be classed as food additives and would be exempt from the pre-marketing clearance requirements. This led to the publication of a list of substances "Generally Recognized As Safe"—the GRAS list. However, in the intervening years tests for toxicity have become more sophisticated, certain GRAS items have been used well beyond the exposure patterns considered in the original development of the GRAS list, and other changes have occurred which have resulted in a reexamination of the criteria used as a basis for classifying substances as GRAS or as Food Additives.[5] During this period several items have been removed from the GRAS list, perhaps the best known being the cyclamates (Sucaryl).[6] Before substances not in the GRAS list may be added directly to foods or to substances likely to contaminate food as a result of their use in processing, or be used in packaging, the manufacturer or producer must demonstrate that the additive may be safely used. If the FDA is satisfied with the evidence presented, an order will be issued permitting its use. The procedure is somewhat different for

[5] Criteria Proposed for Classing Substances as GRAS or as Regulated Food Additives. *FDA Papers*, 5 (1): 33 (1971).
[6] Federal Register 34: 17063–17064 (Oct. 21, 1969).

color additives. Under the Color Additives Amendment of 1960 a color additive may not be used unless the Food and Drug Administration has listed that additive for use and prescribed the conditions for its use. Neither a food nor a color additive may be used to deceive the consumer or be certified as safe if found to induce cancer in man or animals.

The Pesticide Chemicals Act of 1954 prohibits the introduction into interstate commerce of raw agricultural commodities bearing the residue of a pesticide chemical unless the pesticide is safe or the residue is within the tolerance established by the Food and Drug Administration as safe.

Misbranding. The Food, Drug, and Cosmetic Act also prohibits the introduction into interstate commerce of any misbranded food. The Fair Packaging and Labeling Act passed in 1966 was a further endeavor to prevent unfair or deceitful packaging or labeling of consumer commodities. Manufacturers must give careful attention to the labeling requirements to avoid misbranding. Some of the most important requirements are listed below:

1. The label must not be false or misleading in any way.
2. A food must not be offered for sale under the name of another food.
3. Imitations must be so labeled.
4. Containers must be made, formed, and filled in such a way as not to be misleading.
5. If the food is in a packaged form, the label must contain:
   a. The name and place of business of the manufacturer, packer, or distributor.
   b. An accurate statement of the quantity of the contents in terms of weight, measure, or numerical count.
6. Required information must be placed on the label with such conspicuousness and in such terms as to render it likely to be read and understood by the ordinary individual under customary conditions of purchase and use.
7. If a food is one for which a standard of identity, a standard of quality, or a standard of fill of container *has* been adopted, and it does not meet this standard, the label must state that it falls below this standard.
8. If a food is one for which a standard of identity has *not* been adopted, the label must contain the common or usual name of the food; and if made of two or more ingredients, the name of each ingredient must be listed in the order of its predominance by weight. Spices, flavorings, and colorings can be so designated without naming each.
9. If a food bears or contains artificial flavoring, artificial coloring, or chemical preservatives, the label must declare it. This applies to standardized as well as nonstandardized products. However, artificial coloring need not be declared on the labels of butter, cheese, and ice cream.
10. Foods offered for special dietary uses must be labeled with information concerning vitamins, minerals, and other dietary properties.

Small open containers of fruits and vegetables and food which is usually processed further or re-packed later in substantial quantities may be exempt from these labeling requirements. For example, cheese which is produced in large wheels and cut by the retailer later may be exempted.

No matter how exact the labeling requirements may be, the homemaker must read them if she is to get her money's worth and guard her family's health. The Food and Drug Administration in emphasizing the importance of consumer education and understanding says: Read the Label—It's Your Protection.

Definitions and Standards. The Food, Drug, and Cosmetic Act provides that definitions and standards may be formulated. The Congress itself has established the standard of identity for butter and for nonfat dry milk. Presently there are nineteen broad categories of food and more than 270 individual products for which standards of identity have been established. Generally speaking, each identity includes two classes of ingredients: those which are required to be present, often within prescribed limits, and those which are optional. The optional ingredients, if used, must in most instances be declared on the label. The presence of artificial flavor, artificial color (except in butter, cheese, and ice cream), or chemical preservatives must be declared. Standards of identity are subject to change as reading of the *Federal Register* will show, but many of these changes are without appreciable effect on the product.

When the Food and Drug Administration decides to formulate a definition or standard, intensive studies are made. They study the usual composition of the food product, investigate the trade practices followed, and consult consumers to determine what they expect that food product to be. Standards may be standards of identity, standards of quality, or standards of fill of container. Once adopted, these definitions and standards provide the processor, the retailer, and the consumer with a common language—a yardstick of value. Thus when the homemaker selects a food for which a definition or standard has been formulated (Table 2–1) certain ingredients must be present in the food and often in prescribed proportions. Although currently (1971) ingredient listing is not required on the labels of foods for which standards of identity have been established, it is probable that such a requirement will be in force in the near future. A product that imitates a standardized product but does not meet the requirements must be labeled "Imitation." Certain standards of identity recognize that foods can be improved nutritionally by adding vitamins or other supplements. For example, the standard of identity for "enriched" flour specifies the amount of such added ingredients.

Standards of quality are minimum standards only and specify such factors as tenderness, color, and freedom from defects. A standard of quality has been set for many canned fruits and vegetables. If a food does not meet the standard, it must be labeled "Below Standard in Quality, Good Food—Not High Grade" or specify the reason why it does not meet the standard of quality. Because products so labeled are not attractive to the buyer, the consumer seldom sees products labeled sub-standard on the retail market today.

Table 2–1. *Foods for which Standards of Identity Have Been Adopted by the Food and Drug Administration*

Part of Code*	Foods	Part of Code*	Foods
14.	Cacao Products	27.	Canned Fruits and Fruit Juices
15.	Cereal Flours and Related Products	29.	Fruit Butters, Fruit Jellies, Fruit Preserves and Related Products
16.	Macaroni and Noodle Products	31.	Nonalcoholic Beverages
17.	Bakery Products	36.	Shellfish
18.	Milk and Cream	37.	Fish
19.	Cheeses, Processed Cheeses, Cheese Foods, Cheese Spreads and Related Foods	42.	Eggs and Egg Products
		45.	Oleomargarine, Margarine
		46.	Nut Products
20.	Frozen Desserts	51.	Canned Vegetables
22.	Food Flavorings	53.	Tomato Products
25.	Dressings for Foods		

* *Code of Federal Regulations,* Title 21, 1971.

Standards of fill of container tell the packer how full the container must be to avoid deceiving the consumer. They are particularly necessary for products that shake down or settle after filling. If a product does not meet the standard, it must be labeled "Below Standard in Fill."

Seafood. Although shellfish is regulated by the Food and Drug Administration, the Bureau of Commercial Fisheries of the United States Department of the Interior is responsible for the protection of the supply of other fish and fish products. The Food and Drug Administration has adopted standards of identity and standards of fill of container for shellfish. The Bureau of Commercial Fisheries operates a voluntary inspection system for fish and fish products and has adopted standards for such products as frozen fried fish sticks, halibut steaks, and ocean perch fillets. These standards have served to upgrade the quality of the product offered for sale and have provided the industry with a standard measure of quality to follow.

Milk, Shellfish, and Food Service. The Public Health Service, which is concerned primarily with the control of infectious and contagious diseases, has long assisted states and municipalities in the preparation of laws for the prevention and control of diseases, particularly those which may be transmitted through milk, shellfish, and foods served to the public in restaurants, on interstate carriers, and through vending machines.

However, reorganization of the Department of Health, Education, and Welfare in 1968 resulted in the transfer of the milk, shellfish, and food service sanitation programs to the newly formed Division of Sanitation Control in the FDA's Bureau of Compliance and for the first time all major food protection programs of the Department of Health, Education, and Welfare were brought together into a single agency.[7] With the reorganization, the Division of Sanitation Control also assumed the advisory role to state and local authorities concerning the development of recommended sanitation standards, technical procedures, and other program guides. A classic example of the work done by the Public Health Service is the *Grade "A" Pasteurized Milk Ordinance*,[8] a guide which has been widely adopted and which is discussed in Chapter 8.

Interrelationship among Agencies

The programs described here are only some of the activities of the federal government in the protection of the national food supply. Many other agencies are engaged in similar or related activities. For example, the Federal Trade Commission concerns itself with unfair trade practices and with false or misleading advertising; the Federal Communications Commission regulates advertising on radio and television; the Atomic Energy Commission is responsible for the control of radiation in food and food products, but the FDA has the responsibility for approving the marketing of irradiated foods.

This diffusion of responsibility for the regulation of the food supply may present serious problems to manufacturers and producers. The dairy industry provides a good example of the complexity of food regulations today. The Public Health Service developed recommended state milk and frozen desserts codes, both of which have been adopted by many states. The Dairy Division of the Consumer and Marketing Service sponsors a voluntary inspection and grading service and has developed standards for milk used for manufacturing purposes. In addition, the Food and Drug Administration has adopted standards of identity for certain dairy products. Because the array of regulations is puzzling to industry, Congress is studying ways in which these activities can be coordinated with one another as well as with the various state regulatory activities.

State and Local Protection of the Food Supply

Food sold locally or solely within the state may be regulated by state and local laws. The power of the state and local governments to regulate the manufacture and sale of many foods rests upon their police power—the power to protect the health of their citizens. State and local laws may apply to food entering the state in interstate commerce, but not if this would impose an undue burden on interstate commerce or if it would discriminate against goods moving in interstate commerce. Thus, a state may not make

[7] *FDA Papers* 3:4 (Dec. 1969–Jan. 1970).

[8] *Grade "A" Pasteurized Milk Ordinance. 1965 Recommendations of the U.S. Public Health Service.* United States Public Health Service Publication No. 229, 1965.

special labeling requirements which would place an undue burden on national producers by requiring them to make a special label for use within that state.

The consumer will find that several state and local agencies are involved in the protection of the food supply at the state and local levels. Most commonly these activities are carried on by the departments of health and the departments of agriculture. In recent years the development of cooperative agreements between state and federal agencies has increased significantly. For example, the Consumer and Marketing Service has agreements with many states for the grading of poultry under which the overall supervision is done by the federal agency but the actual grading may be by federal or state employees. Federal grades, standards, and regulations are used and inspection for wholesomeness is required. The Wholesome Meat Act, the Wholesome Poultry Products Act, and the Egg Products Inspection Act give the federal government authority to check on the extent to which states are carrying out the provisions of these acts. In cases where the state is failing, the federal agency may assume the responsibility.

In an effort to develop greater uniformity among state food laws, the Uniform State Food, Drug, and Cosmetic Act was adopted in 1940 by the Association of Food and Drug Officials of the United States. The food portions of this Act follow those of the federal Act with respect to definitions, prohibited acts, adulteration and misbranding, and penalties. It also authorizes the state to adopt definitions and standards which conform as far as practicable to those in the federal Act. The Uniform Act was revised in 1961 to incorporate the pesticide chemicals, food additives, and color additives sections of the federal Act. Most states have adopted either the entire Act or a substantial part of it.

It is difficult to make general statements about regulations in states and municipalities because of great variation and rapid changes among them. Instead the consumer must inform herself of the current situation in her own area. In order to assist in evaluating the situation, this section describes certain phases of the state programs for inspection and/or grading of eggs, fruits and vegetables, and seafood.

Eggs

The grading, sizing, labeling, and packaging of shell eggs are controlled on a state-by-state basis in accordance with state egg laws and these may vary from state to state. The federal-state grading service is conducted under cooperative agreements between the USDA and state departments of agriculture. The graders may be either federal or state employees. The official USDA grade shield on a carton of eggs or on the tape that seals the carton means that licensed egg graders have supervised every step of the grading and packaging operations. The USDA's grading program for shell eggs is a voluntary service and only cartons bearing the official USDA grade shield have been government graded. When the Egg Products Inspection Act, mentioned earlier, becomes effective the processing of egg products for both interstate and intrastate commerce will be under continuous inspection and uniform standards, grades, and weight classes will be required for eggs in interstate commerce.[9]

Fruits and Vegetables

Inspection of fruits and vegetables is often a joint venture between the federal and state governments. Standards employed and the training requirements of the inspectors are the responsibility of the USDA. Use of the service by the industry is voluntary and users pay a fee. Some states require that certain products be graded and labeled on the basis of either federal or state grade standards. Federal grades of fresh fruits and vegetables are largely for use in large volume trading. The consumer is much more likely to find U.S. grade labels on processed fruits and vegetables than on the fresh product. However, retail packages of apples, potatoes, onions, carrots, and some other fresh products may be found bearing the U.S. grade label.

Dairy Products

The protection of the public's health with respect to milk is primarily the function of state and local governments. State programs provide for sanitary and quality inspection of dairy products. In most states a state agency is authorized to establish standards of identity and quality for dairy products and to inspect and grade such products. Many states also have specific legislation dealing with ice cream and frozen desserts.

In 1923 the U.S. Public Health Service established an Office of Milk Investigations to assist the states in the development of milk sanitation programs at both state and local level. In 1924 the USPHS published its first Grade A Pasteurized Milk Ordinance. Since that time it has been revised at least thirteen times and has been either adopted or used as a basis for the milk sanitation law or regulation in 39 states and more than 2,000 communities. However, other states and communities have refused to recognize the USPHS standard milk ordinance. The ordinance is the basis for the certification of interstate milk shippers in areas where milk must be imported. The certification, a voluntary program, has grown rapidly with the increased interstate shipment of milk and in 1966 there were 1,429 certified shippers in 46 states and the District of Columbia. The basic provisions of the milk ordinance and code are as follows:

1. Defines milk and milk products.
2. Prohibits sale of adulterated or misbranded milk and milk products.

[9] *Federal Register* 36: 9814–9834 (May 28, 1971).

3. Requires permit for sale or storage of milk and milk products.
4. Requires that the label state the name of contents, grade, whether pasteurized or raw, name of producer if raw, or identity of plant if pasteurized, and certain information about vitamin D, skim, homogenized, reconstituted, concentrated, or recombined milk.
5. Requires frequent inspection of farms and plants.
6. Requires samples to be submitted at intervals.
7. Provides for grading of milk producers and processors.

Seafood

Many coastal states have a program of sanitary inspection of shellfish, and some include other types of seafood. The federal-state program for the certification of interstate shippers of shellfish provides for a voluntary cooperative interstate shippers program designed to insure the safety of shellfish shipped in interstate commerce. In order to be a certified participant in the program, a state must comply with the practices recommended by the federal agency. The reason for having special regulations for shellfish is that they are often eaten raw or only partially cooked, and if grown in sewage-contaminated waters or processed and distributed under insanitary conditions they are potential carriers of disease.

Summary

The alert, informed consumer is a vital part of the federal and state programs designed to protect the nation's food supply. The obtaining of food, including production, processing, and distributing practices and the handling of the food after purchased must all be carefully safeguarded if wholesome food is to be available for all. The need for education, information, and inspection is constantly increasing. However, agencies responsible for inspection of foods, whether federal or state, are seriously limited in their activities due to financial restraints.

In today's self-service markets a consumer has little or no opportunity to check the conditions under which the food has been grown and processed and often cannot find a grocer or meat cutter to answer questions. However, the consumer can be assured concerning the safety and quality of the products purchased for family use by carefully reading the labels on packaged goods and by selecting foods which have been inspected and graded. In the long run the consumer must take some responsibility for her choices and an active part in seeing to it that all food offered for sale is wholesome, nutritious, and palatable. Given the guarantees of purity and safety, her choice is largely dependent upon nutritional needs, how much she has to spend, and factors of personal preference.

Activities

1. Visit three groceries in your community. Determine if the meat sold there is federally inspected or state inspected. Does the store offer more than one grade of beef for sale?

2. What agency is responsible for the administration of the food protection program of your state?

3. Compare labels on several cans of a canned fruit or vegetable. Where possible, use products of varying grades.

4. Are any of the fresh fruits or vegetables currently available in your market marked with U.S. grade?

References

Code of Federal Regulations, Titles 7, *Agriculture;* 9, *Animals and Animal Products;* 21, *Food and Drugs.*

Federal Register.

Food. The Yearbook of Agriculture, 1959. U.S. Dept. Agr., Washington, D.C.: United States Government Printing Office. Pp. 327–458.

FRAZIER, W. C. *Food Microbiology.* 2nd ed. New York: McGraw-Hill Book Company, Inc., 1967.

GUNDERSON, F. K., H. W. GUNDERSON, and E. R. FERGUSON, Jr. *Food Standards and Definitions in the United States.* New York: Academic Press Inc. 1963.

KINDER, F. *Meal Management.* 3rd ed. New York: The Macmillan Company, 1968.

TROELSTRUP, A. W. *The Consumer in American Society.* 4th ed. New York: McGraw-Hill Book Company, Inc. 1970.

3

fruits

Fruits are known to have been included in the diet of man since prehistoric times, and references to their use and the desire of people for them may be found like a bright thread running through the fabric of the religious books as well as the folk legends of all peoples. The story of the forbidden apple in the Garden of Eden and the lamentations of the wandering tribes of Israel when they cried in protest to Moses, "It is no place of seed, or of figs, or of vines, or of pomegranates,"[1] are familiar. It is interesting to note that these early references to fruit include many that are well known today, such as apples, grapes, pomegranates, berries, and melons.

Fruits are widely used and enjoyed throughout the world. United States Department of Agriculture data have shown that in the United States between 1920 and 1970 there was a decrease in the amount of fresh fruit consumed and a substantial increase in the amount of canned and frozen fruit. Because drying is an ancient method of preservation, it is not surprising that the proportion of dried fruit decreased during this period. The use of frozen fruit started in about 1925, but not until 1949 did the amount rise to 9 pounds per person per year. The amount of citrus fruit used per capita by 1970 was, however, more than three times the amount used in 1910, whereas the consumption of apples decreased to about half the 1910 level. This can be attributed to better facilities for shipping citrus fruits, to the popularity of frozen and canned citrus juice, and to emphasis on the high ascorbic acid content of citrus fruits. The amounts of fruit other than citrus fruit and apples and the amount of melons used per capita have not changed greatly over the years.

Classification
Scientifically speaking, the term *fruit* includes a number of foods ordinarily classed as vegetables, nuts, or grains. Most of the foods that are usually listed as fruits are pulpy, in contrast to the legumes, nuts, or grains, which are dry and not generally designated as fruits. This presentation is confined

[1] Numbers 20:5.

to those products commonly classed on the market and in the diet as fruits. These include apples, peaches, pears, plums, citrus fruits such as oranges, lemons, and grapefruit; berries of all kinds, melons, bananas, grapes, dates, figs, and others less well known.

The listing of these foods under a single heading *fruits* is justified because each has grown from the flower of a plant yielding its ripened seed with some edible adjacent or surrounding tissues. Even casual observation shows a wide difference in the structure of the various fruits, and leads to an effort to classify them into groups of similar types.

A botanical classification of fruits is shown in Table 3–1. Plants that have a single flower with one pistil produce simple fruits which may be either dry or fleshy. In simple dry fruits the ovary wall becomes leathery, woody, or papery as it ripens. Examples are cereal grains, legumes, and nuts.

Simple fleshy fruits are those in which the ovary wall is fleshy when it is mature. Berries and drupes are examples of simple fleshy fruits. In the true berry the entire ovary wall ripens into a fleshy, and often juicy, tissue. According to the botanist's definition, avocados, dates, eggplants, grapes, persimmons, red peppers, and tomatoes are all true berries. Botanically speaking, citrus fruits are modified berries, although the pericarp, which is the rind or the peel, is usually not considered edible. Drupes (Figure 3–1) are berries in which the pericarp is divided into three parts: an outer covering, usually a thin skin; the fleshy portion; and an inner part, the stone or pit which encloses the seed. Examples are almonds, apricots, cherries, olives, peaches, and plums. In the almond the seed is eaten, but in the other drupes listed the outer fleshy portion is used as food.

Table 3–1. *Botanical Classification of Fruits* *

	Simple					Aggregate Fleshy	Multiple Fleshy
		Fleshy					
Dry				Accessory			
	True Berries	Modified Berries (citrus)	Drupes	False Berries	Pomes		
Grains	Avocado	Grapefruit	Almond	Banana	Apple	Blackberry †	Breadfruit
Legumes	Date	Lemon	Apricot	Cranberry	Pear	Raspberry	Fig
Nuts	Eggplant	Lime	Cherry	Cucumber		Strawberry †	Mulberry
	Grape	Orange	Olive	Currant			Pineapple
	Persimmon		Peach	Gooseberry			
	Red Pepper		Plum	Muskmelon			
	Tomato			Squash			

* From *Botany*, fifth edition, by Carl L. Wilson, Walter E. Loomis and Taylor A. Steeves. Copyright 1952, © 1957, 1962, 1967, 1971 by Holt, Rinehart and Winston, Inc. Adapted and reprinted by permission of Holt, Rinehart and Winston, Inc.
† Actually an aggregate-accessory because the receptacle is fleshy and edible.

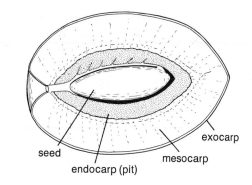

Fig. 3–1. *Simple Fleshy Fruits. Section view of an olive fruit, a drupe.*

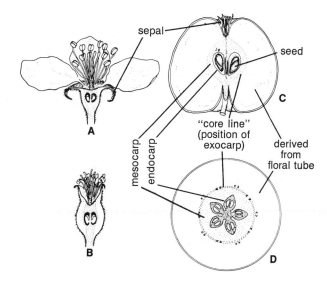

Fig. 3–2. *Development and structure of the apple, an accessory fruit. A, flower of apple. B, older flower, after petals have fallen. Unshaded regions in A and B represent the floral tube. C, D, cross sections.*

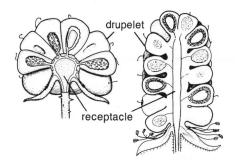

Fig. 3–3. *Aggregate fruits. Left, raspberry. Right, blackberry (aggregate-accessory).*

(Figs. 3–1, 3–2, and 3–3 are from *Botany,* fifth edition, by Carl L. Wilson, Walter E. Loomis and Taylor E. Steeves. They are on pages 318, 319, and 319 respectively. Copyright 1952, © 1957, 1962, 1967, 1971 by Holt, Rinehart and Winston, Inc. Reprinted by permission of Holt, Rinehart and Winston, Inc.)

In accessory fruits other parts of the plant join with the ovary to form the fruit. They are sometimes called "false" berries because the entire fruit is fleshy. False berries can often be distinguished from true berries by the remainder of the flower that can be seen at the tip of the fruit opposite the stem. The group includes fruits that are usually called berries, such as cranberries, currants, and gooseberries, as well as others such as bananas, cucumbers, muskmelons, and squash. In apples and pears, which are accessory fruits classified as pomes, the core, or inner paper-like portion, is the ovary. Around this and adhering to it are other plant parts that become fleshy as the fruit develops (Figure 3–2).

Aggregate fruits develop from flowers that have a number of pistils. Each pistil develops as it might in a separate flower, forming tiny drupes or drupelets, which adhere to one another as in the blackberry (Figure 3–3).

Multiple fruits are formed not from a single flower, but from a cluster of flowers grouped closely together. The pineapple is a typical multiple fruit which develops from several flowers that consolidate into one mass during ripening. Each of the many sections that make up a pineapple is a developed flower, and each one is attached to a center core that has a more or less woody stem structure.

Ripening and Storage

The chemical changes that take place during ripening occur either while on the parent plant or after the fruit is picked. These changes include a decrease in starch and acidity of the green fruit and an increase in sugars, as well as transformations in the pectic substances and aromatic compounds. The pectic substances change gradually from a large molecule called protopectin, characteristic of underripe fruit, to a smaller molecule, pectin, which occurs in ripe fruit and is responsible for the formation of fruit jellies. The softness of overripe fruit is, in part, due to the change of pectin into a still smaller molecule, pectic acid, which is not capable of forming jelly.

Certain fruits such as bananas and persimmons are very astringent when they are underripe because they contain tannins.[2] This astringency disappears during ripening not because the tannins disappear from the fruit, but because they become less soluble and therefore less capable of producing an astringent feeling in the mouth. During ripening the full flavor of the fruit develops. The flavor of a fruit is determined by its content of acids, sugar, and other substances often referred to as aromatic compounds. Changes occur in these compounds during ripening until at a certain stage each fruit is considered most desirable for eating. This stage may vary with the use to be made of the fruit and with individual taste because some people prefer firm tart fruit and others a softer and sweeter fruit. With the exception of a

[2] Tannin is a word loosely applied to a group of astringent substances that occur in certain plants. Chemically, they are phenolic compounds.

few fruits like bananas and pears, fruits are of highest quality if ripened before they are picked.

After fruit is harvested, it is sometimes precooled rapidly to reduce it to refrigerator temperatures. It is shipped, usually under refrigeration, and may be stored for some time before it is sold depending upon the nature of the fruit.

During shipping and storage, controlled temperature, humidity, and atmosphere aid in maximum preservation of freshness and retard postharvest disorders and the growth of spoilage organisms. Exposure to warm temperatures accelerates ripening or maturing and may foster microbiological growth. Exposure to temperatures below the normal physiological range results in chill injury. Poor ventilation or an adverse atmosphere causes an accumulation in the tissues of substances injurious to the fruit. Different species and even different varieties of the same species show differences in the lower limit of temperature to which they can be subjected without showing signs of injury. In general fruits produced in temperate zones can withstand lower temperatures than can those produced in tropical and sub-tropical regions, although there are exceptions. Obvious symptoms of chilling injury are pitting of surfaces and discolorations either at the surface or of deeper-lying tissues.[3]

Although in some cases it is convenient to delay the ripening of fruit after it has been picked, in others it is desirable to accelerate normal ripening. This can be done by ethylene gas, which is given off by fruit during the normal process of ripening and which can be added artificially to the atmosphere in which a fruit is stored. Flavor develops, the texture becomes mellow, and the color is changed from green to the color of the ripe fruit. The vitamin content of the fruit is not injured by the gas. In some instances, however, ripening on the vine or trees is necessary for maximum development of vitamin content. For this reason fruits picked when they are green tend to be lower in vitamin content whether ripened in the air or in an atmosphere containing ethylene gas. Some fruits, such as cantaloupes, do not respond well to ethylene gas treatment. Although the surface color of cantaloupes changes when they are treated with the gas, the flesh remains hard and the flavor undeveloped.

Many fruits and vegetables are now prepackaged, usually in plastic film, before they are sold. Such prepackaging saves the time of clerks and purchasers, decreases damage from consumer handling, and protects food from contamination by dirt and insects. Most fruits and vegetables are packaged in plastic that has tiny holes to allow for the necessary exchange of gases. Good moisture retention is, however, still possible because the perforated area is small compared with the total surface of the package. For this reason moisture loss from the food is low and there is little wilting. Some fruits,

[3] R. B. Duckworth. *Fruit and Vegetables*. Oxford: Pergamon Press, 1966. Pp. 165–181.

such as apples and citrus fruits, are sometimes prepackaged in net bags instead of in plastic.

When fresh fruit is brought into the home, the first step is to sort it, to discard decayed fruit, and to remove injured fruit for immediate use. It can then be stored in a covered container or in perforated plastic bags at a temperature that depends on the type of fruit. Most fruits can be washed and dried before storage, if desired, but berries, cherries, and grapes keep better if washed just before used. Ordinary refrigerator temperatures are best for berries and most types of fruit such as apples, apricots, grapes, peaches, plums, etc. Citrus fruits can be kept for reasonable periods in a refrigerator, but when grapefruit and lemons are held for several weeks at temperatures below 10° C. (50° F.), they may show pitting of the skin and discoloration of the flesh. Other tropical fruits such as bananas, avocados, and pineapples are best stored above 10° C. (50° F.) to avoid chilling injury. Slightly unripe fruits that are sound will ripen if held at room temperature, but they should not be placed in the sun. Cantaloupes will soften at room temperatures but will not improve in flavor. For this reason they are best purchased when ripe or almost ripe.

Selection
Fresh Fruits

Because of modern transportation and the popularity of fruits, a wide variety is now available on the market at all times of the year. It is possible, for instance, to have at one meal a salad or fruit cup containing grapefruit from Florida, bananas from Central America, and grapes from California. Imported fruits are also available, marked with the name of the country in which they were grown. In buying fruits, it is necessary to consider the limitations of the food budget, the tastes of the family, and the season of the year. It is important to know when particular fruits are available and how to evaluate their quality.

The availability of fresh fruits during each month of the year is shown in Table 3–2. Although the seasons for locally grown fruits differ in various parts of the United States, the table can be considered representative of the entire country because of the rapid transportation of fresh produce. It can be seen that some fruits such as apples, bananas, and citrus fruits are in good supply during a large part of the year, whereas others like berries and plums are available only during certain months.

Grades for fresh fruits and vegetables are determined on the basis of color, size, shape, degree of maturity, and freedom from defects. Defects may be caused by dirt, freezing, disease, insects, mechanical injury, or other means. Although there is no marked difference in the nutritive value of first and second grade fruits, there is a difference in appearance and waste. On the wholesale market most fresh fruits and vegetables are sold on the basis of U.S. grades. Premium grades are U.S. Extra Fancy, which applies only to

Table 3–2. *Monthly Availability of Fresh Fruit* * †

	Jan.	Feb.	March	April	May	June	July	August	Sept.	Oct.	Nov.	Dec.
					G = Good Supply	F = Fair Supply	S = Small Supply					
Apples	G	G	G	G	F	S	S	S	G	G	G	G
Apricots					S	G	G	S				
Avocados	G	G	G	G	G	F	F	F	F	F	G	G
Bananas	G	G	G	G	G	G	G	G	G	G	G	G
Berries (Misc.)					S	G	G	G	S	S	S	
Blueberries					S	G	G	G	S			
Cantaloupes		S	S	S	F	G	G	G	G	S	S	
Cherries					S	G	G	S	S			
Cranberries	S								F	F	G	G
Dates	G	F	F	S	S	S	S	S	S	G	G	G
Figs						F	G	G	F			
Grapefruit	G	G	G	G	G	F	S	S	S	G	G	G
Grapes	S	S	S	S	S	F	G	G	G	G	G	F
Honeydews		F	G	F	F	G	G	G	G	G	S	S
Lemons	G	G	G	G	G	G	G	G	G	G	G	G
Limes	S	S	S	S	G	G	G	F	F	F	S	G
Mangoes			S	F	G	G	G	F	S			
Nectarines	S	S				F	G	G	G	S		
Oranges	G	G	G	G	G	F	S	S	S	F	G	G
Papayas	S	S	S	S	F	S	S	S	S	F	S	S
Peaches					S	G	G	G	G	S		
Pears	F	F	F	F	F	S	S	G	G	G	G	F
Pineapple	S	F	G	G	G	G	F	F	S	F	F	F
Plums-Prunes						G	G	G	G	S		
Strawberries	S	S	F	G	G	G	G	S	S	S	S	S
Tangelos	F	S							S	F	G	G
Tangerines	G	S	S	S	S	S				S	G	G
Watermelons	S	S	S	S	F	G	G	G	S	S	S	S

* From *Food for Us All. The Yearbook of Agriculture*, 1969. United States Department of Agriculture, Washington, D.C., p. 161.

† Each year's production will vary. This chart is an estimate of probable availability.

apples, and U.S. Fancy. Other grades include U.S. Extra No. 1, U.S. No. 1, U.S. No. 2, and U.S. Combination.

Some fruits are divided on the basis of size as well as grade. The size and grade designations are independent of one another because fruit of small, medium, or large size can be of top quality. Some fruit, such as apples and citrus fruit, are graded for size according to the number that can be packed in a box of standard size. Of course the larger the number of fruits in the box, the smaller is their size.

Because grades for fresh fruits are often not available on the retail market, some points to consider in the selection of individual fruits are given below.

More detailed suggestions are given by Smith.[4] Although appearance and quality are often closely related, fine appearance does not always mean fine quality. A fruit that looks very attractive may have relatively poor quality because of over-maturity or because of its variety. It is also true that fruit with a poor appearance caused by surface imperfections may be of excellent quality when eaten.

Apples. Apples are best when they are well colored for the variety, free from bruises, fresh and firm. Table 3–3 shows some of the varieties commonly used in the United States, the months when they are available, and the suitability of the varieties for different uses. It will be seen that a variety that is excellent for one purpose may not be equally good for another purpose. Store apples in the refrigerator.

When they are stored, apples become more mature and therefore softer. For this reason apples are likely to be of better quality soon after harvest than they are in the spring. Apples of good harvest quality, however, were acceptable for eating raw when held for as long as five months at 5° C. (40° F.) and for six months or more at 0° C. (32° F.). The same was true in general for apples used in making applesauce and baking.[5]

Apricots. Apricots are best when ripened on the tree to a firm ripe stage. When picked too green, they may not ripen completely in storage. For this reason the color of apricots should be a strong orange or golden yellow when they are purchased. Store ripe apricots uncovered in the refrigerator.

Avocados. When right for eating, avocados are as soft as a ripe pear. The flavor is delicate and nut-like, and the texture soft and buttery. It is interesting to notice that avocados are much higher than most fruits in fat, containing from 5 to 20 per cent, depending upon the variety and time of harvest. Avocados are best purchased when firm and then allowed to soften by keeping at room temperature for three to five days, or for a longer period in the refrigerator at 10° C. (50° F.) or above.

Bananas. Bananas are best when they are harvested in a mature-green stage, then ripened at normal room temperature. Fruit that is yellow or greenish-yellow is selected for cooking or for use within a few days, but for immediate consumption bananas that are yellow with small brown flecks are best. Bananas should not be stored in a refrigerator except for short periods necessary to chill a banana salad or dessert.

[4] M. E. Smith. *How to Buy Fresh Fruits.* Home and Garden Bulletin No. 141. United States Department of Agriculture, Washington, D.C., 1967.

[5] M. E. Kirkpatrick, A. O. Mackey, R. R. Little, R. H. Matthews, and C. E. Falatko. *Quality of Apples for Household Use.* Home Economics Research Report No. 8. United States Department of Agriculture, Washington, D.C., 1959.

Table 3–3. *Know Your Apples* *

Variety	Season	Description (Size, color, and flavor)	Raw	General cooking	Baking whole
Cortland	October to March	Medium to large. Bright striped red. Juicy, moderately tart, crisp, tender, fragrant.	●	●	
Red Delicious	October to April	Medium to large. Deep red, five knobs on blossom end. Sweet, firm, tender, fragrant.	●		
Golden Delicious	October to March	Medium to large. Yellow. Sweet, firm, crisp, tender.	●	●	
Grimes Golden	October to February	Small to medium. Yellow with small dark specks. Moderately juicy, slightly tart, firm, crisp, tender, fragrant.	●	●	
Jonathan	October to February	Small to medium. Deep red. Juicy, moderately tart, tender, crisp, fragrant.	●	●	
McIntosh	October to March	Medium. Bright dark red with stripes. Juicy, moderately tart, tender, crisp, fragrant.	●	●	
Northern Spy	October to March	Large. Bright striped red. Juicy, moderately tart, firm, crisp, tender, fragrant.	●	●	●
Rome Beauty	November to May	Large. Yellow mingled with red. Juicy, slightly tart, firm, rather crisp.	●	●	●
Stayman	November to April	Medium to large. Dull striped red. Juicy, tart, firm, crisp.	●	●	●
Winesap	January to May	Small to medium. Deep bright red with small scattered white dots. Juicy, slightly tart, hard, crisp, fragrant.	●	●	●
Yellow Newtown	February to June	Medium. Yellow. Juicy, moderately tart, hard, crisp.	●	●	
York Imperial	October to April	Medium to large. Light or purplish red over yellow. Lopsided shape, usually. Slightly tart, hard, crisp.	●	●	●

* From *Apples in Appealing Ways.* Home and Garden Bulletin No. 161 United States Department of Agriculture, 1969, p. 4

Berries. Berries are best when they are fresh, clean, firm, plump, and well colored for the type. They should be free of excess moisture, dirt, mold, or decay. Store berries unwashed and uncovered in the refrigerator.

Cherries. Cherries are best when they are fresh, bright, plump, and a good color for the variety. They should not be soft, overripe, or shriveled and should be free from decay, mold, skin breaks, and cracks. Store cherries unwashed and uncovered in the refrigerator.

Citrus Fruits. Oranges and grapefruit make up the bulk of the citrus crop, but this group also includes lemons, limes, tangerines, tangelos, and kumquats. Tangelos are a cross between the tangerine and the grapefruit, whereas kumquats look like tiny oranges. There are two main citrus growing areas in the United States—the southeastern area that includes Florida and the Gulf states and the western area that includes California and Arizona.

Fruit from both areas is excellent in quality although somewhat different in certain characteristics. Because of the bright sunshine and low humidity in California and Arizona, fruit from this area may have a brighter color than fruit from the Southeast. When citrus fruit ripens on the tree, it first turns a ripe color and then if not picked may turn green again, although it is still ripe. Some varieties may show some green even when ripe. The green color of California fruit can be removed by introducing ethylene gas as already described. Florida fruit, however, does not respond well to this treatment and for this reason is sometimes rubbed with color, which does not affect the edible quality of the fruit. If this is done, the fruit must be labeled "color added."

Grapefruit are best when they are firm, heavy for their size, well shaped, and rather smooth. A thick skin is undesirable, but a russet color has little effect on quality. Grapefruit are available with and without seeds and with white or pink flesh.

Most of the lemons sold in the United States come from California, although some are shipped from Arizona, and a few are produced in Texas and Florida for local consumption. Good quality lemons are firm, bright, and heavy for their size, with a reasonably fine textured skin. Light colored fruit is usually highest in acid, while a deeper yellow color indicates less acidity.

Oranges of highest quality are firm, heavy for their size, of good color, and have reasonably fine textured skin. Puffy or spongy oranges are likely to be light in weight, low in juice content, and poor in quality.

Citrus fruit, except tangerines, may be stored in a cool room or uncovered in the refrigerator. Tangerines should be stored covered in the refrigerator.

Grapes. Grapes are sometimes divided into the American type that has a skin that slips off easily and the European type with an adherent skin. The common varieties of American grapes are Concord, Delaware, Niagara, Catawba, and Scuppernong. They are grown in the eastern and midwestern states. The European type, grown in the western states, has a higher sugar and solids content than do most of the American types. Some popular grapes of the European type are Malaga, Muscat, Thompson Seedless, Emperor, Ribier, and Tokay. Grapes of either type are best when they are mature, plump, fresh in appearance, and firmly attached to their stems. High quality for the variety usually indicates good sugar content and flavor. Store grapes unwashed and uncovered in the refrigerator.

Melons. This group includes cantaloupes (also called muskmelons), casaba, cranshaw, honeyball, honeydew, Persian, and watermelons. Selection of these fruits for best quality and flavor is difficult and may test the skill of the most experienced buyer. Except in watermelons, ripeness is indicated by a slight softening of a small area around the "eye" at the blossom end. Evidence of easy, natural separation of the melon from the stem at harvest time indicates ripeness, as does a shift in color from greenish to yellowish in many melons. The distinctive odor of the melon is most pronounced when it is fully ripened. Some types of melons are not available in retail markets fully ripe but are selected when mature enough that they will ripen fully in a few days at ordinary room temperature. It is important, however, that

Fig. 3–4. *Varieties of melons are shown whole and cut into small balls and arranged in a water-melon boat.*

cantaloupes and watermelons be ripened adequately before they are picked because they do not improve in flavor and sweetness after harvest. Store ripe melons in the refrigerator. Place those with a noticeable odor in a plastic bag.

Peaches. Peaches are classified as yellow-flesh and white-flesh, each having both freestone and clingstone varieties. The freestone varieties are popular for fresh dessert use and for freezing, while clingstone varieties are used mainly for commercial canning. Tree-ripened peaches have a better flavor than those ripened in storage but are so perishable that they cannot be shipped for long distances. For this reason they are frequently picked in a mature-hard stage and may be too firm for immediate use. If the color is creamy or yellowish, the peaches will ripen in a reasonably satisfactory manner, but if the peaches are picked so immature that they cannot ripen, they may shrivel or become flabby. High quality peaches are bright in color, plump, fresh looking, fairly firm to firm, and free from bruises. Store ripe peaches uncovered in the refrigerator.

Pears. Of the many varieties of pears grown in the United States, the Bartlett variety, a late summer pear, is one of the most popular for dessert use and also for commercial and home canning. Many other varieties are, however, being grown principally in the western states and are held in cold storage so that pears of some variety are available throughout the year. These are mostly winter pears such as Anjou, Bosc, Winter Nelis, and Comice. Pears are best picked when mature but still hard and green. They are then ripened during transit and in storage. They can be selected before they are fully ripe as they will continue to ripen satisfactorily at room temperature. They are best when plump, fairly firm to firm, and free from bruises. They can, of course, be selected fully ripe for immediate use. Store ripe pears in the refrigerator.

Pineapples. Because pineapples are shipped to the United States from Hawaii, Puerto Rico, Bermuda, Costa Rica, Mexico, and the Bahamas, they are picked when mature but hard so that they will reach the market in good condition. They ripen during shipment and storage, becoming bright and from yellow to reddish-brown in color when they are mature. Good pine-apples have a fragrant odor and are heavy in relation to their size. Store ripe pineapples in the refrigerator.

Plums. A large variety of plums is now grown and used for dessert purposes. The color of the fully ripe plum may be yellowish green, orange red, or purplish blue depending upon the variety. Plums of good quality are plump, clean, fresh in appearance, fully colored for the variety, and soft enough to yield to slight pressure. Store ripe plums in the refrigerator.

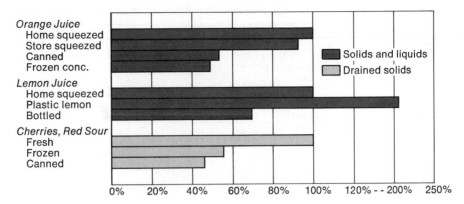

(The 207% for plastic lemon not proportional)

Fig. 3–5. *Comparative cost of fruits which were least expensive in the processed form.* (Calculated from Harp and Dunham, in *Comparative Costs to Consumers of Convenience Foods and Home-Prepared Foods.* Marketing Research Report No. 609, U.S. Department of Agriculture, 1963.)

Processed Fruits

The prices of some of the most popular fruits when purchased in fresh, frozen, and canned form have been compared. Figure 3–5 indicates that the processed fruit juices were cheaper than the freshly squeezed juice with the exception of lemon juice in plastic-lemon containers, perhaps due to the higher cost of the plastic-lemon packaging and a small sales volume. The low retail price for the processed juices is made possible by small retail margins of profit and lower transportation charges for the processed than for the fresh product.

Processed red sour cherries were cheaper than fresh, but the other processed fruit products shown in Figure 3–6 were more expensive in the processed than in the fresh form when the drained solids were compared. When compared on the solids and liquids basis, canned pineapple and grapefruit were less expensive than fresh.

Wise management of expenditures made for fruits and vegetables involves a selection among fresh fruits and those processed by various methods. The relationships shown in Figures 3–5 and 3–6 cannot be expected to represent all possible marketing conditions and they do not include dried fruits, which may sometimes be more economical than fruits processed by other methods. Fresh fruits available in abundance at the height of the season may represent a more economical buy than is shown in the figures.

Grades. United States grades[6] are available for a wide variety of processed fruits and vegetables—canned, frozen, and dried, as well as for related

---

[6] *Food For Us All. The Yearbook of Agriculture, 1969.* United States Department of Agriculture, Washington, D.C., pp. 160–161.

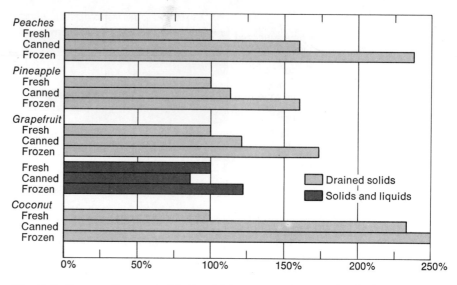

Fig. 3–6. *Comparative cost of fruits which were most expensive in the processed form.* (Calculated from Harp and Dunham, in *Comparative Costs to Consumers of Convenience Foods and Home-Prepared Foods.* Marketing Research Report No. 609, U.S. Department of Agriculture, 1963.)

products such as jams, jellies, olives, peanut butter, and pickles. The same grades are used for most of these products, although for a few products the grade names may deviate slightly from the standard names to conform with commercial practices of long standing.

U.S. Grade A or U.S. Fancy is an excellent quality in which the products are uniform in size and color, practically free from blemishes, and have attained the proper degree of maturity or tenderness. This grade is desirable for use in desserts, salads, and other dishes in which appearance and texture are important.

U.S. Grade B or U.S. Choice (Extra Standard for vegetables) is a good quality that includes a high proportion of processed fruits and vegetables. The products may not be as uniform in size and color or as tender or free from blemishes as Grade A products. This grade is, however, quite satisfactory for most uses.

U.S. Grade C or U.S. Standard is used for processed fruits and vegetables of fairly high quality. They are just as wholesome and may be as nutritious as the higher grades. They are a good buy for use in dishes like puddings or pies for which appearance and tenderness are not of great importance.

U.S. Grade D or Substandard is sometimes used for processed fruits that do not meet the specifications for U.S. Grade C, but which are wholesome food.

The inspection system is not universally used because it is not compulsory except as it may be required for the purchases of certain buyers and of federal and state purchasing departments. Manufacturers must request and pay the cost of inspection. The terms Grade A, Grade B, or Grade C may be used on labels of foods that have not been inspected if the products meet specifications for the grade claimed. Improper use of the grades means that the products are mislabeled and therefore the manufacturer is open to prosecution.

Money can be saved by buying as low a grade as is satisfactory for the use intended and by comparing the price of various brands because some of them may be less expensive for the same quality than others. Savings can sometimes be made by buying large containers. The size of the container purchased must be considered in relation to the amount needed for a meal and the storage facilities available for any excess. Canned or frozen fruit is sometimes put on sale just before the new crop is available. Such merchandise may be a good buy for immediate use but not for holding over a long period of time, because the quality of canned or frozen foods that have been stored for long periods is usually less desirable than that of foods stored for shorter periods.

Canned Fruit. In addition to the grade, the label of canned fruit often indicates strength of the sugar syrup used. The strength of syrup that is desirable depends on the use that is to be made of the fruit and on the personal

Fig. 3–7. *Grades of canned fruits and vegetables help the consumer select the quality which will be satisfactory for the use intended.*

preferences and dietary needs of those who will consume it. Fruit packed in water is available on some markets for use by diabetics and in low calorie diets. The label also may indicate how the fruit has been prepared. Pineapple, for example, may be available as slices, cubes, chunks, spears, tidbits, and crushed.

In buying canned food of any kind, including fruit, it is wise to avoid purchasing dented cans because a small amount of pressure may cause such cans to leak and therefore to spoil. Cans that have bulged should be discarded because bulging usually indicates spoilage that has resulted in the formation of gas. An exception to this rule is cans of carbonated beverages, the ends of which bulge because of the deliberate addition of gas in canning. A discoloration of the inside of the can is frequently observed with certain foods. This discoloration is harmless and can be compared with the discoloration of silver by egg.

When not all of the food has been used for a meal, the remainder can safely be left in the can, covered, and placed in the refrigerator. Because the can and its contents have been rendered sterile in the canning process, there is no harm in such a practice, and it may be safer than transferring the food to another container which is not likely to be sterile.

The volume and weight of foods in cans or jars of various sizes are shown in Table 3–4. The volume held by a can of a certain size is always the same, but the weight varies with the density of the food.

Frozen Fruit. A wide variety of frozen fruits packed in various ways is now available. Paperboard containers holding from 10 to 20 ounces are often used, although packages having a larger capacity are also used. Packages which are stained, evidence of defrosting during transport or storage, should be avoided, as should packages which are not hard frozen. The amount of frozen food that can be purchased conveniently at one time depends upon the storage facilities that are available. Frozen foods should be stored at or near −18° C. (0° F.).

Dried Fruit. Although the per capita consumption of dried fruits has decreased in recent years, important amounts are still used. Dried fruits offer variety and have a distinctive taste and texture that is preferred for some purposes. In drying fruits, much of the water is removed from the mature fruit. The water content is indeed reduced so much that bacteria and molds are unable to grow on dried fruits under ordinary storage conditions. The ease with which fruits can be dried in some climates and with which they can be shipped and stored without special packaging or refrigeration explain why drying has been used as a method of food preservation since antiquity. Usually dried fruits can be stored in a closed container at room temperature, but in especially hot and humid weather it may be best to store them in the refrigerator to prevent the possibility of mold growth.

Table 3–4. *Common Container Sizes for Canned Foods* *

Industry Term	Container		Products
	Consumer Description		
	Approximate Net Weight (check label)	Approximate Cups	
8 ounce	8 oz.	1	Fruits, vegetables, specialties.† 2 servings.
Picnic	10½ to 12 oz.	1¼	Condensed soups, small quantities of fruits, vegetables, meat and fish products, specialties.† 3 servings.
12 ounce (vacuum)	12 oz.	1½	Used largely for vacuum packed corn. 3 to 4 servings.
No. 300	14 to 16 oz.	1¾	Pork and beans, baked beans, meat products, cranberry sauce, blueberries, specialties.† 3 to 4 servings.
No. 303	16 to 17 oz.	2	Fruits, vegetables, meat products, ready-to-serve soups, specialties.† 4 servings.
No. 2	1 lb. 4 oz. or 1 pt. 4 fl. oz.	2½	Juices, ready-to-serve soups, specialties,† and a few fruits and vegetables. 5 servings.
No. 2½	1 lb. 13 oz.	3½	Fruits, some vegetables (pumpkin, sauerkraut, spinach and other greens, tomatoes). 5 to 7 servings.
No. 3 cylinder	3 lb. 3 oz. or 1 qt. 14 fl. oz.	5¾	Fruit and vegetable juices, pork and beans, condensed soup and some vegetables for institutional use. 10 to 12 servings.
No. 10	6½ lb. to 7 lb. 5 oz.	12–13	Fruits, vegetables for restaurant and institutional use. 25 servings.

* From *Canned Food Tables*. National Canners Association, Washington, D.C., Revised 1965.
† Specialties: Usually a food combination such as macaroni, spaghetti, Spanish style rice, Mexican type foods, Chinese foods, tomato aspic, etc.

Fruit can be dried in the sun or by the application of artificial heat and sometimes forced ventilation. It may be dipped in lye to help remove the peel or to make the peel more tender. It is often treated with sulfur dioxide, usually produced by burning sulfur. Sulfur dioxide prevents the darkening of the fruit during drying and also protects certain vitamins from oxidation. Trays of fruit are then dried in the sun or indoors with artificial heat and either natural ventilation or a forced draft of air. The moisture content of most dried fruits varies from 18 to 25 per cent depending upon the fruit. Any sulfur that remains on the fruit after drying goes off in the steam during cooking.

Some dried fruits contain more than the usual 18 to 25 per cent moisture. If the food is sold in a package that is completely sealed and therefore protected from contamination, it may contain more than 25 per cent moisture. Such dried fruit is softer and therefore easier to eat without cooking than ordinary dried fruit. It is also easy to rehydrate and cook.

Vacuum drying is a comparatively new method of drying that results in fruits of very low moisture content, often about 2.5 to 5 per cent, and therefore of excellent keeping qualities. The federal regulations now refer to such foods as "dehydrated" in comparison to food of higher moisture content prepared by conventional drying methods, which is called "dried" fruit. This usage is in contrast to an earlier use of the term dehydration to mean fruits dried by the use of artificial heat, rather than in the sun. Vacuum dried foods are usually of superior quality because the use of a vacuum makes it possible to dry at a low temperature, and the absence of air prevents some of the changes in quality that occur during ordinary drying. Because of their extremely low moisture content, these foods are usually packaged in cans to prevent the absorption of moisture from the air. As might be expected from the description, vacuum drying is a more expensive process than most other forms of drying. It does, however, offer the opportunity to produce dehydrated foods of superior quality. Freeze-drying, a process mentioned on pages 573–574, is used for fruits intended for special purposes.

Dried fruit juices of good quality can be prepared by foam-mat drying.[7] In this process, a foam is prepared by adding a stabilizer to the concentrated juice. The foam is forced through a press into strips like spaghetti, which are then dried to about 1 per cent moisture.

Another new method of drying which is used for fruits like apples and blueberries is explosive puffing.[8] After partial drying, the fruit is heated under pressure and then is ejected from the container. The sudden drop in pressure vaporizes some of the water in the fruit, producing a porous structure. Drying is then continued to the desired moisture content. The puffed fruit dries more rapidly than fruit that has not been puffed.

Nutritive Value

The nutritive value of some common fruits is shown in Table 3–5. The protein and fat are not included because these nutrients are low in most fruits except avocados and olives which contain a higher proportion of fat than other fruits. Fruits contain indigestible fiber in the form of cellulose, which is partly responsible for their characteristic texture. The crispness of

[7] U.S.D.A. Creates Grapefruit Juice Powder. *Food Engineering*, 36: 100–101 (May, 1964).

[8] N. H. Eisenhardt, R. K. Eskew, and J. Cording, Jr. Explosive Puffing Applied to Apples and Blueberries. *Food Engineering,* 36: 53–55 (June, 1964).

apples, the hard, grainy particles in some pears, the rather stringy quality of certain plums, and the characteristic segments of oranges are due to the presence of indigestible fiber and to its arrangement in the specific fruit. This fiber, though present in relatively small proportions, makes possible the retention of the high water content characteristic of fruit. During digestion it tends to absorb more water, thus increasing the bulk of the undigested residue in the intestinal tract.

Fruits vary in their content of minerals, but all fruits supply some of these important nutrients. Oranges stand out among the fruits in Table 3–5 for their calcium content, although it will be observed that all of the fruits listed contribute to the calcium and iron content of the diet.

Fruits are especially important in the diet for the vitamins they contain. The yellow fruits, such as apricots, cantaloupes, and peaches, are high in vitamin A value. The B vitamins—thiamine, riboflavin, and niacin—are present in fruits in relatively small amounts. Vitamin C or ascorbic acid is the vitamin that gives fruits their special importance. It is relatively easy to meet the National Research Council's recommended allowance for ascorbic acid if citrus fruits, cantaloupes, strawberries or tomatoes are included in the diet. For this reason the United States Department of Agriculture's Daily Food Guide (described in Chapter 1) includes a citrus fruit or other fruit or vegetable important for vitamin C. It will be noticed in Table 3–5 that adults can meet their daily allowances of ascorbic acid, which is 55–60 mg., by eating one orange or by drinking about one-half cup of orange juice. Grapefruit and grapefruit juice can also be used to meet this requirement. The citrus fruits are especially important sources of ascorbic acid because they are available throughout the year. There are, however, some other seasonal fruits that contain important amounts of this vitamin. For example, either half a cantaloupe or two-thirds cup of raw strawberries is a good substitute for citrus fruits. Some of the fruits that are lower in ascorbic acid than citrus fruits may still make an important contribution to the diet if eaten in relatively large amounts.

The ascorbic acid of fruit varies with the type of fruit, exposure to the sun, and other growing conditions. It is likely to be higher in early fruits than in late fruits. Ascorbic acid decreases gradually during storage, especially at temperatures above 0° C. (32° F.). Bruising, peeling, cutting into pieces, and exposure to air decrease ascorbic acid retention. Peeling apples may result in the loss of 8 to 25 per cent of their ascorbic acid. Cooking fruits also lowers their ascorbic acid content. The loss may be from 25 to 35 per cent for applesauce and as much as 80 per cent for apple pie. Berries are best kept cold, dry, and whole to retain a maximum amount of ascorbic acid. They lose ascorbic acid rapidly if they are bruised or capped before storage. It is evident that the vitamin retention of fruit varies with the treatment, but in general fruits are valuable when they are used raw and when they have the minimum of bruising, cutting, and exposure to air.

Table 3–5. Nutritive Value of Certain Fresh Fruits and Orange Juice *

Fruit	Approx. Measure	Weight gm.	Food Energy calories	Calcium mg.	Iron mg.	Vitamin A value I.U.	Thiamine mg.	Riboflavin mg.	Niacin mg.	Ascorbic Acid mg.
Apples, raw	1 apple	150	70	8	.4	50	.04	.02	.1	3
Apricots, raw	3 apricots	114	55	18	.5	2890	.03	.04	.7	10
Avocados, raw, California	1 avocado	284	370	22	1.3	630	.24	.43	3.5	30
Avocados, raw, Florida	1 avocado	454	390	30	1.8	880	.33	.61	4.9	43
Bananas, raw	1 banana	175	100	10	.8	230	.06	.07	.8	12
Cantaloupes, raw	½ melon	385	60	27	.8	6540†	.08	.06	1.2	63
Grapefruit, raw, white	½ grapefruit	241	45	19	.5	10	.05	.02	.2	44
Grapefruit, raw, pink or red	½ grapefruit	241	50	20	.5	540	.05	.02	.2	44
Grapes, raw, American type, slip skin	1 cup	153	65	15	.4	100	.05	.03	.2	3
Grapes, raw, European type, adherent skin	1 cup	160	95	17	.6	140	.07	.04	.4	6
Lemons, raw	1 lemon	110	20	19	.4	10	.03	.01	.1	39
Oranges, raw	1 orange	180	65	54	.5	260	.13	.05	.5	66
Orange juice, fresh	1 cup	248	110	27	.5	500	.22	.07	1.0	124
Orange juice, canned	1 cup	249	120	25	1.0	500	.17	.05	.7	100
Orange juice, frozen, concentrate: diluted with 3 parts water	1 cup	249	120	25	.2	550	.22	.02	1.0	120
Orange juice, dehyd. crystals, prepared with water	1 cup	248	115	25	.5	500	.20	.07	1.0	109
Peaches, raw	1 peach	114	35	9	.5	1320‡	.02	.05	1.0	7
Pears, raw	1 pear	182	100	13	.5	30	.04	.07	.2	7
Pineapple, raw, diced	1 cup	140	75	24	.7	100	.12	.04	.3	24
Plums, raw, except prunes	1 plum	60	25	7	.3	140	.02	.02	.3	3
Strawberries, raw, capped	1 cup	149	55	31	1.5	90	.04	.10	1.0	88
Tangerines, raw	1 tangerine	116	40	34	.3	360	.05	.02	.1	27
Watermelon, raw	1 wedge 4 by 8 inches	925	115	30	2.1	2510	.13	.13	.7	30

* From *Nutritive Value of Foods.* Home and Garden Bulletin No. 72, Agricultural Research Service, United States Department of Agriculture, Revised 1971.

† Value for varieties with orange-colored flesh; value for varieties with green flesh would be about 540 I.U.

‡ Based on yellow-fleshed varieties.

Citrus fruits retain ascorbic acid well whether they are raw, canned, or frozen, perhaps because of their acidity. Orange juice, whether freshly squeezed, canned, or reconstituted from frozen concentrate or dehydrated crystals, retains most of its ascorbic acid when stored for several days in the refrigerator.[9] In fact, a few hours outside the refrigerator will not result in serious loss. Storage of orange juice is not recommended, however, because a change in flavor occurs before much of the vitamin value is lost. Although orange juice is usually covered when held in a refrigerator, a lid on the orange juice container makes no important difference in the retention of vitamin C. Canned juice may safely be stored in the can until it has been used.[10] There is a loss of edible material and therefore of nutritive value when oranges are squeezed and the juice strained. For this reason the edible yield of strained juice is only about two-thirds to three-fourths that of the orange eaten as sections.

Although fruits lose some of their vitamin content during canning, the losses are not serious. Losses of ascorbic acid during the storage of canned fruits and vegetables are small at temperatures of about 15° C. (60° F.), but the loss increases as the temperature increases. High storage temperatures also have an unfavorable effect on the palatability of canned foods.

Fruit retains its nutritive value well during freezing and during storage of the frozen food. Ascorbic acid is better retained in fruit frozen with sugar or syrup than in fruit frozen without sugar.

Although fruits do not retain vitamins as well during drying as in other methods of preservation, dried fruits contribute some nutrients to the diet and add variety. Lye-dipping tends to destroy vitamin A activity and ascorbic acid, whereas sulfuring protects these two vitamins, probably by preventing oxidation.

Whatever the method of preparation, the solution of nutrients from fruits is unlikely to be a problem because the liquid in which fruits are cooked is seldom discarded. In fact, some people consider it more tempting than the fruit itself.

Preparation
Raw Fruit

Most fresh fruits, when thoroughly ripe, are suitable for serving raw. This method makes it possible to obtain the full value of the fruit without the loss through cooking of such nutrients as ascorbic acid. The first step in preparation is washing, which is necessary because fruit collects dust and microorganisms while growing and may also carry a residue of the spray used to prevent spoilage by fungi and insects. The Federal Food and Drug Administration requires that raw agricultural products shipped across state

[9] A. Lopez, W. A. Krehl, and E. Good. Influence of Time and Temperature on Ascorbic Acid Stability. *Journal of The American Dietetic Association.* 50: 308–310 (1967).

[10] *Food. The Yearbook of Agriculture, 1959,* United States Department of Agriculture, Washington, D.C., p. 484.

Courtesy of Calavo Growers of California

Fig. 3–8. *Avocados may be cut lengthwise around the seed, peeled, and sliced, or cut crosswise into rings or half rings, and then peeled. The fruit may be halved, the seed removed, and small balls scooped out of the unpeeled halves.*

lines do not contain unsafe pesticide residues but does not, of course, regulate locally grown and marketed produce. Special machines are used to remove spray residue from some of the larger fruits before they reach the market.

When fruit is to be served raw, it is often cut up in some way before it is served. The way in which it is cut depends upon the fruit, and perhaps the only general rules that can be given are that overhandling makes the fruit unattractive and that large pieces of fruit are often preferred to smaller pieces in which the identity of the fruit may be lost. Apples are usually peeled before they are sliced, but if added color is desired, as for a salad, they can be sliced without peeling.

Citrus fruits can be prepared in several ways. The peel can be removed with the fingers and the sections eaten with the adhering membrane. Grapefruit and large oranges can be cut in half, the sections loosened from the membrane with a knife, and then eaten with a spoon. Or the peel and outer membrane can be cut away by a continuous circular method and sections of the fruit then removed with a knife from the membrane between them. If

Fig. 3–9. Grapefruit and large oranges can be cut in half, the central core removed, and the sections loosened from the membranes with a knife.

Courtesy of the Florida Citrus Commission

Fig. 3–10. The peel and outer membrane can be cut away by a continuous circular method and sections of the fruit removed with a knife from the membrane between them. A more rapid method of cutting citrus fruit is to slice the fruit perpendicular to the central core, forming wheel-shaped pieces.

Courtesy of Sunkist Growers, Inc.

a faster method is desired, chunks of the flesh with some of the accompanying membrane can be cut off and away from the membranes in the center of the fruit. The membranes that form a central core in the orange or grapefruit are discarded after most of the flesh has been cut from it. An even more rapid method of cutting citrus fruit is to slice the fruit perpendicular to the central core, forming wheel-shaped pieces.

Some fruits such as apples, bananas, and pears (fruits low in ascorbic acid) darken rapidly when cut because enzymes[11] cause chemical changes in the fruit. As long as adequate ascorbic acid is present the chemical change does not progress to the stage where browning occurs. When the ascorbic acid is exhausted the chemical reaction continues to the place irreversible browning results. Dipping the fruit in citrus juices helps protect it from such discoloration. Solutions of ascorbic acid or of acids such as citric or tartaric are also effective. Other ways to prevent such browning are by the addition of sugar or a syrup to the fruit as is often done before freezing or by heating the fruit to the boiling point. The sugar or syrup slows down the action of the enzymes and protects the fruit from air. Heating fruit prevents discoloration by destroying the enzymes but is undesirable for some purposes because it softens and partially cooks the fruit.

Cooked Fruit

Sometimes fruit is cooked for variety, to make it more palatable, to increase its keeping quality, to soften cellulose, or to cook the starch. Green apples, for example, are much improved by cooking because of their starch content. The storage period for strawberries and the other highly perishable fruits may be extended several days by cooking.

Fruits cooked on top of the range are said to be stewed. They are cooked in water if a soft product is desired, or in a syrup for a firmer product that holds its shape. Stewing is best done slowly for a short time in a small amount of water in a deep, well-covered pan. Rapid cooking tends to break up the fruit and to cause the escape of volatile flavoring compounds. The use of a minimum amount of sugar helps to complement the natural flavor of the fruit.

Apples for sauce are often cooked in water, and sugar is added after cooking. The apples are washed, sliced, and cored before cooking. If desired, they can be peeled and, after cooking, either left in the form of slices or put through a sieve. They can also be cooked without peeling and put through a sieve after cooking. This has the advantages of greater speed, less waste, and a darker color in the finished product because of the color of the peels. In any case, about one tablespoon of water per apple is added, the pan is covered and placed over low heat, and the apples are then cooked until tender. Sugar is added to taste after the apples are cooked and strained.

---

[11] Enzymes are protein substances that are produced by living cells and accelerate specific chemical reactions without being destroyed in the process.

Table 3–6. *Proportion of Sugar to Fruit for Sauces, Compotes, and Preserves*

Fruit	Sauce	Compote	Preserves
Apples, 2 lbs.	$1/2$–1 cup	1–2 cups	3 cups
Cherries, 2 lbs.	1 cup	——	4 cups
Peaches, 2 lbs.	$1\frac{1}{3}$ cups	$1\frac{1}{2}$–3 cups	4 cups
Pears, 2 lbs.	1 cup	$1\frac{1}{2}$–3 cups	4 cups
Plums, 2 lbs.	1 cup	$1\frac{1}{2}$–3 cups	4 cups

If desired, lemon juice can be added to improve the flavor of apples that lack desirable tartness.

Fruit that is cooked in syrup usually maintains its shape better than fruit cooked in water. If the sugar concentration is about the same as the concentration of soluble materials in the fruit, the fruit tends to hold its shape during cooking. If, however, the sugar concentration in the syrup is higher than that of the fruit, water is withdrawn from the fruit by osmosis, the fruit shrinks, and becomes tough. Firm fruit, like the Kieffer pear, may shrivel and become hard if cooked in a syrup. Such firm fruits are best cooked in water until tender before sugar is added. Sugar can be absorbed into the fruit only after the tissues are softened by cooking. While fruit cooked in syrup is sometimes called a compote, fruits cooked with larger amounts of sugar are called preserves or jam. The proportions of sugar required for sauces, compotes, and preserves are shown in Table 3–6, and the times required for cooking various fruit products in Table 3–7.

Baking is another popular method of preparing fruit. Apples are prepared for baking by coring and slitting the skin at right angles to the core around the middle of the apple, to avoid splitting during cooking. The apples are put in a baking dish, sugar and water added, and the apples are baked either covered or uncovered. Other fruits prepared as necessary can also be baked.

Further variety in fruit dishes can be obtained by varying the ingredients. For example, apples may be baked with brown or maple sugar instead of

Table 3–7. *Approximate Time Required for Cooking Various Fruit Products*

Fruit		Sauce	Compote	Baked
Apples		10 minutes	20–30 minutes	45–60 minutes
Bananas		——	——	20–25 minutes
Cherries		10 minutes	——	——
Peaches		10 minutes	15–25 minutes	30–60 minutes
Pears	Soft	10–30 minutes	20–60 minutes	25 minutes
	Hard	$1\frac{1}{4}$ hours	——	$1\frac{1}{2}$ Hours
Plums		10 minutes	20–25 minutes	——

granulated sugar. They may be stuffed with nuts, raisins, or other dried fruits or baked in a sauce made of sugar, water, flour, and butter. They may be seasoned with spices like nutmeg, cinnamon, or cloves. Similar variations are possible with other fruit dishes.

Frozen Fruit

If desired, frozen fruits can be cooked like fresh fruits. They are, however, often eaten without further preparation. They are best thawed in the un-opened package, which protects them from the air. If the fruit is to be eaten without further preparation, allowing a few ice crystals to remain in the fruit results in a firmer texture than if thawing were complete.

Dried Fruit

Dried fruits can be used in many ways. They can be stewed, made into pies, used in puddings, cookies, cakes, candies, breads, marmalades, sieved and used in whips, or in any number of other desserts. The first step in preparing dried fruits is usually to wash them, although this step can be omitted if the package says that it is unnecessary. The dried fruit may, of course, be eaten without further preparation.

Before or during cooking, it is necessary for the dried fruit to absorb some of the moisture lost during drying. When dried fruit is placed in water, some of the water passes through the cell membranes into the dried fruit because the concentration of sugar, salts, and other soluble compounds is greater within the fruit than in the water. This occurs because of the same forces of osmosis that operate, in the opposite direction, when raw fruit is put into a concentrated sugar syrup. In each case water goes from the less concentrated to the more concentrated side of the cell membrane. As it takes up water, dried fruit becomes more plump, and at the same time some of the sugar and other solids within the dried fruit dissolve in the water.

To prepare dried fruits, cover one pound of fruit with a quart of water. Most dried fruit can be cooked immediately, but if necessary the fruit can be soaked for about an hour or until well plumped before cooking. With any of the methods for rehydration and cooking, the same water is used for cooking as for soaking. If sugar is to be added, it is added during the last 5 minutes of the cooking period. Sugar that is added before cooking delays softening by affecting the ability of the fruit to absorb moisture.

Activities

1. List the fresh fruits for sale in several local stores. Record any information available on their grade, size, variety, and place of origin. Note the price and appearance of the fruit.

2. Select a fruit that is frequently canned. Buy as many brands, grades, and can sizes as possible. Turn out of the cans, code the samples to avoid bias, and compare:

a. The amount of fruit in a can. To do this, drain the fruit and measure or weigh the fruit and the syrup.

b. The quality of the fruit.

c. The cost of comparable amounts of fresh and frozen fruit.

3. Buy bananas varying in ripeness—slightly green, yellow, yellow flecked with brown, and overripe. Compare their taste and texture.

4. Buy some bananas that are slightly green.

a. Store some of them in a refrigerator and some at room temperature for several days. Compare their quality.

b. Place several bananas in a paper bag with the top sealed or wrap in newspapers and leave at room temperature several days. Compare with bananas that have stood unwrapped under the same conditions.

5. Prepare oranges for serving by cutting in several ways. Compare the appearance of the product and the time required for each method.

6. Prepare applesauce in several ways:

a. With different varieties of apples.

b. Cook with and without peeling, then sieve and sweeten.

c. Peel, cook, and divide into 2 portions. Sweeten and serve 1 portion. Sieve, sweeten, and serve the other.

d. Prepare sauce as desired, then add different amounts of sugar.

e. Peel, slice, and divide into 2 portions. Cook 1 portion in water and then sweeten. Cook the other portion in water to which has been added the amount of sugar used for the first portion.

f. Cook sliced apples in covered and uncovered saucepans.

7. Compare apples baked in the oven and glazed on top of the range.

8. Select a fruit and purchase it fresh and in as many processed forms as possible. Prepare according to package directions. Compare the palatability, preparation time, and cost of each form. It will be necessary to weigh or measure the products so that the cost can be calculated for equivalent amounts.

References

Apples in Appealing Ways. U.S. Dept. Agr., Home and Garden Bull. No. 161 (1969).

CHAPMAN, V. J., J. P. SWEENEY, M. E. MARTIN, AND E. H. DAWSON. *Fruits: Consumer Quality Characteristics, Yield, and Preparation Time of Various Market Forms.* U.S. Dept. Agr., Home Econ. Research Rept. No. 29 (1965).

Fruits and Tree Nuts—Bloom, Harvesting, and Marketing Dates, and Principal Producing Counties by States. U.S. Dept. Agr., Agr. Handbook No. 186 (1969).

Fruits in Family Meals, A Guide for Consumers. U.S. Dept. Agr., Home and Garden Bull. No. 125 (1970).

SMITH, M. E. *How to Buy Fresh Fruits,* U.S. Dept. Agr., Home and Garden Bull. No. 141 (1967).

Storing Vegetables and Fruits in Basements, Cellars, Outbuildings, and Pits. U.S. Dept. Agr., Home and Garden Bull. No. 119 (1966).

4

cereals

From earliest time, grain has been man's chief means of subsistence. So important was its production that the Romans and ancient peoples of many other lands believed that the protection of grain was the primary concern of Ceres, one of the most powerful Roman goddesses. Thus from the name Ceres came the term cereal. As indicated by its derivation, the term in the broad sense includes those plants belonging to the grass family which produce grains, and it has now been extended to cover in addition the food products from these grains.

Cereals have played an important part in world affairs. The earliest civilizations were founded upon the growing of cereals, and the importance of cereals continues at the present time. Indeed grain now provides roughly half the calories for the world directly, and much of the other 50 per cent of the calories comes indirectly from cereals. Some of the products that can be said to come directly from cereals are breakfast cereals, flour, starches, flavored shaped snack foods, and baked products. Meat, poultry, and dairy products come indirectly from cereal because cereals are fed to animals.

On each continent there is a wide geographic area well adapted to the growth of one or more of the cereals. The golden ripple of broad fields of ripened wheat is well known in Russia, Canada, Argentina, and the United States. Tasseling corn may be seen in South America, Mexico, and the United States, whereas the domain of rice stretches from Japan, China, India, and Africa to the southern portion of the United States. The cereal that is grown in an area depends upon the climatic and soil conditions. In the past, the discovery of the adaptability of certain grains to new areas has affected the migration and colonization of nations. For example, the discovery that rye could be grown in northern Europe led to the development of that territory. The discovery and use of labor-saving machinery for the growth and harvesting of grain have made it possible to produce much more grain with the same amount of labor than was possible without these devices. Improved genetic strains have resulted in increased yields and improved nutritive value.

Although, as indicated above, the local growing conditions determine what cereals can be produced in a country, in turn, the cereals grown locally determine to a very large extent what grains are used in cooking and thereby affect the food customs of a particular area. In the Orient, where rice is the predominating cereal, the mainstay of the diet is a bowl of rice on which a sauce containing vegetables and meat or fish is used. The scarcity of meat in such areas makes it necessary to stretch the limited supplies by using meat in a sauce on rice rather than serving it as a separate course. Wheat is usually the preferred cereal in areas in which it can be grown because it is used to make bread. Bread can truly be called "the staff of life" in wheat-growing countries. Rye bread is used in the countries of northern Europe where rye is grown, and cornbread or other corn products are used in certain areas of the United States and South America where corn grows well.

In the United States during the last twenty years, the amount of cereal products used has decreased, as shown in Figure 6–1 (page 101). This trend has been influenced by the increasing prosperity of the country and also by the decreased activity of the population as a whole and hence a decreased need for calories.

In this chapter, the structure, processing, and selection of cereals will be considered along with their nutritive value and methods of preparation. Starch cookery, flour, and baked products will be discussed in later chapters.

Structure

Kernels of cereals used as foods are, from a botanical standpoint, the simple dry fruits of the grasses. The fruit, or ovary wall, can scarcely be recognized because as it ripens it turns into a papery structure called the pericarp, or bran. The seed consists of the germ, or embryo, and the endosperm, or white starchy portion of the grain. The endosperm furnishes a temporary food supply of starch and protein for the developing germ or embryo until the roots of the plant can obtain nourishment from outside sources.

Rice and oats have a hull, an outer straw-like protective covering, that is always removed before milling. Except for the hull, these two kernels are similar in many ways to the others shown in Figure 4–1. Because of its importance, the wheat kernel has been selected for discussion. The bran, composed largely of cellulose, is made up of several layers that surround the endosperm. Botanically, the aleurone layer is the outer row of thick-walled cells of the endosperm, but it is removed with the bran during the milling process. This layer contains oil and protein but does not contain gluten or starch. The endosperm, which occupies the largest part of the kernel, is composed mainly of starch granules imbedded in a matrix of protein. In milling, the endosperm to be used for white flour is separated from the bran and germ. The germ, found at one end of the grain, occupies only a small portion of the kernel. The outer layer of the germ, which is adjacent

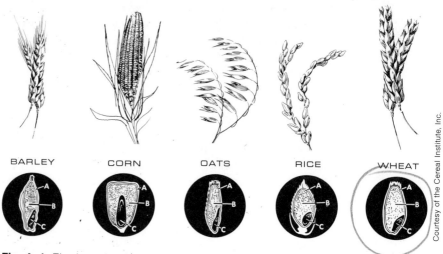

BARLEY   CORN   OATS   RICE   WHEAT

Courtesy of the Cereal Institute, Inc.

Fig. 4–1. *The kernels of the various grains are similar in their structural parts. Shown in the magnified sections are: A, bran; B, endosperm, C, germ.*

to the endosperm, is called the scutellum. It is important because it contains most of the thiamine of the wheat kernel. The entire germ, which is rich in oil and protein, amounts to only 2 to 3 per cent of the weight of the wheat kernel; the bran 14 to 16 per cent; and the endosperm 81 to 84 per cent.

The unbroken kernel of wheat keeps well because its outer layer protects the contents from air and insects. When this protection is destroyed by milling, the fat of the wheat germ tends to become rancid in a short time. Cereal products, such as white flour, that do not contain the germ keep better than whole wheat flour because they are less likely to become rancid or infested with insects.

Processing Breakfast Cereals

Breakfast cereals, now available in bewildering and seemingly ever-increasing variety, can be divided conveniently into hot or ready-to-cook cereals and ready-to-eat cereals. Either type can be made from the whole grain or from the grain that has been refined by removal of the bran and germ. In the latter case, the cereal is often enriched.

Hot Cereals. The grain can be whole, cracked, ground, or rolled for use as hot cereal. Grinding or rolling the grain has the advantage of dividing it into small particles that cook more rapidly than the whole grain. Cracked wheat is made by cracking cleaned wheat into fragments. For farina, the inner portion of the wheat kernel, from which the bran and the germ have been removed, is ground into particles. Some packages of farina[1] carry the statement "Disodium phosphate added for quick cooking." This salt, by making the farina more alkaline, causes the particles to swell faster and to cook in a shorter time. The statement "Enzyme treated for quicker cooking" may also appear on farina packages. This statement means that a protein-splitting enzyme has been added to the farina, which is then moistened and warmed to permit enzyme activity. When the cereal has been changed as much as desired, it is heated to inactivate the enzyme and dried in preparation for packaging and marketing. Farina treated in this way requires substantially less time for cooking than untreated farina.[2]

Oats are usually rolled for use as a breakfast cereal. The outer hull, an inedible straw-like covering, is first removed leaving the bran and germ. The kernel is then steamed for a few minutes, passed through rollers, and dried. Quick-cooking oats are manufactured like regular rolled oats except that the steamed oat kernel is cut into pieces and rolled more thinly than for regular oats. Wheat can also be rolled for use as cereal.

Ready-to-eat Cereals. Ready-to-eat cereals are usually available in great variety. They are made from one cereal or from a mixture of cereals combined with seasonings such as salt, sugar, and malt. They are flaked, granulated, shredded, or puffed, after which they are usually toasted and sometimes coated with sugar. Flakes are prepared by cooking a cereal with flavorings to a heavy paste, forming flakes, and toasting. Shredded wheat is made by cooking a mixture of flour and seasonings, forcing the product through a shredding machine, forming the shreds into a loose biscuit, and baking. Puffed cereals are made by heating the grains under high pressure. When the pressure is released suddenly, the steam within the grain forces out the cell walls and puffs the grain to about eight times its original size.

Like other foods for which there is no federal standard of identity, the ingredients used in cereals must be listed on the package in the order of their predominance by weight. This means that the first ingredient listed is present in the largest amount, the second in the next largest amount, etc. Valuable information concerning the grains and other ingredients used in cereals can be obtained from such labels.

Wheat

Wheat is certainly the most important grain in the United States and in many other countries, but internationally it ranks approximately equal to rice in total output. Varieties of wheat and the milling of flour will be discussed in Chapter 12.

[1] *Code of Federal Regulations,* Title 21, Part 15.140.
[2] *Code of Federal Regulations.*

Bulgur. Probably the oldest ways of using wheat are for making bulgur and porridge. Bulgur was used in Biblical times and remains even today a staple food of the Middle Eastern countries. Bulgur is processed in the United States and is widely available, but often as a gourmet food rather than the staple that it might well be. It is used in this country in combination with meat dishes, as pilaf to accompany meat dishes, in soups, salads, and even desserts. Bulgur may be substituted for rice in many dishes. Bulgur, which is also called "parboiled wheat," is made by heating whole kernels of wheat with water, drying, removing some of the bran, and cracking the kernels. Because it has been precooked, bulgur can be cooked rapidly by the methods used for cooking rice. Bulgur is also sold in canned form.

Macaroni Products. In countries such as Italy macaroni products, also called alimentary pastes or pasta, are at least as important in the diet as bread is in ours. These products are probably of more ancient origin than bread and are widely used because they are simpler to make and can be stored more easily than bread. The most important ingredient in these foods is durum wheat, a hard wheat with a high gluten content and a yellowish color that is highly desirable in macaroni products. In milling durum wheat, the bran and germ are removed and the starchy inner portion is ground coarsely to produce semolina. Semolina is then mixed to a stiff dough with water and forced through a die that shapes the dough. Salt and flavoring are sometimes added. Farina or flour made from wheats other than durum can be used. However, a large proportion of soft wheat produces macaroni that has a dull gray color and a weak pasty structure when cooked. The use of nonfat dry milk (NFDM) in the manufacturing of macaroni was approved a few years ago.[3] Macaroni containing NFDM is said to be more resistant to overcooking and to stickiness when held after cooking than is regular macaroni. It is considered to have texture and flavor characteristics superior to those of standard macaroni.[4]

Macaroni products can be shaped into a wide variety of forms, as shown in Figure 4–2. Macaroni is tube-shaped with a hole in the middle, whereas spaghetti is shaped like a cord with no hole in the center. Vermicelli is like spaghetti except that it has a small diameter. Bow knots, shells, strands, elbows, and other shapes can be made from the same dough. The shaped dough is dried before packaging. Noodles, which are usually shaped like a ribbon, are made from dough similar to that used for macaroni, except that it must contain not less than 5.5 per cent by weight of the solids of egg or egg yolk.

[3] *Code of Federal Regulations,* Title 21, Part 16.13 and Part 16.14.

[4] E. F. Glabe, P. W. Anderson, and P. F. Goldman. Macaroni Made with Nonfat Milk. *Cereal Science Today,* 12: 510–511, 532 (1967).

Courtesy of Durum Wheat Institute

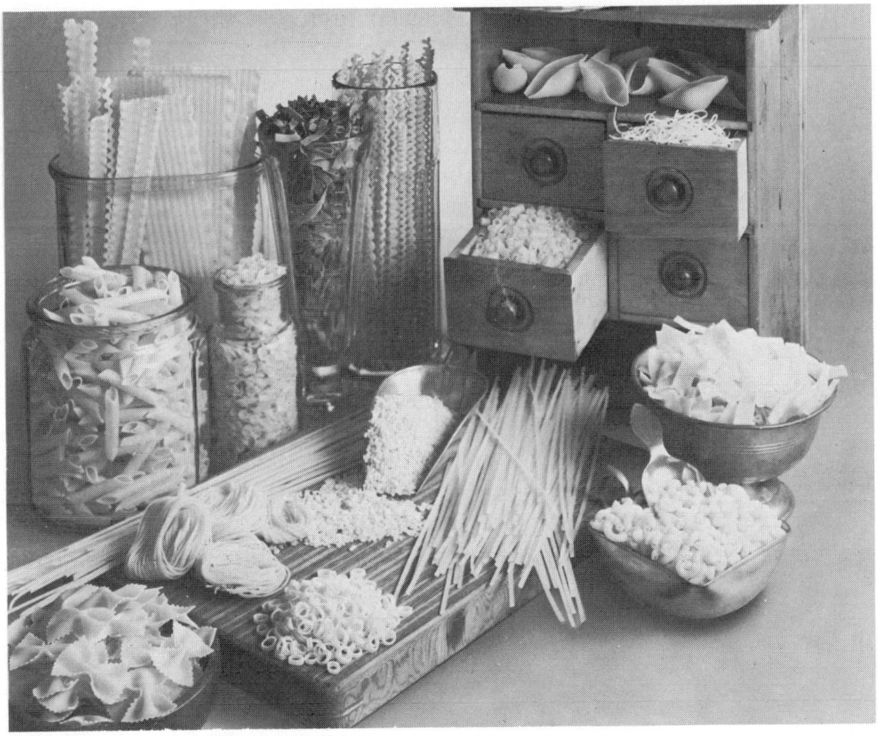

Fig. 4–2. *The well known pastas macaroni, spaghetti, vermicelli, farfalle (butterflies or bows), and conchiglie (conch shells) are shown in this picture as well as many less familiar such as mafalde, tortiglioni, and fusilli (spindles).*

Rice

For many people, rice rather than wheat is the staff of life. Indeed, for about one-half of the world's people rice is the principal food. It is estimated that about 95 per cent of the world's rice crop is produced and consumed in the southeastern part of Asia including adjacent islands.[5] The climate in certain parts of this area is well adapted to the growth of rice, which requires a long growing season with abundant water and relatively high temperatures. The yield of rice per acre is high, especially if two crops a year are grown on the land. In the Orient where labor is cheap, the planting, cultivating, and harvesting are all done by hand.

Most rice is eaten as a boiled grain with seasoning added when available. The whole grain with just the husk removed is known as brown or un-

[5] *Food For Us All. The Yearbook of Agriculture, 1969.* United States Department of Agriculture, Washington, D.C., p. 206.

polished rice. Usually preferred, however, is polished rice, from which the bran has been removed.

To avoid the loss of water-soluble nutrients in the outer layers, brown rice is sometimes parboiled before it is milled. The whole brown rice in the husk is steeped in hot water, steamed, dried, and then milled. During this process water-soluble nutrients in the outer layers and germ diffuse into the kernel where they remain after subsequent removal of the husk and outer layers of the rice. Converted rice is made by a similar process in which both vacuum and pressure are used in addition to steeping and steaming. After milling, parboiled rice contains 70 to 90 per cent of the water-soluble vitamins and minerals that were present in the rough rice. For this reason the nutritive value of parboiled rice is intermediate between that of regular white rice and brown rice. Polished rice can be enriched by a process that will be described in another section. Pre-cooked rice is now available to those who want a product that requires only a few minutes of kitchen preparation. To make it, rice is cooked, rinsed, often enriched, and dried by a patented process.

Many varieties of rice that differ in their characteristics are grown. They are sometimes classified as long-, medium-, and short-grain rice. Long-grain rice produces an especially attractive cooked product with fluffy, dry kernels. The length of the kernel is about four or five times its width, and it is clear and translucent. Long-grain rice is more expensive than medium- or short-grain rice because it requires a long growing season, yields less, and is more expensive to mill than the other products. Medium-grain rice is preferred to short-grain by most consumers. Short-grain rice has a chalky look, rather than the clear translucent look of long-grain, and the grains have a greater tendency to stick together during cooking.

Wild rice is not a true rice but the seed of a grass that grows wild in shallow lakes and marshes along the Great Lakes and the upper Mississippi. It is also known as Indian rice because it was an important food of the American Indian tribes. The Indians harvested wild rice by knocking the ripe grains into their canoes. The kernels are long, narrow, cylindrical in shape, and dark in color. Because it is difficult to cultivate and harvest, only a limited amount of wild rice is available. For this reason its price is far above that of other cereals. It is considered a delicacy by many people, perhaps because of its distinctive flavor, and is much prized as a stuffing for game or as a dish to be served with game.

Corn

After wheat and rice, corn is the third most widely produced cereal, accounting for about 25 per cent of the world's grain. Of this, the United States grows more than 40 per cent, which seems appropriate because corn originated in the new world where the English and European settlers learned of its use from the American Indians and soon made it one of their important crops. Corn is still an important part of the diet of people in Mexico, Central

America, and in the southern United States. Immature ears of corn are used as a vegetable, whereas mature corn is made into uncooked and ready-to-eat breakfast cereals, hominy grits, meal, flour, oil, and starch. Corn is also used for animal feed and industrial purposes.

In the United States the word corn is used to refer to maize or Indian corn. People of other countries refer to the leading cereal crop or crops of the region as corn. For example, in England "corn" refers to wheat or to cereal grains in general that are used as food, whereas in Scotland "corn" usually refers to oats. In the Bible "corn" refers to small cereal grains, probably wheat and barley, that were cultivated in Palestine and Egypt.

Although white corn is favored for hominy and breakfast foods, both yellow and white corn are used for making corn meal. Yellow corn has the advantage of higher vitamin A value because of the carotenoids it contains. Corn meal contains small amounts of crude fiber and fat. Bolted corn meal is similar except that it is ground finer than regular corn meal. Degerminated corn meal is prepared by grinding corn and removing the bran and germ. Corn meal is used for baking and as a hot cereal.

To make hominy, the hull and germ are removed from whole kernels of corn either by soaking in lye or by machinery. That prepared by machinery is called pearl hominy. The endosperm of the corn is left whole for hominy but is broken for grits. Quick-cooking grits can be prepared by lightly steaming hominy grits and compressing them slightly to fracture the particles. Hominy may be cooked in milk or water and served as a vegetable. Corn grits are used for hot cereals and for the preparation of ready-to-eat corn cereals.

Corn oil extracted from the germ by pressure is widely used in salad dressings and other food preparations. Cornstarch obtained from the endosperm of the corn by a wet milling process is the starch most used in household cookery. Cornstarch is also used as a starting material in the production of corn syrup or corn sugar. To make corn syrup, cornstarch is broken down by acid or by enzymes into dextrins, maltose, and glucose. In making corn sugar or glucose, the process is continued longer and the sugar is purified and dried.

Barley

Although barley has been a human food since antiquity and was termed by Pliny as the most ancient food of mankind, it is not widely used at present. Much of the barley now raised is used for feed or for industrial purposes. As a food, barley is consumed in this country mainly as flour or meal for persons allergic to other grains, for infants or invalids, as a breakfast food, and as pearl barley for thickening soups. Pearl barley is the polished grain with the bran removed. Barley lacks gluten to which wheat owes its breadmaking qualities. As a result, a light porous loaf cannot be made from it, but it is possible to combine barley flour with wheat flour in the proportion of one to five and obtain an acceptable loaf of bread. In central and northern

Europe, barley is used in making bread.

Malt is made by sprouting barley. During the process of sprouting, many physical and chemical changes occur within the grain. One of the most important of these is the formation of amylase, an enzyme capable of changing starch to maltose, a sugar that is readily fermented by yeast. Malt is much used with starch in the making of yeast and in the production of fermented products such as certain beverages and bread. Malted barley is also used in malted milk beverages, in coffee substitutes, and in the malt syrup used in bakeries and confectioneries.

Oats

Much of the oats used for human consumption is consumed as oatmeal. The term oatmeal is applied to both ground or cut oats and rolled oats. The preparation of rolled oats has already been described. Oats can also be ground with stones or cut with steel cutters to form a product that re-

Fig. 4–3. *A breakfast of rolled oats is economical and especially appetizing during cold weather.*

Courtesy of The Quaker Oats Company

sembles cracked wheat. The meal can be used for breakfast cereal or in muffins, cookies, cakes, and wafers. Because of its lack of gluten, oatmeal is little used for breadmaking.

Rye

Rye is an important grain in Europe, where it is estimated that in 1970 about one pound of rye was grown for every five pounds of wheat. In the United States, the ratio was about one pound of rye for forty pounds of wheat. Rye is used especially in areas where the climatic conditions are unsuited to the successful growth of other cereals. Much of it is consumed within the country where it is grown. Rye is the only cereal besides wheat that contains protein of such a nature as to make it desirable for breadmaking purposes. The protein of rye doughs is softer, more sticky, and less strong than that of doughs made from hard wheat. For this reason, bread made from rye flour is not so light and porous as that made from wheat flour. Rye flour is often mixed with wheat flour to make a lighter loaf of bread. Only a limited amount of rye is used in breakfast foods.

Buckwheat

Buckwheat is really not a cereal, for it is not the fruit of a grass but the fruit of an herbaceous plant; however, its nature and use so closely resemble that of cereals that it is usually grouped with them. The chief use of buckwheat is for making griddle cakes. It is used in prepared griddle cake flours either alone or in combination with wheat or other flours.

Nutritive Value

Cereal products remain an important food in the United States, even though the amount consumed has decreased considerably during this century. The 1965 nationwide survey of household food consumption showed that 12 per cent of the food dollar was spent for grain products and they furnished 26 per cent of the food energy, 40 per cent of the thiamine, and about 30 per cent of the iron.[6] Cereal products are concentrated foods with moisture contents of less than 15 per cent. Their protein content varies as shown in Table 4–1. Rice contains about 7 per cent; corn 8 or 9 per cent; wheat varies from 9 to 14 per cent depending upon the variety; whereas oatmeal contains about 14 per cent protein. Like other vegetable proteins, those of cereal are incomplete—that is, they do not contain all of the amino acids required by the body. They are, however, well utilized when they are supplemented by the more complete proteins of milk, eggs, or meat. The discovery of "high lysine" corn led to research of other cereals and the finding that large differences exist in the amount and the quality of the protein in all cereal species. This holds great promise for the people whose

[6] S. F. Adelson. Changes in Diets of Households, 1955 to 1965—Implications for Nutrition Education Today. *Journal of Home Economics,* 60: 448–455 (1968).

Table 4–1. Nutrients in Some Cereal Products *

	Approx. Measure	Weight gm.	Food Energy cal.	Protein gm.	Calcium mg.	Iron mg.	Thiamine mg.	Riboflavin mg.	Niacin mg.
Barley, pearled, light, uncooked	1 cup	200	700	16	32	4.0	.24	.10	6.2
Buckwheat flour, light, sifted	1 cup	98	340	6	11	1.0	.08	.04	.4
Bulgur, canned	1 cup	135	245	8	27	1.9	.08	.05	4.1
Corn (hominy) grits †									
Degermed, enriched, cooked	1 cup	245	125	3	2	.7	.10	.07	1.0
Cornmeal †									
Whole-ground, dry	1 cup	122	435	11	24	2.9	.46	.13	2.4
Degermed, enriched, dry form	1 cup	138	500	11	8	4.0	.61	.36	4.8
Degermed, unenriched, dry form	1 cup	138	500	11	8	1.5	.19	.07	1.4
Farina, quick-cooking, enriched, cooked	1 cup	245	105	3	147	.7	.12	.07	1.0
Macaroni, cooked until tender									
Enriched	1 cup	140	155	5	8	1.3	.20	.11	1.5
Unenriched	1 cup	140	155	5	11	.6	.01	.01	.4
Oatmeal or rolled oats, cooked	1 cup	240	130	5	22	1.4	.19	.05	.2
Rice, white									
Enriched, cooked	1 cup	205	225	4	21	1.8	.23	.02	2.1
Enriched instant, ready-to-serve	1 cup	165	180	4	5	1.3	.21	—	1.7
Parboiled, cooked	1 cup	175	185	4	33	1.4	.19	—	2.1
Rice, puffed, added nutrients	1 cup	15	60	1	3	.3	.07	.01	.7
Wheat flours									
Whole-wheat, from hard wheats, stirred	1 cup	120	400	16	49	4.0	.66	.14	5.2
All-purpose or family flour enriched, sifted	1 cup	115	420	12	18	3.3	.51	.30	4.0
Self-rising, enriched	1 cup	125	440	12	331	3.6	.55	.33	4.4
Cake or pastry flour, sifted	1 cup	96	350	7	16	.5	.03	.03	.7
Wheat, puffed, added nutrients	1 cup	15	55	2	4	.6	.08	.03	1.2
Wheat, shredded, plain	1 biscuit	25	90	2	11	.9	.06	.03	1.1
Wheat flakes, added nutrients	1 cup	30	105	3	12	1.3	.19	.04	1.5

* Compiled from *Nutritive Value of Foods.* Home and Garden Bulletin No. 72. Agricultural Research Service. United States Department of Agriculture, 1971. For enriched products, figures are based on minimum levels of enrichment.

† Products made from yellow varieties of corn may contain from 150 to 620 International Units of Vitamin A value; those from white varieties contain only a trace.

diet is largely cereal in nature.[7] In countries that do not have sufficient animal protein, a variety of vegetable proteins can be combined skillfully according to their amino acid content to furnish all of the amino acids that the body requires. Because most of the fat that cereals contain is present in the germ, the fat content of whole grain cereals is greater than that of refined cereals. However, the fat content of cereals in general is low, being about 1 per cent for many of the refined cereals, about 2 per cent for whole wheat, brown rice, or whole grain rye, and about 4 per cent for whole ground corn.

Cereals are high in carbohydrate because the endosperm, which makes up the main part of the grain, is largely starch. The carbohydrate content of most cereals varies from 70 to 80 per cent, being slightly higher for refined cereals than for whole grain cereals, which contain more protein and fat. Most of the food energy in cereals comes from carbohydrates.

The calcium content of most of the cereals is rather low as shown in Table 4–1. Buckwheat appears to be unusually high in this mineral and oatmeal is higher than the other cereals commonly used. Oatmeal, in fact, stands out among the other cereals because it is somewhat higher in protein, calcium, iron, thiamine, and riboflavin, than whole corn, brown rice, or whole wheat.

Because minerals and vitamins are present in higher concentrations in the germ and outer branny layers of the kernel than in the starchy endosperm, refined cereals are lower in minerals and vitamins than whole grain cereals. To improve the nutritive value of the refined cereals, many of them are enriched by the addition of iron, thiamine, riboflavin, and niacin. If the cereal is labeled enriched, the levels of these four nutrients must be between the minimum and maximum levels specified by federal regulations.[8] Enrichment with calcium and vitamin D is optional except that self-rising corn meal and self-rising flour must be enriched with calcium.

Several southern states in which corn meal and grits are staple food for a large part of the population require that these cereals be enriched to the same level as flour and some states even require the enrichment of whole corn meal. The enrichment of corn products is especially important in areas where they are used widely not only because they are often refined but also because even whole corn is lower in some minerals and vitamins, especially in niacin, than whole wheat.

About 80 per cent of the macaroni products now sold in the United States are enriched. Higher levels of nutrients are used than for some of the other enriched cereal products because macaroni products are usually cooked in an excess of water that causes a substantial loss of nutrients.

[7] *Contours of Change. The Yearbook of Agriculture, 1970.* United States Department of Agriculture, Washington, D.C., pp. 326–330.

[8] B. K. Watt and A. L. Merrill. *Composition of Foods—raw, processed, prepared.* Agriculture Handbook No. 8. United States Department of Agriculture, Washington, D.C., 1963, p. 171.

As already indicated, the nutritive value of rice can be improved by parboiling before milling. Such rice, called parboiled or converted, is higher in minerals and water-soluble vitamins than polished rice because these nutrients have been dissolved from the outer coatings and have penetrated the endosperm before removal of the bran and germ. Polished rice can be enriched in two ways. If it is packed in consumer containers and labeled "To retain vitamins do not rinse before or drain after cooking," the rice can be prepared with non-rinse-resistant ingredients. If it is not so labeled or if it is sold in bulk, it must be enriched by a method that will give rinse resistance. This can be done by impregnating a small proportion of the rice with the enrichment ingredients and coating it with water resistant substances. This premix is then added to rice that has not been enriched.

Breakfast cereals that are labeled enriched must follow federal standards for the addition of iron, thiamine, riboflavin, and niacin like other enriched foods. The same minimum levels for these nutrients are used for enriched corn, rice, and farina as for enriched white flour. Many of the breakfast foods now on the market, especially ready-to-serve cereals, contain added nutrients. These usually include one or more of the enrichment nutrients. In some cases calcium, ascorbic acid, or a protein concentrate is also added. There are at present no federal standards regarding the addition of such nutrients in the manufacture of cereals. Information concerning such additions is available on the label. Because some of the additions partially restore losses from milling the whole grain, such cereals have been called "restored." The term is a loose one since the selection of nutrients for addition and the enrichment levels in the final product are determined entirely by the manufacturer.[9]

Because thiamine is more sensitive to heat than the other B-vitamins, its retention during the cooking of cereals has been studied. Thiamine was well retained in most hot cereals cooked for an hour,[10] in cornmeal mush and grits boiled 30 minutes,[11] and in rice cooked in a minimum amount of water.[12]

Selection

Although individual cereal products vary greatly in price, as a group cereals are an economical food that supply about half the calories for the world's three billion people. Because they furnish generous amounts of nutrients at

[9] *Food. The Yearbook of Agriculture, 1959.* United States Department of Agriculture, Washington, D.C., p. 241.

[10] F. Hanning. The Effect of Long Cooking Upon the Stability of Thiamin (Vitamin B_1) in Cereals. *Journal of The American Dietetic Association,* 17: 527–530 (1941).

[11] K. Thomas, J. K. Pace, and J. Whitacre. *Effects of Enrichment on the Thiamine, Riboflavin, and Niacin of Corn Meal and Grits as Prepared for Eating.* Texas Agricultural Experiment Station Bulletin 753 (1952).

[12] M. C. Malakar and S. N. Banerjee. Effect of Cooking Rice with Different Volumes of Water on the Loss of Nutrients and on Digestibility of Rice *in vitro. Food Research,* 24: 751–756 (1959).

low cost, cereals form an even more important part of the food intake in developing nations than in more highly developed nations and in diets of low income families than in those with higher incomes. People tend to substitute more expensive foods for cereals as their income increases.

When selecting cereal products of any type, it is important to select whole grain, enriched, or restored products because of their higher mineral and vitamin content rather than refined unenriched products.

For each of the grains there are usually marketed three forms of cereals: those that are uncooked, those that are partially cooked, and those that are entirely cooked during the process of manufacture. To the first class belong the whole and cracked grains and many of the granular forms. The partially cooked cereals are for the most part rolled or flaked grains although a few of the granular cereals belong in this class.

Although ready-to-eat cereals are often chosen because they are easy to serve, it is pleasant to have at least one hot dish at a meal, especially during the winter months, and often a hot cereal is most satisfactory for this purpose. In addition, uncooked cereals, particularly those that take a long time to cook, are nearly always less expensive per serving than ready-to-eat cereals (Table 4–2).

It is important in buying cereals to notice the weight that is printed on the package, because some small packages, especially of uncooked granular cereals, may weigh more and therefore contain more servings than a bulkier cereal. When the same cereal is offered in packages of several sizes, a large package is likely to be more economical than a small package.

Ready-to-eat cereals vary greatly in their characteristics and also in their price. Those that are advertised as being especially high in certain nutrients are likely to be high priced. Because of this, the consumer may not get any more for her money than when she buys some of the cheaper whole-grain and enriched items. Sugar coated cereals cost more per ounce than many of the common unsweetened cereals.

The period of time during which a cereal can be stored can sometimes be extended by putting it into a tightly covered metal or glass container or into

Table 4–2. *Monthly Cost of Cereals for Family of Five* * *(Each served one ounce daily)*

Type of Cereal	Cost
To-be-cooked	$2.20 to 4.61
Ready-to-eat	$4.02 to 7.52
Sugared	$5.36 to 7.71
Individual packages	$8.18 to 9.49

* Compiled from *Food for Us All. The Yearbook of Agriculture, 1969.* United States Department of Agriculture, p. 282.

a sealed plastic bag. Storage times are shorter for whole grain than for refined cereals. Ready-to-eat cereals that have absorbed moisture from the atmosphere become crisp again if placed in a heated oven for a few minutes.

Preparation

Probably man first consumed cereals as whole grain without preliminary preparation. But after his mastery of fire, he learned that heat increased the palatability of these foods; he parched the grains by heating them over an open flame. Later the discovery was made that the combined application of water and heat improved the cereal further. Cereals today are heated with water either in the process of manufacturing or in the home. Cooking in this way increases palatability, improves appearance, and increases digestibility. Cereals enclosed in bran like whole wheat kernels cannot, of course, be digested. On the other hand, if the grain is crushed or ground, the digestive juices can reach the starch granules and digest them even when they are raw. Digestion of the raw starch is slower than for cooked starch, however, and the raw food is not considered palatable by most people. Heat and moisture soften the cellulose of bran and gelatinize the starch.

Because cereals contain a high percentage of starch, cereal cookery is largely starch cookery. The starch occurs in granules that do not dissolve in cold water but swell when heated with water. On further heating they continue to swell and the starch suspension becomes more clear and thick. Granular cereals, because of the presence of other substances or the size of particles, do not cook so rapidly as do the corresponding starches.[13] The time required for cooking all cereals depends in part upon the size of their particles. Coarse cereals require more time than fine cereals and whole grain such as wheat may even require soaking before cooking. Cooking times are shorter for flaked than for unflaked cereals. Cooking time is also dependent on treatment during processing as enzyme treatment, precooking, or addition of disodium phosphate. The "instant" cereals require only the addition of hot water and they are ready to eat. Those cereals labeled "quick cooking" take 1 to 5 minutes of cooking time in boiling or simmering water—certainly a contrast to the thirty minutes to three hours required for cooking cereals 25 years ago.[14]

Breakfast Cereals

Although the directions on the package are probably the most reliable guide for cooking an individual cereal, some general guides to cookery may prove helpful. It is important to avoid lumps in combining the cereal and the water and in heating the mixture. Three methods are suggested for combining water and cereal without lumping. Any of these methods is suitable for most

[13] O. Hughes, E. Green, and L. Campbell. The Effect of Various Temperatures and Time Periods on the Percentage of Gelatination of Wheat and Corn Starch and of Cereals Containing Those Starches. *Cereal Chemistry,* 15: 795–800 (1938).

[14] *Food For Us All. The Yearbook of Agriculture, 1969,* p. 207.

flake or granular cereals, but for cereals that are ground especially fine Method 2 may be the most satisfactory because lumps sometimes form when such cereals are added to boiling water.

Method 1. Have the salted water boiling rapidly. Slowly add the cereal, stirring the whole or flaked cereals only as much as is necessary, using a fork. This aids in preserving the shape. Cook over direct heat until the cereal has absorbed the water and becomes quite thick.

Method 2. Stir the cold salted water into the cereal. Heat very gradually to the boiling point without stirring. Continue cooking the required time.

Method 3. Stir the cereal into the salted water somewhat below the boiling point. Continue stirring until the boiling point is reached. Continue cooking the required time, stirring occasionally as needed. This method is seldom described but gives excellent results.

After the cereal and salted water have been combined, cooking can be done directly over slow to moderate heat, or the cereal can be cooked indirectly over boiling water in a double boiler. If a partially cooked cereal is being used, a double boiler is usually unnecessary. But for cereals that cook more slowly a double boiler is convenient because less stirring and watching are necessary than when cooking over direct heat. During cooking, changes take place in the flavor as well as in the structure of the cereal. In some cases a better flavor may be obtained if quick-cooking cereals are cooked a few minutes longer than the time given in the directions on the package. However, although it is necessary to cook the cereal long enough for best flavor development, care must be taken not to overcook cereals because they tend to become gummy.

General proportions for use in cereal cookery are shown in Table 4–3. If desired, part or all of the water can be replaced by milk in cooking cereals. If this is done, it is advisable to cook the cereal in a double boiler because the milk is likely to scorch when cooked over direct heat. The milk can be added, of course, in the form of nonfat dry milk. Cereal should not be stirred more than necessary to avoid sticking because excessive stirring tends to break up the structure of cereals and to make them pasty. Keeping the lid on the pan during cooking and serving promptly help to prevent the

Table 4–3. *General Proportions in Cereal Cookery*

Type of Cereal	Amount of Cereal	Amount of Water	Salt
Flaked	1 cup	2 cups	$\frac{1}{2}$ teaspoon
Whole and cracked	1 cup	4 cups	1 teaspoon
Granular	1 cup	5 or 6 cups	$1\frac{1}{4}$ to $1\frac{1}{2}$ teaspoons

formation of the tough dry skin that is caused by loss of moisture from the surface when hot cereal is exposed to the air.

The acceptability of hot cereal is improved by proper service. It is best when served very hot and in moderate rather than in too large servings. Color and contrast can be added in the form of fruits of various kinds. Fruit juices can be substituted for part of the water in cooking, or dried fruits such as figs, raisins, or dates can be added to the cereal early in the cooking process. The proportions usually suggested are one-fourth to one-half cup of fruit to one cup of dry cereal. Fresh, canned, or cooked fruits can also be added to the cooked cereal just before serving. Cream, top milk, or whole milk is usually served with cereals, although for variety butter is sometimes desired.

Rice

Rice that is well cooked is fluffy and dry with each grain separate and firm but tender. Occasionally rice that is more moist is preferred because it packs together easily and holds its shape well in a ring mold or patties. It is necessary to use just the right amount of water in cooking rice because when too little water is used the cooked rice is likely to be hard, brittle, and small

Fig. 4–4. An East Indian specialty consists of fluffy white rice served with accompaniments of shrimp, lobster, bananas, mushrooms, and eggs, seasoned with various spices.

Courtesy of Alcoa Wrap

in volume, but when too much water is used the rice sticks together in a pasty mass formed by the starch of the rice grains and the excess water.

It is important to follow package directions about washing rice because of the danger of losing vitamins that have been added for enrichment. The loss of vitamins and minerals is likewise substantial when rice is cooked in an excess of water but negligible when just sufficient water is used.[15] For this reason and because flavor and texture are better, rice is best cooked in the amount of water that will be absorbed during cooking. Usually two cups of water and a half-teaspoon of salt are enough for one cup of rice, although the amount of water can be increased to two and one-fourth cups if softer rice is desired. The rice is stirred into rapidly boiling water, the pan is covered tightly, and the rice is cooked slowly for 12 to 15 minutes or until tender. It is then removed from the heat and allowed to stand covered for 10 minutes or the length of time recommended on the package. If desired, one-half teaspoon of cooking fat or oil can be added with the rice to prevent foaming. During cooking the heat is turned low because rapid boiling may break the grains or cause the rice to boil over. It is especially easy to cook rice in a double boiler or in the oven. To cook in the oven, two cups boiling water are poured over one cup of rice and one-half teaspoon of salt in a baking dish. The pan is covered and the rice baked at 177° C. (350° F.) for thirty minutes or until tender. During cooking, rice takes up water and swells so that one cup uncooked rice yields about three cups cooked rice.

Although cooking methods and times are similar for regular white rice whether the grains are long, medium, or short, times vary somewhat with the manufacturing process. For example, brown rice takes about twice as long to cook as white rice, and parboiled or converted rice requires about half again as long as regular white rice. Precooked rice is quickly prepared by the method described on the package.

Because it is a bland food, rice can be prepared in many ways and with many flavors. It can be used as an ingredient in dishes such as meat loaf, croquettes, casseroles, cheese dishes, or puddings. Some favorite rice dishes are Spanish rice, which contains onions and tomatoes, or pilaf, for which uncooked rice is fried in a small amount of fat until it is brown and then is cooked in chicken or beef bouillon, tomato juice, or water until the liquid is absorbed and the rice is soft.

Macaroni Products

A package or a fraction of a package of macaroni, spaghetti, or noodles is usually cooked at one time because many of these products cannot be measured accurately in a cup. An eight-ounce package usually furnishes eight to nine servings since these foods swell to about twice their original size when cooked. To cook eight ounces of a macaroni product, add two teaspoons of salt to two quarts of rapidly boiling water, gradually add the

[15] M. C. Malakar and S. N. Banerjee, *op. cit.*

Fig. 4–5. *In making lasagna, line up ingredients for layers in the order they are added.*

Courtesy of U.S. Department of Agriculture

macaroni so that the water continues to boil, and cook uncovered until just tender. The macaroni is then drained and returned without rinsing to the hot pot. Macaroni made with milk cooks in less time than that made with water; cooking time is also shortened when disodium phosphate is added during the manufacturing process. Macaroni products are usually cooked until tender but firm, not pasty or sticky. The strands should be distinct, not matted.

Activities

1. Examine a wide variety of uncooked and ready-to-eat cereals. Among the ready-to-eat cereals include some that have special nutrients added and some that are sugar coated. Make a table listing across the top: Cereal, Type, Weight of Package, Cost of Package, Cost Per Ounce, Approximate Measure of a One-Ounce Portion, Grains Present in Largest Amount. Fill in the table, grouping together uncooked cereals of different types and ready-to-eat cereals of different types. The last column is filled in from the list of ingredients that appears on the package. Note that some cereals contain only one grain while others contain several. Compare the cost per serving of uncooked and ready-to-eat cereals of various types. If desired, 100-calorie portions can be used instead of 1-ounce portions of each cereal. Put out for inspection either 100-calorie or 1-ounce portions of cereals. For this purpose it is best to cook the raw cereal.

2. Cook a portion of rolled oats (not quick-cooking) or cracked wheat over direct heat in a covered saucepan, in a double boiler, and in a pressure saucepan. Compare the finished products. If rolled oats are used, cook a portion according to package directions for comparison.

3. Purchase as many varieties of uncooked and prepared, to-be-cooked rice as are available. Cook according to a standard method and compare the volume increase, appearance, palatability, and cost per serving of the different forms of rice.

4. Prepare rice pilaf and wheat pilaf using bulgur. Prepare dishes with several types of macaroni products.

5. Compare the appearance, texture, and palatability of rice, macaroni, or spaghetti cooked in different proportions of water and for different lengths of time.

References

BATCHER, O. M., P. A. DEARY, AND E. H. DAWSON. Cooking Quality of 26 Varieties of Milled White Rice. *Cereal Chem., 34:* 277–285 (1957).

BATCHER, O. M., K. F. HELMINTOLLER, AND E. H. DAWSON. Cooking Rice for School Lunches. *J. Home Econ., 48:* 36–37 (1956).

Cereals and Pasta in Family Meals. A Guide for Consumers. U.S. Dept. Agr., Home and Garden Bull. No. 150 (1968).

Contours of Change. The Yearbook of Agriculture, 1970, U.S. Dept. Agr., Washington, D.C.: United States Government Printing Office. Pp. 326–330.

Cooking White Rice. U.S. Dept. Agr., ARS 61-2 (1956).

Food and Nutrition Board, NAS-NRC. *Cereal Enrichment in Perspective,* 1958. Natl. Acad. Sci.-Natl. Research Council, Washington, D.C.

HARRIS, R. S., AND H. VON LOESECKE (Eds.). *Nutritional Evaluation of Food Processing.* New York: John Wiley & Sons, Inc. 1960. Pp. 358–369; 492–502.

MATZ, S. A. *Cereal Technology.* Westport, Conn.: The Avi Publishing Company, Inc. 1970. Pp. 221–376.

5

coffee, tea, and cocoa

When they were first introduced into Europe, tea, coffee, and cocoa were cherished commodities which only the wealthy could afford. Today these beverages are standard household items. They not only serve as natural companions to the three meals a day, but give their names to many types of social gatherings, ranging from the neighborhood kaffee-klatsch to the most formal tea. Many a hostess is judged by her ability to make a "good" cup of coffee or tea.

Coffee

Coffee probably grew wild in Africa but was first cultivated in Arabia where a physician wrote of its use toward the end of the ninth century. In about 1500, coffee was introduced into Europe where its use spread from country to country. Tea was more popular than coffee in Colonial America, but both beverages were too expensive for general use.

The United States may owe its coffee-drinking habits to the Boston Tea Party of 1773 because after that event coffee became more popular than tea. The use of coffee increased rapidly in the United States until this country is now the largest consumer of coffee in the world. The English may trace their tea-drinking habits to another quirk of fate. When Ceylon was a good coffee producer, England was one of their best buyers and consumed about as much coffee as tea. A disease of the coffee plant called rust, however, forced the planters in Ceylon to discontinue coffee and replace it with tea. Many of the English then shifted to tea-drinking and now consume much more tea than coffee.

Production

It is estimated that in 1970–71, 17 per cent of the coffee in the world export market was from Brazil, a drop from 50 per cent in 1950. In the meantime, Africa's share had risen from 15 per cent in 1950 to 33 per cent.[1] The United

[1] *World Agriculture Production and Trade. Statistical Report, December, 1970.* Foreign Agricultural Service. United States Department of Agriculture, Washington, D.C., p. 25.

Fig. 5–1. *Since the coffee tree may bear both ripe and unripe cherries at the same time, the crop must be harvested by hand. It takes nearly two thousand cherries to provide enough beans for a single pound of roasted coffee.*

States imports almost 45 per cent of the coffee that enters world trade.[2] This amounts to about fifteen pounds per person or the equivalent of three cups a day for each American over ten years of age. However, since 1962 there has been a slow but gradual decrease in the per capita consumption of coffee in this country.[3]

Coffee is grown on an evergreen shrub that blooms about three years after it is planted and produces a fruit that is often called a cherry. The fruit, a reddish purple when ripe, is picked by hand and depu!ped to expose the two oval coffee beans. These are then dried and hulled to remove the

[2] *Contours of Change. The Yearbook of Agriculture, 1970.* United States Department of Agriculture, Washington, D.C., p. 254.

[3] *National Food Situation.* NFS, 135, 1970. Economic Research Service. United States Department of Agriculture, Washington, D.C., p. 19.

parchment-like covering and the silver skin. The coffee beans are cleaned, graded for weight and size, and finally inspected to remove impurities and imperfect beans. Two major types are imported by the United States— milder flavored Arabica varieties grown in Central and South America, and more strongly flavored Robusta varieties from Africa and Asia. The milder Arabica varieties (about three-fourths of all coffee imports) are used in roasted blends. Robusta varieties are largely used in instant coffee, but recently are being used to some extent in roasted blends.[4]

During roasting flavor develops and the beans change in color from tan to chestnut or dark brown, depending on the degree of the roast. People have different preferences depending upon region and national origin. A dark roast is generally preferred in the South, a light roast along the Pacific coast, and a medium roast elsewhere in the United States, although there are many exceptions.

Most of the caffeine can be removed from coffee by extraction with a solvent. Such decaffeinated coffee is frequently used by people who wish to avoid the stimulating effect of caffeine. A simulated coffee drink made from a preparation of roasted cereals is used sometimes by people who cannot tolerate any caffeine. Such preparations may easily be identified by the labels.

Although experiments on instant or soluble coffee were made before the Civil War, little instant coffee was sold before 1945. Since that time it has become increasingly popular until at the present it accounts for about one cup of coffee in five in the United States. To make it, roasted ground coffee is extracted with water in a percolator or other suitable equipment. The coffee grounds are discarded and the coffee extract is freeze dried or dried on a drum in a vacuum or by spraying it into a heated chamber. Instant coffee is simply dried coffee brew with nothing added. Because it weighs only about one-fourth as much as the corresponding amount of regular coffee, it is easier to ship. Although instant coffee may lack some of the aroma of regular coffee, manufacturers are developing methods for including some of the aroma constituents.

Frozen coffee is also available on some markets. It is a liquid coffee concentrate to which water is added to prepare the beverage.

Selection

Many brands of coffee which represent different blends of coffee beans are available on the market to meet the various tastes and purses of the public. The selection of coffee is largely a matter of choosing the brand most pleasing to the consumer and continuing its use. Price is not always an authoritative guide to the brand that will be preferred. Occasionally an inexpensive coffee proves to be costly when considered on the basis of the amount of beverage that can be made from a pound.

[4] *Food for Us All. The Yearbook of Agriculture, 1969.* United States Department of Agriculture, Washington, D.C., p. 18.

Fig. 5–2. *One of the final steps in coffee processing is taste-testing for grade. In the consuming countries tasting determines blend qualities.*

Courtesy of U.S. Department of Agriculture

The grind must, of course, be selected on the basis of the method that is to be used for preparing the coffee. Regular grind is used for steeped or percolator coffee, drip grind for drip coffee, and fine grind for vacuum coffee. For best yield, it is wise to use as fine a grind as possible for the method because greater surface area exposed to water permits more rapid extraction of coffee flavor during brewing. Freshly ground or vacuum packed coffee is likely to be fresher and have a better flavor than ground coffee that has been kept without vacuum packing. Although coffee is packed under a vacuum, carbon dioxide given off by the coffee soon fills the vacuum and may even exert some pressure on the can. Except for those who buy their coffee in the bean and grind it at home, it is unwise to buy more coffee than will be used in about one week because of staling. Keeping ground coffee in the refrigerator or the freezer retards the loss of flavor and the development of staleness that occur when ground coffee is exposed to air at room temperature.

Instant coffee is less expensive per serving than regular coffee, as indicated in Figure 5–3, which shows the cost per serving of instant coffee on the

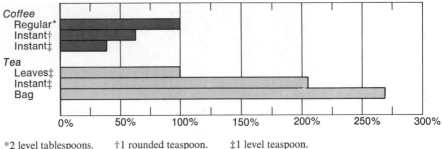

*2 level tablespoons.   †1 rounded teaspoon.   ‡1 level teaspoon.

Fig. 5–3. Comparative cost of a serving of regular and instant coffee and of regular, instant, and bag tea. (Calculated from Harp and Dunham, in Comparative Costs to Consumers of Convenience Foods and Home-Prepared Foods. Marketing Research Report No. 609, U.S. Department of Agriculture, 1963.)

basis of a rounded teaspoon and of a level teaspoon. It may seem surprising that a highly processed food such as instant coffee should be less expensive than regular coffee. This can be explained, however, by the fact that to make equal amounts of beverage, less green coffee is needed for the instant coffee than for the regular roasted coffee. Another factor that reduces the cost of instant coffee is the great reduction in weight and volume that it represents.

Composition

Caffeine, the stimulating principle of coffee, is also present in tea, cocoa, chocolate, and beverages made from them, as indicated in Tables 5–1 and 5–2. Wide fluctuations in the caffeine content of these beverages must be expected due to variations in the caffeine content of the coffee beans, tea leaves, or cocoa and in the strength of the brew. Little difference has been found in the caffeine content of coffee made by the percolator, drip, and vacuum methods.[5]

Table 5–1. The Caffeine and Theobromine Content of Coffee, Tea, and Cocoa *

Product	Caffeine per cent	Theobromine per cent
Coffee, roasted	1.2–1.9	
Coffee, instant	3.0–4.0	
Tea, dry leaves	2.0–4.4	
Chocolate	trace–0.25	0.7–1.5
Cocoa	0.2 ±	1.2–2.1

* Source and treatment play an important part in determining the exact content in the product.

[5] R. G. Martinek and W. Wolman. Xanthines, Tannins, and Sodium in Coffee, Tea, and Cocoa. Journal of the American Medical Association, 158: 1030–1031 (1955).

Table 5–2. *The Caffeine and Theobromine Content of Several Beverages* *

Beverage	Caffeine *mg. in 5 oz. beverage*	Theobromine *mg. in 5 oz. beverage*
Coffee	90–125	—
Tea	30–70	—
Cocoa, breakfast	1.1–3.2	9–55
Chocolate	7.8	125
Cola drink		
Brand A	36.3	—
Brand B	38.9	—

* Data courtesy of the Pan-American Coffee Bureau, New York.

Coffee contains a substance that turns into the B-vitamin niacin during roasting. The niacin content of one cup (175 ml.) coffee is about one milligram.[6] People who drink three and one-half cups of coffee a day, which is considered to be an average amount, secure about one-fourth of their daily allowance of niacin from this source. Niacin is easily extracted during the preparation of coffee since percolation, dripping, or boiling gives over 71 per cent extraction of the niacin present.

The flavor of coffee is due to a complex mixture of organic compounds including some that contain sulfur. These compounds are now being studied with special interest because of the availability of new methods of analysis and because of the problems connected with the production of instant coffee from which some of the more volatile flavors are lost during preparation. The fact that these flavors are volatile means that they evaporate rapidly and are lost when the beverage is heated for a long time.

Coffee owes part of its flavor to the presence of tannins.[7] Tannins are responsible for the astringent flavor of underripe fruits such as persimmons and bananas and also of oak bark. The quantity of tannins in coffee beans is reduced during the roasting process. Because tannins are not as soluble in water as is caffeine, they are less completely extracted during brewing. As the temperature of brewing is increased, however, more of the tannins are dissolved. This is one of the important reasons for using temperatures slightly below the boiling point in brewing coffee, for although the presence of small amounts of tannins gives the brew a pleasant flavor, larger amounts are likely to give it a bitter and undesirable flavor.

Preparation

Coffee can be brewed successfully by a variety of methods, each of which has its advantages and may result in an excellent beverage. Whatever the method used, the best results are obtained when the coffee is fresh and when

[6] R. Bressani and D. A. Navarrete. Niacin Content of Coffee in Central America. *Food Research,* 24: 344–351 (1959). Also, L. J. Teply and R. F. Prier. Nutritional Evaluation of Coffee Including Niacin Bioassay. *Journal of Agricultural and Food Chemistry,* 5: 375–377 (1957).

[7] The most important tannin in coffee appears to be chlorogenic acid.

it is ground suitably for the method. The equipment must be clean with no evidence of a stale coffee odor. Uniform results depend upon accurate measurements. The proportion of coffee to water is about the same for all methods. The amount of coffee suggested is two level tablespoons of coffee for three-quarters of a cup of water, the amount held by many coffee cups. Because people prefer coffee of varying strength, it may be best to try the recommended proportion of coffee and then to adjust it according to taste. It is convenient to work out a formula that requires as few measurements as possible. For example, in preparing four servings of coffee it is convenient to measure one-half a level cup of coffee instead of eight level tablespoons and to measure three cups of water in a pint or quart graduated cup.

Stainless steel, enamel, glass, or porcelain is often recommended for coffee pots rather than aluminum, tin, nickel, or copper because of the possibility that some of these metals may give the beverage an astringent or bitter taste. Aluminum has, however, been used widely and with apparent success in coffee makers. Coffee makers of any type, except some automatic pots, work effectively only if they are three-quarters full or more. The directions given below are for non-automatic coffee makers. For automatic coffee makers it is best to follow the manufacturer's directions.

The quality of the water with which coffee is made is an important factor in the quality of the brew. All tap water contains some dissolved inorganic compounds. If their concentration in the water is so low that they cannot be tasted, they do not affect the taste of coffee, but water in which dissolved chemicals can be tasted will probably impart an undesirable taste to the coffee brewed from it.[8] Fresh, cold water usually makes better coffee than water from a hot water faucet.

Drip or filtered coffee is made by pouring boiling water through drip-ground coffee held in the fine-meshed container of a drip pot. The container in some pots is fine enough to act as the filter and prevent passage of the grounds. A filter paper is used in some drip pots or when very finely ground coffee is used. When dripping is completed, the upper section of the coffee pot is removed and the coffee is served. In this method the water passes over the coffee only once, making it necessary that the beans be finely ground in order to expose as much surface as possible and hence to have a maximum of soluble substances extracted.

When coffee is made by percolation, the coffee of medium or "regular" grind is placed in a perforated container held in the top of the pot. The water is forced by heat through a central tube to the top of the pot where it is sprayed over the coffee and extracts the soluble materials as it drips through the grounds. When this method is used, the ground coffee does not come into contact with boiling water, but unless care is exercised, the beverage boils after it has flowed through the grounds and the flavor is

[8] E. E. Lockhart, C. L. Tucker, and M. C. Merritt. The Effect of Water Impurities on the Flavor of Brewed Coffee. *Food Research,* 20: 598–605 (1955).

Fig. 5–4. *In the drip method a measured amount of boiling water passes through a measured amount of ground coffee.*

1 Measure cold water into kettle and heat to boiling. Meanwhile preheat coffeepot by rinsing with very hot water.

2 Measure drip-grind coffee into cone with filter paper, or filter section of coffeepot, depending on type of drip pot used.

3 Pour measured fresh boiling water into cone or upper container of drip pot. Cover, depending on pot used.

4 When dripping is completed in 4 to 6 minutes, remove upper section. Stir brew and serve.

Fig. 5–5. *In a percolator the water bubbles up through the percolator stem, spraying gently over the coffee grounds. As it seeps through the grounds, the flavor is extracted.*

1 Remove basket and stem and measure fresh cold water into percolator. Place on heat until water boils. Remove from heat.

2 Measure regular-grind coffee into basket.

3 Insert basket and stem into percolator, cover, return to gentle heat and percolate slowly 6 to 8 minutes. (Note: Water level should always be below the bottom of coffee basket.)

4 Remove coffee basket and stem and serve coffee.

These directions are for non-automatic coffee-makers.
Follow manufacturers' instructions for automatic coffee-makers.

Fig. 5–6. *In the vacuum method steam from boiling water creates pressure which forces most of the water up into the top bowl, where it gently bubbles through the coffee grounds.*

1 Measure fresh cold water into lower bowl. Place on heat and bring to boil. Place filter in upper bowl. When water boils, measure fine-grind coffee into upper bowl.

2 Remove boiling water from heat. Insert upper bowl with slight twist to insure tight seal. Return to reduced heat. (When using electric range, turn off electricity.)

3 Most of water will rise into upper bowl. Allow to mix with ground coffee for 1 minute, stirring thoroughly in zig-zag fashion first 20 seconds.

4 Remove from heat. Brew will return to lower bowl within 2 minutes. Remove upper bowl and serve coffee.

Courtesy of Pan-American Coffee Bureau

partially lost. Some electric percolators are so constructed that the water never reaches the boiling point. In most non-automatic percolators it is best to remove the coffee basket before serving.

In vacuum coffee makers, steam from boiling water forces most of the water from the lower into the top bowl where it bubbles through the coffee grounds. When the lower bowl cools, a vacuum is created that pulls the brew through a filter into the lower bowl. Coffee makers of glass, stainless steel, or aluminum are available. The top container, which resembles a funnel, fits tightly into the lower container. A filter of glass, metal, fabric, or other material closes the opening into the upper container. Cold water is measured into the lower container and heated. The filter is placed in the upper bowl, secured if necessary, and fine ground coffee is added. When the water boils, the heat is reduced and the upper bowl is inserted with a slight twist. After the water rises into the upper bowl, the brew is stirred and the coffee pot is removed from the heat. The brew returns to the lower container in about two minutes. The upper bowl is then removed and the coffee served. This method makes an especially clear and sparkling brew. There is some variation from this method among the different vacuum coffee makers, however, and in such cases manufacturer's directions should be followed.

Steeped coffee, which is excellent if properly made, is sometimes convenient for serving a large group because very simple equipment can be used. If the coffee is brewed in an old-fashioned pot, cold water is measured into the pot, brought to a boil, and the heat reduced so that the water is just below the boiling point. A measured amount of coffee of "regular" grind is added and stirred. The pot is set over low heat and allowed to steep six to eight minutes. The water should never reach the boiling point after coffee is added. If grounds have not settled at the end of the brewing period, a small amount of cold water is added. Another way to make steeped coffee is to mix egg white or whole egg with cold water and crushed egg shells if desired. This mixture is combined with the ground coffee. Freshly boiled water is added and the mixture is steeped about three minutes over low heat. It is then cleared by adding a little cold water. One egg white or whole egg is about enough for six cups of boiling water. As the egg coagulates on heating, it encloses the minute particles of coffee which are responsible for the muddy appearance of the unclarified beverage. If a large enough coffee pot is not available, coffee can be brewed in a kettle. Coffee of regular grind is measured into a clean cloth that has been soaked and rinsed for use. The bag should be only about half full so that the coffee can expand and the water circulate. The cloth is tied with a cord long enough to reach the handle of the kettle. Water is brought to a boil in the kettle, the heat reduced, and the bag of coffee attached to the pot handle and dropped into the water. The heat is reduced so that the water does not boil, and the sack is pushed up and down frequently until the coffee has brewed for eight to ten minutes. The sack is removed and the coffee served as soon as possible.

Espresso coffee originated in Italy, where it is very popular and from where it has spread to other countries including the United States. It is made in a special apparatus that passes a mixture of steam and hot water through finely powdered coffee on a filter. Each cup is individually brewed under a spigot. It is usually served in small cups because it is black and strong.

Coffee served in small cups after dinner is sometimes called *café noir* or *demitasse*. It can be made by any method but is usually at least half again as strong as regular coffee.

Coffee, whether it is regular or extra strength, can be served black or with cream and sugar. In Europe, *café au lait* is often served, especially for breakfast; this is made by pouring into the coffee cup equal parts of strong hot coffee and hot milk. In Austria coffee is often topped with a spoon of whipped cream. Some of the more imaginative ways of serving coffee are to put half coffee and half cocoa into the cup and top with whipped cream, to add cinnamon or nutmeg to coffee with or without hot milk, or to add a twist of lemon or orange peel and sugar to espresso or demitasse coffee.

Coffee is best when it is freshly brewed, but if it must be held before serving, it is best to keep it hot for periods up to an hour rather than to cool and reheat it. If the pot is not automatic, it can be set over a very low heat, perhaps on an asbestos pad, on a candle-warmer, or in a pan of hot water.

Iced coffee can be made by mixing twice the usual amount of instant coffee with a little cold water, placing it in a glass, adding ice cubes, and filling the glass with cold water. It can also be made from coffee of regular strength brewed by any method and cooled in a nonmetallic container for not more than three hours. The cold coffee is then poured over ice, made of coffee if desired. Another method is to make hot coffee by using two-thirds the amount of water to the usual amount of coffee. This extra-strength brew is poured hot over ice cubes.

Tea

Tea is said to be the most popular and least expensive beverage in the world except for water. Certainly it is the national drink in the countries of Asia and the Middle East, where tea is produced, and in the United Kingdom, the world's largest importer of tea. In the United Kingdom the annual per capita consumption of tea is nearly ten pounds, but in the United States it is only about 0.7 pound per person. Heavy consumption of coffee and cola drinks in the United States helps to explain the comparatively low consumption of tea.

The use of tea as a beverage probably started in China long before the Christian era. Tea did not become popular in Europe, however, until late in the eighteenth century. As indicated in the section on coffee, tea might have been more popular than coffee in the United States if the English had not levied a duty on tea brought into the Colonies.

Production
and Selection

Most of the world's tea now comes from India, Ceylon, Indonesia, and Africa. China was the world's largest producer before the Second World War but now exports little tea. Tea grows best in a tropical climate where rainfall is abundant. Although it grows from sea level up to 6,000 feet, it does especially well at moderately high altitudes.

Tea is the leaf of an evergreen shrub that resembles a camellia bush. The young unopened leaf bud at the end of the shoot is considered of highest quality and the first and second leaves are of good quality. About 3,200 shoots, picked by hand, are required to make a pound of processed tea. The quality of tea depends not only upon the size of the leaves but also upon the variety of the plant, the place where it is grown, the weather, the time of picking, and the curing method.

The two main types of tea, black and green, are made by different methods from the same type of leaves. For black tea, the leaves are first allowed to wither until soft and then they are rolled with a machine. The rolling releases enzymes that cause the leaf to "ferment." The word "fermentation" in connection with tea means simply that oxygen is taken up by the action of enzymes—not that the more familiar bacterial fermentation occurs. The oxidation which started in the rollers is completed in a fermenting room where the tea leaves are spread out in order to absorb more oxygen. The process is stopped by heating and drying the leaves. For green tea, the leaves are allowed to wither and are then rolled and dried but not fermented. During fermentation some of the aroma of the leaf is evaporated and some of the tannins destroyed. For this reason black tea has a somewhat less fragrant odor and less astringent taste than green tea. About 97 per cent of the tea consumed in the United States is black. Most of the green tea is used in the country where it is produced.

Oolong tea is semi-fermented by a manufacturing process similar to that used for green tea except that the leaf is withered and fermented slightly. Most oolong tea is imported from Formosa. This tea combines the properties of black and green tea.

Black teas from India, Ceylon, and Indonesia are graded by leaf size as described in Table 5–3. As this list indicates, the term "pekoe" denotes only a size of tea leaf and not a type or quality. The broken grades, which constitute about 80 per cent of the total production, make a stronger, darker tea than the leaf grades and are therefore preferred in some countries including the United States. Black tea is sometimes combined with flavoring substances such as jasmine flowers, mint, orange, and a variety of spices. The first grade of green tea is Young Hyson, which forms nearly 90 per cent of the green tea sold. Gunpowder tea is green tea with small round leaves tightly rolled into little pellets. Brick tea, which is used in Russia, is made from either black or green tea. The tea is moistened and pressed into bricks under pressure. For use, tea is whittled from the edge of the brick and ground. Loose tea or tea bags are usually packaged in sealed containers to avoid deterioration.

Table 5–3. *Grades of Black Tea* *

Leaf Size	Description
Orange Pekoe	Long, thin, wiry leaves which sometimes contain yellow tips or bud leaf. The liquors are light or pale in color.
Pekoe	The leaves of this grade are shorter and not so wiry as orange pekoe but the liquors generally have more color.
Souchong	A bold and round leaf, with pale liquors.
Broken Orange Pekoe	Much smaller than any of the leaf grades and usually contains yellow tip. The liquors have good color and strength in the cup and are the mainstay of a blend.
Broken pekoe	Slightly larger than broken orange pekoe with rather less color in the cup; useful as a filler in a blend.
Broken Pekoe Souchong	A little larger or bolder than broken pekoe and in consequence lighter in the cup, but also used as a filler.
Fannings	Much smaller than broken orange pekoe and its main virtues are quick brewing with good color in the cup.
Dust	The name for the smallest grade produced. Very useful for a quick brewing, strong cup of tea; used only in blends of similar sized leaf, generally for catering purposes.

* From *Two Leaves and a Bud (The Story of Tea)*. Tea Council of the U.S.A., Inc. New York, p. 10.

Tea bags have proved so convenient for brewing tea that one-half of the tea drunk in the United States is made from them. Instant tea has become important in recent years, accounting for 33 per cent of the United States sales in 1969.[9] As indicated in Figure 5–3, tea is more expensive when prepared, according to manufacturers' directions, from instant tea or tea bags than from tea leaves.

Composition

The aroma and some of the flavor of tea are due to a complex mixture of compounds not fully understood. Some of the characteristic liveliness is evidently due to its caffeine content. The percentage of caffeine in a pound of processed tea is greater than in a pound of roasted coffee, but because less tea than coffee is used to brew a cup of beverage, a cup of tea usually contains less caffeine than a cup of coffee (200 cups of tea may be obtained from a pound of tea leaves as opposed to 40 cups of coffee from a pound of coffee). However, care must be taken in making such comparisons because of great variations in the strength of the brew. Essentially all the caffeine

[9] *National Food Situation.* NFS, 134, 1970. Economic Research Service. United States Department of Agriculture, Washington, D.C., p. 28.

in tea is extracted in a three-minute brew. If it is brewed longer, more tannin is extracted but very little additional caffeine.

Tea owes much of its characteristic flavor to the tannins that it contains. The tannins, a complex mixture of more than twenty substances, are altered or partially destroyed when tea leaves are fermented and dried to make black tea. Although tannins perform an important function in furnishing strength and body to a tea, excessive amounts give the brew an unpleasant astringency. Boiling tea or extracting it for long periods of time are avoided since these conditions dissolve excessive amounts of tannin. Milk removes some of the astringency of tea because the protein called casein that it contains combines with the tannin.

Although tea contains traces of several vitamins, the amounts are not significant in the ordinary diet. The fresh green tea leaf is very rich in vitamin C, but nearly all of this vitamin is lost during fermentation and drying.

Preparation

The observation of a few simple rules does much to insure success in tea-making. Tea pots made of glass, pottery, or porcelain hold the heat best. Boiling water is poured into the pot to freshen and heat it, and then discarded. The tea can be put into the pot loose, in a tea ball, a piece of cheesecloth or a strainer, or a tea bag can be used. From one-half to one teaspoon of tea is usually allowed per cup. The number of tea bags depends upon the amount and kind of tea in the bag. A tea ball should not be filled more than half full because it is necessary to allow for the swelling of the leaves. Freshly boiling water is added and the pot is tightly covered to prevent the escape of steam carrying the characteristic odor. The tea is allowed to steep for three to five minutes. If the leaves are in a container, they are lifted from the beverage as soon as the desired strength is reached. If the tea has been added loose, the beverage can be strained into a second scalded pot as soon as it has steeped sufficiently. The strength of the tea can be regulated by the addition of freshly boiling water. In making tea, it is always best to use freshly drawn cold water that has just come to a full rolling boil because water that has been reheated makes the tea taste dull and flat. Tea has the best flavor immediately after it has been made. Allowing it to stand lowers its quality. Tea is commonly served with sugar, cream, milk, or thinly sliced lemon or orange. Sometimes candied ginger, cloves, or even jam is added.

Iced tea is popular in the United States, where it accounts for about 50 per cent of the tea used. It can be made from instant tea and cold water, from a regular blend of tea, or from a blend made especially for iced tea. If hot tea is poured over ice cubes, it is made half again as strong as usual to allow for dilution by the melting ice. Iced tea is often made from tea of regular or extra strength that has been cooled, but such infusions sometimes become cloudy because tannins that dissolve in hot water may precipitate out as the water cools. Tea should be kept at room temperature and poured over ice

Fig. 5–7. *Tea is at its best when carefully prepared and attractively served.*

The kettle: wide at base for rapid boiling; heavy in weight to hold heat

The pot: usually porcelain; eight cup capacity encourages fresh brews

The cups: smaller than coffee cups; narrow and deep so tea stays hot

Tea cannister: double lid gives tight seal, retains aroma, flavor

Courtesy of Sunset Magazine.

when ready to serve. Although clouding does not affect the flavor of tea, its clear color can be restored by adding a little boiling water.

Cocoa

Chocolate and cocoa, which originated in the New World, were in common use in the West Indies and in Mexico before the discovery of these countries by the European nations. At present, most of the world's cocoa is produced in Africa and Latin America. Both chocolate and cocoa are manufactured from the cocoa bean, the seed of a fleshy fruit which grows on a tree, the botanical name of which is *Theobroma cacao.* The translation of *Theobroma* is "food for the gods," indicating the esteem in which these products were held.

Cocoa beans are encased in fleshy pods from seven to twelve inches long, each of which contains thirty to forty beans or seeds. The pods are opened

Courtesy of Ewing Galloway

Fig. 5–8. *The pods of the cocoa tree are from seven to twelve inches long and grow close to the trunk or main branches. Within the pod the beans are attached to a central stem.*

and the beans are removed and allowed to ferment for several days. They are then dried, graded, and shipped. The fermented, dried cocoa beans resemble almonds, although they are less pointed. They are surrounded by paperlike skins or shells.

Processing

Most cocoa beans are imported by Western Europe and the United States. They are cleaned and roasted to facilitate the removal of the shell and to develop flavor, color, and aroma. The meat of the bean, known as the nib, is ground by passing it through rollers. During grinding, the heat generated melts the cocoa butter, and the ground nibs form a semi-liquid paste called "chocolate liquor" or "cocoa mass." This material solidifies on cooling to a hard brown block that is sold as bitter chocolate or baking chocolate. Sweet chocolate is made by adding sugar and flavorings to bitter chocolate and milk chocolate by adding milk, sugar, and flavorings.

Bitter chocolate contains 50 to 58 per cent of a fat called cocoa butter that is extracted when chocolate is to be made into cocoa. To make cocoa, some of the cocoa butter is removed by squeezing the chocolate liquor in a hydraulic press. Breakfast or high fat cocoa must contain not less than 22 per cent fat, medium fat cocoa 10 to 22 per cent, and low fat cocoa less than 10 per cent fat.[10] It is easy to understand from this description of the manufacture of cocoa why fat is added when cocoa is substituted for chocolate in a recipe. Three tablespoons cocoa and one tablespoon fat are approximately equivalent to one ounce (one square) of chocolate. Because of its lower fat content, cocoa is less likely to separate in a hot beverage than chocolate and keeps better in hot weather. In the summer, chocolate may show whitish patches because at about 30° C. (85° F.) a little cocoa butter comes to the surface. This change affects only the appearance and involves no loss of flavor. Cocoa is usually less expensive than chocolate because cocoa butter is in demand for use in manufacturing confections as well as pharmaceutical and toilet preparations.

Spices or other seasonings can be added to the cocoa but must be declared on the label. Cocoa is often treated with an alkali during its manufacture to make it darker in color, less acid in flavor, and less likely to settle in the cup. The addition of alkali must also be declared on the label.[11] Alkali-treated cocoa has sometimes been called Dutch process cocoa.

As indicated in Tables 5–1 and 5–2, cocoa and chocolate and the beverages made from them contain theobromine and a trace of caffeine. Although theobromine is a stimulant, more theobromine than caffeine is required to produce the same effect. Because of this fact and because only a small amount of cocoa ordinarily is used in making cocoa or chocolate milk, these beverages are not usually considered harmful for children. Tannins in cocoa and chocolate contribute color and flavor.

Preparation

In contrast to coffee and tea, which are made by extracting the soluble substances with water, a hot beverage is made by incorporating the cocoa or chocolate with milk. The beverage can be made by combining one tablespoon cocoa or one-third ounce chocolate, one tablespoon sugar, a few grains salt, and two tablespoons water, heating and stirring in a small saucepan until the ingredients boil, and adding a cup of hot milk. Boiling the cocoa or chocolate with the sugar and water reduces the tendency for the cocoa to settle and prevents a raw flavor that might occur if the starch in the cocoa were not cooked enough. Beating the cocoa with a rotary egg beater helps prevent the formation of a scum. The preparation of cocoa is simplified by using chocolate syrup that can be purchased or prepared at home. It is easily prepared by combining one cup of cocoa or five to six squares of chocolate, one cup of sugar, one-fourth teaspoon of salt, and one cup of water. These

---

[10] *Code of Federal Regulations*, Title 21, Parts 14.3–14.5.
[11] *Code of Federal Regulations*, Title 21, Part 14.1.

ingredients are brought to a boil, stirring constantly, and boiled for about five minutes. After cooling, a tablespoon of vanilla can be added if desired, and the syrup put in a jar for storage in the refrigerator. Cocoa can be made easily by adding the syrup to hot milk. Cocoa is sometimes garnished in the cup with a marshmallow or whipped cream.

During cookery, cocoa and chocolate are incorporated in different ways. Cocoa is usually sifted with the dry ingredients in baking or combined with sugar and a small amount of liquid for puddings. Chocolate is melted by putting it in milk heated for puddings or pie fillings. For cakes, it is melted before it is added to the batter. Envelopes of cocoa and partially hydro-genated vegetable oil that require no melting can be substituted for chocolate if desired.

Activities

1. Prepare coffee in the following ways and compare the results:
a. Prepare by steeping, in a percolator, and in drip and vacuum pots.
b. Clarify steeped coffee with egg white, egg shells, or a dash of cold water.
c. Use coffee of regular and drip grinds in making both steeped and drip coffee.

2. Compare coffee brewed in the regular way and from instant coffee. Code the samples and taste. Repeat with tea.

3. Compare beverages brewed from coffee of different brands and different prices. Be sure method of making is the same.

4. Prepare after-dinner coffee and *café au lait*.

5. Brew coffee and tea using tap and distilled water. Compare the quality of the brews.

6. Brew coffee and tea using different proportions. Does everyone who tastes the brews agree on the best proportion?

7. Compare beverages made from black, green, and oolong tea and from tea containing flowers such as jasmine or orange blossoms.

8. Prepare hot spiced tea.

9. Compare iced tea made in several ways from tea leaves and from instant tea, using the directions on the package. Code and compare.

10. Prepare and evaluate chocolate and cocoa, using whole fresh milk, dried whole milk, a single and a double portion of nonfat dry milk, and evaporated milk.

11. Make a cocoa mix by combining cocoa, sugar, a few grains salt, and nonfat dry milk. Work out the formula and directions for using the mix.

References

Coffee Consumption in the U.S. 1920–65. U.S. Dept. Commerce, Business-Defense Services Administration (1961).

Coffee, Please. Pan-American Coffee Bureau, New York (1960).

Farmer's World. The Yearbook of Agriculture, 1964. U.S. Dept. Agr., Washington, D.C.: United States Government Printing Office. Pp. 184–194; 200–205.

Food For Us All. The Yearbook of Agriculture, 1969. U.S. Dept. Agr., Washington, D.C.: United States Government Printing Office. Pp. 18–19; 237–243.

POTTER, N. N. *Food Science.* Westport, Conn.: The Avi Publishing Company, Inc. 1968. Pp. 506–522.

SIVETZ, M. *Coffee Processing Technology.* Westport, Conn.: The Avi Publishing Company, Inc. 1963.

WELLMAN, F. L. *Coffee. Botany, Cultivation, and Utilization.* New York: Interscience Publishers, Inc. 1961.

WICKIZER, V. D. *Coffee, Tea, and Cocoa—An Economic and Political Analysis.* Stanford, Calif.: Stanford University Press. 1951.

6

vegetables

A century ago vegetables were regarded as of minor importance in the diet of the people of the United States. The number and quantity produced in the home garden were limited, and few were purchased. Today, because of improvements in production, processing, and shipping, many kinds of vegetables are available throughout the year, even in small markets. General availability, increased knowledge of their nutritive value, and more prepreparation have undoubtedly contributed to increased consumption.

The consumption of vegetables other than potatoes and sweet potatoes has increased during the twentieth century while that of potatoes and sweet potatoes has decreased. However, during the past ten years there has been a reversal in this trend for white potatoes. Many reasons have been suggested for this shift in vegetable consumption. In addition to the greater availability of fresh vegetables, increased buying power, a shift of population from farm to nonfarm areas, and a decrease in the need for energy have no doubt had an influence. Certainly the use of some vegetables has increased greatly because of commercial processing. For example, fresh peas are available for only about one month each summer but when canned or frozen they are available throughout the year. The importance of processing is shown in the increased use of canned vegetables from 23 pounds per capita in 1929 to 52 pounds in 1969. Frozen vegetables, practically unknown in 1929, accounted for 19 pounds of the 212 pounds of vegetables consumed in 1969.[1] The recent increase in potato consumption is attributed to the high acceptability of processed products such as dried potato flakes, frozen potato products, and potato chips. Attitudes have also affected consumption. Tomatoes, which a century ago were regarded as "poisonous love apples," are now an important food throughout the year.

In this chapter a classification of vegetables is first considered, followed by some points on selection and storage. The color, flavor, and nutritive value of vegetables are discussed, as well as various methods for their preparation.

[1] *The Vegetable Situation.* TVS, 178, 1970. Economic Research Service, United States Department of Agriculture, Washington, D.C. P. 15.

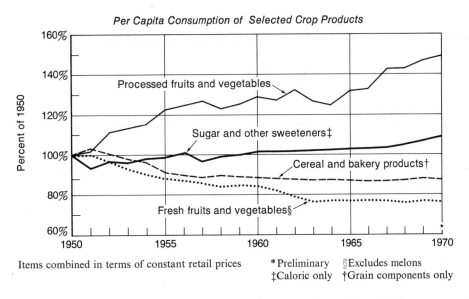

Fig. 6–1. *Per capita consumption of selected crop products.* (From *1970 Handbook of Agricultural Charts.* Agricultural Handbook No. 397, U.S. Department of Agriculture 1971, p. 37.)

Classification

As indicated in the fruit chapter, botanically speaking, a fruit is the ripened ovary of a plant together with any adjacent parts that may be fused with it, whereas a vegetable is some other edible part of a plant. In common practice this classification is not binding and some fruits are referred to as vegetables. Table 6–1 shows the parts of plants usually eaten as vegetables. These parts may be the leaf, stem, flower, fruit, seed, tuber, bulb, or root.

Selection and Storage

The wide selection of fresh and processed vegetables now available throughout the year can add variety and a generous supply of nutrients to the diet. The use of a number of vegetables adds interest to meals and avoids the monotony that results from serving the same vegetable several times a week.

Fresh Vegetables

Because of good transportation and a wide variety of growing conditions in the United States, fresh vegetables are available throughout the year. Some vegetables like beets, cabbage, carrots, lettuce, onions, potatoes, and spinach are readily available every month of the year, but certain other widely used vegetables, like asparagus, lima beans, corn, and peas are available in the fresh form during only a part of the year (Table 6–2) or are available in limited quantities and therefore at high prices.

The grading of fresh and processed vegetables is similar to that of fruits, which has already been discussed. A larger number of grades are used for

Table 6–1. Part of Plant Eaten as a Vegetable

Leaf	Stem	Flower	Fruit	Seed	Stem Tuber	Bulb	Root
Brussels sprouts	Asparagus	Broccoli	Cucumbers	Beans	White potatoes	Garlic	Beets
Cabbage	Celery *	Cauliflower	Eggplant	Corn	Jerusalem artichokes	Leeks	Carrots
Chard		French artichokes	Okra	Peas		Onions	Parsnips
Collards			Peppers			Shallots	Radishes
Dandelions			Pumpkin				Rutabagas
			Snap beans				
Endive			Squash				Salsify
Kale			Tomatoes				Sweet potatoes
Lettuce							Turnips
Mustard							
Spinach							
Watercress							

* Celery is a leaf stem.

less perishable vegetables such as potatoes than for other vegetables. Because grades are not often seen on most fresh vegetables sold on the retail market and because the vegetable may have deteriorated after grading, it is important to know what to look for when shopping for vegetables. A good general rule is to buy fresh vegetables that are firm, crisp, and bright in color but not overripe, decayed, wilted, blemished, dirty, or bruised. Fresh vegetables are usually cheapest and best in quality and nutritive value at the height of their season. Some brief suggestions for the selection of fresh vegetables are given below. More detailed suggestions on selection are given by Smith.[2] The selection of salad greens is discussed in the chapter on salads.

It is often necessary to store vegetables for a period before use. The keeping quality of the vegetable depends upon its nature. Although with a few exceptions vegetables are at their best immediately after they are harvested, most mature roots, bulbs, tubers, and seeds can be stored for varying periods of time without serious injury to quality.

From the standpoint of keeping quality, vegetables are sometimes classed as perishable, semi-perishable, and staple. While the perishable ones have comparatively poor keeping quality even when stored in a refrigerator or in

[2] M. E. Smith. *How to Buy Fresh Vegetables.* Marketing Bulletin No. 13. United States Department of Agriculture, Washington, D.C. 1967.

Table 6–2. *Some Seasonal Fresh Vegetables and Months When They Are Usually Plentiful.**

	Jan.	Feb.	Mar.	Apr.	May	June	July	Aug.	Sept.	Oct.	Nov.	Dec.
Artichokes			•	•	•							
Asparagus			•	•	•	•						
Beans, snap						•	•	•	•			
Beets						•	•	•	•	•		
Broccoli	•	•	•	•						•	•	
Brussels sprouts	•								•	•	•	•
Cauliflower										•	•	•
Corn, sweet					•	•	•	•	•			
Cucumbers					•	•	•	•				
Endive, Belgian		•	•	•	•					•		•
Garlic							•	•	•	•		
Okra					•	•	•	•	•			
Parsnips	•	•	•							•	•	
Peas, Green				•	•	•	•					
Potatoes												
California					•	•	•	•				
Maine	•	•	•	•	•							
Idaho	•	•	•	•							•	•
Pumpkin										•		
Sweet potatoes									•	•	•	•
Tomatoes												
Florida	•	•	•	•	•							•
California							•	•	•	•	•	
Mexico	•	•	•	•	•							
Turnips-Rutabaga	•	•	•							•	•	•

* Although each year's supply will vary, "•" indicates the months when 10 per cent or more of the total annual supply of the fresh vegetable is usually available.

crushed ice, the semi-perishable will keep for some time in a refrigerator, and the staple may be satisfactorily kept for some time without refrigeration.

    To keep the vegetable crisp, it is put into a covered container or plastic bag. Asparagus retains its crispness if set upright in about one inch of water in a wide-mouthed jar after removal of the butt ends. It is sometimes convenient to wash vegetables before storage in a refrigerator unless the vegetable is an especially delicate one like leaf lettuce.

Such staple vegetables as potatoes, beets, carrots, parsnips, rutabagas, cabbage, onions, squash, and pumpkin can be stored in an outside pit, a storage cellar, or a basement storage room. Detailed directions for such storage are available.[3]

Artichokes. As indicated in Table 6–1, there are two types of artichokes. The French or Globe artichoke is the large unopened flower bud of a plant of the thistle type. French artichokes of good quality are compact, plump, heavy in relation to their size, and with large fresh, fleshy, tightly-clinging green leaf scales. With age, the leaf scales become partially brown and tough.

The Jerusalem artichoke is a thick, potato-like tuber that grows underground. It is not often seen on the retail market.

Asparagus. The best asparagus is crisp and firm but tender with closed, compact tips, and smooth round stems. A rich green color should cover most of the spear, which should snap or break easily at or slightly above the white, woody portion. Although size is not directly related to quality, stalks that are at least one-half inch in diameter are usually preferred.

Beans, Snap. There are many varieties and shapes of snap beans. Both green beans and yellow wax beans are popular. Young, tender snap beans have pods of good even color which are slender with no large bumps. The pods are also stringless and straight, not withered, twisted, rusty, or spotty. They snap easily when broken.

Beets. Beets of good quality are firm, round, reasonably smooth, and clean. Small or medium size beets are usually preferred to large or elongated beets, which may be tough or woody.

Broccoli. The edible parts of broccoli consist of the tender leaves and young stalks and branches with their bud clusters or heads. When the broccoli is over-mature, the compact bud clusters open to form flowers that are yellowish. The color of broccoli varies from dark to purplish green. Broccoli of good quality has compact heads that are relatively large in comparison with the leaves. The stems are crisp, short, and tender, not tough or woody. When over-mature broccoli has been purchased, it is best to peel off the outer woody portion of the large stalks before cooking.

Brussels Sprouts. Brussels sprouts should be fresh and bright green in color, hard and compact, with no discoloration or blight.

Cabbage. Much of the cabbage sold has compact heads with greenish or white leaves. The best quality heads are solid, crisp, heavy, and well

[3] *Storing Vegetables and Fruits in Basements, Cellars, Outbuildings, and Pits.* Home and Garden Bulletin No. 119. United States Department of Agriculture, Washington, D.C. 1966.

Courtesy of the United Fresh Fruit and Vegetable Association

Fig. 6–2. *Vegetables of the cabbage family, including cauliflower, broccoli, green cabbage, red cabbage, and Brussels sprouts, can be used in a variety of hot and cold dishes.*

trimmed. The leaves should not be discolored or decayed. Early crop green cabbage may be medium firm, or even soft but is suitable for immediate use if the leaves are fresh and crisp. Some of the other types of cabbage available are red cabbage; Savoy cabbage, which has a loose head with green crinkly leaves; and Chinese cabbage, which has a long tapering head with crinkly leaves on a solid core. Cabbage of all types can be cooked or used as salad greens.

Carrots. Carrots are usually sold in plastic bags with the tops removed, although some unwrapped bunches are also available. Most of the carrots now marketed are harvested before they have reached full maturity. Carrots of high quality are firm, well colored, smooth, and well shaped.

Cauliflower. Heads of good quality are compact, firm, white, or creamy-white in color, and free from soft or wet decay. Yellow leaves and spreading flower clusters are indications of poor quality; a granular or "ricey" texture will not harm the eating quality if the head is compact.

Celery. Much of the celery now marketed is the green, or Pascal type. In some markets white or blanched celery is also available. Celery of high grade is crisp, clean, and of medium length and thickness. The branches should be brittle enough to snap easily but should not be woody or excessively stringy.

Corn. Much of the fresh corn on the market is sweet corn, which usually has yellow kernels but may sometimes have white kernels, as determined by the variety. Early maturing varieties of field corn are sometimes sold as fresh corn. Good corn has plump, milky kernels and husks that are bright green. Over-mature kernels are usually deep in color and excessively firm, whereas immature kernels are very small, soft, and undeveloped. Corn deteriorates rapidly after harvest unless kept cold and moist. Look for stem ends which are not discolored or dried.

Cucumbers. Cucumbers should be fresh, smooth, firm, well formed, and green. A small amount of whitish-green color at the tip is not objectionable, but a yellowish color indicates over-maturity. Cucumbers that are withered, shriveled, soft, or spongy are undesirable.

Eggplant. Eggplant should be firm, heavy for its size, and free from scars or cuts. A uniform deep purple color is preferred. Large, rough, spongy places indicate poor quality.

Greens. The leafy vegetables most often used for cooked greens are spinach, beet tops, kale, turnip tops, leafy broccoli, chard, collards, cress, dandelions, mustard, sorrel, chicory, endive, and escarole, although others may be used

Kale

Kohlrabi

Collards

Beet Tops

Mustard Greens

Spinach

Fig. 6–3. *These leafy green vegetables, often served cooked, are highly nutritious. The kohlrabi may be served either raw or cooked.*

occasionally. Greens of good quality are tender, young, crisp, and green. They should be free from decay, mold, insects, dirt, coarse stems, and yellow leaves.

Mushrooms. Mushrooms are fungi that differ greatly from other vegetables in appearance. Although a wide variety of mushrooms is used in other countries, only one type of mushroom (a form of *Agaricus Campastris*) is cultivated in the United States. Mushrooms of this type are white to creamy-white in color. They should look clean, fresh, and be free of bruises, decay, discoloration, open caps, pitting, and wilting. The fluted formation of "gills" between the cap and stem becomes brown or black when the mushrooms are over-mature.

Okra. The pods of okra should be fresh, tender, meaty, medium in size, and not badly misshapen. They should be bright green in color.

Onions (Green) and Related Vegetables. Green or spring onions may be regular onions harvested when their bulbs have reached a diameter of from one-fourth to one inch. Scallions are very young green onions that show no bulb development. Leeks resemble scallions but are larger and have flat leaves. Shallots are similar to green onions but the bulb resembles garlic in that it is made up of several "cloves." Chives have more slender stems than the other vegetables shown in Figure 6–4. They are often sold in a pot that may be kept in the kitchen and are snipped as needed, usually with scissors.

Onions (Mature). The onions sold on retail markets can be divided into mild and stronger types. The mild flavored onions are usually large and elongated or flat with a white, yellow, or red color. They are either the Spanish or Bermuda type. Onions with a stronger flavor are usually globe-shaped and medium in size with white, yellow, red, or brown skins. They keep very well under proper storage conditions. Onions of either type are best when they are clean, hard, well shaped, and mature with dry skins. They should be free of seedstems and of moisture at the neck, which indicates decay.

Parsnips. Good parsnips are firm, smooth, and well shaped. Those of small to medium size are preferred to larger parsnips which may have tough, woody cores.

Peas. Freshness is especially important in peas because they lose sweetness and flavor rapidly after being picked. The pods should be fresh, slightly velvety to the touch, and fairly well filled with peas. Flat, dark-green pods are likely to contain immature peas, whereas swollen pods that are light in color and flecked with gray may contain peas that are over-mature. The peas should be young, tender, and sweet.

Peppers. Peppers may vary from large bell-shaped peppers to small Chili peppers. Sweet peppers are usually sold when they are green, but peppers of the pungent or hot type may be sold in either the green or the red stage of

Red Globe

Sweet Spanish

Yellow Globe

Shallots

Scallion

Spring Onion

Chives

White Globe

Fig. 6–4. *The onion family, with its distinctive flavor, is valued both as a vegetable and as a seasoning.*

maturity. Whatever the variety, peppers should be well formed with fleshy walls and be glossy, tender, firm, and free from decay or blemish.

Potatoes, White. United States grades are seen more often on potatoes than on other vegetables. The wholesale grades are U.S. Fancy, U.S. No. 1, U.S. Commercial, and U.S. No. 2. Of these grades, U.S. No. 1 and U.S. No. 2 are used most frequently. Small consumer packages may be marked with the retail U.S. Grades A and B or with wholesale grades. Sizes of potatoes are designated as large, medium, or small.

Another way in which potatoes are classified is as "new" or "late crop." New potatoes are dug before they are fully mature and are marketed immediately. The immature skins are easily injured and likely to look discolored, ragged, and feathery. Late crop potatoes are mature and can therefore be shipped and stored from the time of their harvest until spring.

The potato is commercially grown in every state in the Union. The same variety grown in different regions may vary in taste, composition, and texture.[4] The varieties, which are not easy for most consumers to identify, can be grouped under the headings round-white, long-white, russet, and red. It may be advisable to try several of the varieties available on the local market and select one or two that are suitable for the use intended.

For salads or casserole dishes a potato with waxy characteristics is often preferred, while for mashing, baking, or frying a more mealy potato is desirable. A potato that is mealy and dry when boiled is also mealy and dry when mashed or baked. For most cooking methods mealiness is a desirable quality, but some of the most mealy potatoes may be undesirable for boiling because they tend to slough. Potatoes tend to become less mealy on storage and to slough less than when freshly harvested. Potatoes are likely to be waxy if they have a low content of starch and a high content of water, and mealy if they have a high content of starch. Potatoes of these two types can be separated because their specific gravities are different. If one cup of table salt is dissolved in 11 cups of water, the potatoes that are low in solids, and therefore waxy, will float, whereas those that are high in solids, and hence mealy, will sink.

A green color sometimes develops on the surface of potatoes that have been exposed to sun in the field or to natural or artificial light after harvesting. Such greenish discoloration should be trimmed away when present because it gives the potatoes an undesirable bitter taste.

Potatoes are best stored in a cool, dry, dark place with good ventilation and a temperature of 7° to 10° C. (45° to 50° F.). During storage of potatoes some of their starch is converted to sugar. If the storage temperature is 5° C. (40° F.) or below, the sugar accumulates because the metabolic activities of the tuber are too slow to use the sugar. The sugar gives the potatoes an undesirable sweet taste and causes them to brown too much when used for potato chips or French fried potatoes. If such potatoes are held at room temperature for a week or two, however, the excess sugar is used by the potato and cooking quality is improved.

Potatoes, Sweet. There are two types of sweet potatoes, the dry type and the moist sweet type. The dry type has a light colored skin and after cooking has a light yellow or pale orange flesh that is firm, dry, and somewhat mealy. The moist sweet type, sometimes incorrectly called a yam, has deep yellow or orange-red flesh that is soft, moist, and sweet. Good sweet potatoes of either type are clean, smooth, well shaped, firm, and bright in appearance. Those that are badly misshapen or decayed should be avoided because waste in preparation is high.

Radishes. Radishes should be well formed, smooth, firm, crisp, and tender. The color depends upon the variety, but most radishes sold commercially

---

[4] *Toward the New.* Agriculture Information Bulletin, No. 341. United States Department of Agriculture, Washington, D.C. 1970.

are red and round. Radishes that are pithy, spongy, wilted, or unusually large are undesirable.

Rhubarb. The stalks of rhubarb should be of medium thickness, firm, clean, and crisp, with no decay. The hot-house rhubarb that is available early in the year is usually light pink or pale red in color, whereas the field-grown rhubarb that is sold in late spring and early summer has a dark, rich red color.

Squash. There are many varieties of squash which differ widely in color, size, and shape. They are usually divided into summer and winter varieties. The summer varieties, which may be white, yellow, or green, are best when they are immature because the rind and seeds are usually cooked and served with the squash. For this reason a hard rind and well developed seeds are undesirable. Summer squash should be fairly heavy for its size and the skin easy to puncture. Fall and early winter varieties usually have a green or orange rind and are likely to be larger than the summer varieties, although some, such as acorn squash, are rather small. Winter squash should have a hard rind of evenly developed color and should be clean and well shaped.

Fig. 6–5. *Summer and winter squash come in a variety of shapes and colors. Acorn squash provides an appetizing container for a chopped fruit filling.*

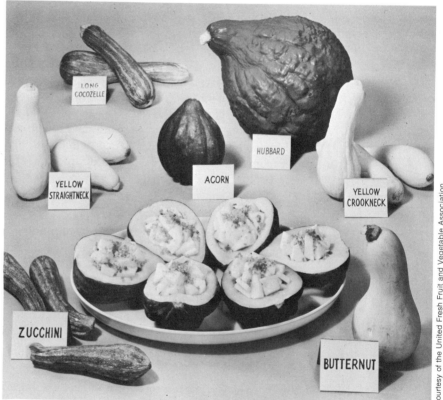

Courtesy of the United Fresh Fruit and Vegetable Association

Tomatoes. Tomatoes of good quality are well formed, plump, fairly firm to firm, and free from bruises. The color is uniform red unless the tomatoes are of a yellow variety. In most markets the tomatoes sold during late fall, winter, and spring are shipped from California, Florida, and Texas or are raised in local greenhouses. If tomatoes are to be shipped long distances, they must be picked while still green or just beginning to change in color, but they must be mature enough to ripen under proper conditions. Unless they are fully ripened tomatoes should not be stored in the refrigerator since the cold temperature may prevent later ripening.

Tomatoes that have been allowed to ripen on the vines have a flavor superior to those that are picked when immature, but such fully ripened tomatoes are available for only limited periods because they must be from sources that are near the market. Ripe tomatoes are especially susceptible to damage by bruising.

Turnips. Turnips of good quality are firm, smooth, and free from decay, cracks, spots, or other blemishes. Early turnips, which are marketed immediately after harvesting, are small and tender. Late or main crop turnips are frequently stored after harvest. Rutabagas, a special variety of turnip, are large, elongated, with a yellow flesh and a flavor that differs from most other turnips. Rutabagas and other turnips are sometimes coated with wax to prevent loss of moisture during storage.

Processed Vegetables

When the costs of fresh, frozen, and canned vegetables are compared throughout the year, the cost per serving in the processed form is lower for some vegetables and higher for others. It may be difficult at first to understand how the fresh vegetables can be more expensive than the frozen or canned vegetables, because freezing and canning involve processing, packaging, shipping, advertising, and other costs. These costs are more than offset, however, by reduced marketing costs due to the great reduction in the bulk and weight of these vegetables on processing. About 50 per cent of the weight as purchased is discarded in preparing these vegetables for cooking. This reduction in weight makes possible substantial savings in packaging, storage, and transportation. The spoilage that occurs in marketing the fresh vegetable is, of course, eliminated when the vegetable is frozen or canned.

Some vegetables are more expensive in the processed than in the fresh form. For some fresh vegetables, such as green beans, there is little waste and hence less saving in marketing in the processed form. Another factor that may explain the slightly higher cost of certain processed vegetables over those in the fresh form is their low sales volume.

Comparisons have been made of the palatability and nutritive value of some fresh and processed vegetables. Although differences were not great, fresh vegetables were generally slightly superior to frozen. Canned vegetables usually were rated lower than fresh or frozen vegetables. Fresh vegetables, both uncooked and cooked, were usually higher in ascorbic acid than frozen or canned forms.[5] Since in canned vegetables the amount of ascorbic acid in the liquid and in the solids was about equal, approximately half of the ascorbic acid is lost if the liquid is discarded.

Potatoes are now available in a variety of forms. In the study of comparative costs to consumers of convenience foods and home-prepared foods, Harp and Dunham[6] found that the cost per serving of the processed product exceeded the cost per serving of the home prepared product. If, however, the homemaker's time was valued at 50 cents an hour, many of the processed products were cheaper than those made from fresh potatoes. Most of the processed potato dishes were rated good in color, texture, and flavor, in some instances as good as the fresh. In overall acceptability, however, products made from fresh potatoes rated better than those made from processed potatoes. In most cases, at least one brand of each processed product was comparable in eating quality to fresh potatoes, but wide differences were observed between brands of processed potatoes, especially dehydrated products. Dehydrated hash browned potatoes and frozen potato puffs received the best acceptability scores for the processed potatoes, whereas canned whole potatoes served without further seasoning received low scores. The quality of frozen French fried potatoes is affected by the length of time and storage conditions during the interval from freezer to "finish frying." Better quality was obtained by "finish frying" the potatoes directly from the frozen state whether the method was a hot oven or hot fat. Potatoes held thawed usually absorbed more fat and had a shriveled appearance.[7]

Vegetables are also frozen with seasonings or sauce, sometimes in a plastic pouch that is dropped into boiling water for cooking. Such convenience products appear to be more expensive than the corresponding vegetable frozen in the usual manner.

Modern processing methods have made it possible to improve the quality of dehydrated vegetables. Such vegetables are widely used in dried soup mixes. Dried processed potatoes and dried onions have also become popular. Dried beans and peas are old favorites that have been available for many years.

A guide for yield of fresh and processed vegetables is given in Table 6–3. For most vegetables one serving is considered to be approximately one-half cup.

[5] H. H. Harp and D. F. Dunham. *Comparative Costs to Consumers of Convenience Foods and Home-Prepared Foods.* Marketing Research Report No. 609. United States Department of Agriculture, Washington, D.C. 1963, pp. 66–67.

[6] *ibid.*, pp. 17–18 and 65–66.

[7] H. K. Burr. Frozen French Fried Potatoes. Effects of Thawing and Holding Before Finish Frying and Their Non-Relation to Starch Retrogradation. *Journal of Food Science,* 36: 392–394. (1971).

Table 6–3. *Approximate Amount of Cooked Vegetable Obtained from Canned, Frozen, and Fresh Market Units.* *

Vegetable	Cans (drained)		Frozen Packages		Fresh (1 lb. as purchased)
	Size of container	Cups	Size of container	Cups	Cups
Asparagus, cut	14 oz.	$1\frac{1}{3}$	10 oz.	$1\frac{1}{4}$	2
Beans, green or wax, cut	$15\frac{1}{2}$ oz.	$1\frac{3}{4}$	9 oz.	$1\frac{2}{3}$	$2\frac{1}{2}$
Beans, lima	16 oz.	$1\frac{3}{4}$	10 oz.	$1\frac{2}{3}$	$\frac{7}{8}-1\frac{1}{8}$ ‡
Beets, sliced, diced, or whole	16 oz.	$1\frac{3}{4}$	—	—	$1\frac{3}{5}-2$
Broccoli, cut	—	—	10 oz.	$1\frac{1}{2}$	$1\frac{1}{4}-2$
Carrots, diced or sliced	16 oz.	$1\frac{3}{4}$	10 oz.	$1\frac{2}{3}$	$2-2\frac{1}{2}$
Cauliflower	—	—	10 oz.	$1\frac{1}{2}$	$1-1\frac{1}{2}$
Corn, whole kernel	16 oz.	$1\frac{2}{3}$	10 oz.	$1\frac{1}{2}$	—
Kale	15 oz.	$1\frac{1}{3}$	10 oz.	$1\frac{1}{8}$	—
Okra	$15\frac{1}{2}$ oz.	$1\frac{3}{4}$	10 oz.	$1\frac{1}{4}$	2
Peas	16 oz.	$1\frac{3}{4}$	10 oz.	$1\frac{2}{3}$	$1-1\frac{1}{4}$ ‡
Potatoes, French fried	—	—	9 oz.	$1\frac{2}{3}$	—
Spinach	15 oz.	$1\frac{1}{3}$	10 oz.	$1\frac{1}{4}$	$1\frac{1}{4}-2$
Summer squash	—	—	10 oz.	$1\frac{1}{3}$	$1-1\frac{1}{2}$
Tomatoes	16 oz.†	$1\frac{7}{8}$	—	—	2

* Data for canned and frozen vegetables from *How to Buy Canned and Frozen Vegetables*. Home and Garden Bull. No. 167, United States Department of Agriculture, 1969; data for fresh vegetables calculated from data in Table 6–8.
† undrained
‡ purchased in pod

Color

The color of vegetables depends upon the pigments they contain. These pigments are important because of the changes they undergo in cooking and because some of the carotenoids can be changed by the body to vitamin A. The effects of various factors on the pigments are summarized in Table 6–4.

Green

The green color of vegetables is due to the pigment chlorophyll, which has an important function in manufacturing carbohydrates in the plant. Chlorophyll is present only when plants are grown in the presence of light; it is absent from plants like blanched celery and white asparagus that are grown in the dark.

Chlorophyll is insoluble in water and therefore in the cooking water. It is changed chemically to an olive-green compound when heated in the small amount of acid that is liberated during cooking from the cells in which it is enclosed within the vegetable. Although this acid is present in the raw vegetable, it cannot affect the chlorophyll until the cell structure is broken down by cooking. If the cooking water is alkaline, as many city waters are, it neutralizes the acid coming from the vegetable. In canned green vege-

Table 6–4. Effects of Various Factors Upon the Pigments of Foods

Pigment	Color	In Water	Acids	Alkalies	Heat	Metals
Chlorophyll	Green	Very slightly soluble	Turn it bronze green	Brighten and intensify	Turns it bronze green	Copper and zinc brighten and intensify
Carotenoids						
Carotene	Yellow	Insoluble	Little effect	Little effect	Little effect	Little effect
Xanthophyll	Yellow					
Lycopene	Red					
Flavonoids						
Antho-cyanins	Red to blue	Soluble	Brighten or turn them red	Dull or turn them blue	Little effect	Tin and iron turn them to purple, blue, or green
Antho-xanthins	White	Soluble	Turn them white	Turn them yellow	Little effect	Iron turns them green or brown

tables, all the chlorophyll is changed to the olive-green compound because of the amount of heat required for canning and the presence of unneutralized acid. Green vegetables cooked in a pressure saucepan usually have a very good color because although the temperature is high, the time is short.

When more alkali is present than is required to neutralize any acid that is released, chlorophyll changes to a bright-green compound that can be dissolved in water. This accounts for the greenish color of the water in which some vegetables have been cooked. Sometimes baking soda is added to the cooking water because soda is alkaline and therefore makes the green color bright. Its use is not recommended, however, because the excess that is usually added destroys ascorbic acid and makes the texture of the vegetable undesirable.

Yellow

Yellow and orange vegetables and fruits owe their color to carotenoids which, like chlorophyll, are insoluble in water. Chlorophyll is accompanied by carotenoids in the ratio of about three or four parts of chlorophyll to one of carotenoids. Because the animal body can convert some carotenoids into vitamin A, yellow vegetables, and those having a dark green color such as the leafy green vegetables, are important sources of vitamin A value. Vegetables having a light green color, such as head lettuce, are not as good sources of vitamin A value as are vegetables like spinach and broccoli that are dark green. It is not correct to speak of the vitamin A content of vegetables because they contain not vitamin A but carotenoids that the body can change into vitamin A. Green and yellow vegetables can be said to contain provitamin A, precursors of vitamin A, or vitamin A value. An exception to the rule that most carotenoids are yellow or orange is the red carotenoid in tomatoes, watermelons, pink grapefruit, apricots, and persimmons.

Red

The other red vegetables and fruits, as well as those that are purple or blue, owe their color to anthocyanins, a group of pigments classed as flavonoids, which are soluble in water, little affected by heat, but sensitive to acidity. They become brighter red when acid is added and bluish in a slightly alkaline medium. Thus, red cabbage has an unattractive blue color when cooked in tap water but turns red when something acid, such as vinegar or apple, is added. Glass jars or enamel-lined cans are used for vegetables and fruits containing anthocyanins because the tin and iron of ordinary cans turns these pigments purple or blue and precipitates them. Otherwise the anthocyanins cause few problems because foods that contain them are sufficiently acid to retain their attractive color during cooking. The pigment of beets, unlike other anthocyanins, changes little during cooking unless it becomes dissolved in the cooking water. This can be avoided by cooking beets without peeling or in a small amount of water.

White

Although it would seem that white vegetables might not contain pigments, some of them contain anthoxanthins, also classed as flavonoids, which are closely related chemically to anthocyanins and are sometimes called flavones. They are soluble in water, colorless when slightly acid but yellow when alkaline. They are widely distributed in plants, often occurring with other pigments like anthocyanins but also found alone in such vegetables as potatoes, white corn, or yellow-skinned onions. They cause few cookery problems except for the yellow to brownish color sometimes seen in yellow onions cooked in alkaline water that contains a trace of iron. The color of these vegetables will be whiter if a little acid such as cream of tartar, lemon juice, or vinegar is added in cooking. Such an addition, however, is likely to make the texture firmer.

Flavor

The flavors of vegetables are due to a complex mixture of compounds that are being studied but are not yet fully understood. All vegetables are acid in reaction, varying from the rather acid tomatoes to the more nearly neutral carrots, potatoes, peas, and corn. The effects of the acid in green vegetables on the retention of their color during cooking has been discussed. Sugars are responsible in part for the flavor of such vegetables as peas and corn when they are freshly harvested. Some of their sugar is lost during storage. Glutamic acid, one of the amino acids (compounds that combine to make protein molecules), may be partly responsible for the superior flavor of young, freshly harvested vegetables, since they contain higher levels of this amino acid than more mature, stored vegetables. The unusually high glutamic acid content of mushrooms may explain their characteristic flavor and their enhancement of the flavor of other foods. Glutamic acid in the form of its salt, monosodium glutamate, is used to enhance the flavor of vegetables as well as of meat, poultry, and fish. It is a constituent of soy sauce, many seasoned salts, and is also sold in the pure form.

Vegetables of the onion and cabbage families (Table 6–5) owe their characteristic flavors to sulfur compounds. In both families, the raw vegetable does not have much odor until it is cut. In onions and garlic, cutting or crushing permits the enzyme and the sulfur compound to be mixed, and the enzyme then acts very rapidly on the sulfur compound to produce the characteristic pungent odor of the freshly cut vegetable. Another enzyme appears to be responsible for the flavor of shredded raw cabbage. The sulfur compounds of the onion and cabbage families differ from each other in their reaction to cooking. Onions become increasingly mild as they are boiled, especially if the volume of water is large, because the sulfur compounds responsible for their flavor are volatile and soluble. The pungent but not unpleasant flavor of raw cabbage, however, changes gradually during cooking to the typical, penetrating flavor of overcooked cabbage. As the sulfur compounds of the cabbage family break down during cooking, hydrogen sulfide is formed. This change can be minimized by starting the vegetable in boiling water and cooking for the minimum length of time.

Nutritive Value

In addition to giving their interesting colors, textures, and flavors to the diet, vegetables contribute minerals, vitamins, and bulk in the form of cellulose and pectic compounds. Most vegetables are low in protein, although immature peas and lima beans and cooked mature legumes contain 6 to 8 per cent. The carbohydrate content is low in most vegetables except seeds and starchy roots that store starch for the germinating plant. For example, the carbohydrate content is less than 3 per cent in lettuce but about 17 per cent in

Table 6–5. *Vegetables in the* Brassica *(Cabbage or Mustard) and in the* Allium *(Onion) Families*

Brassica		Allium
Broccoli	Collards	Chives
Brussels sprouts	Kale	Garlic
Cabbage	Kohlrabi	Leeks
celery or Chinese	Mustard greens	Onions
common	Mustard spinach	Shallots
red	Rutabagas	
Savoy	Turnips	
Cauliflower		

potatoes and 22 per cent in corn and lima beans. Carbohydrates are present chiefly as starch, although some sugar is present in freshly harvested peas and corn. For vegetables low in protein and fat, the food energy content follows closely the carbohydrate content.

The vitamin A value of green and yellow vegetables has already been mentioned. Because the proportion of chlorophyll to carotenoids is fairly constant, dark green leaves have greater vitamin A value than lighter green leaves. Collards, kale, spinach, turnip greens, and broccoli have many times more vitamin A value than lettuce, cabbage, asparagus, peas, or snap beans, and leaf lettuce contains more than head lettuce. Similarly high is the vitamin A value of such yellow vegetables as sweet potatoes, carrots, and winter squash, as shown in Table 6–6.

In fact, it can be said that the greener the vegetable, the higher it is in vitamins and minerals. Greens compare favorably with tomatoes and some of the citrus fruits in ascorbic acid, especially if the leaves are young rather than mature, and are higher than most vegetables in riboflavin. The calcium and iron content of greens are excellent; however, spinach, chard, and beet greens contain oxalic acid, which combines with calcium to form an insoluble compound that is unavailable to the body. For this reason, these vegetables are not as good sources of calcium as some of the other green vegetables. They are, however, valuable in the diet because of other nutrients they contain.

Although some of the nutrients are lost in the cooking of vegetables, it does not necessarily follow that more nutrients will be consumed if a vegetable is eaten raw because of differences in the size of servings. One-half cup of cooked vegetable is usually considered as one serving, but about two and one-half cups of raw greens are required to make this amount of cooked greens.

The cabbage family ranks high in nutritive value. Broccoli, because of its dark-green color, is very good in vitamin A value. It is also high in calcium and ascorbic acid. Although lower than broccoli, the other members of the cabbage family listed in Table 6–6 are good sources of ascorbic acid and other nutrients.

The seed vegetables lima beans and peas are high in thiamine. Mature beans and peas, sometimes called legumes, are often used as a main dish because of their high protein content. Although not a complete protein, the protein of legumes is valuable in a mixed diet. The legumes are also valuable for their content of calcium, iron, and the B-vitamins.

While not strikingly high in any nutrient, white potatoes are important in the diet because they are eaten in larger amounts than many other vegetables and because they contain good amounts of a number of important nutrients, especially ascorbic acid. The outbreak of scurvy that once followed a potato famine in Ireland shows what an important contribution generous amounts of potatoes can make to the ascorbic acid content of the

Table 6–6. *Nutritive Value of Certain Vegetables* *

Vegetable	Approx. Measure	Weight gm.	Food Energy calories	Calcium mg.	Iron mg.	Vitamin A value I.U.	Thiamine mg.	Riboflavin mg.	Niacin mg.	Ascorbic Acid mg.
Asparagus, cooked spears	4 spears	60	10	13	.4	540	.10	.11	.8	16
Beans										
lima, cooked	1 cup	170	190	80	4.3	480	.31	.17	2.2	29
snap, cooked	1 cup	125	30	63	.8	680	.09	.11	.6	15
Beets, cooked, diced	1 cup	170	55	24	.9	30	.05	.07	.5	10
Broccoli stalks, cooked	1 stalk	180	45	158	1.4	4500	.16	.36	1.4	162
Brussels sprouts, cooked	1 cup	155	55	50	1.7	810	.12	.22	1.2	135
Cabbage, green fine shred	1 cup	90	20	44	.4	120	.05	.05	.3	42
Cabbage, red coarse shred	1 cup	70	20	29	.6	30	.06	.04	.3	43
Carrots, raw	1 carrot	50	20	18	.4	5500	.03	.03	.3	4
Carrots, cooked, diced	1 cup	145	45	48	.9	15220	.08	.07	.7	9
Celery, raw, diced	1 cup	100	15	39	.3	240	.03	.03	.3	9
Collards, cooked	1 cup	190	55	289	1.1	10260	.27	.37	2.4	87
Corn, canned solids + liquid	1 cup	256	170	10	1.0	690	.07	.12	2.3	13
Kale, cooked, with stems	1 cup	110	30	147	1.3	8140	—	—	—	68
Lettuce, looseleaf	2 large leaves	50	10	34	.7	950	.03	.04	.2	9
Okra, cooked	8 pods	85	25	78	.4	420	.11	.15	.8	17
Onions, cooked	1 cup	210	60	50	.8	80	.06	.06	.4	14
Peas, canned, solids + liquid	1 cup	249	165	50	4.2	1120	.23	.13	2.2	22
Potatoes										
Sweet, baked, peeled	1 medium	110	155	44	1.0	8910	.10	.07	.7	24
White, baked, peeled	1 medium	99	90	9	.7	trace	.10	.04	1.7	20
Potato chips, medium	10 chips	20	115	8	.4	trace	.04	.01	1.0	3
Spinach, cooked	1 cup	180	40	167	4.0	14580	.13	.25	1.0	50
Squash, summer, cooked, diced	1 cup	210	30	52	.8	820	.10	.16	1.6	21
Squash, winter, baked, mashed	1 cup	205	130	57	1.6	8610	.10	.27	1.4	27
Tomatoes, raw	1 tomato	200	40	24	.9	1640	.11	.07	1.3	42
Tomatoes, canned, solids + liquid	1 cup	241	50	14	1.2	2170	.12	.07	1.7	41
Turnips, cooked, diced	1 cup	155	35	54	.6	trace	.06	.08	.5	34
Turnip greens, cooked	1 cup	145	30	252	1.5	8270	.15	.33	.7	68

* From *Nutritive Value of Foods.* Home and Garden Bulletin No. 72, Agricultural Research Service, United States Department of Agriculture, 1971.

diet. The ascorbic acid content of potatoes and other vegetables decreases during storage, especially if storage temperatures are high. The calorie content per serving of potatoes is similar to that of lima beans, corn, and peas. It is not high unless accompanied by generous amounts of butter, margarine, sauces, or sour cream.

Table 6–6 indicates that some vegetables such as celery, cucumbers, beets, and onions contain only small amounts of nutrients compared with some of the other vegetables. They are valuable, however, because of the flavor, crispness, and color they add to the diet.

In using such data as given in Table 6–6, it must be realized that the exact value of a nutrient depends upon many variables such as variety, growing conditions, maturity, and methods of storage, marketing, and preparation. An effort has been made by the Department of Agriculture to give figures that are representative for the United States throughout the year. The figures should be considered as good averages rather than as absolute values.

Preparation of Vegetables
Preliminary Preparation

Many vegetables which are low in starch are attractive in appearance and are good to eat raw when they are crisp and tender. Raw vegetables generally offer the same problem of preliminary preparation as do raw fruits but require more cleaning. Vegetables commonly grow in or close to the ground and so are exposed to contamination even more than are fruits. All soils contain organisms, many of them pathogenic. Even if the vegetables escape contamination by the soil, they are exposed to dust, insects, and human hands before being brought into the home. Hence careful and thorough washing is essential. All spoiled portions should be removed. Whether the vegetable is washed only, washed and brushed, scraped, or peeled is determined by the vegetable selected, its age, and the method of preparation. Soaking some vegetables may be helpful in removing dirt or insects and in making the vegetable crisp. However, it is better to avoid soaking after cutting the vegetable into pieces because water-soluble nutrients may be lost.

Although some of the outer leaves of such vegetables as cabbage, broccoli, and lettuce must be discarded if they are damaged, wilted, or yellowed, as many of them as possible should be used because they are higher in nutritive value than the inner leaves. The vitamin A value is higher especially in the darker outer leaves which contain more carotene than the inner leaves. Such vegetables as potatoes are often cooked before peeling, because peeled vegetables usually lose more of their nutrients during cooking than unpeeled vegetables. Of course, some vegetables with thick skins, such as turnips, rutabagas, and eggplant, are always peeled before cooking. Stems and even midribs of leaves may be removed before cooking if they are tough, because they contain little nutritive value and require longer cooking than the remainder of the leaf. Therefore, their removal may even improve

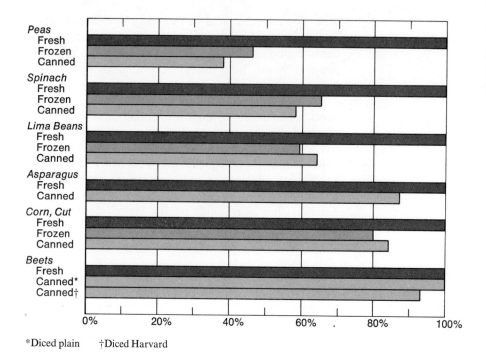

*Diced plain   †Diced Harvard

Fig. 6–6. *Comparative cost of vegetables which were least expensive in the processed form.* (Calculated from Harp and Dunham, in *Comparative Costs to Consumers of Convenience Foods and Home-Prepared Foods.* Market Research Report No. 609, U.S. Department of Agriculture, 1963.)

retention of some nutrients, as indicated in Table 6–7 by the ascorbic acid content of collards.

Cutting the vegetable into pieces increases the surface area from which soluble nutrients can be dissolved, but it also shortens the cooking time. Probably because of a balance between these two factors, nutrients are usually well retained if vegetables are cut into pieces of medium size. Loss of soluble nutrients may become excessive, however, when vegetables are cut into very small pieces, such as green beans cut into thin diagonal strips. Carrots cut lengthwise will lose fewer nutrients than those cut crosswise.

Effects of Cooking

During cooking, the texture of vegetables changes because cooking softens the cellulose, hemicellulose, and pectic substances that make up the cell walls of the vegetables. This softening of the cell walls greatly reduces the bulk of leafy vegetables during cooking, but ordinarily the cell walls will not rupture. The starch granules found in such vegetables as potatoes swell and change to a more soluble form. Microorganisms are destroyed by heat during cooking. Some minerals are dissolved in the cooking water, but fortunately the retention of one of the most important minerals, calcium, is excellent when the water contains calcium. If the water is moderately high

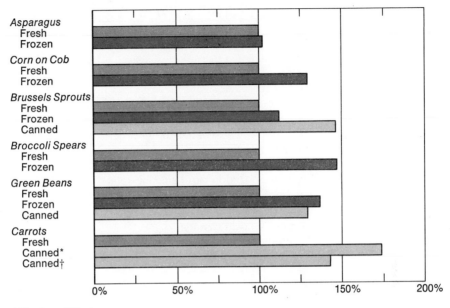

*Sliced   †Diced

Fig. 6–7. *Comparative cost of vegetables which were most expensive in the processed form.* (Calculated from Harp and Dunham, in *Comparative Costs to Consumers of Convenience Foods and Home-Prepared Foods.* Marketing Research Report No. 609, U.S. Department of Agriculture, 1963.)

Fig. 6–8. *Asparagus should be washed carefully to remove sand from the tips. The lower part of the stalk is broken off before the asparagus is cooked.*

Courtesy of Western Growers Association

Table 6–7. *Vitamin Content of Several Vegetables Cooked by Different Methods* *
(Expressed in Mg. per 100 Gm. Edible Portion, Drained)

Vegetable and Method of Preparation	Thiamine mg.	Ribo-flavin mg.	Niacin mg.	Ascorbic Acid mg.
Beans, green snap, boiled in				
small amount of water, short time	0.07	0.09	0.5	12
large amount of water, long time	0.06	0.08	0.3	10
Cabbage				
shredded, boiled in small amount water	0.04	0.04	0.3	33
wedges, boiled in large amount water	0.02	0.02	0.1	24
Collards				
leaves without stems boiled in				
small amount of water	0.11	0.20	1.2	76
large amount of water	0.07	0.14	1.1	51
leaves including stems boiled in				
small amount of water	0.14	0.20	1.2	46
Potatoes				
baked in skin	0.10	0.04	1.7	20
boiled in skin	0.09	0.04	1.5	16
boiled, pared before cooking	0.09	0.03	1.2	16
mashed, milk and table fat added	0.08	0.05	1.0	9
Turnip greens, boiled in				
small amount water, short time	0.15	0.24	0.6	69
large amount water, long time	0.10	0.23	0.5	47

* Compiled from *Composition of Foods—raw, processed, prepared,* by Watt and Merrill. Agriculture Handbook No. 8, Agricultural Research Service, United States Department of Agriculture, Revised 1963.

in calcium, the calcium may remain the same as in the raw vegetable or even increase during boiling. Such waters are found rather frequently in the United States and probably elsewhere.

It has already been noted that carotenoids are insoluble in water. They are also stable to heat and are therefore little affected by cooking. Ascorbic acid and the B-vitamins are affected because they are soluble in water. Ascorbic acid is the most easily lost and is therefore most often studied. In addition to being dissolved in the cooking water, it may be destroyed by enzymes in the vegetable if the vegetable is heated slowly during the early part of the cooking period. Enzymes work more rapidly as the temperature rises but are inactivated before the boiling point is reached. For this reason, it is important always to put the vegetable into boiling rather than cold water when cooking is started so that enzymes can be inactivated as rapidly as possible.

Methods

Vegetables can be well cooked in a variety of ways—a much greater variety, in fact, than is used by many families. They can be boiled, steamed, cooked in a pressure saucepan, baked, or panned. They can be cooked alone or in combination with other vegetables. After cooking, they can be mashed, creamed, fried, or seasoned in a great variety of ways, as by the addition of table fat, bacon fat, salt pork, herbs, vinegar, or lemon juice.

Customs for vegetable preparation vary throughout the world. In England, for example, vegetables are usually served boiled, but in Egypt they are served boiled only to a person who is ill. Other Egyptians prefer their vegetables cooked in the oven or on top of the range with onion, garlic, meat, and other seasonings. In Italy, hot vegetables are often seasoned with olive oil instead of the butter or margarine that is popular in many other countries. On the continent of Europe, vegetables are served in many ways, often beautifully seasoned and garnished. The use of vegetables in soups and the delicious creamed spinach are noteworthy. In the United States there are also such regional preferences as vegetables cooked for a long time with pork meat or fat in the Southeast, or for shorter times in the North and West. It is important that students understand the effects of different methods of cookery on the nutritive value and palatability of vegetables, and be willing to try new methods, but they also should learn respect for the preferences and customs of others.

Boiling. Probably the most commonly used method for cooking vegetables is boiling, and the usual recommendation is to cook in a small amount of salted water in a covered pan until just tender and still slightly crisp. The water is boiling when the vegetable is added and is brought back to the boiling point as rapidly as possible. The heat is then reduced until it is just high enough to keep the water boiling. Vegetables boiled rapidly break up because of mechanical agitation, and cook no more speedily than those boiled slowly. There is no need to avoid the use of water entirely because experiments have shown that the ascorbic acid retention is about the same and palatability is better when vegetables are cooked in half their weight of water as when they are cooked according to the so-called "waterless cooking" method in the minimum of water required to prevent scorching. The reason for the similar retention in these two methods is probably that the greater solution losses with the larger amount of water balance the losses that occur when the vegetable heats through more slowly in the minimum amount of water. One-half to one cup water for four servings of a vegetable is equivalent to about half the weight of the vegetable. About one-half teaspoon salt is needed for this amount of vegetable. The amount of a vegetable required for four servings and the times required for various methods of cooking are shown in Table 6–8. Times are only approximate because they vary with the maturity of the vegetable and other factors. It is best to test

Table 6–8. Characteristics and Preparation of Fresh Vegetables *

Vegetable	Predominating Pigment	Strong or Mild Flavor	Amount to Purchase for 4 Servings	Description	Covered or Uncovered for Boiling	Time for Cooking (Minutes)			
						Boiling	Steaming	Baking	Saucepan Pressure†
Artichokes, French	Chlorophyll	Mild	2 lb.	Whole	Uncovered	35–45	—	—	10–12
Artichokes, Jerusalem	Chlorophyll	Mild	1 lb.	Pared, whole	Covered	25–35	35	30–60	—
Asparagus	Chlorophyll	Mild	1½–2 bunches or 1 lb.	Tips	Uncovered	5–15	7–15	—	½–1½
	Chlorophyll	Mild		Whole or butts	Uncovered	15–25	12–30	—	1–2
Beans, fresh lima	Chlorophyll	Mild	⅘ lb. shelled 1½ to 2½ lb. in pods	Shelled	Covered	20–40	25–40	—	1–3
Beans, green	Chlorophyll	Mild	⅘ lb.	Whole or 1-inch pieces	Uncovered	15–30	20–35	—	1½–3
Beets, young, small	Anthocyanins	Mild	1–1½ bunches	Whole	Covered	30–45	40–60	40–60	5–10
mature, small	Anthocyanins	Mild	1–1¼ lb.	Whole	Covered	45–90	50–90	50–90	10–18
Beet greens	Chlorophyll	Mild	1–1½ lb.	—	Uncovered	5–15	—	—	—
Broccoli	Chlorophyll	Strong	1–1½ lb.	Flowerets	Uncovered	8–20	15–20	—	1½–2½
Brussels sprouts	Chlorophyll	Strong	⅘–1 lb.	Whole	Uncovered	6–15	8–18	—	1
Cabbage, white	Anthoxanthins	Strong	1 lb.	Quartered	Uncovered	12–15	15	—	2–3
white	Anthoxanthins	Strong	1 lb.	Shredded	Uncovered	5–9	10–11	—	1
green	Chlorophyll	Strong	1 lb.	Shredded	Uncovered	3–8	8–10	—	½–1½
Carrots, young	Carotene	Mild	1–1½ bunches	Whole or halves	Covered	15–25	20–30	35–45	3–5
old	Carotene	Mild	¾–1 lb.	Diced	Covered	15–25	20–25	—	2–3
Cauliflower	Anthoxanthins	Strong	1¾–2 lb.	Whole	Uncovered	20–30	25–30	—	3½
	Anthoxanthins	Strong	1¾–2 lb.	Flowerets	Uncovered	8–15	10–15	—	1½
Celeriac	—	—	1¾–2 lb.	Sliced or diced	—	15–20	25	—	—
Celery	Chlorophyll	Mild	1 bunch or 1 lb.	Diced	Covered	15–20	25–30	—	2
Chinese cabbage	Chlorophyll	Strong	¾–1 lb.	Sliced	Uncovered	8–10	—	—	—
Collards	Chlorophyll	Strong	2 lb.	—	Uncovered	10–20	—	—	—
Corn	—	Mild	4 ears	On cob	Covered	5–10	10–15	—	0–1½
Cucumbers	Chlorophyll	Mild	3 medium	Sliced	Covered	5–6	—	—	—
	Chlorophyll	Mild	2 medium	Whole, stuffed	Covered	—	20	20–25	—
Dandelion greens	Chlorophyll	Mild	1¾ lb.	—	Uncovered	15–25	—	—	—

Vegetable	Color pigment	Flavor	Amount to purchase*	Preparation	Covered or uncovered	Boiling	Steaming	Baking	Pressure saucepan†
Egg plant	Chlorophyll	Mild	1 medium	Diced	Covered	8–15	12–20	—	—
	Chlorophyll	Mild	2 small	Whole, stuffed	—	—	—	30–45	—
Kohlrabi	Anthoxanthins	Strong	1 lb.	Pared, sliced	Uncovered	20–30	30	—	—
Mustard greens	Chlorophyll	Strong	1½–2 lb.	—	Uncovered	15–25	—	—	—
Okra	Chlorophyll	Strong	1 lb.	Whole	Uncovered	10–20	20	—	3
Onions	Anthoxanthins	Strong	1 lb.	Large, whole, or partially quartered	Uncovered	20–35	—	45–60	5–8
Parsnips	Anthoxanthins	Strong	1 lb.	Small, whole	Uncovered	15–25	—	30–50	3–4
	Anthoxanthins	Mild	1 lb.	Sliced	Covered	15–25	30–40	—	6
Peas, green	Chlorophyll	Mild	1½–2 lb. in pod	Shelled	Uncovered	8–20	10–20	—	0–1
Peppers	Chlorophyll	Strong	4	Whole, stuffed	Uncovered	10–15	—	25–30	8–10
Potatoes, white	—	Mild	*1–1½ lb.	Whole, small	Covered	25–35	30–45	45–60	6–8
Potatoes, sweet	Carotene	Mild	1–1½ lb.	Quartered lengthwise	Covered	15–25	25–30	—	6–8
Pumpkin	Carotene	Mild	1–1½ lb.	Whole	Covered	25–35	30–35	30–50	8–10
Rutabagas	Carotenoids	Mild	1½–2 lb.	Diced	Uncovered	20–25	25–30	—	8–10
Salsify	—	Strong	1¼ lb.	Sliced	Covered	20–30	—	—	5–8
Spinach	Chlorophyll	Mild	1 lb.	Without stems	Covered or Uncovered	3–5	5–10	—	0–1½
Spinach	Chlorophyll	Mild	1½–2 lb.	With stems	Covered or Uncovered	5–10	6–12	—	0–1½
Squash, summer	Chlorophyll	Mild	1½–2 lb.	Sliced	Covered	5–15	15–20	30	1½–3
Squash, winter	Carotene	Mild	1½–2 lb.	Diced	Covered	25–30	30–40	—	6–12
	Carotene	Mild	1½–2 lb.	1-portion pieces	Covered	—	—	50–70	—
Tomatoes	Lycopene	Mild	1 lb.	Whole	Covered	5–10	10	15–25	—
	—	Mild	1 lb.	Whole, stuffed	—	—	15–25	20–30	—
Turnips	—	Strong	1 lb.	Diced	Uncovered	10–20	20–25	—	1½–3
Turnip greens	Chlorophyll	Strong	1½–2 lb.	—	Uncovered	15–25	—	—	1–1½

* The amount to purchase and the length of time suggested for cooking are approximations only.

† At the end of the cooking period, put the pressure saucepan in cold water or under running cold water to reduce the pressure rapidly.

vegetables with a fork when they are almost done and to continue cooking if necessary. Vegetables cooked only to the crisp stage have better color, better retention of nutrients, and a milder flavor than those cooked until soft.[8]

Some vegetables have a greener color and a milder flavor when they are cooked in an uncovered pan rather than cooked covered in the manner just described. When no cover is used, there should be enough water to cover the vegetable after it has wilted during the first few minutes of cooking. This method is often recommended for members of the cabbage family—broccoli, Brussels sprouts, cabbage, cauliflower, Chinese cabbage, and kohlrabi. Losses of nutrients tend to increase if the amount of water is increased to more than half the weight of the vegetable, but for some people such losses are offset by the greener color and milder flavor of the vegetable. Table 6–7 indicates that although losses of vitamins are greater with larger amounts of water, they are not extreme. In some of the examples in the table it will be noted that two variables are combined so that cooking losses are increased by cooking for a long time and by using more water.

Other experiments have shown that covering the pan does not influence ascorbic acid retention if the same amounts of water and of vegetable are used in both pans. This is logical because ascorbic acid and the other vitamins are not volatile. If, however, the amount of water is small, the pan must be covered so the vegetable that is above the water can cook in the steam. The composition of the cooking utensil, whether aluminum, enamel, Pyrex, or stainless steel, has little effect on the retention of asorbic acid by vegetables boiled in them.

Steaming. Vegetables cooked by this method are placed in the perforated container of a steamer over boiling water and covered tightly. Steaming also applies to the "waterless cooking" method already discussed. The vegetables are placed in a heavy pan with the minimum amount of water to prevent scorching. Salt is sprinkled on the vegetables when they are put into the steamer or pan. The vitamin retention of vegetables cooked in pans of these two types and in a pressure saucepan are similar, as might be expected. From the standpoint of color and palatability, steaming is, perhaps, a better method for such vegetables as potatoes, squash, beets, and carrots than for green vegetables or members of the cabbage family.

Pressure Cooking. Vegetables cooked in a pressure saucepan usually have good color and flavor. The vegetable is often cut into smaller pieces for this method than for boiling so that the heat will penetrate rapidly and uniformly. Solution losses from the cut surface are small because the amount of water is small and the time short. It is not so easy to test for doneness in the pressure saucepan as with the other methods because the pressure must be

[8] I. Noble. Ascorbic Acid and Color of Vegetables. *Journal of The American Dietetic Association,* 50: 304–307 (1967).

reduced and the lid removed before the vegetable is tested. If the vegetable is young, it can usually be cooked successfully for the shorter time given in Table 6–8, and if it is mature, for the longer time. It is especially important to avoid overcooking because of the high temperature being used. The times are for a cooker operating at fifteen pounds pressure, the pressure in pans having only one setting. Some saucepans have settings for 5, 10, and 15 pounds pressure. The directions that came with the saucepan should be followed, with care taken that after cooking the pressure is first reduced to zero by putting the pan in cold water; then the weight is removed from the vent and the cover is removed.

Baking. Some vegetables, such as winter squash, tomatoes, and potatoes, can be baked whole in their skins. They are simply washed thoroughly, put on a baking pan or on the racks of the oven, depending upon the nature of the vegetable, and baked until tender. Baking times are shown in Table 6–8. Because the oven temperature is not critical, vegetables can be baked at the temperature being used for preparing other food for the meal. If only the vegetable is in the oven, temperatures of 177° to 205° C. (350° to 400° F.) are appropriate, although temperatures of 218° to 232° C. (425° to 450° F.) may be preferred for white potatoes. Potatoes are sometimes pricked before baking to avoid bursting the skins, but there may be an advantage in baking them without pricking so that the steam will be retained and help cook the potato. In any case, a slit should be cut in the potato as soon as it is taken from the oven to release steam and prevent the potato from becoming soggy.

Vegetables can also be baked in a casserole. Fresh vegetables cut into small pieces or frozen vegetables that have been thawed partially are put in the casserole with a little table fat, about a tablespoon of water, salt, pepper, and other seasonings if desired, covered, and baked until tender at 163° to 177° C. (325° to 350° F.). An approximate time for most green vegetables is 45 minutes. Another method of casserole cookery is to combine cooked vegetables with a white sauce, put in a casserole, cover with buttered crumbs, and bake at about 205° C. (400° F.) until the crumbs are brown. Vegetables prepared in this way are said to be scalloped.

Stir-Frying. A method of vegetable cookery adapted from the Orient, and one that retains color and nutrients as well, is called stir-frying. It is best used with tender vegetables that are high in moisture. Leafy vegetables are broken into pieces, cabbage is shredded, but such vegetables as asparagus, string beans, or celery are cut into thin diagonal pieces. One or two table-spoons of fat for four servings of vegetable are heated in a fry pan, and the vegetable is added, along with salt and other seasoning if desired. The fry pan is covered and the vegetable is cooked over low heat for a short time with occasional stirring. A small amount of water is added if necessary. Cooking is stopped when the vegetable is still slightly crisp. Although vegetables are cut into small pieces for stir-frying and casserole cookery, losses are not great because no liquid is drained from the vegetable when it is served.

 Electronic Oven. Vegetables cooked by microwaves in an electronic oven compare closely in palatability and nutrient retention to those boiled in a small amount of water. One advantage of baking potatoes in an electronic oven is that the potatoes may be reheated without sogginess.[9]

Frozen Vegetables. It is usually most convenient to cook frozen vegetables without thawing. If they are frozen in a block, cooking is faster when they are broken up with a fork soon after they are put in boiling water. Frozen vegetables that are thick, such as corn on the cob and large stalks of broccoli, may need some thawing so that cooking will be uniform throughout the vegetable. About one-half cup of water is used for each pint of vegetable. The vegetable is dropped into the boiling water, brought back to a boil quickly, and boiled gently until just tender. Cooking times are shorter for frozen than for fresh vegetables because blanching and freezing make vegetables more tender. If a commercially frozen vegetable is being used, the directions on the package furnish a good guide for cooking.

Canned Vegetables. In serving canned vegetables, it is especially important not to discard the liquid because of its high content of nutrients. If there is too much liquid to serve with the vegetable, it can be drained, boiled until it is concentrated to about a third of its original volume, and the vegetable added and heated through. It is important not to concentrate the liquid with the vegetable in it because this over-cooks the vegetable.

Dried Vegetables. Mature peas and beans are often dried. Before cooking, they must be rehydrated. This can be done rapidly by boiling the vegetable in water for two minutes and then allowing it to stand for one hour, or more slowly by allowing it to stand in cold water for fifteen hours or overnight. Dry beans soaked by these two methods absorb the same amount of water and are equally palatable. Dry beans soaked and cooked in hard water do not soften properly because the calcium and magnesium present in the water combine with the pectic substances of the vegetable to form insoluble salts. This undesirable effect can be prevented by substituting soft water or by adding sodium bicarbonate to the hard water. About one-eighth teaspoon of soda for each cup of dry beans is sufficient. An excess of soda will reduce thiamine retention. Rehydrated peas or beans can be cooked in a pressure saucepan in three to ten minutes, depending upon the variety. Care must be taken not to fill the saucepan more than one-third full and to add a little fat to prevent foaming and possible clogging of the vent.

Because of the use of a variety of modern methods of dehydration, the directions on the package should be noted carefully.

[9] A. W. Goldsmid. Microwave Baked Potatoes in Large Scale Food Preparation. *Journal of The American Dietetic Association,* 51: 536 (1967).

Courtesy of the United Fresh Fruit and Vegetable Association

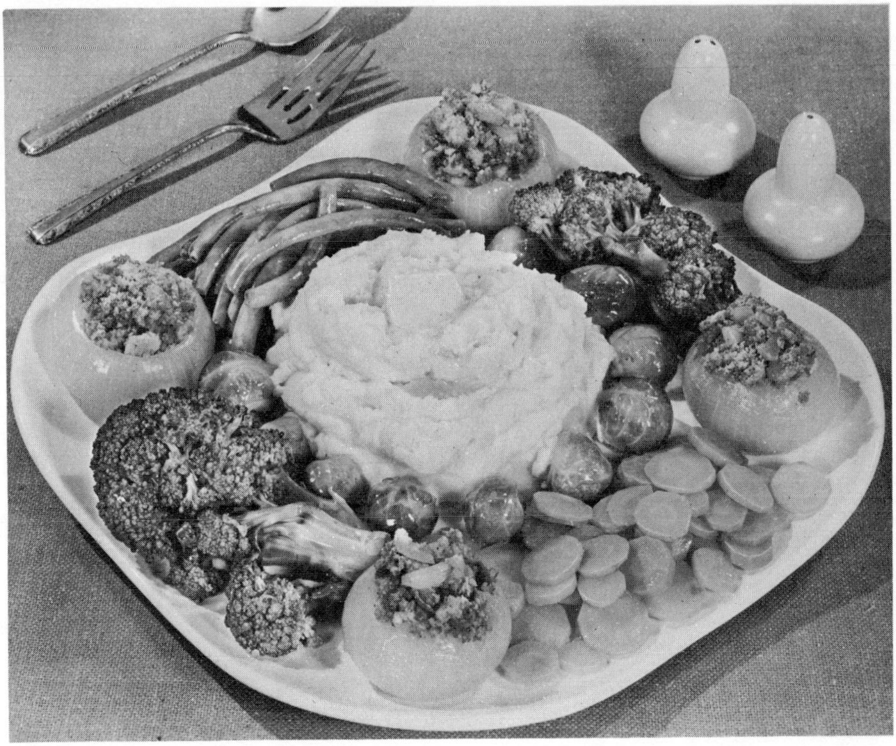

Fig. 6–9. *Variety and contrast add interest to this fresh vegetable meal of mashed potatoes, broccoli with lemon butter, snap beans, baked onions with tomato stuffing, Brussels sprouts, and continental carrots.*

High Altitudes. Because the boiling point of water is lower at high altitudes than at sea level, the boiling times for vegetables will be longer. It may be convenient to accelerate cooking by using a pressure saucepan, but unless the pressure pan is adjusted for the altitude, cooking times must be increased at high altitudes because the temperature within the pan is lower than at sea level with the same pressure. Baking times are the same at high and low altitudes when similar temperatures are used.[10]

Serving

Interest and variety can be added to vegetables with imaginative additions in serving. Seasonings are used sparingly and with care so that they will bring out rather than hide the natural flavor of the vegetables. Salt, pepper, and monosodium glutamate if desired are often added to the drained cooked

[10] L. Garrett. *A Cook's Almanac for Altitude Problems.* New Mexico Extension Service Circular 373 (1964).

vegetable and about one tablespoon table fat, bacon fat, salad oil, or other fat per cup of vegetable. Butter or margarine may be heated until brown before using on vegetables. Toasted bread crumbs added to the browned table fat give variety. Vegetables can be creamed by combining one cup white sauce with about two cups vegetable. A medium white sauce is commonly used, although thin white sauce may be preferred for lima beans, potatoes, or when grated cheese is added. The liquid drained from the vegetable can be combined with nonfat dry or evaporated milk for use in the sauce. It can also, of course, be used for soups or gravies.

Variety can be added to drained vegetables with a little heated cream, either fresh or sour, French dressing, a dash of soy sauce, lemon juice, grated cheese, minced onion, cut chives, green pepper, parsley, or fried mushrooms. An especially interesting texture is produced by adding bits of crisp bacon to greens or slivered almonds or sliced water chestnuts to green beans. The flavor of cut fresh or dried mint leaves and a little sugar is good with carrots and peas, herbs with lima beans and many other vegetables, and nutmeg with asparagus, carrots, snap beans, spinach, squash, or sweet potato. A little vinegar and sugar heated together can be used with beets, cabbage, snap beans, or other vegetables.

Vegetables like potatoes and squash are often mashed and table fat, seasonings, and milk added if desired. However, mashing has been found to decrease the ascorbic acid content of potatoes because it mixes air with the vegetable (Table 6–7).

Activities

1. Select a green vegetable and prepare by each of the basic methods described in the text—boiling, steaming, cooking in a pressure saucepan, baking whole or in a casserole, and stir-frying. Use the same proportion of table fat and salt to vegetable for each method so that the flavor of the vegetable can be evaluated accurately. Repeat, if desired, with a member of the cabbage family, a red vegetable, a yellow vegetable, and a white vegetable.

2. Compare a green vegetable boiled in various amounts of water, covered and uncovered, and cooked for various lengths of time. Repeat with any other vegetable desired.

3. Select one vegetable from each of the groups shown in Table 6–1. Boil in a small amount of water or in chicken broth and serve in as many ways as possible. Serve with various table fats, with lemon juice, herbs, bits of crisp bacon, buttered crumbs, slivered almonds; with white sauce, cheese sauce, tomato sauce, or Hollandaise sauce. Scallop the vegetable with or without cheese and prepare a soufflé.

4. Select a vegetable such as squash, one of the stem tubers or roots, and serve fried in deep or shallow fat and mashed.

5. Stuff and bake a whole tomato. Cut tomatoes in half, add buttered crumbs, then bake or broil.

6. Study a cookbook to find as many ways as possible of preparing white potatoes, both raw and reheated. Prepare as many of the recipes as possible.

7. Select a vegetable and purchase it fresh and in as many processed forms as possible. Prepare according to package directions. Compare the palatability, preparation time, and cost of each form. It will be necessary to weigh or measure the products so that the cost can be calculated for equivalent amounts.

8. List vegetables that are unfamiliar or disliked by several students. Prepare them in attractive ways, and then taste and discuss their appetite appeal.

9. List the fresh vegetables for sale in several local stores. Record any information available on their grade, size, variety, and place of origin. Note the price and appearance of the vegetable.

10. Select a vegetable that is frequently canned. Examine as many brands, grades, and can sizes as possible. Turn out of the cans, code the samples to avoid bias, and compare:
a. the amount of vegetable in a can. To do this, drain the vegetable and measure or weigh the vegetable and the liquid.
b. the quality of the vegetable.
c. the cost of comparable amounts of vegetable.

References

Food for Us All. Yearbook of Agriculture, 1969. U.S. Dept. Agr., Washington, D.C.: United States Government Printing Office. Pp. 174–195.

Green Vegetables for Good Eating. U.S. Dept. Agr., Home and Garden Bull. No. 41 (1964).

Handbook of Food Preparation. American Home Economics Association, Washington, D.C. 1971. Pp. 84–103.

HARRIS, R. S. AND H. VON LOESECKE (Eds.). *Nutritional Evaluation of Food Processing*. New York: John Wiley & Sons, Inc. 1960. Pp. 337–358; 462–484.

How to Buy Fresh Vegetables. U.S. Dept. Agr., Home and Garden Bull. No. 143 (1967).

How to Buy Canned and Frozen Vegetables. U.S. Dept. Agr., Home and Garden Bull. No. 167 (1969).

Potatoes in Popular Ways. U.S. Dept. Agr., Home and Garden Bull. No. 55 (1969).

POTTER, N. N. *Food Science*. Westport, Conn.: The Avi Publishing Company, Inc. 1968. Pp. 464–483.

SWEENEY, J. P., V. J. CHAPMAN, M. E. MARTIN, P. L. KING, AND E. H. DAWSON. *Vegetables—Consumer Quality, Yield, and Preparation Time of Various Market Forms*. U.S. Dept. Agr., Home Econ. Research Rept. No. 17 (1962).

Tomatoes on Your Table. U.S. Dept. Agr., Leaflet No. 278 (1966).

Vegetables in Family Meals. U.S. Dept. Agr., Home and Garden Bull. No. 105 (1971).

7

salads

In many homes the plans for the meals of the day are not considered complete unless at least one salad is included. Whether the salad accompanies a meal of hearty foods or forms the main dish of a luncheon or supper, it can supply vivid color, delicious flavor, and valuable minerals and vitamins. Throughout the year a variety of salad foods are available. In fact, there is hardly a natural food that does not have some place in salad making.

A salad may be considered to consist of a green salad vegetable, with or without other foods, that is served with a tart dressing. A light salad that accompanies a meal of hearty food can be served as a first course, with the meat course, or as a separate course after the meat. Main dish salads are, as the name implies, substantial salads that form the basis for a meal. They are usually a combination of vegetables with a protein-rich food such as fish, chicken, meat, cheese, or nuts. Molded salads can be either light or more substantial, depending upon their ingredients. In this chapter, different types of salad greens and the preparation of various types of salads and salad dressings are discussed.

Salad Greens   Salad greens are used as the basis for practically all salads and may indeed form the entire salad with the addition of a little salad dressing. They are available in great variety, although not all varieties may be available at any one time and place. Their different shades of green and different textures and flavors afford a pleasing contrast when combined in a salad of mixed greens or when used as the basis for salads that include other ingredients. Salad greens that are frequently sold commercially are shown in Table 7–1. Some of these greens can be grown easily in home gardens and, in certain parts of the country, can be grown throughout much of the year, especially if a sheltered spot is chosen. Greens that are usually cooked, such as spinach, turnip greens, mustard greens, and collards, are good salad ingredients when they are young and tender. The selection of cabbage and of the greens that are often cooked has been discussed in the vegetable chapter.

Fig. 7–1. *The greens most frequently used in salad making are often combined to give interesting contrasts in texture and flavor.*

Courtesy of Western Growers Association

Wild greens, such as dandelions, lamb's quarters, poke, and sorrel, are also interesting salad ingredients when they are available. Watercress grows wild in abundance in some areas and is also sold commercially.

Endive or Chicory and Escarole

The terms endive and chicory are sometimes used synonymously. The broad-leaved plant of upright growth is sometimes called Belgian, French, or witloof chicory or endive. The leaves are tightly folded around a core, the color is white to light green, and the flavor slightly bitter. Curly endive or chicory is much greener and its habit of growth more spreading than that of Belgian, French, or witloof chicory or endive.

Escarole resembles curly endive, but its leaves are broader and the spine of the leaves whiter than those of curly endive.

Lettuce

The leading commercial variety of lettuce is iceberg or crisp-head. Heads of good quality are firm, clean, crisp, and tender. They are free from rusty appearance, decay, and excessive outer leaves. The outer leaves are good to

Table 7–1. *Ingredients of Raw Vegetable Salads*

Greens	For Color, Flavor, and Texture Contrast
Lettuce	Bean sprouts
Bibb or limestone	Carrots
Boston or butterhead	Cauliflower
Romaine or cos	Celery
Iceberg or crisp-head	Cucumbers
Leaf or garden	Garlic
Cabbage	Mushrooms
Celery or Chinese	Onions
Green	Chives
Savoy	Green onions
Endive or chicory	Leeks
Belgian, French, or witloof	Mild nature
Curly	Bermuda
Escarole	Spanish or Valencia
Parsley	Scallions
Spinach	Shallots
Swiss chard	Peppers
Watercress	Green
	Red
	Radishes
	Red cabbage
	Summer squash
	Tomatoes
	Turnips

use if not too coarse because they are greener and, therefore, higher in vitamin A value than the inner leaves. Lettuce with seedstems is avoided because it has a bitter flavor. Such heads are likely to have wide spaces between the base portions of the outer leaves and an abnormal swelling of one side of the top of the head.

Boston or butterhead lettuce forms a looser, smaller head than iceberg lettuce. The leaves are relatively smooth, soft, tender, and succulent but not so crisp as those of iceberg lettuce.

Bibb, which is sometimes called limestone lettuce, is a variety of butterhead lettuce. The heads are smaller and more cup-shaped than those of Boston lettuce. The outer leaves are dark-green and the core almost white. The leaves have an interesting crisp texture and an attractive appearance.

Leaf or garden lettuce does not form a head. It is grown extensively in greenhouses and in gardens. Depending upon the variety, the leaf may be curled or smooth and the color may vary from pale-green to dark-green to reddish-rust. Leaf lettuce cannot be shipped long distances.

Fig. 7–2. *Bibb lettuce (right) has a smaller, more cup-shaped head than Boston lettuce (far right). Both have loose heads and smooth, tender leaves.*

Courtesy of H. J. Heinz Co.

Cos or romaine lettuce has a tall cylindrical shape and long, dark-green leaves that are crisper and stiffer than those of most other varieties of lettuce.

Parsley and Watercress

Parsley may have a flat or a curled leaf. It is available throughout the year and can be used as a garnish or as a salad green. Because of the dark-green color, it is unusually high in vitamin A value. Good parsley is bright, fresh, green, and free from yellowed leaves or dirt. Slightly wilted parsley becomes crisp when put into cold water.

Watercress is a pleasantly pungent, dark-green vegetable that can be used as a garnish or as a salad green. It is best when fresh, young, crisp, tender, and free from dirt or yellowed leaves.

Light Salads

Salads used as a dinner accompaniment are intended to stimulate appetite rather than satisfy it. They are, therefore, low in calories and in protein. Raw vegetables and fruits are usually preferred because of their crisp texture, but cooked vegetables or fruits may offer variety, especially at times when only a limited variety of raw foods is available.

Some of the ingredients of raw vegetable salads are shown in Table 7–1. Salads can be made with only one salad green or with a wide variety of the items in the table and perhaps others. Good meal planning suggests that the number of food mixtures in any meal be limited. For this reason if a mixed dish, such as a casserole, is being served, it may be best to serve a simple

Fig. 7–3. These dark green vegetables add accent to salads: top, spinach; bottom, left to right, parsley, watercress, and chives.

Courtesy of H. J. Heinz Co.

salad rather than a salad containing many ingredients. On the other hand, with a roast or steak a tossed salad containing a variety of vegetables may be very attractive.

Greens and other raw vegetables are best served clean, cold, crisp, and dry except for salads of wilted lettuce or spinach in which a hot salad dressing is poured on the raw vegetable. The cleaning of salad vegetables may be a problem because they usually grow close to the ground. They are best washed in running water or in a large container of water. The leaves are removed from the water and, therefore, from any dirt that may remain in the bottom of the container. Cold water is ordinarily used, but lukewarm water can be used for crinkly leaves because it makes the creases in the leaves open so that sand and soil will wash out. Coarse outside leaves are removed and shredded for use in salad or put aside for use in soups or stews. A head of lettuce can be opened by removing the core with a sharp knife and holding the cut portion under cold running water. It is easy to make lettuce cups in this way unless the head is very firm because the water forces the leaves apart without injuring them. After salad greens are washed, the excess water is drained from them on a rack or towel. They are then stored in a plastic bag or hydrator in the refrigerator.

Salad greens can be torn or cut before serving. Some people prefer tearing because they believe that cutting bruises the leaves. Head lettuce can be cut into wedges for a head lettuce salad or shredded with a knife. Perhaps because it is less tender than lettuce, cabbage is usually shredded finely before it is made into a salad. A good general rule in preparing any salad ingredients is to have the pieces small enough that they can be eaten easily and yet not so small that their identity is lost. Fruits and vegetables that are easily cut with a fork can be left in pieces that are larger than bite-size if desired.

Any raw vegetables that are to be used in a salad are best cut immediately before the salad is served because chopping, shredding, or grating raw vegetables releases enzymes that cause substantial losses of ascorbic acid. Cucumbers are usually sliced although they may be cubed or cut into long strips. They may be scored with a fork and either peeled or not peeled.

Fig. 7–4. *To open a head of iceberg lettuce remove the core with a sharp knife. When the cut portion is held under running water, the leaves are forced apart without injury.*

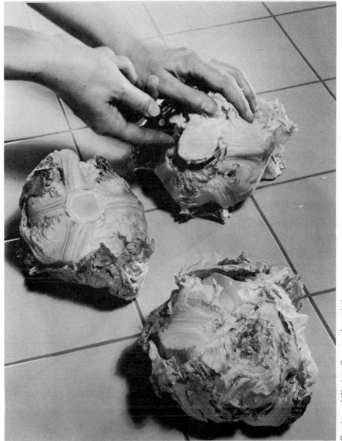

Courtesy of Western Growers Association

Tomatoes can be peeled easily if they are dipped in boiling water for a few seconds or rotated over a hot flame until the skin breaks. They are cut just before they are added to a salad so that juice from the tomato will not dilute the salad dressing. For use in salads carrots can be grated, cut in thin strips with a knife, or in very thin strips or "curls" with a vegetable peeler. Raw cauliflower is cut into small flowerets which can be sliced if desired. Raw mushrooms thinly sliced are an attractive salad ingredient.

Cooked vegetables to be used in a salad are best if they are tender but firm enough to hold their shape. Some of the favorite cooked vegetables are

Fig. 7–5. *Lettuce is often torn apart by hand so as not to bruise the leaves. Cabbage has less tender leaves than lettuce and is usually shredded with a knife.*

Fig. 7–6. *Radish roses and celery and carrot curls are made by placing the sliced vegetables in ice water.*

green beans, asparagus, pickled beets, and whole tomatoes canned with a trace of calcium so they hold their shape better than ordinary canned tomatoes.

Many ingredients are added to vary tossed vegetable salads. Raw fruits, nuts, crisp bacon, anchovies, olives, and croutons (toasted bread cubes) are sometimes added. Onions, cut fine or in rings, are often added. For a mild garlic flavor, cut cloves of garlic are sometimes put in the salad dressing and later removed or rubbed on the salad bowl just before the salad ingredients are added. Generous amounts of garlic or onion are best avoided because they overshadow other ingredients. Herbs, either fresh or dry, add interest to salads.

A great variety of fruit salads is possible, made from raw, canned, and cooked fruits. Fruits that are likely to turn brown after cutting, such as apples, bananas, and avocados, can be dipped in the juice of citrus fruits or pineapple, or in French dressing before they are used. The salad dressings

Fig. 7–7. *Fresh fruit in season is combined to make a refreshing patio salad.*

Courtesy of Western Growers Association

used for fruit salads are usually milder in flavor and sweeter than those used for vegetable salads.

Molded Salads

Salads that contain gelatin are often called molded salads. Those that contain little or no sugar are sometimes called aspics, or savory jellies, perhaps to distinguish them from the sweet gelatin mixtures used for dessert. Molded salads can be light, such as tomato aspic, or main dish salads, such as chicken aspic. From the standpoint of nutrition, some molded salads are not good substitutes for a salad containing fresh vegetables or fruits. For example, a salad made of a commercial gelatin mix to which a very few pieces of fruits or vegetables have been added offers few nutrients except a little sugar. However, tomato aspic that is made with well seasoned tomato juice or a perfection salad that contains generous quantities of shredded raw vegetables such as cabbage, celery, onion, and green pepper compare favorably in nutritive value with many other types of salad. The texture of most molded salads is improved by the addition of crisp ingredients.

Frozen salads can be included under this heading because they also hold their shape. They usually contain fruit, either fresh or canned, and generous amounts of whipped cream and mayonnaise. For this reason they are better accompaniments for a light summer meal than for an ordinary dinner.

Main Dish Salads

Main dish salads are often used for luncheon and sometimes for dinner, especially during hot weather. They usually contain protein in the form of cooked fish, meat, or poultry, hard cooked eggs, or cheese. Blue, Cheddar, cottage, and Swiss cheeses are popular for such salads. Other substantial salads that would make a good meal with the addition of some cold sliced meat are potato or red kidney bean salad. A favorite main dish salad is a tossed salad of raw vegetables with julienne strips of protein foods such as cheese, chicken, ham, and turkey on top.

Salads that consist largely of a soft material such as cooked meat or fish are improved by the addition of something crisp such as celery, pickles, or apples. Meats and sometimes vegetables can be marinated before they are used in salads. A marinade is a savory sauce, such as French dressing, into which the salad ingredients are put for an hour or two before use. They are then drained and put in the salad. If several ingredients for a salad are being marinated at the same time, they are best marinated separately so that their flavors will not blend. Greens are not marinated because contact with an oil wilts them. The flavor of a main dish salad made with meat, poultry, fish, or potato is often improved by allowing it to stand in the refrigerator one to two hours. Greens are added just before serving to avoid wilting.

Salad Dressings

Salad dressings contain acid, fat, seasonings, and sometimes other ingredients. The acids are usually vinegar or lemon juice, and the fat a vegetable oil, although other fats can be used. Some salad dressings are so simple that they are hard to classify. For example, salad can be dressed with lemon juice or vinegar with or without sugar and seasonings. Sour cream, which contains butter fat and an acid that develops during the souring process, can be added plain to fruit salads or combined with crumbled blue cheese to make a cheese dressing for vegetable salads. Sweet or sour cream or evaporated milk is sometimes combined with vinegar or lemon juice and seasonings. A dressing made of hot bacon fat, vinegar, and seasonings is popular for wilted lettuce or hot potato salad.

Three types of salad dressing in common use are French dressing, mayonnaise, and a dressing that is called cooked dressing when made at home or salad dressing when sold commercially.

French Dressing

This dressing has long been a favorite as indicated by the fact that the Romans used a simple mixture of oil and lemon juice or vinegar on their greens, and this dressing is in common use today in Italy, France, and many other countries. The popularity of such a dressing in France undoubtedly explains its name.

Table 7–2. *French Dressing Variations* *

Kind	Amount of Dressing	Suggested Additions	Suggested Uses
Cocktail Sauce	1 cup	1 cup chili sauce	Fish sauce
Russian	1 cup	2 Tbsp. chili sauce 1 Tbsp. chopped onion	Green or vegetable salads
Red	1 cup	2 Tbsp. tomato catsup 2 Tbsp. chopped olives or pickles Sweeten if desired	Green salads Sauces
Roquefort	1 cup	2 to 4 Tbsp. crumbled Roquefort or blue cheese Few drops Worcestershire sauce	Green salads
Martinique	1 cup	2 Tbsp. chopped parsley 2 Tbsp. green pepper	Green salads
Chiffonade	1 cup	2 Tbsp. chopped olives 1 Tbsp. chopped green pepper 1 Tbsp. chopped onion 1 chopped hard-cooked egg	Lettuce or greens
Creamy	1 cup	2–3 Tbsp. cream (shake well)	Greens
Sweet French	1 cup	4 Tbsp. confectioners sugar or 4 Tbsp. honey	Fruit salads

* From Kintner and Mangel, *Vinegars and Salad Dressings*. Missouri Agricultural Experiment Station Bulletin 631, 1954.

French dressing, as made in the home, is usually a temporary emulsion[1] containing three or four parts of vegetable oil to one of vinegar or lemon juice. The dressing can be seasoned simply with salt and pepper or with many other things such as paprika, sugar, honey, and a wide variety of herbs. The amount of sweetening agent added affects not only the flavor but also the consistency of the dressing. A French dressing with a high sugar content may have a jelly-like consistency and remain an emulsion for some time. Variety can be secured in French dressing by the addition of a number of ingredients such as those listed in Table 7–2. Ingredients such as paprika, ground mustard, or tomato soup may aid in stabilizing the emulsion. Although the preparation of French dressing at home is very easy, it can be made even more quickly by the use of prepared mixes and marked bottles that indicate how much oil and vinegar to add.

[1] An emulsion is a dispersion of one liquid within another. The dispersed liquid is in the form of minute droplets. The other liquid forms a continuous phase around the dispersed liquid. Emulsions may be temporary or permanent. A temporary emulsion lasts for a short time, perhaps a few minutes, while a permanent emulsion may last for a long period. A permanent emulsion requires, in addition to the two liquids, an emulsifying agent. This may be egg yolk, whole eggs, egg whites, gelatin, starch, or a variety of gums, or certain other compounds.

(Commercial French dressings must contain not less than 35 per cent by weight of vegetable oil and an acid ingredient that may be vinegar, lemon juice, or lime juice.)They contain seasonings and are usually emulsified with vegetable gums, pectin, or other emulsifying agents. The quantity of emulsifying ingredients used may not exceed 0.75 per cent by weight.(Commercial French dressings are often red or orange because of the addition of paprika or tomato paste.)

A wide variety of vegetable oils is used in French dressings. Some people prefer the taste of olive oil, especially in a simple mixture of oil, vinegar or lemon juice, and a few seasonings. Because of the high price of olive oil, it is sometimes combined with other vegetable oils for use in salads. More often, however, one of the other vegetable oils, such as corn, cottonseed, peanut, or soybean oil, is used. The use of mineral oil in salad dressing or, indeed, in any food preparation is not advisable because it is a laxative and because when taken with a meal it dissolves fat-soluble nutrients such as vitamin A and therefore prevents their absorption.

Mayonnaise

Mayonnaise is an emulsified dressing prepared from vegetable oil, egg yolk or whole egg, seasonings, and an acid ingredient that may be vinegar or lemon or lime juice. It will be seen that the ingredients are those of French dressing except that egg has been added. This makes it possible to form a permanent emulsion of oil droplets in water stabilized by a protein complex of the egg. Although whole egg may be used, egg yolk tends to yield a stiffer, more stable emulsion. Commercial mayonnaise must contain not less than 65 per cent fat.

Mayonnaise can be made at home if desired. The size and shape of the bowl and beater must allow the mixture to be well beaten. Too shallow a bowl will result in spreading the egg into a thin film so that little or no mixing is possible. An electric mixer or a blender is convenient because much beating, especially at the beginning of the process, is necessary for good mayonnaise. Rapid beating is. more effective than slow beating, but pausing for a short time during the process is not harmful to the product. The seasonings and at least part of the vinegar are usually added to the egg. The oil, at room temperature, is then added in very small quantities at first and then more rapidly. The emulsion sometimes breaks during mixing or later during storage, resulting in a curdled appearance. If this occurs, it is necessary to start mixing again with egg or a tablespoon of water or vinegar and to add the curdled mixture slowly while beating. It is of no value to add the egg or liquid *to* the curdled mixture. If desired, a softened solid fat can be substituted for oil in making a product similar to mayonnaise. Hollandaise sauce is similar to mayonnaise except that the fat is butter.

Mayonnaise of high quality is golden yellow, palatable, and stiff enough to hold its shape. Its color is determined largely by the color of the egg yolk, although occasionally the oil has some effect. The flavor and color of mayonnaise change little during storage, and the acidity is high enough to delay spoilage. Excessive stirring of mayonnaise should be avoided because it may break the emulsion and thus cause separation. Storage at too low or at too high a temperature or exposure to air may also cause the mixture to curdle. A variety of salad dressings can be made by adding different ingredients to mayonnaise, as shown in Table 7–3.

Cooked Dressing

A product that resembles mayonnaise can be made by substituting a cooked starch paste for part of the egg and reducing the amount of oil. When this is done commercially, the product may not be labeled mayonnaise but is labeled "salad dressing" or with a trade name. Commercial salad dressing contains vegetable oil, an acid ingredient (vinegar, lemon or lime juice), egg yolk, seasonings, and a cooked or partially cooked starchy paste prepared with a food starch, tapioca flour, wheat flour, or rye flour. Vegetable gums, pectin, or other emulsifying agents can be added if desired. Commercial salad dressings must contain not less than 30 per cent fat. Because of the difference in ingredients, salad dressings are usually less expensive and lower in energy value than mayonnaise. Salad dressings and French dressings contain about 50 to 60 calories per tablespoon, whereas mayonnaise contains about 100 calories per tablespoon. Special low-calorie dressings, which may furnish as few as 10 calories per tablespoon, are usually made with sweeteners other than sugar.

Cooked salad dressing can be made at home using as a basis a sauce containing flour, starch, eggs, or a combination that is thickened by cooking. The ingredients used vary greatly but include liquid, which may be water or milk, an acid ingredient (usually vinegar or fruit juice), and seasonings, which include sugar, salt, and others such as mustard, paprika, celery salt, and onion salt. Table fat or cream is usually added.

Service

Salads of any type are most attractive when they are served immediately after preparation or after chilling for a short time. Excessive handling is best avoided as it often makes an unattractive salad. Salad dressing is usually added just before the salad is served because it wilts greens on which the dressing stands.

The salad bowl, in which the salad foods are lightly tossed with a suitable dressing, makes an attractive addition to any table. The salad may be served at the table and the size of the serving may be as large or small as desired. If preferred, the salad may be served in individual salad bowls or attractively arranged on a cold plate. A lettuce leaf cup or a bed of shredded salad greens usually forms the foundation on which a suitable amount of salad is placed. As a rule the salad covers only about half the plate. Simple salads attractively arranged are desirable. Even for special occasions "candle salad," "butterfly salad," and "rabbit salad" are best avoided. Garnishes

Table 7–3. *Commercial Salad Dressing or Mayonnaise Variations* *

Kind	Amount of Dressing	Suggested Additions	Suggested Uses
Appetizer	1 cup	1 cup French dressing	Vegetable salads
Thousand Island	1 cup	$\frac{1}{3}$ cup chili sauce 1 Tbsp. chopped olives 1 Tbsp. chopped pickles 1 chopped hard-cooked egg	Lettuce
Russian	1 cup	2 Tbsp. chili sauce 1 tsp. sugar	Lettuce Greens
Roquefort	1 cup	2 Tbsp. mashed Roquefort cheese 1 Tbsp. lemon juice	Lettuce or greens
Cream	1 cup	$\frac{1}{3}$ cup cream or canned milk 1 Tbsp. sugar $\frac{1}{2}$ tsp. salt	All types vegetables
Herb	1 cup	2 Tbsp. chopped chive 1 Tbsp. chopped parsley 2 Tbsp. milk	Fish Meat Cabbage
Tart	1 cup	2 Tbsp. horseradish 1 Tbsp. prepared mustard	Potato or starchy vegetable salads
Red	1 cup	4 Tbsp. tomato paste Sugar } to taste Salt	Fish Salad or sauces
Fluffy	1 cup	2 Tbsp. sugar $\frac{1}{2}$ cup cream, whipped	Fruit or sweet salads
Fruit	1 cup	$\frac{1}{4}$ cup fruit juice $\frac{1}{2}$ cup cream, whipped	Fruit
Party	1 cup	2 Tbsp. Maraschino cherry syrup 4 Tbsp. Maraschino cherries $\frac{1}{4}$ cup cream, whipped	Fruit
Hawaiian	1 cup	$\frac{1}{2}$ cup crushed pineapple (slightly drained)	Fruit
Cranberry	1 cup	$\frac{1}{2}$ cup cranberry jelly $\frac{1}{4}$ cup cream, whipped	Turkey, chicken, banana salads
Peanut Butter	1 cup	$\frac{1}{3}$ cup peanut butter 1 Tbsp. sugar 3 Tbsp. cream	Apple or fruit
Gelatin	1 cup	$\frac{1}{2}$ cup stiff gelatin—beaten 2 Tbsp. sugar	Fruit or gelatin salads
Cream cheese	1 cup	6 oz. cream cheese 1 Tbsp. sugar $\frac{1}{2}$ tsp. salt	Fruit or gelatin salads (excellent as spread)

* From Kintner and Mangel, *Vinegars and Salad Dressings*. Missouri Agricultural Experiment Station Bulletin 631, 1954.

may, however, add to the attractiveness of certain salads. A sprig of watercress or parsley, a ripe olive, a small pickled beet, a stuffed prune, or a dark plum may add just the contrast in color or form needed. The garnish should, for the most part, be edible. It may be the salad dressing on which a dash of paprika or a bit of chopped parsley or watercress is sprinkled, or it may be chopped olives, green or red pepper, pimiento, or nuts. Sometimes slices of hard-cooked egg, a ring of green pepper or onion, or a strip of pimiento is placed directly on the salad.

When a salad forms a separate course, suitable accompaniments should be served with it. The simplest of these is saltines or plain salted crackers, which may or may not be sprinkled with cheese and heated. Cheese straws are excellent with fruit salads and may also be used with vegetable salads. Cheese balls, as well as other forms of cheese, are frequently served. Small crisp rolls, dainty sandwiches, unsweetened wafers, salted nuts, olives, and potato chips all have their place as salad accompaniments.

Activities

1. Prepare the following salads and serve with a suitable salad dressing:
a. Greens, individual or combined
b. Shredded cabbage alone and with a variety of other ingredients
c. Mixed raw vegetables
d. Raw vegetables and fruits combined
e. Tomatoes stuffed in several ways
f. Cooked and raw vegetables
g. Raw fruits
h. Main dish salad plates containing meat, poultry, fish, cheese, or eggs.

2. Prepare a variety of molded and of frozen salads.

3. Make French dressing from several recipes and from several mixes. Compare the color, taste, consistency, stability of emulsion, and price with as many commercially prepared French dressings as desired.

4. Buy several brands of mayonnaise and salad dressing. Compare their color, taste, consistency, and price. If desired, homemade mayonnaise and cooked salad dressing can be compared with the commercial products.

5. Prepare a variety of salad dressings using sour cream as a base.

References

SMITH, M. E. *How to Buy Fresh Fruit.* U.S. Dept. Agr., Home and Garden Bull. No. 141 (1967).

SMITH, M. E. *How to Buy Fresh Vegetables.* U.S. Dept. Agr., Home and Garden Bull. No. 143 (1967).

milk and milk products

Although man has been aware of the value of milk for many centuries, it was necessary to learn something about chemistry and nutrition before the real contribution of milk to the diet could be understood. Later the study of microbiology made possible the development of methods for the safe distribution of milk.

It is said that milk and milk products supply almost one-third of the world's intake of animal protein.[1] Cows provide from 90 to 95 per cent of the total supply of milk used for human food. Milk cows, however, produce best in the temperate zones and may not produce well in some climates where other milk-producing animals such as goats, sheep, deer, buffalo, camels, donkeys, mares, and yaks are quite at home.[2]

This chapter describes the different ways that cow's milk is processed, including fluid, concentrated, and cultured milks, cream, and cheese. The selection, storage, nutritive value, and preparation of these products is also considered. Ice cream and other frozen desserts are discussed in a later chapter.

Processing
Although the making of cheese from milk has gone on for many centuries, the processing of fluid milk was of little importance as long as each family owned milk animals. With the growth of cities in comparatively recent times, however, methods of processing fluid milk have been developed. An early solution to the problem of milk transportation was to drive the cow or other milk animal to the customer and to draw the milk there. A later custom, practiced even today in some countries, was to take the milk from house to house in large open containers. At each stop as much milk as desired was dipped out and poured into the container provided by the

[1] J. P. Vickery. Possible Developments in the Supply and Utilization of Food in the Next 50 Years. *Food Technology,* 25: 619–624 (1971).

[2] *Farmer's World. The Yearbook of Agriculture, 1964.* United States Department of Agriculture, Washington, D.C., p. 155.

consumer. A more sanitary alternate to this method was to haul the milk in large closed containers and to draw it out through a faucet as needed. Today large dairy farms often far from the centers of consumption produce milk of high quality. It may be delivered to creameries in huge refrigerated trucks especially equipped with glass-lined tanks, where it is processed and then delivered to the consumer or retailer in sanitary containers of various sizes.

Raw milk usually contains a variety of bacteria. Some of them—like those that cause souring of milk—are not harmful, but others cause disease. Organisms causing diseases such as tuberculosis and brucellosis (undulant fever) may be present in milk as it comes from the cow, whereas those causing diseases such as diphtheria, scarlet fever, septic sore throat, and typhoid fever may find their way into milk because of diseases in the individuals who handle the milk. The systematic testing of cows through federal and state inspection programs has almost eradicated tuberculosis in cattle and is lowering the incidence of brucellosis. Requirements for health examinations, for proper cleanliness of hands and clothes, and other regulations have helped to reduce the possibility of milk contamination by human disease organisms. As explained in Chapter 2, many state and municipal ordinances include some or all of the sanitary standards set forth in the "Grade A Pasteurized Milk Ordinance" recommended by the United States Public Health Service.[3] These recommendations cover the health of the cow, the health and sanitary practices of the milkers and others who handle the milk, the conditions under which the cows are kept, the utensils and rooms used in handling the milk, and the prompt cooling of milk. The ordinance defines milk as the lacteal secretion of cows which contains not less than $8\frac{1}{4}$ per cent nonfat milk solids and not less than $3\frac{1}{4}$ per cent milk fat. The milk ordinance requires the pasteurization of all milk because of the safety that pasteurization affords. Currently much of the milk is subjected to a vacuum treatment prior to pasteurization to reduce unsavory, volatile flavors such as those from grasses, wild onions, or silage eaten by the cow.[4] Whenever applicable the provisions of the milk ordinance will be discussed in this chapter.

Fluid Milk

Pasteurized Milk. Pasteurization destroys all of the disease-producing organisms and usually over 99 per cent of the bacteria found in milk. It is fortunate that the disease-producing organisms are more sensitive to heat than most of the other organisms because if heat enough to kill all of the organisms were required, there would be a greater change in flavor than occurs with pasteurization. Milk is pasteurized by heating it to at least

[3] *Grade "A" Pasteurized Milk Ordinance. 1965 Recommendations of the U.S. Public Health Service.* United States Public Health Service Publication No. 229, 1965. The ordinance was effective July 1, 1967, for milk shipped between states. Adoption in individual states depends upon action of their legislatures.

[4] *Protecting Our Food. The Yearbook of Agriculture, 1966.* United States Department of Agriculture, Washington, D.C., p. 68.

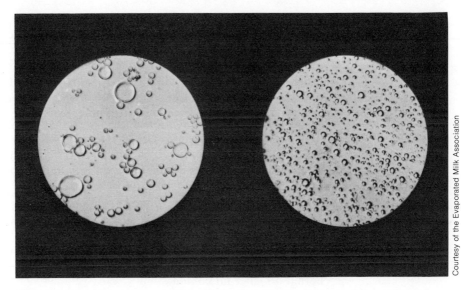

Fig. 8–1. *Homogenization reduces the size of fat globules in milk and thus prevents their separation. At left are butterfat globules in untreated evaporated milk, and right, fat globules in homogenized evaporated milk. Magnified 1000 times.*

63° C. (145° F.) and holding it at that temperature for not less than thirty minutes or by heating to at least 71° C. (161° F.) for not less than fifteen seconds, or by any other procedure shown to be as effective as these treatments.[5] The first of these methods has been called the "hold" method and the second the "high temperature, short time" (HTST) method. Grade A milk must not contain more than 100,000 bacteria per ml. when received at the plant and not more than 20,000 bacteria per ml. after pasteurization.

Pasteurized milk is equal to raw milk in nutritive value except for a slight reduction in the thiamine and ascorbic acid contents. Carefully controlled HTST pasteurization permits maximum retention of these two vitamins.

Homogenized Milk. Most of the fluid milk sold in the United States at present is homogenized. The homogenized milk on the market is pasteurized fluid whole milk in which the fat[6] globules have been divided into many tiny droplets, usually by forcing the milk through small openings under high pressure. Homogenization of milk stabilizes the emulsion so that no cream line is formed upon standing and the milk remains uniform throughout the container. The milk has a smooth, rich flavor that many people find satisfactory for cereals and coffee as well as for a beverage.

---

[5] *Protecting Our Food. The Yearbook of Agriculture, 1966,* p. 68.

[6] When the word "fat" is used in relation to dairy products in this discussion, it refers to milk fat, which is also called butter fat.

Vitamin D Milk. Few natural foods are good sources of vitamin D, which is essential for mineral metabolism. To assure a reliable source of this vitamin milk is often fortified to contain at least 400 U.S.P. units of vitamin D per quart. This can be done by feeding the cow vitamin D concentrates, by irradiating the milk, or by adding vitamin D concentrates to the milk. Milk fortified with vitamin D must be so marked on the label.

Fortified Multiple Vitamin and/or Mineral Milk. Although not a legal market milk in all states, four-fifths of the states either allow or regulate the fortification of fresh pasteurized whole milk with the vitamins A, D, thiamine, riboflavin, and niacin; and the minerals iron and iodine.

Two Per Cent Milk. The fat content of milk labeled as "2 per cent" varies in different states. Fourteen states have established minimum and maximum percentages of fat, which generally range from 1.5 to 2.25 per cent.

Lowfat Milk. Milk of this type is sometimes called "partially skimmed" because its fat content is usually 0.5 to 2.0 per cent, although a few states permit a higher fat content.

Skim Milk. Probably because of the emphasis on low-calorie and low-fat diets in recent years, skim milk has become popular. Skim milk is like fresh fluid whole milk except that its fat content is less than 0.5 per cent. Sometimes additional nonfat dry milk, vitamins, and minerals are added. Fluid skim milk is pasteurized and may also be homogenized.

Fortified Skim Milk. This milk, available on some markets, is fluid skim milk with added vitamins A and D, and usually contains at least 10 per cent nonfat milk solids.

Chocolate Milk. The flavoring ingredients of chocolate milk must be chocolate and sugar. If cocoa is used, the milk is labeled "chocolate flavored." Whole milk must be used in chocolate milk. If some of the fat has been removed, the product can be called "chocolate lowfat milk" or "chocolate skim milk" according to its fat content. These products usually have nonfat milk solids added. Depending on state regulations, some dairies use designations such as "chocolate drink" or "chocolate dairy drink." The nutritive value of these beverages is like that of the milk from which they are made except that chocolate and sugar have been added, making the calorie content higher than that of the original milk. Vegetable gum stabilizers are often used in chocolate milk to maintain the suspension of the chocolate.

Filled or Imitation Milk. In some states filled or imitation milks are permitted, although as of January 1, 1971, filled milk was illegal in 26 states. Filled milk is a combination of skim milk and vegetable fat; or nonfat dry milk, water, and vegetable fat. In either case it is homogenized. Imitation milk is usually made from vegetable fat, protein such as sodium caseinate or soya solids, corn syrup solids, flavoring agents, stabilizers, emulsifiers, and water.[7]

Concentrated Milks

Because fresh fluid milk contains about 87 per cent water, its bulk and weight can be reduced greatly by removal of some of the water.

Concentrated Fresh or Frozen Milk. Concentrated fresh milk is milk from which a considerable portion of the water has been removed. Concentrated frozen milk is produced by freezing concentrated milk. Either of these products can be diluted with water and served as fresh milk. Because of the added processing, they are not competitive in price with fresh fluid milk in areas where fluid milk is plentiful, but they find ready acceptance in areas that lack a supply of fresh milk.

Evaporated Milk. Evaporated milk is whole milk from which about 60 per cent of the water has been removed by heating the milk in a vacuum. The milk is homogenized, cooled, put into cans, and sterilized by heat treatment. Evaporated milk must contain not less than 7.9 per cent milk fat and not less than 25.9 per cent total milk solids. It may contain an added stabilizer. Most evaporated milk on the consumer market contains added vitamin D. Evaporated milk can be reconstituted by adding an equal volume of water. Evaporated skim milk is available on some markets. It is like evaporated milk except that skim milk instead of whole milk has been used in its preparation.

Evaporated Filled Milk. Filled milk is prepared by adding a vegetable fat such as coconut or cottonseed oil to skim milk. The milk is then homogenized and the water evaporated until the concentration is similar to that of evaporated milk. Because of the substitution of fats, this milk is usually less expensive than evaporated milk. The manufacture and sale of filled evaporated milk was illegal in 42 states as of January 1, 1971.

Sweetened Condensed Milk. In making this product, sugar is added to whole milk before evaporation. The finished product contains not less than 28 per cent total milk solids, not less than 8.5 per cent milk fat, and from 42 to 44 per cent sugar. Because the sugar acts as a preservative, the milk can be stored in cans without further heat treatment.

Dried Whole Milk. This is whole milk from which 95 to 98 per cent of the water has been removed. The milk is preheated, concentrated in vacuum pans, and dried either by spraying into a chamber of hot air or on a slowly revolving heated drum. Because of its fat content, which is at least 26 per cent of the dried product, dried whole milk does not keep so well as dried skim milk. For this reason it is packed in tin containers under gas. Its retail

[7] *Food For Us All. The Yearbook of Agriculture, 1969.* United States Department of Agriculture, Washington, D.C., p. 146.

distribution is largely for infant feeding, but it is used commercially in the manufacture of ice cream.

Nonfat Dry Milk. This product is also called dry skim milk, powdered skim milk, or skim milk powder, and contains not more than 1.5 per cent fat in the dry product. It is made by drying skim milk in a manner similar to that used for whole milk. Nonfat dry milk is usually spray-dried for home use because this treatment retains the flavor of the milk better than the more severe heat treatment of roller drying. Most retail nonfat dry milk is processed so that it has a light granular texture and disperses readily in water. This "instant" nonfat dry milk can be produced either by wetting and re-drying spray-dried milk or by direct spray-drying in an apparatus designed to dry and agglomerate the milk at the same time. Package directions for reconstituting nonfat dry milk with water should be followed because the instant dry milk granules are more bulky than conventional powdered milk. Some nonfat dry milk is graded by the U.S. Department of Agriculture, in which case it is labeled U.S. Extra Grade or U.S. Standard. To earn the "U.S. Extra Grade" shield, instant nonfat dry milk must have a pleasing flavor, a natural color, and dissolve instantly when mixed with water.[8]

Nonfat dry milk is now used in the home in large quantities because it is usually the least expensive form in which milk can be purchased, is convenient for storage, and is quite acceptable as a beverage or in cooking. Nonfat dry milk can be added to some foods to supplement their food value.

Cultured Milks

Allowing microorganisms to grow in milk is one of the oldest methods of preserving milk. Although modern methods of preservation have made culturing or "fermentation" unnecessary, milks treated in this way are still in demand because of their altered taste, the sometimes extravagant health claims made for them, and the quality of the foods in which they are used.

Cultured milks are prepared from pasteurized milk to which are added selected microorganisms used to develop the desired flavor and consistency. Most of these organisms change lactose into lactic acid, which then thickens the milk by partially coagulating the protein. The food values of cultured milks are in general equivalent to the milk from which they were prepared.

Cultured Buttermilk. Buttermilk produced in commercial dairies is made by adding a culture of lactic-acid-forming bacteria to pasteurized skim or lowfat milk. By making the milk mildly acid, lactic acid coagulates some of the protein and thus thickens the milk. Butter granules are sometimes added to produce buttermilk that contains 1 per cent or less of milk fat. Buttermilk was originally a by-product of buttermaking, being the liquid that

[8] *How to Buy Instant Nonfat Dry Milk.* Home and Garden Bulletin No. 140. United States Department of Agriculture, Washington, D.C., 1967.

remained after the fat was removed from churned milk or cream. Like cultured buttermilk, it is essentially free from fat.

Buttermilk can be prepared at home by reconstituting but not chilling nonfat dry milk, and adding one-half cup of commercial cultured buttermilk for each quart. The milk is covered and allowed to stand at room temperature until clabbered, or overnight, then stirred and stored in the refrigerator. Buttermilk made in this way can be used as a starter for another batch, although in time off flavors develop and a new starter is needed.

Yogurt. Yogurt is made by adding a culture of acid-forming bacteria to milk that is usually homogenized, pasteurized, and partially concentrated. The product is semi-solid with a fine, smooth texture and a tangy flavor. Buttermilk and yogurt will keep for as long as two weeks if the refrigerator is maintained at 5°C. (40°F.) or below. These fermented products should be returned promptly to the refrigerator and not allowed to sit at room temperature.

Cream and Related Products

Cream can be separated from milk by gravitation. The milk is allowed to stand in shallow containers and the cream, which is lighter than milk, rises to the top and can be skimmed off. A more recent method of separating cream is in centrifugal separators that can be adjusted so that cream of approximately the same fat content is obtained each time. Cream is pasteurized and may be homogenized.

The consumer can obtain light cream by mixing heavy cream and milk. Under some conditions this may be an economical procedure. For use in coffee several dried cream substitutes or "coffee whiteners" are available, some of which contain no dairy products. The ingredients are listed on the containers in which they are sold and are similar to those used for imitation milk.

Half-and-Half. Half-and-half is a mixture of milk and cream which in most states must contain not less than 10.5 per cent fat. It is often homogenized since this process makes it thicker and helps prevent fat separation when it is added to coffee.

Light Cream. Light cream, which is also called coffee cream or table cream, is often used for coffee or cereal. Except for two states that give 16 per cent as the minimum, this cream contains not less than 18 per cent and usually not as much as 22 per cent fat, the minimum required for whipping. It is generally homogenized, which also interferes with formation of a stable whipped foam.

Sour Cream. Sour cream or cultured sour cream is a fluid or semifluid cream resulting from the souring, by lactic-acid-producing bacteria or similar culture, of pasteurized cream. The fat content must be at least 18 per cent.

Whipping Cream. Whipping cream contains not less than 30 per cent fat. Light whipping cream contains 30 to 36 per cent fat whereas heavy cream or heavy whipping cream contains not less than 34 per cent fat. Homogenization of such cream is usually avoided because it interferes with whipping. Sterilized whipping cream can be kept for several months unopened in the refrigerator, but should be used within ten days after opening. Vegetable gum stabilizers in this product improve the stability of the whipped foam but to some this additive has an objectionable mouth feel.

Whips. Pasteurized cream containing sugar, stabilizers, flavoring, and often other ingredients is now sold in pressurized containers. When the valve is pressed, aerated cream comes out because of the pressure of the gas within the container. The foam is less stable and usually more expensive than that produced by whipping cream in the regular way. Products resembling cream that contain non-milk fats and milk solids or no dairy products at all are also dispensed under pressure to give a product resembling whipped cream.

Also available are frozen whipped toppings and dry mixes, which can be combined with milk and whipped to form a stable foam. The ingredients in these are similar to those in imitation milk, though the ratio of ingredients may be altered.

Cheese

The making of cheese is an ancient method of preserving milk. Although it is not known when cheese was first used, legends concerning its origin have been handed down through the centuries. One of these is of an Arab who, setting off on a long journey, took milk in a container he had made from the stomach of a young calf. When he stopped to drink the milk, he noticed that only a small amount of watery substances ran from the bag. One version of the story says that he ripped open the bag and tasted carefully the solidified mass inside, found it had a mild sweet flavor, and ate it immediately. Another version of the story says that he hung his bag in a convenient place and continued his journey without tasting the contents. Weeks later he returned by the same route and remembered the bag he had left. When he stopped, he found the odor of the contents so inviting that he tasted and consumed the firm curd. In any case he told his fellow countrymen of his discovery.

The story about the Arab illustrates the first steps that are necessary in making either uncured or cured cheese. The milk that he carried formed a curd because lactic-acid-producing bacteria increased its acidity and because the enzyme rennin in the calf's stomach that served as a container helped in its coagulation. The enzyme rennin,[9] which even now is obtained from the stomachs of calves, coagulates milk at a temperature of about 37° C. (99° F.). Temperature is important in making rennin curd because no coagulation occurs below 10° C. (50° F.) or above 65° C. (149° F.). When the

---

[9] Trade name for rennin or rennet is Junket.

temperature is slightly high, the curd tends to be tough and stringy, whereas at temperatures slightly below the optimum, the curd is too soft. Previous boiling of milk retards coagulation and makes the curd soft. A rennin gel forms best when the milk is slightly acid, but further increases in acidity tend to inhibit the action of rennin. Raw milk and pasteurized nonhomogenized milk form firm curds, but milk that has been homogenized, boiled, or diluted forms a softer curd. Rennin is sometimes added to sweetened flavored milk to form a dessert that resembles baked custard in its consistency.

In making cheese, the first step is to warm the milk slightly, add a starter of lactic-acid-producing bacteria, and after the acidity has increased slightly, to add rennin. The casein of milk soon coagulates, and the curd that has formed is cut to separate the whey. Whey is a clear liquid that contains some of the water-soluble substances in milk. The curds are left rather moist for soft cheeses, but more whey is removed when hard cheeses are to be made. The removal of whey can be regulated by the amount of the manipulation of the curd and the temperature to which the curd is heated during this process.

Although large amounts of whey are discarded even today, whey in the dry form is being used in certain prepared foods such as starch puddings, cakes, crackers, and whips. Such use seems advisable because whey contains sugar, minerals, water-soluble vitamins, and any soluble proteins of the milk that were not coagulated by heat during the preparation of cheese.

Uncured Cheese. Cottage cheese consists of the curds of pasteurized skim milk. It can be made with only the lactic acid starter, but rennin is often added especially for the cottage cheese that has large curds. The curds are salted, and cream is added for creamed cottage cheese, which must contain not less than 4 per cent fat and not more than 80 per cent moisture.

Cream cheese is made in a similar manner from cream or a mixture of cream and milk. Neufchâtel cheese resembles cream cheese but contains less fat and more protein. All uncured cheeses must be held in the refrigerator and used promptly because they do not keep well.

Cured Cheese. The curd for cured cheese is usually prepared from pasteurized milk; however, raw milk can be used if the cheese is to be stored at least sixty days before use because aging the cheese for a sufficient time destroys any disease organisms that may be present. Yellow color is often added to the milk in making cheeses such as Cheddar. The temperature to which the curd is heated is higher for hard than for soft cheeses. The curds are cut with knives and drained by pushing them to the sides of the container. After the cutting, draining, and heating have been completed, the curd is placed in molds or hoops and pressed to drain out more whey. Salt is added by rubbing it on the surface of the cheese or by floating the cheese in a brine bath. The molded cheese is coated by dipping it in paraffin to delay loss of moisture.

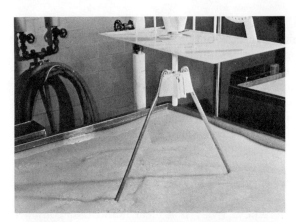

Fig. 8-2. *Many steps are required before milk becomes Cheddar cheese.*

The milk is heated.

A starter curd is added to the milk.

Rennet is used to coagulate the milk.

Every step is accurately controlled.

The curd is matted.

Milling the curd.

Salting the curd.

The cheese is pressed into shape.

Courtesy of Kraft Foods Company

Table 8–1. *Classification of Some Popular Varieties of Natural Cheeses* *

Soft Unripened	Soft Ripened 4–8 weeks	Semisoft Ripened 6 wks.–4 mos.	Firm Unripened	Firm Ripened 1–12 mos.	Very Hard Ripened 5 mos.–2 yrs.	Blue-Vein Ripened 2–12 mos.
Cottage	Brie	Bel Paese	Gjetost	Cheddar	Parmesan	Blue (spelled Bleu on imported cheese)
Cream	Camembert	Brick	Mysost (also called Primost)	Colby	Romano	
Neufchâtel	Limburger	Muenster		Caciocavallo	Sap Sago	
Ricotta		Port du Salut	Mozzarella	Edam		Gorgonzola
				Gouda		Roquefort
				Provolone		Stilton
				Swiss (also called Emmentaler)		

* Adapted from *Cheese Buying Guide for Consumers*, by Small and Fenton. Marketing Bulletin No. 17, United States Department of Agriculture, 1961.

Cheese is ripened in rooms that have the correct temperature and humidity for the type of cheese being made. A low temperature of 2° to 10° C. (36° F. to 50° F.) with a long ripening period tends to produce cheese superior to that ripened at a higher temperature. During ripening, changes are produced in the cheese by the enzyme rennin and by enzymes of the microorganisms that are characteristic of the cheese. The tough rubbery texture of green cheese changes to the smooth tender body of well-ripened cheese, and the flavor changes. Cheddar cheese, which is ripened by bacteria, has a mild flavor at first that changes during curing to the full mellow flavor of well-aged Cheddar cheese. This cheese is named for the village in England in which it was first made. In the United States, where it is the most popular cured cheese, it is often called American cheese. Colby resembles Cheddar cheese but is softer, more open in texture, and milder in flavor. It is not cured so long nor does it keep so well as Cheddar. Edam cheese is similar to Cheddar except that the fat content of the milk is usually reduced to about 2.5 per cent, and the curd is shaped into a flattened ball or a loaf and is often covered with red paraffin.

Swiss cheese has a mild, nut-like flavor and characteristic holes or eyes that develop in the curd as the cheese ripens because gas is given off by the bacteria. Large eyes are considered a characteristic of high quality Swiss cheese.

The mold-ripened semihard cheeses belong to a closely related family. They are ripened with a mold called *Penicillium roqueforti* or a similar mold that forms the blue-green mottling characteristic of blue cheese. Roquefort cheese is an imported product made of sheep's milk. Similar cheeses made of cow's milk are known as Bleu in France, Blue in the United States, Stilton in England, and Gorgonzola in Italy.

Soft cheeses can be ripened with bacteria or mold. In cured soft cheeses, ripening progresses from the rind toward the center of the cheese. Limburger is a familiar example of a soft bacteria-ripened cheese, whereas Camembert is a mold-ripened soft cheese.

Processed Cheese and Related Products. To make processed cheese, several natural cheeses, both fresh and aged, are ground and mixed with the aid of heat and an emulsifying agent. Acid, cream, water, salt, coloring, and spices or flavorings can be added, but the moisture content may not exceed by more than 1 per cent that of the cheese from which it is made. The cheese is then poured into sanitary air-tight packages for retail sale. Heating stops the action of bacteria and enzymes responsible for curing cheese.

Processed cheese foods are similar to processed cheese but contain less fat and milk solids and more moisture. In making this product, cream, milk, skim milk, or whey can be added to the cheese.

Processed cheese spread is similar to processed cheese food except that it contains more moisture and less fat so that it can be spread at room temperature. Fruits, vegetables, or meats may be added. Such ingredients must, of course, be listed on the label.

Coldpack or club cheese is prepared by grinding and mixing without heating one or more varieties of fresh and aged natural cheese. Acid, water, salt, color, and spices may be added, but the moisture content of the finished cheese may not exceed the maximum that is permitted for the variety of natural cheese from which it is made. Coldpack cheese, which often has a sharp cheese flavor, is sometimes made from well-aged Cheddar cheese. Other types of cheese may be included.

Coldpack cheese food is prepared in the same way as coldpack cheese, but many include the additional dairy ingredients used in processed cheese food. Sweetening agents, pimientos, fruits, vegetables, and meats may also be added. Because of its higher moisture content, coldpack cheese food spreads more easily than coldpack cheese.

Whey Cheese. Large quantities of whey are a by-product of the cheese industry. A traditional use for whey is in a cheese called Mysost. To make it, water is evaporated by boiling whey until it is reduced to about one-fourth of its original volume and has the consistency of heavy cream. The cheese, which consists largely of caramelized lactose, is light brown in color

Courtesy of American Dairy Association

Fig. 8–3. *This array of popular cheeses includes: 1. Limburger spread; 2. Liederkranz; 3. Cheddar spread; 4. brick cheese; 5. spreadable cheese food; 6. cottage cheese; 7. cream cheese; 8. packaged processed cheese slices; 9. blue cheese; 10. Edam; 11. Muenster; 12. packaged Cheddar wedge; 13. Mozzarella; 14. Gouda; 15. pasteurized process cheese spread; 16. Cheddar; 17. Camembert; 18. Gouda; 19. grated Parmesan; 20. Parmesan wedge; 21. processed American; 22. Cheddar pineapple; 23. Port du Salut; 24. Swiss cheese; 25. Mozzarella; 26, 27. Provolone.*

with a buttery consistency and a mild sweet flavor. A similar cheese called Gjetost, popular in Norway, is made of the whey of goat's milk or of a mixture of cow's and goat's milk.

Selection and Storage
Milk

The type of milk purchased depends upon personal preference, local availability, and price. In comparing skim milk with whole milk, it must be remembered that skim milk lacks fat and, unless fortified, fat-soluble vitamins. In some diets, however, the lack of fat is an advantage. Fat-soluble vitamins are added to some fluid skim milks, or they can be obtained from other food. In localities where little fresh fluid milk is sold, more dependence must be placed upon processed milks than in areas where plentiful supplies of fresh milk are available. Even when fresh milk is abundant, however, it may be convenient to have a supply of processed milk for emergencies.

Factors influencing the price of milk are supply, size of package, and how obtained. Milk is usually less expensive when packaged in large rather than small containers and when purchased at the store rather than delivered to the home.

Fluid fresh milk, cream, and cultured milk products retain their flavor and nutritive value best when they are kept clean, cold, and tightly covered. Rinse off the bottle or carton, and dry with a clean cloth before placing it in the coldest part of the refrigerator. Milk and cream should not be left exposed to light because this destroys riboflavin and may cause off flavor.

To preserve the quality of these products, the homemaker should place them in the refrigerator as soon as possible after they are purchased or delivered to the home and should remove them from the refrigerator only long enough to pour the amount needed for immediate use. New milk should not be mixed with old unless the mixture will be used immediately, nor should milk be poured back into the original container once it has been removed from it.

Canned milks can be stored at room temperature for long periods of time until opened. However, once opened these should be refrigerated like fresh milk. Dry milk should be stored in a cool dry place at 26° C. (75° F.) or lower, if possible, until reconstituted and then treated like fresh milk. The package should be closed immediately after using because dry powder exposed to moisture in the air during storage may become lumpy and stale.

Milk frozen in a home freezer and held for a month or less can be used, although the flavor and appearance may be changed. Sour cream, yogurt, evaporated milk, and cream cannot be frozen satisfactorily.

Cheese

In the United States, larger amounts of cottage cheese and American-type cheese are sold than any other type. With more than 400 varieties of natural cheeses there are several for every taste. Selection of cheese may be based on flavor, texture, cost, or method of packaging—wedges, oblongs, segments, cubes, slices, blocks, and grated.

American cheese has long been graded for the wholesale trade on the basis of flavor, body, and texture. The United States grades AA, A, B, C, and D are now appearing on some consumer packages. Official grades for Swiss cheese consider eye formation as well as the factors on which Cheddar cheese is judged.

Soft unripened cheeses should be used within a few days after purchase. Cured cheeses can be kept for longer periods in the refrigerator if they are properly wrapped in wax paper, foil, or plastic. The original covering should be left on the cheese if possible. If cheese is to be stored for an extended period, the surface can be dipped in hot paraffin. To protect the flavor of other foods in the refrigerator, cheeses such as Limburger that have a strong flavor are best stored in a tightly covered jar and used within a short time after purchase. Mold that may form on the surface of cheese during storage is not harmful and can be scraped off before the cheese is used. If cheese has become dry and hard in the refrigerator, it can be grated and used in food preparation. Many types of cheese can be frozen successfully, although some may become slightly crumbly or mealy on freezing. Pieces of cheese weighing not more than one pound can be tightly wrapped in moisture-proof freezer wrappings and held in the freezer as long as six months.

Except for cottage cheese, cheeses are best served at room temperature. The amount needed for the meal is cut off and allowed to stand at room temperature for thirty minutes to an hour.

Nutritive Value

Milk is an inexpensive source of some of the most important nutrients in the diet. The amounts recommended in the Daily Food Guide are two to three cups of milk a day for children under 9, three or more cups for children 9 to 12, four or more cups for teenagers, and two or more cups for adults. Because of its high nutritive value, milk is capable of supplementing other foods in the diet and of helping to prevent the occurrence of certain dietary deficiencies. In the United States its contribution to the calcium and riboflavin content of the national dietary is especially important as indicated by the fact that milk and its products provide about two-thirds of the total calcium and nearly one-half of the riboflavin in the diet. Although high in calcium and phosphorus, milk is comparatively low in iron.

Table 8–2, which gives the composition of whole milk, shows that it has a good balance of carbohydrates, fat, and proteins. The carbohydrate in milk is lactose, which is less sweet than the common sugar sucrose. It is also less soluble than sucrose—a characteristic that causes it to crystallize out under some conditions and thus impart a grainy texture to ice cream or condensed milk. During the souring of milk, lactose is changed to lactic acid by bacteria.

Table 8–2. *Composition of Whole Milk* *

Constituent	Per cent
Carbohydrates	4.9
Protein	3.5
Fat	3.7
Water	87.2
Ash	0.7

* Compiled from *Composition of Foods—raw, processed, prepared,* by Watt and Merrill. Agriculture Handbook No. 8, Agricultural Research Service, United States Department of Agriculture, Revised 1963.

The fat content of whole milk varies with the breed of cow and according to the minimum standard established in each state. The minimum standard for the fat content of whole milk in many states is 3.25 per cent.[10] The fat content may, of course, exceed the minimum standards, and a value of 3.7 per cent is considered valid as a national average for milk on the farm production basis.[11]

Skim milk, whether it is fluid or reconstituted from the powdered form, contains all the nutrients of whole milk except the fat and fat-soluble vitamins, but some fluid skim milks are enriched with vitamins A and D. Because of the difference in fat content, whole milk contains 160 calories per cup, whereas skim milk or buttermilk contains only 90 calories per cup. The calorie content of partially skimmed milk containing 2 per cent fat is, of course, higher than that of ordinary skim milk, which contains about 0.1 per cent fat.

Milk contains a plentiful supply of protein of high biological value. The chief protein in milk is casein, which comprises about 80 per cent of the protein. Because it is greatly affected by changes in acidity, it plays an important part in the souring of milk and in the making of cheese. Since much of the casein in fresh milk is combined with calcium salts, it is known as calcium caseinate. This compound is not in solution but is suspended in milk in minute solid particles. Albumin, the protein in milk that is second in importance, is present in much smaller quantity, while the protein globulin ranks third in amount.

Whole milk and other milk products that contain milk fat also contain the fat-soluble vitamins. The most important of these is vitamin A, the amount of which varies with the ration of the cow. During the summer, when the cow has access to green feed, the milk may contain twice as much vitamin A as milk produced during the winter. The yellowish color of milk fat is due to the carotenoids it contains. Other fat-soluble vitamins present in smaller amounts are vitamins D, E, and K. Whole milk, which naturally contains some vitamin D, is often fortified so that it contains not less than 400 U.S.P. units per quart. Milk is only a fair source of thiamine but is a good source of riboflavin, which is responsible for the greenish-yellow color of the whey of milk. Because the riboflavin of milk is readily destroyed by light, the current practice of marketing milk in opaque cartons assists in the retention of this vitamin. Vitamin B_{12} and other dietary essentials are also found in milk.

Imitation milks available in some states may have a nutritive value quite different from whole cow's milk. The non-dairy products and homogenized

[10] *Federal and State Standards for the Composition of Milk Products.* Agriculture Handbook No. 51. United States Department of Agriculture, Washington, D.C. (1971).

[11] B. K. Watt and A. L. Merrill. *Composition of Foods—raw, processed, prepared.* Agriculture Handbook No. 8. United States Department of Agriculture, Washington, D.C., 1963, p. 39.

milk have approximately equal calories; however, studies at Michigan State University showed that non-dairy products contain only about one-fourth as much protein as cow's milk and only one-eighth as much calcium.[12] Plainly the non-dairy products will have the vitamin and mineral content of natural cow's milk only if these nutrients are included in the formulation.

Although all milk products provide some of the nutrients of whole milk, none of them duplicate its high nutritive value (Table 8–3). Cream contains more fat, food energy, and vitamin A value than whole fresh milk but less of such other nutrients as protein, calcium, and the B-vitamins. Cheese made from whole milk is high in protein, fat, calcium, and vitamin A value and contains some of the B-vitamins. Because of its higher moisture content, cottage cheese is a less concentrated food than Cheddar cheese. Its popularity in reducing diets is due to its high protein content and comparatively low calorie content; however, cottage cheese produced by acid coagulation of the skim milk has a lower calcium content than the milk itself.

Preparation
Milk

Although milk is consumed in large quantities as a beverage, it is also important in food preparation. In the preparation of many dishes the milk is first heated or scalded. Sometimes when this is done a film forms on the surface; such a scum is less likely to form if the milk is covered during heating and if a foam is produced by beating the milk. Another problem in heating milk is the formation of a coating on the pan, which becomes visible when the milk is poured from it. This coagulated material, which is probably albumin, is likely to scorch when milk is heated over direct heat instead of over boiling water. The casein of fresh milk is not coagulated by boiling, but if the milk has become slightly acid and high temperatures are used, the casein may coagulate and cause the milk to curdle. This may happen when milk begins to sour or when acid ingredients are added.

The cooking qualities of homogenized milk are slightly different from those of nonhomogenized milk. Some products such as cornstarch pudding and cocoa or chocolate beverages may be thicker with homogenized than with nonhomogenized milk. Curdling due to heat coagulation may occur more readily with homogenized than with nonhomogenized milk because homogenization apparently decreases the stability of the protein in the milk. This is especially evident in making scalloped potatoes. White sauces or gravies made of homogenized milk may appear curdled because the added fat does not combine well with that of the homogenized milk. Baked custards made with nonhomogenized milk cook more rapidly and may be more attractive than those made from homogenized milk.

[12] Homogenized Milk vs. Non-Dairy Products. *Journal of The American Dietetic Association* 54: 224 (1969).

Table 8-3. Nutrients in Milk and Certain Milk and Imitation Milk Products*

Milk or Milk Product	Measure	Weight gms.	Food Energy cal.	Protein gm.	Fat gm.	Calcium mg.	Vitamin A Value I.U.	Thiamine mg.	Riboflavin mg.	Niacin mg.
Milk:										
Fluid, whole, 3½% fat	1 cup	244	160	9	9	288	350	.07	.41	.2
Fluid, skim	1 cup	245	90	9	trace	296	10	.09	.44	.2
Fluid, 2% fat, nonfat milk solids added	1 cup	246	145	10	5	352	200	.10	.52	.2
Evaporated, undiluted	1 cup	252	345	18	20	635	810	.10	.86	.5
Condensed, sweetened	1 cup	306	980	25	27	802	1100	.24	1.16	.6
Cheese:										
Blue or Roquefort type	1 cu. in.	17	65	4	5	54	210	.01	.11	.2
Cheddar	1 cu. in.	17	70	4	6	129	230	.01	.08	trace
Cottage, creamed	1 cup	245	260	33	10	230	420	.07	.61	.2
Cottage, uncreamed	1 cup	200	170	34	1	180	20	.06	.56	.2
Cream, 8-oz. package	1 pkg.	227	850	18	86	141	3500	.05	.54	.2
Process, American	1 cu. in.	18	65	4	5	122	210	trace	.07	trace
Process cheese food, American	1 cu. in.	18	60	4	4	100	170	trace	.10	trace
Cream:										
Half-and-half	1 cup	242	325	8	28	261	1160	.07	.39	.1
Light or coffee	1 cup	240	505	7	49	245	2020	.07	.36	.1
Sour	1 cup	230	485	7	47	235	1930	.07	.35	.1
Whipped topping (pressurized)	1 cup	60	155	2	14	67	570	—	.04	—
Whipping, heavy (unwhipped)	1 cup	238	840	5	90	179	3670	.05	.26	.1
Imitation cream products:										
Creamers:										
Powdered	1 teaspoon	2	10	trace	1	1	trace	—	—	—
Liquid (frozen)	1 tablespoon	15	20	trace	2	2	10	.00	.00	—
Whipped topping:										
Frozen	1 cup	75	230	1	20	5	560	—	.00	—
Powdered, made with whole milk	1 cup	75	175	3	12	62	330	.02	.08	.1
Milk desserts:										
Ice cream, regular (10% fat)	1 cup	133	255	6	14	194	590	.05	.28	.1
Ice cream, rich (16% fat)	1 cup	148	330	4	24	115	980	.03	.16	.1
Ice milk, hardened	1 cup	131	200	6	7	204	280	.07	.29	.1
Ice milk, soft-served	1 cup	175	265	8	9	273	370	.09	.39	.2

* From *Nutritive Value of Foods*. Home and Garden Bulletin No. 72, Agricultural Research Service, United States Department of Agriculture, 1971.

Whipped
Cream

Cream whips best when it is 48 to 72 hours old and when it is cold. A temperature of 7° C. (45° F.) or less is desirable. At about this temperature the butter fat in the cream hardens, which helps to make a stable foam. The cream curdles more readily at higher temperatures, and at 18° or 20° C. (65° or 68° F.) it is impossible to obtain a good whip. The shape and size of the container in which the cream is beaten and the efficiency of the beater affect both the volume obtained and the time required for beating. A chilled bowl with sloping sides and deep enough to permit a rotary or electric beater to incorporate air effectively into the cream is usually recommended. The volume of cream approximately doubles when it is whipped.

Whipped
Evaporated
and Nonfat
Dry Milk

Although the products are quite different from whipped cream, very cold evaporated milk and nonfat dry milk can be whipped. Evaporated milk is first chilled, often in an ice cube tray, until fine ice crystals form. The bowl and beater are also chilled. After whipping, two tablespoons of lemon juice or vinegar may be folded in for each cup of evaporated milk as measured before whipping. This is thought by some to increase the stability of the foam, but it also gives an acid taste which may be undesirable. For nonfat dry milk, one-half cup of the instant milk and one-half cup cold water or fruit juice are beaten until soft peaks form. Two tablespoons of lemon juice are added, if water is used, and beating is continued until stiff peaks form. One-fourth to one-half cup sugar is then added with additional beating.

Cheese

Cheese, like meat and eggs, is high in protein of good quality and in fat. For this reason cheese is best used in place of meat and eggs in the diet rather than in addition to them. Cheese also has the advantage of being relatively low in cost. Since cheese is a concentrated food, it is often combined with a carbohydrate food such as bread, potatoes, macaroni, spaghetti, or rice. The serving of crisp vegetables or fresh fruits with such a cheese dish makes an attractive meal. Some of the popular dishes containing cheese are cheese soufflé, cheese fondue, macaroni and cheese, scalloped vegetables with cheese, fried cheese balls, toasted cheese sandwiches, rarebit, and many others. When cheese is used in cooking, it should blend readily with other ingredients without stringing or matting. To achieve such a result, it is necessary to use a suitable type of cheese for the dish being prepared and comparatively low temperatures for short periods of time because excessive heat causes the cheese to form strings and become tough. Aged natural cheese or processed cheese blends better and is less likely to become stringy than natural cheese that has not been aged sufficiently. The superior cooking quality of aged cheese may be due to changes in the protein during ripening. The good cooking qualities of processed cheese are probably a result of the emulsifying agents it contains.

Activities

1. What regulations and ordinances apply to the production and sale of dairy products in your community? How do these regulations compare with those recommended by the United States Public Health Service?

2. Under code numbers, taste as many of the fluid and reconstituted milks as possible. Have all the milks uniformly chilled. Repeat after making them into cocoa.

3. Tabulate the price per quart of as many kinds of milk as you can find in your local markets. Include in this tabulation the price per quart of various concentrated milks after reconstitution.

4. Prepare buttermilk from nonfat dry milk and compare its taste with that of fresh fluid buttermilk.

5. Purchase a variety of cheeses, bring them to room temperature, arrange them on the table with some plain crackers, and have a tasting party.

6. Compare scalloped potatoes made as follows:
a. Put layers of sliced potatoes, flour, salt, pepper, and dots of table fat in two baking dishes. Over one dish pour nonhomogenized milk and over the other pour homogenized milk.
b. Put sliced raw potatoes in two baking dishes. Over one of them pour a white sauce made of table fat, flour, salt, pepper, and nonhomogenized milk in the same proportions used in item 6a. Over the other dish of potatoes pour a white sauce made in the same way from homogenized milk.
c. Mix nonfat dry milk, flour, salt, and pepper in a clean paper bag. Toss sliced raw potatoes in this mixture and put in a baking pan. Dot with table fat and add hot water to cover.

7. Compare the quality and price of whips made with:
a. Light whipping cream
b. Heavy whipping cream
c. Cream in a pressurized container
d. Evaporated milk
e. Nonfat dry milk
f. Non-dairy whipped topping
In what products could each of these whips be used successfully?

8. Prepare cheese sauce or rarebit with young Cheddar cheese, well-aged Cheddar cheese, and processed American cheese.

References

Cheese Buying Guide for Consumers. U.S. Dept. Agr., Marketing Bull. No. 17 (1961).

Cheese in Family Meals. A Guide for Consumers. U.S. Dept. Agr., Home and Garden Bull. No. 112 (1970).

Cheese Varieties and Descriptions. U.S. Dept. Agr., Agr. Handbook No. 54 (1969).

Federal and State Standards for the Composition of Milk Products. U.S. Dept. Agr., Agricultural Handbook, No. 51 (1971).

Grade "A" Pasteurized Milk Ordinance. U.S. Dept. Health, Education and Welfare. Public Health Service Pub. 229 (1965).

GRISWOLD, R. M. *The Experimental Study of Foods.* Boston: Houghton Mifflin Company. 1962. Chapter 4.

HARRIS, R. S. AND H. VON LOESECKE (Eds.). *Nutritional Evaluation of Food Processing.* New York: John Wiley & Sons, Inc. 1960. Chapter 4.

KON, S. K. *Milk and Milk Products in Human Nutrition.* Food and Agr. Organ. U.N., Nutritional Studies No. 17 (1959).

Milk and Its Products. Facts for Consumer Education. U.S. Dept. Agr., Agr. Info. Bull. No. 125 (1954).

Milk in Family Meals. A Guidebook for Consumers, U.S. Dept. Agr., Home and Garden Bull. No. 127 (1967).

Newer Knowledge of Milk, 3rd ed. National Dairy Council, Chicago (1965).

Newer Knowledge of Cheese, 2nd ed. National Dairy Council, Chicago (1967).

9

eggs

It is not surprising that eggs have had symbolic importance to many peoples because the fertile fresh egg, which seems to be inanimate, yields a fully developed chick after only twenty-one days of incubation. To many primitive people, eggs signify the return of life following the winter season. Eggs are offered to the idols at spring festivals among certain tribes in Africa and South America. To the Egyptians, eggs signify the restoration of mankind after the deluge; the Jews use them in the Passover Feast as a symbol of happy deliverance from bondage and to celebrate their departure from Egypt, whereas the Hindus hold eggs to be the source of all life and refrain from eating them. The use of eggs by Christian people in celebrating Easter may be a tradition handed down from earlier festivals.

In this chapter, the structure, nutritive value, preservation, and selection of eggs, their functions in cookery, and preparation are considered.

Structure

Some of the important parts of the hen's egg are shown in Figure 9–1. Because the shell is porous, it allows an exchange of moisture and gases with the surrounding air—a feature which is of value to the developing embryo but which decreases the keeping quality of the egg. On the outside of the shell is a thin film sometimes called the cuticle or "bloom" that prevents excessive loss of moisture through the shell and protects the contents of the egg from contamination. The color of the shell, which varies from brown to white, depends upon the breed of chicken. It is unrelated to the color of the yolk or to the food value and quality of the egg.

Between the shell and the egg white are two membranes which separate as the egg cools after it is laid. The inner membrane contracts, leaving an air space in the large end of the egg between the two membranes. The fresh egg contains both thick and thin white. The thin white is in two layers—one surrounding the yolk and the other just under the shell. The remaining egg white is thick.

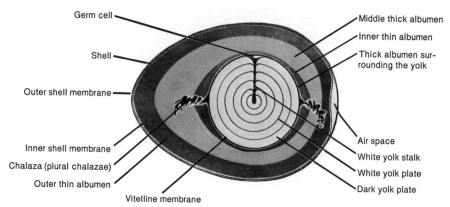

Germ cell

Shell

Outer shell membrane

Inner shell membrane

Chalaza (plural chalazae)

Outer thin albumen

Vitelline membrane

Middle thick albumen

Inner thin albumen

Thick albumen surrounding the yolk

Air space

White yolk stalk

White yolk plate

Dark yolk plate

Fig. 9–1. *This diagram shows the structure of an egg.*
Courtesy of the Poultry and Egg Institute of America

A high proportion of thick white is an indication of quality in an egg, for a thick white keeps the yolk centrally placed within the shell and makes the egg stand up well when it is turned out of the shell. Such an egg makes a more attractive fried, poached, or hard-cooked product than does an egg with a larger proportion of thin white. The thickness of the white of egg varies among individual hens. Eggs of young hens are likely to contain more thick white than those of older birds.

The yolk is surrounded by a membrane known as the vitelline membrane. Attached to the vitelline membrane on each side are dense, cordlike layers of white called chalazae or yolk anchors, which hold the yolk as near the center of the egg as possible. When the white becomes thinner during storage it does not anchor the yolk as effectively as in a fresh egg, and the yolk rises in the egg. There is a germ spot on the yolk of both fertile and infertile eggs. It is light in color and on the upper side of the yolk. The color of the yolk depends upon the food of the hen. A deep yellow yolk results from a diet high in carotenoids because carotenoids from the feed are deposited in the yolk.

Nutritive Value

Although proportions vary among eggs, the white is usually about 58 per cent of the weight of the whole egg, the yolk 31 per cent, and the shell 11 per cent. As shown in Table 9–1, about three-quarters of the weight of whole eggs is water. The yolk is a more concentrated food than the white since egg yolks contain only about 51 per cent water, whereas egg whites contain over 87 per cent. The yolk also contains more protein, fat, minerals, and vitamins than the white, which is almost devoid of fat. Because the proteins of the eggs are of excellent biological value, eggs can be used instead of meat, poultry, or fish in the diet. The fat in egg yolk is present in an emulsified form, and the yolk is used as an emulsifying agent in cookery.

Table 9-1 *Composition of Edible Portion of Whole Egg, Whole Yolk, and Egg Whites* *

Constituent	Whole Egg per cent	Egg Yolk per cent	Egg White per cent
Water	73.7	51.1	87.6
Protein	12.9	16.0	10.9
Fat	11.5	30.6	trace
Ash	1.0	1.7	0.7

* Compiled from *Composition of Foods—raw, processed, prepared*, by Watt and Merrill. Agriculture Handbook No. 8, Agricultural Research Service, United States Department of Agriculture, Revised 1963.

In addition to protein and fat, eggs contain all of the other nutrients such as minerals and vitamins that are required by the developing chick. Although eggs also provide many of the nutrients necessary for the human body, they are not a complete food. They are especially valuable as a source of iron, but a large proportion of the calcium of the egg is found in the shell and therefore is not available as human food.

Egg yolks resemble butter in their vitamin A value. However, the vitamin A value of both of these foods depends upon the amount of carotenoids and vitamin A in the feed consumed by the chicken or cow and deposited as either vitamin A or provitamin A in the egg yolks or the milk fat. The vitamin A value of egg yolk, however, cannot be predicted on the basis of the depth of yellow color because vitamin A is colorless and because hens that do not have access to green or yellow feed may be given adequate amounts of vitamin A through supplements. In such cases the yolks might be light in color but high in vitamin A. Conversely, very deep color may result from large concentrations of xanthophylls, carotenoids that have no vitamin A value.

Eggs also contain vitamin D and the B-vitamins. In fact, they are among the few food sources of vitamin D. The amount of this vitamin in eggs depends, however, upon the ration of the hen and her exposure to sunlight. Both egg yolks and whites are good sources of riboflavin, the vitamin that gives a slightly greenish tint to egg whites. Eggs are a fair source of thiamine and contain a trace of niacin. They are deficient in ascorbic acid.

Preservation

Even though the production of eggs is less seasonal now than it was a few years ago, there is still a lowered production from May to October. There is also an increased seasonal demand often associated with certain holidays. To provide shell eggs at a reasonable price in all seasons and to provide processed eggs for institutions and industry, eggs are preserved by different methods for later use. In addition to cold storage, it is estimated that approximately one-tenth of the eggs produced in the United States today are processed to give liquid, frozen, or dried eggs. Prompt refrigeration of newly laid eggs is desirable whether they are to be marketed soon or preserved for later use.

Changes During Storage

As soon as an egg is laid, some changes in its composition begin and continue during storage. As previously mentioned, probably the first change is the appearance of an air cell at one end of the egg as soon as the contents of the egg are cool. This air cell usually increases in size during storage because moisture is evaporated through the porous egg shell. This loss of moisture can be decreased by increasing the humidity of the room in which the eggs are held. During storage the white of eggs becomes thinner. In addition, some water from the white gradually passes into the more concentrated yolk. As a result of this gain in water and of a weakening in the vitelline membrane, the yolk gradually flattens. If the process goes far enough, the membrane may break when the egg is opened.

Eggs become more alkaline during storage because carbon dioxide is lost. The increased alkalinity has an undesirable effect on the protein of the egg. Sometimes carbon dioxide is added to the atmosphere of the storage room to reduce the loss of this gas from the egg and also to delay microbial growth.

Although most eggs are sterile when they are laid, they may become infected with microorganisms that enter the egg through the porous shell or cracks in the shell. Such infection is more likely to occur in dirty eggs or eggs washed by undesirable methods. The egg has natural defenses against microbial invasion that help reduce the frequency of such infections.

The methods used for the preservation of eggs retard or prevent the undesirable changes that have been discussed. In the past, eggs were stored at home in water glass (sodium silicate), which closed the pores of the shell and thus helped keep the eggs. This method has been replaced by the more effective techniques of cold storage, freezing, and drying.

Cold Storage

In areas where there is adequate refrigeration, cold storage is the method most commonly used for preserving eggs. However, the quantity of eggs kept by this method declined from 102 million dozen in 1952 to 9 million dozen in 1969.[1] The success with which eggs can be held in cold storage is indicated by the fact that equally good soft-cooked eggs were obtained from eggs held fifteen weeks in cold storage as from those held one week at room temperature.[2] In fact, Grade A quality can be maintained for as long as six months in cold storage. A temperature of −1.5° to 0° C. (29° to 32° F.) is recommended. At −2.5° C. (27.5° F.) eggs freeze. A relative

---

[1] *The Egg Products Industry: Structure, Practices, and Costs, 1951–1969.* Marketing Research Report No. 917. United States Department of Agriculture, Washington, D.C., 1971, p. 26.

[2] E. H. Dawson, C. Miller, and R. A. Redstrom. *Cooking Quality and Flavor of Eggs as Related to Candled Quality, Storage Conditions, and Other Factors.* Agriculture Information Bulletin No. 164. United States Department of Agriculture, Washington, D.C., 1956, p. 18.

humidity of 85 to 90 per cent helps to reduce moisture loss from the eggs; however, if the relative humidity is over 90 per cent or if the air circulation is not adequate, mold growth may appear on the eggs or on the box that contains them. The addition of carbon dioxide to the atmosphere in the storage room prevents the growth of some microorganisms and helps delay some undesirable changes in the interior quality of eggs. High concentration of carbon dioxide, however, increases the tendency of thick white to become thin.

Eggs keep better in cold storage if they are pretreated. Dipping eggs in mineral oil or plastic seals the pores of the shell, thus reducing loss of moisture and carbon dioxide from the contents. The retention of carbon dioxide within the egg has an effect similar to that of adding a small amount of carbon dioxide to the atmosphere of the store room. An even more effective method of treating eggs before they are put into cold storage is to dip them for a few minutes in a hot liquid, either water or oil. This heat treatment pasteurizes the shells, reduces the number of microorganisms, and causes a thin film of egg albumin to be coagulated on the inner surface of the shell. Such heat treatment, which has been called thermostabilization, increases the length of time that eggs maintain Grade A quality in cold storage, but the eggs tend to stick to the shell when broken out and do not whip to a good foam.

Freshly laid eggs or stored eggs of high quality deteriorate rapidly if held at room temperature in the store or home. Refrigerated storage is essential at all times. At home, eggs can be stored in the refrigerator in the carton in which they were purchased or can be transferred to another container. It is best to store them with the blunt end up to avoid movement of the air cell and yolk.

Freezing

Eggs are now frozen for bakeries, institutions, and food industries where large quantities of eggs are used. Small packages of frozen eggs for consumer use are not available at present commercially, but eggs can be frozen at home if desired.

When liquid eggs are frozen commercially in federally inspected plants, they must be pasteurized by flash heating to 60° C. (140° F) and held at this temperature for not less than three and one-half minutes.[3] This treatment destroys disease-producing microorganisms such as *Salmonella* that may be present in liquid egg, usually from the shell or other surfaces with which the egg comes into contact. Careful sanitation during preparation for freezing and prompt use after thawing are also essential.

Eggs are not frozen in the shell because expansion of the water of the egg on freezing usually breaks the shell. Before freezing, eggs are broken and may also be separated. The individual egg is examined as it is broken and before it is combined with other eggs. Only eggs of high quality can be used

[3] *Code of Federal Regulations.* Title 7, Part 55. Effective June 1, 1966.

because even one inferior egg would result in an undesirable product. Care is taken not to expose the eggs to contamination when they are removed from the shell. Egg whites can be frozen successfully without any addition; however, if egg yolks are frozen without any addition, the yolks become gummy and lumpy after thawing and do not blend well with other ingredients. To prevent such changes, a small amount of salt, sugar, or other edible ingredient may be added to the egg yolks before freezing. Whole eggs also may have a stabilizer added before freezing. The choice of an additive depends upon the use to be made of the eggs after they are thawed. Salt can be added if egg yolks are to be used for mayonnaise or noodles, but sugar would be more appropriate if the eggs are to be used in confections or baked goods. The addition of combinations of liquid skim milk, salt, and sucrose or dextrose followed by homogenization before freezing was found to be a desirable treatment for eggs to be scrambled.[4]

It may be convenient to freeze eggs when the supply is abundant or when the homemaker wishes to use only the yolks or whites and save the other part of the egg for future use. Each cup of egg yolks should be blended with one tablespoon of sugar or corn syrup or one-half teaspoon salt. One-half tablespoon corn syrup or sugar or one-half teaspoon salt is added to each cup of blended whole eggs. Eggs should be frozen in the amounts that will be used at one time. If desired, they can be frozen in a grid or ice cube tray so arranged that each cube is equivalent to one whole egg, yolk, or white.

Drying

Although dried eggs are not commonly available in packages of retail size, they are used by homemakers in angel food, cake, and other mixes. They are widely used commercially and to some extent in the Donated Foods Program administered by the United States Department of Agriculture. The small amount of glucose that occurs naturally in egg whites is removed by an enzyme process or by microbial fermentation before drying because the presence of this sugar in egg white causes an unpleasant flavor and a brown color to develop during the storage of the dried egg white. Sugar is sometimes removed from whole eggs before they are dried. As with frozen eggs, all liquid eggs used in federally inspected plants must be pasteurized before they are dried, except that dried whites may be heat-treated in the dried form instead of being pasteurized in the liquid form.[5] Liquid eggs and egg yolks are usually spray-dried in a manner similar to that used for drying milk, but egg whites may be dried in pans. Dehydrated egg products keep best when they are dried to a low moisture content and packed in an inert gas such as nitrogen. Precaution against contamination is mandatory for all egg products, whether frozen, chilled, or dried.

[4] K. Ijichi, H. H. Palmer, and H. Lineweaver. Frozen Whole Eggs for Scrambling. *Journal of Food Science.* 35: 695–698 (1970).

[5] *Code of Federal Regulations.*

Selection

The Egg Products Inspection Act passed by Congress in December, 1970, became effective for egg products July 1, 1971, and for shell eggs July 1, 1972. This regulation, administered in the United States Department of Agriculture, assures the consumer that eggs and egg products distributed to them and used in products consumed by them are wholesome, otherwise not adulterated, and properly labeled and packaged.

All eggs offered for sale in most retail stores are graded. Because eggs are also sold on the basis of weight, the consumer must consider both grade and weight in relation to the price of eggs. Grade and size are independent factors since Grade A eggs have the same quality whether they are small or large.

Grades

Eggs are graded by candling, which means they are passed before a bright light. This makes it possible to judge the thickness of the egg white and the size, mobility, and location of the egg yolk. The light makes visible any abnormalities in the shell, the size of the air cell, or defects such as blood or meat spots, spoilage, and development of the embryo. Because such development soon renders eggs inedible, infertile eggs are preferred to fertile eggs for market use. Eggs that are dirty, that have checked or cracked shells, or that leak are so labeled during grading. These should be used promptly and only for dishes that are thoroughly cooked since they may contain disease microorganisms. Because of possible deterioration in eggs after they are graded, and of variations between individual graders, federal regulations permit that 20 per cent or less of the eggs in a package may be below the specified grade. For Grade AA eggs 15 per cent of this tolerance may be Grade A or B, not more than 5 per cent Grade C and not more than 0.5 per cent leakers or dirties.

Some characteristics of quality are shown by the appearance of eggs of U.S. Grades AA, A, B, and C in Figure 9–3. As illustrated here, eggs of superior quality are higher in relation to their width than eggs of poorer quality. This is true of both the white and the yolk, and is evident in poached

Fig. 9–2. *U.S. grade marks used for shell eggs of all sizes indicate specific conditions of shell, air cell, yolk, and white.*

Courtesy of the U.S. Department of Agriculture

Fig. 9-3. *U.S. Standards for Quality for Each of the Four Grades of Eggs.*

U.S. Grade AA. An egg of AA quality covers a small area; the white is very thick and stands high; the yolk is firm, high and well-centered.

U.S. Grade A. An egg of A quality covers a moderate area; the white is reasonably thick, stands fairly high; the yolk is firm, high, and well-centered.

Raw

Poached

Fried

Hard-cooked

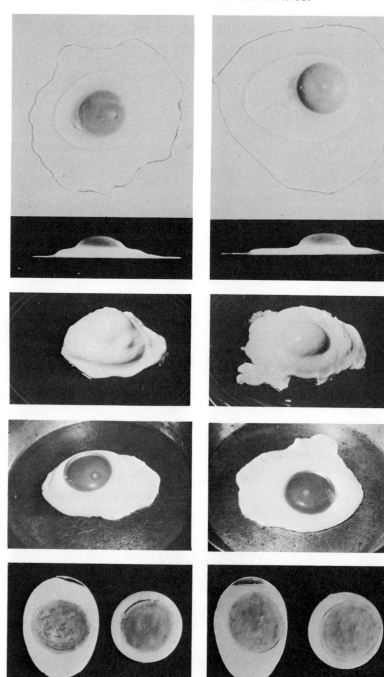

U.S. Grade B. An egg of B quality covers a wide area; has a small amount of thick white; the yolk is somewhat flattened, enlarged, and off center.

U.S. Grade C. An egg of C quality covers a very wide area; the white is thin and watery; the yolk is flat, enlarged, off center, and breaks easily.

Raw

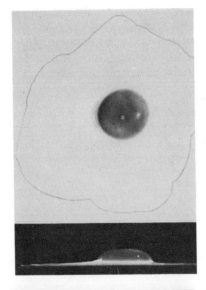 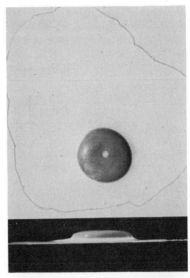

Poached

Fried

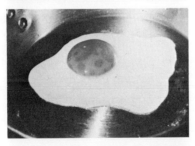 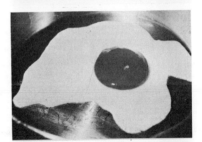

Hard-cooked

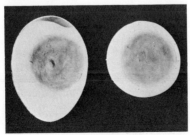 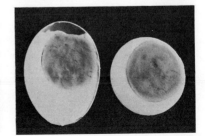

Courtesy of the U.S. Department of Agriculture

and fried eggs as well as in raw eggs. In lower grades the yolk is flatter and the white thinner than in higher grades. For this reason, it is not possible to obtain an attractive poached or fried egg from an egg of C quality because of excessive spreading of the yolk and white. The increased size of the air cell in low grades is evident in the photographs of hard-cooked eggs.

The characteristics of eggs of U.S. grades are described in Table 9–2. In addition to the characteristics already mentioned, eggs of top quality must

Table 9–2. *United States Consumer Grades for Shell Eggs* *

Factor Quality	AA Quality	A Quality	B Quality	C Quality
Shell †	Clean. Unbroken. Practically normal.	Clean. Unbroken. Practically normal.	Clean; to very slightly stained. Unbroken. May be slightly abnormal.	Clean; to moderately stained. Unbroken. May be abnormal.
Air cell	$\frac{1}{8}$ inch or less in depth. Practically regular.	$\frac{3}{16}$ inch or less in depth. Practically regular.	$\frac{3}{8}$ inch or less in depth. May be free or bubbly.	May be over $\frac{3}{8}$ inch in depth. May be free or bubbly.
White	Clear. Firm. (72 Haugh units †† or higher.)	Clear. May be reasonably firm. (60–71 Haugh units.)	Clear. May be slightly weak. (31–59 Haugh units.)	May be weak and watery. Small blood clots or spots may be present.‡ (Less than 31 Haugh units.)
Yolk	Outline slightly defined. Practically free from defects.	Outline may be fairly well defined. Practically free from defects.	Outline may be well defined. May be slightly enlarged and flattened. May show definite but not serious defects.	Outline may be plainly visible. May be enlarged and flattened. May show clearly visible germ development but no blood. May show other serious defects

* From *Shell Egg Grading and Inspection of Egg Products.* Marketing Bulletin No. 30, United States Department of Agriculture, 1964.

† For eggs with dirty or broken shells, the standards of quality provide three additional qualities. These are: Dirty (unbroken but may be dirty); Check (checked or cracked but not leaking); Leaker (broken so contents are leaking).

†† Haugh units indicate the height of the thick white.

‡ If they are small (aggregating not more than $\frac{1}{8}$ inch in diameter).

Table 9–3. *United States Weight Classes for Shell Eggs*

Size or Weight Class	Minimum Net Weight per Dozen ounces
Jumbo	30
Extra Large	27
Large	24
Medium	21
Small	18
Peewee	15

have a clean, unbroken, and normal-appearing shell. Shells that are dirty, abnormal in any way, or that show abnormality in shape, such as an unusually round or pointed egg, are graded down.

Eggs of Grade AA or A are especially good for poaching, frying, and cooking in the shell. Eggs of Grade B or C are more suitable for cookery purposes in which appearance and delicate flavor are less important. Eggs with small blood or meat spots can be used for cookery because the spots can be removed easily.

Size

The size of eggs is classified on the basis of weight per dozen, as indicated in Table 9–3. Eggs of Jumbo and Peewee size are not ordinarily found on the retail market. The fact that Jumbo eggs weigh twice as much per dozen as Peewee eggs underlines the fact that uniform results in baking cannot be expected if a specified number of eggs is used per recipe unless the size of eggs is controlled. It is usually assumed in such recipes that the egg size is either medium or large. If eggs of other sizes are available instead, the amount of eggs can be adjusted according to the information in Table 9–4. Variation due to egg size is avoided in some household recipes by using a measure of eggs, such as a cup of egg whites for angel food cake. For research purposes eggs are usually broken, blended, and weighed.

Table 9–4. *Number of Whole Eggs, Whites, and Yolks per Cup* *

Size	Number per Cup		
	Whole Eggs	Whites	Yolks
Extra Large	4	6	12
Large	5	7	14
Medium	6	8	16
Small	7	10	18

* From *Food and Home Notes*. Agricultural Research Service, United States Department of Agriculture, September 8, 1965.

Price

The price of eggs fluctuates during the year due to differences in seasonal production and also differences in demand. Some eggs go into cold storage at times of peak production. This helps to equalize prices throughout the year. Price also depends upon the grade and size of the eggs. Although small eggs cost less per dozen than larger eggs they may or may not be a better buy. Already mentioned is the fact that most recipes are based on the volume of large or medium eggs. The purchase of smaller eggs at lower cost for individual servings may mean the purchase of less nutritive value.

In communities where eggs having either white or brown shells sell at a premium price, money can be saved by buying the shell color for which there is less demand because shell color is not related to egg quality. It may be good economy to use eggs freely when they are inexpensive and to limit their use when their price is high. Purchases should usually be limited to a week's supply because eggs deteriorate and require refrigerator space for storage.

Functions in Cookery

Because of their many important functions, eggs are widely used in cookery. Perhaps their most important function is the contribution of nutrients—a point that hardly needs further elaboration. It is also easy to realize that they add flavor and color to any dish in which they are used. For example, desserts, sauces, and similar dishes seem to be more palatable when they are thickened at least in part with eggs. The functions of eggs that require discussion are coagulation, leavening, and emulsification.

Coagulation

When eggs are heated, their proteins coagulate. Coagulation gives firmness to breakfast eggs, thickens custards and pie fillings, helps form the outer walls of cream puffs and popovers and the cell walls of cakes, binds together the ingredients of meat loaves and croquettes, coats and helps brown foods that are dipped in egg before frying, and clarifies broths and coffee by enclosing particles present in the liquid. Egg yolk and beaten whole eggs begin to coagulate at about 65° C. (149° F.) but continue to thicken until a temperature of about 70° C. (158° F.) is reached. Undiluted egg white begins to thicken at a lower temperature, about 60° C. (140° F.), and continues to thicken until the temperature reaches 64° or 65° C. (147° to 149° F.). Such factors as the addition of other substances to the eggs and the temperature and length of time of heating affect these coagulation temperatures. Although the protein of eggs is usually coagulated by heat, it may be coagulated by other means. Acids, alkalies, and salts influence the heat coagulation of eggs and may bring about their coagulation without heat when used in quantities larger than are commonly used in foods. The whipping of egg white causes a slight coagulation of the proteins because they are dried out and stretched when they are beaten.

During the coagulation of protein by heat, new bridges are formed between the chains of molecules that make up the protein. These chains of molecules can be thought of as a series of strands that interlace to form a network in which liquid is held. The amount of liquid may be small as in the case of hard-cooked eggs or larger as in scrambled eggs or custards. Heating results first in the formation of a homogeneous mass, but if heating is continued the network contracts and squeezes out the enclosed liquid leaving a dry, tough, solid protein mass. Over-coagulation can be brought about by using too high a temperature or a low temperature for too long a time. Although comparatively high temperatures can be used successfully in egg cookery if the time is short, their use may be difficult because careful watching is required. Over-coagulation of an egg simply results in a tough white and a mealy yolk with no separation of liquid, but when a substantial amount of liquid has been added, over-coagulation may result in a curdled appearance, as in stirred custard or scrambled eggs. Examples of coagulation will be discussed throughout the section on preparation of eggs.

Leavening
The effectiveness of eggs as a leavening agent depends upon the amount of air beaten into them and retained. Although egg yolks form a fine, thick, lemon-colored foam when beaten long enough, they are seldom used for leavening because the foam is small in volume. The white of egg is used more frequently as a source of leavening than either the yolk or the whole egg because it forms a stable foam more readily. When egg white foam is heated, the air bubbles expand, the egg white stretches, and then coagulates to give a light, porous structure to the product. Factors influencing such foam will be discussed in connection with puffy omelets, soufflés, and meringues.

Emulsification
Egg yolk acts as an emulsifying agent because a protein complex that it contains forms a thin film around tiny globules of oil to make an emulsion stable. Eggs, especially egg yolks, act as emulsifying agents in many foods including shortened cakes, but their functions are less fully understood in such complex systems than in the simpler system of mayonnaise, which is discussed in Chapter 7.

Preparation of Eggs
Although eggs may be prepared and served uncooked in a few products such as eggnog and frozen desserts, recognition of eggs as possible carriers of infective organisms that can cause disease in man has tended to discourage the serving of uncooked eggs. During cooking by any method, eggs are coagulated—sometimes only slightly and at other times more thoroughly. Eggs may also perform some of the other functions discussed in the previous section. They are often cooked with little or nothing added as when they are cooked in the shell, baked, fried, poached, scrambled, or served as an

omelet. They are the principal ingredient of custards, soufflés, and meringues but only one of many ingredients in some of the baked foods that will be discussed in chapters to follow. When eggs are the sole or principal ingredient of a dish, it is especially important to use eggs of high grade so that the dishes will taste good and so that poached and fried eggs will have a good shape.

In the Shell

High temperatures are best avoided when cooking eggs in the shell because of possible over-coagulation and toughness. At the other extreme, eggs held in water at 70° C. (158° F.) may not become sufficiently firm. An easy way of cooking eggs in the shell that avoids possible breaking of the shell by heat is to put them in a pan and cover completely with cold water. The pan is covered and the water is then heated slowly to a simmering temperature (simmering means that the temperature is just below the boiling point). For soft-cooked eggs, the pan is removed from the heat and allowed to stand for three to five minutes. The longer time is used for a large number of eggs. Hard-cooked eggs are started in the same way and then simmered for twenty to twenty-five minutes but not allowed to boil. If the eggs are not served hot, they are put into cold water so that they will cool rapidly.

Another way of cooking eggs in the shell is to heat to boiling in a deep saucepan enough water to cover the eggs. Put the eggs into the saucepan gently, one at a time, with a tablespoon; cover, remove from the heat, and allow the pan to stand in a warm place four to ten minutes for soft-cooked eggs, according to the consistency desired. For hard-cooked eggs, after adding the eggs, cover and reduce the heat so the water is just below the boiling point. Cook twenty-five to thirty minutes.

The surface of the yolks of hard-cooked eggs sometimes appears dark green. This color is believed to result from ferrous sulfide formed by a combination of the iron of the yolk and the sulfur of either the white or the yolk. The greenish color is more likely to occur when eggs have been over-cooked or allowed to cool slowly in the cooking water. Cooking the eggs for the minimum length of time required to make them hard and cooling them in cold running water help to prevent this color formation.[6] A greenish color is more likely to form with eggs that have been stored a long time than with fresh eggs. The darkening of silver that has come into contact with egg is attributed to the formation of silver sulfide.

Hard-cooked eggs can be used as a basis for a variety of dishes. They can be used in sandwiches, salads, or "deviled" by cutting in half lengthwise and seasoning the yolk with mayonnaise, mustard, salt, and pepper. They can be cut in quarters lengthwise and added to plain white sauce or white sauce to which curry powder, fried mushrooms, grated cheese, ham, or dried beef has been added.

[6] R. C. Baker and J. Dorfler. Discoloration of Egg Albumin in Hard Cooked Eggs. *Food Technology*, 23: 77–79 (1969).

Poached

It is especially important to use eggs of high quality for poaching so that the poached egg will be compact in shape and the yolk will be veiled with white. In the usual method of poaching eggs, enough water to cover the eggs completely is brought to a boil in a shallow pan, an egg is broken into a cup, and is dropped gently into the water. After all of the eggs are added, the water is reheated to simmering, removed from the heat, covered, and allowed to stand about three to five minutes or until the eggs are firm but not hard. Salt or vinegar is sometimes added to the water in which eggs are poached because they hasten coagulation and thus may improve the shape of poached eggs that have thin whites. They tend, however, to make the surface of the poached egg less shiny than if cooked in plain water. If desired, eggs can be poached in milk. Eggs are sometimes poached in pans made especially for the purpose. The pans have several small cups that are greased, filled with an egg, covered, and held over simmering water until the eggs are of the desired consistency.

Fried

The shape of a fried egg depends upon the quality of the raw egg. The usual method of frying eggs is to put a thin layer of table fat or bacon drippings into a fry pan. The fat should be just hot enough to make a drop of water

Fig. 9–4. *Fried eggs that are not to be turned can be cooked to the desired firmness by spooning hot fat over the tops of the eggs.*

Courtesy of the Poultry and Egg National Board

sizzle so that the eggs will set within a few seconds but not become brown or tough. The eggs are slipped into the fat and cooked slowly until the white is set. The top of the egg can be cooked by dipping a little hot fat over it or by covering the pan.

If desired, eggs can be fried—or perhaps fried-poached is a better word—with only a little fat. About a teaspoon of fat is put into a fry pan, the heat is kept low, and eggs are added one at a time. About two tablespoons of water are added, the pan covered, and the eggs are steamed until they are done.

Baked

Eggs can be baked or "shirred" in individual dishes, or several can be baked together in a large, shallow dish. The eggs are broken into the greased baking dish, and one tablespoon of milk is added for each egg. The eggs are dotted with table fat, sprinkled with salt and pepper, and the pan is covered. The eggs are baked in an oven at 163° C. (325° F.) for twenty to twenty-five minutes or until they are firm. This method is especially desirable if eggs are to be prepared for a large group or if the oven is being used for other purposes. When individual baking dishes are used, the eggs are served in the dish in which they are cooked. Interesting variations of baked eggs are possible. They can be baked in a nest of hash; cream or a variety of sauces can be added; or the bottom of the baking dish may be covered with crumbs,

Fig. 9–5. *Baked or shirred eggs may be prepared in individual baking dishes.*

the eggs added, and covered with additional crumbs. Another variation is to separate an egg, beat the salted white until stiff, put it into a baking dish, and place the yolk into a depression made in the egg white.

Scrambled

Scrambling is a method of egg cookery that permits many variations. Usually one teaspoon or less of table fat or bacon drippings for each egg is heated gently in a fry pan. One-eighth teaspoon of salt, a dash of pepper, and one tablespoon of liquid are added for each egg. The liquid is usually milk but can be cream, water, tomato juice, or other liquids. The mixture can be beaten with a fork only long enough to break up the yolks and leave streaks of white and yellow in the cooked product or, if desired, more thoroughly with a rotary or electric beater. The eggs are then poured into the fry pan and cooked over low heat. They are stirred slowly so that the thickened portions are lifted from the bottom of the pan and the uncooked portion allowed to run down. Constant stirring is avoided so that a large soft mass will be obtained rather than a mass of tiny curd-like particles. Cooking is discontinued when the eggs are coagulated and before they become dry. Scrambled eggs can also be cooked in a double boiler. If this is to be done, one or two tablespoons of milk can be added for each egg. The mixture is cooked over simmering water without stirring. Because heated fat is not used in this method, the flavor of the eggs is slightly different from those cooked in a fry pan.

Omelets

French or plain omelets are made without separating the eggs, but eggs are separated for puffy omelets. French omelets can be made from the mixture used for scrambled eggs or from seasoned eggs to which no liquid is added. A fry pan of the correct size [7] for the number of eggs is selected. About one teaspoon of fat for each egg is melted in the fry pan. The egg mixture is added and the pan placed over moderate heat. As the omelet cooks and the eggs coagulate, the omelet is lifted from the edge toward the center and the pan tipped so that the uncooked mixture flows under the cooked portion. When the whole mixture is creamy and the bottom is slightly browned, the omelet is rolled or folded in half by lifting the handle of the pan and manipulating the omelet with the aid of a spatula. It is then turned onto a warm platter. If desired, grated cheese, chopped meat or fish, creamed vegetables, fruit, jelly, a sauce of tomatoes, onions, and green pepper, or fried mushrooms can be put on the omelet before it is folded.

Puffy or foamy omelets are made from separated eggs. One tablespoon of liquid, which can be water, milk, fruit or tomato juice; an eighth teaspoon of salt; and a dash of pepper are added to the yolks for each egg. The yolks are beaten and folded gently but thoroughly into egg whites that have been beaten until stiff but not dry. This mixture is put into a heated fry pan that

---

[7] The top diameter of the pan is about $5\frac{1}{2}$ inches for one egg, 7 or 8 inches for two or three eggs, and 10 inches for six eggs.

Fig. 9–6. *To make a puffy omelet:*
Beat together egg yolks, liquid, and seasoning and fold into stiffly beaten egg whites. Pour the mixture into a greased skillet, and cook slowly until the omelet has browned on the bottom. Place the skillet (a heat-proof or removable handle is necessary) in a moderate oven. Cook until the top is light brown and a spatula inserted in the center comes out clean.

Remove the omelet from the oven and make a shallow crease across the middle of the omelet. Fold over and roll the omelet from the skillet onto a serving platter.

Courtesy of the Poultry and Egg National Board

contains about one teaspoon of table fat for each egg. The mixture is spread over the pan and cooked slowly without stirring until delicately browned on the bottom. It is then put into an oven at about 177° C. (350° F.) until the top of the omelet is dry and firm. If desired, the omelet can be cooked in the oven for the entire period. The omelet is folded in half with a spatula and turned onto a warm platter. Any of the additions suggested for French omelets can also be used for puffy omelets. If water or fruit juice is used as the liquid in a puffy omelet, it may be added to the egg white before beating instead of to the egg yolk. In other details the method is the same. Milk or any other liquid that contains fat cannot be added to the egg white because the fat interferes with whipping. Sometimes water is preferred to milk or cream whether it is added to the yolk or to the white because an omelet containing water is usually larger than one made with milk or cream. Proper beating of the egg whites is important because the lightness of the omelet depends upon the amount of air incorporated with them. Overbeating is avoided because over-beaten egg whites do not combine well with other ingredients and do not stretch well during the baking process. Loss of air while folding in the remaining ingredients must also be avoided.

Soufflés

Soufflés are closely related to puffy omelets except that a thick white sauce is added to the beaten egg yolks before the beaten egg whites are folded in. Often some other ingredient such as grated cheese, chopped meat, fish, or vegetables is added which makes it possible to turn leftover foods into a glamorous dish. To make a soufflé, the white sauce (see Chapter 12) and the chopped food are cooled slightly, mixed thoroughly with the beaten egg yolks, and folded gently but thoroughly into egg whites that have been beaten until stiff but not dry. The mixture is placed in an ungreased baking dish so that the soufflé can cling to the sides and attain as much volume as possible. A baking dish that has straight sides and that is full at the end of the cooking process is best.[8] The dish is set in a pan of hot water and baked in a moderate oven (177° C., 350° F.). The soufflé is done when a knife inserted into the center comes out clean. Care must be taken to cook soufflés the right length of time since over-cooking toughens the product, while under-cooking results in excessive shrinkage when the soufflé is taken from the oven. Because any soufflé shrinks to some extent even when it is thoroughly baked, it is best removed from the oven after the guests are seated at the table. An especially impressive soufflé can be made by filling the baking dish more than two-thirds full and tying firmly around it a collar of aluminum foil or heavy wax paper within which the soufflé can rise. The collar comes two or three inches above the rim of the dish and is removed when baking is completed.

Dessert soufflés can also be made by adding sugar and flavoring such as vanilla, coffee, chopped nuts, orange marmalade, or chocolate to the basic

[8] A one and one-half quart dish is usually adequate for a soufflé containing three or four eggs.

Fig. 9–7. *An impressive soufflé can be made by wrapping aluminum foil around the baking dish, with a 3-inch collar above the rim.*

soufflé ingredients. The word "soufflé" is also applied to a baked mixture of fruit pulp or fruit pulp and juice with sugar and stiffly beaten egg whites.

One type of fondue resembles a soufflé except that bread or bread crumbs are used as the thickening agent instead of flour. To make cheese fondue, scalded milk, bread crumbs, cheese, table fat, and seasonings are combined, added to egg yolks that have been beaten, and folded into egg whites beaten until stiff but not dry. The mixture is baked like a soufflé. Bread crumbs give the fondue more body than a soufflé so that fondues are less delicate and, therefore, less likely to fall before they are served.

Custards

Custards are among the most popular dishes that are thickened with egg. Frozen, dried, or shell eggs can be used to make custards.[9] A custard can be thought of as milk thickened with egg and sweetened and flavored if used for a dessert or left unsweetened for a main dish. The consistency of cooked custard depends upon the proportion of eggs to milk and upon the addition of other ingredients. The method of cooking a custard greatly affects the finished product. Soft or stirred custards are cooked over hot water or low heat with constant stirring. They do not set to form a gel like

[9] D. M. Downs, D. A. Janek, and M. E. Zabik. Custard Sauces Made with Four Types of Processed Eggs. *Journal of The American Dietetic Association,* 57: 33–37 (1970).

baked custard, and even when they are quite thick they can be poured from the container. Their consistency resembles that of heavy cream that has not been whipped. Baked custards are cooked without stirring. The finished product is a delicate jelly that usually holds its shape when turned from the baking dish.

The usual proportions for stirred or baked custards are one or one and one-half eggs and two tablespoons of sugar for each cup of milk, but as many as four eggs and four tablespoons of sugar may be used. One and one-half to two eggs per cup of milk are sometimes used for custard pie, and even larger amounts of egg per cup of milk are used when making custards that are to be turned out of a large mold or cut into fancy shapes and used as garnishes. Two egg yolks can be substituted for one egg in making custard. Although two egg whites thicken custard about as much as one whole egg, they are seldom used because they add no color to the mixture and do not give the usual custard flavor. One tablespoon of flour can be substituted for one egg in making custard or cream pie fillings without too great a sacrifice of flavor and texture. Starch and eggs are both used for thickening such desserts as bread pudding, rice custard pudding, tapioca cream, and similar products.

Fig. 9–8. *Baked custards may be turned out of their cups and served with a fruit sauce.*

To make custard, the eggs are beaten slightly, sugar and a dash of salt are added, and scalded milk is added very slowly at first and then more rapidly. This mixture is cooked either over hot water or low heat or in the oven. For the former method, the mixture is cooked with constant stirring over water that is simmering but not boiling or over very low heat until the custard coats a metal spoon. The custard is removed immediately from the heat, set in cold water, and stirred until slightly cool. Then the custard is flavored, usually with vanilla extract. When custards are to be baked, flavoring is added to the same mixture used for stirred custards. The mix is poured into custard cups or other baking dishes that are set in a pan of hot water and baked in an oven at 177° C. (350° F.) until a knife inserted in the center of one of the custards comes out clean. If preferred, the custard can be covered with aluminum foil to keep out excess moisture and cooked in a steamer until firm.

Cooking custard for too long a time over-coagulates the egg protein. In stirred custard this results in a curdled appearance. If this condition should occur, the custard can be improved by beating with a rotary beater. Over-cooking baked custards causes the appearance on the side of the baking dish of "bubbles" which can be seen readily when glass dishes are used. Over-cooked baked custards are likely to have a porous structure, and when cut, liquid separates from the cut surface as it does from some jellies.

Thermometers can be used to determine when custards are done. The thermometer is suspended so that the bulb is in the center of the custard. It has been found that an increased proportion of eggs or the addition of acid fruits lowers the coagulation point and makes the custard firmer. Increasing the amount of sugar or dilution of the eggs by adding more milk raises the coagulation temperature and may increase the cooking time. Custards made with egg yolks coagulate at a higher temperature, whereas those made with egg whites coagulate at a lower temperature than those made with whole eggs. If the cooking temperature is high, heating is rapid and thickening occurs at a higher temperature than usual, but over-coagulation occurs so soon after maximum coagulation that it is very difficult to cook the custards properly.

Custards lend themselves to many variations. Soft custards can be served alone or as a sauce over fresh or canned fruit, cake, gelatin desserts, and a variety of puddings. Soft custards may also be garnished with whipped cream, tiny cubes of jelly, bits of colored fruits, nuts, or shredded coconut. Floating island is made by poaching spoonfuls of meringue in hot water and putting them on soft custard. The custard is usually thickened with egg yolks so that the egg whites can be used for the meringue.

Baked custard can be varied in many ways. Before baking, the top of the custard is frequently sprinkled with nutmeg. Coconut can be added before baking, or the custard mixture can be flavored with instant coffee or chocolate. When chocolate is used, additional sugar may be necessary. Caramel custard is one of the most popular desserts in Europe. To make it, about two tablespoons of additional sugar per cup of milk are caramelized by heating in a pan. This melted caramel is then poured while still hot into the bottom of the mold or molds in which the custard will be baked. When the baked custards are turned out of their molds, the caramel forms a sauce over the custard.

A custard mix without sugar can serve as the basis for a main dish. Seasonings, grated cheese, corn, or other foods can be added to the eggs and milk, and the mixture cooked as for a baked custard. A mixture of eggs and milk poured over layers of bread and cheese in a pan and baked makes an attractive luncheon dish. A custard mixture is the basis of the popular French dish Quiche Lorraine for which a mixture of crumbled crisp bacon, eggs, milk, and sometimes cheese is baked in a pan lined with plain pastry.

Egg White Foams

When egg whites are beaten, air is incorporated to form a foam. Such foams are used in puffy omelets, soufflés, and in many other foods such as meringues, shortened cakes, angel food cakes, and sponge cakes. These foods depend at least in part upon the leavening furnished by air beaten into the whites and retained during preparation of the food. When heat is applied, the foam expands, the egg white stretches, and then "sets" or coagulates to give a light, porous structure. A number of factors affect the amount of air that can be beaten into an egg white and the stability of the foam. A stable foam is one from which little liquid separates on standing.

When a rotary beater or electric mixer with twin beaters is used, thin whites are beaten to a larger volume than thick whites. Because the whites of eggs tend to become thinner on storage, the age of an egg has sometimes been associated with ease of whipping. Egg whites at room temperature whip more quickly than those at refrigerator temperature and yield a larger volume.

Beating. The shape of the bowl affects the ease of whipping egg whites and also the type and volume of foam produced. A bowl with a small rounded bottom that slopes out to a wider top is usually considered best. The beater should fit the bottom of the bowl. The type of beater also affects the characteristics of the beaten egg white. Rotary beaters turned by hand have proved less effective in producing a stable foam than an electric mixer with twin beaters, each of which revolves around a stationary axis. Still better results have been achieved with a beater that moves around a bowl that is stationary. A beater of this type produces a larger, more stable foam with thick rather than thin whites. Results are variable with old-fashioned flat wire whips.

Whatever the type of beater, the extent to which the egg white is beaten is very important. After a little beating, the egg white looks frothy or slightly foamy with large air bubbles on the surface. As beating is continued, the foam becomes stiffer and the air cells smaller. At first the foam is very shiny and flows when the bowl is tipped. The foam forms rounded peaks when the beater is withdrawn and held upside down. Further beating produces smaller air cells, a whiter foam, and a moist appearance. At this stage the foam is considered to be stiff but not dry and is ideal for use in cakes, omelets, soufflés, and similar products. Additional beating produces a dry foam that is rigid and almost brittle. The appearance is very white but dull, and the egg whites are over-beaten for most purposes. Such egg whites do not blend well with other ingredients and do not expand well in the heat of the oven because their cell walls are too rigid.

Additions. Acid, usually in the form of cream of tartar, is often added to egg whites for such products as meringue and angel food cake because it makes the foam more stable. Fat, whether it is from yolk, milk, or some other source such as a greasy bowl or beater, interferes with the whipping of egg white, and if present in sufficient quantity may prevent whipping entirely. One drop of egg yolk may reduce the volume of whipped egg white to less than one-third of the volume that would otherwise be obtained. Although many people believe that salt aids in the whipping of egg whites, experimental evidence indicates that the addition of salt appears to decrease the volume and stability of beaten egg whites or whole eggs. Additional study is needed before the effects of salt are completely understood. Sugar is often added to egg whites in making meringues and cakes. It has been found best to beat the egg whites until they form a soft peak and then to add the sugar gradually. More beating is required when sugar is present than when egg whites are beaten alone. The foam produced with sugar can be spread easily and is more stable than foams that contain no sugar.

Meringues. Superior soft meringues have been produced when the egg whites were beaten at high speed throughout the beating period [10] and when two and one-half tablespoons instead of two or three tablespoons of sugar [11] were used for each egg white. Spreading the meringue on hot cream filling has some advantages over spreading it on cold filling. A cream pie covered with soft meringue can be baked at temperatures as high as 218° C. (425° F.) if the time is short. High temperatures have the advantage of producing less sticky and more tender meringue than that baked at lower temperatures [12] but one with greater leakage. A temperature of 177° C. (350° F.) for a longer time is frequently recommended. The lower temperature more nearly assures heating the meringue all the way through.

Hard meringues are made from a mixture that contains more sugar than is used for soft meringues. Cream of tartar is usually added to the egg whites

[10] A. M. Briant, M. V. Zaehringer, J. L. Adams, and N. Mondy. Variations in Quality of Cream Pies. *Journal of The American Dietetic Association,* 30: 678–681 (1954).

[11] J. N. Gillis and N. K. Fitch. Leakage of Baked Soft-Meringue Topping. *Journal of Home Economics,* 48: 703–707 (1956).

[12] E. E. Hester and C. J. Personius. Factors Affecting the Beading and the Leakage of Soft Meringue. *Food Technology,* 3: 236–240 (1949).

when they are foamy, and about one-fourth cup of sugar is used for each egg white. The additional sugar prolongs the beating time required to make a stiff foam. If the hard meringues are to be served with ice cream or sweetened fruit, they are shaped on a piece of ungreased paper laid on a cookie sheet. The mixture can be baked as a pie shell and filled with a whipped cream mixture to make "angel pie." The meringue mixture can also be combined with chopped nuts, chopped dates, and even ready-to-eat cereal and baked as cookies or "kisses." Hard meringues are baked at a low temperature for a long time to dry out the mixture and make it crisp.

Activities

1. Using a table of food values, find the protein content of one serving of beef. Calculate the size serving of each of the following that would give an equivalent amount of protein:
a. Eggs
b. Bacon and eggs
c. Cheese and eggs

2. Compare frozen and dried eggs, if available, with fresh eggs in several cooked products.

3. Examine some eggs against a light. If no candler is available, improvise one by cutting a $1\frac{1}{4}$ inch hole in a piece of cardboard and hold it near a light bulb in a darkened room. Hold the egg in the light which comes through the hole and examine for size of air cell, and location and mobility of the yolk.

4. Break out on a plate several eggs of varying grades. Compare their appearance, including the height of the yolks and of the thick white.

5. Find out what grades of eggs are available in your local stores. If eggs of several sizes are available, compare their prices.

6. Compare the tenderness of eggs hard-cooked 30 minutes in water at 80° C. (176° F.), 13 minutes in boiling water, and 7 minutes in a pressure saucepan at 15 pounds pressure.

7. Prepare a puffy omelet and a French omelet.

8. Prepare and compare a variety of egg dishes based on hard-cooked eggs, poached, fried, baked, scrambled eggs, omelets, and soufflés. Sauces can be used for added variation. Estimate the cost per serving.

9. Prepare some dessert soufflés.

10. Prepare and compare a variety of custards including custard sauces and desserts thickened with eggs and a starchy thickening agent.

References

DAWSON, E. H., C. MILLER, AND R. A. REDSTROM. *Cooking Quality and Flavor of Eggs.* U.S. Dept. Agr., Agr. Info. Bull. No. 164 (1956).

Egg Grading Manual. U.S. Dept. Agr., Agr. Handbook No. 75 (1968).

Eggs in Family Meals. A Guide for Consumers. U.S. Dept. Agr., Home and Garden Bull. No. 103 (1971).

EVERSON, G. J. AND J. J. SOUDERS. Composition and Nutritive Importance of Eggs. *J. Am. Dietet. Assoc.,* 33: 1244–1254 (1957).

GRISWOLD, R. M. *The Experimental Study of Foods.* Boston: Houghton Mifflin Company. 1962. Chapter 3.

How to Buy Eggs. U.S. Dept. Agr., Home and Garden Bull. No. 144 (1968).

The Egg Products Industry—Structure, Practices, and Costs. U.S. Dept. Agr., Marketing Research Report No. 917 (1971).

Shell Egg Grading and Inspection of Egg Products. U.S. Dept. Agr., Marketing Bull. No. 30 (1964).

10
meat

Meat has long had an important place in the diet. In the prehistoric days of the cave-dweller, man's diet was composed largely of meat. Records of dinners served in Medieval England showed that sometimes as many as five or six different meat dishes were served at one meal. Settlers in the American Colonies ate an abundance of deer, bear, buffalo, and turkey. Extension of the United States westward to include the prairie section which was suitable for cattle grazing resulted in rapid expansion of beef production.

The United States has more than 25 per cent of the world's meat supply although it has less than 6 per cent of the world's population. As a result, people in the United States consume more meat than people in any other country except New Zealand, Australia, Uruguay, and Argentina, all of which are important meat-producing countries. It is, of course, easier to plan a diet of high nutritive value when an abundance of animal foods is available.

In this chapter the structure, aging, prepackaging, curing, selection, and nutritive value of meat will be considered. This material will be followed by a discussion of the preparation of meat by various cooking methods. So much more research has been done on beef than on other animals that when the type of meat is not specified it can be assumed to be beef. Differences in the handling of veal, lamb, and pork will be considered when sufficient data are available.

Structure
Wholesale and
Retail Cuts

A beef carcass is first cut in half through the backbone to form two "sides" of beef. The side of beef is next divided into two quarters and then into wholesale cuts that can be handled more easily than a side or quarter. The nature of these wholesale cuts varies in different countries and in different sections of the United States. For example, different methods of making the wholesale cuts are used in New York, Boston, Philadelphia, and Chi-

195

cago. Diagrams of these four systems are shown by Kotschevar.[1] To avoid confusion, only the Chicago or Midwest method is shown in Figure 10–1. According to this method, the side of beef is cut between the twelfth and thirteenth ribs into a hind quarter that includes the hind shank, round, rump, loin end, short loin, and flank, and a fore quarter that includes the rib, chuck, plate, brisket, and fore shank.

The hind leg may be cut as indicated into a round and rump or left as a full round. The rump is sometimes tied into a roast after removal of the large bone that it contains. Part of the round steak is called top round because when the wholesale round is put on the butcher's block it is at the top. In the New York method of cutting, the round may be divided into the sirloin tip and the top and bottom round. Care is necessary to distinguish between the sirloin tip of the round steak and the sirloin steaks that are cut from the wholesale loin end. The hind shank, one of the least tender cuts, is used for soup, stew, or ground beef. As can be seen from the diagram of wholesale cuts of beef, the flank steak is an abdominal muscle.

The loin end is cut into sirloin steaks that vary considerably in their appearance. Such variations can be accounted for by the fact that sirloin steaks contain different bones and their muscles run in different directions; some of them lie parallel to and others perpendicular to a knife that divides the steaks. This is in contrast to the short loin in which the muscle fibers are perpendicular to the cut surfaces of the steaks. Although the sirloin steaks are not quite so tender as those from the short loin, they are tender enough to broil and, with the possible exception of the pin bone sirloin, which has a large proportion of bone and fat, are a good buy when priced below steaks from the short loin.

The short loin is usually considered the choicest wholesale cut because it contains two tender muscles. The larger one is called the rib eye or loin muscle *(longissimus dorsi)*, and the other is called the tenderloin or fillet *(psoas major)*. Although the rib eye extends almost the entire length of the body, the major part of the tenderloin is in the short loin. These two muscles are often boned out of over-aged cows and bulls because they are relatively tender even though the meat of the entire carcass of such animals is too tough to use as ordinary steaks and roasts. The boned rib eye steak is called by various names such as "Kansas City steak," "New York steak," "loin strip steak," and "top loin steak." Restaurants sometimes bone the short loin of a high grade animal, but retail stores usually do not because the customer expects to find the tenderloin on any T-bone or porterhouse steak that she buys.

The porterhouse steak is taken from the short loin near the loin end. In this steak the size of the tenderloin is maximum, approaching that of the rib eye. The T-bone steaks are so called because their bone is shaped like

[1] L. H. Kotschevar. *Quantity Food Purchasing.* New York: John Wiley & Sons, Inc., 1961, pp. 486–487.

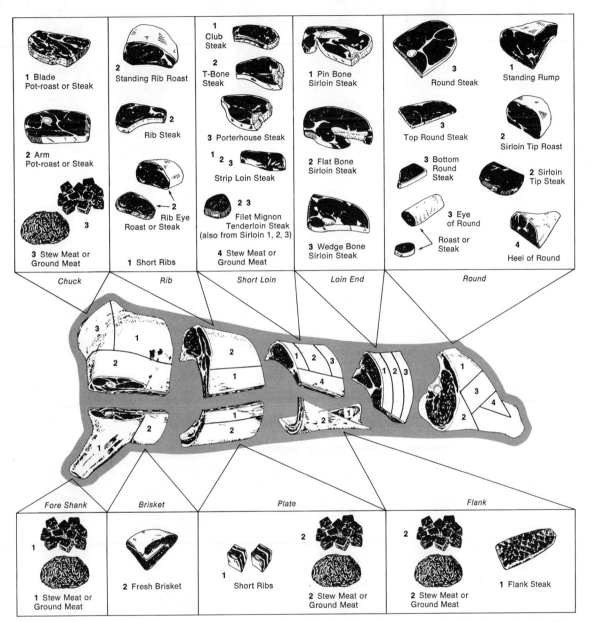

Fig. 10–1. *Wholesale and retail cuts of beef are shown in this chart. Familiarity with these facilitates the buying of beef.* (From *How to Buy Beef Steaks.* Home and Garden Bulletin No. 145, United States Department of Agriculture, 1968).

a T. The tenderloin of the T-bone is smaller than that in the porterhouse steak. Some markets use the words "T-bone steak" to cover all steaks with a bone of this type including the porterhouse steak. The club steaks are taken

Fig. 10–2. *These beef steaks are popular on the retail market. Those from the loin are tender enough to be broiled.* (From *How to Buy Beef Steaks.* Consumer Marketing Service, Home and Garden Bulletin No. 145, February, 1968.)

Porterhouse Steak. Cut from the short loin, this is often the most desirable but most expensive steak. The tenderloin portion can be removed and served as filet mignon.

Sirloin Steak. Cut from the loin end, these steaks vary in tenderness and in bone content. When buying sirloin steak, select one with a small amount of bone.

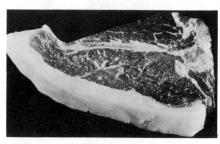

T-Bone Steak. This cut is also from the short loin but has a smaller amount of tenderloin than the porterhouse.

Club Steak. This cut, too, comes from the short loin, but it usually sells for a little less than porterhouse or T-Bone.

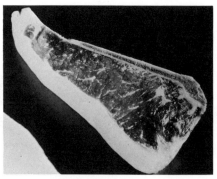

Strip Loin Steak. This steak is the same as the large muscle in both the porterhouse and the T-Bone. It is a very flavorful, tender steak which may be broiled or pan-broiled in the Prime, Choice, and Good grades.

Sirloin Tip. This is a boneless steak, less tender than the regular sirloin. Can be broiled or pan-broiled in Prime and Choice grades. Braise in lower grades. Allow 6 to 8 ounces per person.

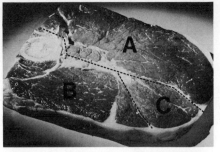

Round. Because it has little waste, the round steak is an economical buy. It is not as flavorful and juicy as some of the other steaks because it lacks marbling. The full round contains three muscles which vary in tenderness. It can be divided as shown.

a. top round, the tenderest of the three muscles, can be broiled or pan-broiled in Prime and Choice grades; braise the lower grades. Also called **inside round.**

b. bottom round, not as tender as top; cook with moist heat in all grades. Also called **outside round,** bottom round is often sold with the **eye-of-the-round** attached.

c. eye-of-round, also a less tender cut, but when sliced thin, Prime and Choice grades can be pan-broiled; cook with moist heat in other grades.

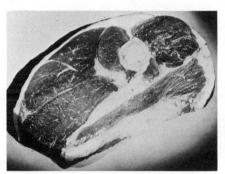

Arm Chuck. Sold as steak in some stores, this cut is best used as Swiss steak or braised. It is a less tender cut but has a well-developed flavor. It can be identified by the round arm bone and has little waste. Also called **arm steak.**

Flank. Boneless steak, with very little fat. Definitely a less tender cut, but it has a well-developed flavor. Braise, cook with moist heat, in any grade.

from the end of the short loin that is near the wholesale rib cut. Most of the club steaks have no tenderloin, but sometimes the term is applied to steaks that have a small piece of tenderloin.

The wholesale rib can be cut into roasts or steaks. Such steaks, when boned, are called "Delmonico," "Spencer," or "rib eye" steaks. The more tender end of the wholesale rib is adjacent to the short loin and this side of the rib resembles in appearance the club steak. The rib eye is large at the twelfth rib, where it adjoins the short loin. As the cuts of the rib approach the chuck, the size of the rib eye decreases and additional, less tender muscles make their appearance. The ends of the ribs that are trimmed from rib roasts and the short plate can be cut into short ribs.

The chuck is a large wholesale cut that is about the size of the round. Like the sirloin, it contains muscles that run in different directions. Chuck that is cut adjacent to the rib section is called blade-bone chuck because it contains part of the shoulder blade. Cuts in which the blade bone is shaped like the number seven are sometimes called seven-bone pot roasts. Pot roasts can also be cut from the chuck adjacent to the fore shank. These are called shoulder arm or arm pot roasts because they contain a piece of the bone of the fore leg. This cut is smaller and differs in appearance from the round steak which contains bone of the hind leg. The brisket, which lies under the chuck, is often used for making corned beef. The fore shank, or fore leg, like the hind shank, is a less tender cut and is used for soup, stew, and ground beef.

The ability to recognize the retail cuts of beef is especially valuable in these days of prepackaged meat because it permits the consumer to recognize the meat she wishes to buy and to know how to cook it.

For comparison, the wholesale cuts of beef, veal, pork, and lamb are shown in Figure 10–4. In the figures these carcasses are all about the same size, but in reality the size of the animals differs greatly as shown by the carcass weights that are above the diagrams. Perhaps the most obvious difference between the diagrams is that the smaller animals are cut into fewer wholesale cuts than is beef. This is hardly surprising since the entire lamb carcass may weigh about the same as a wholesale beef round. Another conclusion that can be drawn is that the animals are cut to give as large a proportion of the cuts demanded by the consumer as possible. For instance, much of the pork carcass goes into the leg or ham, the loin, and bacon. Lamb is cut to yield a large proportion of leg and chops, both loin and rib. The anatomy of the four animals is so similar that the location of the retail cut in the animal can be recognized easily by a person thoroughly familiar with beef cuts. The sizes of the retail cuts depend upon the size of the animal. For example, cuts corresponding to beef steaks are sometimes called chops in the other animals, and are so much smaller than beef steaks that more than one chop may be necessary to serve one person. Slices of the round called round steak for beef are called cutlets for veal and lamb. The plate and brisket of beef correspond to the breast of veal and lamb and the belly

Fig. 10–3. *The beef shown here includes both tender and less tender cuts. Recommended methods for cooking these cuts of beef include roasting, braising, or cooking in liquid. (From Consumer and Marketing Service, Home and Garden Bulletin No. 146, January 1968.)*

Rib Roast. These roasts should be at least two ribs thick for oven roasting. Steaks cut from ribs of higher grades are tender and flavorful.

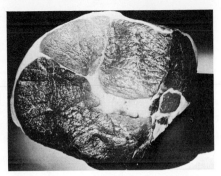

Rump Roast. A very flavorful cut, but less tender than the rib; has considerable bone. Prime, Choice, and Good grades can be oven-roasted; pot roast the lower grades. Often sold boned and rolled, for easier carving.

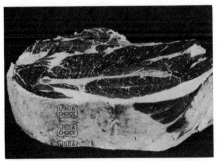

Blade Chuck. An economical roast, with excellent full beef flavor, it can be oven-roasted in the Prime and Choice grades, although it has several muscles that vary in tenderness. All grades make excellent pot roast.

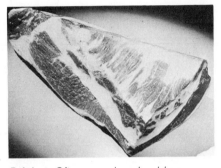

Brisket. Often cured and sold as corned beef, the brisket is also sold fresh, usually with bones removed. Definitely a less tender cut, it must be cooked with moist heat (pot roasted) in all grades.

Heel of Round. A boneless, less tender cut from the round, this roast contains several muscles, of varying tenderness, It should be pot roasted regardless of grade.

Shoulder Arm. Contains less bone than the blade chuck, but this cut is less tender. It has the same well-developed flavor, however. Pot roast in all grades.

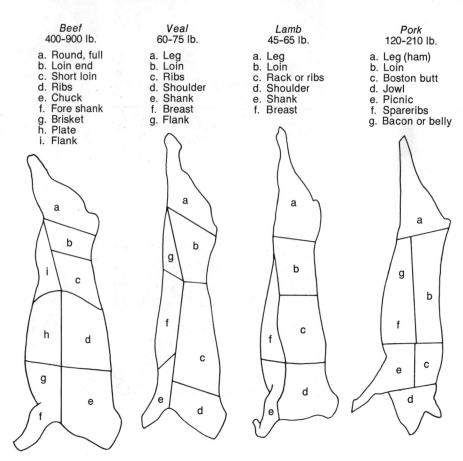

Beef 400–900 lb.	Veal 60–75 lb.	Lamb 45–65 lb.	Pork 120–210 lb.
a. Round, full	a. Leg	a. Leg	a. Leg (ham)
b. Loin end	b. Loin	b. Loin	b. Loin
c. Short loin	c. Ribs	c. Rack or ribs	c. Boston butt
d. Ribs	d. Shoulder	d. Shoulder	d. Jowl
e. Chuck	e. Shank	e. Shank	e. Picnic
f. Fore shank	f. Breast	f. Breast	f. Spareribs
g. Brisket	g. Flank		g. Bacon or belly
h. Plate			
i. Flank			

Fig. 10–4. *In this diagram the wholesale cuts of beef, veal, lamb, and pork are about the same size, but actually the animals differ greatly in size as indicated by the carcass weights above the diagram.*

of pork. The meat of younger animals tends to be lighter in color than that from older animals. For this reason the flesh of veal is much lighter than that of beef. Meat from young animals also tends to have less flavor but to be more tender than that from older animals. In pork, the shoulder, called the Boston butt, and the fore leg, called picnic shoulder, are often cured. Sometimes the rib eye or loin muscle is boned out of pork and smoked to give Canadian-style bacon. The belly, from which the spare ribs and breast bone are removed, is smoked to give bacon. The hind leg of pork is familiar as smoked ham. Any cut of pork can, of course, be used either fresh or smoked.

Muscle and Connective Tissue

Most cuts of meat consist of muscle combined with some connective and fatty tissues. Muscle tissue is made up of bundles of muscle fibers. The fibers are long and slender, with dimensions similar to those of a human hair. The muscle fiber, composed largely of protein and capable of contracting, is enclosed in a very thin skin. Individual muscle fibers are made into bundles by a thin network of connective tissue. A sheet of connective tissue surrounds the bundle and forms the tendon that attaches a muscle to a bone. Such tendons are easily seen in a chicken leg or the hind shank of beef.

Connective tissue contains the proteins collagen and elastin. Tendons and the tissues that surround muscles are rich in collagen. The connective tissue that connects one bone to another (ligaments), and that occurs in cartilage and in blood vessels, is rich in elastin. Connective tissues high in elastin are called elastic fibers because they stretch and return to their original shape in contrast to connective tissues that are rich in collagen which are flexible but offer great resistance to a pulling force.

Tough cuts of meat tend to have more collagen and elastin than do the more tender cuts, probably because connective tissue is thicker and more developed in the muscles that are used frequently, such as the neck and the fore legs. Cooking makes tissues that contain collagen more tender by changing collagen into gelatin, which is soluble and offers little or no resistance to chewing. The amount of collagen converted to gelatin increases with the length of the cooking period. However, some collagen is changed to gelatin even during the broiling of beef to the rare stage. Although water is required for this conversion, there is enough water in the meat to form gelatin even in cooking methods for which no water is added. Cooking causes some softening of elastin but not nearly so much as in collagen. Fortunately the elastin content of most muscles is low.

As animals are fattened, fat is deposited in connective tissues—first around certain organs such as the kidney and under the skin of the animal, and later as marbling within the muscles. A generous amount of marbling appears only after enough fat has been deposited outside the muscles to cause considerable waste in cutting and cooking the meat. Some fat is desirable in any case because it increases the palatability of meat and aids in retaining the moisture of muscles during cooking.

Aging

A few hours after death, the muscles of animals become stiff, a change known as rigor mortis. A day or two after the stiffening has occurred, the muscles become soft again. These changes are important to the consumer because of the effect they have on the tenderness of meat. Meat that is cooked while it is in rigor is likely to be exceedingly tough. It becomes more tender after rigor has passed. Meat of all types is held in cold storage during the short period required for rigor to pass and for the meat to become chilled so that cutting is easy. Pork is usually not aged beyond this point because the ease with which pork fat becomes rancid gives the meat an unpleasant flavor when it is aged. Veal and lamb can be aged for brief periods, beef and mutton for longer periods, because an outer layer of fat protects the lean from microbial growth. Tenderness increases during the aging of meat, probably because enzymes in the meat affect muscle protein. Most of the increase in tenderness of beef occurs during the first ten days to two weeks of storage. Beef usually reaches the consumer by the time it has been aged ten days, but beef that has a good covering of fat can be aged for longer periods if desired. Beef aged longer than two weeks becomes slightly more tender and develops a "gamey" flavor preferred by some people to the milder flavor of beef aged for a shorter time.

Prepackaging

In many retail markets meat is prepackaged to facilitate self-service and to delay moisture loss. Such packages usually carry a label that identifies the cut of meat and tells its weight and price. The plastic films used for fresh red meat are not perforated like those used for fruits and vegetables but are permeable to oxygen so that the color of the meat will remain red. If red meat is packaged in a film that is not permeable to oxygen, its color may be purplish. The purple color will change to red again as soon as it is exposed to the air. Meats such as poultry and cured meat are often vacuum-sealed in a plastic film that is impermeable to gases. Sliced cured ham is often covered with an opaque paper, usually printed with a picture of sliced ham. This covering is to protect the characteristic pink color from darkening caused by the bright lights over the meat counter. Packaging materials for any meat should not absorb grease or water. Fresh meat so packaged may be kept in the home refrigerator in its original wrapper if the meat is to be used within one or two days. If kept longer, the wrapper should be loosened at both ends.

Curing
Meats

The process of curing meat was developed originally so that meats could be stored without refrigeration. In its simplest form, curing means the addition of a liberal amount of salt (sodium chloride). Drying, an even older method of preservation, and the addition of salt were for centuries the only artificial methods of preserving meat and fish.

Variations in the basic salting process have been made gradually. At present, few meats except "salt pork," made from the bellies and fat backs of hogs, are treated by the addition of salt alone. Sugar is added to improve the flavor and to counteract the hardening effect of salt, and salts called nitrites and nitrates are added to alter the color of meat and make it stable during cooking. Some cured meats are also smoked, a process that gives the meat a pleasant flavor and helps prevent spoilage by drying the surface partially and depositing products that inhibit microbial growth. Pork and beef are the meats most often cured.

A dry cure is made by mixing common salt, sugar, and the salts that fix color. It can be added to ground meat for sausage or other prepared meats. Pieces of meat such as bacon, Canadian bacon, and certain types of hams are first rubbed with the dry cure and then packed tightly in layers in a box, where they remain for three or four weeks before they are smoked. Dry cure penetrates more slowly than brine cure.

The ingredients used in a dry cure can be dissolved in water to form a brine cure. Meat can either be soaked in the brine, sometimes for several weeks, or the brine can be injected into the meat, which results in a more rapid and complete penetration of the curing ingredients. In cuts such as hams, briskets, and tongues that have their vascular system intact, the curing brine is often pumped into the arteries. Brine is injected into cuts such as bacon with needles, a process called "stitch pumping." Often several methods of applying the curing ingredients are combined. For example, a ham may be artery-pumped, stitch-pumped, and then either rubbed with the dry curing salts or immersed in a curing brine.[2] Corned beef, usually made from brisket, plate, or round, is cured but not smoked. Most other meats, including hams, are smoked after they have been cured.

Modern processing methods may produce ham quite different from that with the traditional heavy cure. Only enough of the curing ingredients are used to give the desired flavor, rather than enough to preserve the meat. For this reason, such meats require refrigeration. Pumping the curing solution into the ham makes it possible to market a cured or even a cured-cooked product that weighs more than the fresh uncured meat. Because of possible deception of consumers, it is now required that ham be labeled "Water Added" if the ham weighs up to 10 per cent more than the uncured meat and "Imitation Ham" if it contains more than 10 per cent water. These requirements apply, of course, only to inspected meat. Although the addition of water to ham has obvious economic implications for consumers, cured hams containing more moisture than fresh hams were found by many people to have eating quality as good or better than those processed to the original weight. More specifically, this experiment indicated that cured hams weighing 108 and 117 per cent of the weight of the fresh hams were more tender and juicy and better in flavor than those weighing 93 and 100 per cent of the fresh weight.[3]

Hams of the traditional type, called country style or "Virginia type" hams are prepared with a dry cure instead of being pumped with a brine cure. The dry cure, sometimes containing black pepper, is rubbed into the meat, which is then piled and cured for a period of about one day per pound of ham. The hams are smoked intermittently for about thirty days and aged for seven to eleven months. The heavy salt cure makes it possible to keep such hams without refrigeration. They are usually soaked in water and boiled before they are baked.

Before discussing the treatment required of all pork products that may be eaten without further cooking, it is necessary to explain that some hogs suffer from a disease called trichinosis. This disease, which is not detected when the carcass of the hog is inspected, is caused by thread-like worms

[2] American Meat Institute Foundation. *The Science of Meat and Meat Products.* San Francisco: W. H. Freeman and Co., Publishers, 1960. Chapter 10.

[3] O. M. Batcher, G. L. Gilpin, N. R. Duckworth, and P. W. Finkel. Eating Quality of Quick-Cured Hams. *Journal of Home Economics,* 56: 758–762 (1964).

Courtesy of the National Live Stock and Meat Board

Fig. 10–5. *This selection of sausages includes, reading clockwise from far left: veal loaf, New England ham, boiled ham, peppered loaf, souse, pickle and pimiento loaf, summer sausage, bologna, liver sausage.*

called trichinae. The technical name of the organism is *Trichinella spiralis.* Although this organism occurs in only a small proportion of the hogs killed each year, it is a potential danger because the organisms are in the muscles of infected pork; and if they have not been destroyed by heat during cooking, or by some other means, the person who eats the pork may acquire trichinosis. This disease, which is not contagious, is contracted only by swallowing living trichinae. The seriousness of the disease depends upon the number of trichinae that have been eaten.

Trichinosis in humans can be prevented by making sure that all fresh pork and fresh pork products such as sausage are adequately cooked.

When prepared under official meat inspection, all products containing pork that are to be eaten with little or no additional cooking must be heated to an internal temperature of at least 58.5° C. (137° F.) or treated by approved methods of freezing or drying and curing to destroy any trichinae that may be present.[4] This requirement applies to prepared products including ham and sausage, except fresh unsmoked sausages.

Sausages

Many types of sausages are made from chopped or ground meat to which seasonings and often curing ingredients have been added. The meat may be pork or pork with beef, veal, lamb, or mutton. A few sausages are made without pork. Sausages may contain extenders such as cereal, starch, soy

[4] *Code of Federal Regulations,* Title 9, Part 318.10.

Table 10–1. *Classification of Some Popular Sausages*

Types	Examples
	Uncooked *
Not smoked	Bratwurst
	Bockwurst
	Pork sausage
	Weisswurst
Smoked	Kielbasa
	Smoked pork sausage
	Cooked †
Cured and uncured	Blood sausage
	Liver sausage or Braunschweiger
Smoked	Berliner-style
	Bologna
	Frankfurters (wiener, Vienna)
	Knackwurst
Semi-dry and dry	Cervelats
	Soft-summer sausage
	Hard
	Pepperoni
	Salami
	Thuringer ‡

* Must be cooked before eating.
† Must be safe to eat as cold cuts when federally inspected.
‡ Another type of Thuringer is classified as uncooked.

flour, or dry milk, but if the sausage is federally inspected, such an addition must be declared on the label and may not exceed 3.5 per cent.[5] They may also contain up to 3 per cent added water except that frankfurters, Vienna sausages, bologna, and others of their type may contain up to 10 per cent added water.[6] A list of ingredients in order of their predominance by weight must be shown on the package.

Sausage can be sold in bulk or packed into casings. It can also be treated in various ways by cooking, curing, and smoking as indicated in Table 10–1. Probably the favorite uncooked sausage in the United States is ground pork that is seasoned and sold in bulk, packages, or in casings, either linked or unlinked. It must be refrigerated and cooked thoroughly before it is eaten.

Under the classification of cooked sausages in Table 10–1, blood sausage and liver sausage or Braunschweiger are listed as "cured and uncured" because they may contain meats of both classifications. Liver sausage usually contains fat pork, pork liver, and gelatinous material seasoned with onion and spices. When it is smoked, it is often called Braunschweiger.

[5] *Code of Federal Regulations,* Title 9, Part 317.8(16) and Part 319, Subparts E and G.
[6] *Code of Federal Regulations.*

Frankfurters, which are cooked smoked sausages, are especially popular in the United States. These sausages are also called wieners or, when put into small casings, Vienna sausages. The meat mixture used for frankfurters is often 60 per cent beef and 40 per cent pork, although other meats may be used. Some frankfurters are made with all beef. Bologna is similar to frankfurters except that the spices are different, and larger casings are used. With both, the meat mixture is ground, seasoned, stuffed into casings, smoked, and cooked. Skinless frankfurters are stuffed into cellulose casings that are removed after processing. Dry and semidry sausages are of European origin. Some of them are smoked and dried, whereas others are dried without smoking. They are sometimes called summer sausages because they keep well.

Cooked meat specialties are not usually encased like sausages. Luncheon meats include meat loaf, ham loaf, liver loaf, and loaves that contain such ingredients as cheese, macaroni, pimento, pickles or olives. There also are liver pastes, liver spreads, deviled ham, minced ham, ham spread, and many others. Some of these products are often canned. Souse, scrapple, and head cheese are made from pork products or pork meat.

Selection
Inspection

In the earlier chapters on milk and eggs the need for sanitation in handling foods high in protein was discussed. Meat also is high in protein and in water, conditions which are optimum for microbial growth; therefore, careful handling of meat is necessary to assure wholesomeness. Meat from diseased animals is not considered fit for human consumption. The consumer can be sure the meat comes from a healthy animal if it carries the stamp "Inspected and Passed." Meat and meat products from plants that do not ship out of state may not be federally inspected. However, as a result of the Federal Wholesome Meat Act of 1967, the states must provide an inspection service equal to federal standards for plants that sell within the state or these plants will become subject to federal inspection.[7]

When butchering is done at home it is possible that meat of diseased animals may be used as food. Some states regulate the procedure for handling "game" animals, if these carcasses are taken to the commercial locker plant or to the meat retailer for cutting and packaging. This regulation is to prevent the possible spread of contamination from these animals to inspected meat.

Inspection includes examinations of the live animal and of the glands, viscera, and carcass after slaughter. Each stage of any processing, such as curing or canning, is supervised; a sanitary inspection of the entire plant is made; and accuracy of labeling is confirmed. Any unhealthy animals or carcasses showing signs of disease are condemned. The stamp for fresh

[7] *Food For Us All. The Yearbook of Agriculture, 1969.* United States Department of Agriculture, Washington, D.C., p. 94.

Fig. 10–6. *USDA meat grader rolling a Choice veal carcass. The grade and the letters "USDA" are enclosed in a shield and the word "veal" also is included. (From* Food for Us All. *The Yearbook of Agriculture, 1969, U.S. Department of Agriculture, p. 99.)*

meat, which must appear on every wholesale cut, assures that the meat was wholesome when it left the plant. It is not necessary to cut the stamp off before cooking because the vegetable dye used is harmless.

Grading

Meat grades are an indication of the quality of the meat in contrast to inspection, which indicates only whether the meat is wholesome. The only connection between inspection and grading is that meat that is graded must first be inspected. The packer who wishes to sell graded meat requests and pays for the grading service, which is performed by the United States Department of Agriculture. The grades used for various animals are shown in Table 10–2. The grade is marked on meat with a roller stamp that leaves a ribbon-like imprint of the grade that can be seen on most retail cuts. As with the inspection stamp, the grades are marked with a harmless purple vegetable dye that need not be cut from the meat before cooking. Some packers use their own systems in which grades are designated by such terms as Star, Quality, and Banquet, or Premium, Select, and Arrow instead of by the grades of the United States Department of Agriculture. It is unlikely that

Table 10–2. *United States Department of Agriculture Quality Grades for Meat*

Beef	Veal and Calf	Lamb	Yearling Mutton	Mutton
Prime	Prime	Prime	Prime	—
Choice	Choice	Choice	Choice	Choice
Good	Good	Good	Good	Good
Standard	Standard	Utility	Utility	Utility
Commercial	Utility	Cull	Cull	Cull
Utility	Cull			
Cutter				
Canner				

any one store will carry all of the possible grades of meat because the owner usually stocks only the grade or grades that will satisfy the majority of his customers.

Beef can now[8] be graded for either or both of two factors called "quality" and "cutability" that are considered important to consumers. The "quality grade" is based on conformation and palatability indicating characteristics of the lean. The grades that result from a consideration of quality are shown in Table 10–2. Good conformation for beef as for other meat means that carcasses have a high proportion of meat to bone and that as much as possible of the carcass weight is composed of the more valuable parts such as the loin and round. Animals of good conformation have full, thick muscles in relation to their length, whereas those of inferior conformation are thinly muscled, narrow and thin in relation to their length, and have an angular, thin, sunken appearance (Fig. 10–7). Beef of high grade comes from a young animal. The lean is well marbled, fine in texture, and normal in color. Texture becomes coarser and color darker as the animal ages. Maturity is indicated most accurately by evaluating the condition of the bones and cartilages. Young animals have bones that are reddish in color and slightly soft, with cartilages on the ends. The bones of older animals are white, flinty, and completely ossified. The Prime, Choice, Good, and Standard grades are restricted to beef from young cattle and the Commercial grade to beef from cattle too mature for Good and Standard. The Utility, Cutter, and Canner grades include beef from animals of all ages. Beef of Utility grade is the lowest that is commonly sold in the carcass. Some of the tender cuts such as the rib and the tenderloin are removed from Cutter beef. The remainder of the Cutter carcass and all of the Canner carcass are used in processed meat products.

The second factor on which beef can be graded is called "cutability," a term that indicates the proportion of edible meat available in the cut. The cutability groups are denoted by numbers 1 through 5 with Group 1 repre-

---

[8] Effective June 1, 1965.

Fig. 10–7. *USDA studies have shown that among lambs of the same degree of fatness those that have higher leg conformation grades have higher yields of retail meats. Yield grade descriptions apply primarily to carcasses, but the yield grade standards apply also to wholesale cuts which include either the hotel rack or loin.* (From *USDA Yield Grades for Lambs.* Marketing Bulletin 52. U.S. Department of Agriculture, 1970, p. 6.)

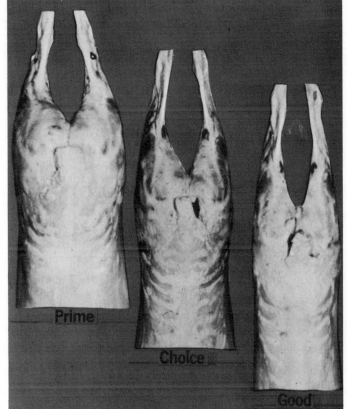

senting the highest degree of cutability. To be classified in Group 1, beef must have a large proportion of muscle as indicated by a relatively large rib eye area, a thin layer of external fat, and small deposits of fat around the internal organs. Beef that is graded for both quality and cutability allows the consumer to select high quality beef without excess fat.

The animals other than beef shown in Table 10–2 are to some extent classified according to age by their names. Veal usually comes from animals three months old or less which have subsisted largely on milk. Calves' meat usually comes from animals which are three to eight months old and have consumed feeds other than milk for a substantial period of time. Veal and calf are grouped together for convenience in Table 10–2 because the grades used for them are the same and the meat of calves is sometimes sold as veal.

Meat that is marked "spring lamb" is from the carcasses of new-crop lambs slaughtered during the period beginning in March and terminating the week containing the first Monday in October. Meat marked simply "lamb" may be as old as fourteen months, whereas yearling lamb is usually one to

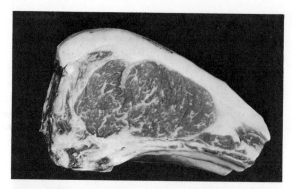

Fig. 10–8. *U.S. Grades for Beef.*

USDA Prime. Prime grade beef is the ultimate in tenderness, juiciness, and flavor. It has abundant marbling—flecks of fat within the lean—which enhances both flavor and juiciness. A U.S. Prime rib roast is considered by many as the finest meat dish available.

USDA Choice. Choice rib, rump, round, and sirloin tip roasts can also, like Prime, be oven roasted. They will be quite tender, juicy, and flavorful. Choice grade beef has slightly less marbling than Prime, but still is of very high quality.

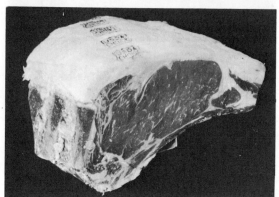

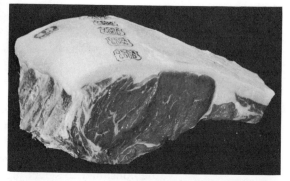

USDA Good. Good grade beef often pleases thrifty shoppers because it is somewhat more lean than the higher grades. It is relatively tender, but because it has less marbling it lacks some of the juiciness and flavor of the higher grades. Some stores sell this quality of beef under a "house" brand name rather than under the USDA grade name.

USDA Standard. Standard grade beef has a high proportion of lean meat and little fat. Because it comes from young animals, beef of this grade is fairly tender. But because it lacks marbling, it is very mild in flavor and most cuts will be somewhat dry unless prepared with moist heat.

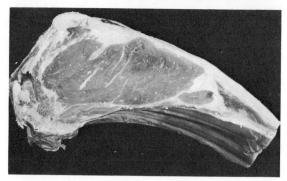

two years old. Carcasses from sheep more than two years old are called "mature mutton." Although popular in England, very little yearling lamb or mature mutton is sold in the United States. This is probably unfortunate, since meat from lambs eleven to twelve months old has a higher proportion of lean, more marbling, and is juicier, more tender, and has better texture and flavor than meat from lambs five and one-half months old.[9]

"Mutton" and "chevon" are terms sometimes used in the southwestern states for meat from young goats popular for barbecues.

Pork is not included in Table 10–2 because federally graded pork is not available to most consumers. The grades are similar to the yield grades for beef in that they identify carcasses for differences in yield of trimmed wholesale cuts.[10] In selecting pork, plump full muscles with a high proportion of lean to fat and bone are desirable. The flesh should be firm and fine-textured and may range from grayish pink to red in color. Breeding studies have resulted in a meat-type hog that produces more lean pork and less lard than was produced by the fat-type hog previously available.[11] Most pork is from hogs six months to one year old.

Amount and Cost Per Serving

In the United States from one-fourth to one-third of the average food budget is spent for meat, more than for any other food group. It is therefore essential that care be used in its selection so that the choice will be satisfying and the cost within the limits prescribed by the budget.

An average serving of cooked boneless meat weighs about three ounces. Because of loss in cooking, it is usually necessary to start with approximately four ounces of raw meat. Table 10–3 indicates that three to four servings per pound may be obtained from boneless meat. Five servings are usually available only when some other ingredients are added as for meat loaf or stew. In other cuts the number of servings per pound depends upon the proportion of bone and fat in the meat. Meat of high grades has more fat and, therefore, fewer servings per pound than meat of lower grades, except that pork of low grade may be high in fat. Meat that has little bone yields three to four servings per pound; meat with a medium amount yields two to three servings; and meat with large amounts of bone and gristle yields only one to two servings per pound. In some cuts of meat, part of the lean meat does not slice well and is therefore more usable in hash, stew, salad, or a creamed dish than as sliced meat. For this reason a larger roast than the minimum, calculated on the basis of servings per pound, may be a good buy. The homemaker would then plan to use the remnants of meat from the roast at another meal.

[9] P. C. Paul, J. Torten, and G. M. Spurlock. Eating Quality of Lamb. 1. Effect of Age. *Food Technology,* 18: 1779–1782 (1964).

[10] *Food For Us All. The Yearbook of Agriculture, 1969.* United States Department of Agriculture, Washington, D.C., pp. 103–104.

[11] *Food. The Yearbook of Agriculture, 1959.* United States Department of Agriculture, Washington, D.C., pp. 331–334.

Table 10–3. *Buying Guide for Meat* *

Food Item and Form	Market Unit	Approximate Volume or Number of Servings per Market Unit †	Approximate Weight per Cup	
Meat, fresh or frozen				
boned or ground meat	1 lb		227 g	8.0 oz
cooked		3 to 4 servings		
diced		1½ to 2 c	142 g	5.0 oz
meat with minimum amount of bone (steaks, roasts, chops, etc.)	1 lb			
cooked		2 to 3 servings		
diced		1 to 1½ c	142 g	5.0 oz
meat with large amount of bone (shoulder cuts, short ribs, neck, etc.)	1 lb			
cooked		1 to 2 servings		
diced		1 c	142 g	5.0 oz
Cured and/or smoked				
ham, ground	1 lb		170 g	6.0 oz
cooked, ground		2½ to 3 servings	109 g	3.8 oz
diced		1½ to 2 c	147 g	5.2 oz
bacon	1 lb	24 slices		
frankfurters	1 lb	8 to 10 sausages		
luncheon meat, sliced	12 oz	8 slices		
diced			141 g	5.0 oz
Canned				
corned beef	12 oz	4 servings		
ham, smoked	1½ lb	6 to 8 servings		
diced		3¾ to 4½ c		
luncheon meat	12 oz	4 servings		
sausage, Vienna	4 oz	8 to 10 sausages		
Dried				
chipped beef	4 oz	1⅔ servings		

* *Handbook of Food Preparation.* American Home Economics Association, Washington, D.C. 1971, p. 69.
† Three ounces of cooked meat is the usual amount for one serving.

The cut or type of meat that is the best buy depends upon the cost per pound and upon the amount of waste. A rough estimate can be made from the data in Table 10–3. For example, a homemaker can afford to spend twice as much per pound for meat that gives four servings as for meat that gives only two servings per pound.

It is important to realize in buying meat that its price per pound reflects both supply and demand. In beef, the cuts in most demand are probably those from the wholesale cuts called loin end, short loin, and rib, which together make up about 26.5 per cent of the beef carcass. It is reasonable to expect that the remaining 73.5 per cent of the carcass will sell at a lower price per pound with the possible exception of some preferred cuts such as the center round slices and the rump. It is possible to save money by buying the less tender cuts of beef and the less popular cuts of pork, lamb, and veal. Picnic shoulders and Boston butts are likely to be less expensive than ham. Most variety meats are reasonably priced and offer excellent nutrition. A few variety meats, such as calves' liver and sweetbreads, may be quite high in price. Another way of saving money in buying meat is to purchase the lower grades, which not only cost less per pound but also have less waste than the higher grades.

The cost per serving of meat dishes is altered when meat is made into convenience foods that require little or no preparation. Harp and Dunham found in their study of the cost per serving of some main dishes containing beef that, except for canned beef stew, the convenience items were more expensive than the home-prepared items.[12] Frozen beef patties cost about two and one-half times as much per serving as beef patties prepared from fresh ground beef. Frozen beef and meat loaf dinners that contained meat and two vegetables cost twice as much as similar home-prepared dinners. Canned beef patties and frozen beef pie cost about one and one-half times as much per serving as the home-prepared foods. The canned beef stew and frozen beef pies contained less beef per serving than standard home recipes. Canned beef stew contained the equivalent of about 2 ounces of raw beef per serving, whereas the frozen beef pie contained about 2.5 ounces of raw beef per serving. When the amount of meat in the home recipes was reduced to that in the commercial products, the cost per serving of canned stew was 6 per cent higher than home-prepared stew, and the frozen beef pie was 84 per cent more expensive than home-prepared beef pie. A meal in which the main dish contains only 2 or 2.5 ounces of meat might be improved by the addition of some other high protein food such as cottage cheese salad or custard dessert.

The results of a more recent survey of costs of meat dinners and entrees in one city are shown in Figure 10–9. As was found in the earlier study, most convenience meat items cost more than the home-prepared.

Nutritive Value

Meat is an important source of good quality protein, iron, and B-vitamins, all of which occur in the lean part of the meat. Much of the fat in meat forms a layer around the muscle and is sometimes removed before cooking or on the plate. This is called "separable" fat. The lean that remains may contain

[12] H. H. Harp and D. F. Dunham. *Comparative Costs to Consumers of Convenience Foods and Home-Prepared Foods.* Marketing Research Report No. 609. United States Department of Agriculture, Washington, D.C., 1963.

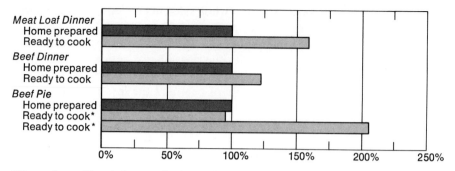

* Range of cost of brands that contain widely different proportions of meat.

Fig. 10–9. *Retail cost per serving of dinners and entrees containing meat. The dinners had the same amount of meat and of potatoes and a second vegetable.* (From *Family Economics Review.* June, 1971. Consumer and Food Economics Research Division, Agricultural Service, U.S. Department of Agriculture.)

some fat as marbling. Because of variations in the amount of fat removed from meat before it is eaten, some of the figures in Table 10–4 are for lean and fat, and others are for lean only. The data in Table 10–4 are for individual servings containing 3 ounces of cooked lean and fat. If only the lean is eaten, the fat and hence the calories are lower, but other nutrients are about the same, except for a small amount of vitamin A that is in the fat. Thiamine is higher in pork than in most other meats. Because the figures in Table 10–4 are for cooked meat only, it should be added that the nutrients of meat are well retained during cooking except that thiamine, being more sensitive to heat than the other vitamins, undergoes greater losses during cooking. This vitamin is better retained in meat cooked to low rather than high end point temperatures and in meat roasted at low rather than high oven temperatures. The drippings of braised and stew meat contain a substantial amount of the B-vitamins of the meat. This is not a problem because they are used with the meat as gravy. Losses of nutrients during the cooking of meat are in general not high enough to cause concern.

Compared with muscle meats, liver, which is a gland, is very high in minerals and vitamins. Indeed it acts as a reservoir of nutrients in the body and even includes carbohydrate in the form of glycogen. It is an excellent source of vitamin A and a good source of niacin and ascorbic acid. Ascorbic acid was not included in Table 10–4 because the other meats shown do not contain it. The nutrients in some of the other variety meats, such as tongue, resemble those of muscle meat more closely than they resemble liver.

Preparation

During cooking, many changes take place in meat. One of the most obvious is the changed color of the meat pigments. Rare beef is bright rose-red; medium beef is pink; and well-done beef is brownish-gray. Lamb can be

Table 10–4. Composition of One Serving of Cooked Meats *

Meat	Amount oz.	Amount gm.	Food Energy calories	Protein gm.	Fat gm.	Calcium mg.	Iron mg.	Vitamin A Value I.U.	Thiamine mg.	Riboflavin mg.	Niacin mg.
Beef roast, oven-cooked: Relatively fat, such as rib:											
Lean and fat	3.0	85	375	17	34	8	2.2	70	0.05	0.13	3.1
Lean only	1.8	51	125	14	7	6	1.8	10	0.04	0.11	2.6
Relatively lean, such as heel of round:											
Lean and fat	3.0	85	165	25	7	11	3.2	10	0.06	0.19	4.5
Lean only	2.7	78	125	24	3	10	3.0	Trace	0.06	0.18	4.3
Lamb leg, roasted:											
Lean and fat	3.0	85	235	22	16	9	1.4	—†	0.13	0.23	4.7
Lean only	2.5	71	130	20	5	9	1.4	—†	0.12	0.21	4.4
Pork roast, oven-cooked:											
Lean and fat	3.0	85	310	21	24	9	2.7	0	0.78	0.22	4.7
Lean only	2.4	68	175	20	10	9	2.6	0	0.73	0.21	4.4
Veal roast, medium fat, medium done:											
Lean and fat	3.0	85	230	23	14	10	2.9	—†	0.11	0.26	6.6
Liver, beef, fried	2.0	57	130	15	6	6	5.0	30,280	0.15	2.37	9.4
Frankfurter	2.0	56	170	7	15	3	0.8	—	0.08	0.11	1.4

* From *Nutritive Value of Foods*. Home and Garden Bulletin No. 72, Agricultural Research Service, United States Department of Agriculture, 1971.

† No basis found for imputing a value, although it is believed a measurable amount of the constituent might be present.

cooked to a pink or gray color depending upon whether medium or well-done lamb is wanted. Veal and pork should be cooked until well done as indicated by a light gray color of the lean. Cooking the meat to the recommended temperature as indicated by a thermometer inserted into the center of the cut assures that the desired degree of "doneness" is reached.

During cooking, some of the muscle proteins coagulate. With certain cooking methods, the muscle fibers become tougher, but under other circumstances heat seems to soften the coagulated proteins. Such changes will be studied in the sections to follow. The connective tissue protein called collagen does not coagulate on cooking, but instead some of it changes to gelatin. Fat melts and makes the meat seem juicier and more tender. Moisture is evaporated from meat during cooking. The drippings of meat consist of water and melted fat with some dissolved constituents of the meat.

Some of the methods used for cooking meat are summarized in Table 10–5. This table does not imply that methods of cookery other than those suggested should not be used. Indeed there are many other possibilities. The table may serve as a reminder that many cuts of meat can be used with success in planning palatable meals. The pleasure of eating is unnecessarily limited in homes where only a small variety of meats or other foods is served. The table also gives an indication of speed of cooking because broiling and pan-frying are much more rapid methods of cooking than are roasting, braising, and simmering. Under some conditions, preparation time must be the deciding factor in choosing a cut of meat.

Broiling

Broiling is a process of dry heat cookery in which heat is applied to meat directly from its source, which may be the broiling unit of a gas or electric range or hot coals. If the heat remains constant, its intensity is regulated by the distance of the meat from the source of heat. Enough heat is necessary to produce good browning in a short time. Broiling at too low a temperature is unsuccessful because the meat is likely to be gray and liquid cooks out of it. The cuts used for broiling are beef steaks from one to two and one-half inches thick, beef tenderloin, lamb chops, smoked ham, Canadian or regular bacon, veal liver, and ground meat. Broiling is not usually recommended for fresh pork or veal cuts other than liver.

To broil meat, the broiler is preheated and the rack greased lightly. It is necessary to put meat on a rack during broiling so that the fat can drip away from the meat. If the fat is held in a pan or on aluminum foil with the meat during broiling, the character of the meat is changed, and there is danger of burning the fat. The door of a gas range is closed during broiling, but the door of an electric range is left open so that steam will not accumulate in it during cooking. The fat around the outside of the meat is often slashed before broiling to prevent curling. It is easy to tell when meat has broiled long enough if a thermometer is inserted before cooking. The thermometer is placed so that the center of its bulb is in the center of the largest muscle and the thermom-

Table 10–5. *Methods of Cooking Various Cuts of Meat**

Method	Beef	Veal	Lamb	Pork
Broiling	Thick steaks Sirloin Porterhouse T-bone Club Rib	Liver	Chops Ground lamb	Smoked ham slices Canadian bacon Bacon
Pan-broiling and frying	Thin steaks Top round Sirloin T-bone Club Rib Cube steaks Ground beef Liver	Cube steaks Ground veal Liver	Chops Ground lamb Liver	Smoked ham slices Canadian bacon Bacon Thin steaks Thin chops Liver
Roasting	Rib, standing or rolled Sirloin tip Rump	Large loin Leg Shoulder	Loin Leg Shoulder Rib	Fresh and smoked ham Fresh and smoked shoulder Loin Spareribs
Braising	Rump Chuck Heel of round Short ribs Round steaks Flank steaks Liver	Round Shoulder Rump Loin chops Rib chops Cutlets	Shoulder cuts Shanks Neck slices Breast Short ribs	Ham slices Thick chops Thick steaks Tenderloin Spareribs Hocks Liver
Simmering, stewing	Heel of round Brisket Shank Short ribs Corned beef	Shanks Breast	Shanks Neck slices Breast	Smoked ham Smoked shoulder Spareribs

* Compiled from *Food. Yearbook of Agriculture, 1959.* United States
Department of Agriculture, pp. 525–526.

Courtesy of the National Live Stock and Meat Board

Fig. 10–10. *Bacon is broiled on a rack so the fat can drain away during cooking.*

eter is horizontal when the meat is on the broiler rack. If necessary, the thermometer can be rotated for easy reading when the meat is turned. The broiler pan is placed according to the manufacturer's directions. Usually the surface of the meat is two to five inches from the heat. Thin steaks are placed closer to the heat than thick steaks. The meat is broiled until one side is browned, seasoned with salt and pepper, and turned by sticking a fork into the fat rather than into the lean. It is then browned on the other side and seasoned when done. The meat is cooked until the desired temperature, as shown in Table 10–6, is reached. If a thermometer has not been used, doneness can be tested by making a small cut with a paring knife along a bone near the center of the meat and judging the color of the meat. Broiling times vary greatly according to the thickness of the meat and the degree of doneness required. A timetable for broiling and other methods of meat cookery is given in the *Handbook of Food Preparation*.[13]

Pan-Broiling

Pan-broiling resembles broiling except that heat is applied by means of hot metal rather than from a direct source. The cuts of meat used for pan-broiling are shown in Table 10–5. Most of them are the same as used for broiling but are cut thinner because it is easier to broil the thicker cuts and pan-broil the thinner ones. Pan-broiling is usually carried out in a heavy fry pan greased lightly and heated thoroughly. The meat is browned quickly on both sides. If desired, the meat can be held on its edge to brown the fat. The heat

[13] *Handbook of Food Preparation.* American Home Economics Association, Washington, D.C., 1971, p. 73.

is reduced to a moderate temperature and the meat turned several times. No water is added, and the pan is not covered at any time. As fat accumulates in the pan, it is poured off. Chops three-fourths to one inch thick require ten to fifteen minutes for cooking.

Frying

Like broiling and pan-broiling, frying is a dry heat method because the cooking is done in an open pan without the addition of water. Meats can be pan-fried in a shallow layer of fat or deep-fat fried. Sometimes meat to be fried is first rolled in flour or in egg and crumbs to give a brown crust and to protect the meat from the intense heat of the fat. As indicated in Table 10–5, the cuts used for pan-broiling can also be fried.

Roasting

Originally, roasting referred to the cooking of a large cut of meat before an open fire. The meat was held on a spit and rotated slowly so that all parts were evenly cooked. Today, meat is roasted in an oven, and the term "roasting" is used in much the same sense as baking. Roasting is a dry heat method in which meat is cooked in an open pan without added water. On the other hand, pot roasts are cooked by braising, a moist heat method that will be discussed in another section. At one time, meat to be roasted was first seared by putting it into a hot oven for a few minutes before reducing the oven temperature. Although searing makes the outside of the meat brown, it is no longer recommended because it increases cooking losses and requires readjustment of the oven temperature soon after the meat is put into the oven.

Constant temperatures of 110° to 260° C. (230° to 500° F.) have been tested for roasting meat.[14] The lower temperatures were found to cause less weight loss during cooking and to produce meat that was more uniformly done, more tender, juicier, and better flavored than that produced by the higher temperatures. Roasting times are long, however, at the lower temperatures. For convenience, a temperature of 163° C. (325° F.) is now recommended[15] for roasting tender cuts such as those shown in Table 10–5 under roasting.

Meat requires little preparation before it is roasted. The meat can be seasoned if desired, but salt penetrates only a short distance, and most of it is found in the drippings. The meat is placed fat side up on a rack in an open pan. The rack can be omitted if the bones of a roast such as the standing rib hold the meat up out of the drippings. The advantage of having the fat side of the meat up is that some of the fat melts into the meat during roasting. Strips of bacon or other fatty tissue is sometimes put over the top of meat such as veal roasts that have little fat. A meat thermometer is inserted so that the center of the mercury bulb is in the center of the largest muscle and

[14] J. A. Cline, E. A. Trowbridge, M. T. Foster, and H. E. Fry. *How Certain Methods of Cooking Affect the Quality and Palatability of Beef.* Missouri University Agricultural Experiment Station Bulletin No. 293, 1930.
[15] *Handbook of Food Preparation*, p. 73.

Fig. 10–11. To prepare a rib roast the meat is placed fat side up on a rack in an open pan and a meat thermometer is inserted so that the bulb is in the center of the largest part.

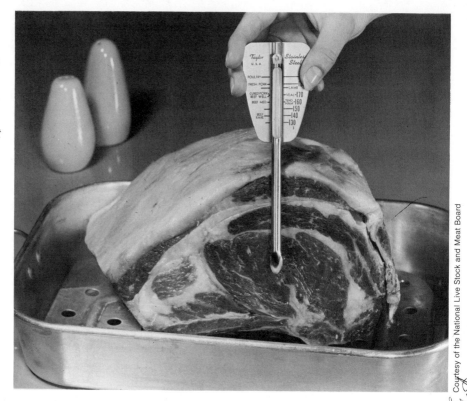

does not touch bone or fat. The pan is not covered during roasting because covering increases cooking losses and cooks the meat by moist rather than by dry heat. Basting meat by spooning drippings over it during cooking probably has little advantage and requires added time and effort.

When the desired end point or internal temperature is reached, the placement of the thermometer can be tested by moving it. If the temperature drops, the meat is put back into the oven for additional cooking.

The end point temperature of the meat is a more reliable guide to degree of doneness than minutes per pound. The time required to cook a roast is affected not only by the weight of the roast but also by its shape and the proportion of bone. There is, for example, little difference in the total cooking time for a standing rib roast and a matching rib roast that has been boned and rolled, although it is obvious that the time per pound would be considerably greater for the rolled roast than for the standing roast because of the weight of the bone. The proportions of fat, connective tissue, and muscle tissue also affect cooking time. Small roasts require a longer cooking time per pound than do large roasts. For all these reasons, tables [16] are used

[16] *Handbook of Food Preparation*, pp. 72–73.

to estimate the total cooking time of meat, but the end point temperature is used to indicate when meat is done. It is advisable to plan the cooking schedule so that the meat is taken from the oven twenty to thirty minutes before the meal is served. This makes the meat easier to carve and allows time for making gravy.

After meat has been removed from the oven, its temperature usually rises several degrees over a period of 15 to 45 minutes. Because this rise of temperature is due to penetration of heat from the outside to the cooler inside of the meat, the rise is greater for rare than for well done roasts, for roasts cooked at high oven temperatures, and for large roasts.

Beef can be roasted rare, medium, or well done. The decision about how well done to cook the meat is usually made on the basis of individual preference. Research has shown, however, that if tender beef is cooked rare the cooking time is shorter, the cooking losses lower, and therefore there are more servings per pound. In addition, rare meat is more tender and juicier than well done meat. On the other hand, less tender cuts than those mentioned under roasting in Table 10–5 may be more tender if cooked well done, as will be discussed in the sections to follow.

Although veal is relatively high in connective tissue and low in fat, the meat is likely to be tender because it comes from a young animal. It can be roasted successfully in an uncovered pan, especially if the oven temperature is low. It is often desirable to add fat either by inserting the fat into the roast with a larding needle or by fastening bacon, slices of salt pork, or suet on the surface of the veal with skewers. Veal is usually cooked well done, although there is no reason why it should not be cooked to a lower end point temperature than listed in Table 10–6 if preferred.

Pork is cooked well done so that any trichinae that may be present will be destroyed by heat. In the past an end point temperature of 85° C. (185° F.) was recommended. This temperature seems unnecessarily high, however, compared with the temperature of 58.5° C. (137° F.) that is accepted in the

Table 10–6. *End Point Temperatures for Cooking Meat*

Meat	Degree Cooked	End Point Temperature
Beef	Rare	60° C. (140° F.)
	Medium	71° C. (160° F.)
	Well done	77° C. (170° F.)
Veal	Well done	74°–77° C. (165°–170° F.)
Lamb	Well done	82° C. (180° F.)
Pork		
Fresh	Well done	77° C. (170° F.)
Smoked ham	Well done	71° C. (160° F.)
Smoked picnic	Well done	77° C. (170° F.)

meat inspection regulations as safe for cooking raw pork. When rib and loin pork roasts were cooked to 77° C. (170° F.), cooked meat yields were greater and the meat was more juicy and comparable in flavor and tenderness to roasts cooked to 85° C. (185° F.).[17] Pork roasts were equally good when roasted at 149°, 163°, and 177° C. (300°, 325°, and 350° F.), but cooking time was reduced as temperature increased. When the oven temperature was 190° C. (375° F.), however, the roasts appeared overcooked and the oven was spattered.[18] It is evident that fresh pork can be roasted in an oven at 163° or 177° C. (325° or 350° F.) to an internal temperature of 77° C. (170° F.) if desired.

As indicated in Table 10–6, smoked hams are cooked to an internal temperature of 71° C. (160° F.) and smoked picnics to 77° C. (170° F.). Fully cooked or canned ham may, of course, be served without further heating, or it can be warmed to an internal temperature of about 54° C. (130° F.).

Cuts of beef such as chuck, round, and rump are usually considered to be less tender and therefore not suitable for roasting. It has been found, however, that they can be roasted successfully if oven temperatures are low and the meat is cooked well done. For example, chuck and rump roasts were much more tender when cooked in an oven at 125° C. (257° F.) than at 225° C. (437° F.). At the lower oven temperature, cooking times were long, ranging from 52 to 90 minutes per pound for chuck and 46 to 77 minutes per pound for rump. In this study there was little difference between the tenderness of naturally tender cuts cooked at the low and at the high oven temperatures.[19] In another experiment[20] even lower oven temperatures were used and were found to result in further increase of tenderness of less tender cuts. Beef chuck and round were roasted until well done at 80° C. (176° F.) and at 125° C. (257° F.). This experiment shows that low oven temperatures result in more tender meat than higher oven temperatures. The study is, however, more valuable in proving a point than it is for practical application, because total roasting times at the lower oven temperature ranged from 21 to 43 hours and, in addition, few ovens can be regulated to such a low temperature. Oven temperatures ranging from 93° to 121° C. (200° to 250° F.), however, may be practical for homemakers who wish to start less tender cuts of meat before going to work. Average cooking times were about two hours per pound for four-pound cuts of blade or rump roasted at 107° C. (225° F.) to an end point temperature of 71° C. (160° F.).[21]

[17] A. F. Carlin, D. M. Bloemer, and D. K. Hotchkiss. Relation of Oven Temperature and Final Internal Temperature to Quality of Pork Loin Roasts. *Journal of Home Economics*, 57: 442–446 (1965).

[18] *ibid.*, Carlin, Bloemer, and Hotchkiss.

[19] S. Cover. *Effect of Temperature and Time of Cooking on the Tenderness of Roasts.* Texas Agricultural Experiment Station Bulletin No. 542 (1937).

[20] S. Cover. Effect of Extremely Low Rates of Heat Penetration on Tendering of Beef. *Food Research*, 8: 388–394 (1943).

[21] M. M. Nielsen and F. T. Hall. Dry-Roasting of Less Tender Beef Cuts. *Journal of Home Economics*, 57: 353–356 (1965).

When the speed of heat penetration during cooking is increased, it usually causes the meat to be less tender than when the heat penetrates more slowly. For example, the insertion of heavy metal skewers in meat causes the meat to cook more rapidly but to be less tender than without the skewers. Because heat penetrates faster through meat in water or steam than in air, moist heat cooking is more rapid than dry heat. Aluminum foil acts like a covered roasting pan in retaining steam. Meat cooked in foil required a shorter cooking time but was less tender, less juicy, and of less satisfactory flavor than matching roasts cooked by dry heat.[22] A cooperative study has shown that when corresponding cuts of beef round were cooked to the same end point temperature by the dry heat methods of broiling and roasting and the moist heat method of braising, any differences that were found in scores for tenderness and flavor were in favor of dry heat cooking.[23]

Braising

Braising is a popular moist heat method of meat cookery. As indicated in Table 10–5, it is used for a wide variety of cuts. When braised, thinner cuts of beef are often called Swiss steaks, whereas larger pieces of beef may be called pot roasts. The first step in braising is usually to brown the meat in a small amount of fat. It can be dipped in flour and seasoned before browning if desired. A small amount of liquid may be added, or the meat may cook in its own juices. It is then covered and simmered on top of the range or in an oven at 121° to 163° C. (250° to 325° F.). Thin cuts like chops or steaks from lamb, pork, or veal cook in about 45 minutes, but as long as four hours may be required for a large pot roast of beef. If vegetables are to be added, they are added just long enough before the meat is to be served so that they can be properly cooked and ready to serve with the meat. Although browning usually improves the color and flavor of braised meat, it is an optional step in the process. The essential step is that meat is cooked slowly in a covered utensil either on top of the range or in the oven.

Meat is sometimes cubed or pounded with a special instrument or the edge of a plate before it is braised. Such treatment makes the meat more tender.

The cuts of beef most often braised are the round and chuck. At home, they are usually braised until tender to a fork. In the laboratory, fork-tenderness can be produced by cooking meat to an end point temperature of 100° C. (212° F.) and holding at that temperature for 25 minutes. In a series of studies[24] on beef round and loin cooked by dry heat to an end point temperature of 61° C. (142° F.) and 80° C. (176° F.) and by moist heat to 100° C. (212° F.) for 25 minutes, it was found that the connective tissue of loin was tender when cooked to 61° C., whereas that of the round was tough at that

[22] M. P. Hood. Effect of Cooking Method and Grade on Beef Roasts. *Journal of The American Dietetic Association*, 37: 363–365 (1960).

[23] E. H. Dawson, G. S. Linton, A. M. Harkin, and C. Miller. *Factors Influencing the Palatability, Vitamin Content, and Yield of Cooked Beef.* Home Economics Research Report No. 9. United States Department of Agriculture, Washington, D.C., 1959.

[24] S. Cover, S. J. Ritchey, and R. L. Hostetler. Tenderness of Beef. I., II., and III. *Journal of Food Science*, 27: 469–488 (1962).

temperature but more tender at the higher temperatures. The juiciness of both muscles decreased as temperature increased. Round became softer to the teeth and tender to the point of mealiness when braised to 100° C. and held for 25 minutes. The loin, however, became harder and tougher with increased temperature. The reasons for these differences, which are not fully understood, may lie in changes in the protein of the muscle tissues. As degree of doneness increases, the muscle fibers of the round change in such a way that they seem mealy because they are easily broken or fragmented by the teeth. The muscle fibers of the loin, by contrast to those of the round, become harder, tougher, and adhere together as temperature increases.

It is evident from these studies and from the work on low temperature roasting that the less tender cuts of meat can be made tender by cooking until they are well done either by dry heat at a low temperature or by moist heat. Of these two methods, moist heat is the more rapid. By contrast, more tender cuts, such as a loin, are most tender when cooked by dry heat to a rare or medium done stage but become tougher when cooked by moist heat.

Cooking in Liquid

To make a stew, pieces of meat may be rolled in flour and browned in fat if desired. Whether or not the meat is browned, enough liquid is added to cover the meat, the pan is covered tightly, and the meat is simmered until tender to the fork. Large pieces of meat can also be cooked in liquid. Corned and smoked meats, such as corned beef or ham, are not browned before

Fig. 10–12. To braise a pot roast, the meat, which may first be browned, is placed in a pot with a small amount of liquid, covered, and simmered slowly.

cooking, but large cuts of other types of meat such as beef heel of round, can be browned if desired. The meat is covered with water and cooked like a stew. Total cooking times vary from one and one-half hours for lamb stew to about five hours for an eight-pound piece of beef. As in braising, any vegetables that are to be used are added just long enough before the meat is to be served so that they can be properly cooked. It is important to distinguish between cooking meat in enough liquid to cover and braising; in braising, a very small amount or no liquid is added, but the meat is covered to keep steam in the cooking dish.

Electronic Cooking

In electronic ovens electricity is changed into microwaves. The absorption of microwaves agitates the molecules of food. The friction produced thereby heats the food. Electronic cookery has the advantage of great speed but also certain disadvantages. As microwaves penetrate the food, they are absorbed, sometimes before they reach the center of the food. This may result in meat that is unevenly done. Cooking losses may be larger and retentions of thiamine lower in meat cooked by electronic compared with conventional cooking. In one study[25] all the meat products prepared in the electronic range had lower total palatability scores than similar products prepared in conventional gas ovens.

Some of the disadvantages of the electronic oven can be overcome by adding a conventional broiling unit to the oven that will brown steaks, roasts, and other products during the cooking process, thus avoiding the gray crust of meat cooked in the electronic range.

Variety Meats

Variety meats, sometimes called sundry edible parts, include edible organs that have not been classified elsewhere in the discussion of meats. Most of them are listed in Table 10–7. The names of some of them—like liver, kidney, heart, tongue, brains—are self-explanatory. Sweetbreads are the thymus glands of young beef, veal, and lamb. This gland disappears as the animal matures. Tripe is the inner lining of the stomach of beef.

Variety meats deserve an honored place in menu planning because they are high in nutritive value and can be used for many delicious meat dishes. It is hard to make a generalized statement about cooking these meats because they differ greatly in tenderness and their size depends upon that of the animal from which they come. Sliced liver and the kidneys of young animals cook quickly. Heart, tongue, and tripe usually require longer cooking to make them tender. Brains and sweetbreads are usually precooked in water containing salt and lemon juice or vinegar, then broiled, fried, or heated in a sauce. Oxtails, the tails of beef, are sometimes listed with variety meats, although they are not included in Table 10–7. Because oxtails require a long slow cooking, they are often used for soup or braising.

[25] A. M. Kylen, B. H. McGrath, E. L. Hallmark, and F. O. Van Duyne. Microwave and Conventional Cooking of Meat. Thiamine Retention and Palatability. *Journal of The American Dietetic Association,* 45: 139–145 (1964).

Fig. 10–13. *These variety meats include, left to right: liver, heart, tongue, kidney, and brain.*

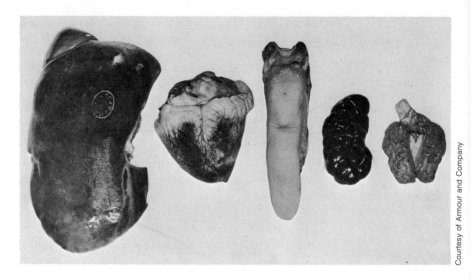

Courtesy of Armour and Company

Enzymes

Meat can be made more tender by treating it, while raw, with enzymes that split proteins. The enzyme most commonly used is papain from a tropical plant called papaya, although other enzymes can be substituted. These enzymes affect both the muscle and connective tissue of the meat and, when properly applied, make it more tender. At home, the enzyme is applied to the surface of the meat as a dry powder or a liquid, and the meat is pierced repeatedly with a fork to make the enzyme penetrate it. The meat is sometimes held for several hours before cooking, but this is probably unnecessary because most of the enzyme action occurs during cooking.[26]

Such enzymes are also used commercially. Steaks can be dipped in a papain solution before they are frozen. An even more promising method of application is to inject an enzyme solution into the veins of the animal a few moments before it is slaughtered. The enzyme is then distributed through the meat by the animal's own circulatory system.[27] Beef treated in this way is sold under the trademark ProTen. It is claimed[28] that this treatment makes it possible to use dry heat with cuts such as chuck that might otherwise be cooked by moist heat.

Although certain enzymes are capable of making meat more tender, it is necessary to use them with care because they may also decrease juiciness or make meat so tender that its texture is mushy or crumbly. The use of enzymes on meat that is already tender or the use of excessive amounts of enzymes on any meat should be avoided.

[26] A. L. Tappel, D. S. Miyada, C. Sterling, and V. P. Maier. Meat Tenderization. II. Factors Affecting the Tenderization of Beef by Papain. *Food Research*, 21: 375–383 (1956).

[27] H. E. Robinson and P. A. Goeser. Enzymatic Tenderization of Meat. *Journal of Home Economics*, 54: 195–200 (1962).

[28] *ibid.*, Robinson and Goeser.

Table 10–7. *Timetable for Cooking Variety Meats* *

Kind	Broiled	Braised	Cooked in Liquid
Liver			
Beef			
3- to 4-pound piece		2 to 2½ hours	
Sliced		20 to 25 minutes	
Veal (Calf), sliced	8 to 10 minutes		
Pork			
Whole (3 to 3½ pounds)		1½ to 2 hours	
Sliced		20 to 25 minutes	
Lamb, sliced	8 to 10 minutes		
Kidney			
Beef			1 to 1½ hours
Veal (Calf)	10 to 12 minutes		¾ to 1 hour
Pork	10 to 12 minutes		¾ to 1 hour
Lamb	10 to 12 minutes		¾ to 1 hour
Heart			
Beef			
Whole		3 to 4 hours	3 to 4 hours
Sliced		1½ to 2 hours	
Veal (Calf)			
Whole		2½ to 3 hours	2½ to 3 hours
Pork		2½ to 3 hours	2½ to 3 hours
Lamb		2½ to 3 hours	2½ to 3 hours
Tongue			
Beef			3 to 4 hours
Veal (Calf)			2 to 3 hours
Pork } usually sold			
Lamb } ready-to-serve			
Tripe			
Beef	10 to 15 minutes †		1 to 1½ hours
Sweetbreads	10 to 15 minutes †	20 to 25 minutes	15 to 20 minutes
Brains	10 to 15 minutes †	20 to 25 minutes	15 to 20 minutes

* From *Lessons On Meat*. National Live Stock and Meat Board, Chicago, Illinois. Copyright © 1964. Reprinted with permission.

† Time required after precooking in water.

Frozen Meat

Frozen meat can be cooked equally well with or without thawing. If cooking is started when the meat is frozen, a longer cooking time must be allowed. Large frozen roasts, for example, may take one and one-half times as long to cook as an unfrozen roast of the same size. Thick frozen steaks and chops may be broiled at a lower temperature than defrosted ones to ensure that the meat will be cooked to desired doneness without becoming too brown on the outside. Small roasts and thin cuts require less extra time when they are cooked without thawing, depending upon the size and shape of the cut. If meat is defrosted before cooking, it should remain in its original wrappings and be cooked soon after thawing. Meat varies little in palatability, nutritive value, or shrinkage whether it is thawed as part of the cooking procedure, at room temperature, or in the refrigerator.

Activities

1. Compare the size, color, and appearance of the same cut from beef, veal, lamb, and pork. Cuts such as the rib, loin, or round would be suitable, but all should be from the same location in the animal.

2. Using a beef shank, hock, or a chicken leg, examine the way that the muscles are surrounded by connective tissue and attached to the bone.

3. Study the labels of the sausages sold in your local stores.

4. What grades of meat are available in your market?
a. If more than one grade is available, compare the price per pound of the same cut in different grades.
b. Is the meat inspected by a federal or by a state agency?

5. Make two patties from $\frac{1}{2}$ pound of ground beef. Broil one and pan fry the other. Do you consider the cooked patty a small, average, or large meat serving?

6. Cook weighed amounts of meat with small, medium, and large amounts of bone and study the size servings suggested in the text.

7. Prepare a meat loaf mixture using all beef and a minimum of added ingredients. Divide the mixture among four small baking pans or use custard cups. Bake in an oven at 163° C. (325° F.). Remove the pans at end point temperatures of 63° C. (145° F.), 71° C. (160° F.), 77° C. (170° F.), and 85° C. (185° F.). Compare size of the cooked loaves, the palatability of the meat and the amount of liquid cooked out. To what temperature should meat loaves containing pork be cooked?

8. Cook both tender and less tender cuts of beef in several ways.

9. Cook veal, lamb, fresh and smoked pork in several ways.

10. Prepare variety meats in several ways. Calculate the cost per serving.

11. Prepare leftover meats in several ways.

References

American Meat Institute Foundation. *The Science of Meat and Meat Products*. San Francisco: W. H. Freeman & Co., Publishers. 1960.

Answers to Questions Consumers Ask About Meat and Poultry. Finished Foods Committee, Home Economists in Business, P.O. Box 178, Western Springs, Ill. (Not dated).

Beef and Veal in Family Meals. A Guide for Consumers. U.S. Dept. Agr., Home and Garden Bull. No. 188 (1970).

Bull, S. *Meat for the Table*. New York: McGraw-Hill Book Company. 1951.

Food For Us All. The Yearbook of Agriculture, 1969. U.S. Dept. Agr., Washington, D.C.

GRISWOLD, R. M. *The Experimental Study of Foods.* Boston: Houghton Mifflin Company. 1962. Chapter 5.

HARRIS, R. S. AND H. VON LOESECKE (Eds.). *Nutritional Evaluation of Food Processing.* New York: John Wiley & Sons, Inc. 1960. Pp. 261–277; 376–381; 442–460.

How to Buy Beef Roasts. U.S. Dept. Agr., Home and Garden Bull. No. 146 (1968).

How to Buy Beef Steaks. U.S. Dept. Agr., Home and Garden Bull. No. 145 (1968).

Inspection, Labeling, and Care of Meat and Poultry. A Consumer Education Guide. U.S. Dept. Agr., Agricultural Handbook No. 416 (1971).

KINDER, F. *Meal Management,* 3rd ed. New York: The Macmillan Company. 1968. Appendix C: "Carving Meat and Poultry."

Lamb in Family Meals. A Guide for Consumers. U.S. Dept. Agr., Home and Garden Bull. No. 124 (1967).

Meat and Poultry. Labeled for You. U.S. Dept. Agr., Home and Garden Bull. No. 172 (1969).

Meat and Poultry. Standards for You. U.S. Dept. Agr., Home and Garden Bull. No. 171 (1969).

Meat and Poultry. Wholesome for You. U.S. Dept. Agr., Home and Garden Bull. No. 170 (1969).

Money-Saving Main Dishes. U.S. Dept. Agr., Home and Garden Bull. No. 43 (1970).

Pork in Family Meals. A Guide for Consumers. U.S. Dept. Agr., Home and Garden Bull. No. 160 (1969).

POTTER, N. N. *Food Science.* Westport, Conn.: The Avi Publishing Company, Inc. 1968. Pp. 373–389.

Trichinosis. U.S. Dept. Agr., Leaflet No. 428 (1963).

11

poultry and fish

It is logical to discuss poultry and fish in the same chapter because both are excellent alternates for red meat. They contain protein in an amount comparable in quality and quantity to red meat. They have the advantage of furnishing variety in the diet, especially as both can be prepared in a great number of ways. In addition, poultry and fish sometimes may be more readily available than other meat. In this chapter the selection and storage, nutritive value, and preparation of poultry are discussed followed by similar considerations for fish.

Poultry

Poultry, once a Sunday treat, is now an everyday, low cost meat because of revolutionary changes in its production. Much of the progress, due to research and breeding, has taken place in the last twenty-five years. The reduction in the amount of feed needed to produce a pound of lean meat and the development of breeds which grow rapidly are responsible for the abundant supply of poultry currently enjoyed. The scale of production has also changed greatly. Instead of keeping a few chickens on every farm in order to supply the family with eggs and poultry meat, production is now a large-scale, heavily capitalized operation that permits efficient production of high quality, low priced poultry.

Improved breeding has resulted in changed conformation as well as a higher meat to bone ratio for turkeys and ducks. A turkey has been developed by the Department of Agriculture at Beltsville, Maryland, that is meaty and small, so that it is easily used by small families. The efficient large-scale production of turkeys has changed their meat from a holiday treat to a year-round staple food. The production of ducks in the United States is far lower than that of chickens or turkeys. Improvements have been made in breeding ducks that are more uniform in size and have a higher ratio of meat to bone and fat. A few geese, guineas, and pigeons or squabs are also produced. It is hardly surprising that the consumption of poultry in the United States has doubled in the last twenty years (Figure 11–1), a much greater increase than for other meats.

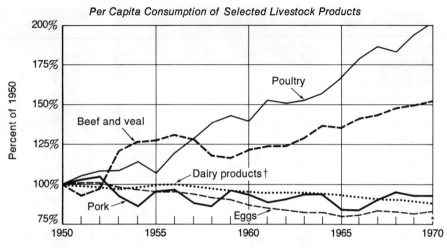

Per Capita Consumption of Selected Livestock Products

Items combined in terms of constant retail prices   *Preliminary   †Includes butter

Fig. 11–1. *Per capita consumption of selected livestock products.* (From *1970 Handbook of Agricultural Charts.* Agricultural Handbook No. 397., U.S. Department of Agriculture, November, 1970, p. 37.)

Selection and Storage

Inspection. The Wholesome Poultry Products Act passed by Congress in 1968 requires that all poultry sold in the United States meet a uniform standard of wholesomeness whether inspected by federal or by state inspectors. Inspection of poultry begins with the live birds and continues through slaughter, evisceration, and packaging. Because the inspection process includes examination of the eviscerated carcass, all poultry marketed under the Wholesome Poultry Products Act is dressed and drawn. Inspection marks used on poultry and poultry products are shown in Figure 11–2. Traditionally this circular mark has been an assurance of wholesome meat and poultry for consumers.

Fresh poultry meat for use in prepared foods such as frozen chicken and turkey dinners, pot pies, soups, and other canned and frozen products is inspected again at the time of processing to make sure it is still wholesome. The Consumer and Marketing Service of the U.S. Department of Agriculture must approve labels for products processed under federal inspection. These labels, denoting supervision and approval of the processing or preparation, assure the consumer that the product is wholesome and provide correct information about the product—from the proper name to a complete list of ingredients.

Grading. Unlike inspection, which is mandatory, the grading of poultry is optional; however, much of the poultry on today's market is graded. The poultry grader, federal or federal-state, examines each bird for conformation, meatiness, amount of fat, and defects such as torn skin or discolora-

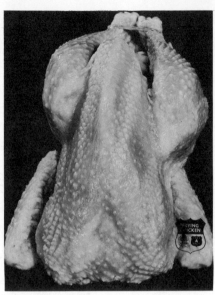

Fig. 11–2. *Look for the USDA Shield. You may find it and the inspection mark on the poultry label or on a wing tag.* (From *How to Buy Poultry*. Home and Garden Bulletin No. 157, U.S. Department of Agriculture, 1968.)

tion, before assigning a grade.[1] Poultry Graded A, the highest grade, is attractive, well finished, full fleshed, and meaty. Poultry of Grade B is of good table quality but slightly lacking in fleshing, meatiness, and finish, or it may have some dressing defects. This grade is seldom printed on poultry labels, and this quality bird is usually sold without a grade mark. Grade C poultry may have less meat in proportion to bone, lack adequate fat covering, and have crooked or misshapen bones. Birds graded C quality are usually used in the production of processed foods.

These grades apply to chickens, turkeys, ducks, geese, or guineas. The inspection mark may be combined with the grade shield as indicated in Figure 11–2. These combined or separate marks may appear as part of the label printed on a wrapping film for frozen birds or may be a wing tag clipped or tied to a wing (Figure 11–2). The grade may also be used for poultry parts and for raw, ready-to-cook poultry rolls, roasts, or bars, if they meet the standards for the grade.[2]

Classes of Poultry. Tenderness of poultry is generally associated with the age of the bird. Young, tender-meated birds should be chosen for barbecuing, frying, broiling, or roasting. Mature, less tender-meated classes are

[1] *Food For Us All. The Yearbook of Agriculture, 1969.* United States Department of Agriculture, Washington, D.C., p. 118.

[2] *Food For Us All. The Yearbook of Agriculture, 1969*, p. 119.

Fig. 11–3. *A U.S. Grade A chicken is shown at left, a U.S. Grade B chicken is on the right.*

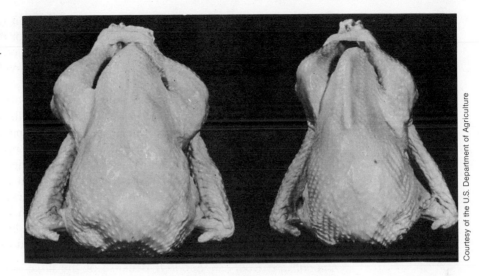

Courtesy of the U.S. Department of Agriculture

appropriate for fricasseeing and for stewing, for use in soups, salads, and other prepared dishes containing chicken. Chicken, turkey, and duck are the most popular poultry meats on the retail market, with little goose or guinea available. In Table 11–1 terms are listed for young and for mature classes of the popular birds. The choice of a class of poultry depends upon the use intended. The broiler-fryer chicken dominates the market through-

Table 11–1. *Terms Used to Identify Young and Mature Classes of Poultry* *

Species	Young	Mature
Chickens	Young chicken	Mature chicken
	Rock Cornish game hen	Old chicken
	Broiler	Hen
	Fryer	Stewing chicken
	Roaster	Fowl
	Capon	
Turkeys	Young turkey	Mature turkey
	Fryer-roaster	Yearling turkey
	Young hen	Old turkey
	Young tom	
Ducks	Duckling	Mature duck
	Young duckling	Old duck
	Broiler duckling	
	Fryer duckling	
	Roaster duckling	

* Compiled from *Food For Us All. The Yearbook of Agriculture, 1969.* United States Department of Agriculture, p. 119.

out the year. For roasting, either a roaster or a capon (an unsexed male chicken) is usually chosen. For stewing, a mature hen or male chicken may be used although young birds are satisfactory. As with other animals, older birds are usually fatter and are thought by many to have more flavor than young poultry.

Turkeys of excellent quality are now available. Turkey fryer-roasters are young birds of a small breed such as the Beltsville White. They can be broiled, fried, or roasted. Roasters are tender young birds usually five to six and a half months old. A hen turkey of a small breed may weigh as little as five pounds, but a broad-breasted tom may weigh over twenty-four pounds. It is easy to understand from these figures that the age of a turkey cannot be estimated from its weight. Fully mature turkeys, which can be identified by their hardened breastbones and coarse skin, are not often found on the market. Such turkeys are best cooked by moist heat either by braising or in the oven in a covered roaster or tightly wrapped with aluminum foil.

Amount and Cost per Serving. Because of the large amount of bone and skin more ready-to-cook poultry must be provided per serving than for

Table 11–2. *Price per pound of whole chicken fryers, ready to cook, and of chicken parts providing equal amounts of edible meat for the money* *

If the price per pound of whole fryers, ready to cook, is—	Chicken parts are an equally good buy if the price per pound is—				
	Breast half	Drumstick and thigh	Drumstick	Thigh	Wing
Cents	Cents	Cents	Cents	Cents	Cents
27	38	35	33	36	21
29	41	37	36	39	23
31	44	40	38	41	25
33	47	42	41	44	26
35	49	45	43	47	28
37	52	47	46	49	29
39	55	50	48	52	31
41	58	53	50	55	33
43	61	55	53	57	34
45	63	58	55	60	36
47	66	60	58	63	37
49	69	63	60	65	39
51	72	65	63	68	41
53	75	68	65	71	42
55	78	71	68	73	44

* From *Family Economics Review*, Consumer and Food Economics Research Division, Agricultural Research Service, United States Department of Agriculture, Washington, D.C., September 1969, p. 22.

some other meats. When ready-to-cook poultry is used, from three-fourths to one pound per person is allowed for broiled or fried chicken and for roast chicken, turkey, duck, or goose. When chicken is stewed, about half a pound of ready-to-cook poultry is required per person. Sometimes a more practical method of estimating the quantity required is to realize that a small broiler weighing about one and a half pounds will yield two servings, and a fryer of two and a half pounds will yield four servings. When poultry is roasted, additional servings beyond those estimated may be available as chunks of cooked meat for use at another meal. An approximate yield of one cup of diced, cooked meat per pound of ready-to-cook bird is a useful guide when using fresh or frozen poultry to prepare casseroles and salads.

Chicken and turkey are sold whole or cut up, and chicken is often available as packages of pieces, such as breasts, legs, wings, or backs and necks. The price for a whole bird is usually less per pound than for a cut up bird. In comparing prices for whole or cut up birds versus prices for pieces the yield of edible meat must be considered. When whole fryers are 39 cents a pound, chicken breasts are an equally good buy at 55 cents a pound (Table 11–2); that is, breasts provide more meat for the money at prices less than 55 cents a pound and less meat for the money at prices over 55 cents a pound.

The comparative cost of home-prepared, ready to cook and ready to serve poultry dinners and entrées is shown in Figure 11–4. As is pointed

Fig. 11–4. *Retail cost per serving of dinners and entrees containing poultry meat.* (From *Family Economics Review.* June 1971. Consumer and Food Economics Research Division, Agricultural Research Service, U.S. Department of Agriculture.)

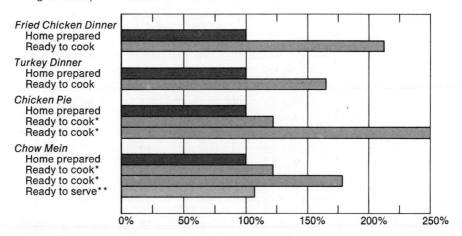

*Range of cost of brands that contain widely different proportions of meat.
**Canned.

out, the range in cost of both the chicken pie and the chow mein is due in part, at least, to the different amounts of poultry meat contained.

Harp and Dunham in an earlier study on the retail cost per serving of some home-prepared and convenience forms of chicken found that fried chicken cost about 5 per cent more per serving when the chicken was purchased cut up than when it was purchased whole.[3] The cost was considerably higher when fried chicken was prepared from breaded raw chicken or prefried chicken. Frozen chicken dinners cost about two and a half times as much as home-prepared dinners. The cost comparison was similar for turkey dinners. Canned chicken meat was about double the cost of the home-prepared product. The low cost of several of the processed products can be explained by the fact that they contain less meat than the home-prepared foods. For example, home-prepared chow mein contained about 30 per cent chicken, whereas canned or frozen chow mein contained only about 3 per cent of lean chicken meat per serving. The canned fricassee had 38 per cent as much lean chicken meat as the home-prepared product. Home-prepared chicken pie also contained more meat than the frozen product. Cost per serving of home-prepared forms decreased when the amount of meat in them was decreased to match the frozen products. Poultry pies that are federally inspected must contain in each eight-ounce pie one and one-eighth ounces or 14 per cent of cooked poultry meat, which is equivalent to two ounces of raw de-boned poultry meat.

The yield of lean meat from cooked poultry varies with the type. When roasted, chicken broilers, fryers, and roasters yield 41 per cent lean meat based on ready-to-cook weight; turkey fryers or roasters 46 per cent; and ducklings only 22 per cent, due in part to their high proportion of fat.[4] Large turkeys yield more lean meat than small turkeys. For this reason, and because of their low price per pound, half a large turkey may be a better buy than a small turkey of the same weight.

Storage. All poultry is perishable. Fresh chilled poultry should be stored loosely wrapped in the refrigerator at 3° C. (38° F.) or lower and should be used within one to two days. The giblets should be removed from the internal cavity of whole birds and wrapped separately. The wrapped bird and giblets should be placed on a container with a rim or raised edge to prevent juices from dripping and possibly contaminating other foods. Special care and cleanliness is important in handling uncooked poultry to prevent possible cross-contamination to other foods. The hands and all utensils and work surfaces in contact with fresh poultry should be thoroughly

[3] H. H. Harp and D. F. Dunham. *Comparative Costs to Consumers of Convenience Foods and Home-Prepared Foods.* Marketing Research Report No. 609. United States Department of Agriculture, Washington, D.C., 1963.

[4] E. H. Dawson, G. L. Gilpin, and A. M. Harkin. Yield of Cooked Meat from Different Types of Poultry. *Journal of Home Economics,* 52: 445–447 (1960).

washed and sanitized after the contact. Wooden cutting boards need special attention such as scrubbing with a stiff bristled brush dipped into hot detergent water followed by a hot water rinse. It is not advisable to partially cook poultry, store, and finish cooking at a later time since heat penetration may not be sufficient during the initial cooking period to destroy bacteria that may be present.

Frozen uncooked poultry may be kept in the freezer at −18° C. (0° F.) for up to one year, although quality deteriorates with longer storage time; fat birds store well for only a few months. The birds or pieces should be packaged in a moisture and vapor resistant wrapping or container and kept solidly frozen. Cooking may be started from the frozen state or the meat may be allowed to thaw—usually until pliable. The two methods most frequently recommended for thawing frozen poultry are: 1) in the refrigerator, still in the original wrap, placed on a container as for fresh poultry, and 2) in cold water, still in the original wrap. Thawing at room temperature in a heavy paper bag is sometimes recommended[5] but many workers believe this is not a desirable practice because of danger of spoilage. Thawing in cold running water takes the least time. A 12 to 16 pound turkey thaws in 6 to 7 hours in cool water and in 2 to 2½ days in the refrigerator.

Nutritive Value

Like red meat, poultry contains an abundance of high quality protein. Young poultry such as the broiler-fryer is lower in fat and therefore in calories than most meats, especially if the skin is not eaten (Table 11–3). Older birds contain more fat than young birds, but much of it is located under the skin and around the giblets where it can be removed if desired. The fat content of poultry also depends upon the method of preparation. It is lower in roasted or broiled poultry than in fried poultry. Light meat is lower in fat and also in iron, thiamine, and riboflavin than dark meat. Turkey meat is similar to chicken meat in composition, but ducks and geese are higher in fat than chickens and turkeys. The mineral and vitamin content of poultry is similar to that of red meat.

Preparation

Like other meats, poultry tends to be tough if it is cooked while in rigor, but it requires only about four hours for rigor to pass in chickens and about twelve hours in turkeys.

Broiling. Usually the smallest of the broiler-fryers are selected for broiling. A popular size is two and a half pounds or under, although young chickens of any weight can be broiled. Depending upon size, the chickens are split in half lengthwise, or quartered, and placed skin side down in a broiler pan or other shallow pan one layer deep without crowding. The use of a rack is optional. The chicken is brushed with melted fat, seasoned with salt, pep-

[5] *Food For Us All. The Yearbook of Agriculture, 1969,* p. 121.

Table 11–3. Composition of Cooked Poultry and Fish *

	Weight gm.	Food Energy cal.	Protein gm.	Fat gm.	Calcium mg.	Iron mg.	Vitamin A Value I.U.	Thiamine mg.	Riboflavin mg.	Niacin mg.
Poultry										
Chicken, cooked										
Flesh only, broiled	85	115	20	3	8	1.4	80	.05	.16	7.4
Breast, fried, ½ breast †	94	155	25	5	9	1.3	70	.04	.17	11.2
Drumstick, fried †	59	90	12	4	6	0.9	50	.03	.15	2.7
Potpie, baked, 1 pie	227	535	23	31	68	3.0	3020	.25	.26	4.1
Fish										
Clams, raw, meat only	85	65	11	1	59	5.2	90	.08	.15	1.1
Fish sticks, breaded, cooked, frozen, 10 sticks	227	400	38	20	25	0.9	—	.09	.16	3.6
Haddock, breaded, fried	85	140	17	5	34	1.0	—	.03	.06	2.7
Ocean perch, breaded, fried	85	195	16	11	28	1.1	—	.08	.09	1.5
Oysters, raw, meat only, 1 cup	240	160	20	4	226	13.2	740	.33	.43	6.0
Salmon, pink, canned	85	120	17	5	167 †	0.7	60	.03	.16	6.8
Shrimp, canned	85	100	21	1	98	2.6	50	.01	.03	1.5
Tuna, canned in oil, drained solids	85	170	24	7	7	1.6	70	.04	.10	10.1

* Compiled from Nutritive Value of Foods. Home and Garden Bulletin No. 72, Agricultural Research Service, United States Department of Agriculture, 1971.
† Bone included.

per, and any other desired seasonings, and placed in the broiler so that the highest part of the chicken is 4 to 5 inches from the heat. As the pieces brown, they are turned and basted with drippings or added fat. The total cooking time is 35 to 45 minutes. If preferred, young chickens prepared as for broiling can be cooked in the oven at 205° C. (400° F.) allowing 45 minutes to one hour. The chicken is turned once.

Frying. Young chicken of any weight and cut in any way desired can be fried. It can be cooked with or without flouring. A convenient way to flour chicken is to put about half a cup of flour, one teaspoon salt, paprika and pepper, or other seasonings if desired, into a clean paper or plastic bag. The chicken is then shaken a few pieces at a time in the flour mixture. Enough fat to make a layer about one-half inch deep is placed in a fry pan and heated until a drop of water sizzles, or until the recommended temperature is reached in an electric skillet. The pieces of chicken are browned in the fat, turning as necessary with kitchen tongs or two spoons to avoid piercing the meat. Chicken cooks best if it is not crowded in the pan. It is cooked slowly without a cover until tender, usually twenty to thirty-five minutes. Chicken can also be fried in deep fat at 177° C. (350° F.). The chicken is removed when properly browned. The cooking time may be about ten minutes for smaller pieces and fifteen for larger pieces. If desired, pieces of chicken that have been browned in shallow or deep fat can be transferred to a shallow uncovered pan and placed in an oven at 350° F. until tender.

When raw chicken is dipped in a batter, the coating sometimes comes off during deep fat frying because evaporation of moisture causes the meat to lose about one-fourth of its weight and to shrink away from the batter that has coagulated in the early part of the frying process. This can be avoided by frying the chicken, then dipping it in batter, and frying it again in deep fat just long enough to brown and cook the coating.

A comparison of skillet-fried, deep-fat-fried, and oven-fried chicken has been made.[6] Deep-fat-fried chicken was brown and crisp but high in fat content. Chicken that was oven-fried at 190° C. (375° F.) in a pan containing about one-third cup hydrogenated fat was crisp, brown, and lowest in fat content of the three methods. Skillet-fried chicken that was covered during the last half of the cooking period was not so crisp as that cooked by the other two methods but was more moist.

Roasting. Tender chickens, turkeys, and ducks can be roasted on a rack in a shallow uncovered pan. The body cavity can be stuffed, or not, as desired. The bird is usually trussed by fastening the neck skin to the back with a skewer, turning the wing tips back of the shoulders, and tying the drumsticks to the tail. This procedure prevents the wings and legs from

[6] A. A. Smith and G. E. Vail. Yield and Composition of Broiler-Fryers Fried by Three Methods. *Journal of The American Dietetic Association,* 43: 541–544 (1963).

becoming too brown during roasting and makes a more attractive product for serving. If desired, a meat thermometer can be used in roasting turkeys. It is placed one-half to one inch deep in the breast or in the center of the inner thigh muscle. The muscles of other poultry are not usually large enough for a thermometer. Drying of the skin during roasting can be prevented by brushing it with soft fat or oil. No water is added and no cover used. Excessive browning of the breast of large birds can be prevented by putting a piece of thin cloth moistened with fat or a piece of aluminum foil loosely over the breast. An oven temperature of 163° C. (325° F.) is used for stuffed poultry; 205° C. (400° F.) for unstuffed chicken broilers, fryers, or roasters. If poultry is roasted at 121° C. (250° F.), the roasting time is long, and the period during which food-spoilage microorganisms may grow is increased. Roasting at the high temperature of 232° C. (450° F.) is undesirable because the meat may be dry and the skin charred. Other disadvantages at this high temperature are the unevenness of heat penetration, which results in uneven cooking of the bird and inadequate heating of the stuffing.[7]

Roasting turkey in the plastic film in which it was sold or tightly wrapped in aluminum foil has been found undesirable because juice cooks out of the meat and causes the meat to stew. The cooking time is shortened, but the meat and skin are likely to split.[8]

Poultry can be basted with pan drippings or melted fat several times during roasting, and the string may be cut to release the legs when roasting is half or two-thirds done. Poultry is done when the leg joints move easily and the meat of the drumstick is soft when pressed. If a thermometer is used, the turkey is removed from the oven when the temperature is 82° C. (180° F.) in the thigh or 71° C. (160° F.) in the breast. If the turkey is small, the end point temperature in the breast should be higher, about 78° C. (173° F.).[9] Poultry is usually cooked well done, but overcooking is undesirable because it results in loss of juiciness.

Stuffing a turkey and refrigerating or freezing it at home is not recommended. To avoid the possibility of food poisoning, turkey should not be stuffed until just before it is to be roasted; if the stuffing is prepared in advance it should be refrigerated separately. Commercially frozen stuffed turkeys should be bought only if they are hard-frozen and should not be thawed before cooking.[10]

Giblets and neck are usually simmered in water. The liver cooks quickly and can be broiled or fried instead of simmered. The other giblets are cooked

[7] M. Woodburn and A. E. Ellington. Choice of Cooking Temperature for Stuffed Turkeys. Part II. Microbiological Safety of Stuffing. *Journal of Home Economics,* 59: 186–190 (1967).

[8] W. B. Esselen, A. S. Levine, and M. J. Brushway. Adequate Roasting Procedures for Frozen Stuffed Poultry. *Journal of The American Dietetic Association,* 32: 1162–1166 (1956).

[9] V. D. Bramblett and K. Fugate. Choice of Cooking Temperature for Stuffed Turkeys. Part I. Palatability Factors. *Journal of Home Economics,* 59: 180–185 (1967).

[10] *Turkey on the Table the Year Round.* Home and Garden Bulletin No. 45. United States Department of Agriculture, Washington, D.C., 1961.

Fig. 11–5. *To roast a whole turkey:*

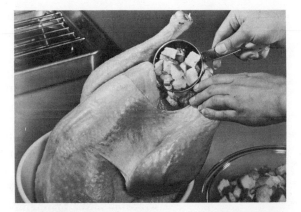

Place the turkey, neck down, in a large mixing bowl to simplify stuffing. Insert stuffing by cupfuls and shake the drumsticks so the bird will be lightly stuffed.

To prevent overbrowning, tuck each leg, one at a time, under a band of skin. Thus no sewing or skewers are needed. The wings are turned back of the shoulders.

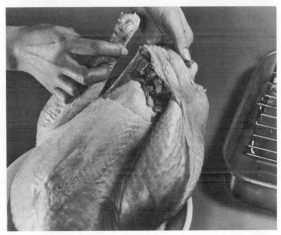

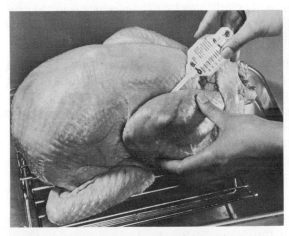

Place the bird on a rack in a shallow baking pan. Insert a thermometer in the thickest part of the inside thigh muscle, avoiding the bone.

When the bird is half to two-thirds roasted, cut the band of skin at the tail. Place a loose tent of aluminum foil over the bird and continue roasting until done.

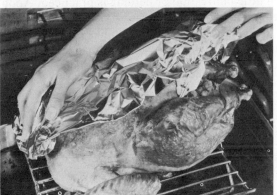

Courtesy of the Poultry and Egg National Board

until the gizzard is fork-tender. If preferred, the giblets can be salted, sealed in aluminum foil, and put on a rack as poultry is roasted.

Moist Heat. Older poultry such as mature hens is often cooked by moist heat. Such poultry can be fricasseed, a word frequently used in poultry cookery, although it means the same as braised. It can also be steamed by cooking in a perforated pan or rack over boiling water, or simmered in water to cover. Two and a half to three hours are usually required for mature chickens that weigh three to four pounds. Chicken cooked in this way is the basis for a wide variety of dishes such as salads, casseroles, creamed chicken, and sandwiches. If broiler-fryers are more easily available and less expensive than hens, they can be cooked by moist heat for a short period of time or roasted without stuffing for use in such dishes.

Frozen. Frozen poultry can, of course, be substituted for fresh. Turkey is often sold in the frozen form, but chickens of the broiler-type are most often sold unfrozen. There is distinct consumer preference for fresh rather than frozen fryers.[11] probably because of the ready availability of fresh fryers at low prices. Evidence also indicates that changes occur in the proteins of frozen chicken.[12] When chicken is cooked before freezing, it becomes less tender than similar meat cooked but not frozen.[13]

Color Changes. Two color changes that are occasionally seen in chicken deserve comment. The darkening of the bone that occasionally occurs in frozen poultry is due to liberation of the blood pigment hemoglobin from the bone marrow on freezing and thawing.[14] This harmless change can be reduced by cooking chicken for a brief period before freezing. The pink color that sometimes appears in poultry meat heated in an oven or over a wood fire is probably due to the presence of substances used in curing meats. This pink color does not affect quality.

Fish

A readily available high-protein food, fish is the one major category of food consumed by man for which little cultivation or herding is practiced. About 90 per cent of the catch comes from oceans, seas, and tributary waters. The remainder are caught in rivers, lakes, or other bodies of fresh water. Whether from ocean, coastal, or inland waters fish for human consumption should be taken from uncontaminated water. Fish can be taken from the

[11] A. W. Brant, R. H. Forsythe, and M. H. Swanson. Consumer and Retailer Attitudes Toward "Fresh" Versus Frozen Fryers. *Food Technology,* 19: 661–665 (1965).

[12] A. W. Khan, L. VanDenBerg, and C. P. Lentz. Effects of Frozen Storage on Chicken Muscle Proteins. *Journal of Food Science,* 28: 425–430 (1963).

[13] W. C. Mickelberry and W. J. Stadelman. Effect of Cooking Method on Shear-Press Values and Weight Changes of Frozen Chicken Meat. *Food Technology,* 16(8): 94–97 (1962).

[14] A. W. Brant and G. F. Stewart. Bone Darkening in Frozen Poultry. *Food Technology,* 4: 168–174 (1950).

ocean most efficiently with large factory-ship fleets that make huge catches and then clean and process the fish by freezing, curing, or canning on board ship. Such equipment makes it possible to bring the fish to the market in excellent condition and at low prices. Japan and Russia are leaders in this field of large-scale fishing.

Compared with many other countries, the United States is a relatively small consumer of fishery products. The per capita consumption, which has changed little since 1930, was 11.4 pounds edible weight in 1970, less than one-fourth the amount of poultry consumed. Production of fishery products has not surged ahead in the United States in recent years as it has in other countries. Indeed almost half the fish consumed in the United States is imported.

Fish is a food source not dependent upon farm land which is in short supply throughout the world. Also, the supply of fish tends to be self-replenishing and, with the exception of a few types of fish that are eagerly sought, has shown little sign of exhaustion until recently. Only a few types of fishing, such as that done in farm ponds and oyster farming, require cultivation.

Selection and Storage

Varieties. The two major groups of fish are finfish and shellfish. Fish with fins vary enormously in size and in variety. Out of about two hundred commercial species of fish, most people are familiar with fewer than twenty. Some of the common varieties of salt water and fresh water fish as well as shellfish are listed in Table 11–4. The usual market size, forms, and the principal areas where the fish are available are also given. Some of the forms in which fresh fish are sold are shown in Figure 11–6. Whole or round fish are marketed as taken from the water. Drawn fish have had the internal organs removed, whereas dressed or pan-dressed fish have also had the scales, head, tail, and fins removed. Steaks are cross-section slices from a large dressed fish, and fillets, which are practically boneless, are the sides of a fish cut lengthwise away from the backbone.

Good whole fresh fish have bright, clear, bulging eyes and reddish-pink gills, are free from slime or unpleasant odor, and exhibit a firm elastic flesh that springs back when pressed. Flesh of frozen fish should be solidly frozen when purchased. There should be no discoloration or freezer burn, and little or no odor. A strong odor indicates poor quality.

Shellfish are an especially popular type of fish that can be divided into two groups. One group has a soft body protected by a shell, such as oysters, mussels, clams, and scallops. The other has a segmented crust-like shell and includes lobsters, crabs, shrimp, and crayfish. Oysters, clams, scallops, and crabs are available in all coastal areas of the United States, although they differ in size and other characteristics. Large quantities of oysters are produced by oyster farming in submerged land along the Atlantic seaboard. Shrimp are caught in southern waters—both in the Gulf and in the Pacific.

Table 11-4. A Guide for Buying Fish and Shellfish *

Species	Fat or Lean	Usual Market Range of Round Fish in Pounds	Usual Market Forms	Main Market Areas †
Salt Water:				
Bluefish	Lean	1—7	Whole and drawn	Middle and South Atlantic
Butterfish	Fat	$1/4$—1	Whole and dressed	North and Middle Atlantic
Cod	Lean	3—20	Drawn, dressed, steaks, and fillets	Entire United States
Croaker	Lean	$1/2$—$2^1/2$	Whole, dressed, and fillets	Middle and South Atlantic; Gulf
Flounder	Lean	$1/4$—5	Whole, dressed, and fillets	Entire United States
Grouper	Lean	5—15	Whole, drawn, dressed, steaks, and fillets	South Atlantic; Gulf
Haddock	Lean	$1^1/2$—7	Drawn and fillets	Entire United States
Hake	Lean	2—5	Whole, drawn, dressed, and fillets	North and Middle Atlantic; Midwest
Halibut	Lean	8—75	Dressed and steaks	Entire United States
Herring, sea	Fat	$1/4$—1	Whole	North Atlantic; Pacific
Lingcod	Lean	5—20	Dressed, steaks, and fillets	Pacific
Mackerel	Fat	$3/4$—3	Whole, drawn, and fillets	North and Middle Atlantic; California
Mullet	Lean	$1/2$—3	Whole	Middle and South Atlantic; Gulf; Midwest
Pollock	Lean	3—14	Drawn, dressed, steaks, and fillets	Entire United States except Pacific
Rockfish	Lean	2—5	Dressed and fillets	Pacific and Midwest; Gulf
Rosefish	Lean	$1/2$—$1^1/4$	Fillets	Entire United States
Salmon	Fat	3—30	Drawn, dressed, steaks, and fillets	Entire United States
Scup (Porgy)	Lean	$1/2$—2	Whole and dressed	Middle and South Atlantic
Sea Bass	Lean	$1/4$—4	Whole, dressed, and fillets	Middle and South Atlantic; Pacific
Sea Trout	Lean	1—6	Whole, drawn, dressed, and fillets	Middle and South Atlantic; Gulf
Shad	Fat	$1^1/2$—7	Whole, drawn, and fillets	North, Middle and South Atlantic; Pacific
Snapper, red	Lean	2—15	Drawn, dressed, steaks, and fillets	Middle and South Atlantic; Gulf
Spanish mackerel	Fat	1—4	Whole, drawn, dressed, and fillets	Middle and South Atlantic; Gulf
Spot	Lean	$1/4$—$1^1/4$	Whole and dressed	Middle and South Atlantic
Whiting	Lean	$1/2$—$1^1/2$	Whole, drawn, dressed, and fillets	Entire United States except Pacific

Fresh Water:				
Buffalofish	Lean	5—15	Whole, drawn, dressed, and steaks	Midwest
Carp	Lean	2—8	Whole and fillets	Midwest; Middle Atlantic
Catfish	Fat	1—10	Whole, dressed, and skinned	Middle and South Atlantic; Midwest; Gulf
Lake herring	Lean	$1/3$—1	Whole, drawn, and fillets	Midwest
Lake trout	Fat	$1\frac{1}{2}$—10	Drawn, dressed, and fillets	Midwest
Sheepshead	Lean	$\frac{1}{2}$—3	Whole, drawn, dressed, and fillets	Midwest
Suckers	Lean	$\frac{1}{2}$—4	Whole, drawn, dressed, and fillets	Midwest
Whitefish	Fat	2—6	Whole, drawn, dressed, and fillets	Midwest
Yellow perch	Lean	$\frac{1}{2}$—1	Whole and fillets	Midwest
Yellow pike	Lean	$1\frac{1}{2}$—10	Whole, dressed, and fillets	Midwest
Shellfish:				
Clams	Lean		In the shell and shucked	Entire United States
Crabs	Lean		Live, and cooked meat	Entire United States except Midwest
Lobsters	Lean		Live, and cooked meat	North and Middle Atlantic; Midwest
Oysters	Lean		In the shell, and shucked	Entire United States
Shrimp	Lean		Headless, and cooked meat	Entire United States
Scallops	Lean		Shucked and cleaned	Entire United States

* From *Basic Fish Cookery*. Test Kitchen Report No. 2, Bureau of Commercial Fisheries, United States Department of the Interior, 1959.
† North Atlantic Area includes the coastal states from Maine to Connecticut; Middle Atlantic Area, New York to Virginia; South Atlantic Area, North Carolina to Florida; Gulf Area, Alabama to Texas; Pacific Area, Washington to California (North Pacific, Washington, Oregon, and Alaska); and Midwest Area, central and inland states.

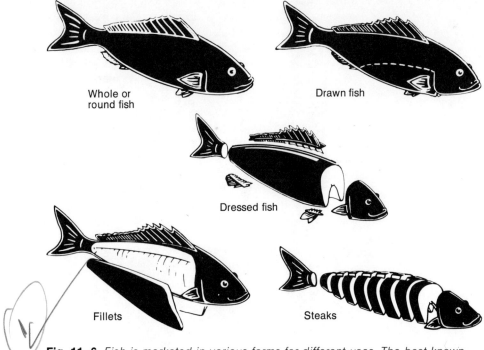

Fig. 11–6. *Fish is marketed in various forms for different uses. The best known forms are shown above.*

Courtesy of the Bureau of Commercial Fisheries, U.S. Department of the Interior

The northern lobster is found in the cold waters of the North Atlantic Ocean near the shores of North America and of Europe. The type of lobster that is often available in frozen form in the United States is the spiny lobster. It comes from southern waters such as those of Florida, southern California, the Bahamas, South Africa, and Australia. Almost all of the meat of the spiny lobster comes from its broad tail, and therefore only the tail is frozen. The meat of the northern lobster is more widely distributed throughout the body than with the spiny lobster, and the choicest meat of the northern lobster is in its large claws. For convenience, frog legs, turtle, octopus, and squid are often classified with shellfish.

About half of the fish consumed in the United States is in the fresh or frozen form and the other half is canned. Fresh fish are readily available to those who live on the ocean or inland waters but may not be obtainable far inland because they deteriorate rapidly. Unlike most foods, the enzymes of fish operate at about 5° C. (40° F.), the temperature of the water from which they came. In order to keep fish for any length of time, they must be frozen, canned, or cured. Freezing has made a wide variety of fish available wherever there is adequate refrigeration. All types of fish are frozen, usually in the most compact form such as fish fillets or peeled shrimp. During frozen storage, fish may become slightly dry and tough compared with the corresponding fresh fish. Research is being done on methods of preventing these changes which are probably due to slight alterations in the protein.

Convenience forms of frozen fish have also become available. Fish sticks are made by cutting pieces of fish from blocks of frozen fillets into portions that weigh about one ounce. Frozen fried fish sticks have been breaded, precooked, and frozen. They require only heating before serving. Frozen fish soups are another convenience form of fish that has become popular recently. The purchase of canned fish is often advantageous because it may be used as it comes from the can in any recipe that calls for cooked fish. Tuna, sardines, and salmon are most commonly purchased, but many other types are available.

Only small amounts of cured fish are used in the United States, but much larger quantities are used in many other countries. Fish can be cured by salting, drying, pickling, or smoking. The addition of salt to fish draws water from their flesh. Fish allowed to remain in the salt solution are said to be pickled. Some examples are pickled herring, sprats, mackerel, and salmon. Fish may also be salted and then dried in the sun or by artificial heat. Salt cod is often prepared in this way. Salt dried fish are more widely used in the countries of southern Europe, South America, and the West Indies than in those countries that have ample refrigeration. Smoked fish are popular in some parts of the United States, especially among people of Scandinavian origin. Smoking and salting may be combined, as in the production of "finnan haddie" from haddock.

Inspection and Grading. The sanitary quality of shellfish is especially important because some of them are eaten raw and few are subjected during

Fig. 11–7. *The meat of the northern lobster is distributed throughout the body with that in the claws being the choicest; almost all of the meat in the spiny lobster is in the tail.* (From *Food for Us All, the Yearbook of Agriculture,* 1969. U.S. Department of Agriculture, p. 129.)

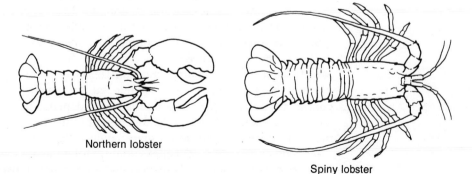

Northern lobster

Spiny lobster

cooking to a temperature high enough to destroy microorganisms. Shellfish produced in polluted water are therefore a possible source of infection. For this reason, many coastal states have a program for the sanitary inspection of shellfish, as explained in Chapter 2. In addition, the Bureau of Commercial Fisheries has a voluntary system for inspection of fish and fish products for wholesomeness. Government grades for quality are available for certain fish products. This inspection and grading are indicated by shield symbols and are established by the Fish and Wildlife Service of the United States Department of the Interior.

Amount and Cost per Serving. The amount of fish required per person depends upon the form in which it is bought. For one serving, about one pound of whole fish, one-half pound dressed fish, or one-fourth to one-third pound of steaks, fillets, or sticks is required. In other words, enough to make three to three and one-half ounces of cooked fish is needed per serving.

The price of fish varies greatly with the variety. For example, lobsters, oysters, and salmon may cost as much as the choicest meat cuts, whereas cod, haddock, herring, and mackerel may be much less expensive. Other varieties of fish that are sometimes discarded by fishermen can be used for attractive but very inexpensive dishes. Hence, it is possible to spend as much or as little as one wishes for fish.

Frozen fish sticks were slightly more expensive and the haddock dinner considerably more expensive than the corresponding home-prepared products. There was little difference between the cost of home-prepared or canned salmon. Canned fish flakes were less expensive than home-prepared haddock, but slightly more expensive than home-prepared cod.

Storage. The procedures and precautions pertinent to poultry are also valid for fish and shellfish. If there are any differences fish are even more perishable than poultry and should be cared for accordingly.

Nutritive Value

The nutritive value of cooked fish is shown in Table 11–3. The calorie content of most fish is somewhat lower than that of meat and poultry because fish usually contains more moisture and less fat. All types of fish, including shellfish, are high in protein that is completely adequate for nutritional purposes. The fat content of raw fish is considerably less than that of most types of raw meat and poultry. In fact, the fat content of shellfish and many of the common finfish is less than 5 per cent. Some fish have more than 5 per cent fat, but none ordinarily exceeds 16 per cent fat. Fish are high in the unsaturated fats that are recommended for some therapeutic diets. Of course, the fat content of cooked fish also depends upon the amount of fat added in cooking as well as the fat content of the raw fish. As with chicken, the skin of fish is higher in fat than the flesh.

The mineral content of fish is variable. Like meat, many types of fish are poor sources of calcium. Those canned with bones, however, are an excellent source of calcium if the bones, which become quite soft in canning, are eaten with the fish. The data for salmon in Table 11–3 reflect this fact. Calcium is unusually high in oysters and shrimp. Most fish are not high in iron, but oysters contain an abundance of this mineral and are also unusually high in copper. Fish from the sea are high in iodine content because of the presence of this element in sea water.

The vitamin content of most fish is comparable to that of meat except that the fatter fish are comparatively high in vitamin A. The livers of fish are used as a source of vitamins A and D.

Preparation

Fish cookery differs from meat cookery in that both dry and moist heat methods can be used with fish of any type. One of the reasons is that connective tissue in fish muscle is different in structure and lower in concentration than that of red meats and poultry and does not present a problem in cooking. Muscle fibers of fish separate readily after a rather short cooking period, which may prevent the retention of the shape of the fish during cooking. Cheesecloth is sometimes tied around fish to keep it from breaking during cooking and while being removed from the cooking medium. Also because it is tender and the muscle fibers separate easily, it is especially important not to overcook fish. Fish is usually cooked until it flakes when tested with a fork. A thermometer can be used in cooking thick cuts of fish. Too much heat either in the form of high temperatures or low temperatures for too long a time increases cooking losses and is likely to produce a dry, firm, and tasteless product.

The cooking method for fish is sometimes determined by its fat content. Broiling and baking are considered to be especially suitable for fat fish because their natural fat content keeps them from becoming dry when cooked. Lean fish are less likely to fall apart on boiling or steaming than are fat fish. Lean fish can also be broiled or baked, especially if fat is added to keep them from becoming dry. It is possible, however, to cook fish of varying fat contents by any method desired. The low fat content of fish accounts for the frequent use of fat during fish cookery or the use of melted butter or rich sauces with fish.

Although the flavor of a few fish is quite distinctive, that of most fish is rather mild. Methods of preparation are chosen to bring out the delicate flavor of the fish, and accompaniments are planned that offer a distinctive, often tart, flavor and a contrast in color. Lemon is often used in cooking or as a garnish. Some of the popular garnishes are beets, carrot sticks, celery, green peppers, cranberry sauce, parsley, lettuce, watercress, paprika, pickles, radishes, sliced cucumbers, tomatoes, or hard-cooked eggs. Crisp vegetable salads are attractive with a meal centered around fish.

Broiling. Serving-size fillets or steaks of fish are sprinkled with salt and pepper on both sides and placed on a greased broiler pan in a preheated oven about two inches from the heat. Fillets from which skin has not been removed are placed skin side up. If the fish is frozen, it is placed lower than thawed fish in the oven to prevent overcooking the surface before the in-

Fig. 11–8. *Pan-dressed sea trout, dipped first in egg and then rolled in crumbs, is placed in a fry pan containing ⅛ inch of melted fat and fried at moderate heat.*

Fig. 11–9. *Serving-size portions of cod fillets are breaded, placed in a frying basket, lowered into a kettle containing enough fat to cover the fish, and cooked until an even golden brown.*

Courtesy of U.S. Department of Commerce National Marine Fisheries Service

terior is cooked. As with meat, the door of an electric oven is left open for broiling, but that of a gas oven is closed. Broiling is continued for five to eight minutes or until the fish is slightly brown. It is then brushed with melted fat, turned, brushed with fat on the other side, and broiled until it is lightly browned and flakes easily when tested with a fork. Fish can be broiled successfully outdoors if held over hot coals in a hinged wire grill that has been well greased.

Frying. Frying is one of the most popular methods of cooking fish, probably because it adds fat and crispness, while masking quality defects that might

Fig. 11–10. *Before baking, the cavity of a fish may be filled with stuffing and the edges sewn together or closed with skewers.*

Courtesy of U.S. Department of Commerce National Marine Fisheries Service

show up in baking or steaming.[15] Small whole dressed fish, fish fillets, or steaks are first seasoned with salt and pepper. They can then be dipped in milk or a mixture of one egg beaten slightly with a tablespoon of milk or water and then in fine crumbs, cornmeal, or flour. Fat or oil about $\frac{1}{8}$ inch deep is heated in a heavy pan until it is hot but not smoking, and the fish is cooked until browned on the under side, turned and cooked until the second side is browned and the fish flakes readily, about 10 minutes.

Fish prepared as for pan-frying can be fried in deep fat heated to 190° C. (375° F.). A deep kettle not more than half full of fat should be used, and only one layer of fish placed in the frying basket. The fish is cooked three to five minutes or until it is golden brown, the basket removed, and the fish drained on absorbent paper.

An especially quick and easy method of cooking fish is called oven-frying, although it might be argued that the method is really baking. One pound of fillets or steaks cut in serving portions is dipped in one-half cup of milk to which one and one-half teaspoons of salt have been added. The fish are then rolled in one-half cup of fine bread crumbs, placed in a greased baking dish, and two tablespoons of melted fat or oil are poured over them. They are cooked on a shelf near the top of a very hot oven 260° C. (500° F.) for about ten minutes or until tender and brown. Fish cooked in this way are lower in fat than those fried in a skillet or in deep fat.

Baking. Fish can be baked whole or as fillets or steaks. The whole fish is sprinkled with salt and pepper and placed on a greased baking pan with or

[15] W. J. Dyer, D. I. Fraser, R. G. MacIntosh, and M. Myer. Cooking Method and Palatability of Frozen Cod Fillets of Various Qualities. *Journal of the Fisheries Research Board of Canada,* 21(3): 577–589 (1964).

Fig. 11–11. *To steam fish, place in a well-greased steamer insert pan. Sprinkle with salt. Cover and cook over boiling water until fish flakes easily when tested with a fork—5 to 10 minutes. (From* Let's Cook Fish. *Fishery Market Development Series No. 8, U.S. Department of Commerce National Marine Fisheries Service.)*

without stuffing. If it is stuffed, the opening is sewn together or closed with skewers. The top of the fish is brushed with melted fat, or strips of bacon are placed over the top. The fish can be basted during baking if desired. Fillets or steaks are salted and may be baked either plain, after dipping in a sauce such as melted table fat and lemon juice, or after stuffing is placed between two fillets or steaks. As with whole fish, the top is brushed with melted table fat or bacon slices are put on top. If the baking time is adjusted, a wide variety of oven temperatures can be used. In many recipes, 177° C. (350° F.) is recommended. This temperature or 205° C. (400° F.) was found more satisfactory than 232° C. (450° F.) or 260° C. (500° F.) for baking two-pound pieces of salmon to an internal temperature of 70° C. (158° F.).[16] Sometimes the presence of skin or bone in a fish has been thought to make a difference in its taste. An experiment has indicated, however, that the

[16] H. Charley and G. E. Goertz. The Effects of Oven Temperature on Certain Characteristics of Baked Salmon. *Food Research*, 23: 17–24 (1958).

acceptability of fish was not affected by the presence of bone or skin during baking.[17]

Moist Heat. Fish cooked by moist heat is often served plain or with a sauce, in casseroles, or in salads. To cook fish in water, it can be placed in a wire basket or on a plate tied with a piece of cheesecloth. The fish is lowered into the boiling water and simmered about ten minutes. The flavor is improved by adding three tablespoons of lemon juice or vinegar and one and one-half teaspoons of salt to each quart of water.

Fish can be steamed on a well-greased steamer pan over boiling water for about ten minutes. An alternate way to steam fish is to season with salt and pepper and wrap tightly in aluminum foil. All the folds are doubled and pinched together to make them steam tight. The wrapped fish is put on a pan and baked in an oven at about 232° C. (450° F.).

Another popular moist-heat method of preparing fish is in chowder. Many types of fish can be used for chowder, and vegetables are usually added. The liquid may be water, milk, tomato juice, or a combination of liquids.

Cooking shellfish. Shellfish may be cooked by many of the methods used for fish. High temperatures and long cooking should be avoided because they have a toughening effect on most shellfish. Specific directions or recipes are usually followed for each kind of shellfish because each varies greatly in size and in general characteristics.

Activities

1. a. What classes of poultry are available in the local stores?
b. Is this poultry inspected?
c. Is it graded? If so, what grades are available?

2. Compare the palatability and cost in both time and money of some home-prepared and convenience forms of poultry and of fish.

3. Prepare broiled, fried, and baked chicken.

4. Prepare a variety of poultry casserole dishes.

5. Calculate the cost per pound of lean, boneless meat for chicken, turkey, and selected cuts of beef and pork. Use local prices and the data on yields in Chapters 10 and 11.

6. What weight of chicken would you buy if you needed 1 pound cooked cut meat for a chicken casserole?

7. List the varieties of fresh, frozen, and cured fish in your local stores. Are any of them inspected or graded?

8. Calculate the cost per serving of some of the more and some of the less expensive varieties of fish and compare with the cost per serving of some selected poultry and meat dishes.

[17] R. E. Baldwin, D. H. Strong, and J. H. Torrie. A Study of the Influence of Selected Preparation Procedures on Flavor and Aroma of Fish. *Food Technology,* 16(7): 115–118 (1962).

9. Find an inexpensive finfish that is readily available in the fresh or frozen form in your stores and prepare it in as many ways as possible.

References

After a Hundred Years. The Yearbook of Agriculture, 1962. U.S. Dept. Agr., Washington, D.C.: United States Government Printing Office. Pp. 304–309.

Canadian Fish Cook Book. Ottawa: Department of Fisheries. 1959.

Cooking the Turkey. Poultry and Egg National Board, 18 S. Michigan Avenue, Chicago, Ill. (not dated).

FINN, D. B. *Fish . . . The Great Potential Food Supply*. Food & Agr. Organ. U.N., World Food Problems, No. 3, Rome (1960).

Food. The Yearbook of Agriculture, 1959. U.S. Dept. Agr., Washington, D.C.: United States Government Printing Office. Pp. 353–370.

Food for Us All. The Yearbook of Agriculture, 1969. U.S. Dept. Agr., Washington, D.C.: United States Government Printing Office. Pp. 127–138.

GILPIN, G. L., E. W. MURPHY, S. C. MARSH, E. H. DAWSON, and F. BOWMAN. *Meat, Fish, Poultry, and Cheese, Home Preparation Time, Yield, and Composition of Various Market Forms*. U.S. Dept. Agr., Home Economics Research Report No. 30 (1965).

HARRIS, R. S. and H. VON LOESECKE (Eds.). *Nutritional Evaluation of Food Processing*. New York: John Wiley & Sons, Inc. 1960. Pp. 277–280; 283–300; 381–385.

How to Buy Poultry. U.S. Dept. Agr., Home and Garden Bull. No. 157 (1968).

KERR, R. G. *Basic Fish Cookery*. U.S. Fish & Wildlife Serv., Test Kitchen Series No. 2 (Reprinted 1964).

Let's Cook Fish. A Complete Guide to Fish Cookery. U.S. Dept. Int., Fishery Market Development Series, No. 8 (not dated).

POTTER, N. N. *Food Science*. Westport, Conn.: The Avi Publishing Company, Inc. 1968. Pp. 389–396; 404–418.

Poultry in Family Meals. A Guide for Consumers. U.S. Dept. Agr., Home and Garden Bull. No. 110 (1971).

Turkey on the Table the Year Round. U.S. Dept. Agr., Home and Garden Bull. No. 45 (1961).

12

flour and starch

The structure and use of cereals of various types have been discussed in Chapter 4. Because of its importance, wheat flour was reserved for discussion in this chapter in which milling, quality, and nutritive value of different types of flour are considered. Starch cookery, especially of sauces and desserts, is also included. Since the protein of flour is so important in flour mixtures, the discussion of this component of flour is included in Chapter 13.

Flour

The terms hard and soft, used to distinguish between kinds of wheat, are also used to describe the flour produced by the milling of wheat. Hard wheat, which is higher in protein and better for making bread than soft wheat, has a vitreous endosperm that tends to break between the cells, thereby producing a granular free-flowing flour. Soft wheat has a more mealy endosperm that tends to be pulverized in milling to a flour with few whole cells. When rubbed between the fingers, the granular texture of hard wheat flour and the soft talcum-like feeling of soft wheat flour are easily distinguishable. Flour from soft wheat is especially good for cakes, pastry, cookies, and crackers. Soft wheats are usually grown in places of abundant rainfall, whereas hard wheats are grown in areas of more limited rainfall and greater extremes of temperature. Only limited areas are capable of producing good quality strong, hard wheats. Such areas are found in the northern Great Plains of the United States, in the prairies of Canada, and in certain areas of the Soviet Union, Australia, and South America, mainly in Argentina. Durum wheat is a very hard wheat that belongs to a botanical species different from that of the common wheats. It is grown in areas that produce hard wheat.

Wheat is also classified as spring or winter wheat, depending upon the time of planting. Wheat must be planted in the spring in areas where the winters are very cold. In milder climates wheat is often planted in the fall so that it can develop a root system before cold weather. Winter wheat grows rapidly in the spring and is harvested in early summer, giving higher yields than spring wheat. Although spring wheat is usually harder than winter wheat, winter wheats may be either hard or soft depending upon the variety.

Milling

The purpose of milling is to break apart the wheat kernels and to separate the endosperm from the bran and germ of wheat, thus producing white flour. This is possible because the bran and germ tend to form flakes, which can be separated from the smaller pieces formed from the inner, more granular endosperm. The two major steps of milling are the gradual grinding of the wheat kernel and the separation of particles of various sizes and characteristics that are produced from the kernel. Both the traditional method of roller milling, which was introduced about 1880, and new methods introduced in the late 1950's and early 1960's will be described. The literature indicates that the new methods are being adopted widely although it is difficult to know how much the older methods are being displaced. In some cases the new and old methods are being used to supplement each other in a single mill.

Grinding. The earliest method of milling was simply to grind the wheat kernels between two stones. At first the stones were shaped like a mortar and pestle. Later two flat circular mill stones with furrowed surfaces were used. They were rotated at first by men or animals and later by wind or water power. Usually grain was passed only once between the stones. The meal that resulted was sometimes sifted to remove coarser particles of bran and germ or tossed into the air so that the wind would remove the lighter particles of bran, but even when this was done the flour resembled whole wheat more closely than the white flour we know today.

The introduction of roller milling around 1880 made possible whiter flour with better baking qualities than had been available before that time. In this method the wheat kernels are passed between fluted steel break rolls that open up the kernels and release the contents. The size of the particles is reduced gradually by passing them between rolls that are set closer and closer together and finally between smooth steel reduction rolls. The grinding must be gradual and the material must be separated between grindings in order to produce white flour. If the material were ground fine in one operation, whole wheat flour would result, and effective separation of the white flour would be impossible.

Further reduction of particle size may be accomplished by impact milling. However, this method has not been highly successful and attrition grinding seems to be more widely used.

Separation. In the roller milling process, ground material from each roll is passed through a series of sieves of different sizes usually made of silk or nylon fabric. The germ and bran are removed from particles of medium size, called middlings, by further sifting and by the application of suction in a middlings purifier to remove the lighter particles.

Air classification is a relatively new method for separating flour particles.[1] The air classifier contains a unit that rotates fast enough to set up very strong

[1] N. N. Potter. *Food Science*. Westport, Conn.: The Avi Publishing Company Inc., 1968, p. 446.

Fig. 12–1. *Wheat passes through a number of stages in the milling process, each of which results in a typical product such as these shown here, top to bottom: after the break, purified middlings; the finished product.*

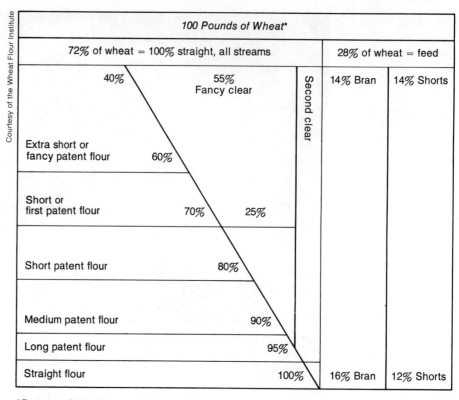

Courtesy of the Wheat Flour Institute

100 Pounds of Wheat*		
72% of wheat = 100% straight, all streams	28% of wheat = feed	

40% · 55% Fancy clear · Second clear · 14% Bran · 14% Shorts

Extra short or fancy patent flour   60%

Short or first patent flour   70%   25%

Short patent flour   80%

Medium patent flour   90%

Long patent flour   95%

Straight flour   100%   16% Bran   12% Shorts

*Swanson, C.O., Wheat and flour quality

Fig. 12–2. *Many different grades of flour may be milled from one hundred pounds of wheat, as indicated in this graph.*

circular air currents. When a mixture of flour and air is introduced, the slightly finer particles are blown to the top and the larger, heavier particles remain at a lower level. This method of separation can be applied either to flour milled by the conventional roller milling process or by attrition grinding. It has been found that the finer flour particles separated by air classification are higher in protein and the larger particles are lower in protein than the average for the parent flour. The air classifier offers a powerful method of improving flours by the removal of a fraction that may detract from baking quality. For example, the removal of a high-protein fraction from a sample of soft wheat flour may improve its cake-making ability, whereas the addition of this high protein fraction to another sample of soft wheat flour may improve its bread-baking quality. Air classification offers great flexibility in the use of wheats of different types and is finding increased application.[2]

[2] E. L. Griffin, Jr. and V. Pfeifer. Multiplies Flour Varieties. *Food Engineering,* 37: 86–88 (January, 1965).

Final Steps. No matter what method has been used for grinding and separating the flour, the miller has many streams of material coming from the different steps in the process. A combination of all these streams in the original proportions results in whole wheat flour. As indicated in Figure 12–2, 100 pounds of wheat results in a maximum of about 72 per cent white flour. The remainder, which contains almost all the bran and germ of the wheat, is used as feed. When all streams of white flour are combined, straight flour results. Frequently the streams are divided to give patent and clear flour. Patent flour is made from the most refined streams of flour. The extra short patent is made up of from 40 to 60 per cent of the white flour, whereas the long patent may contain as much as 95 per cent of the white flour. The flour that remains after the removal of the patent flour is called clear. Patent flours are commonly used for household and bakery needs, whereas clear flour is employed in products such as rye or whole wheat bread and pancake flour for which its creamy to grayish color is not a disadvantage.

Freshly milled flour has a creamy color because it contains carotenoids, the same pigments that make certain fruits and vegetables yellow. When such flour is stored for several months, it becomes whiter and its baking qualities improve because of oxidation by air. This process is usually accelerated by the addition of certain oxidizing agents that are permitted for use in flour. Flour treated in this way must be labeled "bleached." An enzyme called amylase is sometimes added in the form of sprouted wheat or barley to flours low in this enzyme. In the dough, this enzyme converts starch to maltose, a sugar that can be used by yeast. If the flour is to be enriched, premixed concentrates of vitamins and minerals are added. This process will be discussed more fully in another section.

Types

Whole Wheat Flour. Whole wheat flour, also called graham flour or entire wheat flour, must contain all the natural constituents of wheat in unaltered proportions. Its quality is best when it is freshly ground because the high fat content of the germ is subject to the development of rancid flavors and odors.

Bread Flour. Bread flours are milled from blends of hard wheats and are usually available only to bakers.

All-Purpose Flour. Much of the flour used in the home is all-purpose flour, also called general-purpose or family flour. As the term indicates, this flour is intermediate to bread flour and cake flour in its characteristics and is intended for all cookery purposes. It is usually made from a blend of wheat, sometimes both hard and soft wheats, that contains less protein than bread flour. Investigation of the properties of family flour from retail markets in Atlanta, Boston, Charlotte, Chicago, Dallas, and San Francisco showed considerable variation in the properties of the flour marketed in each city.[3]

[3] R. H. Matthews, Starch Gelatinization and Some Physical Properties of Selected Wheat Flours. *Cereal Science Today,* 15: 78–80 (1970).

Instant Blending Flour. Instant blending, agglomerated, instant, or instantized flour is characterized by a granular texture and relatively uniform particle size. It is free flowing, disperses quickly in cold water, is dust free, and does not pack down, hence requires no presifting.[4] The ease with which it can be wet is explained by its open, porous structure which is similar to that of instant nonfat dry milk. Instant blending flour is manufactured by adding moisture to all-purpose flour so the surfaces of the flour particles become sticky and adhere to form agglomerates which are then dried to a moisture content of 14 per cent or less.[5]

Self-Rising Flour. In areas such as the South where hot breads are popular, self-rising flours are frequently sold. Because they contain salt and the ingredients of baking powder, one measurement can be used instead of three. Self-rising flour is usually not used for making yeast breads or as a thickening agent for sauces, gravies, and puddings.

Cake Flour. Cake flour is a short patent flour made of soft wheat. It has a low protein content and fine uniform granulation. It is usually possible to distinguish between all-purpose and cake flours by their appearance and physical characteristics. The all-purpose flour feels somewhat granular when rubbed between the fingers, and when pressed lightly in the hand it will not hold its shape. Cake flour is very white and fine—almost powdery—and holds its shape when pressed lightly.

Pastry Flour. Pastry flour has properties intermediate between those of all-purpose and cake flours. It is usually made of soft wheat and is designed for making pastry, cookies, and similar products.

Nutritive Value

Because of the uneven distribution of nutrients within the wheat kernel, many of the minerals and B-vitamins are lost during milling, as can be seen in Table 12–1. The protein content of white flour is similar to that of whole wheat because most of the protein is in the endosperm. On the other hand, the aleurone layer, which is just under the bran, contains many of the minerals and much of the niacin, while the scutellum, which lies between the germ and the endosperm, contains most of the thiamine. Riboflavin is more evenly divided within the wheat kernel than the other nutrients. During milling, much of the calcium and iron and many of the B-vitamins present in whole wheat go into the feed portions with the bran and germ.

To improve the nutritive value of flour and bread, which form so large a proportion of the caloric intake of many people, an enrichment program was started in 1941 in the United States. The enrichment of flour and bread is now required by more than half of the states, but in actuality much of

[4] H. C. Black and W. Bushuk. A Laboratory Flour Agglomerator. *Cereal Science Today,* 11: 517 (1966).

[5] W. S. Claus and E. M. Brooks. Some Physical, Chemical, and Baking Characteristics of Instantized Wheat Flours. *Cereal Science Today,* 10: 41–43, 52, 62 (1965).

Table 12–1. *Nutrients in 100 Grams of Wheat Flours* *

Flour	Food Energy calories	Protein gm.	Calcium mg.	Iron† mg.	Thiamine† mg.	Ribo-flavin† mg.	Niacin† mg.
Whole wheat	333	13.3	41	3.3	0.55	0.12	4.3
80% extraction	365	12.0	24	1.3	0.26	0.07	2.0
All-purpose							
Unenriched	364	10.5	16	0.8	0.06	0.05	0.9
Enriched	364	10.5	16	2.9	0.44	0.26	3.5
Self-rising, enriched	352	9.3	265	2.9	0.44	0.26	3.5
Bread flour, enriched	365	11.8	16	2.9	0.44	0.26	3.5
Cake or pastry flour	364	7.5	17	0.5	0.03	0.03	0.7

* Compiled from *Composition of Foods—raw, processed, prepared,* by Watt and Merrill. Agriculture Handbook No. 8, Agricultural Research Service, United States Department of Agriculture, Revised 1963. Minimum and maximum levels of enrichment are shown on p. 171 of this publication.

† For enriched products, figures are based on the minimum level of enrichment.

the white bread and all-purpose flour sold in the United States is enriched because most of the large manufacturers of bread and all-purpose flour produce only enriched products. Products labeled "enriched" and sold in interstate commerce must meet the standards of identity set by the Federal Food and Drug Administration. These standards require that enriched flours contain amounts of thiamine, riboflavin, niacin, and iron between the prescribed minimum and maximum levels. In addition, calcium and vitamin D may be added within stated limits if desired. As can be seen in Table 12–1, enrichment raises the levels of iron, thiamine, and niacin approximately to the levels of whole wheat flour, whereas the riboflavin content of enriched flour exceeds that of whole wheat. Enrichment does not change the physical character or taste of white flour but does assure a food product that is high in nutritive value. It does not require changing food habits, and white flour is less subject to the development of rancidity and to insect infestation than is whole wheat flour. As explained in Chapter 4, cereal products other than wheat flour are also often enriched.

Starch

Starch is important in food preparation whether it is used in a purified form like cornstarch or as flour, which contains a large proportion of starch as well as protein and other components. Starches from different sources have the same chemical composition and all can be broken down into dextrose. The number of dextrose units and the way they are joined differ. The dextrose units may be joined in a straight chain or they may combine to form complicated chains with many side branches. The ratio of these molecular forms, for a given starch, is determined by genetic factors. As starch occurs naturally the molecules aggregate into granules. In this section, the function of starch as a thickening agent in such foods as sauces, gravies, puddings, and pie fillings will be discussed. Starch also has important functions in breads and cakes, which will be discussed in another chapter.

Types

Cornstarch is the most widely used of the purified starches. It is made by a process of wet milling in which the hull and germ are removed, the corn ground, and mixed with water. The semi-liquid material is separated by passing it over sieves or centrifuging it. The starch settles out while most of the protein remains suspended. The starch is then washed, dried, and powdered. Cornstarch is widely used because it is inexpensive, lacks characteristic flavor, and cooks to a smooth and almost clear paste in water or other clear liquid.

Wheat starch is little used in food preparation, but wheat flour is extensively used as a thickening agent. Flour has less thickening power and makes a more opaque gel than cornstarch, but its characteristic flavor is preferred by many to that of other thickening agents. Although either hard or soft wheat flour can be used, soft wheat flour makes a sauce with characteristics intermediate between those of sauces thickened with cornstarch and hard wheat flour.

Arrowroot starch is obtained from the roots of a plant grown in the West Indies. It resembles cornstarch in being white, fine, and powdery. It is an excellent thickening agent for starch puddings, gravies, sauces, and pastries and is used in cookies.

Rice starch and flour are used in products such as pancake flour and by persons who are allergic to wheat. Potato starch, although extensively used abroad, finds limited use in this country in food preparation. It thickens at a lower temperature than cornstarch, becomes thinner on further cooking, and does not form a gel on cooling as does cornstarch.

Tapioca is made from starch obtained from the tuberous roots of cassava or manioc, a woody tropical plant native to Central America. The starch, also known as tapioca flour, is used to mix a dough from which commercial tapioca is prepared. For pearl tapioca, the moist dough is forced through a sieve the size of which determines whether the pearls will be coarse, medium, or fine. The little pellets are then subjected to high temperature. Flake tapioca is made by baking the moist starch in thin sheets which are then ground to give the quick-cooking, "minute," or granular tapioca. Granular is more popular than pearl tapioca because it requires no soaking, whereas pearl tapioca must be soaked at least an hour before using. Tapioca, like the other root and tuber starches, tends to become "ropey" if over-cooked.

Waxy starch is obtained from special species of rice or corn that have a waxy endosperm. The starch they contain is made up of branched molecules, whereas regular starch contains molecules having straight as well as branched chains. Waxy starch forms a smooth paste when cooked with water but does not gel on cooling unless used in very high concentrations. These properties make it ideal for use in thickening the filling of fruit pies. Sauces or gravies made with waxy starch have the advantage of remaining thick during freezing and thawing, in contrast to sauces made with regular starch which tend to separate on thawing. For this reason, waxy starches are often used in prepared foods that are to be frozen.

Starches can be modified either chemically or physically. Acids, numerous other chemicals, and enzymes may be used to bring about chemical modifications that change hot paste viscosity, ability to gel, and other properties. The ability to tailor-make a starch for any specific application is extremely useful to the food industry. The pregelatinized starch in instant puddings is an example of physical modification. Starch, either untreated or chemically modified, is gelatinized and then dried on hot rolls or drums. The resulting powder is porous and is so rapidly rehydrated when combined with cold liquid that thickening occurs almost immediately.

In making substitutions, it is sometimes convenient to know that one tablespoon flour is equivalent to about one-half tablespoon cornstarch, potato starch, rice starch, or arrowroot starch or to one tablespoon of quick-cooking tapioca. It is not surprising that smaller amounts of most purified starch products are required for thickening than of flour, which contains protein and other constituents in addition to starch.

Changes on Cooking

Dry Heat. When starch or flour is heated without moisture, it first becomes brown and later black because carbon is formed. If the heating is continued beyond this stage, the carbon is burned off as carbon dioxide. Flour is sometimes browned on a pan in the oven or in a skillet over direct heat and used to add color to gravy although it does not have as much thickening power as the original flour. During heating the starch molecules are broken into smaller fragments called dextrins. The change in color as well as in molecular size is referred to as dextrinization. It is this process which is responsible, in part, for the browning of toast and the crust of breads and cakes. Dextrins have molecular weights that vary widely but are lower than those of the original starch and higher than those of sugar. During the digestion of starch in the body, dextrins are formed from starch by the action of enzymes. Dextrins are also formed when corn syrup is made from cornstarch, although this is not a dry heat process but results from acid or enzymatic hydrolysis of cornstarch.

Moist Heat. Starch granules do not dissolve in cold water but instead form a suspension. When heated, the granules swell suddenly over a temperature range characteristic of the particular starch. As heating continues, the suspension becomes thicker and more translucent. This process is often called gelatinization. Starch suspensions must be heated beyond the temperature at which thickening begins to obtain a firm gel. During the usual cooking procedures, most foods high in starch reach a temperature of 95° C. (203° F.) or above. Starch mixtures are usually cooked for a short period after thickening occurs to improve their flavor. During ordinary cooking, most of the starch remains in the swollen granules and only a small amount goes out of the granules into the solution. The swollen granules can, however, be broken by excessive stirring or heating to high temperatures.

When the cooked suspensions of corn and some other starches are cooled, they form gels, if sufficiently concentrated. A gel is an elastic solid like baked custard, fruit jelly, or cornstarch pudding. The terms gelatinization and gelation are easily confused, however, these terms apply to quite different phenomena. Gelatinization involves all the changes that occur when an aqueous starch suspension is heated, whereas gelation is the solidification of a suspension which usually occurs with cooling.

When starch or flour is mixed insufficiently with cold liquid or added directly to hot liquid, lumps are likely to form. The granules on the outside of the lump swell as a result of taking up water, whereas those on the inside remain dry or swell only slightly. Sometimes when a large lump is cut, raw starch can be seen in the center. In addition to giving sauce or gravy an unpleasant consistency, such lumps decrease thickening because the starch within the lump is not available for thickening the sauce. To prevent lumping, starch granules are separated by mixing them with fat, a small amount of cold liquid, or sugar, depending upon the recipe. The liquid, either hot or cold, is then added and the mixture is cooked. The direct addition of dry starch or flour to hot liquid must be avoided because it causes lumps to form.

Preparation

Sauces. In some cultures sauces play or have played a more important part in cookery than they do in the United States at the present time. They were evidently important in England during medieval times as indicated by the following quotation:

Our ancestors, as we have found, did not highly esteem simple dishes, and a cook of any reputation aimed as far as possible . . . to transform one thing into another quite different, since as a rule it was beneath his dignity to offer food that had cost but slight effort. The most effective way to remove the stigma of simplicity . . . was to employ a sauce made hot with spices and condiments.[6]

The sauces were thickened with flour, broken bread, or eggs. French cookery owes much of its special quality to the many sauces that are used. As in all their cookery, the French do not spare time or effort in the preparation of sauces that are especially appropriate to individual foods.

In the United States, white sauces and gravies are probably the most frequently used. A thorough understanding of the proportions, methods, and possible modifications of a basic white sauce are necessary fundamentals

[6] W. E. Mead. *The English Medieval Feast.* Boston: Houghton Mifflin Company, 1931, pp. 96–97.

of food preparation, for white sauce "is the basic king of sauces, which lends triumph and lustre to plain foods when smooth and creamy; but leads to depression and indigestion when greasy and lumpy."[7]

White sauces are sometimes called cream sauces because the consistency of medium white sauce used for creamed vegetables is about the consistency of thick cream. The proportions used in white sauces are shown in Table 12–2. Skillful use of this table makes possible the preparation of many dishes such as cream soups, cream gravy, scalloped dishes, soufflés, and croquettes.

Several methods can be used for preparing smooth white sauces. In each method the separation of dry starch granules is accomplished by coating the granules with fat or by suspending them in cold liquid. Probably the most used method is to melt the fat and stir in the flour or starch until all particles are coated with fat. The hot or cold liquid is then added. If hot liquid is used it should be added gradually with constant stirring until gelatinization occurs. The thickened mixture is then heated until no raw starch taste remains. If cold liquid is used it may be added as described for hot liquids or the starch-fat mixture may be removed from the heat, liquid added all at once, heating resumed with constant stirring and the sauce completed as when hot liquid is used. In a second method, flour is mixed with a small amount of cold milk, the remaining milk and fat are heated together in a double boiler, and the flour mixture is added gradually with stirring. The mixture is then boiled for two minutes with constant stirring over direct heat or cooked for a longer time in the top of a double boiler. In a third method, the flour and fat are combined, added to the hot liquid, and the cooking is finished as in the second method.

Another way of making white sauce is from a mix that can be prepared easily at home. One cup of all-purpose flour, 1 cup of table fat, 4 teaspoons of salt, and $2\frac{1}{2}$ cups of nonfat dry milk are mixed with a pastry blender or fork until crumbly. The mixture is stored in a covered jar in the refrigerator. To make white sauce, 1 cup of liquid is combined with $\frac{1}{4}$ cup of mix for thin sauce, $\frac{1}{2}$ cup of mix for medium sauce, or $\frac{3}{4}$ cup of mix for thick sauce. The liquid can be water, broth, or the liquid in which vegetables have been cooked. The mix is put into a saucepan and the liquid is added slowly with constant stirring. It is cooked until thickened and seasoned to taste.

The basic recipe can be varied in many ways. For instance, onion, celery, mushrooms, or almonds can be cut and browned in the fat before the flour is added. Bouillon, stock, or the liquid in which vegetables have been cooked can be substituted for part or all of the liquid. To the finished sauce, herbs, curry powder, or other spices, capers, mint, parsley, pimento, grated cheese, or hard-cooked eggs can be added.

Cream soups are thin sauces in which part or all of the liquid is vegetable juice, pulp, or broth from meat, poultry, or fish. Vegetables for cream soups

[7] Alma McKee. *To Set Before a Queen.* New York: Simon and Schuster, Inc., 1964, pp. 17–18.

Table 12–2. Proportions for White Sauces *

Kinds	Proportions for Making			Uses	Proportions for Use
	Liquid	Thickening Agent	Fat†	Seasoning or Flavoring		
Very thin	1 cup milk	½ tablespoon flour	1 tablespoon	½ teaspoon salt	Cream soups made from starch foods	Allow ¼ to 1 cup cooked, strained vegetable or other pulp to 1 cup sauce. The average amount is ½ cup.
Thin	1 cup milk	1 tablespoon flour	1 tablespoon	½ teaspoon salt	Cream soups made from non-starch foods	
Medium	1 cup milk	2 tablespoons flour	2 tablespoons	½ teaspoon salt	Creamed dishes, scalloped dishes, gravies	Allow 2 to 3 cups vegetable, meat, or fish—cut into suitable pieces—to 1 cup sauce for creamed or scalloped dishes.
Thick	1 cup milk	3 to 4 tablespoons flour	2 tablespoons	½ teaspoon salt	Soufflés	Allow 3 eggs and from ¾ to 1 cup other ingredients to 1 cup sauce.
Very thick	1 cup milk	4 to 5 tablespoons flour	2½ tablespoons	½ teaspoon salt	Croquettes	Allow 1 to 3 cups finely divided ingredients to 1 cup sauce.

* Adapted from *Practical Cookery*, 23rd ed., by the Department of Foods and Nutrition, Kansas State University. Courtesy of John Wiley & Sons, Inc., 1966.

† Butter or margarine is preferable for many sauces.

Fig. 12–3. *To make a white sauce, melt the fat in a saucepan or in the top of a double boiler. Add the flour and stir to a smooth paste.*

Remove from the heat and pour in the liquid; cold liquids may be added at once, hot liquids should be stirred in gradually.

Stir slowly but steadily and cook until the sauce is thick and smooth.

are cooked in a small amount of water until tender and then put through a strainer. The cooking water, as well as the pulp, is used in the soup. Leftover vegetables can be used in this way if desired. From $\frac{1}{2}$ to 1 cup of the cooked strained vegetable can be added to 1 cup of sauce as indicated in Table 12–2. The proportions used depend upon the flavor and concentration of the vegetable material. For nonstarchy vegetables such as celery or spinach a thin white sauce is used, but for starchy vegetables like potatoes, peas, beans, or lentils a very thin white sauce is preferred. Flour is not omitted even from cream soups made with starchy ingredients because it helps prevent settling of the vegetable pulp. If desired, the soup can be made by melting 1 tablespoon of fat, stirring in 1 tablespoon of flour, adding 1 cup of liquid, which is a combination of milk and vegetable juice, and seasoning to taste. Cream soup can also be made by grating a raw vegetable such as potato directly into white sauce. The soup is then brought to a boil and served immediately. To make cream of tomato soup, seasoned hot tomato juice or sieved canned tomatoes are added gradually with stirring to hot, thin white sauce. If desired, the tomato juice can be thickened and added gradually to hot milk. No soda is necessary to prevent curdling, but the soup should be served soon after it is mixed. Soups should be well flavored either by adding ingredients such as onion, celery, parsley, herbs, or spices to the vegetable while it cooks or by adding flavorings to the finished soup. In any case, the soup should be salted and flavored to taste before serving. Soup can be garnished with chopped parsley, grated cheese, toasted bread crumbs, popcorn, or many other garnishes.

Gravies are made in the same way as white sauce, but the fat and often part or all of the liquid are from the cooked meat. It is important to measure the fat and juices to obtain the right proportions, and to prevent greasy gravy if the drippings contain much fat. Juices may be extended with bouillon or milk if the volume is too low from the drippings. The proportions of a thin or medium white sauce can be used as preferred. If desired, the flour can be browned in the fat to develop color, but in this case a higher proportion of flour must be used because of the formation of dextrins.

Desserts. Dessert sauces are made in the same way as white sauce but in these, sugar is often added and the liquid may be fruit juice or water plus flavoring. Starchy desserts are usually named according to the thickening agent and flavoring used. For example, cherry tapioca is a dessert of cherries thickened with tapioca, whereas chocolate cornstarch pudding contains milk, chocolate or cocoa, cornstarch, and sugar. Cornstarch pudding is often called blanc mange from the French phrase meaning "white eating." Although blanc manges can be thickened with a variety of starches, cornstarch is so frequently used that the terms blanc mange and cornstarch pudding are now used interchangeably.

As can be seen in Table 12–3, a wide variety of cornstarch puddings is possible depending upon the ingredients used. They are usually mixed by

Table 12–3. *Common Variations of Cornstarch Pudding*

Product	Liquid	Starchy Agent	Sugar	Other Ingredients
Plain blanc mange	1 cup milk	1½–2 Tbsp. corn-starch	2 Tbsp.	½ tsp. vanilla
Chocolate blanc mange	1 cup milk	1½–2 Tbsp. corn-starch	3 Tbsp.	½ sq. chocolate † ¼ tsp. vanilla
Chocolate cream pudding	1 cup milk	1½–2 Tbsp. corn-starch	3 Tbsp.	1 stiffly beaten egg white ½ sq. chocolate † ¼ tsp. vanilla
Coconut blanc mange	1 cup milk	1½–2 Tbsp. corn-starch	2 Tbsp.	½ tsp. vanilla ½–1 cup shredded coconut
Fruit blanc mange	1 cup milk	1½–2½ Tbsp. cornstarch	2 Tbsp.	½ cup dates, pine-apple, bananas, cherries, prunes or other desired fruit
Nut blanc mange	1 cup milk	1½–2 Tbsp. corn-starch	2 Tbsp.	½ tsp. vanilla ¼–½ cup chopped nuts
Caramel blanc mange	1 cup milk	1½–2 Tbsp. corn-starch	2 Tbsp.	½ tsp. vanilla 2 Tbsp. caramel syrup
Maple blanc mange	1 cup milk	1½–2 Tbsp. corn-starch	2 Tbsp. maple sugar	
Fruit tapioca	1 cup fruit juice and water	2–2½ Tbsp. quick-cooking tapioca	3 Tbsp.	½–1 cup fruit
Indian pudding	1 cup milk	1 Tbsp. corn meal	1½–2 Tbsp. molasses	¼ tsp. ginger

† Or 1½ tablespoons of cocoa and 1½ teaspoons of table fat.

combining cornstarch with sugar and adding a small amount of cold milk. The remaining milk is scalded and thickened by adding the cornstarch mixture. The mixture is boiled over direct heat for about 2 minutes with constant stirring. An additional 5 to 10 minutes of cooking over hot water in a double boiler may improve the flavor of the pudding. When chocolate is used, it is melted in the hot milk, but cocoa is combined with the starch-sugar mixture to prevent lumping. Flavoring extracts are added at the end of the cooking period. The pudding is poured into containers and covered to prevent the formation of a skin due to evaporation during storage in the refrigerator.

Table 12–4. *Proportions of Cornstarch Required for Desserts of Different Consistency*

Type	Amount Liquid	Amount Cornstarch
Sauce	1 cup	$\frac{1}{2}$–$\frac{3}{4}$ tablespoon
Cup dessert	1 cup	1–$1\frac{1}{2}$ tablespoons
Small mold	1 cup	$1\frac{1}{2}$ tablespoons
Large mold	1 cup	2–$2\frac{1}{2}$ tablespoons

The amount of thickening in a cornstarch pudding can be varied according to the use that is to be made of it, as shown in Table 12–4. Less cornstarch is needed for a sauce that is to be poured over pudding or cake; more is needed if the pudding is to be turned out of a mold, especially if the mold is large.

The amount of sugar in cornstarch puddings affects their consistency. As more sugar is added, the gel becomes more tender, until with excessive amounts a thick syrup is formed instead of a gel. This is probably because the water required to dissolve excess sugar is not available for gelatinization of the starch.

Acid ingredients such as the lemon juice added to certain puddings may affect the thickness of the starch gel. Such ingredients are sometimes added to the cooked starch paste because if they are added before cooking, modification of the starch molecule may cause the gel to be softer.

Table 12–3 shows proportions for puddings thickened with tapioca or corn meal as well as with cornstarch. Fruit tapioca can be prepared by cooking the tapioca and sugar in liquid until the mixture is clear, pouring over the prepared fruit, and baking until fruit is tender. Tapioca cream is prepared by adding eggs, sugar, and flavoring to tapioca that has been cooked in milk. Pudding thickened with corn meal, called Indian pudding, is popular in New England.

Starch puddings can also be made from mixes. Commercial mixes that require cooking yield a pudding much like those made from original ingredients. Instant puddings, which have pregelatinized starch as the thickening agent, require only cold liquid and rapid beating to form a tender, soft gel. However the texture of instant puddings is somewhat granular.

Activities

1. Prepare and evaluate several types of cream soup.

2. Prepare gravy by several methods. If meat drippings are not available, bouillon cubes or canned bouillon and cooking fat can be used. Brown the flour used to thicken one of the gravies. Compare the ease of making gravy with regular and with instant flour.

3. Prepare and evaluate starchy sauces suitable for serving with cake, fruit, or pudding, such as vanilla sauce, raisin sauce, chocolate sauce, and lemon sauce.

4. Prepare and evaluate a variety of starchy desserts. Some possibilities are:
a. Vanilla cornstarch pudding using the recommended amount of sugar and smaller and larger amounts of sugar.
b. Chocolate cornstarch pudding made with chocolate and with an equivalent amount of cocoa and fat (see Table 12–3).

5. Prepare a vanilla pudding with original ingredients, with a commercial mix which requires cooking, and with an instant mix. Compare cost, time required for preparation, and quality of the pudding.

References

BORGSTROM, G. *Principles of Food Science*. New York: The Macmillan Company. 1968. Vol. I, pp. 347–349; 363–364; Vol. II, pp. 5–7.

FOOD AND NUTRITION BOARD, NAS–NRC. *Cereal Enrichment in Perspective, 1958*. Natl. Acad. Sci.–Natl. Research Council, Washington, D.C.

GREWE, E. Variation in the Weight of a Given Volume of Different Flours. I. Normal Variations. II. The Result of the Use of Different Wheats. III. Causes for Variation, Milling, Blending, Handling, and Time of Storage. *Cereal Chem.,* 9: 311–316; 531–534; 628–636 (1932).

GRISWOLD R. M. *The Experimental Study of Foods*. Boston: Houghton Mifflin Company. 1962. Chapter 9.

HEID, J. L. and M. A. JOSLYN (Eds.). *Fundamentals of Food Processing Operations: Ingredients, Methods, and Packaging*. Westport, Conn.: The Avi Publishing Company, Inc. 1967. Pp. 107–129.

POTTER, N. N. *Food Science*. Westport, Conn.: The Avi Publishing Company, Inc. 1968. Pp. 440–463.

WHISTLER, R. L. Alsberg-Schock Lecture: Starch and Polysaccharide Derivatives in the Food and Non-Food Industries. *Cereal Science Today,* 16: 54–59, 73 (1971).

WILDER, R. M. and R. R. WILLIAMS. *Enrichment of Flour and Bread. A History of the Movement*. Natl. Acad. Sci.–Natl. Research Council Publ. No. 110, Washington, D.C. (1944).

13

introduction to flour mixtures

Flour mixtures include a large variety of baked foods such as quick breads, yeast breads, cakes, and pastry. They also include other products, such as steamed puddings and breads, and doughnuts and fritters that are fried. Needless to say, these flour mixtures have an important role in the diets of most peoples.

Flour mixtures exist not only in many varieties, but also in many qualities. Quality is usually judged by the appearance, flavor, odor, and other characteristics of the product. It will be important in the chapters that follow to learn what factors affect quality and the characteristics of a product made in different ways. It is sometimes more important to learn what characteristics in a product are preferred and how they may be achieved than to center attention on a "standard" product. The use of the word "standard" implies that we know what the product should be. This is, however, a matter of opinion that varies with the individual and with the region or country in which he lives. A broad tolerance for differences in food preparation must not, however, be used as an excuse for poor food preparation. It might be impossible to find anyone who preferred lumpy cornstarch pudding, tough pastry, or fallen cake.

In this chapter the proportion of ingredients and mixing methods will be discussed as they apply to a wide variety of flour mixtures. Characteristics of specific baked products will be presented in the chapters that follow. The functions of the principal ingredients of baked products will also be discussed. Special attention will be given to proteins in flour, leavening agents, and fats because they are not discussed in other chapters.

Proportion of Ingredients

The proportion of ingredients is all-important in determining the nature of the product. The proportion of liquid to flour influences the thickness of the uncooked flour mixture. In Table 13–1, baked flour mixtures are classified as batters and doughs, according to the amount of flour and liquid they contain. The proportions shown are only rough approximations because

Table 13–1. *Classification of Batters and Doughs According to Proportion of Flour to Liquid* *

Type	Approximate Proportions by Volume		Consistency	Examples
	Liquid	Flour		
Pour batters	1 part	1 part	Thin enough to pour a steady stream	Popovers, griddle cakes, waffles, and cream puffs
Drop batters	1 part	2 parts	Breaks into "drops" when poured	Muffins, fritters, cake, gingerbread, drop biscuits, and drop cookies
Soft doughs	1 part	3 parts	Soft but can be handled on board	Baking powder biscuits, yeast rolls, and bread
Stiff doughs	1 part	4 parts	Firm to touch and can be rolled easily on board	Pie crust, noodles, and rolled cookies

* Adapted from *Practical Cookery*, 23rd ed., by the Department of Foods and Nutrition, Kansas State University. Courtesy of John Wiley & Sons, Inc., 1966, and the Kansas State University Endowment Association.

of variations between recipes and because of the effects of other ingredients such as egg, sugar, fat, and baking powder on the characteristics of the mixture. Batters that pour contain about one cup liquid to one cup flour, whereas those that break into drops when poured, such as muffin or cake batters, contain about one cup liquid to two cups flour. Doughs do not pour; they are stiff enough to knead or roll on a board. Soft doughs, such as those used for baking powder biscuits and certain yeast products, contain about one cup liquid to three cups flour, whereas a stiff dough for pie crust contains about four cups flour for each cup of liquid.

Measuring

Baking success depends upon the proportions of ingredients used and upon the techniques of mixing and cooking. It is true that some successful cooks do not measure or weigh their ingredients in the usual way. It is probable, however, that all of them measure in some way, perhaps visually with a long used utensil such as a teacup or a bowl or by touch, adding ingredients until the batter or dough has certain characteristics. Such procedures make it difficult to teach another person, or to try new recipes, and may fail completely if the favorite measuring utensils are broken. Accurate measurements or weights are therefore recommended, especially for the beginning cook.

Americans usually measure ingredients in standardized measuring cups and spoons; however, workers in research, commercial food preparation, and homemakers in many other countries more often weigh than measure ingredients. Weighing is usually more accurate than measuring because it is not affected by the packing of such foods as flour or by the way in which the measuring cup is filled. Errors in measuring may be due either to inaccurate measuring utensils or to the way in which they are used. The accuracy of a measuring cup, which should hold 236.6 ml. water, can be tested with a graduated cylinder. Although it is not likely that a cup full of water will measure exactly 236.6 ml. it should be approximately that amount and 236.6 ml. of water measured in a graduate cylinder should "fill" the measuring cup. Liquids are measured in a graduated cup. It is helpful if the rim of the cup extends above the one-cup level and is shaped into a pouring lip to avoid spilling when the cup is moved and emptied. Foods that are not liquid are measured in fractional household dry measures also called individual fractional cups. The cup is filled and leveled with the straight edge of a spatula which, to avoid packing the food, is held at right angles to the top of the cup. Dry or solid foods should not be measured in a measuring cup designed for use with liquids because there is no accurate way of leveling the surface. Shaking flour into a measuring cup is especially undesirable because it packs flour into the cup. Measuring spoons are used for small amounts of all foods. In measuring foods, it is important to know the following volume equivalents:

1 quart	= 4 cups
1 pint	= 2 cups
1 cup	= 16 tablespoons
1 tablespoon	= 3 teaspoons

Care must be taken in comparing weight and volume measurements because foods vary in density as shown by their weight per cup.[1] One pound of water, milk, fresh liquid eggs, and table fat measures about two cups, but the same weight of flour measures about four cups. Flours of different types vary in their weight per cup.

Liquid such as milk, water, oil, or syrup is measured by pouring into a graduated cup placed on a level surface until the liquid reaches the desired mark. The level of liquid is checked by having the eye at the level of the mark. If the eye is above or below the mark, the reading is likely to be inaccurate. Other foods are measured in individual fractional cups. Only two foods, solid fat and brown sugar, are packed into the cup. Solid fat is pressed firmly to eliminate air bubbles within the fat. When the cup or a measuring spoon is full, it is leveled with the straight edge of a spatula or knife. Table fat in $1/4$-pound sticks is easily measured because $1/4$ pound is

[1] *Handbook of Food Preparation.* American Home Economics Association, Washington, D.C., 1971.

Fig. 13–1. *Accurate measuring is essential for consistent baking success.*

Courtesy of the Rice Council

equivalent to $\frac{1}{2}$ cup of fat. Brown sugar is packed into individual fractional cups firmly enough that the sugar keeps the shape of the cup when it is turned out. If brown sugar is lumpy, it is rolled and sifted before measuring. Free-flowing brown sugar is simply poured into a cup and leveled. However, free-flowing and regular brown sugar are not interchangeable in recipes, by volume, for one cup of free-flowing or granulated weighs 152 grams and one cup of the regular brown sugar, packed, 200 grams. White sugar is spooned into individual fractional cups until the cup overflows before the cup is leveled with a straight edge. Dry milk is measured in this way or by pouring it into a cup from the spout of the package.

White flour presents more of a problem in measuring than other ingredients because of its tendency to pack. Sifting before measuring has been recommended for many years because it gives more uniform results than measuring without sifting. Flour is sifted once, placed lightly without shaking into a measuring cup with a spoon until the measure is overflowing, and then leveled with a straight edge. Flour should not be sifted directly into a cup because flour measured in this way weighs less than flour measured by the recommended method. Recently, in an effort to simplify household practices, the measurement of flour without sifting has been suggested. In making this recommendation, manufacturers have claimed that their flour was presifted—certainly a safe claim since all flour is sifted many times during milling.

Fig. 13–2. Correct measurement of flour is essential in the production of high quality batters and doughs.

Sift a portion of flour once. Waxed paper may be used to hold the flour as it is sifted.

Spoon flour into dry measuring cup; level. Do not scoop.

With the straight edge of a spatula, level the top of the cup.

Courtesy of the Wheat Flour Institute

Table 13–2. *Weight Per Cup of All-Purpose and Cake Flours Measured in Different Ways* * †

Flour	Weight of 1 cup gm.	Increase Over Sifted, Spooned per cent
All-purpose flour		
Sifted, spooned	115	—
Unsifted, spooned	126	10
Unsifted, dipped	137	19
Instant ‡	129	12
Cake flour		
Sifted, spooned	96	—
Unsifted, spooned	109	14
Unsifted, dipped	118	23

* All data except that for instant flour compiled from Matthews and Batcher, in *Journal of Home Economics,* 55: 123–124, 1963. Courtesy of the authors and the American Home Economics Association.
† In all cases the cup was leveled with the straight edge of a spatula.
‡ From *Handbook of Food Preparation,* Revised 1971. Courtesy of the American Home Economics Association.

The real problem in measuring flour without sifting is that flour so measured weighs more than flour that is sifted before measuring and that recipes in most cookbooks are intended for use with sifted flour spooned into a measuring cup. Table 13–2 indicates that unsifted flour weighs even more when a cup is dipped into the flour container than when unsifted flour is spooned into the cup. In obtaining the data for Table 13–2, it was found that the results of many measurements were most uniform when the flour was sifted before measuring, intermediate when unsifted flour was spooned into the cup, and least uniform when the cup was dipped into the flour container. These results are reflected in the product, since less acceptable muffins and cakes were obtained from measured unsifted flour than from the same volume (lower weight) of sifted flour.[2]

Good results with conventional recipes can be insured by sifting the flour before it is measured or by removing two tablespoons of flour from unsifted flour that has been spooned into the cup. This procedure may, however, result in spilling the flour and may be awkward when fractional parts of a cup are involved. Another obvious solution is to develop recipes that are intended for use with unsifted flour. This was done at the time "pre-sifted" flour was promoted with the pre-sifted flour plainly designated, usually also identified by brand name. However, with passing time and the exchange of recipes it would seem easy to omit the qualification thus causing a distortion of the original ratio.

[2] R. H. Matthews and O. M. Batcher. Sifted Versus Unsifted Flour. *Journal of Home Economics,* 55: 123–124 (1963).

Whole-grain flours and meals are not sifted before they are measured because sifting might remove some of the larger particles. Instead, they are stirred to lighten them and then spooned into a measuring cup and leveled. Instant flours do not pack so they are not sifted before they are measured, but as noted in Table 13–2 instant flour weighs more per cup than all-purpose flour. In addition, instant flour takes up liquid at a faster rate than does conventional flour. Tests with ten products showed that the imbalance of ingredients can be corrected if two tablespoons of flour are removed from each measured cup.[3]

Leavening agents and other dry ingredients used in small quantities are stirred and then measured by dipping a heaping measuring spoon from the container and leveling it with a straight edge. Because eggs vary widely in size, it is important to select those of medium or large size for use in recipes that call for a particular number of eggs. If a balance is not available, one-half egg can be measured by beating one egg slightly and putting it into two glass custard cups or similar utensils so that the levels are the same.

Mixing Methods

Mixing methods for specific foods will be described in the chapters to follow. Most foods can be mixed effectively either by hand or with an electric mixer. Emphasis will be given in this book to mixing by hand because electric mixers are not always available, especially to each student in a class, and because something is learned in mixing by hand that may be missed when mixing is done by machine.

Mixing by hand is greatly facilitated by the proper utensils. A bowl with sloping sides and one that is about half full allows for the most effective mixing with the least time and effort. Proper mixing is hindered if the bowl is so full that the contents spill over the sides when stirred or so large that the mixture just covers the bottom. For stirring, a wooden or plastic spoon, as opposed to a metal one, is usually easier on the hand and less likely to scratch the bowl or discolor the mixture.

It may be helpful at this time to consider the definition of words used in explaining how to mix ingredients.

Beat. To use an over and over motion to smooth a mixture and to incorporate air, using a spoon or a wire whisk; or to use an electric mixer or rotary beater.

Cream. To work one or more foods until soft and creamy, often a fat to which sugar is added. A wooden spoon or an electric mixer is often used.

Cut in. To distribute a solid fat in dry ingredients, using a rocking, cutting motion with a pastry blender, or two knives held flat sides together. The size of the particles desired is dependent upon the product to be made.

[3] *Agricultural Research,* 15: (10), April 1967. United States Department of Agriculture, Washington, D.C., p. 16.

Fold. To combine ingredients, usually with a foam. Folding is done with a spoon, a wire whisk, or flat scraper using a down-across-up-and-across-the-top motion without lifting the tool out of the foam. The bowl is rotated during folding.

Knead. To manipulate a dough with a gentle push (with the heel of the hand), pull (with the fingers curled), and turn motion. When referring to a candy, kneading is to work or manipulate the mixture with the hands.

Stir. To mix by a circular or figure eight motion, to blend or combine the mixture.

Whip. To beat rapidly with an electric mixer, a rotary beater, or a whisk to incorporate air to form a foam.

Ingredients

Formulas or recipes have evolved that express the proportion and type of ingredients found to produce desirable products for each of the various types of food mixtures. It is helpful to learn something about these ingredients, their interactions, and their effects upon the flour mixture.

Flour

The type of flour is usually specified in the recipe because it affects the characteristics of the product. Differences between flours were discussed in Chapter 12 but protein is discussed here because of its importance in baked products. Flour is an important ingredient because it forms part of the structure or framework of the finished product.

The protein of flour absorbs large amounts of water, a quality that is important in forming an elastic dough. The importance of protein in water absorption is indicated by the fact that the protein of flour absorbs up to about 200 per cent of its weight of water, whereas starch absorbs only about 15 per cent of its weight. Starch does, however, have an important role in absorbing water because it is present in flour in much larger proportions (about sevenfold larger) than protein. The hydration capacity of flour, which is obviously greatly influenced by its protein content, is important in determining the yield of bread from a given amount of flour. The yield of bread from hard wheat flour is, therefore, greater than from soft wheat flour.

Many of the properties that have just been described are due to gluten that is formed from the protein of flour when water is mixed with it. Gluten can be prepared by adding enough water to flour to make a stiff dough, kneading the dough, and then washing out the starch and water-soluble substances by squeezing the dough under a stream of running water or in a bowl of water. The sticky, elastic residue is gluten, which is shown before and after baking in Figure 13–3. Although the same amount of flour was used for all the gluten balls in this picture, the ball formed from cake flour is smallest, that from all-purpose is next, and the ball from bread flour is the

Fig. 13–3. *Characteristic gluten balls are formed from each kind of flour. These expand with baking as shown here from left to right: cake flour, all-purpose flour, bread flour.*

Courtesy of the Wheat Flour Institute

largest. The quality of gluten from these flours is also different. That from cake flour is soft in texture and likely to tear, whereas gluten from all-purpose flour or bread flour is more elastic and can be stretched without tearing or breaking.

These qualities are related to the performance of the flour; for bread a large amount of elastic gluten is desirable, whereas for cake a small amount of softer gluten may be desirable. In making bread, the gluten forms a continuous network throughout the dough and coagulates during baking to form the structure of the loaf. The starch is imbedded in the gluten meshwork. When CO_2 is formed during the fermentation process, the dough expands and the strands of dough are stretched. Strong gluten is necessary so that the cell walls can stretch without breaking during rising and baking. Because of the smaller amount of softer gluten that it forms, soft wheat flour is less suitable for bread than hard wheat flour. The soft wheat flour does, however, give the light, porous structure that is desirable in cakes, pastries, and even quick breads. It is better than hard wheat flour for many products in which baking powder or soda is the leavening. However, all-purpose flour, with in-between qualities, may be successfully used for most home-baked products. In the South, where quick breads are frequently baked, a softer blend is sold; in the North, where yeast breads are more popular, a harder blend. All-purpose flour is also used for cakes, cookies, and pastries.

Liquid

Flour and liquid both affect the consistency of flour mixtures. Too much liquid or too little flour results in a thin mixture and a product that spreads too much, tends to fall, and is soft, moist, or sometimes even soggy. The product that contains too little liquid or too much flour has a dry, harsh texture and may be uneven in shape due to failure to spread and difficulty in handling.

The liquid used in flour mixtures is usually either milk or water. Milk is preferred for most recipes because of its greater food value and its contribution to the flavor and the browning of the product. Because milk contains about 13 per cent solids, slightly more milk than water is used in a recipe. The liquid hydrates or moistens the flour and proteins, dissolves the sugar and soluble salts, and is essential for the release of carbon dioxide from baking powder (soda) and the gelatinization of starch by heat.

Eggs

In addition to adding structural support, flavor, color, and nutritive value to foods, eggs help retain steam and the gas formed by leavening agents during baking. This property, which can be attributed to the heat coagulation of the protein, is especially marked in thin batters. For example, if popovers are made without eggs, a solid mass instead of a light shell results after baking. Air can be introduced into a batter by means of beaten eggs or egg whites. The careful balance that is necessary in a recipe is illustrated by the fact that an increased amount of egg makes cakes tough unless it is counterbalanced by increasing the amount of ingredients that make a product more tender, such as sugar and fat.

Sugar

Sugar adds flavor or sweetness to flour mixtures and helps the crust to brown during baking. Sugar makes baked foods more tender because it has a softening effect on gluten, the protein formed when flour and water are mixed, and because sugar raises the coagulation temperature of egg. This softening effect of sugar on gluten will be noticed in muffins, yeast bread, and cake. The effects of sugar on the coagulation point of eggs are especially noticeable in baked custards but are probably important in cakes also. Increasing the amount of sugar in cakes without changing the proportions of other ingredients may result in coarse large cells, thick cell walls, and a shiny crust that is crystalline in appearance. Such cakes usually crumble easily.

Leavening Agents

Gas is needed in baked products to make them larger, less compact, and softer in texture than they would be if no gas were present. Gas expands the soft batter or dough which is later set by the heat of the oven. In other words, a leavening agent, sometimes called leaven, is used to make foods light. The common leavening agents are steam, air, and carbon dioxide. In some products, one of these predominates and in others two or three are important.

During cooking, steam is formed by vaporization of water as the temperature inside the baked product rises. Steam is an effective leavening agent because it may occupy a volume from 1600 to 1800 times the volume of the water from which it was formed. Steam is the principal leavening agent in popovers and cream puffs. In both of these products, steam expands a hollow shell formed by the flour and egg of the mixture. Steam undoubtedly contributes to the expansion of baked products in which other leavening agents are used.

Fig. 13–4. *The cavities of cream puffs, which are formed by steam, provide space for generous amounts of filling.*

Air beaten into a mixture expands in volume during baking and therefore leavens the products. Air beaten into egg whites is the principal leaven of omelets, soufflés, sponge cakes, and angel food cakes. It is also important in other products such as shortened cakes and waffles to which beaten egg whites are added. Air cells surrounded by fat form an important part of the structure of shortened cake batters. These air cells are nuclei into which both carbon dioxide and steam find their way during mixing and baking.

The third leavening agent, carbon dioxide, can be formed either by the action of yeast on sugars or by the action of acid on baking soda. Acid can be added to baking soda in the form of sour milk or other acid ingredient, or a dry acid or acid-reacting salt can be combined with baking soda to make baking powder.

Yeast. Leavened bread was used by the Egyptians before 3000 B.C. and later by the Greeks and Romans. In ancient times, a liquid mixture that contained starch, sugar, or both was allowed to stand in the air. Yeast microorganisms soon found their way into the mixture, which then began to ferment. Part of this liquid mixture, called a "starter," could be used in bread dough in the liquid form or could be dried for future use. Liquid starter or a piece of bread dough was saved, preferably in a cold place, from one baking to the next. Starters contain wild yeast and usually bacteria that are, of course, variable in their bread-making ability.

The strain of yeast now sold commercially has been selected carefully for its bread-making ability. Its scientific name is *Saccharomyces cerevisiae.* For household purposes, yeast can now be purchased in the form of active dry yeast or a compressed cake. Because of its low moisture content, active dry yeast keeps much better than compressed yeast. It can be kept for several weeks without refrigeration, and still longer if kept in a cold place, but should be used before the expiration date printed on the package. Compressed yeast is a moist mass of yeast mixed with cornstarch. It keeps for only a week or two in a refrigerator but for several months in a freezer. Fresh compressed yeast is grayish in color, rather brittle, and breaks sharply. If it crumbles easily, it is still good even though it shows a slight brownish color.

Yeast is a living organism that changes sugars to carbon dioxide gas and forms alcohol which is driven off by the heat of baking. In addition to sugar, which may be added as such or formed from starch, yeast requires moisture and a few minerals. Yeast is able to use as food any sugars that are likely to be present except lactose, the sugar of milk. One reason milk helps to make the crust of bread brown is that its lactose is not used by the yeast as the bread rises. Enzymes present in yeast are able to split sucrose and maltose to simple sugars, and another enzyme in yeast breaks down the simple sugars to carbon dioxide and alcohol. Amylolytic enzymes, either present in the flour or added, are able to split the starch of flour to sugar.

Because yeast is a plant, it is sensitive to changes in temperature. Probably the best temperature for the rising of yeast bread is 27° to 29° C. (80° to 85° F.). Although higher temperatures may cause dough to rise faster, they may also encourage the growth of undesirable microorganisms. Rising slows down above 35° C. (95° F.), and the yeast is destroyed at about 54° C. (130° F.). Optimum conditions for rehydrating the two forms of yeast differ. Active dry yeast is best rehydrated in water, not milk, between 40° and 45° C. (104° and 113° F.). Compressed yeast, on the other hand, can be crumbled into lukewarm water or other liquid at about 35° C. (95° F.). The temperature during rehydration seems to require more careful control for active dry yeast than for compressed yeast. However, active dry yeast is frequently added directly to about one-third of the flour and the other dry ingredients and stirred to blend, before adding to all of the liquid which has been warmed. If the yeast is blended dry before rehydration the temperature of the liquid is less precise but may be quite warm, as high as 49° to 54° C. (120° to 130° F.) being recommended. The two forms of yeast, when handled correctly, act at about the same speed in doughs.

Baking Soda. Yeast forms carbon dioxide gas rather slowly in doughs. The same gas can be formed much more quickly by chemical means. This is carried out by allowing an acid to react with baking soda, which is also called sodium bicarbonate ($NaHCO_3$). The reaction of baking soda with an acid can be written in this way:

$$NaHCO_3 \quad + \quad HX \quad \longrightarrow \quad CO_2 \quad + \quad NaX \quad + \quad H_2O$$

soda   acid   carbon   salt   water
                                    dioxide

The student who is familiar with chemistry will understand the chemical formulas in which HX stands for any acid. Those who have not studied chemistry may prefer the words with the explanation that an acid is a sour substance like vinegar that reacts with a basic substance like baking soda to form a salt. When the basic substance is baking soda, carbon dioxide is also formed.

When soda is mixed with an acid substance like sour milk, bubbles of carbon dioxide appear immediately, go off into the air, and therefore cannot leaven the mixture. If soda is to be used as a leavening agent, it must be sifted with the dry ingredients so that carbon dioxide is released in the batter or dough during mixing and baking. One problem with using soda is that acid ingredients vary in degree of acidity. Sour milk varies so much that the right proportion of soda is difficult to determine. Milk that has just "turned" neutralizes very little soda, whereas milk that is very sour will neutralize several times as much. The general rule is one-half teaspoon of soda to one cup milk of average sourness, with modifications depending upon the sourness of the milk. There is more danger of adding too much soda than too little. If the sour milk is not neutralized completely, the flavor may not be objectionable, but too much soda gives a bitter flavor and is likely to cause a yellowish color in the product. Fruit juices and molasses can also be used as a source of acid. Because of variations in the acidity of molasses, one teaspoon soda is used with one to two cups of molasses.

Before baking powders were available, soda and cream of tartar were often added as leavening agents. Cream of tartar is an acid salt of tartaric acid which does not vary in strength, as do sour milk and molasses. One teaspoon of soda reacts with about two and a half teaspoons of cream of tartar.

Baking Powder. Baking powder is a mixture of baking soda and a dry acid or acid-reacting salt. Cornstarch or flour is added to these ingredients to separate them and prevent their reaction in the dry baking powder. Baking powder, one of the early convenience foods, was developed so that one measurement, that of baking powder, would replace two, those of baking soda and an acid. Carbon dioxide is formed from baking powder according to the equation given above.

The use of baking powder is much more recent than that of baking soda and an acid ingredient. In the United States, the first baking powder was developed in 1850.[4] The acid salt, cream of tartar, was used in this baking powder.

The acid constituents of retail brands of baking powders are shown in Table 13–3. Baking soda (sodium bicarbonate) and starch or flour are constituents of each of these baking powders. It will be seen that only one acid, tartaric acid, appears in the list of acid constituents. The others are salts that have an acid reaction in water and are therefore able to release carbon dioxide from baking soda. All of these baking powders must yield at least

[4] L. H. Bailey. *Development and Use of Baking Powder and Baking Chemicals.* Circular No. 138. United States Department of Agriculture, Washington, D.C., 1940.

Table 13–3. *Acid Constituents Used in Retail Brands of Baking Powders* *

Type of Baking Powder	Acid Constituents	Formulas of Acid Constituents	Retail Brands of Baking Powder
Tartrate	Cream of tartar and tartaric acid	$KHC_4H_4O_6$ and $H_2C_4H_4O_6$	Royal Swansdown
Phosphate	Monocalcium phosphate monohydrate	$Ca(H_2PO_4)_2 \cdot H_2O$	Dr. Price Rumford
Anhydrous phosphate	Monocalcium phosphate anhydrous	$Ca(H_2PO_4)_2$	Happy Family Jewel
SAS-phosphate	Sodium aluminum sulfate and monocalcium phosphate monohydrate	$Na_2SO_4 \cdot Al_2(SO_4)_3$ and $Ca(H_2PO_4)_2 \cdot H_2O$	Calumet † Clabber Girl Crescent ‡ Davis OK Hearth Club KC ‡

* All baking powders contain the alkaline constituent sodium bicarbonate, $NaHCO_3$.
† Contains calcium sulfate.
‡ Contains calcium carbonate.

12 per cent available carbon dioxide. Available carbon dioxide is the amount given off under ordinary conditions of baking. The four groups of baking powders differ not in the amount but in the speed with which they give off carbon dioxide. Tartrate baking powder, in which the acid constituents are cream of tartar and tartaric acid, and phosphate baking powder, which contains monocalcium phosphate monohydrate act more rapidly than the other two groups. The acid salt of phosphate baking powder contains water of crystallization whereas anhydrous monocalcium phosphate contains no water and has been manufactured in such a way that the surface is "glazed." Because the anhydrous salt dissolves more slowly, it reacts more slowly in dough than the hydrated form. Anhydrous phosphate is more widely used in mixes than in baking powders. The last group of acid constituents listed in Table 13–3 is used most frequently in household baking powders. Sodium aluminum sulfate (SAS) reacts slowly at room temperature but rapidly in the oven. It is therefore combined with phosphate so that there will be both a rapid and a slow reaction. For this reason, SAS-phosphate baking powder is sometimes called double-action or combination baking powder.

The list of acid-reacting constituents available for use in baking powders has increased beyond those listed in Table 13–3. It is therefore possible for the baker or the manufacturer of self-rising flour, mixes, and refrigerated batters to obtain the type of leavening he wants for his products.

Experience in the laboratory indicates that good results can be obtained with any of the household baking powders when they are properly used. Over-mixing can be expected to have a more harmful effect on batters made with fast- than with slow-acting baking powders, but cream of tartar and phosphates seem to strengthen the gluten of a batter or dough. Sodium aluminum sulfate, on the other hand, may have an undesirable tightening effect on the gluten of the flour. When a high oven temperature is used with a slow-acting baking powder, a crust may form during baking before rising is complete. Further rising then causes cracks to appear on the product that can sometimes be seen on the sides of biscuits and on the tops of muffins, cakes, or quick loaf breads. Careful studies with tartrate, phosphate, and SAS-phosphate baking powders indicate that satisfactory muffins and cakes can be made by using one and one-half teaspoons of any of the three types of baking powder per cup of flour. The amount of baking powder for cakes depends in part upon the proportion of eggs, as less baking powder is required when the proportion of eggs is high than when it is low. Other evidence suggests that the volume of baking powder may be increased about one-fourth when tartrate or phosphate baking powder is substituted for SAS-phosphate. Little information is available on the optimum levels of anhydrous monocalcium phosphate baking powder because this type is not as widely distributed and was developed more recently. Optimum levels of this type baking powder are probably similar to those of SAS-phosphate.

Sometimes it is desirable to substitute sour milk for sweet milk in a recipe. If 1 cup of fully soured milk or buttermilk is substituted for 1 cup of sweet milk, $\frac{1}{2}$ teaspoon of soda is added to the dry ingredients in place of 2 teaspoons baking powder. If sweet milk is used in a recipe that calls for sour milk or buttermilk, enough sweet milk is added to 1 tablespoon vinegar or lemon juice, or to $1\frac{3}{4}$ teaspoons cream of tartar, to make 1 cup.

Fats and Oils

Fats and oils are important ingredients in most baked products. Fats like lard, hydrogenated shortening, butter, and margarine are solid at room temperature, whereas vegetable oils are liquid. They are alike in being mixtures of compounds of glycerol (a trihydroxy alcohol sometimes called glycerin) with three fatty acids.[5] These compounds are called triglycerides. In fats

[5] Students who have had chemistry may find these formulas helpful:

$$H_2COH$$
$$H\ COH \qquad \text{glycerol}$$
$$H_2COH$$

$$CH_3(CH_2)_nCOOH \qquad \text{a saturated fatty acid}$$

$$CH_3(CH_2)_7CH{=}CH(CH_2)_7COOH \qquad \text{oleic acid, a monounsaturated fatty acid}$$

$$CH_3(CH_2)_4CH{=}CHCH_2CH{=}CH(CH_2)_7COOH \qquad \text{linoleic, a polyunsaturated fatty acid}$$

$$H_2COOC(CH_2)_nCH_3$$
$$H\ COOC(CH_2)_nCH_3 \qquad \text{a saturated fat}$$
$$H_2COOC(CH_2)_nCH_3$$

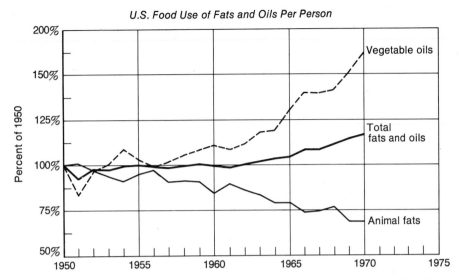

Fig. 13–5. *The per capita consumption of fats and oils was estimated to be 44 pounds in 1950 and 53 pounds in 1970—39 pounds vegetable oils and 14 pounds animal fats.* (From *Fat and Oil Situation*, FOS–257, April 1971, USDA, p. 29.)

that are solid at room temperature, many of the fatty acids are saturated, which means that their carbon atoms have all the hydrogen that will combine with them. Fats that are liquid at room temperature, often called oils, contain some fatty acids that are either smaller in size or more unsaturated than those in solid fats. Monounsaturated fatty acids have one link in the carbon chain that lacks two hydrogen atoms, and polyunsaturated fatty acids have two or more such linkages, which means that they lack four or more hydrogen atoms. The unsaturated linkages are more reactive than saturated linkages—that is, they can be hydrogenated and they react with oxygen from air in oxidative rancidity. It can be seen from this discussion that differences between fats and oils are of degree rather than kind because all oils contain some saturated fatty acids and all solid fats contain some unsaturated fatty acids.

Processing. The methods of processing fats and oils depend upon their source. Lard is made by heating fatty tissues trimmed from market cuts and stripped from the internal organs of pork. At present, most lard is steam rendered, that is, rendered in an enclosed kettle containing steam under pressure and then refined. Leaf lard is rendered in open kettles at low temperatures from the high-quality fat that lines the abdominal wall. Lard may have an antioxidant added to delay rancidity and may be treated in other ways to improve its baking quality. Oleo stock is prepared by heating the internal fatty tissues of beef. Other rendered beef fat is called tallow. Oleo products are sometimes used in blended shortenings. Their former use in

Fig. 13–6. *These charts show the comparative use of butter and margarine during the past twenty years and the expanding use of soybean oil in margarine.* (From *Fat and Oil Situation*, FOS–257, April 1971, USDA, p. 35.)

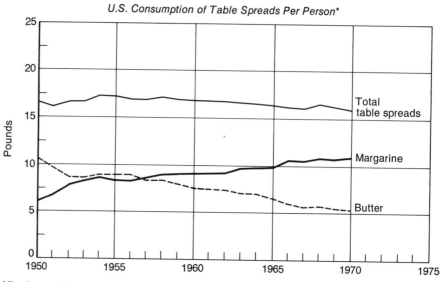

*Product weight

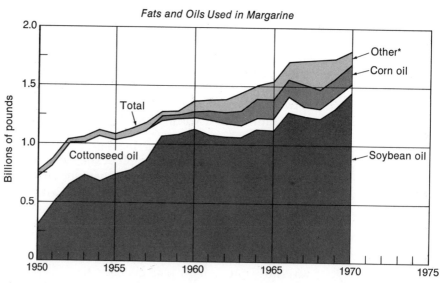

*Mainly lard, but also includes beef, fats, peanut oil, coconut oil, and safflower oil

margarine accounts for the name oleomargarine. Butter is churned from sweet or sour cream (a process that causes the fat particles to clump together) and washed with water. The addition of salt and coloring is optional. Butter must contain at least 80 per cent milk fat.

Vegetable oil was first made from olives but is now made from a wide variety of plant products such as corn, cottonseed, peanut, safflower, and soybean. Oil is pressed or extracted by solvents from the oil-bearing portion of the seed. The oil is then purified by a variety of methods so that the product is light in color and bland in flavor. The oil can be used for salad dressings, frying, and baking. It can also be made into a solid fat known as hydrogenated shortening. This is done by adding hydrogen gas under pressure to the heated oil in the presence of a metal called a catalyst. This process adds hydrogen to some of the unsaturated linkages in the fatty acids, thus saturating them and changing the oil to a fat. The fat is deodorized by treating it with steam and an emulsifier[6] is often added to improve the baking quality. In addition to changing the consistency of the fat, hydrogenation changes the color, flavor, odor, and improves the keeping quality. Lard may also be hydrogenated to improve its baking quality. Many hydrogenated fats are now sold under various trade names. The label indicates whether hydrogenated shortenings are made from vegetable oils or from a combination of vegetable and animal fats.

Margarine is a product that resembles butter except for the nature of the fat. Some animal fat may be used but most margarines are made from vegetable oils, some or all of which may have been partially hydrogenated. Partially hydrogenated oils are used because complete hydrogenation would form a product too firm to use. Many margarines on the market today contain liquid oils also. Labels for margarine must state the types of fat used, in order of predominance and by common name, as well as treatment of fat such as "hydrogenated," "partially hydrogenated," or "hardened" whichever is factual.[7] The manufacture of margarine includes churning together liquid or liquefied oils and pasteurized milk (usually skim) or soy milk. Almost all margarines are now enriched with vitamins to make their nutritive value equivalent to that of butter. In addition salt, emulsifiers, flavor, color, and preservatives may be added and if so must be included in the list of ingredients. Like butter, margarine must be at least 80 per cent fat. Desirable qualities in margarines are firmness at serving temperature, ease of spreading when cold, and "melt in the mouth" characteristics.[8] Whipped margarines have a larger volume, usually six bars per pound rather than four;

[6] The emulsifiers usually added to fats are mono- and diglycerides. The chemical formulas of these compounds are like those of fats except that only one or two instead of three fatty acids are attached to glycerol.

[7] *Federal Register,* 36: 11521–11522 (June 15, 1970).

[8] D. Melnick. Development of Organoleptically and Nutritionally Improved Margarine Products. *Journal of Home Economics,* 60: 793–797 (1968).

however, it is obvious that the increased volume is air and these bars or sticks are not interchangeable with the more solid regular margarines or butter. Low calorie margarines, plainly marked "Imitation," have greatly decreased fat content and increased water content bound together with emulsifiers. It is well to keep in mind that diet margarines are an expensive source of water and that the use of these margarines as an integral part of flour mixtures does not produce acceptable results. In purchasing margarines a wise shopper reads the list of ingredients and makes her choice according to the contents listed.

The consumption of vegetable oils, including those that have been hydrogenated, has increased sharply since 1950, whereas the use of animal fats, including butter, lard, and beef fats, has declined. This trend has been influenced by the substitution of margarine made of vegetable oils for butter and the use of hydrogenated vegetable shortening instead of lard. The annual per capita consumption of edible fats and oil is now about 53 pounds in the United States.

Keeping Quality. Changes in fats, frequently referred to as rancidity, may be a problem when fats or foods containing fats are stored. Rancidity may be due to oxidation or to hydrolysis of the fats. Oxidation is the more common problem. It is encountered in many fat-containing foods such as pork, poultry, fish, and even cereal products as well as in fats. It can be delayed by adding a substance called an antioxidant and by avoiding exposure to air, heat, light, and certain metals such as copper, iron, and nickel. Hydrolytic rancidity sometimes occurs in the storage of dairy and meat products. It is due to an enzyme in the food or in microorganisms that are present. Fats may acquire an unpleasant flavor because they absorb foreign flavors such as those of fish, onions, and flowers. Such changes are not related to rancidity.

Nutritive Value. Fat is a concentrated food that yields nine calories per gram in contrast to the four calories per gram of carbohydrates and protein. It supplies over 40 per cent of the calories in the average American diet.[9] The high energy value of fats and the slowness with which they are digested give "staying qualities" to the diet. Fats also supply several polyunsaturated fatty acids which, in small amounts, are considered essential for normal nutrition. They carry the fat-soluble vitamins A, D, and E, which are needed in normal nutrition.

Cookery Functions. Fat has many functions in food preparation. It adds flavor and also blends other flavors that are soluble in fat, such as those of spices, herbs, and vanilla. Butter or margarine—often referred to as "table fat"—may be preferred for products like white sauce and butterscotch and chocolate sauces in which the fat not only adds flavor but also modifies

[9] *Food. The Yearbook of Agriculture, 1959.* United States Department of Agriculture, Washington, D.C., p. 75.

texture. In salad dressings, some people prefer the flavor of olive oil, while others use vegetable oils that have almost no flavor of their own. Fats that are sometimes discarded, such as chicken fat, bacon fat, or drippings from other meat, are excellent for some cookery purposes.

In addition to contributing flavor in foods, fats are important in food emulsions such as mayonnaise. They help make baked goods tender by "shortening" the strands of gluten in batters and doughs. The shortening values of different fats will be discussed in Chapter 15 under pastry, a product in which such effects are easily compared. Fats are important in the aeration of shortened cakes because air beaten into cakes is held in the batter by the fat.

Fat is also important in food preparation as a frying medium. Frying changes the appearance of foods and may also change their textures. The crisp brown crust usually developed is attractive, and the characteristic flavor and odor are inviting. Foods such as potato and corn chips develop an appealing crisp texture.

Food fried in a small amount of fat is said to be pan-fried or sautéed. The temperature of the fat can be regulated by heating the pan on a controlled heat unit or by using an electric skillet. If an ordinary burner is used, it should be regulated so that the fat does not smoke at any time.

For deep-fat frying, a heavy, flat-bottomed kettle with a wire basket or an electric deep fryer is filled one-third to one-half full of fat and heated to the desired temperature before the food is added. Temperature is checked with a thermometer unless an automatic electric deep fryer is used. The temperatures appropriate for deep-fat frying are shown in Table 13–4. To avoid large temperature fluctuations, it is desirable to add a relatively small amount of cold food at one time. It has been found that the addition of about two ounces of sliced potatoes may lower the temperature of four pounds of fat as much as 9° C. (16° F). If food is added in such large amounts that the fat is cooled greatly, it must be cooked longer and thus absorbs more fat than when temperature fluctuations are smaller. If the fat is too hot during frying, the food becomes deep brown in color and hard on the surface but may not be cooked in the center. Over-heating also causes undesirable chemical changes in the fat. On the other hand, the food may be soggy, grease-soaked, and generally unattractive if the fat is not hot enough.

Table 13–4. *Temperatures for Deep-Fat Frying*

Product	Temperature of Fat	
	degrees F.	degrees C.
Chicken	350	177
Doughnuts, fish, fritters	350 to 375	177 to 190
Cauliflower, croquettes, egg-plant, onions	375 to 385	190 to 196
French fried potatoes	385 to 395	196 to 201

For deep-fat frying, fats are preferred that do not break down at the temperature used for frying. Decomposition of a fat occurs when smoke is given off from the fat during heating. The odor of such fat is sharp and the fumes irritating. Food fried in smoking fats is likely to have an unpleasant flavor, and the fat itself becomes rancid sooner than fat that has not reached such a high temperature.

The smoke point varies with the type of fat.[10] Those with the highest smoke point are usually the vegetable oils or hydrogenated vegetable fats to which no emulsifier has been added. Emulsifiers that improve the cake-baking qualities of fats lower their smoke points. Although some people prefer the flavor of lard for deep-fat frying, its smoke point is comparatively low because it contains more free fatty acids than some of the other fats.

The smoke point of a fat is affected by the way in which it is used as well as by the nature of the fat. The fact that the smoke point is lowered if a large surface of fat is exposed to air during frying explains the use of a deep kettle with a small surface. Smoke point is also lowered by the presence of foreign particles such as crumbs, bits of food, and flour. To remove such particles, fat is filtered through facial tissue or a soft paper towel supported by a strainer before it is stored in a refrigerator. Occasionally it is desirable to also clarify the fat. Solid fats are clarified by adding a cup of hot water for each cup of fat and heating the mixture slowly for ten minutes. The fat and water mixture is filtered so that small charred particles will be removed. The water is drained from the fat after the mixture is chilled enough to make the fat firm. Oils or soft fats are clarified by adding four or five thin slices of raw potato for each cup of fat and heating slowly for twenty minutes. The fat is then filtered and cooled.[11] The frying kettle and basket need frequent washing with soap and water to avoid the accumulation of products of fat decomposition. A frying fat should be discarded when its color has darkened considerably or if it foams severely when food is added to it. Foaming is an indication that the fat has begun to break down. Butter and margarine are not used for deep-fat frying because of the 15 per cent water content and emulsifiers present. Butter and many margarines also contain milk solids.

Although some fat absorption is normal in fried foods, an excessive amount is undesirable because it results in grease-soaked, unattractive food. The technique used in frying affects the amount of fat absorbed. For example, less fat is absorbed at high than at low frying temperatures, but temperatures that are too high cause excess surface browning. A drop in temperature due to the addition of a large amount of cold food can be avoided by adding a small amount at a time. An excessive amount of fat may be absorbed if the cooking time is long or if the surface area of the food is large. Immediately after frying, food is drained on absorbent paper to remove excess fat.

[10] B. Lowe, S. Pradhan, and J. Kastelic. The Free Fatty Acid Content and the Smoke Point of Some Fats. *Journal of Home Economics*, 50: 778–779 (1958).

[11] *Food. The Yearbook of Agriculture, 1959*, pp. 504–505.

All of the factors that have been mentioned affect fat absorption in doughnuts. The frying temperature and time require careful control, and the dough should be rolled and cut so that an excess surface area is not exposed during frying. Fat absorption may be excessive if the dough is made more moist by adding extra liquid or by substituting a softer flour. Fat absorption is also increased when extra sugar or fat is added to the recipe. Increased mixing time, on the other hand, develops gluten and decreases both fat absorption and tenderness.

Baking at High Altitudes

If cake recipes developed at sea level are used at altitudes over 3,000 feet, the results may be disappointing. The reason is that as atmospheric pressure is reduced by increased altitude, gas expands more readily than at lower altitudes. In addition, steam is formed earlier in a baked product because water boils at a lower temperature than at sea level. The expansion of a cake may therefore be excessive in the early part of the baking period before the heat of the oven has coagulated the proteins and gelatinized the starch enough to stabilize its structure. The use of sea-level cake recipes at high altitudes is likely to result in a small, heavy product.

Research on this problem done in states where altitudes are high indicates satisfactory products may result if the amount of baking powder is reduced, and the liquid is increased. It may also be necessary to strengthen the cell structure by reducing the amount of sugar and sometimes the fat. A table of suggested adjustments [12] is available for those who wish to adapt a favorite recipe for use at high altitudes. Recipe booklets for use at high altitudes are listed at the end of this chapter. Boxes of cake mix often include suggestions for altitude adjustment.

Usually adjustments for altitude are not necessary for yeast products, pastry, or cream puffs. The amount of leavening in biscuits and muffins may be decreased slightly at high altitudes and the proportion of egg in popovers increased to help retain steam during baking.

Activities

1. Obtain a container of flour that holds at least 2 pounds, 3 bowls, a one-cup household dry measure, and a spatula or knife with a straight edge.
a. Dip the cup into the flour, level with a straight edge, and put the flour into a bowl. Repeat until 5 cups have been measured.
b. Measure the flour that is in the bowl by spooning it lightly into a cup and leveling with a straight edge. Put 5 cups of flour measured in this way into a second bowl. If any flour remains from the amount measured in 1a, weigh or measure with measuring spoons the remaining flour. If additional flour is required for measuring 5 cups in 1b, obtain it from the original container.
c. Sift approximately half of the flour measured in 1b onto a piece of wax paper. Sift the remainder onto another piece of wax paper. Measure 5 cups of the sifted flour by spooning it lightly into a measuring cup, leveling with a straight edge, and

[12] *Handbook of Food Preparation*, p. 4.

putting it into a third bowl. Weigh or measure as in 1b the amount of flour that remains.

2. If a graduated cylinder is available, check the capacity of the measuring utensils available. Include if possible a graduated measuring cup, household dry measures, and measuring spoons. If preferred, capacities can be checked by weighing the amount of water that these measuring utensils hold because one milliliter of water weighs approximately 1 gram.

3. To one cup of all-purpose flour in a bowl add enough water to form a stiff dough ($\frac{1}{4}$ to $\frac{1}{3}$ cup). Stir the flour and water until a ball forms and the dough leaves the side of the bowl. Take up the mixture and work with the hands until a smooth, elastic dough is formed. Wash in cold water until water squeezed from the dough ball is clear. Use care to retrieve any fragments of dough which are loosened from the mass. Bake the residue at 205° C. (400° F.) for 10 minutes. Reduce oven heat to 149° C. (300° F.) and bake until gluten shells are dry.

a. Repeat with cake flour.

b. Repeat with whole wheat flour.

4. Into a one-pint glass measure put 1 cup buttermilk, sour milk, or 1 tablespoon vinegar plus enough sweet milk to make 1 cup. Add $\frac{1}{2}$ teaspoon baking soda and watch the gas bubbles escape from the milk. Would this gas be effective in leavening a dough? If not, how could it be made to leaven the dough?

5. Compare the appearance of active dry yeast and compressed yeast. Put $\frac{1}{4}$ cup of water in each of 2 custard cups. Have the water at about 35° C. (95° F.) for the cake of compressed yeast and between 40° and 45° C. (104° and 113° F.) for the package of active dry yeast. Note the speed with which both types of yeast form a suspension that can be added to dough.

6. Fry a variety of foods in deep fat.

7. French fry some potatoes in fat at different temperatures and compare their quality.

8. Find a recipe for doughnuts and try some of the methods of varying fat absorption that are suggested in the text.

References

American Standard Dimensions, Tolerances, and Terminology for Home Cooking and Baking Utensils. American Standards Association, Z61.1, New York (1963).

BAILEY, L. H. *Development and Use of Baking Powder and Baking Chemicals.* U.S. Dept. of Agr., Circ. No. 138 (1940).

GRISWOLD, R. M. *The Experimental Study of Foods.* Boston: Houghton Mifflin Company. 1962. Chapters 8 and 10.

JOSLIN, R. P. Taking the Chemistry Out of Chemical Leavening Systems. *The Bakers Digest* 34(5): 58–62 (1960).

MATZ, S. A. *Cereal Technology.* Westport, Conn.: The Avi Publishing Company, Inc. 1970. Pp. 1–73.

POTTER, N. N. *Food Science.* Westport, Conn.: The Avi Publishing Company, Inc. 1968. Pp. 440–447; 456–463.

TRACEY, M. V. Gluten: New Light on an Old Protein. *Cereal Science Today.* 12: 193–197, 214 (1967).

Baking at High Altitudes

BOWMAN, F., and E. DYAR. *Quick Mixes for High-Altitude Baking.* Colo. Agr. Exp. Sta. Bull. No. 45-A (1958).

BOYD, M. S., and M. C. SCHOONOVER. *Baking at High Altitude.* Univ. Wyoming Agr. Exp. Sta. Bull. No. 427 (1965).

DYAR, E., and E. CASSEL. *Mile-High Cakes. Recipes for High Altitudes.* Colo. Agr. Exp. Sta. Bull. No. 404-A (1958).

GARRETT, L. *A Cook's Almanac for Altitude Problems.* New Mexico, State Univ. Coop. Ext. Serv. Circ. 373 (1964).

14

breads

Preferences for different breads vary with the country, the region, and even within the family. In the British Isles breads of many types are enjoyed, especially at afternoon tea. Tugby voiced the English preference when he said: "I'm glad we had muffins. It's the sort of a night for muffins. Likewise, crumpets and also Sally Lunn."[1] Crumpets resemble English muffins and Sally Lunn a sweet yeast bread. On the continent of Europe rye breads, hearth breads, and coffee cakes are popular.

Both quick and yeast breads can be varied widely depending upon the type of flour and upon other ingredients in the recipe. White flour, whole wheat flour, or rye flour can be used; and cereal products such as corn meal, bran, or oatmeal can be substituted for part of the flour.

In this chapter, the preparation of quick breads and yeast breads from the original ingredients and from mixes will be discussed.

Quick Breads
Proportions

In Table 14–1, breads are classified according to their proportions of flour and milk as pour batters, drop batters, and soft doughs. All of the amounts are based on one cup of flour so that they can be compared easily. The range given for some of the ingredients includes many but not all of the variations in recipes that are possible. Some possible additions to the basic recipe will be given under the discussion of specific breads.

Muffins

Muffins will be discussed first because of the wide use of the muffin method of mixing. Good muffins have a rounded pebbled top and a symmetrical shape. The crust is golden brown, crisp, and tender. The muffin feels light in the hand. A cross section shows a moist crumb, medium-fine, evenly distributed air spaces, and no long, narrow tunnels. The muffin is tender and has a good flavor. It varies in richness according to the recipe. The richer muffins tend to be finer in grain than those containing less sugar and shortening.

To mix muffins, the dry ingredients are sifted together into a mixing bowl of suitable size, and a well is made in the center of the flour mixture. The

[1] Charles Dickens. *The Chimes.*

298

Table 14–1. *Proportions Used in Breads*

Product	Oven Temp. degrees F.	Flour, All-Purpose Sifted	Liquid	Fat or Oil	Eggs	Salt	Sugar	Baking Powder	Other Ingredients
Pour batters									
Griddle cakes		1 cup *	3/4–1 cup	1 Tbsp.	0–1	1/2 tsp.	0–1 Tbsp.	1 1/2–2 tsp.	
Waffles		1 cup *	3/4–1 cup	1–3 Tbsp.	1–2	1/2 tsp.	0–1 Tbsp.	1 1/4–2 tsp.	
Popovers	†	1 cup	1 cup	0–2 Tbsp.	2–3	1/2 tsp.			
Cream puffs	400	1 cup	1 cup	1/2 cup	4	1/2 tsp.			
Drop batters									
Muffins	400–425	1 cup *	1/2 cup	1–3 Tbsp.	1/2	1/2 tsp.	1–2 Tbsp.	1 1/2 tsp.	
Soft dough									
Biscuits	425–450	1 cup *	1/3–1/2 cup	2–3 Tbsp.		1/2 tsp.		1 1/2–2 tsp.	
Yeast Bread	375–400	1 cup	1/3 cup	0–1 Tbsp.		1/4 tsp.	1 tsp.–1 Tbsp.		1/3 package active dry yeast or 1/3 cake compressed yeast

* If self-rising flour is used, omit baking powder and salt.   † 425° F. for 20 minutes, then 350° F., or 400° F. for entire time.

Fig. 14–1. *A properly mixed muffin is shown at top, and an overbeaten muffin below. Both sides of the same half are shown in each case.*

eggs are beaten and milk, which has been brought to room temperature, is added, followed by oil or melted fat. The liquids are poured into the well in the center of the dry ingredients and mixed without hesitation just enough to dampen the dry ingredients but not enough to produce a smooth batter. Fifteen or sixteen mixing strokes are usually enough. If preferred, plastic fat[2] can be cut into the dry ingredients rather than melted and added to the liquid ingredients. Excess mixing, by developing gluten and causing loss of carbon dioxide, results in a product that has long, narrow tunnels extending from the bottom toward a peaked top. The muffin is tough, heavy, and uneven in grain. The proportion of flour to liquid in muffins is suitable for gluten development. Because extra sugar and fat interfere with gluten formation, the effects of over-mixing are less evident in using rich rather than plain muffin recipes. Rich muffins are likely to be made in institutions because

[2] A final step in the manufacture of hydrogenated shortening is plasticizing. The purpose is to produce the characteristic soft, creamy product which may be molded or shaped. Fats which are plastic over a fairly wide range of temperatures are easily handled in the making of pastry and cakes by conventional methods.

over-mixing is difficult to avoid when quantities are large. The effects of over-mixing are also less pronounced with cake or pastry than with all-purpose flour. Care should be taken in dipping the batter into the oiled muffin pans to avoid extra mixing. A scraper aids in slipping the batter into the cups of the muffin pan. Muffins should not be "dropped" from the spoon because this stretches the gluten. After the batter has been put into pans, it can be covered with a plastic or foil wrap and stored in a refrigerator for as long as 45 minutes before baking. Quick loaf breads, usually flavored with fruit and/or nuts, are mixed by the muffin method and similar precautions are needed in mixing and panning.

If desired, any one of the following additions may be made to a muffin recipe that contains 2 cups of flour, 2 tablespoons of fat, and 2 tablespoons of sugar:

$\frac{1}{2}$ cup minced crisp bacon
$\frac{1}{2}$ cup minced ham
1 cup grated cheese and $\frac{1}{4}$ cup milk
$\frac{1}{2}$–$\frac{3}{4}$ cup nuts
1 cup apples, chopped fine, $\frac{1}{4}$ cup sugar, $\frac{1}{2}$ teaspoon cinnamon
1 cup cooked dried apricots, well drained and chopped
1 cup blueberries, drained. Increase shortening to 4 tablespoons
    and sugar to 4 tablespoons
$\frac{3}{4}$ cup currants
$\frac{1}{2}$ cup dates and $\frac{1}{2}$ cup nuts, chopped
1 cup candied orange peel
1 cup raisins
Sprinkle with cinnamon and sugar.

Griddle Cakes

Griddle cakes, which are also called pancakes, usually contain ingredients similar to those in muffins. Although they are not always used in the batter, eggs improve the product. If the batter is to stand before it is cooked, it is desirable to use a double-action baking powder. If other ingredients are kept constant and the baking powder is increased, the batter appears progressively drier because of the many gas bubbles present. Griddle cakes are mixed in the same way as muffins. The batter should be stirred no more than necessary, even when dipping or pouring it onto the griddle.

Griddle cakes are cooked on a griddle if possible because they are more difficult to turn if cooked in a pan that has sides. The griddle may not require greasing, but if it does little fat should be used. The griddle is heated until it is hot but not smoking. A drop of water will dance on the griddle when the suitable temperature is reached. Batter is poured onto the griddle and cooked until the surface is full of bubbles that have opened and the batter has lost its sheen. The griddle cake is turned only once, and the other side is browned. The technique of cooking is largely responsible for producing griddle cakes that are evenly browned on both sides, of uniform thickness, and of fairly regular shape. Good griddle cakes are also light and tender, moderately moist but not sticky, and have a smooth tender crust, an even grain, and a pleasing flavor.

Substitutions and additions to the recipe produce a wide variety of griddle cakes. Frequently, sour milk and soda are substituted for sweet milk and baking powder; corn meal, oatmeal, whole wheat, or buckwheat are substituted for part of the flour; apples or blueberries may be added to the batter.

The French or Swedish pancakes—sometimes called crêpes, the French word for pancakes—are quite different from the pancakes that have been described. The mixture is about the same as that for popovers in that the batter is thin, high in egg, and lacks baking powder. Some of the batter is poured into a small griddle or fry pan which is tilted to allow it to spread in a thin layer over the entire surface of the pan. It is then turned and, when done, either rolled or folded into quarters. Crêpes can be served for break-

Fig. 14–2. *Pancakes are ready to be turned when the surface is full of bubbles and the underside is evenly browned.*

Courtesy of The Quaker Oats Company

Fig. 14–3. *When no more steam comes from the iron, waffles should be crisp and brown and ready to serve with a favorite fruit and syrup.*

fast with syrup or sweetened fruit, for lunch with a meat or mushroom filling, or for dessert with confectioners' sugar, fruit, or nuts.

Waffles

The batter for waffles is similar to that for griddle cakes but is usually higher in eggs and fat. Fat is needed in the batter because the waffle iron is not usually greased. In some recipes for waffles, especially those high in the number of eggs used, the eggs are separated, and the beaten whites are folded in after all other ingredients have been added. Yeast is substituted for baking powder in some waffle recipes, and the batter is allowed to rise before it is baked.

Waffles are quite different from griddle cakes because of the method of cooking. Waffle irons are made in such a way that a large surface of the batter is exposed to the heat of the iron and thus becomes crisp. The heat of the waffle iron must be right and just enough batter used to fill the iron. If the iron is opened before steaming stops, the waffle is likely to be torn and limp.

Popovers

Popovers are hollow shells leavened with steam held in by a crust made of flour and egg. The crust is golden brown, crisp, tender, and irregular in shape. Inside the shell are a few thin partitions that are slightly moist. Popovers are served like any other hot bread with butter and jam or honey if desired. They are not filled in the manner of cream puffs. They merit wider use than at present because they are easy to make, high in nutritive value, and attractive in appearance and texture. They are a feature attraction in some fine restaurants. To make them, the ingredients shown in Table 14–1 are simply beaten together until smooth. The long beating sometimes recommended for this product is not necessary. The volume of the popovers tends to increase with the amount of egg. Three eggs per cup of flour make a larger popover than two eggs, while one egg produces a small, muffin-like product. Fat is not essential but may be added for extra tenderness. An excessive amount of fat, especially in greasing the pans, is avoided because melted fat on the surface of the batter permits the escape of steam from the popover during baking and thus decreases volume. The pans used for baking popovers can be made of any oven-proof material but should, if possible, be deep and have rather straight sides. Deep custard cups are satisfactory and can be used easily if put in the oven in a wire rack. A hot oven is used so the popovers will expand rapidly. Temperature may be reduced during baking to permit the product to dry out and to prevent collapse of the popover after it is taken from the oven. Popovers are ready to remove from the oven when they feel quite firm to the touch. If they brown too much before becoming firm, the heat can be turned off and the baking finished in the cooling oven. Possible sogginess can be prevented by piercing the popovers with the tip of a paring knife as they come from the oven.

Yorkshire pudding is the traditional English dish served with roast beef. The ingredients are the same as those for popovers but without fat. Some fat from the drippings of the meat is poured into a baking pan, muffin pans, or custard cups. The batter is added and baked as for popovers. The Yorkshire pudding is served with the roast and gravy.

Cream puffs and eclairs are similar to popovers in that both products are leavened with steam, have a crisp outer shell and a hollow, slightly moist interior. However, the method of mixing the ingredients is quite different. The water and fat are heated to boiling, the flour and salt added all at once and the mixture stirred until a stiff paste forms which leaves the sides of the pan. The mixture is then removed from the heat and allowed to cool slightly. It should be cool enough not to coagulate the eggs when they are added. The eggs are added one at a time and beaten in thoroughly. There is no danger of overbeating and it is important to incorporate the eggs so there is no suggestion of lumpy spots. The eggs add structure and help to emulsify the fat in the paste. When ready for baking the mixture should be smooth with a slight sheen. Cream puffs are shaped into rounds and eclairs into oblongs on an oiled baking sheet. After baking 35 minutes at 205° C. (400° F.) the heat is turned off and the puffs left to dry for about 20 minutes.

Biscuits

At least two types of biscuits are popular in the United States. A biscuit with a large volume and a crumb that will peel off in flakes is obtained by using all-purpose flour, mixing and kneading the dough enough to develop the gluten, and rolling it about one-half inch thick. The preparation of this type is stressed because it seems to be a majority choice. The other type of biscuit is crusty, with a soft, tender crumb that is not flaky. Such biscuits are made from a soft flour, handled as little as possible to avoid gluten development, and usually rolled less than one-half inch thick. Buttermilk or sour milk with baking soda is frequently used. Good biscuits of either type are golden brown with a fairly smooth, level top. They are symmetrical in shape and uniform in size. The crust is crisp, tender, and free from excess flour. The crumb of biscuits is creamy white, slightly moist, tender, and light. The flavor is pleasing.

As indicated in Table 14–1, biscuits are made from a soft dough. Fresh whole milk proved to be better for making biscuits than diluted evaporated milk, reconstituted dry whole milk, or water.[3] An investigation of shortening agents indicated that hydrogenated vegetable oils produced more tender biscuits than vegetable oils or lard, although all of these fats could be used successfully for biscuits.[4] In this study, three tablespoons of fat per cup of flour proved satisfactory.

To prepare biscuits the dry ingredients are sifted into a bowl of suitable size, and the cold fat is added and cut into the dry ingredients with a pastry blender, two knives, a fork, or the fingers until the mixture resembles coarse corn meal. The liquid is added all at once and stirred vigorously with a fork until the mixture stiffens and leaves the sides of the bowl, which usually requires about 20 strokes. The dough is turned out on a lightly floured pastry cloth, board, or a piece of waxed paper and kneaded lightly about 15 strokes, then rolled until it is about one-half inch thick. It is usually cut with a biscuit cutter floured between each cut and pushed straight down without twisting so the biscuits will be symmetrical. Scraps are combined, rerolled, and cut. An alternate method is to cut the entire dough into square, rectangular, or diamond shapes. In this method all the dough is cut at one time. The cut dough is lifted with a wide spatula and placed about one-half inch apart on an ungreased baking sheet. The cut biscuit dough can be allowed to stand on the baking sheet about one-half hour at room temperature or longer in a refrigerator before it is baked. Drop biscuits can be prepared more rapidly

[3] A. M. Briant and M. R. Hutchins. Influence of Ingredients on Thiamine Retention and Quality in Baking Powder Biscuits. *Cereal Chemistry*, 23: 512–520 (1946).

[4] R. H. Matthews and E. H. Dawson. Performance of Fats and Oils in Pastry and Biscuits. *Cereal Chemistry*, 40: 291–302 (1963).

Fig. 14–4. To prepare biscuits: Stir dry ingredients together, and then cut in the fat with a pastry blender.

Blend in enough milk to make a soft dough.

Stir with a fork until the mixture thickens.

Turn out the dough onto a lightly floured board and knead lightly.

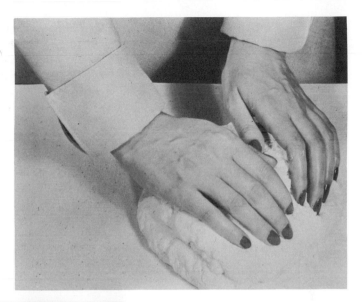

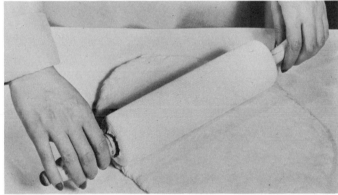

Roll out the dough until it is about ¹/₂ inch thick.

Cut into rounds with a floured cutter and place ¹/₂ inch apart on an un-greased baking sheet.

than biscuits made in the manner just described. Enough milk is added in making the biscuits to form a thick batter which is then dropped onto an oiled baking sheet or into oiled muffin pans and baked. Such biscuits are irregular in shape but have an attractive crisp crust.

The basic biscuit recipe containing two cups of flour can be varied by mixing any one of the following into the dry ingredients:

$\frac{1}{2}$ cup grated cheese
$\frac{1}{3}$ cup minced crisp bacon
$\frac{1}{2}$ cup crushed potato chips
4 tablespoons minced chives
$\frac{1}{2}$ cup chopped nuts
$\frac{1}{2}$ cup raisins
$\frac{1}{2}$ cup dates
$\begin{cases} 1 \text{ tablespoon orange marmalade, } \frac{2}{3} \text{ cup orange juice, 1 egg,} \\ \frac{1}{2} \text{ cup chopped nuts. Omit milk.} \end{cases}$
$\begin{cases} \frac{1}{4} \text{ teaspoon dry mustard, } \frac{1}{2} \text{ teaspoon dry sage, } 1\frac{1}{4} \text{ teaspoon} \\ \text{ caraway seeds, } \frac{1}{4} \text{ teaspoon curry powder.} \end{cases}$

Probable Causes for Deviations

If the quality of quick breads is unsatisfactory, it may be possible to find the cause in the following tabulation:

Product	Deviation	Cause
Muffins	Unevenly browned	Too hot an oven
		Oven does not heat uniformly
		Pans filled too full
		Wrong proportions
		Too much beating
	Peaks	Pans filled too full
		Heat uneven
		Too much stirring
		Insufficient leavening
		Too stiff a mixture
		Too hot an oven
	Tough	Wrong proportions
		Too much mixing
	Heavy and irregular in grain. Tunnels.	Insufficient leavening
		Too much mixing
	Smooth crust	Too much mixing
	Hard crust	Too long baking
		Too high a temperature
	Harsh, dry crumb	Too stiff a batter
		Overbaked

Product, cont.	*Deviation*, cont.	*Cause*, cont.
Griddle cakes	Tough	Too much mixing
		Insufficient leavening
		Too slow cooking
		Wrong proportion of ingredients
	Not thoroughly cooked	Batter too stiff
		Griddle too hot
	Unevenly browned	Griddle too hot
		Griddle of uneven heat
	Poor flavor	Ingredients with "off flavor"
	Heavy	Too much mixing
		Standing too long before cooked
		Insufficient leavening
	Pale color	Griddle not hot enough
	Too thick	Batter too stiff
	Too dark a brown	Overcooked
Waffles	Tough and wilted	Same as for griddle cakes
	Irregular in shape	Not enough batter in iron
	Run out of iron	Too much batter in iron
	Stick to iron	Batter not the correct consistency
		Iron not properly cared for
		Iron not proper temperature
		Lack of fat in batter
	Poor flavor	Same as for griddle cakes
	Heavy	Same as for griddle cakes
	Pale color	Same as for griddle cakes
	Too dark a brown	Same as for griddle cakes
Popovers	Tough	Not baked long enough
		Oven not hot enough
	Hard	Baked too long
		Oven temperature too high
		Oven temperature not reduced when sufficiently browned
	Fail to "pop"	Wrong proportion of ingredients
		Not mixed sufficiently
		Oven not hot enough
Cream puffs	Collapsed walls	Not baked long enough
	Small volume	Water and fat boiled too long
		Not enough egg due to use of small eggs
	Fail to puff	Water, fat, and flour cooked too long

Product, cont.	*Deviation,* cont.	*Cause,* cont.
Biscuits	Tough	Lack of fat
		Too much mixing
	Pale crust	Too slow an oven
		Too stiff a dough
		Flour on surface
	Uneven shape	Carelessness in handling
		Uneven heat
	Uneven brown	Uneven shape
		Uneven heat
	Flat and heavy	Wrong proportion of ingredients
		Improper mixing
	Coarse, porous grain	Improper mixing
	Harsh, dry, crumb	Same as for muffins
	Hard crust	Same as for muffins
	Crumbly and oily	Too high a proportion of fat

Yeast Breads

A wide variety of yeast products is possible—much greater than many of us realize. Some of the variations are due to the ingredients used. White flour of varying strengths, whole wheat flour, rye flour, and other cereal products such as oatmeal, bran, or corn meal can be used. The ratio of ingredients also affects the product. Such large amounts of fat, eggs, and sugar can be added that the product is more like cake than bread, or the ingredients can be reduced to the four essential ones, which are flour, water, yeast, and salt, to make what is often called a "lean" bread.

Yeast doughs can be shaped in many different ways. Hearth breads, which are more widely used in Europe than in the United States, are traditionally baked on the hearth of the oven. In a bakery, the hearth of an oven is usually a piece of flat metal, whereas in Colonial homes it was brick. Hearth breads can be baked in the home on a cookie sheet sprinkled with corn meal. Hearth breads such as those used in France and Italy are usually lean so that the crust of the bread will be crisp. Steam or a pan of water is put into the oven to improve the crust. Other hearth breads such as braided breads have a soft crust and therefore may be high in sugar, fat, milk, and even egg. Many rolls are also baked like hearth bread.

In the United States, most bread is baked in a bread pan and made from a formula such as that shown in Table 14–1. Unless otherwise stated, the discussion that follows will apply to bread of this type.

Ingredients and Proportions

Flour. The flour in bread is important because, as explained in the previous chapter, it forms gluten when mixed with liquid. The framework of dough consists of gluten which expands as carbon dioxide is released by the yeast. Gluten, when coagulated by the heat of the oven, also forms the framework of the finished loaf. Bakers prefer to use bread flour because it gives a large loaf of good quality. Homemakers are more accustomed to using all-purpose flour, which requires less mixing and rising than bread flour. Flour from soft wheat is sometimes used for bread in areas where it is produced. Bread recipes may require adjustment when this is done because soft wheat flour absorbs less moisture and forms gluten of softer quality than hard wheat flour. To avoid overextending the gluten, mixing and rising times are reduced. The amounts of yeast and sugar may be increased slightly so the dough will rise rapidly.

Whole wheat flour or rye flour can be substituted for part or all of the white flour in bread. Either of these flours reduces the volume of bread, and for this reason they are usually combined with white flour. Whole wheat flour that is fresh and ground fine usually makes better bread than whole wheat flour that has been stored or ground coarsely.

Liquid. The liquid in bread dough may be milk, tap water, or water in which potatoes have been cooked. Potato water seems to accelerate the action of yeast but may make the bread dark in color. Milk improves the food value and quality of pan bread and may also delay its staling. Fresh fluid milk is scalded and cooled before it is used in bread to improve its baking quality. Evaporated milk requires no further heat treatment. Nonfat dry milk is sometimes used by homemakers without scalding but it is generally recommended that it be stirred into boiling water. The proportion of liquid to flour must produce a dough of the correct consistency. More liquid is required with flour from hard than from soft wheat.

Yeast. Either active dry or compressed yeast may be used. Although a starter is effective in making bread, it is seldom used today because of the availability of commercial yeast products of high quality. As explained in Chapter 13, active dry yeast may be blended with the dry ingredients using part of the flour, or it may be reconstituted in water between 40° and 45° C. (104° and 113° F.), and compressed yeast is crumbled into water or other liquid at about 35° C. (95° F.). The speed of fermentation can usually be increased by a modest increase in the amount of yeast but a point is soon reached when further increase in the amount of yeast does not accelerate fermentation but simply gives the bread a yeasty flavor. Recipes are more likely to recommend less yeast than shown in Table 14–1 rather than more.

Sugar. The action of yeast can also be accelerated by the addition of sugar to the dough because sugar is a ready source of food for the yeast. When doughs are made without sugar, the yeast first uses the small amount of sugar normally present in flour, and then an enzyme in the flour called diastase or amylase acts on the starch to form sugar. This enzymatic action takes time and thus delays rising. Although the addition of a small amount of sugar to the dough makes the dough rise faster, increasing the level of sugar beyond a certain point delays rising because a large amount of sugar acts as a preservative and thus delays the action of the yeast. When sugar is increased much beyond the upper level shown in Table 14–1, it may be necessary to increase the amount of yeast. Large amounts of sugar also soften the gluten. Doughs for sweet rolls or coffee cake sometimes contain rather high levels of sugar, yeast, and fat. In addition to supplying food for the yeast, sugar adds flavor to the bread and contributes to the browning of the crust during baking.

Salt. Salt is essential to the normal flavor of bread but is sometimes omitted from bread that is to be used in special diets. Salt tends to control the action of the yeast and strengthens the gluten.

Fat. Although fat is not an essential ingredient of bread, it improves the quality of pan bread when used in moderate amounts. It adds flavor to the bread, makes it more tender, and perhaps even more important, may delay staling. Although large amounts of shortening are used in some specialty breads such as Danish pastry, they are not used in pan bread because they interfere with the formation of gluten.

Eggs. Eggs, an optional ingredient, add color, flavor, and nutritive value. Eggs also aid in formation of a fine crumb and tender crust.

Other ingredients. Seasonings such as spices and herbs add zest to bread particularly if it is necessary to make salt-free bread. Fruits and nuts add color, texture, and flavor.

Mixing

Most homemade bread is mixed as a straight dough, which means that all of the ingredients are added before the dough is allowed to rise. The yeast may be reconstituted or, if active dry yeast is used, mixed with a part of the flour before adding it to the liquid. The milk is cooled after scalding so it will not inactivate the yeast. It is convenient to add the flour to the liquid so the dough can be adjusted to the correct consistency. It is often recommended that the ingredients be beaten well after about one-half of the flour has been added. At this point it is easy to beat the mixture thoroughly either by hand or with a household-type electric mixer. All of the flour for bread can be added in the mixers used for institutional cookery and in a few heavy duty household mixers that have a dough hook. Kneading is unnecessary after dough has been mixed adequately on such a machine. When an ordinary household electric mixer is used, mixing cannot be completed by machine because the motor is likely to overheat. The remaining flour is stirred in, and then the dough is kneaded. At the beginning of the kneading period, dough tends to cling to the board, but as it is worked, water is taken up by the gluten and the dough becomes stiffer. Care should be taken not to add too much flour. After the dough has reached the correct consistency, only a light film of flour is used on the board to avoid making the dough too stiff. If kneading is done with a light

Courtesy of the Wheat Flour Institute

Fig. 14–5. *Dough formation parallels the developing of gluten, as shown here from left to right: flour moistened and stirred; gluten partly developed; gluten fully developed.*

motion and tearing the dough is avoided, the dough does not stick to the board after it has been kneaded a few strokes. The dough is kneaded lightly but thoroughly until the gluten is well developed and the dough feels soft and pliable. A definite kneading time cannot be given because it depends upon the experience of the person making the bread, the size of the recipe, and the quality of the flour. Soft wheat flours require only a short kneading period, whereas all-purpose and bread flours require more kneading. Dough that has been kneaded sufficiently is satiny and smooth and silvery blisters may be noted just under the surface when the ball of dough is turned in the light. When mixing is done by hand, it is much more likely that the dough will be undermixed than overmixed. It is easy to over-mix a dough only when a heavy duty mechanical mixer is used.

Fermentation   When kneading is completed, the dough is formed into a round ball with a smooth surface, placed smooth side down in a greased bowl, and immediately turned over so that the surface of the dough is lightly greased. The dough is allowed to rise at a temperature of 27° to 29° C. (80° to 85° F.). Drying of the surface can be prevented by putting the dough in a cabinet or unlighted oven with a pan of hot water or in a large pan of warm water that is covered. If the surface of the dough dries out during rising, a crust is formed that can be seen as a streak in the loaf. Temperatures higher than those suggested are avoided because they may encourage the growth of undesirable microorganisms or even destroy the yeast.

During fermentation, carbon dioxide formed by the yeast causes the dough to rise, the acidity of the dough increases slightly, flavor develops in the bread, and the character of the gluten is changed. The dough is allowed to rise until it has approximately doubled in bulk, as indicated by the fact that when the dough is pressed lightly with a finger the impression remains after the finger has been withdrawn.

If the dough has been made with bread flour, it is "punched down." This is done by putting the hand in the center of the dough, folding the edges of the dough to the center, turning it over to form a new ball, and placing it in a warm place to rise. If the dough has been made with all-purpose flour, a second rise usually makes little difference in the quality of the bread and can be omitted. If it is not convenient to shape the dough for the pan immediately, it should be punched down rather than allowed to rise too long. The motions used in punching dough or later in molding it for the pan should be light, because vigorous manipulation after the dough has risen is likely to injure the gluten and result in a loaf that has a coarse grain and thick cell walls. If dough rises in the bowl a second time, it is allowed to rise until the impression of a finger remains in the dough.

If enough dough has been made for more than one loaf, it is cut into portions of the desired size, made into round balls, and allowed to stand for about fifteen minutes. A shallow bread pan is chosen if possible because the volume of bread baked in a deep pan is smaller than that of bread baked in a pan with lower sides. Several methods can be used to form the loaf. Two that are easy to describe start with flattening the dough into a rectangular shape with the hands or with a rolling pin. The width of the rectangle should be slightly less than the length of the baking pan. The dough can then be rolled, starting on the narrow side, like a jelly roll, the edges sealed, and placed with the sealed side down in a greased baking pan. An alternate method is to fold two sides of the dough so that the dough is in the form of a triangle. Then, starting with the apex of the triangle, the dough is rolled and shaped into a loaf. The dough is allowed to rise in the pan at the same temperature used for the first rise. Bakers speak of "proofing" rather than rising when the dough is in the pan. Proofing continues until the dough has approximately doubled in bulk. If desired, a finger can be pushed gently into one end of the dough near the edge of the pan to check the degree of rising. The amount of rising in the pan does much to determine the size of the loaf. Dough that has not risen long enough makes a small, compact loaf. Dough that has risen too long, however, may rise and then fall, thus causing the bread to have an open, crumbly texture.

Baking

The risen dough is baked in an oven preheated to a temperature of 190° to 205° C. (375° to 400° F.). The baking time is usually 35 to 45 minutes for a one-pound loaf but varies with the oven temperature, the size of the loaf, the composition of the dough, and the type of crust desired. Long baking thickens the crust and decreases the thiamine content of the bread because this B-vitamin is sensitive to heat. During baking, rising continues until the dough becomes hot enough to inactivate the yeast. If bread must be baked before it has risen fully, the temperature of the oven may be lower for a brief period to permit the dough to rise. The best volume is obtained, however, if fully risen dough is put into a hot oven because the heat of the oven causes a rapid expansion of the gas in the dough called "oven spring." It is interesting to watch the dough through a glass oven door, but the oven door should not be opened during this period; the resulting temperature drop would prevent some of the increase in volume. Oven spring is greater when a hard wheat flour has been used because the gluten of such flour more effectively retains the expanding gas than that of soft wheat flour. During baking, gluten coagulates and starch is gelatinized to form the structure of the loaf.

The bread is removed from the oven as soon as tapping the crust produces a hollow sound, taken out of the pans, and put on a wire rack to prevent steaming and softening of the crust. The loaves are cooled uncovered, and the tops brushed with fat if a soft crust is desired.

Sponge Method

Although the straight dough method is the usual one for bread baked at home, other methods are sometimes used. In the sponge method the yeast, the liquid, part of the flour, and often some of the sugar are mixed together to form a drop batter. This "sponge" is allowed to rise until it is full of bubbles, which requires from three hours to overnight. The rising time need not be controlled carefully. The spongy appearance of the risen mixture accounts for the name of the method. The remaining ingredients for the bread are then added and the dough allowed to rise as for the straight dough method. The rising time of this dough is usually shorter than that for dough made by the straight dough method. The sponge method was almost universally used by homemakers before good commercial yeast was widely available. It may be convenient for homemakers who wish to start their bread in the evening and finish it the next morning.

Probable Causes for Deviations

White bread of high quality is large for its weight. The top of the loaf is well rounded and free from cracks or bulges. The crust is an even golden brown and is relatively thin. The grain is fine and even because the cells are small and the cell walls thin. The crumb is smooth, soft, elastic, creamy white, and has a silken sheen in the light. The bread does not crumble enough to make cutting difficult. The flavor is sweet and nutty; the odor is pleasant with no suggestion of a sour or yeasty aroma.

Homemade bread is more similar in volume and texture to the compact loaves now sold at premium prices in some stores than to most commercial bread, which is large in volume and soft in texture. Most of the bread on the market is made from flour higher in protein than the all-purpose used at home and includes softeners such as the mono- and diglycerides used as emulsifiers in hydrogenated vegetable fats. Some of these agents are so effective in softening the crumb of bread that their use is limited by federal regulations[5] so that customers will not be deceived about the age of bread.

If the quality of yeast bread is unsatisfactory, it may be possible to find the cause in the following tabulation:

[5] *Code of Federal Regulations,* Title 21, Part 17.1.

Deviation	*Cause*
Uneven shape	Improper molding Too much dough for pan Insufficient proof
Heavy	Low-grade flour Insufficient or excessive proof
Crackled crust	Too rapid cooling in a draft
Crust bulges and cracks	Too stiff dough Uneven heat in baking Insufficient proof
Thick crust	Too slow baking
Tough crust	Insufficient proof Low grade flour Too much handling of risen dough
Pale crust	Too slow an oven Too much salt Drying of dough during rising Too little sugar
Dark crumb	Kind of liquid or flour used Unfavorable conditions, as insufficient or excessive proof, wrong temperature while rising, too cool an oven, or old or stale yeast
Streaked loaf	Poorly mixed Addition of flour during molding Drying of dough on top before shaping
Crumbly loaf	Weak flour Wheat flour substitutes Excessive or insufficient proof
Coarse-grained	Inferior yeast Low-grade flour Excessive proof Wrong temperature and other unfavorable conditions
Sour taste	Poor yeast or flour Rising too long Too high a temperature while rising Too slow baking Incomplete baking

Specialty Yeast Products

Rolls and Coffee Cake. Rolls and coffee cake are often made from a dough that is sweeter, richer, and softer than that used for loaves of bread. Such doughs often contain eggs. The process of making these products differs little from that of making bread. Adequate development of gluten either by kneading or beating helps make a satisfactory product.

Dough for rolls or coffee cake is usually allowed to rise in the bowl and always allowed to proof after it has been shaped. Great variety is possible by shaping the dough in different ways, by additions to the dough, and by the frostings and decorations used. Rolls from plain bread dough can be baked quickly in an oven at 219° C. (425° F.). Rich doughs, however, are baked at lower temperatures, 177° to 190° C. (350° to 375° F.), to prevent excessive browning of the crust.

Roll doughs are sometimes stored in a refrigerator so that portions of the dough can be baked at intervals. Care must be taken to prevent crust formation, and the storage time should be limited to less than one week. It may be easier in homes where there is adequate freezer space to bake all the rolls at once and store some of them in the freezer until they are needed.

English muffins can be made from the dough used for yeast bread or rolls. After the dough has risen, it is turned out on a board that has been sprinkled generously with corn meal and is turned so that all surfaces are covered with the meal. It is then rolled out about one-half inch thick and cut with a round cutter or tumbler about three inches in diameter. The cut dough is placed on a baking sheet covered with corn meal, allowed to rise, and cooked on a moderately warm 171° C. (340° F.) griddle for about fifteen minutes. It is turned several times.

Pizza. Pizza, originally an Italian dish, has become popular in the United States since the Second World War. Although pizzas are often purchased frozen, in some other convenience form, or ready-to-eat, they can be made at home rather easily. Bread dough is rolled into a circular shape and put on a cookie sheet or in a layer cake pan. The edges are raised slightly. After the dough has risen about fifteen minutes, it is covered with the filling, which usually includes tomato sauce, fresh or drained canned tomatoes, onion, cheese, herbs such as oregano or basil, and anchovies or meat. The favorite cheese is Mozzarella. The pizzas are baked in a hot oven (218° C. or 425° F.). Many variations of fillings are possible with such ingredients as green or black olives, different sausages, mushrooms, shrimp, green peppers, raw spinach, and even such fillings as fruits and nuts that make the pizza suitable for dessert. Small pizzas can be made rapidly from English muffins split in half, toasted, covered with the desired filling ingredients, and topped with a slice of cheese. The pizza is placed under the broiler until the cheese is melted.

Convenience Forms

Both quick and yeast breads are now available in a wide variety of convenience forms including ready-to-serve, brown-and-serve, frozen, refrigerated, and mixes. It is not always easy to evaluate the quality and the cost in money and time of using the available forms.

Without question active time required for the preparation of homemade products is greater than that required for the convenience forms. Active time includes the time necessary for preparation, assembling ingre-

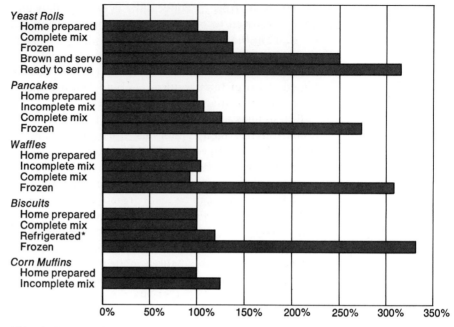

*Chemically leavened

Fig. 14–6. *Comparative cost per serving of breads.* (Calculated from Harp and Dunham, in *Comparative Costs to Consumers of Convenience Foods and Home-Prepared Foods.* Marketing Research Report No. 609, U.S. Department of Agriculture, 1963.)

dients, and equipment but not for cleaning up. Total time is active time plus the time required for thawing, rising, baking, or cooking the foods.

Although results of a survey of the retail cost per serving of bread in various forms reported in 1963[6] indicated waffles made from a complete mix were less costly than home-prepared forms, and the cost of biscuits in these two forms was the same, a more recent publication[7] shows waffles prepared from a mix cost 9 per cent more and biscuits from a mix cost 22 per cent more. Ready-to-serve waffles cost 191 per cent more and ready to cook biscuits 177 per cent more (see Table 19–1). The 1963 report showed incomplete mixes, which generally require the addition of egg and at least

[6] H. H. Harp and D. F. Dunham. *Comparative Costs to Consumers of Convenience Foods and Home-Prepared Foods.* Marketing Research Report No. 609, United States Department of Agriculture, Washington, D.C., 1963.

[7] *Family Economics Review.* June, 1971. Consumer and Food Economics Research Division, Agricultural Research Service, United States Department of Agriculture, Washington, D.C., p. 11.

one other ingredient, were more expensive than the corresponding home-prepared products. Because of high processing and distribution costs, and in some cases low sales volume, pancakes, waffles, and biscuits were most expensive in the frozen form. Frozen yeast rolls and refrigerated biscuits were somewhat more expensive than their home-prepared counterparts. The most expensive forms of yeast rolls were brown-and-serve and ready-to-serve.

The baked products prepared from mixes were often softer than home-prepared baked products. This was true of some of the corn muffin and yeast roll mixes. Ready-to-serve rolls were as soft as home-prepared rolls, but the brown-and-serve rolls were firmer. Home-prepared and frozen baking powder biscuits were about equally tender, whereas those prepared from the other commercial products, especially refrigerated biscuits, were less tender than the home-prepared biscuits.[8]

Mixes can be made at home by sifting together the dry ingredients and cutting in the shortening. Such a mix may be made in quantity and stored for periods up to six weeks without refrigeration or longer in the refrigerator. Probably the mix most often prepared is one from which biscuits can be made by adding milk and other products such as muffins, griddle cakes, waffles, and coffee cake by using a few additional ingredients. Mixes containing corn meal are popular in some areas. Because of the time required to make the mix, homemade mixes do not always save time; however, they can be made at the homemaker's convenience, and they do permit rapid preparation of quick breads at meal time.

Breads can also be frozen at home. Skillful use of the freezer makes it possible even for a small family to enjoy a great variety of breads. Home baking is often more feasible if part of the products can be frozen for use at a later date. Muffins, biscuits, popovers, and all yeast products can be frozen after baking. Batters for popovers and muffins cannot be successfully frozen, but yeast doughs can be frozen. Yeast doughs are frozen more successfully before than after shaping. Storage times are no longer than six weeks for dough but three to nine months for the baked products. Because of the short storage time, the long thawing period, and shaping, rising, and baking that are necessary, it usually seems easier to freeze yeast products after they have been baked rather than as dough.

Activities

1. Make from the original ingredients quick breads of several types with and without variations.
a. Compare and score the products.
b. Estimate the cost per serving and compare with that of yeast bread.
c. Repeat with a variety of yeast breads and rolls.

[8] H. H. Harp and D. F. Dunham.

2. Make several yeast products by the batter or no-knead process.

3. Compare biscuits made from all-purpose flour, pastry flour, self-rising flour, a mix, refrigerated dough, and frozen dough if available. Compare the quality and cost of the products.

4. Compare the quality and cost of rolls, biscuits, muffins, griddle cakes, and waffles made from the different convenience forms and home-prepared. When comparing cost, calculate for equal weights of the baked products. Select recipes for the home-prepared products that will give products as similar as possible to the convenience forms.

5. Use hot roll mix or biscuit mix to make several products. Shape in different ways and glaze, or frost, and trim with sugar, nuts, candied fruit, or coconut.

6. Compare the quality and cost of ready-to-serve pizza and pizza made from the frozen product, a mix, and the original ingredients.

References

GRISWOLD, R. M. *The Experimental Study of Foods.* Boston: Houghton Mifflin Company. 1962. Chapter 11.

HALLIDAY, E. G. and I. T. NOBLE. *Hows and Whys of Cooking.* Chicago: The University of Chicago Press. 1946. Chapters 3 and 6.

POTTER, N. N. *Food Science.* Westport, Conn.: The Avi Publishing Company, Inc. 1968. Pp. 24–30.

Convenience Bread Products

Finished Foods—a Fourth Report. Refrigerated Biscuits, Sweet Rolls, and Dinner Rolls. *J. Home Econ.,* 56: 735–738 (1964).

Finished Foods—a Fifth Report. Pancakes and Quick Breads from Mixes. *J. Home Econ.,* 57: 117–120 (1965).

Finished Foods—a Sixth Report. Coffeecake and Gingerbread from Mixes. *J. Home Econ.,* 57: 357–360 (1965).

FISHER, E. J. *Creative Baking with Mixes.* Oregon State Univ. Coop. Ext. Serv. Ext. Circ. 697 (Reprinted 1962).

The History of Mixes. Ten-Year Success Story. *Prac. Home Econ.,* 4: 76, 160 (1958).

SNOW, P. R. and G. ARMBRUSTER. Management Aspects of Convenience Foods. *J. Home Econ.,* 53: 442–446 (1961).

Homemade Mixes

AMICK, G. and C. RODGERS. *Missouri Mix for Home Baking.* Univ. Missouri Agr. Exp. Sta. Bull. 748 (1960).

DEPARTMENT OF FOODS AND NUTRITION, KANSAS STATE UNIVERSITY. *Practical Cookery.* New York: John Wiley & Sons, Inc. 1966. P. 52.

GOTHARD, M. The Quality and Practicability of a Refrigerated Prepared Dry Corn Meal Muffin Mix. *J. Home Econ.,* 43: 713–715 (1951).

HINDMAN, M. S., M. J. MARBUT, and J. H. MITCHELL, JR. *Corn Meal Mixes. Preparation and Use in Breads, Cakes, and Other Products.* South Carolina Agr. Exp. Sta. Clemson Agr. College Bull. 493 (1961).

Homemade Mixes for Convenience. Oregon State Univ. Coop. Ext. Serv. Ext. Cir. 715 (1962).

SUNDERLIN, G. *Master Mix.* Purdue Univ. Coop. Ext. Serv. H.E. 511(1971).

15

cakes and pies

Cakes and pies are considered together in this chapter because they are flour mixtures that are used for dessert. Both are favorites in American homes, although pies are more likely to occur on restaurant menus than cakes. The opposite is true in Europe where the array of cakes is bewildering and pies are less frequently offered for dessert than cakes, although they may appear as a main dish when made with meat or poultry.

Cakes

Cakes include both shortened and foam cakes. Shortened cakes contain a chemical leavening with the exception of pound cake for which the leavening is air beaten into eggs and shortening. Foam cakes are high in egg into which air is beaten. True angel food and sponge cakes contain neither shortening nor chemical leavening, although some sponge cakes contain small amounts of baking powder. Chiffon cakes have been placed under foam cakes, but since they contain oil they could also be considered as shortened cakes.

Shortened Cakes

Proportions for shortened cakes are shown in Table 15–1. Variations from these figures are possible since cakes may vary from plain ones that are muffinlike to rich cakes that are high in fat, sugar, and eggs, but as a rule proportions of two or more ingredients are varied in order that a suitable balance among ingredients is maintained. Rich cakes have the advantage of good keeping qualities. Plain cakes are often served on the day they are baked and frequently while still warm. They may be accompanied by soft custard or a sweet sauce such as chocolate, vanilla, or fruit.

The shortened cake formula in Table 15–1 is for yellow cake in which the whole egg is used. White cakes contain only egg whites, whereas gold cakes, which are less frequently used than yellow or white cakes, contain only egg yolks. Many variations of shortened cakes can be made, such as spice cake, chocolate cake, marble cake, gingerbread, and many others.

Ingredients. Accurate measurements of the ingredients used for cakes are especially necessary because recipes are carefully balanced and may fail if correct measurements are not used. Cake ingredients should be at room

Table 15-1. Proportions Used in Cakes and Pastry *

Product	Oven Temp. degrees F.	Sifted Flour	Liquid	Fat or Oil	Eggs	Sugar	Salt	Baking Powder	Other Ingredients
Shortened cakes	350–375	1 cup cake or all-purpose	1/4–1/2 cup	2–4 Tbsp.	1/2–1	1/2–3/4 cup	1/8–1/4 tsp.	1–2 tsp.	Flavoring
Angel food cake	350–375	1 cup cake			1–1 3/4 cups whites	1 1/4–1 1/2 cups	1/2 tsp.		Flavoring 3/4–2 tsp. cream of tartar
Sponge cake	350–375	1 cup cake	0–3 Tbsp.		5–6	1 cup	1/2 tsp.	0–1/4 tsp.	Flavoring 0–3/4 tsp. cream of tartar
Chiffon Cake	325	1 cup cake	3/8–1/3 cup	1/4 cup salad oil	3	2/3 cup	1/2 tsp.	1 1/4–1 1/2 tsp.	Flavoring 1/4 tsp. cream of tartar
Pastry	400–450	1 cup all-purpose	2–3 Tbsp.	4–5 Tbsp.			1/2 tsp.		

* In general, proportions found in recipes for cakes and pastry fall within the limits shown in this table. However, for special products they may differ considerably.

temperature so that air can be incorporated into them easily by beating and so that they blend well.

Cake flour usually produces larger, softer, and more velvety cakes than all-purpose flour. If all-purpose flour is substituted, the volume of flour is reduced by about one-eighth because two cups of cake flour weigh about the same as one and three-fourths cups of all-purpose flour (see Table 13–2). Adjustment of the volume is also necessary if instant flour is used.[1] The liquid in shortened cakes is usually milk, although in some recipes it may be water, fruit juice, sour milk, or buttermilk. Although diluted evaporated milk or reconstituted nonfat dry milk can be substituted for fresh whole milk, other substitutions should be avoided because water gives a more moist product than an equal volume of milk; and fruit juice, sour milk, or buttermilk requires the substitution of baking soda for part of the baking powder.

Hydrogenated fats are commonly used for making cakes. The emulsifiers they contain help in distributing the ingredients evenly throughout the batter and in retaining air by reducing the size and increasing the number of air cells in the batter. This helps to produce a cake with fine even grain. Butter and margarine are sometimes used in cakes because of their flavor, but their creaming qualities are not quite so good as those of hydrogenated fats that contain emulsifiers. Neither lard nor vegetable oils hold air well in cake batters. They can, however, be used for cakes if air is incorporated by folding into the batter eggs or egg whites beaten with or without sugar.

Before fats containing emulsifiers were available, the weights of flour and sugar in cakes were approximately equal, which means that about two cups of flour were used for each cup of sugar. The use of emulsifiers has made possible "high-ratio" cakes that contain higher proportions of sugar than cakes made from shortenings without emulsifiers.

When a certain number of eggs is specified in the cake recipe, it is assumed that medium or large eggs will be used. To avoid variations in size of eggs, the amount of whites for angel food cakes is usually given in cups. Frozen or dried eggs can be substituted for fresh eggs. Any type of baking powder can be used successfully in cakes.

Chocolate cake is better when made from a special recipe rather than by modifying one of the formulas in Table 15–1. Cocoa is sifted with the dry ingredients, whereas chocolate is melted over hot water before it is added to the batter. Although small amounts of soda improve the quality of chocolate cake, large amounts give it an undesirable flavor. The color of chocolate cake is redder if soda is used and redder with phosphate or tartrate than with double action baking powder.[2]

[1] *Agricultural Research,* 15: (10), April 1967. United States Department of Agriculture, Washington, D.C., p. 16.

[2] A. M. Briant, L. L. Weaver, and H. E. Skodvin. *Quality and Thiamine Retention in Plain and Chocolate Cakes and in Gingerbread.* Cornell University Agricultural Experiment Station Memoirs No. 332, 1954.

Mixing Methods. Several methods, which vary in the time required for mixing and in the quality of the cake produced, are now used for combining the ingredients of cakes. Any one of the methods must be followed carefully in all its details to insure success.

One of the most rapid but least satisfactory methods of making cake with plastic shortening is the muffin method. The dry ingredients including the sugar are sifted together; the beaten egg, milk, and melted fat are combined, added to the dry ingredients, and beaten until smooth. Cakes made by this method are usually acceptable when warm, especially if they are served with a sauce, but do not keep so well as cakes made by some of the other methods.

Oil can be used in cakes by a modification of the muffin method.[3] The flour, sugar, baking powder, and salt are sifted into a bowl; and the oil, egg yolks, liquid, and flavoring are added in the order mentioned. They are mixed thoroughly, and then the batter is folded into stiffly beaten egg whites. Sometimes only part of the sugar is sifted with the flour, while the remainder is beaten into the egg whites.

The conventional method of mixing requires more time than the other methods discussed in this section. A solid fat such as hydrogenated fat is creamed until soft and plastic. Sugar is then added gradually with much creaming and mixing until the mass is light, fluffy, and of about the consistency of whipped cream. Many air bubbles are beaten into the mixture during this process. For yellow cake, either beaten eggs or egg yolks are added to and thoroughly blended with the creamed fat and sugar. The flour, baking powder, and salt are sifted together, and about one-fifth of these dry ingredients is added and mixed thoroughly for about half a minute. Flavoring is blended with the milk, which is added to the creamed mixture alternately with the dry ingredients in about four portions. After each addition of milk, the mixture is stirred slightly. After each addition of flour, it is mixed thoroughly but for no longer than about ten seconds. After the last portion of flour has been added, the mixture is beaten for about fifteen seconds if a tartrate or phosphate baking powder is used and for about one minute if a SAS-phosphate baking powder is used. If the eggs were separated or if white cake is being made, whites beaten stiff but not dry are folded into the batter after all the other ingredients have been added. The egg whites are mixed thoroughly for about one-half minute so that they will be well blended with the other ingredients. When an electric mixer is used, gradual addition of the ingredients is less important than in hand mixing. The fat, sugar, and eggs can be put into the mixing bowl at once and beaten together thoroughly, or the fat and sugar can be beaten together before the eggs are added. Sifted dry ingredients are added alternately with milk as when a cake is made by hand. Egg whites are folded into the batter by hand or for a short time at a low speed with a mixer.

[3] H. B. Ohlrogge and G. Sunderlin. Factors Affecting the Quality of Cakes Made with Oil. *Journal of The American Dietetic Association,* 24: 213–216 (1948).

Fig. 15–1. To make a cake by the conventional method:

Measure the fat into a mixing bowl and cream it until soft and plastic.

Add the sugar, salt, and vanilla to the fat, creaming until fluffy and light.

Add the eggs and blend thoroughly into the creamed mixture.

Sift together the flour and baking powder onto waxed paper. Add a little at a time to the fat-sugar-egg mixture and blend well. Small portions of flour blend in more smoothly than large portions.

Pour in part of the milk. Stir until the batter is smooth. Continue to add the flour and milk alternately, blending the mixture well after each addition. Add the flour mixture last so the ingredients will blend into a smooth finished batter.

Pour equal amounts of batter into prepared cake pans.

Stagger the pans on one rack in the oven. Allow at least an inch of space between pans and between pans and sides of the oven. The cake is done when the center springs back leaving no fingerprint when touched lightly and when the cake shrinks slightly from the edge of the pan.

Remove the cakes from the oven and set them on racks to cool. Let them stand for 10 to 15 minutes. Then loosen the cake completely from the sides of the pan by running a small spatula up and down around the pan. Place a rack over the pan. Invert.

Courtesy of Swift and Company

3   The "one-bowl" or "easy mix" method of mixing cakes has become popular since its introduction to homemakers in 1943. Because recipes developed for the one-bowl method usually contain higher proportions of sugar and liquid than recipes for the conventional method, the one-bowl method should not be used for recipes intended for another mixing method. The dry ingredients including the sugar are sifted together into a mixing bowl. Plastic fat at room temperature is added, part or all of the milk, and the flavoring. The ingredients are beaten vigorously with a spoon or with an electric mixer at slow to medium speed for two minutes. The bowl is scraped frequently. Any remaining liquid and the unbeaten eggs are added, and beating is continued for two more minutes. In some recipes all of the ingredients are put into the bowl together. When mixing is done by hand, beating must be hard and continuous. If time is required for rest, it is not included in the total mixing time.

The pastry-blend or dough-batter method is not usually suggested for home use because it is not suitable for hand mixing. In this method the flour, baking powder, salt, and fat are beaten together first; then a mixture of the sugar and one-half of the milk is blended in, followed by the egg and the remaining milk.

The conventional, one-bowl, and pastry-blend methods have been compared using an electric mixer and formulas with three levels of sugar.[4] The one-bowl and pastry-blend methods compared favorably with the conventional method. The one-bowl method was better with medium and high than with low sugar formulas.

Baking. For satisfactory results in baking cakes, it is necessary to select the right size, shape, and material in a baking pan, to bake the cake at a satisfactory temperature for the right length of time, and to exercise care in cooling the cake. The pan must be of the size specified in the recipe because cake baked in too large a pan does not brown well and may be dry, whereas cake baked in too small a pan often rises to a peak in the oven and then falls. If a pan of the type recommended is not available, another with approximately the same capacity is substituted. One of the best indications that the pan is the right size is that the baked cake just fills it.

An experiment[5] in which the amount of cake batter used in the pans was proportional to their capacity but the pans varied in shape has revealed that shallow cake pans produced larger and more tender cakes with flatter tops than deep pans. In deep pans the batter near the sides of the pan becomes firm during the early part of the baking period, and the softer center of the batter expands to form a humped crust that usually shows

[4] M. B. Hunter, A. M. Briant, and C. J. Personius. *Cake Quality and Batter Structure. Effects of Formula, Temperature of Ingredients, Kind of Fat, and Method of Mixing.* Cornell University Agricultural Experiment Station Bulletin No. 860, 1950.

[5] H. Charley. Effects of the Size and Shape of the Baking Pan on the Quality of Shortened Cakes. *Journal of Home Economics*, 44: 115–118 (1952).

a crack. Cakes baked in round and square pans of the same depth are similar when the pans are of equal capacity; however, in making such substitutions of shape it is necessary to remember that a square pan has more area than a round pan. For example, a pan 8 inches square has an area of 64 square inches, while that of a pan with a diameter of 8 inches is 50 square inches. Corresponding figures for a 9-inch pan are 81 square inches for a square pan and about 64 square inches for a round pan 9 inches in diameter.

In another study,[6] baking was faster in pans with a dark color or a dull finish than in metals with a bright surface or in glass. Although the cakes that baked faster had larger volume and better crumb quality, they were not quite so attractive because their tops were more rounded and their sides browner than those baked more slowly. Aluminum pans are widely and successfully used for cakes. Those that are shallow and not shiny on the outside bottom are a good choice.

After the cake pan has been chosen, it must be prepared for the batter before mixing is started. Pans used for homemade shortened cakes are often lined with a piece of waxed paper. The pan is put on top of several layers of waxed paper, marked with the point of a pair of scissors, and then cut along the marked line. The bottom of the pan is greased before the paper is put in, but the sides may be left ungreased so the cake can cling to the sides of the pan during baking.

Layer cakes or cupcakes are usually baked in an oven at 190° C. (375° F.) for 15 to 20 minutes and loaf cakes at 177° C. (350° F.) for 45 to 60 minutes. Oven temperatures that are too low result in small volume and poor texture. Ovens should be preheated and if possible tested with an oven thermometer before cakes are baked in them. If the oven racks are not level, the cake will be thicker on one side than on the other. Cake is placed as near the center of the oven as possible and away from the sides so that air can circulate around it. If several layers are baked at once, the pans are not placed directly over each other on the shelves, and air spaces are left between those on the same shelf. Cakes are done if they spring back when pressed with a finger and an inserted toothpick comes out clean. Care should be taken not to overbake cakes.

When cakes are removed from the oven, it is best to place them right side up on a wire rack for ten or fifteen minutes before removing them from the pan. As the cake cools, it becomes firmer and easier to remove from the pan without breaking than when it is first taken from the oven. When removed from the pan, the cake is placed on a wire rack, and any waxed paper that has been used for lining the pan is removed. The cake is then placed right side up on another rack.

[6] H. Charley. Effect of Baking Pan Material on Heat Penetration During Baking and on Quality of Cakes Made with Fat. *Food Research,* 15: 155–168 (1950).

Characteristics. Although some of the qualities of shortened cakes depend upon the ingredients used, all shortened cakes have certain characteristics in common if their quality is good. Externally, the cakes are symmetrical in shape and slightly rounded, although layer cakes may be almost flat on top. The crust is soft, golden brown in color, with no suggestion of sugar crystals. The cake feels light because it has risen well during baking. When cut, the cake holds its shape without excessive crumbling. It is tender, the grain fine and uniform, and the color in keeping with the ingredients and without discoloration from utensils. The odor and flavor are characteristic and pleasing. If the cake is unsatisfactory, a study of the following tabulation may reveal the cause:

Deviation	*Cause*
Sugary or sticky crust	Too much sugar or leavening
	Improper method of mixing
	Underbaking
Uneven browning	Insufficient leavening
	Undermixing
	Uneven heat of oven
Uneven shape	Uneven heat of oven
	Uneven oven, cake not level, pan warped
Falls, low in center	Too thin a batter
	Too much sugar, fat, or leavening
	Undermixing
	Too much batter in pan
	Moving the cake during baking
	Oven temperature too low
	Underbaking
Coarse	Too much sugar or leavening
	Undermixing
	Incorrect oven temperature
Heavy	Insufficient leavening
	Too much fat, sugar, or liquid
	Overmixing
	Pan too heavily greased
	Too much batter in pan
	Incorrect temperature for baking
	Underbaking
	Incorrect cooling
Peaked	Insufficient fat or leavening
	Too much flour
	Oven temperature too high

Deviation, cont.	*Cause,* cont.
Tough	Insufficient fat, sugar, or leavening Too much flour Overmixing
Cracks on top	Too stiff a batter Baking pan too deep Too hot an oven at first of baking
Dry	Not enough fat, sugar, or liquid Too much flour or leavening Addition of chocolate with no increase in liquid or decrease in flour Egg whites beaten too much Overbaking
Soggy	Too much sugar, liquid, or leavening Undermixing

Cookies. Although there are a few exceptions, such as kisses made like hard meringues and lady fingers made from a sponge cake batter, most cookies can be considered a modified shortened cake. Although cookies are usually made from a special recipe higher in fat and lower in sugar and liquid than cakes, cookies can be made by decreasing the liquid or increasing the flour in a cake recipe. The dough can be varied by the addition of nuts, fruits, flavorings, chocolate, or coconut. They can be shaped and decorated in different ways. Drop or sheet cookies are made from a batter somewhat thicker than cake batter. Batter is either dropped from a spoon onto a cookie sheet leaving space between for the cookies to spread or it is poured into a greased pan, baked, and then cut into rectangles, squares, or diamonds.

Rolled or refrigerator cookies are made from a stiffer dough than drop cookies. The dough is rolled and cut with a cookie cutter or knife before baking. A similar dough, usually one that is moderately high in fat, can be shaped into a roll, stored in the refrigerator to chill, sliced, and then baked. The high fat concentration helps the dough stiffen in the refrigerator.

The baking temperature and time for cookies varies with the ingredients and the method of shaping the dough, but it is often 190° C. (375° F.) for about ten minutes. It is usually necessary to lift cookies from the baking pan to a wire rack with a thin spatula while they are still warm so that they will not break during the transfer. If cookies are cooled on the pan and are difficult to transfer, the pan may be replaced in the oven long enough to warm and soften the cookies.

Foam Cakes

Foam cakes depend at least in part upon air beaten into eggs for leavening. Usually most of the air is beaten into egg whites, although, as will be explained, air can also be beaten into whole eggs or yolks for sponge cakes.

Steam formed during baking helps to leaven foam cakes; however, some recipes call for the addition of baking powder. True sponge cakes, which contain neither shortening nor chemical leavening, are divided into two classes, angel food or white sponge cake which contains egg whites and yellow sponge cake which contains whole eggs (Table 15–1). Chiffon cakes, which are included in this section for convenience, depend upon eggs for much of their leavening but also contain oil and baking powder.

For foam cakes of all types, cake flour produces a more tender, moist cake than all-purpose flour. Flour is sifted twice—once before measuring and again to mix in any other dry ingredients like sugar and salt which are to be added with the flour. Additional siftings do not increase the amount of air incorporated into the flour. The leavening of foam cakes that contain no baking powder depends upon beating the eggs so that they incorporate a large amount of air. Folding should be done with extreme care so that the air bubbles are fine and evenly distributed throughout the batter without loss of air during the process. As explained in the chapter on eggs, eggs can be beaten more readily at room temperature than at refrigerator temperature. The bowl and beater must fit each other and be well chosen for the amount of material.

Angel Food Cakes. Cream of tartar, one of the acid salts used in tartrate baking powder, is added to egg whites because its acidity helps to stabilize the egg white foam and therefore to hold the air until the egg white is coagulated by the heat of the oven. Cream of tartar also increases the whiteness of angel food cake. Angel food cakes are made less tender by increasing the amount of flour and more tender by increasing the amount of sugar. Excessive amounts of sugar cause the cakes to fall. All utensils with which the cake is mixed and the pan in which it is baked must be free of any traces of grease.

One of the satisfactory methods of making angel food cake will be described briefly. One-third of the sugar is sifted with the flour because a mixture of flour and sugar blends more easily with beaten egg whites than flour alone. Egg whites are beaten with a rotary beater until they are foamy, salt and cream of tartar are added, and beating is continued until the egg whites hold a soft peak. The sugar that was not added to the flour is beaten into the egg whites gradually, and the flavoring is added. The flour-sugar mixture is sprinkled or sifted in a thin layer over the egg whites and then folded in lightly with a wire whip or a rubber or metal spatula. Folding is done by bringing the instrument down through the mixture almost parallel to the side of the bowl. The utensil is then turned until almost parallel to the bottom and is brought up the other side. When it is at the surface of the mixture, the instrument is turned again so that it is parallel to the surface of the mixture. During the operation the whip or spatula has a circular motion and the bowl is turned slightly. Folding is continued until all of the flour-sugar mixture has been added and then for two minutes more. The batter is poured into an ungreased tube pan. Large air bubbles can be removed by tapping the pan on the table or by moving a spatula through the batter. Angel food cakes can be mixed successfully with an electric mixer if high speed is used in beating the eggs and low speed for folding in the flour-sugar mixture. Oven temperatures of 177° to 190° C. (350° to 375° F.) give a tender, moist cake of good volume. Angel food cake is best if baked only until it shrinks slightly from the sides of the pan, is a delicate brown, and the surface springs back when pressed lightly with a finger. Overbaking toughens such cakes greatly. When the cake is taken from the oven, it is turned upside down until it is cool. Angel food cakes may collapse if they are removed from the pan while hot.

Angel food cake of good quality is symmetrical in shape, evenly and slightly rounded, and delicately browned. The crust is tender but not sticky. The texture is silky, tender, moist, and resilient. The color is white and the grain is fine and uniform. The odor and flavor, which should be delicate and inviting, are affected by the flavoring and the other ingredients used.

Angel food cakes are so delicate in texture that they are not usually covered with a thick layer of frosting. If any frosting is used, it is usually a light covering. Angel food cakes can be served as accompaniments to fruits and frozen desserts. A slice of cake may be covered with crushed fruit such as strawberries and garnished with whipped cream, or topped with ice cream and crushed fruit. Two thin slices may be used as the basis for a sweet sandwich filled with either ice cream or whipped cream and garnished with nuts or fruits. It may also be used in refrigerator pudding. Angel food cake can be cut easily with a wet, sharp knife.

Sponge Cakes. Whole eggs are used in most sponge cakes, although sometimes more egg whites than egg yolks are used, and a few sponge cakes are made with egg yolks only. As shown in Table 15–1, liquid is sometimes added. Added liquid is believed to make a softer, more tender cake; however, too much may cause separation of the cake into layers during baking. Sometimes the liquid is lemon juice which, like cream of tartar, furnishes acid and, in addition, adds flavoring and moisture to the cake.

Whole eggs are usually separated before they are used in sponge cakes. The whites are beaten until they stand up in soft peaks, and then part of the sugar is beaten in as for making angel food cakes. No salt is added at this time. Egg yolks and lemon juice are beaten together until thick and lemon-colored. Part of the sugar is then beaten into the yolk mixture, which is poured over the beaten whites and folded gently until the mixtures are well blended. The flour and salt, with or without about one-third of the sugar, are then folded into the eggs. Folding must be carefully and quickly done to avoid losing air and stirring or beating avoided. An electric mixer can be used successfully with high speed for beating the egg yolks and egg whites and with low speed for folding the ingredients together. A beater that has been used for egg whites can be used for egg yolks without washing, but thorough washing is required if whites are beaten after yolks. Recipes for sponge cakes vary in the order of adding ingredients and in the method of adding sugar. If lemon juice is omitted, cream of tartar is added to the egg whites as for angel food cake.

If an efficient electric mixer is available, sponge cakes can be made in one bowl without separating the eggs.[7] Eggs, lemon juice, and grated rind are beaten together at highest speed until soft peaks are formed, which takes from twelve to sixteen minutes. Sugar is then added gradually while beating at high speed. The flour and salt are sifted over the surface of the mixture and are blended with the eggs at lowest speed.

The same temperatures and precautions apply in baking, cooling, and serving sponge cakes and angel food cakes.

Chiffon Cakes. It has already been said the chiffon cakes have characteristics of both shortened and foam cakes. Although they are made by a modified muffin method, they are more closely related to sponge cakes than are most shortened cakes. The dry ingredients, including part or all of the sugar, are sifted into a mixing bowl; the oil, unbeaten egg yolks, liquid, and flavoring are added and beaten until smooth. The egg whites are beaten until foamy, cream of tartar is added, and beating is continued until the egg whites form soft peaks. If part of the sugar has been retained, it is beaten into the egg whites gradually, and beating is continued until the mixture forms stiff peaks. If sugar has not been retained, the egg whites are beaten until stiff. It will be noted that egg whites are beaten longer for chiffon cakes than for angel food or sponge cake. The mixture containing egg yolks is added a little at a time and is gently folded into the egg whites. After the two mixtures have been combined, the batter is poured into an ungreased pan. A tube pan is often used, although pans of other types can be substituted. The baking temperature is usually 163° to 177° C. (325° to 350° F.).

Pies

Pies are a favorite American dessert that appear in many forms. Fruit pies are usually made with double crusts, although single crusts with a topping can be used, or the fruit can be put into a baking dish and only a top crust used to form a deep dish pie. Custard, pumpkin, chess, and pecan or other nut pies are often baked in a single unbaked crust. Baked pie shells can be filled with chiffon mixtures containing gelatin, ice cream, or cream fillings of many types, often topped with a soft meringue or whipped cream. It might be said that Americans prefer their puddings in a pie shell since any of the fillings mentioned, including those used for fruit pies, can be served as a dessert without pastry.

[7] A. M. Briant and A. R. Willman. Whole-Egg Sponge Cakes. *Journal of Home Economics,* 48: 420–421 (1956).

Plain Pastry

The word "pastry" applies to a wide variety of baked products high in fat, including cream puffs, puff pastry, and even some types of cookies, cakes, and yeast products. In this section only plain pastry that is used for pie crust will be considered.

Ingredients. As shown in Table 15–1, the only ingredients ordinarily used in pastry are flour, fat, liquid, and salt. The flour is usually all-purpose. If pastry or cake flour is substituted, more flour or less fat can be used for an equally tender pastry because these flours weigh less per cup and contain less protein than all-purpose flour. When instant flour is used, the taste and appearance of pastry is improved by adding more fat.[8]

The amount of fat necessary to produce tender pastry depends upon the ability of the fat to coat the flour particles. The most effective shortening agents are unsaturated fats like salad oils which cover a greater area than more highly saturated fats or fats such as lard, which are plastic over a wide temperature range. When one-fourth cup of fat was used per cup of flour (the lower amount of fat suggested in Table 15–1), pastry made from cottonseed, corn, or soybean oils was most tender; that made from lard was next; and that made from two brands of hydrogenated vegetable fat was least tender.[9] The amounts of water were the same for all pastries. With one-third cup of fat per cup of flour, there was less difference in the tenderness of pastry made from the different fats than when lower proportions of fat were used.

Butter and margarine are not often used for plain pastry because they produce less tender pastry than most other fats. They are less plastic at some temperatures than hydrogenated fats and they contain slightly over 80 per cent fat, whereas hydrogenated vegetable oil, lard, and oil contain 100 per cent fat. The tenderness of pastry increases with the proportion of fat until the pastry is too tender to remove from the pan and has an unpleasant fatty consistency. For home use, one-fourth to one-third cup of fat per cup of flour is the usual recommendation (Table 15–1). With hydrogenated fat the higher level, one-third cup, may be safer for the beginner because differences in technique are less likely to result in a tough pastry than when smaller amounts of fat are used. With lard or oil one-fourth cup of fat per cup of flour is usually adequate.

About two tablespoons of water are used for each cup of flour. The amount of water depends upon the type of flour and fat, the temperature, and the mixing technique. It is important to add the right amount of water because an excess makes the pastry tough and insufficient water makes the dough crumbly and difficult to roll. The substitution of milk for water is likely to make the pastry browner. Although oil appears to moisten the flour in

[8] *Agricultural Research.* 15: (10), April, 1967, p. 16.

[9] R. H. Matthews and E. H. Dawson. Performance of Fats and Oils in Pastry and Biscuits. *Cereal Chemistry,* 40: 291–302 (1963).

Fig. 15–2. *To make pastry dough: Measure sifted flour and salt into a mixing bowl. Cut in the shortening with a pastry blender until no particles are larger than peas.*

Sprinkle water, a little at a time, over different parts of the flour mixture. Toss together lightly with a fork. Use only enough water to just moisten the dough.

Place the dough on waxed paper and gently press the dough into a ball inside the paper. Open up the paper and knead the dough 2 or 3 times with the palm of the hand. Let the dough stand for 15 to 20 minutes and it will roll out easily.

Courtesy of Swift and Company

making pastry, the addition of water or milk is essential for proper development of the dough. Salt is added to pastry for flavor. Adding baking powder or substituting self-rising flour for regular flour is not usually recommended.

Mixing. Several methods can be used successfully for mixing the ingredients of pastry. In all of them a "light hand" is necessary for tender pastry. Ingredients at room temperature have been found to produce more tender pastry than cold ingredients. An exception to this general rule is the boiling water used in one mixing method. In the conventional method of mixing pastry, hydrogenated shortening or lard is cut into the flour and salt with a pastry blender or two knives until no particles are larger than peas. Water is then sprinkled over the mixture a little at a time and mixed lightly with a fork. An effort is made to distribute the water evenly by sprinkling it on dry portions and by pushing aside any moist lumps that form. Over-mixing is avoided after water has been added because it toughens the dough. Enough water is added to permit the dough to stick together with gentle pressure and to be flattened slightly without broken edges.

Several variations of the method just described are possible. The mixing can be carried out at low speed on an electric mixer. Mixers are used almost universally for making pies in large quantities and in research so that the amount of mixing can be controlled precisely. They are not often used at home where the amounts are small and hand mixing is quick and easy. Another variation that some homemakers find especially easy has been called the paste method. Two tablespoons of flour are removed for each cup of flour used in the recipe. Fat is cut into the remaining flour and salt. The reserved flour is added to all the water to make a paste and stirred *immediately* into the fat-flour mixture.

Crusts made by any of the methods described above should be flaky as well as tender. Crusts that are flaky have many thin layers that can be seen and even peeled off when the pastry is broken. This flakiness often gives the crust a blistered appearance. Crusts made by the hot water method or with oil instead of plastic shortening are sometimes less flaky and more mealy than those made with plastic shortening at room temperature.

For the hot water method, a measured amount of boiling water is poured over shortening or lard and whipped with a fork. The flour and salt are added and the dough mixed until it clings together. Over-mixing should be avoided. The dough may be chilled before rolling so that it can be handled easily.

When oil is used for making pastry, the oil and water are often shaken or stirred together and then added to the flour and salt. Other recipes suggest that the oil and then the water be stirred into the flour. In any case the dough is mixed lightly with a fork until it holds together. As mentioned above, the amount of water called for in the recipe must be added even though the oil appears to have wet the dough.

Rolling. Dough rolls out more easily if it is allowed to stand a few minutes to hydrate before it is rolled. Only enough dough for one crust is rolled at a time. To avoid toughening the pastry, the dough is handled as little as possible and is never kneaded. The addition of flour during rolling is avoided as much as possible because such flour also toughens the pastry. Dough can be rolled without the addition of flour if it is placed on a piece of waxed paper or plastic film and covered with another sheet of the same material. With some doughs it may be helpful to loosen the paper on each side of the dough several times during the rolling. The paper will not slip during rolling if the counter is dampened slightly. This method is especially effective with oil pastry, which is difficult to handle on a board. If preferred, pastry dough can be rolled on a lightly floured pastry cloth or board. When this is done, the rolling pin, which may be covered with stockinette, is also floured lightly. In any case, rolling is started in the center of the dough and is stopped at the outer edge of the dough. The rolling pin is then lifted for another stroke. Dough is rolled with short, light strokes into a circle about one and one-half inches larger than the top of the pie pan or until the crust has the desired thickness, usually about one-eighth inch.

If a two-crust pie is being made, the lower crust is placed inside the pan. It can be transferred from the board by folding in half or by rolling it lightly around a rolling pin. The sides of the dough are lifted, and the dough is eased into the bottom of the pan without stretching and without creating air bubbles. Stretching is avoided because it causes the dough to shrink during baking. If the dough has been rolled between two pieces of paper, the top piece is pulled off gently, the dough is placed paper side up in the pan, the paper is removed, and the dough fitted into the pan. The crust is cut off at the edge of the pan. The top crust is rolled in the same way as the bottom crust except that it needs to be only slightly larger than the top of the pan. Several slashes are cut to allow the escape of steam formed by the filling during baking. After the top crust has been rolled, the filling is placed in the bottom pastry, and the rim of the bottom crust is moistened with water. The top crust is then placed loosely over the filling. To make a fluted edge, the top crust is trimmed with scissors or a knife so that it extends about one-half inch beyond the edge of the pan. It is then folded under the bottom crust and fluted between the index finger of one hand and the thumb and index finger of the other hand. If preferred, the edges can be pressed together with a fork at half-inch intervals around the pie. A variety of other designs is possible, but in any case the top and bottom crusts should be sealed together firmly to avoid the escape of juice during baking.

For a one-crust pie that is to be baked with the filling, pastry is fitted into the pan and trimmed about one inch beyond the edge of the pan. The excess pastry is folded under and shaped as desired. Filling is added and the pie is baked.

If a one-crust pie shell is to be baked without filling, some precaution must be taken to prevent the pastry from puffing up during baking. This can be done by pricking the pastry with a fork before baking so that air and steam can escape. If preferred, the pastry can be placed on the bottom of an inverted pie pan and pricked. Another device is to fit the pastry inside of a pan leaving the edge flat and placing another pie pan of the same size inside the crust. If this is done, pricking is unnecessary because the second pan prevents puffing during baking. Individual pie shells can be made in tart shells, shallow custard cups, or on the back of muffin pans. If the dough is to be baked unfilled, it is always pricked.

The student will note that pie shells are pricked before they are baked to prevent puffing. The bottom crust of one- or two-crust pies that are to be baked after filling are not pricked because the small holes made by pricking would permit filling to flow under the crust and make it soggy.

Pie pans of dull aluminum or glass cook the bottom crust of pie more effectively than shiny pans which reflect the heat and result in a pale bottom crust.

Baking. Pastry shells or pies are placed in the center or slightly below the center of a preheated oven. If more than one pie is baked at a time, the same precautions are observed as in baking layer cakes. Unfilled pastry shells are usually baked at 219° to 232° C. (425° to 450° F.) for 10 to 15 minutes. The same oven temperatures can be used for two-crust pies containing cooked filling, but the time is 30 to 45 minutes. One- or two-crust pies containing uncooked fillings are baked at the temperature specified by the recipe or at 205° to 219° C. (400° to 425° F.) for 40 to 50 minutes. If excessive browning of the edge of the crust is noticed, it can be covered with a strip of aluminum foil or with pie tape. When pies are removed from the oven, they are placed on a cooling rack. Cream or custard pies are refrigerated as soon as they are cooled.

Characteristics. Good pastry is crisp and tender with a blistered rather than a smooth surface. The edges are well browned, but the center is browned more delicately. It is easily cut with a fork but not so tender that it breaks when served. The flavor is pleasing and delicate and adds to the palatability of the filling. If the pastry is unsatisfactory, it may be possible to find the cause in the following tabulation:

Deviation	*Cause*
Tough crust	Insufficient fat
	Too much water
	Overmixing
	Too much flour on molding board
	Kneading
Crumbly crust	Too little water
	Too much fat
	Self-rising flour used
	Insufficient mixing

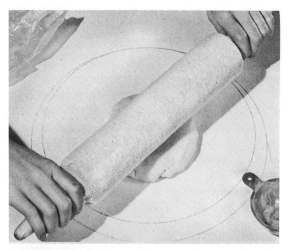

Fig. 15–3. *For a one-crust pie:*
Lightly flour a pastry cloth or board. The rolling pin, which may be covered with a stockinette, is also lightly floured. Place the dough, shaped as a flattened ball, on the cloth. Roll the crust gently from the center out in all directions to form a circle. Lift the rolling pin at the edges to keep a uniform thickness.

Invert the pie pan on top of the dough to be sure the crust extends at least an inch beyond the edge of the pan. Fold the rolled-out dough over the rolling pin and lift onto the pan. Fit the pastry into the pan without stretching it. Trim off any crust that hangs over the edge of the pan more than an inch.

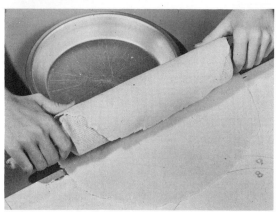

Fold the edge of the pastry under to fit the rim of the pie pan. Flute the edge with a spoon and fingertips. Add filling to the unbaked pie shell, or if baking before filling, prick the sides and bottom of the pastry dough with a fork so it will not puff or shrivel during baking.

Fig. 15–4. *For a two-crust pie:*
Divide the dough in half. Roll out the dough for the bottom crust as for a one-crust pie, but trim the pastry at the rim of the pan. Add the filling.

Roll out the dough for the top crust so that it extends beyond the edge of the rim of the pan. Cut a few slits in the crust to allow steam to escape and place it loosely over the filling. Fold the top crust under the bottom one and flute the edges, sealing together firmly so juice won't leak out during baking.

For a lattice-topped pie, roll out and fit the lower crust into the pan. Roll out the top crust and cut into strips $\frac{1}{2}$ inch wide. Lay the strips about one inch apart over the filling. Turn back alternate rows of pastry and place strips diagonally across, starting from the center. Cut strips even with the edge of the pan. Fold the lower crust over these ends. Press together lightly to form a standing edge.

Courtesy of Swift and Company

Deviation, cont.	*Cause*, cont.
Crust does not brown	Too little fat
	Too much water
	Too much flour on board
	Overmixed
	Rolled too thick
	Oven temperature too low
Soggy lower crust	Filling too moist
	Bottom crust torn or broken
	Soaked before baking starts
	Using shiny pie pan
	Placing pie pan on cookie sheet or aluminum foil
	Oven temperature too low or time too short
Shrinks in pan	Unbalanced recipe
	Too much handling
	Pastry stretched tightly in pan
	Dough stored too long in refrigerator
	Dough uneven in thickness
Pastry shell blisters	Pastry fitted too tightly in pan
	Not pricked enough
	Oven temperature too low

Fillings

Fruit. Although fruit pies are usually made with two crusts, they can be varied by making a lattice top or a deep dish pie. To make a lattice top, pastry is rolled into a rectangle and cut into half-inch strips with a knife or pastry cutter. The strips are placed across the top of the filling in either a square or diamond pattern. The strips can be woven or coiled if desired. Instead of putting the filling into a pan lined with pastry, it can be put into a deep dish or into individual baking dishes and topped with pastry.

The fruit can be fresh, frozen, canned, or dried and cooked. The beginner will probably find it easier to follow a specific recipe than to use any proportions that might be given here. In general it can be said that enough raw fruit is put into a pie shell to fill it and be slightly rounded in the center. A mixture of sugar and a thickening agent such as flour, cornstarch, or tapioca is combined with the fruit. Cornstarch or tapioca produces a clearer filling than flour, but some people prefer the flavor of flour. The amounts of sugar and thickening depend upon the sweetness and juiciness of the fruit. A small amount of salt is often added, and the fruit can be dotted with about one tablespoon table fat. Cinnamon, nutmeg, or lemon juice may be added to apples. When cooked or canned fruits are used, drained fruit can be put into the pastry and treated like fresh fruit, or part or all of the juice can be mixed with sugar and a thickening agent, brought to a boil, and combined with the fruit. Less sugar is used with sweetened frozen or canned fruit than with fresh fruit. Recipes often recommend that the mixture be cooled before it is put in the crust. This probably aids in obtaining a flaky crust.

Cream. For cream pies the filling is a pudding mixture thickened by starch and egg. The starchy ingredient is usually flour. Egg yolks are used in most recipes instead of whole eggs so that the whites can be made into meringue. The flavor of cream pies is varied by the addition of bananas or other fruit, nuts, flavorings, coconut, or chocolate, or by the substitution of brown for white sugar to make butterscotch pie. Lemon pie, for which a special recipe is needed, is a member of this family.

Cream filling can be made by mixing the flour, sugar, and salt and adding scalded milk to them while stirring. This mixture is brought to a boil over direct heat. Part of the hot mixture is then added slowly with stirring to beaten egg yolks and returned to the pan. Cooking is continued with stirring over direct heat for five minutes. Many recipes suggest that cream filling be made in the top of a double boiler, and this can be done if desired. Research[10] has indicated, however, that fillings cooked over direct heat were thicker than those cooked in the double boiler and required less time and flour. Less flour was required when scalded milk was used rather than cooler milk. When the mixture was cooked for five minutes after adding the egg yolk, the hot fillings were more runny than those cooked for only one minute but were more firm when cold. This indicates that the consistency of a hot filling is not always a reliable indication of the firmness of the cold filling. Cream pie fillings are best if they are just thick enough so they do not run when cut.

Variations in the thickness of lemon pie fillings have been observed. They can usually be avoided by adding the lemon juice to the cooked starch paste after it has been removed from the heat so that the starch is not cooked in the presence of acid. The thickness of fillings also varies with the length of the cooking time after egg yolk is added. Such variations can be avoided by cooking long enough after the egg yolk is added to make the filling definitely thicker than the original starch paste. Water is often used instead of milk for lemon pie to make a clear filling and to avoid the possibility of curdling.

Immediately after the cream filling has been cooked, the meringue can be made. Egg whites are beaten until foamy, cream of tartar (one-quarter teaspoon for three egg whites) and a dash of salt are added if desired, and beating at high speed is continued until soft peaks are formed. Sugar is then added gradually while beating continues. As explained in Chapter 9, meringues made with two and a half tablespoons of sugar have been found superior to those made with two or three tablespoons. Beating is continued until the meringue forms stiff peaks. The meringue is then spread over the pie filling which may vary from warm to hot. Care is taken to have the meringue touch the edge of the crust all around the pie. Swirls can be made in the meringue, but they should not be so high that their tops brown excessively in the oven. The meringue is browned in an oven at 219°C. (425° F.) for four or five minutes or at 177° C. (350° F.) for 10 to 12 minutes. The

[10] A. M. Briant, M. V. Zaehringer, J. L. Adams, and N. Mondy. Variations in Quality of Cream Pies. *Journal of The American Dietetic Association,* 30: 678–681 (1954).

higher temperature gives a less sticky, more tender meringue but one that tends to have greater leakage. The short time required at the higher temperature may not permit adequate heating of the meringue.

Custard. Custard pies are usually made by putting a custard mixture that is high in eggs, often three eggs for two cups milk, into an unbaked pastry shell. The preparation of custard has been discussed in Chapter 9. Some soaking of the under crust of custard pie is to be expected, but it can be reduced or almost eliminated by certain precautions. A pie pan of dull aluminum or of glass cooks the bottom crust better than shiny metal because it absorbs the heat of the oven instead of reflecting it. Special care should be taken that there are no cracks or holes in the pastry through which the filling could seep. The pastry shell can be refrigerated while the filling is being prepared. The custard mixture is poured while still hot into the pastry in order to shorten baking time. Although it is usually recommended that pies be baked in the center of the oven, custard pie may be baked on a shelf near the bottom of the oven so that the crust will receive more heat than the filling. Custard pies are usually baked at 205° to 219° C. (400° to 425° F.) for 30 to 40 minutes. The pie is baked until a knife inserted halfway between the center and side comes out clean. The center of the pie will coagulate as it cools. Overbaking causes the custard to curdle. The pie is cooled on a rack for two to three hours before serving.

Soaking of the bottom crust can be avoided completely by baking a pastry shell and the custard mixture separately. The custard mixture is poured into a greased pie pan of the same size as that used for the shell. It is put in a shallow pan of hot water and baked at 177° C. (350° F.). After the custard and crust are cool and just before serving, the custard is loosened around the edge with a small spatula, the pan is shaken gently to loosen the custard, and the pan of custard is tilted so that the edges of the custard and pie shell away from the worker are close together. The custard is shaken and the pan containing it is pulled toward the worker as the custard slips into the shell. If the edge of the custard looks ragged, coconut or chopped nuts can be sprinkled around it.

Pumpkin pie is a variation of custard pie in which pumpkin and spices are added and brown sugar substituted for part or all of the sugar. Sweet potatoes or squash can be used instead of pumpkin to produce a similar pie. Nut pies, such as pecan pies, are rich mixtures containing eggs, sugar, corn syrup, table fat, nuts, and salt. In some recipes milk and flour are added to make a less concentrated mixture.

Undesirable bacteria may grow in cream or custard pies held at room temperature. For this reason, they should be refrigerated as soon as cool.

Convenience Forms

In recent years the use of convenience forms of cakes and pies has increased greatly as indicated by the shelf space devoted to them in most grocery stores. The convenience forms include commercial and homemade mixes,

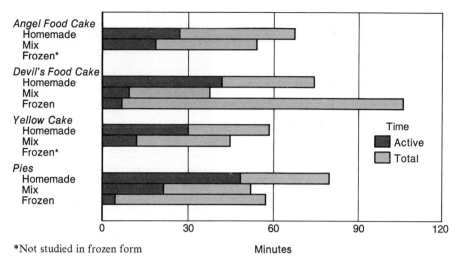

Not studied in frozen form   Minutes

Fig. 15–5. *Preparation times, including active and total time, for angel food, devil's food, and yellow cakes, and pies.* (From Matthews, Murphy, Marsh, and Dawson, in *Baked Products: Consumer Quality, Composition, Yield,* and *Preparation Time of Various Market Forms.* Home Economics Research Report No. 22, U.S. Department of Agriculture, 1963.)

products frozen commercially and at home, and bakery products that are ready-to-serve.

Cakes

Active time, the time that requires the constant attention of the homemaker, is saved by using commercial cake mixes or frozen cakes (Figure 15–5). Total time includes active time plus the periods required for thawing, baking, and cooling the products.

The relative economy of the convenience forms varies with the product. Harp and Dunham[11] reported that angel food cake when made from a complete mix cost about the same as when home-prepared if the cost of the whole egg was included, but cost more than the home-prepared when the cost of the whites was calculated as 60 per cent of the cost of the eggs. The use of angel food mix would be more economical during seasons when the cost of eggs is high than when it is low. Ready-to-serve angel food cake was the most expensive of the preparations studied. The same workers reported that devil's food cake cost more when home-prepared than when made from a mix, probably because chocolate was used for the former and cocoa for the latter. Pound cake prepared from a mix cost less than the home-prepared (Figure 15–6) and the ready-to-serve cost more, the frozen product costing 227 per cent as much as the home-prepared.

[11] H. H. Harp and D. F. Dunham. *Comparative Costs to Consumers of Convenience Foods and Home-Prepared Foods.* Marketing Research Report No. 609, United States Department of Agriculture, Washington, D.C., 1963.

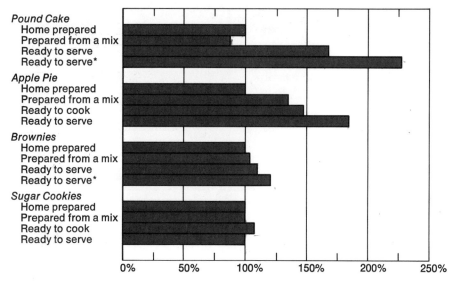

*Higher cost product is frozen.

Fig. 15–6. *Retail cost per serving of some baked goods.* (From *Family Economics Review*, June 1971. Consumer and Food Economics Research Division. Agricultural Research Service, U.S. Department of Agriculture.)

Palatability comparisons are not available for the studies that have been discussed except that some of the cakes made from mixes were softer than those made at home because low-protein flour and emulsifiers are used in the mixes. Softness varied, however, with the mix, some of which were firmer than the homemade products. The quality of cakes made from various mixes and by different homemakers varies greatly. It is quite possible that a mix would produce a better cake than one made at home by an inexperienced person, but the same mix might produce a cake inferior to one made from a recipe by an experienced cook. When comparisons are made, the recipe used for the homemade cake should produce a product similar in quality to the commercial mix.

When cakes are made with mixes, the best results are obtained if all instructions, including those about the preparation of the pans, are followed carefully. Added ingredients as flavoring extracts, spices, finely chopped nuts, coconut, or raisins may be used. Many variations are possible in frostings, fillings, and decorations.

Cake mixes can be made at home by combining the shortening with the sifted dry ingredients until the fat particles are as fine as corn meal. Sometimes the shortening is creamed with part of the sugar before it is added. Mixing of the shortening with the dry ingredients can be done with a pastry blender, the fingers, or the detached beater of an electric mixer. Cake is then made by combining eggs, milk, and flavoring with a measured amount of the mix. If the mix is made specifically for cakes, it contains cake flour and a high level of sugar. If preferred, an all-purpose mix such as that used for biscuits can be used for cakes with the addition of the ingredients mentioned and sugar. Directions for making cake mixes are available from several of the state extension offices, from commercial shortening manufacturers, and in textbooks. Some references to them are included at the end of this chapter. As with biscuit mix, homemade cake mix does not always save time but may be convenient.

Shortened cakes can be frozen either in the batter form or after they have been baked, although volume may be slightly less when cake is made from frozen batter than from fresh batter. Angel food cake batter can be frozen in the baking pan but not batter for sponge cake. Either cake can be frozen after it has been baked. It is evident that all cakes can be frozen successfully after they have been baked but that some difficulties may be encountered in freezing the batter. Frosted cakes should be frozen before they are wrapped so that the frosting will not stick to the paper. Butter cream frostings can be frozen more successfully than seven-minute or boiled frostings.

Pies

Figure 15–5 indicated that active preparation time is saved by baking pies from a mix and even more time is saved by using frozen pies. Figure 15–6 indicates that apple pies prepared at home cost less than those prepared from a mix, those ready to cook cost more and the ready-to-serve cost the most of the four. Harp and Dunham [12] reported that cherry pie was slightly more expensive when prepared from a complete mix than from the original ingredients, whereas coconut pie cost a little more when made from an incomplete mix, and still more when made from a complete mix than from the original ingredients. Both pies were more expensive in the frozen or ready to serve form than in other forms.

Pastry mix can be made at home by sifting flour and salt together, blending in fat, and storing in a covered container in a cool place. It is necessary to add only enough water so the dough will hold together and roll to make a crust. Pudding mixes are sometimes used for pie fillings.

Although fruit pies can be frozen either before or after baking, the quality seems to be better when they are frozen unbaked because the bottom crust of prebaked pies tends to become soggy. Whether the fruit pie is frozen before or after baking, it is put hard-frozen into a heated oven to either bake or thaw. Ascorbic acid may be added to the sugar to prevent browning of light-colored fruits during freezing. Chiffon pies can also be frozen successfully, but freezing tends to toughen meringues and to cause custard or cream pies to separate.

[12] Ibid.

Pastry shells can be frozen either baked or unbaked, but shells and pies may be inconveniently bulky in the freezer. Space can be saved by rolling pastry into circles of the size required and stacking them on a cardboard or cookie sheet with a double thickness of paper between each two. The stack is wrapped in freezer paper or put into a large plastic sack. Sheets of pastry can be removed as needed, thawed ten to fifteen minutes, shaped, and baked.

Activities

1. Find a yellow cake recipe for which the conventional method is recommended and another for which the one-bowl method is recommended. The proportion of eggs to flour should be as similar as possible. Make the cakes, compare, and score the products. How does the proportion of sugar to flour compare in the two recipes?

2. Prepare and score an angel food cake, a sponge cake, and a chiffon cake.

3. Cut down a pastry recipe so that about $\frac{1}{2}$ cup of flour is used. Plan several variables in the proportion of ingredients, in mixing method, and in baking temperature. Roll the pastry flat, put it on a cookie sheet, prick, and bake. Compare and score the products.

4. Prepare cream pies of several types with meringue.

5. Prepare several 2-crust fruit pies using fresh or canned fruits as available.

6. Compare the quality and cost of cakes of several types and of pastry made from mixes and home-prepared. Select recipes for the home-prepared products that will give foods as similar as possible to the convenience forms. Homemade mixes can be included in the comparison if desired. When comparing cost, calculate for equal weights of the baked products.

References

Finished Foods—a First Report. Cake-Mix Cakes—Shortening Type. *J. Home Econ.*, 53: 281–284 (1961).

Finished Foods—a Second Report. Cake-Mix Cakes—Foam Type. *J. Home Econ.*, 53: 759–762 (1961).

Finished Foods—a Third Report. Pie Crusts—From Recipe and Mix. *J. Home Econ.*, 54: 767–771 (1962).

Food for Us All. The Yearbook of Agriculture, 1969. U.S. Dept. Agr., Washington, D.C.: United States Government Printing Office. Pp. 223–224.

GRISWOLD, R. M. *The Experimental Study of Foods.* Boston: Houghton Mifflin Company, 1962. Chapter 12.

OWEN, R. F., J. T. CHASE, B. H. McGRATH, and F. O. VAN DUYNE. *Freezing Cooked and Prepared Foods.* Univ. of Illinois Ext. Serv. Circ. 835 (1961).

SNOW, P. R. and A. M. BRIANT. Frozen Fillings for Quick Lemon Meringue Pies. *J. Home Econ.*, 52: 350–352 (1960).

Homemade Mixes

DEPARTMENT OF FOODS AND NUTRITION, KANSAS STATE UNIVERSITY. *Practical Cookery.* New York: John Wiley & Sons, Inc. 1966. P. 184.

KNICKREHM, M. E., K. W. HARRIS, and K. LONGREE. Formula and Methods for Preparing a Cake Mix in Quantity. *J. Am. Dietet. Assoc.,* 28: 723–725 (1952).

MORRISON, M. H. B. Ready Mixes for Chocolate Cake. *J. Home Econ.,* 49: 283–285 (1957).

STEVENSON, G. T. and C. MILLER. *Introduction to Foods and Nutrition.* New York: John Wiley & Sons, Inc. 1961. Pp. 482–484.

SUNDERLIN, G. *Master Mix.* Purdue Univ. Coop. Ext. Serv. H.E. 511 (1971).

16

sugar, candy,
frozen desserts

In this chapter several products that are sweet and in which crystallization or lack of it is important are grouped together. The manufacture of sugar of different types will be considered and the preparation of candy and frozen desserts.

Sugar

The consumption of sugar in the United States climbed from forty pounds per person in 1875 to about 100 pounds in 1922 and has remained almost constant since that time.[1] About three-fourths of the sugar is used by industry,[2] and reaches the consumer in the form of candy, soft drinks, ice cream, baked goods, canned fruit, and other manufactured products. The average American thus consumes almost 500 calories per day in the form of sugar. Diets containing this amount of sugar are satisfactory if they contain adequate amounts of all the nutrients required by the individual and if the total calorie content of the diet is not excessive. When calories must be reduced, however, better nutrition results when "empty calories" or foods which contribute few nutrients other than calories are eliminated.

Sucrose

The product called sugar, which is known to the chemist as sucrose, is produced either from sugar cane or from sugar beets. Sugar cane is a perennial grass that grows in the tropics and sugar beets do best in the temperate climates. Although sugar cane grows in Louisiana, Florida, Hawaii, and Puerto Rico, and sugar beets in various parts of this country, almost one-half of the sugar used in the United States is imported.

To make cane sugar, the cane is crushed between rollers and the juice is strained. Impurities are removed by heating the juice with lime, and

[1] *National Food Situation.* NFS 136, 1971. Economic Research Service United States Department of Agriculture, Washington, D.C., p. 9.

[2] *National Food Situation.* NFS 136, 1971, p. 17.

water is evaporated from the juice until sugar crystallizes. The material is centrifuged to separate crystals of raw sugar from the syrup, which is called molasses. As will be discussed in a succeeding section, molasses can be evaporated again to remove more sugar. The raw sugar, which is light brown in color because a thin film of molasses clings to the crystals, is then refined to remove practically all of the impurities.

Sugar beets, which grow in climates as found in the United States, Europe, and the Soviet Union, supply about 42 per cent of the world's sugar. Beet sugar is made by cutting the beets into thin strips and soaking them in water to produce raw juice. The methods used for removing impurities, water, and crystallized sugar are similar to those used for juice from sugar cane. Cane and beet sugar are identical in chemical composition and can be used with equal success for all purposes including candy, frosting, and jelly. Granulated sugar from either source contains about 99.5 per cent sucrose, making it one of the most chemically pure substances used in foods.

The size of the sugar crystals is regulated carefully during manufacture because if they are too fine sugar is lost in the syrup and if they are too large they do not dissolve properly during cooking. Regular sugar is rather uniform in granulation. Sugar with smaller crystals is especially screened, uniformly fine-grained sugar for use in cakes, dry mixes, and other products in which quick creaming or rapid solution is desirable. Coarsely granulated sugars are also available for special uses. Granulated sugar is crushed and screened to make powdered or confectioners' sugar. The degree of fineness is sometimes indicated by the number of x's—for example, Fine or Confectioners' 4x type, Very Fine or Confectioners' 6x type, and Ultra Fine or Confectioners' 10x type. These are used for icings, frostings, uncooked candies, and for dusting on foods. Powdered sugar is often mixed with cornstarch to prevent caking. Pressed tablets or cubes of sugar are made by compressing moist white granulated sugar into molds and then drying. Cut tablets are made from sugar that is molded into slabs and cut.

Brown sugar is cane sugar that has not been refined as highly as ordinary granulated sugar. The color of brown sugar varies from almost white through various shades of brown to a color almost as intense as that of roasted coffee. The color depends upon the degree of refinement—in other words, upon the amount of molasses left on the sugar crystals. Light brown and light medium brown sugar are most frequently found on the market. Because brown sugar is more moist than granulated sugar, it often dries out and cakes after the package has been opened. Moisture can be restored by putting brown sugar in a tightly sealed container with a slice of apple or piece of bread to furnish moisture. A free-flowing or "granulated" brown sugar that will not cake is now available.[3] Each granule of free-flowing brown

[3] M. D. Miller and G. E. Spaulding, Jr. Free-Flowing Brown Sugars Ease Handling Problems. *Food Engineering,* 37: 110–112 (May, 1965).

Table 16–1. *Sweetness of Various Compounds Relative to Sucrose* *

Compound	Comparative Sweetness
Saccharin	30600
Calcium cyclamate	3380
Fructose	115
Sucrose	100
Glucose	64
Galactose	59
Maltose	46
Lactose	30

* From Schutz and Pilgrim, in *Food Research,* 22: 206–213, 1957. Courtesy of Institute of Food Technologists.

sugar consists of many tiny crystals lightly bound together into a porous, sponge-like structure. Recipes may require adjustment because a cup of free-flowing brown sugar weighs less than a cup of moist brown sugar.

Other Sugars
The word "sugar" usually refers to sucrose, a sugar that contains twelve carbon atoms. It is easily hydrolyzed[4] by enzymes or by boiling with a little dilute acid into equal parts of the two six-carbon sugars glucose and fructose, a mixture called invert sugar.[5] Lactose, a sugar found only in milk, is obtained from whey, a by-product of cheese manufacture. Lactose, which is used mainly for infant feeding, can be hydrolyzed into the two six-carbon sugars glucose and galactose. Maltose, one of the products of the hydrolysis of starch, is found in corn syrup and in malt. It contains twelve carbon atoms and can be split into two molecules of glucose.

Partial hydrolysis of cornstarch to produce corn syrup and complete hydrolysis to produce glucose will be discussed in another section. Glucose, also called dextrose, is found in fruits, honey, and certain vegetables. Fructose, also called levulose, is widely distributed in fruits. Although pure fructose is at present prohibitive in cost, it can be added to foods in the form of honey or molasses, or formed by the hydrolysis of sucrose. Fructose helps keep food moist because it absorbs water readily. This is an especial advantage in making cookies that are to be stored for a long time.

Although the comparative sweetness of different sugars varies with the method of determination, the high sweetening value of fructose and the low sweetening value of lactose are always apparent as shown in Table 16–1. Because of its high sweetening value and moisture-retaining properties, fructose would probably find wide use if it became available at a reasonable cost. The solubility of fructose in water is greater and that of lactose,

[4] Hydrolysis is a reaction in which a molecule is split with the addition of water.
[5] Invert sugar is so called because the rotation of a beam of plane-polarized light is inverted (changed from right to left) when sucrose is hydrolyzed.

less than sucrose. Lactose crystallizes so easily that crystals are sometimes found in ice creams containing high levels of concentrated milk products.

Syrups

Syrups are sweetening agents in liquid form. When they are substituted for sugars, recipes may need adjustment because most syrups contain 20 to 30 per cent water.

Molasses is the mother liquor left after much of the sugar has been crystallized from the concentrated sap of sugar cane. Because molasses may be high in sugar after the first crystallization, a second and third crystallization may be made. The molasses on the market is usually divided into two grades known to the consumer as "light" or table molasses and "blackstrap" or cooking molasses.

Cane syrup is obtained by boiling down the juice of the sugar cane until it has the consistency of syrup. No sugar is removed in making this product. Cane syrup has a pungency associated with molasses but a delicacy that molasses lacks.

Sorghum syrup is made from sorghum, a large coarse grass that can be grown in temperate climates. Sorghum syrup is produced from the juice of sorghum without extracting sugar from the juice. It is made in small quantities in areas where sorghum is grown.

Maple syrup and maple sugar were made in North America by Indians before the early settlers came to the country. The sap of the sugar maple tree is collected from a hole or gash in the tree trunk and concentrated to the desired consistency by boiling. The sap is collected late in the winter when the nights are cold and crisp with temperatures near −7° C. (20° F.) and daytime temperatures are about 5° C. (40° F.). Maple syrup of highest grade is light in color without cloudiness or an "off" flavor. Darker, stronger flavored maple syrup of lower grade is made from the last of the run of sap. Maple syrup contains not more than 35 per cent water. Maple sugar is produced by further cooking of the syrup to drive off more of the water. The total production of maple syrup and maple sugar in the United States and Canada is small compared with that of other syrups and sugars. Most of the sugar in maple syrup is sucrose, but small amounts of invert sugar, about 6 per cent, may be present. Unlike pure sugar, molasses and cane, sorghum, and maple syrups contribute calcium and iron to the diet.

Honey is one of the oldest sweets. The flavor and composition of honey vary, depending on the source of the nectar (clover, alfalfa, orange blossoms, tupelo, sourwood, etc.). The Federal Food and Drug Administration has set limits of 25 per cent water and 8 per cent sucrose for honey, although analyses usually show 18 to 20 per cent water and 2 to 3 per cent sucrose. The remaining sugars are fructose and glucose with more fructose than glucose. It is the high percentage of fructose, the soluble sugar, which gives honey the property of retaining or attracting moisture when used in food products. There are small amounts of ash and acid and minute amounts of vitamins present. Over half the honey produced in the United States comes from the flowers of clover and alfalfa. Honey may be purchased in the comb in the wooden frames as taken from the hives or the combs may be cut into chunks and packed in containers with extracted honey poured over them. Most of the honey sold in the United States is extracted, which means that the liquid honey has been separated from the comb. Some honey is crystallized and may be called creamed, candied, fondant, or spread. Honey in this form has a fine texture, spreads easily, and does not drip. Honey bought in liquid form may crystallize on standing, especially if it is kept in a refrigerator. It may be used in the crystalline form or brought back to the liquid form by placing the container in a pan of warm water.

Corn syrup is made by treating cornstarch with acid, alkali, or enzymes that hydrolyze the starch molecules to dextrin, maltose, and glucose. The liquid is neutralized, clarified, and concentrated. Light corn syrup is decolorized and may be mixed with sucrose. Dark corn syrup is a mixture of corn syrup and refiner's syrup, which is a by-product of the refining of raw cane sugar. If the hydrolysis of cornstarch is carried to completion, only glucose, which is also called cerelose, corn sugar, or dextrose, remains. The degree of hydrolysis is expressed as the "dextrose equivalents" (D.E.), which is in effect a measure of the sweetness of the syrup.

Synthetic Sweeteners

Although compounds other than sugar are capable of sweetening foods, not all synthetic sweeteners have been approved for food use. Saccharin is widely used by those who must restrict their intake of sugar. As indicated in Table 16–1, saccharin is about 300 times as sweet as sucrose. The sweetening effect differs with the food in which it is used and some people detect a bitter aftertaste. Saccharin may be used successfully in foods that do not depend upon the other functions of sugar such as: crystallization, caramelization, and preservation. Recipes for frozen desserts, custards, and cakes must be reformulated if synthetic sweeteners are used because sugar adds body, makes baked foods more tender, raises the coagulation temperature of egg, and contributes to color. In candies sugar furnishes most of the structure of the product.

Candy

Sugar and to a lesser extent other sweetening agents such as corn syrup, corn sugar, maple syrup, molasses, and sorghum are used in the preparation of candy. Candies are divided into two classes—crystalline or creamy, and noncrystalline or amorphous. The first group includes candies that have a distinct crystalline structure such as fondants, fudge, penuche, and divinity. The noncrystalline group includes caramels, butterscotch, hard candy, lollipops, marshmallows, and gum drops. The type of candy made is determined by the ingredients used, the degree of cooking, and

Fig. 16–1. *To frost a cake with seven-minute icing:*

From a piece of waxed paper cut out a circle one inch smaller than the size of the cake being frosted. Set the bottom layer of the cake over the hole in the waxed paper, with paper extending beyond the edges of the cake. Spread frosting over the top and sides of the bottom layer with a spatula.

Place the second layer on top of the first. Add more frosting and spread evenly around the sides of the cake. With scissors slit the waxed paper on four sides and pull out carefully from under the cake.

Place spoonfuls of icing on top of the cake and spread it carefully to the edges. Not a cake crumb should show. When the top is covered, add more frosting and use the spatula to make swirls.

Courtesy of Swift and Company

manipulation after cooking. Sugar—or some substance high in sugar—is the basis of all common candies. Other ingredients such as chocolate, nuts, and flavoring material alter the flavor and may also alter the texture. Practically all solids that dissolve or mix intimately with the sugar syrup alter the texture.

Like candies, cake frostings are concentrated sugar mixtures. Many of them such as fudge, seven-minute, and boiled frostings are related to the crystalline candies. Uncooked frostings are made of table fat or cream cheese, powdered sugar, flavoring, and a small amount of liquid or egg white. Successful frostings are soft enough to spread easily on the cake but firm enough that they do not run off the cake. They remain soft and creamy during the time the cake retains its freshness.

Crystalline Candies

To make crystalline candies, sugar is dissolved and then crystallized under conditions that make small crystals. Small crystals have a creamy feeling in the mouth, whereas large crystals feel sharp and grainy. The size of the crystals is determined by the ingredients, the extent of cooking, and the conditions under which the candy is beaten after cooking.

Fondant. Fondant is the simplest of the crystalline candies because it can be made, although not always successfully, from sugar and water. Creamy fondant can be made more easily if corn syrup or an acid is added to the sugar and water. Corn syrup contains various substances that interfere with the formation of sucrose crystals. Acid, which is usually added in the form of cream of tartar, splits some of the sucrose molecules into glucose and fructose. These smaller sugars crystallize with difficulty and as a result prevent or delay the union of sucrose molecules to form crystals. An excess of either corn syrup or acid must be avoided because it might prevent crystallization of fondant entirely. When acid is added, the amount of sucrose that is split depends upon the amount of acid, the alkalinity of the water which would neutralize some of the acid, and the length of cooking; slow cooking gives the acid a longer time in which to act. Even though the addition of acid requires careful control of cooking conditions, fondant made with cream of tartar has the advantage of being white in color, creamy in texture, and moist during storage. Its slightly tart flavor helps to balance the sweet flavor of the sugar.

The mixture of sugar, water, and either corn syrup or cream of tartar is cooked to the temperature specified in the recipe. At high altitudes, the temperature is reduced about 1° C. for each increase of 900 feet or 1° F. for each increase of 500 feet in elevation. If crystals appear on the sides of the pan during cooking, they can be removed by covering the pan for a short time so that the crystals can be dissolved by the steam, or removed with a clean, wet cloth wrapped around a fork. To obtain a true temperature reading, it is necessary that the bulb of the thermometer be completely immersed in the boiling liquid, yet not resting on the bottom

Fig. 16–2. *Sugar crystals in fondant are large if the syrup is beaten when it is still hot (103° C. or 217° F.)*

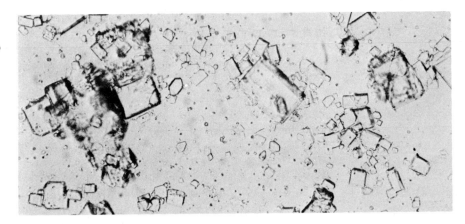

Fig. 16–3. *Medium-sized crystals form in fondant when the syrup is beaten at 60° C. (140° F.).*

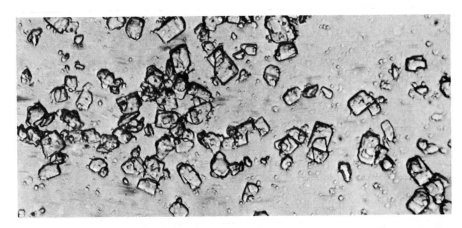

Fig. 16–4. *Small sugar crystals are highly desirable in fondant and are obtained when the syrup is cooled to 40° C. (104° F.) or when it feels just warm to the hand before beating.*

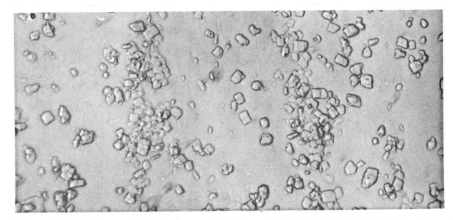

(Figs. 16–2, 16–3, and 16–4 are reprinted from Halliday and Noble, *Hows and Whys of Cooking,* by permission of the University of Chicago Press. Copyright 1926, 1933, and 1946 by the University of Chicago.)

of the utensil. Readings should be made with the eye level with the mercury in the thermometer.

After the syrup has been cooked, it is cooled undisturbed until its temperature is 60° C. (140° F.) or less. The syrup, which was saturated when cooking stopped, becomes supersaturated during cooling, meaning that it contains more sugar than could be dissolved in water at the temperature to which the syrup has been cooled. Because supersaturated solutions have a strong tendency to crystallize, jarring the syrup or introducing crystals from the thermometer or the sides of the pan may start crystallization, which is undesirable at this time because the crystals would be large. When the syrup has cooled sufficiently, beating the solution causes the simultaneous formation of many small crystals. If the syrup is beaten without sufficient cooling, a few crystals are formed at first which grow to very large size and result in grainy fondant. Beating must be continued vigorously until all of the crystals are formed. The extent of crystallization can be judged by the appearance of the syrup, which was viscous, shiny, and smooth when beating started. As crystals begin to form, heat is given off, making the mixture warmer and thinner. On further beating it cools and stiffens rapidly, becoming creamy, dull, and lighter in color as crystallization is completed. Fondant is often kneaded after it has been beaten to help insure a creamy consistency.

Fondant is composed of crystals separated from each other by a highly concentrated syrup. The presence of corn syrup or of glucose and fructose in solution thickens the syrup and thus makes it difficult for the crystals to grow rapidly. Such fondant retains its fine crystals on ripening. On the other hand, fondant made from sugar and water has larger crystals, becomes grainy in a short time, and therefore has a short shelf life. The use of heavy cream instead of water produces opera or cream fondant. This candy has a cream color, a rich flavor, and smooth texture, all due to the high fat content of the cream, although the milk solids also aid in keeping the crystals small. Usually no flavoring is added to cream fondant.

Unlike other candies, fondant requires further treatment before it is ready to use. It is usually allowed to ripen for twelve to twenty-four hours so that it will be plastic and easy to handle. It can be flavored with substances such as peppermint, spearmint, wintergreen, or vanilla. Both flavoring and coloring should be added carefully and in small quantities. The material is worked into the fondant, and centers for bonbons and chocolate creams are shaped with the fingers. Chocolate creams are made by dipping the shaped fondant into dipping chocolate that has been melted and held at a temperature of about 29° C. (85° F.). Bonbons are made by dipping fondant centers into fondant that has been melted over warm water with stirring. Mints are made by dropping melted fondant from a teaspoon on waxed paper.

Other Crystalline Candies. Chocolate fudge is a crystalline candy that is cooked to about the same temperature as fondant, then cooled and beaten to produce fine crystals. It contains more substances that interfere with crystallization than does fondant. These include corn syrup, milk solids, fat, and chocolate. Penuche, sometimes called brown sugar fudge, resembles chocolate fudge except that brown sugar is substituted for white sugar and no chocolate is used. It is usually necessary to stir fudge during cooking because both milk and chocolate tend to stick to the bottom of the pan. Table fat is added after the fudge has reached the desired temperature. Vanilla is added during beating so that its delicate flavor will not be driven off by the heat of the mixture. After the fudge has been beaten until it is thick and creamy but no longer glossy, it is poured into a buttered pan and cut into squares when cool.

Divinity fudge is a crystalline candy that is light in weight and delicate in texture. It can be white or creamy in color depending upon whether white sugar or brown sugar is used. Sugar and water with either corn syrup or acid are cooked to a higher temperature than for fondant or fudge. Before cooking is complete, egg whites are beaten until stiff. The hot syrup is poured slowly over the egg whites, while beating continues until the candy begins to hold its shape. Flavoring and nuts, if desired, are added at this time. The candy is either dropped from a teaspoon on waxed paper or spread in a buttered pan and cut into squares.

Before thermometers were widely used for cooking, sugar mixtures were cooked until they gave a certain test. Some of these tests are shown in Table 16–2 with the corresponding temperatures and products for which they are used. At the lowest temperature given, the syrup will spin a two-inch thread when dropped from a fork or spoon. At higher temperatures when dropped into very cold water, the syrup forms a soft, a firm, and later a hard ball. As the temperature increases, the syrup separates into threads when dropped into very cold water. At first the threads are hard but not brittle; however, as the temperature increases, the threads become brittle. If white sugar is heated slowly, it becomes liquid at about 160° C. (320° F.). At 170° C. (338° F.) it begins to turn brown and is said to have caramelized. This temperature is considerably higher than that used for cooking caramels, which brown at a lower temperature because of interaction between the simple sugars and the milk they contain. At excessively high temperatures, syrups burn to form carbon dioxide and water.

With the exception of the temperatures given in Table 16–2 for liquefying and caramelizing sugar, a range of temperatures is shown. This is done because the temperature to which candy should be cooked for best results varies with the ingredients used. For example, the boiling point is lower for a solution of sucrose than for one containing partially hydrolyzed sucrose because of the larger number of molecules present in the second solution.

Table 16–2. Stages of Sugar Cookery

Stage	Temperature at Sea Level, Sugar and Water Mixture		Product
	degrees C.	degrees F.	
Thread	110–113	230–235	Syrup
Soft ball	113–116	235–240	Fondant, fudge, penuche
Firm ball	119–121	246–250	Caramels
Hard ball	121–129	250–265	Divinity, marshmallows, popcorn balls
Soft crack	132–143	270–290	Butterscotch, taffies
Hard crack	149–154	300–310	Brittles, glacé
Sugar liquefies	160	320	Barley sugar
Liquid becomes brown	170	338	Caramelized sugar

For this reason it is better to use the temperature suggested in the recipe than those given in a table. It can be concluded that cooking temperature rises as sugar concentration increases (and water decreases) and as the number of molecules increases.

Uncooked Candies

Confectioner's sugar can be used as the main ingredient to make uncooked candies similar to fondant and fudge. The sugar is combined with table fat and ingredients such as corn syrup, concentrated milk products, cream, water, fruit juice, melted chocolate, coconut, peanut butter, chopped nuts or other foods, and a variety of flavorings.

Recipes for candies that might be called semicooked are also available. Granulated sugar, table fat, and evaporated milk can be boiled for a definite period such as four to six minutes and then poured over cold ingredients such as chocolate, marshmallow cream, and nuts. Such methods may be more convenient, especially for beginners, than traditional candy recipes.

Noncrystalline Candy

After they have been cooked, candies in this group become firm without forming crystals. In contrast to the crystalline candies, which have been discussed, the noncrystalline candies are sometimes said to be amorphous or "without form." Most of them are not worked after they are cooked.

Candies like caramels are more chewy than butterscotch or brittles, which are cooked to a higher temperature (Table 16–2). However, the noncrystalline nature of these candies depends not only upon the temperature to which they are cooked, but also upon substances in the recipe that help prevent crystallization or upon compounds formed from sucrose when it is heated to a high temperature.

The ingredients depend upon the nature of the candy. In addition to sugar, caramels contain corn syrup, fat, and comparatively large quantities of cream or evaporated milk. Marshmallows are made by cooking a sugar solution to the temperature indicated in Table 16–2, adding soaked gelatin, and beating to give the mixture a fluffy consistency. Sometimes egg white or soy protein is added. Taffy is made from a sugar solution containing acid, corn syrup, or both cooked to a comparatively high temperature, cooled on an oiled surface, and pulled until it is light-colored and porous. Marshmallows and taffy are exceptions to the general rule that noncrystalline candies are not worked after they are cooked. Butterscotch, brittles, and toffee usually contain table fat and sometimes nuts. They are poured without beating after they have been cooked to the necessary temperature.

In these candies and in plain hard candy or lollipops, which are not often made at home, some decomposition of the sucrose is known to occur at the high temperatures used for cooking. These decomposition products help prevent crystallization. Hard candies are usually cooked to a higher temperature than butterscotch. They are usually colored and flavored, often with acid and fruit flavors. Such candies are sometimes said to be in a solid-liquid state because the mass of melted sugar hardens as it sets without the formation of crystals. Because the final moisture content of such candies is very low, they tend to pick up moisture from the atmosphere if they are exposed to humid air. When this happens, some of the sugar they contain may crystallize. They are usually wrapped or packed in a tight container to exclude moisture.

Frozen Desserts

Frozen desserts are popular in many forms such as ice cream, similar products containing less milk fat (ice milk), or another fat (mellorine). Sherbets and water ices made with fruits are also popular. Such desserts can be purchased commercially or made at home. Frozen desserts can be served plain or in many forms such as sodas, milk shakes, malted milks, cones, or with sauce (sundaes).

Frozen desserts are crystalline, but the crystals they contain are of ice, whereas those in creamy candies are sugar crystals. Although the nature of the crystals in these two foods is different, some of the same factors involved in making creamy candy apply to frozen desserts because it is desirable to have small crystals in both products. The nature of the ingredients, the rate of crystal formation, and the rate and amount of stirring in both cases affect the character of the product.

Commercial

Commercially made frozen desserts are now widely used because their quality is usually good and their price is reasonable. The annual consumption of ice cream in the United States increased from 11.4 pounds in 1920 to 18 pounds per person in 1970.[6] Ice milk, mellorine, and sherbet, which con-

[6] *Statistical Abstracts of the United States, 1970.* United States Department of Commerce, Washington, D.C., p. 83.

tain less milk fat than ice cream, accounted for 22, 4, and 5 per cent of the frozen desserts produced in 1968.

Ice Cream. The composition of ice cream is defined by a federal standard of identity.[7] These standards apply to frozen desserts sold in interstate commerce and have also been adopted by many states. In states where they have not been adopted they are not, of course, mandatory for ice cream manufactured and sold within the state.

According to the federal standard, plain ice cream must contain not less than 10 per cent milk fat and 20 per cent total milk solids, which include milk fat and solids not fat. Such ice cream may contain limited amounts of egg yolk solids and certain stabilizers, and emulsifiers that have been recognized as safe. Frozen custard, which is sometimes called French ice cream or French custard ice cream, is subject to the same requirements and in addition must contain not less than 1.4 per cent egg yolk solids. Because the manufacturer often adds bulky ingredients such as chocolate syrup, fruit, nuts, or confectionery to his basic ice cream mix, the requirements for milk fat and total milk solids are reduced to 8 and 16 per cent in such ice creams. The manufacturer can use a variety of dairy products like fluid, evaporated, condensed, dry, or frozen milk and cream, sometimes with butter, to meet these requirements. The ingredients must be pasteurized and are usually homogenized and aged a few hours before they are frozen. By reducing the size of the fat globules, homogenization makes it easier to beat air into the ice cream during freezing and thereby produces a smooth product. The mix is frozen in a freezer equipped with a refrigerant, a scraper, and a beater or dasher. Agitation is essential during freezing to keep the ice crystals small and to incorporate air. The scraper removes frozen material that is adjacent to the cold wall of the freezer, and both the scraper and the beater break up ice crystals and incorporate air into the mixture. Beating continues until the desired volume has been reached. Usually the volume of commercial ice cream is about twice that of the mix, which means that the increase of volume during freezing or overrun, as it is often called, is about 100 per cent. When the desired overrun has been reached, the soft mixture is drawn from the freezer and is placed in a hardening room where freezing continues.

Ice cream that does not contain enough air is heavy, soggy, and coarse in texture, whereas ice cream that contains an excessive amount of air is too fluffy. To prevent the incorporation of an excessive amount of air, the federal standard of identity requires that ice cream weigh at least 4.5 pounds per gallon and contain at least 1.6 pounds total solids per gallon. These figures correspond to an overrun of about 100 per cent. The ability of the mix to incorporate air depends in part upon its content of nonfat milk solids, egg yolk, and emulsifying agents, which include the mono- and diglycerides. Ice

---

[7] *Code of Federal Regulations*, Title 21, Part 20.

cream with a comparatively low overrun often seems to be richer than ice cream with a higher overrun even though the composition of the mix is identical.

Small ice crystals are essential for smooth ice cream. When ice crystals become large, the ice cream seems coarse because the large crystals can be felt by the tongue and palate. All of the solids in the mix help keep the ice crystals small by reducing the amount of water present and by interfering mechanically with the association of water molecules to form ice crystals. Both homogenization of the mix and the air cells help keep the crystals small because small fat globules and air cells interfere with crystallization. The tendency of ice crystals to grow in size during storage can be reduced by the maintenance of a uniformly cold temperature and by the presence of stabilizers such as gelatin or vegetable gums. There are no sugar crystals in ice cream of good quality. Occasionally the inclusion of large amounts of nonfat milk solids results in the crystallization of lactose. The resulting "sandiness" has become unusual in commercial ice creams because of the use of stabilizers that prevent it. Sandiness is unlikely to develop in homemade ice creams because they are seldom stored for long periods and do not usually contain large amounts of nonfat milk solids.

Ice Milk. Like ice cream, ice milk is covered by a federal standard of identity. Minimum requirements for milk fat and total milk solids are less for ice milk than for ice cream, being 2 to 7 per cent for milk fat and 11 per cent for total milk solids. Although the minimum weight per gallon is the same for ice milk as for ice cream, the minimum total solids per gallon can be slightly less for ice milk. Other requirements are the same for these two frozen desserts except that artificial color must be declared on the label for ice milk but not for ice cream. Under the federal regulations artificial flavor must be declared on the label for all frozen desserts in which it is used.

As shown in Table 8–3, ice milk contains less fat than ice cream. Many people think that because ice milk is low in fat it is also low in calories. This is not necessarily true because in order to make ice milk as similar to ice cream as possible manufacturers are likely to put in more sugar and to incorporate less air in ice milk than in ice cream. As a result, although the calorie content per 100 grams of ice milk is lower than for a corresponding weight of ice cream, the calorie content of these two frozen desserts is almost the same when equal volumes are compared (Table 16–3).

Soft-Serve. Although either ice cream or ice milk can be sold in the soft form directly from the freezer, ice milk accounted for 82 per cent of the soft frozen dairy products sold in 1963. The formulas and manufacturing processes for soft-serve frozen desserts are similar to those for standard frozen desserts except that the product is not hardened after freezing.

Sherbets and Water Ices. Sherbets and water ices are similar in that both frozen desserts contain fruit or fruit juices but differ in that sherbet that

Table 16-3. Nutrients in Ice Cream, Ice Milk, and Sherbet * (Approximate measure, 1 cup)

Product	Weight gm.	Food energy calories	Protein gm.	Fat gm.	Carbohydrate gm.
Ice cream:					
Regular (approx. 10% fat)	133	255	6	14	28
Rich (approx. 16% fat)	148	330	4	24	27
Ice milk:					
Hardened	131	200	6	7	29
Soft-serve	175	265	8	9	39
Sherbet	193	260	2	2	59

* From *Nutritive Value of Foods*. Home and Garden Bulletin No. 72, United States Department of Agriculture, 1971.

meets federal specifications contains 1 to 2 per cent milk fat and 2 to 5 per cent total milk solids, whereas water ice contains no dairy products. To give fruit sherbet and water ice a pleasing texture, a lower overrun is used for them than for other frozen desserts. This is reflected in the federal regulation that fruit sherbet and water ice should weigh at least 6 pounds per gallon, whereas ice cream and ice milk weigh at least 4.5 pounds per gallon. As a result, the calorie content per cup of sherbet is not below that of ice cream and ice milk, as might be expected from the low fat content of sherbet (Table 16-3).

Mellorine. Mellorine, a widely used term for "Imitation" ice cream, is a frozen dessert in which butter fat is replaced by another fat such as hydrogenated vegetable oil. It resembles either ice cream or ice milk depending upon its total fat content. It is not covered by a federal standard of identity, and its sale is permitted in only a few states. Most states in which it is sold do not permit its sale in the soft form.

Homemade

Frozen desserts can be made at home by using an ice cream freezer in which the mixture is stirred during freezing or by putting a container of the ice cream mixture in a freezer, in the freezing compartment of a refrigerator, or in packed ice and salt to freeze without stirring.

Stirred Ice Cream. In its simplest form the ice cream mixture that is frozen at home can be said to be sweetened light cream. Products of similar fat content can, of course, be prepared from light cream or a mixture of whipping cream and milk. It is advisable to add a concentrated milk product in the form of evaporated, condensed, or dry milk to improve the whipping quality and nutritive value of the ice cream. Since it is impossible to homogenize a mix at home, it is desirable to incorporate a homogenized dairy product like half and half, evaporated milk, or homogenized whole milk. Pasteurized dairy products are essential to insure the sanitary quality of the product. The mixture is often thickened slightly by cooking part or all of the mixture with egg or flour. Gelatin may be used to keep the ice crystals small during freezing and subsequent storage. An excessive amount of gelatin, however, produces an unpleasantly gummy product that does not melt normally. It is necessary to use the correct amount of sugar in an ice cream mix because, since sugar lowers the freezing point of the mix, an excessive amount may prevent normal freezing.

The ice cream mix is frozen in a container equipped with a dasher turned by hand or by an electric motor and surrounded by a mixture of ice and salt. Before they are used, all pieces of the freezer that come into contact with the mix should be scalded and cooled to insure a low bacterial count in the ice cream. The freezing container is filled not more than two-thirds full to allow for the expansion or overrun produced by beating in air. If before freezing the container is two-thirds full of mix and is completely full of ice cream after freezing, it means that the overrun is 50 per cent. The expansion of homemade ice cream on freezing is seldom as great as that of commercial ice cream.

After the ice cream mix has been put into the can, it is placed in position in the freezer and the crank adjusted to see that it turns properly. Alternate layers of crushed ice and coarse ice cream salt are placed in the outer container. Coarse salt is used because ordinary salt dissolves too rapidly for efficient freezing. The proportions are about one part salt to eight parts ice by measure. If preferred, salt and ice can be mixed before they are packed around the container. During freezing the heat of the mixture is absorbed by the melting ice. The mix does not freeze if ice alone is used. The salt dissolves in the film of water on the surface of the ice, depresses the freezing point of the brine, and thus produces a low temperature. Within limits, the higher the proportion of salt, the lower the temperature reached. Although rapid crystallization is sought in making candy and ice cream that is not stirred during freezing, it is better to freeze stirred ice cream at a moderate rate and therefore to avoid the use of a large amount of salt. Too rapid freezing of the ice cream prevents the breaking up of ice crystals and the incorporation of sufficient air. During freezing, liquid is not drained from the ice-salt mixture unless there is danger that it will seep into the frozen mixture, because the brine increases the speed of melting the ice and causes the mixture to freeze more rapidly.

The mixture is allowed to stand five minutes and then is stirred slowly until it is thoroughly chilled. Rapid stirring of the warm ice cream mix is avoided because it may cause butter to separate as in churning. Stirring should be vigorous after the mixture has become viscous so that ice crystals are broken up as they form and air is beaten into the mixture. When this is done, stirring increases the volume and makes the texture velvety.

Courtesy of the American Dairy Association

Fig. 16–5. *This home ice cream freezer has ice and salt packed around the inner can which holds the ice cream mix. The dasher is lifted out when the ice cream is so firm it can no longer be stirred.*

After the ice cream mix has been frozen enough, it is almost impossible to stir it. At this point the dasher is removed, the ice cream is leveled, and the container is covered tightly and repacked with ice and salt. A larger proportion of salt is used at this time than during freezing, approximately one part of salt to four parts of ice by measure. Any excess of water is drained from the ice, but it is not necessary to draw off all the water. The ice is packed down firmly and the ice cream allowed to stand for at least thirty minutes before serving. During this ripening, the ice cream hardens and becomes smoother.

Refrigerator Ice Creams. Although ice creams that are not stirred continuously during freezing can be packed in a tight container and frozen in a mixture of one part salt to one or two parts ice by volume, this method has been almost entirely replaced by freezing in the ice cube section of a refrigerator or in a freezer because of the wide availability and convenience of such equipment. It is more difficult to prepare ice cream without continuous stirring because the ice crystals tend to grow to undesirable size and air is not incorporated during freezing. For this reason the mixture must be different from that used for ordinary ice cream.

Two desserts that can be frozen successfully without stirring are mousses and parfaits. Mousses are sweetened, flavored whipped cream, whereas parfaits are made by pouring hot syrup over beaten eggs or egg whites and blending with whipped cream. The use of a large proportion of whipping cream, however, results in a dessert that is expensive as well as high in fat and calories. High levels of whipping cream may be unpalatable to some people, especially if the fat has clumped due to excessive beating. For these reasons it is desirable to find a mixture not much higher in fat than standard ice cream that can be frozen without stirring. Refrigerator ice creams that are not excessively rich may contain whipped evaporated or nonfat dry milk, beaten egg white, and moderate amounts of whipped cream to incorporate air. Combinations of stabilizers like agar, pectin, or gelatin—plain or in the form of marshmallows—may be used. Because of their acidity, fruits or fruit juices may help stabilize beaten egg whites, whipped cream, or evaporated milk. The sugar content of refrigerator ice cream mixes cannot be so high that freezing is prevented. Sugar lowers the freezing point of mixtures to which it is added and in too large amounts may prevent freezing entirely.

Refrigerator ice creams should be frozen as rapidly as possible because slow freezing results in the formation of large ice crystals. For this reason the controls of the refrigerator or freezer are set to lower the temperature as much as possible, and a shallow layer of the mixture is put in a metal container which is placed on a surface in the freezer that is chilled by the refrigerating coils. The occasional removal of the mixture to scrape ice crystals from the sides of the container accelerates freezing. Air can be incorporated in mixtures such as those high in evaporated or nonfat dry milk by beating them vigorously when partially frozen. However, after air cells have been incorporated by folding in beaten egg whites, whipped cream, or whipped evaporated milk, beating would remove air from the mixture.

Refrigerator ice creams are usually better in quality when eaten soon after they are frozen than after they have been stored. Although acceptable refrigerator ice creams can be made, it seems unlikely at present that a dessert frozen without stirring can be produced that has the quality of ice cream that is stirred during freezing.

Activities

1. Prepare fondant using corn syrup, cream of tartar, and cream as crystal inhibitors; let ripen until the next laboratory period, evaluate crystal size, then flavor and shape it as desired.

2. In a small pan place about twice as much sugar as is required to cover the bulb of a thermometer. Heat the sugar gradually and notice the temperatures at which it liquefies and at which it caramelizes.

3. Compare the taste of hot or iced tea or coffee sweetened with sugar and with as many synthetic sweeteners as can be obtained.

4. Prepare chocolate fudge according to a standard and an uncooked or semi-cooked recipe.

5. Prepare penuche and divinity candies.

6. Prepare typical noncrystalline candies such as nut brittle, butterscotch, caramels, marshmallows, toffee, and taffy.

7. Prepare vanilla ice cream with and without stirring. Compare the quality and price per serving with commercial vanilla ice cream and also with ice milk and mellorine if these products are available.

8. Prepare orange milk sherbet according to this recipe of the U.S. Department of Agriculture: Combine one $14\frac{1}{2}$-ounce can of evaporated milk, 1 cup of sugar, and $\frac{1}{8}$ teaspoon of salt. Gradually stir in $\frac{1}{2}$ cup of orange juice and $1\frac{1}{2}$ tablespoons of lemon juice. Pour into a refrigerator tray and freeze until firm. Remove to a chilled bowl and beat until smooth and fluffy. Return to the tray and freeze until firm again. Pineapple sherbet can be made by substituting $\frac{1}{3}$ cup of unsweetened pineapple juice for the orange juice. In addition, prepare sherbets in a freezer and purchase commercial sherbet of the same flavor. Compare the quality and price per serving of the sherbets.

References

BROEG, C. B. Sweeteners: Natural and Synthetic. *Food Eng.*, 37: 66–68 (January, 1965).

Farmer's World. The Yearbook of Agriculture, 1964. U.S. Dept. Agr., Washington, D.C.: United States Government Printing Office. Pp. 177–184.

Food for Us All. The Yearbook of Agriculture, 1969. U.S. Dept. Agr., Washington, D.C.: United States Government Printing Office. Pp. 151–152, 232–236.

GOTT, P. P. and L. F. VAN HOUTEN. *All About Candy and Chocolate.* National Confectioners' Assoc. of the U.S., Inc. Chicago (1958).

GRISWOLD, R. M. *The Experimental Study of Foods.* Boston: Houghton Mifflin Company. 1962. Chapter 13.

HEID, J. L. and M. S. JOSLYN (Eds.). *Fundamentals of Food Processing Operations. Ingredients, Methods, and Packaging.* Westport, Conn.: The Avi Publishing Company, Inc. 1967. Pp. 30–77.

Honey . . . Some Ways to Use It. U.S. Dept. Agr., Home and Garden Bull. No. 37 (1964).

POTTER, N. N. *Food Science.* Westport, Conn.: The Avi Publishing Company, Inc. 1968. Pp. 343–353, 523–538.

17

seasonings, nuts, and gelatin

Some of the substances which are used in small quantities to alter the flavor or consistency of foods have been grouped together. Among the seasonings considered are salt, vinegar, extracts, spices, herbs, and flavor potentiators. Nuts are included for convenience and because they are often used in small quantities to add flavor and texture to other foods. Because of their high nutritive value, however, they can be used in the more important role of meat alternates. Gelatin, a protein capable of changing a liquid into an elastic solid, is also included.

Seasonings
Salt

Salt can be regarded as an indispensable food adjunct. Known to the chemist as sodium chloride, its importance in the diet is demonstrated by the fact that wild animals frequently travel miles to a "salt lick" to satisfy their craving. Man's insistent desire for the savor of salt has led governments to establish monopolies on its sale as a means of obtaining a constant income. The human requirement for sodium chloride is usually more than met in the average diet by the natural salt content of the food we eat and the additional salt we add to it. Sometimes the intake of salt is decreased sharply in the therapeutic diets prescribed for those who tend to hold an excess of water in their tissues.

Salt can be obtained by allowing salt water from seas or salty lakes to evaporate in shallow pools or in shallow heated pans. Although the evaporation of brines is an important source of salt in some countries, salt can be obtained more easily from inland deposits where they are available. Underground deposits of salt that have resulted from the evaporation of prehistoric seas are present in many areas. Salt can be mined like coal, or a well can be dug and fresh water introduced. Water dissolves the salt, and the brine is pumped to the surface. Salt obtained from any source is refined, prepared for the market, and packed in cardboard containers. Table salt is fine-grained and contains a harmless chemical that prevents caking caused by the absorption of moisture from the air. Both plain salt and salt to which a small amount of potassium iodide has been added are available on the market. Such "iodized" salt is essential in areas of the United States where the soil and therefore the food grown on it is deficient in iodine. The incidence of goiter in certain low-income areas as reported by the National Nutrition Survey is causing concern. This situation raises questions about the availability and use of iodized salt. As a caution for all consumers it should be noted that iodized salt is not used in prepared salted foods.[1]

Salt can be said to bring out the flavor of foods rather than to add a distinctly new flavor. Even the flavor of sweet foods such as candy or ice cream is improved by the addition of a few grains of salt. Because people vary in the amount of salt they prefer, care must be taken not to add an excessive amount during food preparation. Salt is sometimes combined with herbs, spices, or other flavorings to make celery salt, garlic salt, smoke salt, and seasoned salt. Salt is also used in curing meats and fish and in the making of pickles, butter, and cheese.

Vinegar

Vinegar has been used since ancient times as a flavoring agent and as a preservative of foods. Indeed it has probably been in use as long as wine, because when wine is stored exposed to air and to the action of microorganisms over a period of time it becomes sour—in other words, it becomes vinegar. The word "vinegar" comes from two French words *vin* and *aigre,* meaning "sour wine." Vinegar can be made from a wide variety of carbohydrate-containing foods like cider, malt, grape juice, and occasionally peaches, apricots, or pineapple. Red wine vinegar is made by allowing dark-colored grapes to ferment, whereas yellow or white wine vinegar is made from white grapes or colored grapes from which the skins have been removed. Distilled or white vinegar made from dilute distilled ethyl alcohol is inexpensive and adds no color to a food but may have a harsh acid taste.

Vinegars usually contain 4 to 6 per cent acetic acid, an organic acid responsible for the acidity of vinegar. It is formed when a microorganism called *acetobacter aceti* acts on ethyl alcohol in the presence of oxygen. Although the acid is the same in vinegar from any source, the flavor, odor, and color of the vinegar depend upon the material from which it is made. In Europe wine vinegar is popular, but cider vinegar seems to be preferred in the United States. Flavored vinegars can be purchased or made at home[2] by bringing one pint of vinegar to the boiling point and pouring it over one of the following:

---

[1] *Family Economics Review.* December 1969. Consumer and Food Economics Research Division, Agricultural Research Service, United States Department of Agriculture, Washington, D.C., p. 12.

[2] T. C. Kintner and M. Mangel. *Vinegars and Salad Dressings.* Missouri Agricultural Experiment Station Bulletin No. 631 (1954).

$^1/_2$ teaspoon of dried herbs (rosemary, basil, tarragon, dill seed)
2 tablespoons of fresh herbs (rosemary, sage, sorrel)
$^1/_2$ cup of chopped mint leaves (or chives)
1 head of dill seed
1 small clove of garlic slashed

Cider vinegar is often used in making flavored vinegar; however, malt vinegar is commonly used when tarragon is to be added. Because of its heavy lemon-like flavor, malt vinegar can be used instead of lemon in many dishes including sauces for fish.

One of the most important uses of vinegar is in salad dressings, which were discussed in Chapter 7. Vinegar is used as a preservative in pickles, catsup, relishes, green olives, pickled vegetables, and spiced fruits. It can be used to change sweet milk to sour and was used in pies by the American pioneers, probably when no acid fruit was available.

Extracts

Flavoring extracts are usually solutions of aromatic oils or essences in ethyl alcohol. Natural flavorings are made from the roots, bark, fruit, sap, or leaves of aromatic plants, whereas "artificial," "imitation," or "synthetic" flavorings are prepared from synthetic chemicals to simulate the desired aroma or taste. Vanilla is the extract most familiar to homemakers, but almond, lemon, orange, peppermint, rose, rum, spearmint, or wintergreen extracts may also be used. Many other extracts are used by food manufacturers.

Pure vanilla extract is made from vanilla beans, the fruits of a climbing orchid native to Mexico and Central America. About two-thirds of the world's vanilla crop is grown on islands off the southeastern coast of Africa. Vanilla extract is made by cutting cured vanilla beans into small pieces which are placed in a solution of not less than 35 per cent ethyl alcohol and heated in a percolator. Dextrose, sucrose, or glycerin may be added at the end of the extraction process to prevent precipitation and to preserve the flavor and aroma.[3]

Lemon extract is an alcoholic solution of oil of lemon. Oil of lemon is expressed from fresh lemon peel without the aid of heat. The oils of peppermint and spearmint are obtained by distilling the macerated mint leaves. Full flavor fruit concentrates that include volatile aroma can be made from fruits such as apples and cherries.

Herbs and Spices

"Flavor," a famous gourmet once said, "is the soul of food." He might have gone one step farther by adding, "and spices and herbs are the soul of flavor." Historical records give evidence of the use of herbs in early times

[3] *Farmer's World. The Yearbook of Agriculture, 1964.* United States Department of Agriculture, Washington, D.C., p. 197.

Courtesy of H. J. Heinz Co.

Fig. 17–1. *The vanilla bean yields an extract used in flavoring many desserts.*

as shown by the writings of Pliny, Aristophanes, Virgil, and Horace. Spices may indeed have been even more important in the rather monotonous diets of ancient peoples than they are now because countries have been discovered and wars fought in the search for spices. Although they have little or no food value, spices add interest to a meal and often provide the dash of seasoning that makes the difference between an ordinary dish and a famous dish of distinctive flavor.

In its botanical sense, the term "herbs" is a broad one, and the distinction between herbs and spices is frequently obscure. For practical purposes, however, most people have come to think of herbs as the leaves of aromatic annual or perennial plants grown in the temperate zone and of spices as the products of tropical plants. Spices may come from the bark (cinnamon), berry (pepper), flower bud (clove), root (ginger), or seed (nutmeg). The American Spice Trade Association has suggested as a modern definition of spice, "Products of plant origin which are used primarily for the purpose of seasoning food." [4] If one accepts this definition of spice, and it is becoming more and more accepted, the term includes the tropical spices and also herbs, aromatic seeds, and such blends as curry powder and poultry seasoning. However, in the discussion that follows, the traditional use of the terms "herbs" and "spices" will be used.

In colonial days herbs were important. There was hardly a home without its herb garden in which could be found sage, mint, thyme, and other herbs now nearly forgotten. Recently there has been a revival of interest in herbs among those who realize that their subtle flavors have often been lacking in modern cooking. Many of the savory herbs can have a place in the modern garden. Those easily grown from seed are sage, dill, parsley, chives, basil, thyme, savory, mint, and marjoram. Chives and parsley can be grown in flowerpots on a sunny windowsill during the winter months.

Fresh herbs can be stored in a refrigerator for as long as two weeks if they are placed upright in a tightly closed container with about one-quarter inch of water in the bottom. The older leaves are stripped from the bottom of the stem before it is put into the jar.

Herbs can be preserved by either drying or freezing. Herbs are best dried as rapidly as possible away from direct sunlight. Leaves or seeds in prime condition are scattered on a surface through which air can circulate. After the herbs are dry, the leaves are crushed between the fingers or with a rolling pin, twigs and stems are discarded, and the herbs are tightly covered in a container like a glass jar. For freezing, herb leaves are washed, patted dry, spread in a single layer on freezer paper, rolled, and the ends sealed with freezer tape. Although the flavor of frozen herbs is good, the leaves become limp and begin to darken soon after they have thawed. Mint is sometimes frozen in ice cubes for use in beverages. Other herbs like rosemary, thyme, and basil can be frozen in ice cubes and added to cold soups, broth, or tomato juice. A layer of water is frozen in an ice cube tray, the herb is placed in the center of each cube, more water is added, and the tray is returned to the freezer.

Herbs and spices should be purchased in small amounts so that they may be used before they become stale. Because they contain volatile materials known as essential oils, which give them their characteristic flavor and odor, herbs and spices become stale on standing exposed to the air or when stored in a warm place, as over a range, and lose their valued flavor and odor. Whole spices like nutmeg, stick cinnamon, and peppercorns lose flavor less rapidly than the corresponding ground spice. The shaker tops on spice containers should be closed except when in use. Flavor is released from the whole dried herbs and spices as the exposed surface is increased by crushing the leaves between the fingers or by grinding spices that consist of woody plant parts.

[4] Is It a Spice or Herb? *Journal of The American Dietetic Association*, 57: 419 (1970).

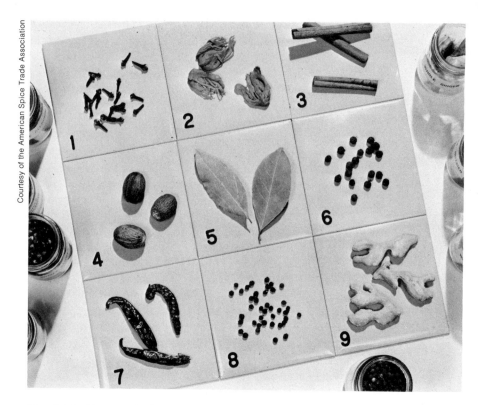

Courtesy of the American Spice Trade Association

Fig. 17–2. *Unground whole spices: 1. cloves; 2. whole mace; 3. cinnamon sticks; 4. whole nutmeg; 5. bay leaf; 6. whole allspice; 7. whole red pepper; 8. whole pepper corn; 9. whole ginger root.*

The essential oil is sometimes extracted from spices like cloves and nutmegs in order to flavor manufactured foods. Essential oils are prepared by suspending the plant material in water and allowing steam to pass through it. The essential oils are distilled, condensed, and separated by this process of steam distillation.

Only enough herb or spice is used in a dish to enhance the natural flavor of the food. Excessive amounts overpower the natural flavor of the food and make the taster conscious of the specific herbs or spices used. Although several may be added to one dish, it is better not to use too many nor to serve too many herb dishes in one meal. Because dried herbs are more compact than fresh, one teaspoon of dried herb is equivalent to about three teaspoons of the fresh herb. Herbs are often added during the last minutes of cooking to avoid driving off their flavor by heat. When herbs are used in uncooked dishes like salads, however, they are added as long as possible before serving so that their flavors will have a chance to blend with those of the other foods.

Although it sometimes seems that there is no limit to the possible combinations of herbs, spices, and foods, some concrete suggestions for their use are given in Table 17–1. In using herbs and spices, it is often convenient to remember that their flavors are more easily dissolved in fat than in water. For this reason herbs are often added to salad dressing. A delicious accompaniment to hot vegetables, cooked eggs, meats, or fish, or for making sandwiches is a combination of one well-packed, level tablespoon of fresh green herbs or one-half teaspoon of dried herbs with four tablespoons butter, margarine, or rendered chicken fat. The mixture can be stored several days in a small covered jar in the refrigerator. Unfamiliar herbs or spices can be tested before using by combining them with butter or cream cheese and spreading on a piece of bread or a plain cracker. Whole fresh or dried herbs and spices like bay leaf and peppercorns are often tied in a piece of cheesecloth, added to soups, stews, or gravies about one-half hour before cooking is finished, and the bag removed before serving.

Flavor Potentiators

In contrast to the herbs and spices, which have a pronounced flavor of their own, small amounts of potentiators enhance the natural flavor of other foods, perhaps by acting on the sensory mechanisms. The first flavor potentiator to be developed was monosodium glutamate or MSG. It is the sodium salt of glutamic acid, an amino acid that occurs in proteins. It is often prepared from wheat gluten, soybeans, or from the waste of the sugar beet. It was discovered in 1908 by a Japanese research worker who was curious to know why the addition of dried seaweed enhanced the natural flavor of many foods, especially those high in protein. MSG is available for home use in purified form,[5] is found in many convenience foods, in certain seasoned salts, and is an important constituent of soy sauces. As mentioned in Chapter 6, glutamic acid has been found in several young, freshly harvested vegetables and is especially high in mushrooms, which may explain why mushrooms enhance the flavor of many dishes to which they are added. The quantity of MSG added to a food depends upon the particular food and the amount being prepared. For example, one-fourth to one-half teaspoon may be added to a recipe for 4 to 6 or one teaspoon or less to a pound of ground beef. Excessive amounts of MSG are avoided because they give the food an unpleasant taste. Most people find that when used in adequate but not excessive amounts, MSG enhances and blends the flavors of foods like meat, seafood, and vegetables. It lessens saltiness in some foods but increases it in others. It reduces the sour taste of tomato products and represses certain undesirable flavors. MSG added to soups and broths may give the feeling of more body and satisfaction after eating. A rough rule for the use of MSG in cooking is to add it to foods with which salt is used. MSG does not replace salt but can be used in a similar way.

[5] A trade name is Ac'cent.

Table 17–1. *Spices, Herbs, Seeds, Blends, and Their Uses*

Spices

Allspice

Comes from West Indies, resembles a blend of cinnamon, cloves, and nutmeg.
USES: Whole: pickling, meats, gravies.
Ground: baked goods, puddings, relishes, fruit preserves.

Cayenne

Spicy small peppers. Most pungent.
USES: Meats, sauces, fish, eggs.

Cinnamon

Bark of tree grown in Indonesia, China, Ceylon, Indochina.
USES: Whole: pickling, preserving, puddings, stewed fruits, hot drinks.
Ground: baked goods, mashed sweet potatoes.

Mustard

Small seed but dry ground mustard is classed as a spice. Grown in U.S., also imported from Europe.
USES: Whole seed: garnish for salads, pickled meats, cucumber pickles, fish, hamburgers.
Dry: meats, sauces, gravies.

Nutmeg

Kernel of nutmeg fruit, grown in Grenada, India, Indonesia.
USES: Whole: pickling, also grated as needed.
Ground: baked goods, sauces, puddings, topping for eggnog, custard, cauliflower, fruits, doughnuts.

Paprika

Grown in U.S., also imported from Spain and Central America.
USES: Colorful red garnish for many foods; also used with chicken, fish, salad dressings, vegetables, meat, gravies, canapes.

Pepper

Small dried berry of a vine native to East Indies. Also comes from India, Indonesia, Borneo, and British Malaya.
USES: Whole: pickling, soups, and meats. Ground (black and white): meats, sauces, gravies, many vegetables, soups, salads, eggs. Our most important spice.

Saffron

Dried stigmas of plant of the crocus family. The world's most expensive spice. Grown in Mediterranean area.
USES: Baked goods, rice, rice and chicken dish of Spain (arroz con pollo).

Tumeric

Root of plant of ginger family. Ingredient of curry powder. Grown in India, Haiti, Jamaica.
USES: Meats, dressings, salads, usually in combination with mustard. Also used in pickling and for relishes, eggs, fish, seafood.

Cloves

Bud of clove tree grown in Indonesia, Madagascar, and Zanzibar.
USES: Whole: pork and ham roasts, stews, pickled fruits.
Ground: baked goods, puddings, vegetables.

Ginger

Root of tuberous plant grown in Asia, Africa, West Indies.
USES: Whole or cracked: chutneys, conserves, pickling, dried fruits, applesauce. Ground: baked goods, pies, puddings, canned fruits, pot roasts, other meats.

Mace

Fleshy, orange-red material between nutmeg shell and outer husk. Grown in Grenada, Indonesia, India.
USES: Whole: fish sauces, pickling. (Also called "blade.")
Ground: cakes, chocolate desserts, noodles.

Table 17–1 (continued)

Herbs

Basil
Also known as sweet basil. Leaves and stems of plant of mint family. Imported from North Mediterranean shore, some grown in U.S.
USES: Tomato dishes, peas, squash, string beans, turtle soup, lamb chops.

Parsley
Dried leaves of parsley, also known as parsley flakes. Grown in U.S.
USES: Soups, salads, meat, fish, sauces, vegetable dishes, also used as garnish.

Bay Leaves
Aromatic leaves of laurel tree grown in Eastern Mediterranean area. Sold whole or crushed.
USES: Pickling, stews, sauces, soups, fish, chowder, meats.

Rosemary
Dried leaves of evergreen shrub of the mint family. Sweet and fresh-tasting, like pine needles in shape. Imported from France, Spain, Portugal.
USES: Lamb dishes, soups, stews, beef, fish, meat stocks.

Chervil
Leaves of an herb that grows in many countries in the temperate zone.
USES: Soups, salads, egg dishes, French dressing, fish, chicken.

Sage
Dried leaves of herb of mint family. America's most popular herb. Imported from Yugoslavia, some grown in U.S.
USES: Pork, pork products, sausages, meat stuffings, fish and poultry, green salad.

Savory

Dried leaves of herb of mint family. Imported from France and Spain.
USES: Meats, meat dressings, chicken, fish sauces, eggs.

Tarragon

Dried leaves and flowering tops of herbs, tastes similar to anise.
USES: Sauces, salads, chicken, meats, eggs, tomato dishes. Also in tarragon vinegar.

Thyme

Pronounced "time." Dried leaves of plant of mint family. Imported from France, some grown in U.S.
USES: Stews, soups, poultry stuffings, clam and fish chowders, meat and fish sauces, croquettes, chipped beef, tomatoes.

Marjoram

Herb of mint family. Imported from France, Chile, Peru.
USES: Stews, soups, sausage, poultry seasonings, fish, fish sauce, lamb.

Mint

Dried leaves, strong sweet flavor. Grown in U.S.
USES: Flavoring soups, stews, beverages, jellies, meat, fish, sauces.

Oregano

Dried leaves of herb of mint family. Imported from Mexico, Italy, Greece, Chile, and France. Similar in flavor to marjoram but stronger.
USES: Pork, beef stews, meat sauces, gravies, omelet, chili con carne.

Table 17–1 *(continued)*

Seeds

Anise

Licorice-flavored fruit of small plant grown in Spain, Syria, China.
USES: Cookies, candies, sweet pickles, coffeecake, and rolls.

Caraway

Dried fruit of plant of parsley family. Imported from the Netherlands.
USES: Baked goods, cabbage, noodles, soft cheese spreads.

Cardamom

Dried fruit of plant of ginger family. Also spelled cardamon. Imported from Guatemala, India, and Ceylon.
USES: Whole (in pod): used in mixed pickling spice.
Seed: used in demitasse.
Ground: Danish pastry, rolls, breads, coffeecake, grape jelly.

Cumin

Small dried fruit of plant of parsley family. Also known as cumino seed; sometimes spelled cummin. Imported from Iran and French Morocco.
USES: Whole or ground: soups, cheese, pies, eggs. An ingredient of curry and chili powders.

Dill

Small dark seed of dill plant imported from India.
USES: Pickling, sauerkraut, salads, soups, fish and meat sauces, gravies, spiced vinegars, green apple pie.

Fennel

Small seedlike fruit with sweet taste somewhat like anise. Imported from India and Romania.
USES: Sweet pickles, boiled fish, pastries, candies.

Poppy

Tiny seed of poppy plant. Blue-colored seed imported from Holland.
USES: Breads, rolls, cookies, salads, noodles.

Sesame

Small oval honey-colored seed, similar to the tomato seed in shape. Imported from Turkey, India, and the Orient.
USES: Gives nut-like flavor to breads, rolls, and cookies.

Curry Powder

Blend of many spices. Important ingredient in dishes of India.
USES: Curry sauce for eggs, vegetables, also used in French dressing, fish, meat, clam and fish chowders.

Celery

Seed of member of parsley family, not same as celery used as vegetable.
USES: Pickling, salads, fish, salad dressings, vegetables.

Coriander

Dried ripe fruit of herb of parsley family. Imported from Yugoslavia and French Morocco.
USES: Whole: mixed pickles, cookies, biscuits, poultry stuffings, mixed green vegetables.
Ground: sausage, rolls.

Blends

Chili Seasoning

Blend of chili peppers and other spices.
USES: Chili con carne and other Mexican dishes, shellfish, oyster cocktail sauces, eggs, gravies, stews.

An even more powerful flavor potentiator than MSG has been found by the Japanese in seaweed and dried fish—products that they have used for centuries to enhance the flavor of sauces served with rice. These potentiators became available commercially in purified form to the Japanese in 1960 and more recently in the United States. They can best be described to the nonchemist as compounds[6] called nucleotides formed from nucleic acid. Nucleic acid is present in the nucleus of all living things where it forms part of the genetic material. At present the flavor nucleotides, either alone or mixed with MSG, are available only for commercial use. They are being added to foods like soups, gravies, and meats and are capable of replacing part of the beef extract used in some products. They give body and smoothness to foods even though they are added in amounts of only about one-tenth the levels of MSG frequently used.

Nuts

As explained in Chapter 3, most nuts are simple dry fruits like cereal grains and legumes. In nuts of this type, the fruit has become hard, stony, or woody on ripening. There are a few exceptions to this general rule, however. For example, Brazil nuts are seeds that grow within the fruit which forms a shell around twelve to twenty-four nuts, each of which has a woody seed coat. Peanuts are seeds that grow underground within a fibrous, woody shell. Cashews are kidney-shaped nuts that protrude from the end of an enlarged fleshy stalk known as the cashew apple.

Almonds and coconuts are classified as drupes, a group of fruits that also includes cherries, olives, peaches, and plums. In almonds the outer structure is discarded when the fruit is harvested, leaving the edible seed. In coconuts the seed is surrounded by a hard, woody shell. The seed contains the edible portion or coconut meat, which provides food for the germinating tree.

The preference for tree nuts has changed with their availability. At the end of the 19th Century wild nuts like hickory nuts and black walnuts were used widely. Because it is difficult to crack the shells and remove the edible portion of these nuts, their popularity declined as nuts that are more easily shelled became available. At present the easily shelled nuts dominate the market. In the United States, the favorite tree nut is the pecan, followed by English walnuts[7] and almonds. The English walnut is grown in the warm climates of California, Oregon, and Washington, as well as in France, Turkey, and Italy. Most of the almonds used in this country come from California, whereas pecans are grown in the southern states. Some of the nuts

---

[6] Disodium inosinate and disodium guanylate which are 5'-nucleotides sold under the trade name Mertaste.

[7] Walnuts of this type are sometimes called Persian because they originated in Persia or neighboring countries. They are called European walnuts in Europe and English walnuts in the United States because during colonial days they were imported from European countries through English ports.

grown in the United States in smaller amounts are filberts or hazelnuts, hickory nuts, pine nuts, and butternuts. Brazil, cashew, and pistachio nuts are imported. Coconuts, the seed of a palm tree, are imported from the West Indies and Central America. Coconuts can be purchased fresh but more often are sold in the flaked or shredded form after being frozen, canned, or dried. Shredded coconut is prepared by removing the husks, grating the coconut meat, and usually adding sugar, salt, and glycerin to help retain moisture. Before canning, coconut is partially dried. The cans of coconut are exhausted, filled with carbon dioxide, sealed, and processed. Coconut is dried further for use as dessicated coconut. Coconut is also imported into the United States as copra, a dried form of coconut meat from which coconut oil is made.

In the United States, more peanuts are used than any other nut. Peanuts, which are also called ground nuts, are a legume. The pods that contain peanuts mature under the ground. The plant is a low branching annual vine. In the fall the vines are loosened from the soil with a plow, and the pods are allowed to partially dry before they are harvested. Peanuts are cooked before they are eaten because they are quite unpalatable raw; they are usually roasted or fried. Peanut butter is made by grinding roasted blanched peanuts and adding salt. Stabilizers may be added to retard oil separation.

In addition to their use as salted nuts, in confections, and as pastes and butters, nuts are used in nut loaves, croquettes, and fillings, in nut breads, cakes, and pastry, and in salads, sandwich fillings, and ice cream. Nuts may be added to salads, sauces, and vegetables but should be added at the last minute so that they retain as much of their crispness as possible.

Selection

Nuts can be marketed shelled or unshelled with the exception of cashews, which are always marketed shelled. Unshelled nuts keep longer than shelled nuts unless special precautions are taken to prevent rancidity. Because of their convenience, however, many nuts are sold in the shelled form and are sometimes cut ready for use. Table 17–2 has been included so that comparisons can be made of the price of nuts purchased in the shell and as nut meats. Shelled nuts are often packed in tin cans and sterilized. An antioxidant is sometimes added to salted nuts because rancidity develops more rapidly in salted than in unsalted nuts. The development of rancidity is delayed by keeping nuts in airtight containers under refrigeration. They can be stored for longer periods in a freezer than at higher temperatures.

Nutritive Value

Nuts, like dried beans and peas, are concentrated sources of many nutrients. Because nuts are one of the richest common sources of protein among foods of plant origin, they are used as a meat alternate. They are also high in fat and therefore in energy value. Except for chestnuts, nuts are not high in carbohydrates. Peanuts are an excellent source of niacin, and most nuts are very good sources of thiamine.

Table 17–2. *Quantity of Nuts to Yield One Pound of Nut Meats*

Nut	Amount to give 1 pound of nut meats	Measure of 1 pound of nut meats
	lb.	cups
Almonds	$3\frac{1}{2}$	3
Brazil nuts	$2\frac{1}{2}$	$3\frac{1}{2}$
Chestnuts	$1\frac{1}{2}$	3
Filberts	$2\frac{1}{4}$	$3\frac{1}{3}$
Peanuts	$1\frac{1}{2}$	$3\frac{1}{4}$
Pecans		
halves	$2\frac{1}{2}$	$4\frac{1}{4}$
chopped		$3\frac{3}{4}$
Walnuts, black		
halves	$5\frac{1}{2}$	4
broken		3
Walnuts, Persian, English		
halves	$2\frac{1}{2}$	$4\frac{1}{2}$
chopped		$3\frac{2}{3}$

Gelatin

Gelatin is formed from collagen, a protein in the connective tissue of animals. Conversion of collagen to gelatin causes the connective tissue of meat to soften during cooking. The formation of gelatin from the collagen present in a soup bone or in poultry often causes homemade broth to have a jelly-like consistency after it has been cooled. Gelatin is made commercially from bones or hides. Fat is first removed from the material. Bones are then treated with acid to remove calcium phosphate, and hides are treated to remove the hair. The material is then heated with water and a small amount of acid or alkali. As the connective tissue cooks, the large protein molecules of collagen are hydrolyzed to the smaller molecules of gelatin. The gelatin-containing broth is drawn off, filtered, concentrated by the evaporation of water, allowed to gel, and then dried into glossy, brittle sheets of pure gelatin. High-speed mills break the brittle sheets into tiny granules. Gelatin used in foods must meet high standards of purity and therefore must be manufactured under sanitary conditions. Glue owes its adhesive qualities to the presence of gelatin but may contain impurities that are not permitted in gelatin.

Nutritive Value

Although gelatin is a pure protein that consists of seventeen amino acids, it is not a protein important in the diet because it is used in small quantities and is incomplete. In fact, gelatin is the only food from an animal source that does not contain complete proteins. It has only traces of the four essential amino acids—tryptophan, threonine, methionine, and isoleucine.[8] Since it is a dry protein, its energy content, which is four calories per gram, is the same as that of flour and dry cereals. Because of these facts, the food value of products in which gelatin is used can be said to depend largely upon the other ingredients included. Gelatin desserts have the advantage of being easily digested, bland in flavor, and acceptable to most people. A one-cup serving of plain, ready-to-eat gelatin dessert contains about 140 calories and four grams of protein.

Uses

The principal use of gelatin is to change a liquid into an elastic solid. In the briefer terms of the colloid chemist, a sol is changed into a gel. This reaction is reversible for gelatin since the gel can be heated to form a sol and then chilled to produce a gel again. The word gel can also be applied to foods like baked custards which are made semisolid by coagulation of egg protein and to fruit jellies and jams in which the gel is formed by pectin, a substance related to carbohydrates that occurs in fruit juice. Fruit jellies are reversible and baked custards irreversible gels.

Gelatin is also used as a foaming agent in marshmallows, some types of nougat, and in some whipped salads and desserts. Gelatin helps keep sugar crystals small in candy and ice crystals small in ice cream by interfering with the union of small crystals to make larger ones. Gelatin concentrates on the surface of air bubbles in whipped desserts or whipped cream and thus stabilizes them.

Gelatin is the basis for a wide variety of salads and desserts that bring sparkle and color to meals. Gelatin dishes of high quality have good flavor, are attractive in appearance, and are firm without being stiff. The flavor and color of the products depend upon added ingredients because gelatin changes consistency without changing taste.

Preparation

Granulated, unflavored gelatin is often packaged in envelopes that contain one tablespoon, enough to gel one pint of liquid. The liquid can be fruit or vegetable juice, water, broth, milk, or other liquids. The gelatin is mixed with a small amount of cold liquid and allowed to stand for a few minutes to soften. The softened gelatin is then dispersed by placing it over hot water or by adding hot liquid and stirring it until the mixture is clear and no granules of gelatin remain. Ingredients such as sugar and salt are added. If not all the liquid was used to disperse the gelatin, the remainder may be added at room temperature or as frozen juice or as ice. However, if the temperature is reduced too much, the mixture may set before all ingredients are added. If the gelatin is to be served plain, the mixture is poured into molds or a serving dish and chilled until set. If fruits or vegetables are to be added, the mixture is chilled to the consistency of thick unbeaten egg white before

[8] *Food. The Yearbook of Agriculture, 1959.* United States Department of Agriculture, Washington, D.C., p. 66.

the well-drained solids are added. Fruit or vegetables added when the gelatin mixture is still a liquid will often float. On the other hand, adding them after the gelatin has set makes it necessary to break up the gelatin, and often a uniform mass is not formed again. Although gelatin dishes form a gel rapidly if they are packed in ice, they do not usually stand up as well when served as do those formed more slowly at ordinary refrigerator temperatures. Two to four hours are usually required for a pint of mixture to gel, although this time can be shortened by adding part of the liquid as frozen juice or ice cubes.

Although one envelope or one tablespoon of gelatin for two cups of liquid is a reliable general rule, the gelatin may be increased or the liquid decreased when a large mold is used, when the product must be held at room temperature in hot weather, when the mixture is high in acid, when a whip is being made, or when large amounts of other ingredients such as fruits, vegetables, egg white, or whipped cream are added. When in doubt, it is better to use too little than too much gelatin because a stiff, rubbery product is unattractive, whereas a soft gelatin dessert can be served in a dessert dish instead of as a mold.

Gelatin is unmolded by dipping the mold in warm water and loosening the gel around the edge with a paring knife. Water that is too hot is avoided because it would melt the gel. The serving dish is placed on top of the mold, and both are turned upside down and shaken while the dish is held tightly to the mold. If the gelatin does not unmold readily, the process is repeated.

Plain gels made with gelatin and sweetened liquid can be used for a variety of desserts. Fruits can be added as already described. Light but elegant desserts may come from the basic recipe for plain gel. When it has attained the consistency of thick unbeaten egg white, the mixture may be beaten until it is light, fluffy, and about twice the original volume to form whips. Sponges or snows can be made by adding unbeaten egg whites to the basic gel mixture, chilled as just described, and beating the mixture until it is light and fluffy, or by beating the chilled gel and the egg whites separately and combining. The filling for chiffon pies is made from a chilled custard or fruit mixture containing gelatin into which beaten egg whites and sometimes whipped cream are folded. Spanish cream is a chilled egg-yolk custard containing gelatin into which beaten egg whites are folded. Bavarian creams are gelatin desserts into which whipped cream is folded. Charlottes are similar to Bavarians but may be higher in whipped cream and are usually molded with ladyfingers. Whipped evaporated milk is sometimes substituted for whipped cream in gelatin desserts.

Molded salads have been discussed in Chapter 7. Main dishes can be prepared from a mixture of gelatin and liquid to which are added poultry, fish, meat, cheese, or hard-cooked eggs. Whipped cream, salad dressing, and vegetables may also be added.

Fig. 17–3. *To make a molded summer fruit dessert:*
Arrange a small amount of fruit in the bottom of the mold to form a design. Spoon on enough gelatin mixture to cover the bottom of the mold. Chill until almost firm.

Chill the remaining gelatin mixture until the consistency of unbeaten egg white. Fold in the remaining fruit and spoon on top of the almost firm layer. Chill until firm. Unmold and garnish with frosted grapes if desired.

Courtesy of Knox Gelatine

Factors Affecting Gelation

Gelation is affected by several factors. One of the most important is the concentration of the mixture because a desirable gel will form only within certain limits. If the concentration of gelatin is excessive, the gel is stiff, whereas with too low a concentration the gel may be soft or no gel forms. The concentration of gelatin also affects the time required for setting. Mixtures of high concentration set more rapidly than those of low concentration. The proportion of gelatin is sometimes increased for mixtures high in acid because increased acidity reduces gel strength. Although a large quantity of sugar may retard the formation of a gel, the amounts of sugar ordinarily used have little effect on gel strength. Gelation does not occur above 35° C. (95° F.). Gels form more rapidly as the temperature decreases. Gels formed at unusually low temperatures may melt more readily, however, than gels formed more slowly.

Fresh and frozen pineapple contain an enzyme, bromelin, that breaks down protein and thereby prevents gelation. Pineapple in these forms can be added after it has been boiled two minutes to inactivate the enzyme. Canned pineapple can be added to a gelatin mixture without further treatment.

Convenience Forms

Dessert mixes that contain gelatin are so familiar that they hardly seem like convenience foods. The ingredients of the mixes, which are listed on the label, usually include sugars, gelatin that may be ground finer than the unflavored gelatin sold for home use, organic acids, flavorings, which may be artificial, and color. Sodium citrate is sometimes added to regulate the acidity. The mix is likely to contain about 10 per cent gelatin. Mixes are now available with vegetable flavors suitable for making salads as well as in a variety of fruit flavors.

Activities

1. Prepare a bowl of mixed raw vegetables for tossed salad. Remove to several smaller containers and sprinkle each with herbs or spices suggested for salad in Table 17–1.
a. Add a simple French dressing made of oil, vinegar, salt, and pepper. Compare the taste of the salads.
b. Repeat, omitting herbs and using French dressing made with different types of vinegar.

2. Compare the taste of cornstarch puddings or custards made with pure and artificial vanilla extracts.

3. Sprinkle salt on some celery sticks, MSG on others. Compare the taste.

4. Prepare homemade soup, creamed chicken, stew, or a dish containing meat, fish, or poultry. Do not include convenience foods because they are likely to contain flavor potentiators. Divide the product into several parts after it has been flavored to taste with salt and pepper. Compare the taste of products containing no MSG and several levels of MSG.

5. Compare the following:

a. The appearance, texture, and taste of several types of shelled, unsalted nuts.

b. Roasted salted nuts prepared according to directions in a cookbook.

6. Compare the unwhipped gelatin products made in parts *a* and *b*.

a. Prepare one package of orange flavored gelatin mix as directed on the package. Chill.

b. Soften 2 tablespoons of unflavored gelatin in $\frac{1}{3}$ cup of cold water. Add $1\frac{1}{3}$ cups of boiling water and stir in 1 cup of sugar. When the sugar has dissolved, add $\frac{1}{4}$ cup of lemon juice and 2 cups of freshly squeezed or reconstituted frozen orange juice. Put half the mixture in the same type container as used for the orange flavored gelatin mix and the remainder in a bowl. Chill.

c. When the mixture in the bowl is slightly thicker than unbeaten egg white, beat with an electric mixer or a rotary beater and chill again.

d. Compare the whipped and plain gelatin made with orange juice.

7. Compare the following:

a. Put 2 tablespoons of cold water in a small bowl, add $1\frac{1}{2}$ teaspoons of gelatin, and soak for 5 minutes. Place the bowl over a pan of boiling water and add 2 tablespoons of sugar. Heat until the mixture is clear and add $\frac{1}{2}$ cup of cold water and 2 tablespoons of lemon juice. Pour the mixture into molds and chill.

b. Make the recipe as in *a*, except add the gelatin to 2 tablespoons of boiling instead of 2 tablespoons cold water.

8. Make the recipe given in *7a* three times using 1, $1\frac{1}{2}$, and 2 teaspoons of gelatin. Compare the products.

9. Find a recipe for a sponge or snow. Make it by adding unbeaten egg white to the chilled mixture before beating, and by folding beaten egg white into the whipped gelatin mixture. Compare the two products.

10. Find recipes in a cookbook and prepare Spanish cream, charlotte russe, and any Bavarian cream.

References

BRONSON, W. F. Technology and Utilization of Gelatin. *Food Tech.*, 5: 55–58 (1951).

DAY, A. and L. STUCKEY. *The Spice Cookbook*. New York: David White Company. 1964.

Farmer's World. The Yearbook of Agriculture, 1964. U.S. Dept. Agr., Washington, D.C.: United States Government Printing Office. Pp. 195–200.

Flavor Potentiators. *Food Eng.*, 36: 62 (May, 1964).

Food for Us All. Yearbook of Agriculture, 1969. U.S. Dept. Agr., Washington, D.C.: United States Government Printing Office. Pp. 249–252.

Handbook of Food Preparation. American Home Economics Association. Washington, D.C. 1971. P. 95.

HAYES, E. S. *Spices and Herbs Around the World*. Garden City, N.Y.: Doubleday & Company, Inc. 1961.

LOWMAN, M. S. *Savory Herbs: Culture and Use.* U.S. Dept. Agr., Farmers' Bull. No. 1977 (1946).

MELNICK, D. Monosodium Glutamate—Improver of Natural Food Flavors. *The Scientific Monthly,* 70: 199–204 (March, 1950).

MERORY, J. *Food Flavorings: Composition, Manufacture, and Use,* 2nd ed. Westport, Conn.: Avi Publishing Company, Inc. 1968.

The New York Academy of Sciences. Flavor Potentiators. *The Sciences,* 4: 19–23 (May, 1965).

Nuts in Family Meals. A Guide for Consumers. U.S. Dept. Agr., Home and Garden Bull. No. 176 (1970).

PARRY, J. W. *Spices.* Vol. I. New York: Chemical Publishing Co. 1969.

Peanut and Peanut Butter Recipes. U.S. Dept. Agr., Home and Garden Bull. No. 36 (1966).

ROSENGARTEN, F., JR., *The Book of Spices,* Wynnewood, Pa.: Livingston Publishing Company. 1969.

WEBSTER, M. W. *Peanut Marketing.* U.S. Dept. Agr., Marketing Bull. No. 29 (1964).

the planning, preparation, and service of meals

18
meal planning

Three meals a day, with or without "snacks," is the most widely accepted pattern of food consumption for many families in this country. However it is recognized that some individuals and even some families tend to skip meals entirely and consume "snacks" throughout the day. Perhaps one of the strongest recommendations for meals is that they give us a "guide to eat by." Well-established meal patterns go far in assuring a similar food intake from day to day and can be a definite aid in selecting food to meet daily nutritional needs.

The three meals of the day may be breakfast, luncheon, and dinner; or breakfast, dinner, and supper, depending on local customs and family activities and traditions. These meals differ from those described in the literature as served in the mid-nineteenth century and even later, not only in the variety of dishes served, but also in the amount of food regarded as a portion.

There are many reasons for the changes in meal patterns. Increased knowledge of and concern for adequate nutrition have led to more careful evaluation of the diet. Along with the change from a predominantly active to a more or less sedentary population has come a corresponding interest in the effect of excess calories upon health and this has led to modifications in food consumption. There is greater abundance and variety of foods and more money in family food budgets than ever before. Changes in kitchen plans and equipment, in sanitary standards, and in the personnel responsible for food preparation and service have influenced our dining habits. Today it is usually the homemaker or some other member of the family who prepares and serves the meals with whatever assistance may be available from other members of the family. She does, however, have available a wide variety of prepared and partially prepared foods, as well as such labor-saving devices as automatic cookers, electric beaters and blenders, ranges, and refrigerators ready for instant use.

General Considerations in Meal Planning

Many factors must be considered in planning and preparing meals to be served in the home. The homemaker is not only responsible for these meals, but through them she also influences the eating habits of her family when they are no longer at home. Food selection and food habits may be influenced greatly by the meals served in the home during the growing-up years.

Although three meals a day may be traditional, they may vary in food content, hour and place served, and the way they are served. For some families, meals are simply a time of consuming food; frequently no two members eat together. Other families find meals, especially the evening meal, a social hour—a time when the family enjoys a bit of leisure and exchanges news and relates happenings of the day. Frequently a simple meal may be one which is most conducive to good fellowship, for if carefully planned, not much time and thought need be given to its preparation and service.

The kind of meals planned will depend, to some extent at least, upon the importance the homemaker and the family place upon meals. Usually the homemaker has an important part in deciding the place of meals in family life, although other factors may enter in which modify her plans. In general, money, time, energy, knowledge, skills, and abilities influence the type of food prepared, and the way it is served.

It is seldom wise to allocate a disproportionate amount of the income to food. However, a family that prefers meals served in an attractive setting, with time enough to enjoy good food, well prepared, may tend to spend more on food and entertaining, for example, and forego an expensive trip. Another family may decide to economize on food—although not at the expense of adequate nutrition—in order to save for a second car. The way the family chooses to use its money is influenced largely by its own values and goals.

Time spent on meals should be carefully evaluated. Sometimes an attempt to reduce the cost of food may lead to an increase in the time spent in preparation. However, with careful planning no more time need be spent in preparing low-cost meals than those of medium cost. The ease with which the homemaker prepares a meal may depend to a great extent upon her experience and upon her willingness to spend time in planning. Many homemakers derive such satisfaction from the preparation of food that they are willing to spend both time and energy in the production of good food. For some, the preparation and service of meals is a creative outlet, and the delight they experience in serving tasty, attractive foods in an appropriate setting is adequate recompense for energy expended.

Today's modern equipment, used in a well-planned kitchen, may greatly reduce the energy required to prepare and serve food. Added to these conveniences are the many processed, partially processed, ready-to-cook, and ready-to-serve foods available in every market.

Knowledge and the application of this knowledge to meal planning is of utmost importance. It may determine the adequacy of the meal planned, the kind of food purchased, its quality and cost, and the way it is stored, prepared, and served.

In recent years great stress has been placed on the importance of good nutrition with emphasis on the foods to be included to insure an adequate diet. What in some countries is regarded as technical information, known only by the specialists in physiology and nutrition, is commonplace among American homemakers. The widespread instruction carried on by the home economics extension service, the contributions made by mass media including radio and television, and the lessons on foods and nutrition given in the schools, have informed people generally of their food needs and how to meet them. In spite of this widespread effort to inform the public concerning nutritional needs, nationwide household food consumption surveys made in 1955 and 1965 show that whereas six out of ten households surveyed in 1955 had diets rated good, only five out of ten in 1965 rated good.[1] To rate good the diet met allowances for all seven nutrients considered. The meat group was the only one of the four food groups that had increased in use during this period. The other three had decreased, the bread and cereal group the least of the three.

There are, then, large numbers of people in the United States who do not get enough of the essential foods even though the study shows many of them could well afford to buy them. The challenge is to discover a successful approach to nutrition education which will result in changes in food selection and food practices acquired through a lifetime of eating experience. Food fads and fallacies often receive more publicity than sound nutrition information. Some, eager to adopt every new fad, ignore their common sense which tells them that it is not a sound nutritional practice. Perhaps the worst offenders are the teenage girls who endanger their health by inadequate food intake, irregular meals, no breakfasts, and other poor dietary practices. Studies indicate, too, that some mothers of teenage girls have equally bad food habits. It is evident, therefore, that knowledge of nutrition and sufficient money for food, while of utmost importance in dietary improvement, are not enough. To be effective, this knowledge and purchasing power must be used to provide nutritionally adequate meals which will be consumed by those for whom they are provided.

Skills and abilities may determine the type of meal planned. The homemaker lacking the skill to prepare simple breads and pastries may do well to use mixes or bakery produced products. Avoiding elaborate "made dishes," she concentrates on simple, well-prepared meats, vegetables, salads and desserts until she has gained both skill and confidence.

Meal planning—whether for the simplest family meal or for an elaborate company dinner—involves consideration of a number of factors: adequacy and availability of foods, traditions and customs, economic resources, personal likes and dislikes, suitable combinations, seasonability, staying quality of food, ease of food preparation and meal patterns. When the consideration

[1] S. F. Adelson. Changes in Diets of Households, 1955 to 1965—Implications for Nutrition Education Today. *Journal of Home Economics*, 60: 448–455 (1968).

of each of these factors has become a habit, the serving of three meals a day, 365 days a year, may soon become routine.

Adequacy of Food

The first responsibility of the homemaker in feeding her family is to make sure that nutritional needs are met. The same nutrients are required by all persons throughout life, but in varying amounts.

The Daily Food Guide, mentioned in Chapter 1, was developed as a simple, easily remembered way to plan appetizing meals containing the nutrients needed for good health. This Guide is for use in the United States and includes only those foods found in the daily diet of a high proportion of the population. Other countries may have equally simple guides, which take into consideration the foods consumed in the area. If the Daily Food Guide is followed and the amount of food recommended from each of the four food groups—milk and milk products; meat, poultry, fish, eggs and dried legumes; fruits and vegetables; and cereals and bread—is included daily, the food needs should be met.

Patterns for meals may vary widely, but a well-planned meal provides its share of the daily food needs of the group to be served. When some guide is not followed, studies indicate a tendency to make inadequate provision for certain food essentials. Sometimes there is a noticeable lack of protein in the diet, accompanied by a deficiency of iron. A surprising number of diets are low in calcium because of the almost complete absence of milk. Although it is not expected that any single meal will contain in exact proportion the foods which the diet for the day should provide, an effort should be made to keep individual meals as nearly balanced as possible. The inclusion of fruit, milk, and whole-grain or enriched cereal in the breakfast makes meeting daily food needs easier. On the other hand, a breakfast of sausages, griddle cakes, and syrup may make it difficult to plan the other meals without exceeding the energy requirement. A good menu is a planned one; not only does it provide for adequate calories and protein through the use of carbohydrate, fat, and protein foods, but also for an optimum amount of those mineral elements and vitamins essential for physical well-being.

Availability of Foods

Formerly, dietary practices depended largely upon the type of food produced in the community. In a locality where rye was the only cereal readily grown, it was included almost to the exclusion of all other cereals in the diet. Similarly, in countries or localities where rice was produced in large quantities, it was the chief cereal in the daily fare. The same held true for highly perishable fruits and vegetables. Today, with improved methods of food preservation and distribution, even the most perishable foods are available over large areas of this country. Fresh meat, milk, and vegetables are obtainable in cities remote from the sources of their production. Inland towns of the Northwest and Midwest, for instance, have citrus fruit available at reasonable cost throughout the year. The improvement in canning and dry-

Fig. 18–1.

A Daily Food Guide

Meat Group
Foods Included

Beef; veal; lamb; pork; variety meats, such as liver, heart, kidney.
Poultry and eggs.
Fish and shellfish.
As alternates—dry beans, dry peas, lentils, nuts, peanuts, peanut butter.

Amounts
Recommended

Choose 2 or more servings every day.
Count as a serving: 2 to 3 ounces of lean cooked meat, poultry, or fish—all without bone; 2 eggs; 1 cup cooked dry beans, dry peas, or lentils; 4 tablespoons peanut butter.

Vegetable-Fruit
Group

All vegetables and fruits. This guide emphasizes those that are valuable as sources of vitamin C and vitamin A.

Sources of
Vitamin C

Good Sources. Grapefruit or grapefruit juice; orange or orange juice; cantaloupe, guava; mango; papaya; raw strawberries; broccoli; Brussels sprouts; green pepper; sweet red pepper.

Fair Sources. Honeydew melon; lemon; tangerine or tangerine juice; watermelon; asparagus tips; raw cabbage; collards; garden cress; kale; kohlrabi; mustard greens; potatoes and sweet potatoes cooked in the jacket; spinach; tomatoes or tomato juice; turnip greens.

Sources of
Vitamin A

Dark-green and deep-yellow vegetables and a few fruits, namely: apricots, broccoli, cantaloupe, carrots, chard, collards, cress, kale, mango, persimmon, pumpkin, spinach, sweet potatoes, turnip greens and other dark-green leaves, winter squash.

Amounts
Recommended

Choose 4 or more servings every day, including:
1 serving of a good source of vitamin C or 2 servings of a fair source.
1 serving, at least every other day, of a good source of vitamin A. If the food chosen for vitamin C is also a good source of vitamin A, the additional serving of a vitamin A food may be omitted.
The remaining 1 to 3 or more servings may be of any vegetable or fruit, including those that are valuable for vitamin C and for vitamin A.
Count as 1 serving: 1/2 cup of vegetable or fruit; or a portion as ordinarily served, such as 1 medium apple, banana, orange, or potato, half a medium grapefruit or cantaloupe, or the juice of 1 lemon.

Milk Group
Foods Included

Milk—fluid whole, evaporated, skim, dry, buttermilk.
Cheese—cottage; cream; Cheddar-type, natural or process.
Ice cream.

*Amounts
Recommended*

Some milk every day for everyone.
   Recommended amounts are given below in terms of 8-ounce cups of whole fluid milk:

Children under 9	2 to 3	Adults	2 or more
Children 9 to 12......	3 or more	Pregnant women......	3 or more
Teenagers	4 or more	Nursing mothers......	4 or more

   Part or all of the milk may be fluid skim milk, buttermilk, evaporated milk, or dry milk.
   Cheese and ice cream may replace part of the milk. The amount of either it will take to replace a given amount of milk is figured on the basis of calcium content. Common portions of cheese and of ice cream and their milk equivalents in calcium are:

   1-inch cube Cheddar-type cheese = $\frac{1}{2}$ cup milk
   $\frac{1}{2}$ cup cottage cheese   = $\frac{1}{3}$ cup milk
   2 tablespoons cream cheese   = 1 tablespoon milk
   $\frac{1}{2}$ cup ice cream   = $\frac{1}{4}$ cup milk

**Bread-Cereal
Group**
Foods Included

All breads and cereals that are whole grain, enriched, or restored; *check labels to be sure.*
   Specifically, this group includes: breads; cooked cereals; ready-to-eat cereals; cornmeal; crackers; flour; grits; macaroni and spaghetti; noodles; rice; rolled oats; and quick breads and other baked goods if made with whole-grain or enriched flour. Bulgur and parboiled rice and wheat also may be included in this group.

*Amounts
Recommended*

Choose 4 servings or more daily. Or, if no cereals are chosen, have an extra serving of breads or baked goods, which will make at least 5 servings from this group daily.
   Count as 1 serving: 1 slice of bread; 1 ounce ready-to-eat cereal; $\frac{1}{2}$ to $\frac{3}{4}$ cup cooked cereal, cornmeal, grits, macaroni, noodles, rice, or spaghetti.

Other Foods

To round out meals and meet energy needs, almost everyone will use some foods not specified in the four food groups. Such foods include: unenriched, refined breads, cereals, flours; sugars; butter, margarine, other fats. These often are ingredients in a recipe or added to other foods during preparation or at the table.
   Try to include some vegetable oil among the fats used.

ing processes, the development of the frozen food industry, and the extension of the list of foods preserved in these and other ways, place a wide variety of foods at the disposal of people throughout the United States. The availability of a large number of foods at prices people can afford to pay markedly influences the daily diet and its adequacy.

The wide variation in dietary patterns throughout the world depends largely upon the available food supply. This is true with respect to both the quantity of calories provided and the nutritive quality of the diets. In countries where food is abundant, the dietary patterns show a distinct trend toward adequacy. In countries where the food supply is limited, the dietary patterns may show a lack in both quantity and quality. War and other catastrophes such as floods, droughts, and earthquakes may make drastic changes in peoples' dietary patterns, usually due to a reduction in the food supply. When followed over extended periods of time such patterns often result in malnutrition, reduced physical vigor, and lowered resistance to disease.

Tradition and Customs

National and religious traditions are often important in determining the food included in the diet. Many descriptions of the customs of different nations are available to students. For example, Pearl V. Metzelthin describes many in her cookbook.[2] Of Sweden she writes, "Dill and fennel sauce are frequently used with mutton, lamb, and beef. The fennel sauce is bottled commercially and is as familiar in Sweden as our catsup bottles here. Small new potatoes brushed and scraped, never peeled, are boiled and then sprinkled with melted butter and finely chopped parsley or dill. Fresh cucumbers, cut lengthwise, the seeds removed and mustard flavored are pickled every summer and are eaten with many Swedish dishes, also. Veal roasts are usually served with a cream gravy as are the Kaldolmar, cabbage rolls stuffed with meat. Pork is the Christmas meat and Julskinka, fine ham, with a fresh cabbage soup, apple tart and a multitude of Smörbakelser (Christmas butter cookies) are usually eaten on Christmas Day."

In describing the Danes Miss Metzelthin writes, "Like their Swedish neighbors, the Danes like clabbered milk, served like the Filbunke (with sugar, ground ginger, rye bread crumbs or finely ground pepper nuts). Danish Buttermilk Soup, a recommended Danish soup for school children, is made by boiling the buttermilk, then thickening it with rice flour and sweetening it with sugar. Grated lemon peel, a few raisins, and a garnish of whipped cream add flavor to the dish. Barley and Apple Soup is another favorite of the rosy-cheeked Danish country folk, with always a dash of raspberry sirup in it."

Norwegian food customs are also mentioned: "A delicious Kylling (roast chicken) with cream sauce or rice crust, or duck stuffed with prunes, are

[2] P. V. Metzelthin. *World Wide Cook Book.* New York: Julian Messner, Inc., 1939, pp. 29, 46, 57.

Nordic specialties often found in Norwegian holiday menus. Ryper (grouse) is so well prepared in Norway that the method easily can be adapted to our native pheasant and partridge as well as grouse.

"The country families in Norway eat Bygg-grynsmelkesuppe (milk soup with barley-groats), some salted pork, potatoes, mashed turnips, sweet or sour milk, or clabber, and a cup of coffee, for an ordinary meal. Ertesuppe (pea soup) and Fleske-pannekake (pancake with pork), followed by coffee, is a popular peasant repast.

"Flatbröd, thin, cracker-like bread wafers made of oats, barley and rye into dry, oblong pieces is the nourishing Norwegian staple. Fancy breads and filled buns are made for special occasions. Shaped like Kvalknuten (whaleknot), Luciekronen (crown), Halvmaanen (half moon) or Napoleons-

Fig. 18–2. *A typical meal on Christmas Eve in a Finnish farmhouse consists of ham with a crust (lower right corner), buttered turnips (in casserole dish at back), rice with a good luck almond (in center of table), and bread without yeast, called rieska.*

Courtesy of the Finnish National Travel Office

hatter (Napoleon hats), they are often filled with raisins, currants, or almonds, and are as good to look at as they are to eat."

Although these customs of the Scandinavian countries were selected just as an example, quotations might have described the poi or the Macadamia nuts of Hawaii, the Dobosh Torte, a ten-thin-layer cake with chocolate filling that melts in the mouth, from Austria; the flaming desserts of France; the Siskebabs of Turkey; the many rice dishes of Japan; the olives, nuts, feta (goat cheese), and sweets of Greece; or the Feijoada, a dish of rice, black beans, meats of many kinds, and seasonings, of Brazil.

In addition to its national dishes, each country also exhibits a characteristic meal pattern. The Norwegians, the Danes, and the Dutch normally eat four to seven meals a day. The Greeks are accustomed to two substantial meals daily. In the United States we announce our pattern as "three square meals a day," but the validity of such a statement can be questioned when viewed against the widespread practices of skipped breakfasts, coffee breaks, and after-school and evening snacks. Actually, there is no valid reason why three meals a day should be served. The important consideration is whether food containing needed nutrients without an excess of calories is provided adequate for the day's activities. Whether this food is consumed as three meals, or three meals plus snacks, is probably of minor importance.

Often religion prescribes or prohibits the eating of certain foods. For example, pork, including lard, is prohibited by the orthodox Jewish faith, which also decrees that milk and meat not be served in the same meal. Most followers of Hinduism eliminate meat entirely from their diet. Other groups prohibit the drinking of coffee or tea as well as alcoholic beverages.

Family custom frequently determines the type of meal as well as the characteristic dishes included. If, in earlier times, ham and eggs were included in the breakfast and a number of heavy foods in the other meals, these foods may well continue as a component part of the family diet. Thus meals may remain heavy long after the changed daily routine of the family makes their inclusion unnecessary or even undesirable. In many midwestern homes, the custom of serving codfish balls on Sunday morning, observed in the family home on the Atlantic seaboard many generations ago, still is followed in a locality far from the habitat of the cod. Some families serve jelly with every meal; others consider hot bread essential.

Economic Considerations

In the United States, with its great range of family incomes, there are wide variations in food budgets for families of the same size, which contributes to differences in expenditures for particular foods. These differences are minimized and tend to disappear with marked downward shifts in food prices, just as they are accentuated with marked upward trends in the cost of certain foods. In affluent homes, fruit out of season may be served for breakfast as a matter of course. Imported relishes and pickles may comprise the hors d'oeuvres, and expensive roasts the main course. Although the budget of a family of moderate means may not provide for foods of the luxury class, it can still offer variety and opportunity for choice. Food budgets of lower income families permit even more limited choices, and it may become increasingly necessary to depend on cereal foods for the main or a substantial part of the meal. The problem then becomes one of supplementing the cereal with foods necessary for an adequate diet although there may be increased difficulty in providing palatable meals. When the allowance for food is limited, it is especially important to know the less expensive alternates for the more expensive recommended foods.

Individual Likes and Dislikes

Although the recommended daily allowances for each of the food groups should be followed, there is room for individual preferences among the classes of foods. However, many people make personal likes and dislikes the only basis for the inclusion or exclusion of a food in their meals. The failure to include milk or other nutritious foods in the diet for such a reason is far too common. With few exceptions, a person can learn to eat any wholesome food with enjoyment despite notions to the contrary.

Suitable Combinations of Foods

The goal in food combinations has been summarized as follows:

The ideal meal is a simple one—whether of one or many courses—in which the different types of food are harmoniously represented, but not repeated, and in which food accessories, such as pickles, spices, preserves, and the like, are little needed because the foods themselves are well cooked and each contributes its own characteristic flavor, texture, form, and color to the making of a well-blended whole.[3]

Interesting contrasts in texture, flavor, and color help determine the attractiveness of a meal. A plate served with creamed codfish, mashed potatoes, and buttered turnips or one served with buttered beets, sliced tomatoes, and salmon has little appeal. A meal in which all of the foods included seem alike in either the smoothness or the roughness of their texture will not be pleasing despite other contrasts.

Flavor contrasts may mean the inclusion of sweet and sour foods or even some bitter and salt. Too many highly seasoned foods at one meal are undesirable; usually one is enough. Likewise, food mixtures should be limited. With a casserole of meat and vegetables, a slice of head lettuce may be more acceptable than a mixed vegetable salad.

Variation in shapes, too, make for interest. Frequently this can be introduced by the way the vegetable or fruit is cut or served. Potatoes, for example, may be served mashed, whole, or as slices, quarters, or strips.

[3] M. S. Rose. *Feeding the Family.* New York: The Macmillan Company, 1929, p. 238. By permission of the publishers.

Fig. 18–3. *A holiday meal of turkey pie, cranberry and lettuce salad, and buttered broccoli has variety in color, flavor, and texture.*

Courtesy of the Wheat Flour Institute

Some contrast in temperature is also desirable. Even in warm weather, at least one hot dish seems to add interest to the meal and to make it more acceptable. Chilled or even frozen foods are sometimes served with the main course.

A meal is more pleasing if it does not contain an excess of protein, carbohydrate, or fat, but inclusion of some of each usually results in a more palatable and satisfying meal and one which is also better from a nutritional point of view.

To a large extent, tradition seems to shape our concept of acceptable food combinations. Baked beans and brown bread; wieners and sauerkraut; roast pork with apple sauce; turkey, dressing, and cranberry sauce; waffles and smoked sausages are well-known examples of food combinations widely accepted as "right and proper" for major parts of meals.

It is unwise, however, to so limit combinations that there is never variety. Baked beans may be equally good with corn bread or whole wheat bread, and waffles with peanut butter and jelly.

Seasonability of Foods

Today, season plays a less important role in meal planning than in former times. Buildings warmed in winter and cooled in summer, and a variety of fresh, frozen, or canned foods available throughout the year have greatly reduced the importance of season. Nevertheless, we continue to associate certain foods with certain seasons, for example, watermelon with late spring and the summer months, and mince meat pie with winter. Furthermore, many foods are more plentiful during certain seasons when they tend to be higher in quality and lower in cost. In spite of the comforts of rather uniform temperatures in homes and offices throughout the year, and of generally reduced physical activity for most persons, there is still a tendency to serve more fruits, leafy vegetables, and salads during hot weather. A seasonal menu for summer provides these foods and protein, simply prepared. Hot breads, rich sauces, pastries and other rich desserts are served less frequently.

During the winter months richer foods and those higher in calories are likely to be served. Pork, fried foods, suet pudding, and hard sauces are traditional cold weather foods—and continue to be served, in spite of the fact that the rationale for a higher calorie intake during the winter months no longer applies. Table 18–1 shows menus typical of those served in summer and winter, including foods often associated with those seasons.

Table 18–1. *Suggested Menus for Summer and Winter Months*

Summer	Winter
Breakfast	
Strawberries and Powdered Sugar Shredded Wheat Milk Plain Omelet Toast Butter Coffee	Grapefruit Oatmeal Milk Small Breakfast Steak Toast Jam Coffee
Luncheon	
Cheese Soufflé Garnished with Crisp Bacon and Asparagus Tips Whole-Wheat Bread and Lettuce Sandwiches Lemon Sherbet Macaroons Milk	Creamed Sweetbreads with Toast Points Lettuce Salad Gingerbread Applesauce Cocoa
Dinner	
Chicken Tetrazzini Broiled Tomatoes Buttered String Beans Bibb Lettuce with Buttermilk Dressing Hard Rolls Butter Melon Iced Tea	Baked Sugar Cured Ham Pineapple Slices Sweet Potatoes Buttered Spinach Celery Curls Green Pepper Rings Bread Butter Steamed Cranberry Pudding with Hard Sauce Coffee

Staying Quality of Foods

In planning meals it is also important to include foods that will give a feeling of satisfaction until almost time for the next meal. Both the form and the composition of the food influence the staying quality, which is believed to depend largely upon the rate of digestion of the food consumed. A breakfast composed of orange juice, unbuttered toast, and coffee may pass from the stomach in a short time with the probable early recurrence of hunger and attendant discomfort. Such a meal is said to possess low staying quality. One including fruit, cereal, egg, and buttered toast is rated as having moderate staying quality; whereas one that includes ham and eggs and fried potatoes, is rated as having high staying quality. As mentioned in Chapter 1, fat affects the rate at which food leaves the stomach; even on a low calorie diet it is probable that some fat should be included because of its staying quality. For indoor workers including students, teachers, homemakers, or persons whose next meal will follow in four hours or less, food having moderate staying value would seem a wise choice. For out-of-doors workers, or for persons who may go six hours between meals, it is desirable to include some foods of high staying quality.

Luncheons or suppers served by American families are often light to moderate in staying value. A meal of low staying quality comprised of bouillon followed by fruit salad without dressing, wafers, and tea can be

Fig. 18–4. *A breakfast of fresh orange juice, followed by French toast, honey butter, sausage, and a beverage should satisfy a hearty eater.*

Courtesy of Western Growers Association

changed to one of moderate staying quality by the addition of a slice of cheese and a glass of milk.

Ease of Food Preparation

Increasingly in this country the ease of preparation is having a marked influence upon the types of foods that people eat. Along with the widened interest and participation of women and girls in community activities and the increased employment of women outside the home has come an emphasis upon ease in food preparation. There is a tendency to keep the time required for preparing a meal to a minimum, and foods are selected and menus planned with this in mind. Contributing to this trend are the rapid changes in food technology, the development of simplified methods of food preparation, the increased use of raw vegetables and fruits, and the availability of a wide range of convenience products that are quickly and easily prepared, including mixes of all types, instant beverages, brown-and-serve foods, frozen pre-cooked foods, and ready-to-serve foods. Ease of food preparation, however, should not be emphasized to the extent that nutrition is impaired, or the total family food budget unbalanced.

Meal Patterns

In a country as large as the United States with the wide disparity in daily meal schedules, in the foods produced and consumed locally, and in family food budgets, there are conspicuous differences in the menus served. However, such differences can only be evaluated in terms of the whole situation that their use is planned to meet.

Each person who plans meals for a family or selects foods for his own consumption tends to follow a pattern from day to day. If, in the beginning, a well-defined plan is followed, it soon becomes almost automatic to select foods that supply the needed nutrients.

The Daily Food Guide indicates the foods to be included in daily food plans. The four food groups can be easily remembered and included in the day's meals. In its simplest form, the Guide recommends that meals be planned around these foods:

> 2 cups of *milk;* more for children
> 2 or more servings of *meat* or alternate
> 4 or more servings of *vegetables* and *fruits*
> 4 or more servings of *bread* and *cereals*

It further recommends "other foods for complete and satisfying meals." A more detailed explanation of the Daily Food Guide is given in Table 1–2. Simple patterns which include these recommended foods are:

> *Breakfast*
> Fruit or Juice
> Cereal and/or Egg
> Toast or Roll
> Milk, Other Beverages

Lunch or Supper
Protein Food—Casserole, Soup, or Sandwiches
Vegetable or Fruit
Bread and Butter (may be in the sandwiches)
Milk, Other Beverages

Dinner
Protein Food—Meat or Alternate
Potatoes, Rice, Macaroni, or Noodles
Two Vegetables or One Vegetable and One Fruit
(One Green or Yellow)
Bread or Rolls and Butter or Margarine
Dessert (may be fruit listed above)
Milk, Other Beverages

Breakfast

Breakfast, the meal which starts the day, is emphasized by nutritionists as being particularly important.[4] Unfortunately, it is frequently omitted because of lack of time, lack of appetite, or some other reason. Perhaps no other meal has become so nearly standardized both in food content and in nutritional value. This standardization makes possible the classification of breakfasts into types: very light, light, medium, and heavy. Each type may function acceptably under certain conditions, and each may satisfy differing food needs. Among the factors that determine the type of breakfast provided in the diet are: the activities and tastes of the persons served, the menus for the other meals, the money available for food, and family customs.

The list of foods commonly used for breakfast is relatively small. Traditionally, certain foods have come to be thought of as breakfast foods, and many others which are equally nourishing and which might be more acceptable to some people are not served. Possibly the teenager, in too big a hurry to eat breakfast, would find time if he could drink it in the form of an orange milk shake with an egg added, or if it were a tasty hamburger with a glass of orange juice and one of milk, or even a bacon and tomato sandwich. Apple pie or baked beans, left-over from the night before, could well form a substantial part of the breakfast. There is no reason why the list of foods served for breakfast is more limited than that served for other meals. Because of lack of time, more careful planning may be necessary than for other meals, but a variety of foods is certainly worth considering.

Fruit or fruit juice is usually an important breakfast item. It serves as an appetizer and may make a substantial contribution of ascorbic acid. The food that follows, whether it be food commonly served for breakfast

[4] *Eat a Good Breakfast.* Leaflet No. 268. United States Department of Agriculture, Washington, D.C., 1969.

Table 18–2. *Typical Breakfast Menus*

Very Light	*Light*	*Medium*	*Heavy*
Baked Apple Toast Jelly Milk Coffee	Half Grapefruit Poached Egg on Toast Milk Coffee	Strawberries Puffed Cereal Milk French Toast Sandwiches with Peanut Butter Filling Pineapple Jam Milk Coffee	Sliced Oranges Rolled Oats Milk Broiled White Fish Hashed Brown Potatoes Biscuits Butter Plum Jam Milk Coffee

or something quite foreign to the usual idea of "breakfast foods," should be determined by the energy needs of the group served and by the portion of the day's food to be included in each meal.

Luncheon

The influence of custom is much less obvious in the luncheon or supper plans than in the breakfast, and a much wider variety of foods is used. Cream soups, chowders, fruit and vegetable salads, "made dishes" such as macaroni and cheese, meat soufflés, sandwiches of all kinds, and cocoa

Fig. 18–5. *This cold-weather luncheon makes good use of left-overs.*

Table 18–3. *Typical Luncheon Menus*

Light	Medium	Heavy
Cream of Tomato Soup	Egg Timbales with	Liver Loaf with
Salmon-Radish Sandwiches	Cheese Sauce	Spanish Sauce
Green Pepper Rings	Water Cress Salad	Baked Potatoes
Sliced Peaches	Buttered Toast Strips	Tossed Vegetable Salad
	Half Grapefruit	Ice Cream Cake
	Milk	Fruit Beverage

are all popular foods for this meal. Variety and interest can be introduced into the luncheon menu by offering pleasing combinations of flavors, colors, and textures. The amount of food included in the luncheon, like that in the breakfast, depends upon the part this meal plays in meeting the day's food requirement.

Dinner

Dinner remains, as it has long been, the chief meal of the day. If it is planned first, decisions can be made more readily in regard to what the breakfast and luncheon should contribute to the day's requirements. Although many dinners include one course of meat, vegetables, and salad and one of dessert, some homemakers like to begin the meal with an additional course which is an appetizer, such as soup, fruit juice, or fruit cocktail. As a rule if meat is included in only one meal of the day, it is for dinner and is the main dish with which the other foods are to be satisfactorily combined. The variety of foods used in the dinner makes possible pleasing contrasts in color, form, and texture. Like breakfast and lunch, dinners are usually more appealing if there is variety from day to day. This might be the meal in which to introduce new foods and different methods of preparation. The menu planned for dinner as well as that of other meals may be light, medium, or heavy, and these menus will be acceptable if each supplements the other meals of the day in order to make adequate provision for the food needs of those to be served.

Table 18–4. *Typical Dinner Menus*

Light	Medium	Heavy
Meat Loaf	Broiled Lamb Chops	Baked Heart
Fresh Mustard Greens	Browned Potatoes	Dressing Gravy
Apricot, Celery, Nut Salad	Asparagus Tips	Mashed Potatoes
Baked Custard with	Mixed Vegetable	Broccoli Almond
Caramel Sauce	Salad	Grapefruit, Orange,
Milk Coffee	Hard Rolls Butter	Avocado Salad
	Ginger Cream	Sesame Seed Rolls
	Milk Coffee	Butter
		Apple Pie Cheese
		Milk Coffee

Application of General Rules

Now, having considered the general aspects of meal planning, let us consider some specific problems faced by the homemaker.

The planning of meals for the family can be one of the homemaker's most interesting and challenging responsibilities. Her success may be greatly influenced by her attitude. Education, either formal or based on a conscious use of available information, should help in the selection and preparation of food which will meet the nutritional needs of her family.

Food Requirements

The first step in planning and preparing meals is to determine the daily food requirements of the individuals to be served. The energy requirement can be fairly accurately determined by totaling the estimated caloric needs of these individuals. For example, a family group might be composed of father, mother, college daughter, and son of high-school age. The three meals of the day must furnish from 2200 to 2900 calories for the father, from 1600 to 2100 calories each for the mother and the college daughter, and 3000 to 3400 calories for the son. The total daily caloric requirement for the family would thus range from 8300 to 11,000 calories. Or another group might be composed of four college girls, with a total requirement ranging from 7000 to 9000 calories. In such a group there may be some variation in individual needs, although probably much less than in many other groups. A daily checking of the calories provided would be laborious and pointless, but an occasional evaluation is valuable, especially for the novice to whom the differing energy values of various foods may not seem real.

The meal should be planned so that individual needs may readily be met by varying the size of portions, by second servings, or by the use of foods rich in calories as spreads or desserts. An additional glass of milk accompanied by a second slice of buttered toast with jam may expand a breakfast adequate for the mother to one adequate for her growing son. The plans for each meal should be flexible enough to allow readily for such adjustments.

The next step in meal planning is to determine whether the foods necessary to meet the body's needs for protein, minerals, vitamins, and roughage are included. The observation of guides, which offer an easy means for such checking, is as important in the planning of meals for the family as in the selection of food for oneself. Nutritionists recommend that the planning of the day's meals begin with provision for foods included in the Daily Food Guide and that other foods be added as needed and desired.

Food Costs

The food budget upon which meal plans should be based is determined by the family income, the number in the family, and their ages and activities. For a family of four, father, mother and two preschool children, with an income of $5,000 per year, 28 per cent of the income or approximately 27 dollars per week could provide good nutrition but would require careful planning. Thirty-four dollars or 37 per cent would provide for a moderate

Table 18–5. *Record of Food Costs*

Food	Amount	Cost per Unit	Cost for Amount Needed (4 persons)

cost food plan as estimated by the U.S. Department of Agriculture in March, 1971.[5] Families with lower incomes may have to use 50 to 60 per cent, or even more. As the income increases, the percentage required for the food budget decreases. Computations based on the food budget are of two types, those that are made to determine the amount allowed "per person per day" and even per meal, and those that are made among the various groups of food to ascertain the adequacy of the diet. The amount "per person per day" is determined by dividing the food allowance for the year by 365 and then dividing by the number of persons in the group. The cost of food for a man 20 to 35 years old, prepared and served at home in March, 1971 was estimated at approximately $1.30 per day on the low cost plan, $1.65 on the moderate cost plan, and $2.04 on the liberal plan.[6]

When the daily food allowance has been determined, the amount for each meal should be determined and the menu planned on this basis. The money expenditure for a given meal should be in keeping with the amount for the entire day's food. An undue expenditure for one meal will play havoc with the food plans for the remainder of the day. The division for meals on the basis of $1.65 for the day might provide 40 to 45 cents for breakfast, 45 to 50 cents for luncheon, and 70 to 80 cents for dinner.

If a check of the day's menus reveals that the cost has greatly exceeded the food allowance, less expensive foods of similar nutritive value should be substituted. Seasonal fruits and vegetables, home-grown products, and less costly cuts of meat can be used. Margarine can replace butter. In some cases it may be necessary to replan and reorganize a particular menu and possibly those of the entire day in order to keep within the budget allotment. An occasional stocktaking of the total for food used in a day may be helpful to the homemaker as a check on food expenditures. A suggested form for such accounting is given in Table 18–5. Since many foods are used and the

[5] *Family Economics Review*. June, 1971. Consumer and Food Economics Research Division, Agricultural Research Service. United States Department of Agriculture. Washington, D.C., p. 27.
[6] *Family Economics Review*. June, 1971.

amount is often small, calculation of the cost should be made to two decimal places.

The dispersion of expenditures among the various groups of foods has been given much study, particularly for the low income levels. Fairly firm recommendations for the division of money among food groups have often been made. But the emphasis now seems to be on meeting the recommendations for the Daily Food Guide within the total amount that can be spent on food. This may require substitution of less expensive foods for those originally planned.

Reducing the Food Bill

There are many ways of reducing the cost of the foods within the four food groups. The following suggestions are adapted from two U.S. Department of Agriculture publications.[7]

Milk Group. Evaporated and nonfat dry milk are usually considerably cheaper than fluid milk and supply comparable amounts of calcium and protein. If the family prefers fluid milk for drinking, processed milks may be used in cooking. For baking, nonfat dry milk need not be reconstituted. From the nutritional standpoint, the following substitutions are considered equivalent to one quart of fresh whole milk:

> 1 quart skim milk plus $1\frac{1}{2}$ ounces butter or margarine
> 17 ounces of evaporated milk
> $4\frac{1}{2}$ ounces dried whole milk
> $3\frac{1}{2}$ ounces dried skim milk plus $1\frac{1}{2}$ ounces butter or margarine
> 5 ounces Cheddar cheese

Meat Group. Eggs may often be a less expensive source of nutrients than meat. Grade B and Grade C eggs may be cheaper than Grade A and just as nutritious.

Dry beans and peas are inexpensive alternates for meats.

When buying meat, consider the amount of bone, gristle, and fat. The cost per serving may be more important than cost per pound.

Meat grades may greatly affect price. Good and Standard grades may be "best buys" for certain meat dishes.

Variety meats such as beef, pork, and lamb liver, heart, kidneys, and brains are usually reasonably-priced sources of minerals and vitamins as well as of protein. A few of the other variety meats such as calves liver and sweetbreads may be higher in price.

Chicken and turkey are often bargains compared with other meats, even though they have a high proportion of bone to lean. Buying dressed chickens whole rather than cut up usually saves a few cents.

Fish is frequently an economical source of protein.

[7] Adapted from *Family Food Budgeting for Good Meals and Good Nutrition.* Home and Garden Bulletin No. 94, United States Department of Agriculture, Washington, D.C., 1969; and from *Food for the Family with Young Children.* Home and Garden Bulletin No. 5. United States Department of Agriculture, Washington, D.C., 1970.

Vegetable and Fruit Group. Dark-green and yellow vegetables give good value in minerals and vitamins. Choose those which are in season and most plentiful. Make use of leafy tops of young beets and turnips. Learn to use a variety of leafy, green vegetables. They are often cheap sources of vitamin A and also contain other vitamins and iron.

Compare costs of canned, frozen, and fresh citrus and tomato juices and citrus fruits and tomatoes. It takes two and one-half to three times as much tomato as citrus juice to give the required amount of vitamin C.

Raw cabbage and some dark-green vegetables are good sources of vitamin C.

Cereal Group. Read labels before you buy. Buy by the weight, not by the size of the loaf or package.

Look for bread that is whole-grain or enriched and made with milk.

Buying cereal in multipacks of small boxes may cost two or three times as much per ounce as the same cereal in a larger box.

Sugar-coated cereals cost more per ounce than many common unsweetened ones, supply more calories, but less of other nutrients.

Cereals cooked in the home are usually less expensive than the ready-to-eat kinds.

Miscellaneous Suggestions. Fat drippings from meat and poultry may be used for cooking and seasoning.

When buying canned goods, buy the lowest grade which will be satisfactory for the dish being prepared. For example, the lowest market grade of canned tomatoes may be used for stews and casseroles.

Consider time and the quality of the finished product when deciding whether to use prepared, partially prepared, or unserviced foods. Compare the cost of prepared and partially prepared foods with similar ones made from ingredients; sometimes prepared foods cost little or no more. Also, consider whether or not you enjoy cooking.

Different Food Cost Levels

Menus and accompanying market orders have been carefully worked out by the consumer service of the U.S. Department of Agriculture for different cost levels. These will be discussed a little more fully in the following chapter. Table 19–1 lists food for a week's menus for a family of four at three cost levels. It will be noted that in many instances the quantities do not vary greatly for the different cost levels.

The money spent by families with liberal food allowances for some food groups obviously will not be much more than that spent by lower income families. More may be spent for fresh fruits and vegetables, milk, meat, eggs, and food accessories, and the use of the highest grades and special packaged products is another way in which food expenditures are increased. A liberal or very liberal food allowance gives much leeway in choices and should make obtaining an adequate diet fairly simple.

Although food prices fluctuate in any locality and also vary substantially in different parts of the country, as a rule they tend to maintain a somewhat constant relationship. Below are examples of a day's menus for each of three different levels of food allowance.

Menus
*Limited Food
Allowance*

Breakfast

One-Fourth Cantaloupe
(In Season)
Hot Whole-Wheat Cereal   Milk
Toast   Margarine
Milk

One-Half Grapefruit
Soft-Cooked Eggs
Toast   Margarine
Coffee

Luncheon

Cottage Cheese
Combination Vegetable Salad
Graham Muffins with Raisins
Butter
Cocoa

Peanut Butter Sandwiches
Cabbage Salad
Prune Whip and Lemon Sauce
Milk

Dinner

Tamale Pie
Lettuce and Carrot Salad
White Bread   Margarine
Rosy Apples
Coffee

Rice, Tomato, and Beef Stew
Baked Onions
Whole-Wheat Bread
Margarine   Jelly
Plain Custard

*Moderate Food
Allowance*

Breakfast
Orange Juice
Toasted Cottage Cheese Sandwiches
Uncooked Strawberry Preserves
Cocoa

Luncheon
Meat Casserole
Endive Salad
Biscuits   Marmalade   Butter
Sliced Peaches with Cream
Wafers

Dinner
Breaded Veal Cutlets
Creamed Carrots and Onions   Buttered Zucchini Squash
Apple and Raisin Salad
Buttered Rolls
Cherry Upsidedown Cake
Coffee

Liberal Food
Allowance

Breakfast

Raspberries   Powdered Sugar
French Omelet   Canadian Bacon
Date Muffins   Butter   Preserves
Cocoa

Luncheon

Curried Shrimp and Mushrooms on Rice
Avocado and Grapefruit Salad
Lemon Angel Cream   Cinnamon Crisps
Milk

Dinner

Leg of Lamb
Parsleyed New Potatoes
Fresh Asparagus with Hollandaise Sauce
Bibb Lettuce
with
Hearts of Artichokes
Finger Rolls   Apricot Preserves
Fresh Blueberry Pie
Coffee

Guides for Planning Meals

The selection of food combinations for desirable menus may be easier if certain guides for meal planning are observed.

1. Select food that meets the nutritional needs of those for whom the meal is planned, using the Daily Food Guide as a basis.
2. Consider food for each meal in relation to food plans for the day.
3. Keep the food value of any given meal essentially the same, day after day.
4. Select food suitable for the meal.
5. Consider the personal likes and dislikes of the group.
6. Select foods that combine pleasingly.
7. Have contrast in the food in color, texture, form, and temperature.
8. Have daily variety.
9. Select foods in season when possible.
10. Avoid serving more than two dishes of concentrated food in any one meal.
11. Select food that is readily prepared.
12. Select food that is easily served.
13. Select foods after due consideration of the equipment on hand.
14. Consider the cost in relation to the food allowance for the day.

Menu Forms

To facilitate the planning of both the individual meal and the meals for the week, a record of the menus chosen should be made. In the customary manner of writing menus, foods are listed in the order served. Spacing is important. Formerly, those foods eaten together as courses were grouped together; today, however, the extra space between courses is frequently omitted. A well-spaced menu is symmetrical. The beverage is usually the last item on the menu. The first letter of all words except prepositions and conjunctions is capitalized.

A breakfast menu would appear thus:

Tangerine Sections
Cracked Wheat with Whole Milk
Scrambled Eggs   Bacon Curls
Toast   Butter
Cocoa

A luncheon menu would be written as follows:

Cheese Fondue
Buttered Green Beans   Carrot Strips
Rolls   Butter
Greengage Plums   Cookies
Milk

A dinner menu would be written as follows:

Tomato Bouillon
Wafers
Standing Rib Roast of Beef
Stuffed Baked Potatoes
Lemon Buttered Carrots
Crisp Green Salad
with
Blue Cheese Dressing
Popovers   Butter
Raspberry-Glazed Chiffon Cake
Coffee   Tea

Activities

1. Observe breakfasts eaten by college women and describe the typical breakfast of such a group. How does it measure up to accepted dietary standards?

2. What changes, if any, are needed to make the meal acceptable? List the changes made in your meal patterns since you came to college. Have the changes been "for better or for worse"? Upon what bases have you made these changes?

3. Suggest a menu of the light type for each of the three meals of one day. What changes would you suggest to make them into the medium type? Into the heavy type?

4. Check a list of daily menus which you have been served recently. Note the regularity with which certain foods recur. Indicate how these could be replaced with foods similar in value to give variety and interest.

5. Obtain and score menus from magazines, newspapers, eating places, and other sources. What modifications do they often require to be satisfactory menus?

6. Evaluate the food you consumed yesterday in terms of the Daily Food Guide. Show how your diet could have been improved. What did snacks contribute?

7. Plan menus for three days for a family of four as described in the section on Food Costs for (a) moderate cost level, and (b) liberal cost level.

8. Plan menus for a day for two different seasons, making use of seasonal foods.

9. List food practices in your family which reflect traditions, customs, or religious restrictions. Obtain menus from a family of a different national background; can you identify any national influences?

References

BOGERT, L. J., G. M. BRIGGS, and D. H. CALLOWAY. *Nutrition and Physical Fitness,* 8th ed. Philadelphia: W. B. Saunders Company. 1966.

Family Fare. A Guide to Good Nutrition. U.S. Dept. Agr., Home and Garden Bull. No. 1 (1970).

Food. The Yearbook of Agriculture, 1959. U.S. Dept. Agr., Washington, D.C.: United States Government Printing Office.

Food for Us All. The Yearbook of Agriculture, 1969. U.S. Dept. Agr., Washington, D.C.: United States Government Printing Office.

KINDER, F. *Meal Management,* 3rd ed. New York: The Macmillan Company. 1968.

LOWENBERG, M. E. Socio-cultural Bases of Food Habits. *Food Technology,* 24: 751–756 (1970).

LOWENBERG, M. E., E. N. TODHUNTER, E. D. WILSON, M. C. FEENEY, and J. R. SAVAGE. *Food and Man.* New York: John Wiley and Sons, Inc. 1968.

MARTIN, E. A. *Nutrition in Action,* 3rd ed. New York: Holt, Rinehart & Winston. 1971.

MCLEAN, B. B. *Meal Planning and Service,* rev. ed. Peoria, Ill.: Chas. A. Bennett Co., Inc. 1964.

WILSON, E. D., K. H. FISHER, and M. E. FUQUA. *Principles of Nutrition,* 2nd ed. New York: John Wiley & Sons, Inc. 1965.

19

food purchasing

During the pioneer days of this country each home met its food needs largely through its own production. Wheat and corn from the fields supplied the flour and meal. Beef and pork were furnished by the farm animals. Orchards yielded fruit both for immediate consumption and for preservation for winter months. Vegetable gardens provided summer fare and supplied cucumbers for pickling, sweet corn and beans for drying and "salting down," as well as potatoes, sweet potatoes, carrots, turnips, and onions to be stored for winter use.

Based on past experiences, each family decided upon the varieties and quantity of each product that would best meet its yearly needs. The food purchases then might include seeds for planting, and the sugar, salt, spices, coffee, and flavorings that could not be produced at home. From the raw foodstuffs of the farm, the homemaker prepared cakes, pies, bread, salad dressings, cured meats, and many other food products in her own kitchen under conditions of sanitation for which she was responsible. Whenever a product fell below her standard, she knew the reason; perhaps "the cream was too sour," "the oven was too hot," or "the sugar was too scant." Her family accepted her handiwork, presumably with understanding and appreciation.

Recent years have brought radical changes in the activities of the home. Relatively little food is produced at home for family needs. The availability of breads, cakes, desserts, and other foods of many types—ready-to-eat, ready-to-thaw, ready-to-bake or -heat, or as mixes—testify to the marketing changes that have taken place, as does the growth of the canned and frozen food and the meat packing industries. The homemaker and her family no longer have personal knowledge of the soundness of the original food, of the sanitary conditions under which it was prepared, of other substances that may have been added as adulterants or preservatives, or of the length of time that may have elapsed between the processing and preparation of a given food and its appearance upon the table. In today's supermarket consumers find an overwhelming array of some ten thousand separate grocery items. With such variety from which to choose, the homemaker or other member of the family who purchases the food for family meals must know a great deal about both food quality and nutritive value in order to purchase wisely. Intelligent shopping habits in the purchasing of the family's food are indeed necessary in this complex market if the food dollar is to be expended wisely.

Woman's Responsibility as a Buyer of Food

The comparative importance of the producer, the transporter, the wholesaler, the retailer, the advertiser, and the consumer in determining the foods available may be argued. Each plays an important part, yet in this day of plenty, the consumer may well play the major role. Although more and more meals are eaten away from home, women still determine to a large extent the quantity and quality of food available in retail stores.

The Food Dollar

The value of the food consumed in the United States in 1970 was estimated to be 113 billion dollars. This amounted to approximately 16.5 per cent of the disposable income. In 1960 it was estimated that 20 per cent of the disposable income went for food.[1] Although year after year an increased amount of money is spent for food, the percentage of the disposable income has decreased, indicating that prices for other goods and services have increased more than those for food.

The many meanings now given to the term "convenience foods" make it difficult to determine how much of the 113 billion dollars was spent on convenience foods. However, it was estimated that in 1965 of the 77.6 billion dollars spent on food that originated on the farm, 52.1 billion went for marketing services.[2] Thus the steps from the farm to the consumer—transportation, processing, advertising, and merchandising—took more than two-thirds of the consumer's dollar spent on farm-produced foods. For this the purchaser received the many conveniences offered her on the grocer's shelf, whether it be flour, cake mix, brown-and-serve rolls, dressed and cut up chicken, canned peas, frozen vegetables in a sauce, or a complete frozen beef or turkey dinner.

The 1965 nationwide food survey showed that expenditures for food were related to income. Families with an annual income of $10,000 or more spent, on the average, eleven dollars per person for food during the survey week as compared with seven dollars spent by families with incomes under $3,000. Families on low incomes averaged more food value for the dollar than did those on higher incomes.[3]

[1] *National Food Situation NFS 133,* Economic Research Service. United States Department of Agriculture, Washington, D.C. August, 1970, p. 8.
[2] *National Food Situation* NFS *133.*
[3] *Toward the New.* Agriculture Information Bulletin, No. 341. United States Department of Agriculture, Washington, D.C., 1970, p. 7.

Whether the family spends less than one-fifth or more than one-half of the money available for living expenses on food, wise choices of the kinds and quantities selected are important responsibilities of the food purchaser.

Wise Purchasing

The general well-being of the family depends to a large extent on an ample supply of nourishing, palatable, wholesome food. The tastes of the various members of the family must be considered, but at the same time the diets furnished should be nutritionally adequate. Knowledge of the amount of each food needed to serve the family is one aspect of this responsibility. Buying more than the family actually needs is wasteful, and the excess expenditure gives little satisfaction to anyone.

Obtaining variety is another phase in the homemaker's planning of food purchases. Her choice of foods influences the food habits of her family, and ultimately affects the market for various foods in the community. If the homemaker buys only "meat and potatoes," the family usually accepts her choice, and its food habits are thus established. But if she buys to meet dietary needs, and frequently purchases vegetables and fruits, including new and different kinds, the food habits of the family will reflect her wisdom. The homemaker thus has a responsibility to use her power to change, through a wider use of different foods, a provincial and inadequate diet into a more cosmopolitan and adequate one. Similarly the demands of the buyer are of great importance in determining the market. When customers demand a variety of convenience and gourmet foods, these become available. When demand for certain foods drops, they soon disappear from the grocery shelves.

The woman shopper may also influence the sanitary conditions in the stores or markets of her community. If she is satisfied with low standards, she may have only a low-grade market in which to buy. If she insists on high standards, markets will meet her demands in order to retain her trade. Likewise, the buyer influences the quality of food available. Whether a high or low quality is available depends upon the shopper's demand. However, the choice between different qualities of food should always be made in relation to the intended use of the food.

Making good buys in purchasing food, an important responsibility of the homemaker, involves making effective use of the family's food money. Certain foods tend to be reasonable in cost much of the time, but many foods will vary frequently in cost. The wise buyer tries to be well informed in order to make the majority of purchases "good buys." This means not only considering cost in relation to quality but also the likes and dislikes of the family, the nutrients supplied, the use to be made of the foods, the ease of preparation, and the available space for storage.

Weights and Measures

The woman buyer has the further responsibility of seeing that she receives the correct weight or measure of the food she buys. The federal government has established legal standards for weights and measures, and in each state and in large cities there are inspectors whose duty it is to see that these standards are maintained. It is only good business practice for the purchaser to insist that she receive the amount for which she pays. As both a home-maker and a citizen, she should see that the regulations really function in her community.

In addition to making occasional checks of her purchases on reliable scales in her own home, the homemaker should observe whether the grocer's scales are balanced before he begins to weigh her purchase, and check whether his hand, a paper tray, or a heavy sack is included in the weight ascribed to the food she is buying.

The practice of prepackaging many of the fresh fruits and vegetables as well as much of the meat contributes to the difficulty of checking actual weights. Some stores mark only the price on the package, which makes it almost impossible to check cost per pound, much less value received. Some fresh fruits and vegetables lose weight when held, and therefore at the time of purchase may weigh less than the stated amount even though the original weight was accurately recorded. This may also occur with frozen foods, especially fruits packed in syrup or with sugar. Juices are drawn from the fruit with resulting loss of weight in the fruit and gain in the syrup.

Fig. 19–1. *Many foods are now pre-packaged and so the buyer does not have a chance to check their weight before purchasing them. An occasional check of weights at home is a wise plan.*

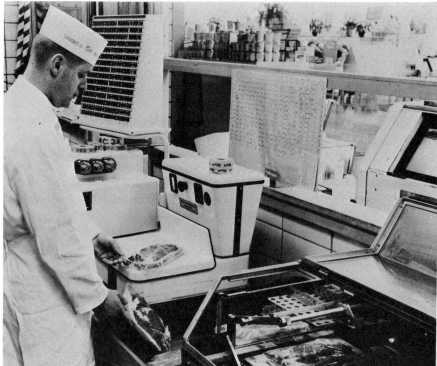

Plentiful Foods

Careful planning of meals is based upon consideration of the foods which may be in plentiful supply because of season, growing conditions, or other causes. Although improved facilities for storing and shipping fresh foods and extensive preservation of foods by canning, freezing, and other methods have helped to minimize its importance, the season remains a factor in the range and price of available foods. In recent years the food price index has tended to reach its highest peak in either July or August. This is largely because the price of meat is highest during the summer. Since more beef, pork, and lamb are marketed in the fall or winter months, the supply is greatest during these seasons and the prices are at their lowest. Fish, shellfish, poultry, and eggs are also more abundant and lower in price at certain seasons.

Fruits and vegetables are most plentiful in the summer and generally are least expensive in the locality where produced. The wise buyer will watch for peak supplies and make generous use of these foods to the extent that they fit into a well-planned diet. Careful study of advertisements in the local newspapers is often helpful in determining what foods are abundant at a given time.

Foods such as oranges, lettuce, and snap beans are grown the year round in one section or another in the country—fresh strawberries may now be available every month of the year—but source and season may make a great deal of difference in supply and price and often in quality.

Weather, insufficient help at harvest time, or strikes may limit the availability of a food on a local and even on a national basis. When a food is in short supply, it may be desirable or even necessary to replace it with one which is readily available, making such adjustments in the menus as are necessary to provide an adequate diet. It may be unwise, from both the personal and the national viewpoint, to maintain the accustomed use of a food that must be obtained at an extremely high cost instead of replacing it with an equivalent inexpensive food readily at hand.

Local marketing conditions or even those in a given store may lead to reduced prices which the careful shopper will note. "Specials" may be offered to lead people into the store—a form of advertising—or they may result from planned special purchases; both will make certain foods available in generous supply for short periods. These may be good buys which justify changes in the food plans for the following week. However, judgment is needed to determine the quality of the food, how soon it will be used, and whether or not it will keep until used.

Quality

Quality has many meanings. It may refer to the wholesomeness, cleanliness, or freedom from undesirable substances. More frequently it connotes a degree of perfection in shape, uniformity of size, and freedom from blemishes of a given food, or the extent of its desirable characteristics of color, flavor, aroma, texture, tenderness, and maturity.

The quality of food affects its price. Since food of highest quality is limited, its price is naturally more than that of lower qualities, of which the supply is greater. If the homemaker always purchases the highest quality of all foods, her grocery bill will be needlessly large. A low-quality food does not necessarily mean one unfit for consumption; it may be unsuited for certain purposes but still be desirable for other uses. For example, a low quality meat may be unsatisfactory for broiling and yet very usable for making soup or stews. Sometimes a lower quality may give just as good a finished product as the higher. Salads or pies can be just as good when made from apples with a few blemishes as from apples graded "top quality." However, apparent economy in the purchase of the lower qualities may sometimes be offset by waste due to poor condition, to the increased time required for preparation, or to the greater amount of fuel used in cooking. Food of low quality at a seemingly low price may often prove to be an expensive purchase in the long run, or may, on the other hand, represent a real economy. It is necessary to evaluate both the food and its proposed use in deciding whether or not it is a good buy.

Packaged Foods

Most food purchased in stores today is packaged in some form or other. This may increase the price, but often the cost of packaging is offset by lower costs in selling at retail and by savings because less trimming and handling are required. Packaging of food offers advantages which consumers seem to regard as worth the additional cost. Packaged food may be cleaner, more attractive in appearance, and more uniform in quality. Packaging may reduce or delay spoilage and often provides a convenient container for storing food. A disadvantage for some buyers is that the amount in the package may not be the quantity desired at a given time. This may be especially true of fresh fruits and vegetables.

The size of the package often affects the price of the product as in the case of cereal packed in individual servings. Homemakers purchasing their cereals in this form pay two or three times more per ounce than if they were buying the same product in a larger box.[4] Fancy packaging, too, usually adds to the price of a food. Packages of similar foods may vary only a small amount in size or weight of contents making it difficult to compare prices unless paper and pencil arithmetic is used. The Fair Packaging and Labeling Act of 1966 gave the government authority to establish and define standards for describing package sizes. This was an attempt to reduce the confusion due to the great number of different package sizes for the same type of product, but a variety of package sizes are still found on the grocer's shelves. However, some stores are now posting the cost per unit near the food, making a comparison easy. For example, one may note at a glance that an ounce of canned shrimp of Brand #1 costs 11.6 cents whereas the

[4] *Family Food Budgeting.* Home and Garden Bulletin No. 94. United States Department of Agriculture, Washington, D.C., 1969.

cost of a like amount of Brand #2 is 17.3 cents; or that one ounce of de-hydrated potatoes costs 4.7 cents when purchased in a 3-ounce package, 3.6 cents when purchased by the pound, and 2.91 cents when a two-pound package is purchased.

Factors Affecting the Price of Food

The prices of food may vary by the year, month, season, and locality. Fluc-tuations may be large or small; for example, if the price of lemons today is compared with that of a year ago, the increase may be as great as 100 per cent or as low as one per cent. Butter and frozen orange juice may vary lit-tle from month to month. Tomatoes may be most expensive in December and cheapest in September. In some localities a head of lettuce may sell for 25 cents, in others for 49 cents. Oranges may cost more in one city than apples, and in another city apples may be more expensive.

Because of these variations in cost, the homemaker has an added prob-lem in meeting her responsibility as an intelligent buyer for her household. She must be informed on current food prices and their relative values. She also should try to understand, to some extent, the reasons for price fluctua-tions in order to purchase intelligently.

Supply and Demand

The price of any commodity is affected by its supply and demand. Other things being equal, the greater the supply, the lower will be the price, and the greater the demand, the higher will be the price. Because many factors influence supply and demand, the problem is much more complicated than it first appears. Also, the influence of supply and demand upon price may be modified or limited in varying degrees by government subsidies, price con-trols, and other regulations.

An increased demand for a product may result from advertising by the producer or distributor and from the public's awareness of its nutritive value. This demand may last for a short time only, or it may be relatively permanent. Recognition of the importance of advertising in increasing de-mand is seen in the yearly expenditure of millions of dollars for the adver-tising of food products. More than fifty years ago L. D. Edie wrote of ad-vertising: "There is no other means by which to single out a particular dealer's goods from the general run of goods and attract unusual permanent attention to them. The tactics of creating demand for high-priced goods by use of advertised brands is mainly a matter of understanding social psy-chology. Dealers who can cultivate shrewdly the instinctive demands of people who are heavily susceptible to psychological traits of display, imi-tation, rivalry, pride, vanity, ostentation, and suggestion hold a clue to the building of a market for their wares at prices well above the general market level."[5]

[5] L. D. Edie. *Principles of the New Economics*. New York: Thomas Y. Crowell Company, 1922, pp. 326–327.

Common knowledge that a food is rich in certain nutrients often increases the demand for it and frequently the price. For example, liver trebled in price when it was found to be especially high in nutritive value and important in the treatment of pernicious anemia. There are many inexpensive foods of high nutritive value that have not been so affected.

Although cost of production, difficulty of production, weather, and tastes may seem to be factors of a different kind, a careful study shows that they are really a part of supply and demand and cannot be considered separately. One of the first factors of importance in controlling price is the size of the crop or the amount of the commodity produced. An abundance of even a much desired product means a somewhat lowered price. This is particularly true when the total world supply is considered. It is possible for a food to have a low price in a community where an abundance is produced and a high one in distant markets because the total crop is short. Especially is this the case in localities which have an abundant supply but inadequate means of bringing it to the markets where the supply is scarce and the demand is great. Then, too, some products cannot be transported easily. Adequate facilities for transportation and refrigeration have tended to equalize the price of foods throughout the civilized world but may also have added to the price of food. If the products are difficult and costly to transport, the selling price must cover this expense.

General Market Conditions

General market conditions have a decided effect upon food prices. This is especially evident on foods of general consumption. Prices of flour, eggs, meat, oil, milk, potatoes, and the like all tend to follow prevailing market prices. As mentioned earlier, government programs of price support, quotas, subsidy payments, and other controls have tended to reduce price fluctuation in foods. Only when there is an actual shortage of a product for which there is a demand, as when a freeze destroys a large portion of the crop or when strikes prevent the harvesting of an entire crop in a certain area is the price likely to be completely out of line.

The Store

At one time the contrast in cost and convenience between the "charge and deliver" and the "cash and carry" stores was an important consideration in deciding where to buy. Today the choice is largely between the grocery store and the specialty store. The modern grocery store may stock in excess of 25,000 items and it is not uncommon to find 10- or 15,000. In contrast to grocery stores where one may purchase every food item found in the average home plus alcoholic and non-alcoholic beverages, household supplies, tobacco products, pet foods, health and beauty aids, magazines and newspapers, phonograph records, toys, greeting cards, and other miscellaneous items, specialty stores, as the name implies, offer a limited number of foods. The most common specialty stores are meat and fish markets, bakery products stores, fruit and vegetable markets, and candy, nut, and confectionery stores. In some areas "farmers markets" and roadside stands may provide high quality produce, at least during certain seasons of the year. Selecting the store or stores from which to buy involves consideration not only of the price of the food but also of its quality. The variety of foods carried may also be a factor. Some grocery stores cater to a clientele willing to pay for specialty and out-of-season foods. The price of staples and other foods found in these stores may be competitive with other markets. Specialty stores probably continue in business because of some unique quality either in products handled or in services rendered, for which the shopper is willing to spend time and energy to go to more than one store to make her purchases.

Partially Prepared and Prepared Foods

The demand for foods that are easily and quickly prepared has resulted in a wide array of partially prepared and prepared foods that are constantly increasing in kinds and quantity. On the shelves of every grocery store are mixes of all types, which with a little time and effort can be made into cakes, breads, icings, puddings, sauces or even main dishes. The variety of canned main dishes and specialty items from all over the world is almost endless. In the freezer cabinets are frozen foods ready for a few minutes of boiling or steaming, frying in deep fat, or oven browning or baking, and frozen meals requiring only oven heating for a brief period to be ready for eating. Frozen and canned fruit juices that are practically ready for serving are favorite choices of shoppers. Salad dressings once made in every home have taken their place along with bread, cakes, and a great variety of other foods now purchased at the store. The availability of potatoes in a variety of partially prepared and prepared forms is believed to account, in large part, for the increased use of potatoes in recent years.

The 1965 nationwide food consumption survey showed an increased use of these foods as compared with 1955. However, some convenience foods decreased in use and were replaced by others with greater convenience, lower price, or better flavor. For example, there was a tendency for flour mixes to be replaced by canned biscuits, chilled dough, brown-and-serve rolls, and fully baked products, and for dried fruits and vegetables and fresh juices to be replaced by canned and frozen.[6] This may well raise the question "What is a convenience food?" How many of the 10,000 or more food items available in the modern supermarket are *not* convenience foods? There seems to be little or no agreement, even in the food industry, as to just what constitutes a convenience food but surely if one were to take the meaning of convenience literally, practically all foods used today are convenience foods. Whether the terms "partially prepared" and "prepared" are more definitive one cannot be sure. As mentioned earlier, some con-

[6] S. F. Adelson. Changes in Diets of Households, 1955 to 1965—Implications for Nutrition Education Today. *Journal of Home Economics,* 60: 448–455 (1968).

venience foods cost no more than the same foods prepared at home from similar ingredients, some cost less, while others are higher in price (Table 19–1). There are advantages in the use of these products, but the homemaker who frequently purchases such foods should determine which may be really good buys in terms of the family needs and which are definitely luxury purchases.

Grades and Brands of Foods as Aids

Consumers today find themselves almost in a maze when they go to the market to purchase foods. Confronted with row upon row of canned foods, tray after tray of fresh foods, and with numerous packages of dried and frozen foods, cereals, and condiments, they may feel bewildered when they attempt to make their selections from the vast array. What grade of pineapple should they buy? What form should it be? Broken slices or whole ones? Which of the many brands of peas will best meet their need for quality? The consumer who understands the significance of grades and brands is better able to answer these questions and to choose foods wisely.

Grades

Numerous laws passed during the twentieth century purport to give the consumer protection in the buying of foods. The Federal Food, Drug, and Cosmetic Act of 1906 was an early attempt to give such assurance. Since that time numerous amendments and modifications have been made in an attempt to provide adequate consumer protection as the production and processing of food moved from the home to industry. This is discussed in some detail in Chapter 2. The Food and Drug Administration does not grade foods, but when it establishes a standard of identity, a standard of quality, or a standard of fill for a container, foods shipped beyond the state boundaries should meet these standards or be labeled "below standard," "substandard," etc. This is an attempt to provide the consumer with wholesome food properly identified.

Grades based on standards have been established by state and federal agencies and by some industries and producers. Most products that bear a U.S. grade must be inspected before they are graded, thus the consumer has assurance of wholesomeness as well as information concerning the quality if the product bears a U.S. grade. Today there are well-established grades for foods that represent more than half of the nation's food bill including milk, butter, cheese, eggs, meat, chicken, turkey, and fresh, canned, and frozen fruits and vegetables. Many of these are discussed in the chapter dealing with the particular food. By means of grades, products are classified and standardized according to size, maturity, color, and other attributes that determine quality.

Grade terminology varies widely, even within a given agency. Products graded under the auspices of the Consumer and Marketing Service of the U.S. Department of Agriculture may be USDA Prime, U.S. Grade A, U.S.

Table 19–1. Cost of a serving of foods partly or entirely prepared commercially and of similar foods prepared from family-type recipes *

Food	Size of serving	Cost of a Serving				Cost Relative to Cost of Home Prepared			
		Home prepared†	From a mix	Ready to cook	Ready to serve‡	Home prepared	From a mix	Ready to cook	Ready to serve‡
	Ounces	Cents	Cents	Cents	Cents	Percent	Percent	Percent	Percent
Dinners									
Meat loaf	11.0	39	—	62	—	100	—	159	—
Beef	11.0	45	—	56	—	100	—	124	—
Fried chicken	11.0	25	—	53	—	100	—	212	—
Turkey	11.5	34	—	56	—	100	—	165	—
Main dishes									
Beef pie	8.0	23	—	22–47 §	—	100	—	96–204	—
Chicken pie	7.7	18	—	22–45 §	—	100	—	122–250	—
Chow mein	6.6	27	—	33–48 §	29‖	100	—	122–178	107
Cheese pizza	8.3	27	30	43	—	100	111	159	—
Bakery products									
Apple pie	4.7	7.0	9.4	10.3	12.9	100	134	147	184
Pound cake	1.1	3.0	2.6	—	5.0–6.8 #	100	87	—	167–227
Brownies	.7	3.5	3.6	—	3.8–4.2 #	100	103	—	109–120
Sugar cookies	.5	1.5	1.5	1.6	1.5	100	100	107	100
Waffles	3.3	4.4	4.8	12.8	—	100	109	291	—
Biscuits	1.4	1.8	2.2	2.4	5.0	100	122	133	277

* From *Family Economics Review.* Agricultural Research Service, United States Department of Agriculture, June 1971, p. 11. Prices from three Washington, D.C., supermarkets, March 1971.
† Family-type recipes used. May differ from formulas used in preparing commercial products.
‡ May require heating but not cooking.
§ Range of costs of brands that contain widely different proportions of meat or poultry.
‖ Canned.
Higher cost product is frozen.

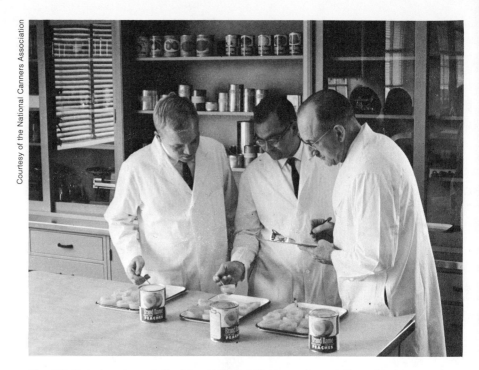

Courtesy of the National Canners Association

Fig. 19–2. *Laboratory staff of the National Canners Association check canned peaches for color, odor, appearance, and uniformity. This type of frequent sampling and inspection assures the homemaker of uniform quality.*

Grade AA, U.S. Fancy, or U.S. No. 1, all for the top quality or grade. Butter graded U.S. Grade AA, U.S. Grade A and U.S. Grade B seems to follow a straightforward pattern, but apples with U.S. Extra Fancy as top grade followed by U.S. Fancy, U.S. No. 1, and U.S. Utility as fourth, indicate the need to know the meaning of the terms, even for products carrying U.S. grades. Terminology used by trade associations as Fancy, Extra Standard, and Sub-standard may be even more confusing and vague than those used by the C&MS. The general adoption of the letter terminology, or the number, by all agencies would greatly aid the homemaker and other consumers in making their food purchases. Furthermore, consumer grades and wholesale grades may differ for the same product, which only adds to the confusion of the consumer if she is aware of the grades for these products—and there are indications that the average consumer knows little about federal grades.[7]

The Consumer and Marketing Service administers extensive inspection and grading programs. Unlike the inspection that is compulsory for certain

[7] *Consumer's Knowledge and Use of Government Grades for Selected Food Items.* Marketing Research Report 876. Economics Research Service. United States Department of Agriculture, Washington, D.C., 1970.

products, use of the federal grading service is, for the most part, on a voluntary basis. However, there is an ever increasing demand for U.S. graded food. The value placed upon such service is evident in food advertisements in the daily newspapers where one often finds the emphasis placed on grades, especially of meats. Because grading of food tends to identify certain standards of quality and to establish uniformity within a particular grade, it enables the consumer to purchase foods that meet her specific needs and to make repeated purchases with confidence.

Brands

Often better known, and sometimes fallaciously regarded as of equal importance with government grading of food, is the practice by a private organization of labeling food under a trade name or brand. Through his brand names, the producer, processor, or distributor hopes to establish the commodity as a standard product and to develop demands specifically for his brand rather than for a certain grade. National advertising campaigns concerned with processed foods are centered on brands and rarely mention the grade of a product. Great sums of money are spent annually to boost products through their brand names and to sell consumers the idea of buying entirely by this means. Products bearing a store's own brand, sometimes referred to as a "house brand" may cost less than the nationally advertised product and may or may not be of equal or better quality. For example, 5 pounds of all-purpose flour bearing a store brand cost 41 cents and two nationally advertised brands each were priced at 57 cents for 5 pounds. The wise purchaser will consider both cost and quality when she chooses a brand. If the product meets a need and has consistently satisfactory quality, the consumer may continue to buy a given brand over a period of time. If the quality is not as represented and the consumer is disappointed, she may try another brand when the time comes to again purchase the item.

Often a company puts out a number of brands of a product, each varying in price from the others and representing a particular quality or grade. The reliability of the brand depends upon the reliability of the company. Sometimes a product of a given brand is widely advertised as being of exceptional quality and grade when it is in fact mediocre. Such practices jeopardize the business life of a company. Reliable producers, distributors, and dealers, realizing the menace of dissatisfaction thus produced, endeavor to make their brands represent products of a relatively definite standard. The brand protects the producer, processor, or distributor by indicating the quality of his product. It may explain the differences in price between various products and safeguard a producer against unscrupulous competition. This is especially true when standards for a brand are definitely stated on the label.

Some knowledge of trade and brand names is essential in the identification of food products in our present merchandising system. The purchaser needs to be familiar with a number of brands and their qualities and to know generally which grade a brand represents. The identification of a brand with a grade is sometimes difficult because not all producers have the same standards for grading. By indicating to some extent the quality, the brand helps the buyer to make a more intelligent purchase; but such assistance is obviously inadequate. There is a growing sentiment for supplementing the brand by definite statements about the characteristics and standards of the product. Although some firms are using both grade and brand names on their products, consumers must depend upon brand names in making many of their food purchases. Until the standards of brands are respected by the distributor and are known by the purchaser, the supposed advantage of obtaining predictable quality through their use is not assured.

Labels

Closely related to grades and brands are the labels of products. Great emphasis is being placed upon labels and their use, and the consumer is urged again and again to read the labels when she buys. From these she should be able to obtain needed information about the product she is considering for purchase. The extent to which this is possible depends upon the type of label and upon the use producer and consumer make of it.

The Fair Packaging and Labeling Act passed in 1966 became effective July 1, 1967. This was intended to prevent unfair or deceitful packaging or labeling of consumer commodities. Among other things under the provisions of this act the label must identify the commodity; carry the name and address of the manufacturer, packer, or distributor; accurately state the net contents in terms of weight, measure, or numerical count; give statement of weight in conspicuous and legible type so located that it is easily read; in no way qualify the statement of quantity; and define the size of serving in terms of weight, measure, or numerical count if the number of servings in a package is suggested. It has long been recommended that the label have a picture of the product reproduced as accurately as possible; that it indicate, in addition to net contents, the number of portions, number of pieces, number of cupfuls, size of can, etc.; that it give a brief description of the raw product and possibly of the method of processing; that it furnish directions for use of some products; and that it make mention of recipe books or other available literature.

Labels may be classified as descriptive, grade, and informative. A descriptive label, as the term indicates, carries a description of the product and may give general information, standardized information, or both. The description may contain few or many facts, and may be helpful or meaningless in helping the customer to evaluate the product or to decide upon its purchase. A grade label bears a grade symbol—letter, word, number, or score—that indicates the rank of the product according to established grade standards. An informative label gives adequate information in simple terms regarding the quality, use, and care of the product, so that the purchaser is able to judge the quality or value in terms of her own needs, and to compare

Fig. 19–3. *Sample label for retail container complying with the FDA's Fair Packaging and Labeling Regulations. Left to right, consumer panel use shown, alternate use as duplicate principal display panel; principal display panel; information panel.*

this quality and value with other grades of the product and with the same grade of product offered under other brand names. This type of label includes the data given by both grade and descriptive labeling, along with other information that is important to the consumer. Informative labeling is advocated not only by many consumers but by many producers as well.

Although the labels on food products are not perfect, progress is being made in the right direction. Good labels make the marketing of food easier for the consumer, the producer, and the middleman. To encourage the development of better labeling practices, consumers must make use of labels and demand informative ones of high quality.

Determining the Food to Be Purchased

In purchasing food for a family a basic consideration is the food needs of the group. These are determined, first, by the composition of the family, including the number, age, and size of persons comprising it; second, by the activities of the various members of the family as these affect food needs; and third, the condition of health of the members of the family. It is obvious that the food needs of a group of six adults engaged in sedentary work differ markedly from those of a family made up of a father engaged in outdoor labor, the mother, two sons of high-school age, a ten-year-old daughter, and a two-year-old son. The food needs of any family can be determined with some degree of exactness. They do not vary with differences in incomes, with the type of dwelling, nor with the success of investments. Within certain limits, these needs tend to remain somewhat constant, the changes as a rule being more or less gradual.

Table 19–2. *Adequate Food for One Week at Different Expenditure Levels for a Family of Four* *†

Food	Low-Cost Diet	Moderate-Cost Diet	Liberal-Cost Diet
Leafy green and yellow vegetables	2.00 lbs.	2.00 lbs.	2.25 lbs.
Citrus fruits and tomatoes	7.50 lbs.	8.75 lbs.	10.00 lbs.
Potatoes	7.25 lbs.	6.25 lbs.	5.50 lbs.
Other vegetables and fruits	16.00 lbs.	19.00 lbs.	21.25 lbs.
Milk, cheese, ice cream (1 oz. cheese or 2–3 large dips of ice cream equal 1 cup milk)	18.00 qts.	19.00 qts.	20.00 qts.
Meat, poultry, fish	9.00 lbs.	13.75 lbs.	16.00 lbs.
Eggs	21	25	27
Dried beans and peas, nuts	.81 lbs.	.50 lbs.	.44 lbs.
Cereals and cereal products (count 1½ lbs. of "baked foods" as 1 lb. of flour)	10.00 lbs.	9.00 lbs.	8.25 lbs.
Fats, oils	1.75 lbs.	2.12 lbs.	2.25 lbs.
Sugar, syrup, preserves	2.25 lbs.	3.00 lbs.	3.63 lbs.

* From *Family Food Budgeting for Good Meals and Good Nutrition.* Home and Garden Bulletin No. 94, United States Department of Agriculture, 1971, pp. 7, 9, 10.
† Family composed of moderately active parents and two preschool children.

Resources

The food actually purchased to meet the food needs depends upon the income. Families with low incomes have less to spend for food than those with moderate or high incomes, and it is estimated that they may need to spend 50 to 60 or even 70 per cent of the income for food; even then the food budget will probably be less than that of families of moderate means, spending 20 per cent of the income for food.

The way the food needs of a family of four may be met at different cost levels is shown in Table 19–2. As one examines the table it is evident that there are not great differences in quantities recommended for the three cost levels. However, great differences in actual cost may result from the type of food purchased, the season, and possibly the extent to which the food is ready-prepared. It is relatively easy to plan meals for a family of four showing how the cost can vary from $4.00 to $11.00 per day (June, 1970).[8]

Further differences in expenditure levels may be the result of the quality of food purchased. However, higher quality foods are not always more costly for although they cost more per pound or unit, the fact that there may be less waste may result in a less expensive product in the end. Certain foods in a given group cost more than others. For example, cauliflower is more expensive than cabbage, and a rib roast more expensive than chuck.

[8] *Your Money's Worth in Foods.* Home and Garden Bull. No. 183. United States Department of Agriculture, Washington, D.C., 1970, p. 7.

Food produced at home may affect the expenditures for different items. Some farm families as well as a few living in towns and villages may produce a substantial part of their food.

Another resource to be considered is the time and skill available to prepare the food. The use of expensive cuts of meat which can be prepared in a few minutes, ready-to-eat gourmet dishes, and frozen breads and pastries may be a great saving of time but may add materially to the cost of the food. However, prepared or partially prepared foods do not always cost more than similar foods prepared from ingredients in the home. Each should be considered not only for cost but also for quality, including nutritive value, whenever possible.

Storage Space   The kind and amount of storage space are important in determining the amount of different kinds of food to be purchased. Studies show that the majority of homes have limited food-storage space. There is no longer the potato cellar, carefully banked in the back yard. The basement, once an admirable cold-storage place, now houses a furnace and may be too warm

Fig. 19–4. *The sliding shelves of this cabinet make effective use of a small amount of space to store fruits and vegetables.*

Fig. 19–5. *Adequate storage space contributes to wise buying.* (Space Design for Household Storage by Helen McCullough, Illinois Agricultural Experiment Station.)

for storing vegetables and fruits. The pantry or buttery with its tiers of shelves has disappeared from the modern house.

The former custom of buying one to three months' supply of staple groceries, vegetables, and fruits has yielded to weekly, bi-weekly, or even daily purchasing. Though the lack of storage space in the home is partially responsible for this shift in buying habits, the improved market, with food of all kinds readily available, is also a factor. With the improved modes of transportation that shorten the trip to the market from an all-day journey to one of an hour or less, the need for food-storage space has become less acute for most families.

The increased use of frozen foods makes home freezers or refrigerators with adequate freezer storage desirable assets to many homes. Quantity buying of frozen foods may result in a financial saving. There is need for a wise balance between the semi-annual buying of pioneer days and the twice-daily shopping trips of some present-day apartment dwellers. Storage space of all kinds should be provided to make possible efficient and economical purchasing of food.

The question of what constitutes adequate food-storage space in the home is not an easy one to answer; families differ in their needs, practices, and desires. Many homemakers are dissatisfied with the food-storage space in their homes and want more than they have. Families should give more consideration and study to the matter. In any home, provision should be made for cool-storage, dry-storage, refrigerator and freezer space, and for the storage of other foods not so included. This space should be as adequate for the family's need as is possible.

In many homes the existing food-storage space could be better utilized if a little time and thought were given to the matter. Some improvements might readily be effected with the expenditure of little or no money, as for example: ridding shelves of needless clutter; storing food more efficiently in the available space; and increasing surface storage space by putting new shelves between present shelves which are often so far apart that potential storage space is entirely wasted. In any case, food purchasing must be planned in relation to the available storage space.

Prices and Price Trends

Prices and price trends exert an influence on decisions in the buying of food. In general, lower prices tend to encourage and higher prices tend to discourage the purchase of a food. It is important, then, that essential foods should not be priced too high for the majority of people to purchase. The government has therefore found it necessary at various times to use price controls, price ceilings, and subsidies as means of keeping the prices of various essential foods at reasonable levels. Often larger amounts of a food may be purchased if the price is reduced for a short period than if it remains constant. Sometimes a probable upward trend in the price of a commodity also makes a larger purchase desirable. When there is adequate storage space and the food is one with excellent keeping quality, quantity buying may be wise. The decision in each case should depend upon the kind of food to be purchased as well as upon existing general business and home conditions.

Keeping Quality of Food

The tendency of food to keep or to spoil should be considered in the light of storage facilities and the probable rapidity of consumption by the family. Loss through spoilage may offset any advantage of large quantity purchasing.

The season influences the quantity of certain foods that may be advantageously purchased. Frozen and canned foods are often available at reduced prices in late spring or early summer just before the new crop reaches the market. These may be wise purchases if they will be used in a reasonable length of time. However, it is well to remember that these have already been held almost a year, so long storage should not be planned. Apples, potatoes, and sweet potatoes, when mature and of high quality, may be purchased in much greater quantities in the fall and early winter than in late spring.

Menus

Menus provide plans for meeting the food needs of the body, listing specific foods to be served at definite times. These lists indicate the kinds of foods to be used and form the basis for planning the market order. Menus should take into consideration the food already on hand, as well as the foods available on the market, the current prices, the needs and likes of the family, and the ease of preparation. By careful checking of the recipes to be used and the number of persons to be served, the homemaker can determine the amount of food needed.

The following moderate-cost food plan is suggested for a family of four—father, mother, boy of two and girl of four.[9] The approximate amounts of food required for the week are listed immediately following the menus.

Menus

Sunday

Breakfast	*Dinner*
Orange Juice	Pot Roast with Carrots, Potatoes,
Scrambled Eggs	and Onions
Toast Preserves	Sliced Tomatoes
Milk for children	Hot Biscuits
	Two-Egg Sponge Cake with
	Ice Cream
	Milk

Supper
Welsh Rarebit on Toast
Shredded Cabbage and Raisin Salad
Fruit in season
Milk for children

Monday

Breakfast	*Luncheon*
Orange Juice	Omelet Green Beans
Hot Oatmeal with Milk	Celery Strips
Toast	Bread
Milk for children	Baked Indian Pudding
	Milk

[9] *Food for the Family with Young Children.* Home and Garden Bulletin No. 5. United States Department of Agriculture, Washington, D.C. 1970.

Dinner
Beef Casserole with Mounds of Mashed Potatoes
(beef left from Sunday roast)
Sliced Beets   Fruit Salad with Cottage Cheese
Cornbread
Sponge Cake with Honey Sauce
Milk for children

Tuesday

Breakfast
Grapefruit Sections
Soft-Cooked Eggs
Rye Toast
Milk for children

Luncheon
Baked Macaroni and Cheese
Green Beans   Carrot Strips
Bread
Oatmeal and Prune Pudding
(oatmeal left from Monday
breakfast)
Milk

Dinner
Broiled Liver or Liver Pattie
Baked Potato   Baked Corn Pudding
Tossed Green Salad with Chopped Crisp Bacon
Bread
Fruit in season
Milk for children

Wednesday

Breakfast
Orange
Ready-to-eat Cereal with Milk
Toast   Preserves
Milk for children

Luncheon
Apple-Cabbage Salad
Beef Salad Sandwich
(beef left from Sunday)
Baked Indian Pudding
Milk

Dinner
Pork Chops   Potatoes Boiled in Jackets
Homemade Vegetable Relish
Creamed Peas   Celery Strips
Rye Bread
Fruit Cup   Milk for children

Thursday

Breakfast
Tomato Juice
Hot Oatmeal with Milk
Toast
Milk for children

Luncheon
Creamed Eggs on Toast, or
Soft-Cooked Eggs with Toast
Jellied Fruit Salad
Milk   Cookies

Dinner
Baked Shoulder of Lamb   Rice
Chopped Broccoli   Cole Slaw
Bread
Canned Peaches   Graham Crackers
Milk for children

Friday

Breakfast
Prunes with Orange Slices
Hot Wheat Cereal with Raisins
and Milk
Toast
Milk for children

Luncheon
Cream of Tomato Soup
Minced Lamb Sandwich
Peach Salad
Nut Cookies
Milk

Dinner
Baked Fish (haddock, cod, or halibut)
Green Lima Beans   Baked Potato   Celery Strips
Bread
Orange Compote
Milk for children

Saturday

Breakfast
Tomato Juice
Ready-to-Eat Cereal with Milk
Toast   Preserves
Milk for children

Luncheon
Peanut Butter and Celery
Sandwiches
Vegetable Salad
Floating Island or Junket
Milk

Dinner
Fried Chicken   Riced Potatoes   Spinach
Hearts of Lettuce with Cottage Cheese Dressing
Prune Pudding with Nut-Graham Cracker Topping
Milk for children

A 6-ounce serving of milk is planned for each of the children at every meal. If they sometimes want more, they are given it at the end of the meal; they usually have additional milk as an afternoon snack. The parents have tea or coffee at their meals, if they choose, in addition to the milk they drink. Butter or margarine is served with breads.

**Food Supply
For a Week** [10]

Milk, Cheese, Ice Cream

14 quarts fluid whole milk
1 14½-ounce can evaporated milk
½ pound Cheddar-type cheese
1 12-ounce package cottage cheese
1 pint ice cream

Meat, Poultry, Fish

2½ pounds chicken
1½ pounds pork chops
3½ pounds chuck roast of beef
4 pounds shoulder of lamb
¾ pound liver
1 pound fish fillet
¼ pound bacon

Eggs

2 dozen

Dry Beans and Peas, Nuts

3 ounces shelled nuts
⅓ pound peanut butter

Grain Products

3 loaves enriched white bread
3 loaves whole-wheat bread
1 loaf rye bread
1 pound rolled oats or whole-wheat cereal
12-ounce package ready-to-eat cereal
1 pound enriched flour
½ pound enriched cornmeal
¼ pound enriched macaroni
¼ pound rice
1-pound box graham crackers

Citrus Fruits, Tomatoes

3 pounds oranges
2 6-ounce cans frozen concentrated orange juice
1 large grapefruit
1 pound tomatoes
1 46-ounce can tomato juice
1 10½-ounce can tomato soup

Dark-Green and Deep-Yellow Vegetables

1 10-ounce package frozen broccoli
1 pound carrots
¼ pound salad greens
1 pound fresh spinach

Potatoes

6 pounds potatoes

Other Vegetables and Fruits

1 10-ounce package frozen green lima beans
1 pound green snap beans
1 pound beets
1 pound (head) cabbage
1 bunch celery
1 8¾-ounce can corn
2 small heads lettuce
⅓ pound onions
1 No. 2 can peas
2 pounds apples
1 No. 2½ can fruit salad
1 No. 2½ can peaches
1 pound prunes
¼ pound raisins
3 pounds other fruit

[10] Some of the staple foods are purchased in larger quantity than listed here to save time and money. They will keep for later use if properly stored. In addition to the foods listed above, coffee, tea, salt, flavorings, gelatin, junket powder, etc., are purchased as needed.—*Food for the Family with Young Children.*

Fats, Oils	*Sugars, Sweets*
1½ pounds butter or margarine	2 pounds sugar
⅓ pound lard or other shortening	1 pint molasses, honey, jelly, or preserves
⅓ pound salad dressing or salad oil	

If a family has less money to spend on food and must plan for a low-cost diet, modifications may be made in the type of food or in quality, or both. The modified plan will not necessarily be more or less nutritious than the one shown, for with care low-cost menus will meet the nutritional needs as they are known today. Likewise, a high-cost food plan will not automatically be more nutritious than a moderate or low-cost one. It was estimated in Dec., 1971, that the cost of food for a family of four with preschool children would be $27.60 for the low-cost plan. For the moderate-cost plan the estimate was $35.10 and for the liberal plan $43.00.

Regardless of cost plan followed, staple foods more frequently used in the preparation of all meals should be purchased in larger quantities than are required for a few days or a week. Examples of such foods are flour, sugar, cocoa, and vinegar. It is relatively much more expensive to make frequent purchases of staples in small lots than to stock them in quantity.

The following suggestions will be found helpful by those responsible for the purchasing of food for a family or other group.

Fig. 19–6. *The cost of the recommended dietary allowance of protein for a day can vary more than eleven-fold.* (From Handbook of Agricultural Charts. Agricultural Handbook No. 397. U.S. Department of Agriculture, November, 1970, p. 61.)

Cost of ⅓ of a Day's Protein*
Meats and Meat Alternates, June 1970

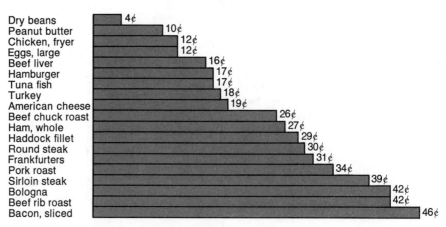

*⅓ of recommended dietary allowance (1968) for 20-year-old man.
BLS prices. Averages for U.S. cities.

1. Plan menus one week in advance.
2. When planning the menus
    a. make list of foods and amounts needed
    b. provide for utilization of left-overs.
3. Make plans flexible enough to take advantage of special sales.
4. Watch advertisements for food specials.
5. Check the "plentiful foods" list weekly.
6. Know the USDA system of grade labeling.
7. Plan and buy, at one time, food for no less than one day's meals.
8. Use foods that are in season.
9. Know the quantity and quality required.
10. Purchase by grade whenever possible.
11. Determine the price before buying.
12. Purchase by weight whenever possible.
13. Observe the scales during weighing and frequently check weights at home.
14. Be familiar with the types of information given on labels.

In making out a market order it is helpful to know the number of servings yielded from a specific unit measure of each of the foods included in a menu. This makes it easier to purchase an amount which assures plenty of food for the meal, but with no unnecessary waste. Labels on frozen foods and on many other packaged foods indicate the approximate number of servings in the package. Many canned foods also have such information on the labels. Table 6–8 gives the quantities of fresh vegetables needed for four servings and Table 10–3 suggests the number of servings obtained from one pound of various cuts of beef. A purchasing guide that includes this information for a number of other commonly served foods is given in Table 19–3. By adding information about other foods to this list from time to time, the homemaker can build up a fairly complete buying guide for easy reference when the need arises.

Table 19–3. *Guide for Purchasing Foods*

Food	Unit Measure	Number of Servings
Bread	1 lb. loaf	12–16 slices
Butter or margarine	1 lb. (2 cups)	48 pats
Cheese:		
American or brick	1 lb. (2⅔ cups cubed, or 4 cups grated)	14–16 slices
Cottage	1 lb. (2 cups)	6–8
Chocolate (beverage)	1 lb. (16 squares)	60
Cocoa (beverage)	1 lb. (4 cups)	100
Coffee (beverage)	1 lb. (5 cups)	50
Crackers, soda	1 lb. (small, square)	108 crackers
Farina and other granular cereals	1 lb. (3 cups)	25

Table 19–3 *(continued)*

Food	Unit Measure	Number of Servings
Fruits:		
Apples	1 lb.	3–4
Apricots		
Fresh	1 lb.	4–6
Dried	1 lb.	12
Bananas	1 lb.	3
Berries	1 qt.	6–8
Cherries	1 qt. (2 cups, pitted)	4–5
Grapefruit	1	2
Grapes	1 lb.	4
Lemons	1 doz.	1 pt., juice
Oranges	1 doz.	1 qt., juice
Peaches		
Fresh	1 lb.	4
Dried	1 lb. (3 cups)	12
Pears	1 lb.	4
Pineapple	2 lbs. (1 medium)	6
Prunes (dried)	1 lb. (2½ cups)	8–9
Rhubarb	1 lb. (4–8 stalks)	4–5
Gelatin:		
Flavored	3 oz. pkg. (1 pt. jelly)	4–6
Unflavored	¼ oz. pkg. (1 pt. jelly)	4–6
Ice Cream	1 qt.	6–8
Macaroni, spaghetti, or noodles	1 lb.	18
Marshmallows	1 lb.	60–80 marshmallows
Milk:		
Dry, Nonfat	1 lb.	Equals 4¼ qts. skim milk
Dry, Whole	1 lb.	Equals 3½ qts. milk
Evaporated	1 can (14½ oz.)	Equals 3⅓ cups milk
Liquid	1 qt.	4 cups
Oats, rolled	1 lb. (5 cups)	12–13
Rice	1 lb. (2¼ cups)	12–14
Tea	1 lb. (6–8 cups)	300
Vegetables (dried):		
Beans		
Kidney	1 lb. (2⅓ cups)	11–12
Lima	1 lb. (2½ cups)	10–11
Navy	1 lb. (2⅓ cups)	10–11
Peas, split	1 lb. (2 cups)	10

Activities

1. Make a list of desirable practices to follow in purchasing food. What are the characteristics of "good buys" in foods?

2. Determine the types of aids available to people buying food for personal and family use. Decide what use homemakers should make of each of these.

3. Compare the prices for a number of foods at different stores. How much do these vary? What are some probable reasons for this? How many of the stores have "weekend specials"?

4. Select two or three food items and determine the number of different package weights or sizes for each in two or three stores. Compare the prices per unit for one food item packaged:
a. in different size packages or containers,
b. in different types of packages or containers.

5. Cite instances when the national food situation affected the purchasing of food. Give an example of how the food situation in another country affected the purchasing of food in this country.

6. Prepare a 5 to 10 minute talk in which two or more of the following questions are considered:
a. What foods do you purchase by grade? By brand? Why? Would you do otherwise if you could?
b. What foods are sold by grade in your community? Would you like to see the number increased? What advantages would you take of such increases?
c. What experiences have you had in buying food by grade? To what extent do these warrant buying by grade?
d. What satisfactions and difficulties have you had in buying food by brand? Do you prefer this plan? Why?
e. The Fair Packaging and Labeling Act of 1966—its success and failure.

7. Discretionary provisions of the Fair Packaging and Labeling Act of 1966 permit the government to issue regulations concerning bargain price labeling such as "cents off." How many examples can you find in a supermarket near you of "cents off" labels? Is the price less than that of unmarked items otherwise apparently identical?

8. Obtain the brand names used for food products of several packers or distributors and show how these are related to grades.

9. Classify a number of labels of food products. Evaluate each in terms of its value to a homemaker. Which type of label predominates in the labels being studied?

10. Participate in a class discussion on ways to reduce food expenditures without lessening the adequacy and attractiveness of the food.

References

Consumers All. The Yearbook of Agriculture, 1965. U.S. Dept. Agr., Washington, D.C.: United States Government Printing Office.

Food. The Yearbook of Agriculture, 1959. U.S. Dept. Agr., Washington, D.C.: United States Government Printing Office.

Handbook of Food Preparation. American Home Economics Association, Washington, D.C. 1971.

KINDER, F. *Meal Management,* 3rd ed. New York: The Macmillan Company. 1968.

Storing Perishable Foods in the Home. U.S. Dept. Agr., Home and Garden Bull. No. 78 (1971).

TROELSTRUP, A. W. *The Consumer in American Society.* 4th ed. New York: McGraw-Hill Book Company. 1970.

WRIGHT, C. E. *Food Buying.* New York: The Macmillan Company. 1962.

Your Money's Worth in Foods. U.S. Dept. Agr., Home and Garden Bull. No. 183 (1970).

20

facilities for
meal preparation

The time required for the preparation of a meal depends to an extent upon the arrangement and equipment of the kitchen. Although certain guides can be given in planning efficient kitchens, there will necessarily be many variations in actual requirements for kitchen space, arrangement, and equipment, since no two families are identical in size, age groups, and activities. The homemaker who stays at home with three children under five years of age may desire quite a different kitchen set-up from the working wife whose homemaking activities are restricted to the after-five hours. The rural homemaker who must prepare three meals a day for a family of eight of course has different needs from those of an urban wife whose family is composed of a retired husband and herself. Extensive use of prepared and partially prepared foods may demand quite different facilities from those required for meals prepared from the basic ingredients. Regardless of the kind of food served, however, a kitchen with equipment so arranged that the meal may be prepared with the minimum expenditure of time and energy results in greater satisfaction to the one in charge of meal preparation.

The Kitchen

The plan as well as the size may affect the efficiency of the kitchen. Types of plans most used are the U, the broken U, and the L; but the one wall, the corridor, and the island are also common plans. As the terms imply, the U-plan has appliances on three adjacent walls with continuous counter space, while the broken U-plan has a door or passageway in one side. The L-plan uses two adjacent walls and the corridor, two opposite walls. The island plan may be found in any type. A kitchen 10 by 12 feet is considered an average size by many workers; one 8 by 10 feet small in size, and one 12 by 14 feet large. Kitchens vary widely both in shape and dimensions. Whether a small, average, or large size is most desirable will be influenced by the number of meals served, the kinds of food used, and the other activities carried on in the kitchen. In some households the kitchen serves not only as a place for the preparation, but also for the eating of meals, and it may become the center for the preservation of food, laundering, and even the social life of the family. Ultimately the choice of plans depends largely upon personal preference; an efficient arrangement is possible in any type of kitchen.

The floor of the kitchen should be resilient and easy to clean and care for. The walls also should be easy to clean and should add to the cheerfulness of the room. Adequate ventilation and lighting should be provided. The whole area should be lighted so that the worker's shadow never falls upon her work. An illumination value of 70 footcandles is recommended for the sink area and of at least 50 at the range and the work counter.

Arrangement of Equipment

Regardless of the type of kitchen plan used, the arrangement of the equipment should contribute to efficient work procedures. The work done in the kitchen centers on the preparation and serving of meals, the clearing away and washing of dishes, and the storage and care of equipment, food, and other supplies. All of the equipment related to one activity should be grouped together in as convenient and compact an arrangement as possible. The large farm kitchen in which more than one person works needs just as careful planning as the tiny wall-kitchenette of an urban apartment.

The equipment for the preparation and serving of food and for the clearing away and the washing of dishes can well be arranged into three centers: the *mixing* center, the *cooking* and *serving* center, and the *cleaning* and *washing* center. Storage should be provided in each center for all the equipment and supplies commonly used there, with additional storage elsewhere as needed. The arrangement should be such that each activity can be completed in its own place, with the work proceeding in an orderly way and generally from right to left. For example, the steps in preparing a soft custard might include mixing, cooking, stacking the soiled dishes and utensils, washing the dishes and utensils, and putting them away. An arrangement that permits the work to move easily from right to left is convenient for most right-handed workers.

An exact description of what equipment should be located in each center cannot be given because not all people make the same choices nor work in the same ways, but there are certain items upon which there is agreement. In the mixing center a work counter is necessary, and storage cabinets should be provided both above and below. Pans, bowls, cups, spoons, forks, knives, and similar utensils used in the preparation of the food may be located in this center. Certain frequently used foods such as flour, sugar, baking powder, and spices may be kept here also.

The center where the food is cooked is focused about the range. Here there should be storage space for utensils and dishes needed at the range

Fig. 20–1. *Sliding shelves in the cooking area hold the most frequently used pots and pans.*

Courtesy of St. Charles Manufacturing Company

and possibly a small serving table, wheel tray, or shelf. A kitchen arranged with no utensils for cooking near the range is inefficient.

The cleaning and washing center, sometimes called the sink center, includes the sink, the food waste disposer unit, drainage boards, a dishwasher (if included in the plan), the small equipment to be used here, and usually a work counter. Utensils and supplies for washing vegetables and fruits and for preparing uncooked vegetables and fruits should be at hand, as well as those for dishwashing and other cleaning tasks.

Although not classed as a work center, the storage spaces are important in the arrangement of the kitchen. Articles to be stored include those in constant use, those for seasonal or occasional use, and those rarely used. Each work center should provide storage space for equipment and supplies which are in frequent use. The cold storage space or the refrigerator should be placed proximate to both the mixing center and the sink. Storage for vegetables and fruits which do not need refrigeration but require washing and peeling can be located near or in the cleaning and washing center. Some dish storage may be above the drain board in the cleaning and washing center.

Every effort should be made to make storage space truly functional. In addition to the placement of articles at the point of first use, functional storage also involves clear visibility and easy and quick accessibility. Ways of providing for convenient storage include vertical files for flat and shallow utensils and dishes; horizontals and slanting files for trays, covers, and the like; pull-out panels and shelves; bins for the storage of vegetables and fruits; and revolving shelves of the Lazy Susan design for corners.

Orderly arrangement and availability of small equipment are also important. Nothing hinders efficient meal preparation more than having to spend time looking for misplaced utensils. Pieces of equipment that are often used together should be kept near each other and some plan for their arrangement should be made. Some workers prefer all the knives together, and all the spoons in another place and all cups in a third. Others prefer the bread knife near the bread box, the pancake turner near the griddle, and the measuring cup near the sugar and the flour. Personal preference is so important that it seems best for the worker to plan her own kitchen arrangement and to use its resources consistently.

When it is realized that more than a thousand meals are prepared each year by the homemaker whose family eats most of its meals at home, consideration of the relation between work centers becomes a matter of impor-

Fig. 20–2. *A space-saving peg board can be used to hold small equipment where it will be handy to the mixing area.*

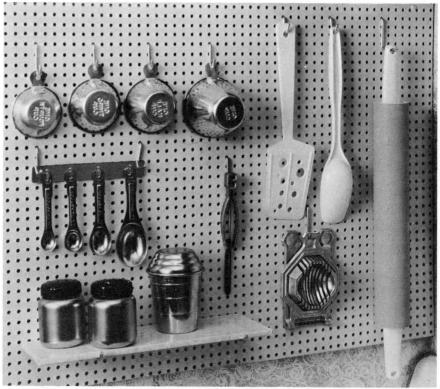

tance. These should be located and organized so that in preparing a meal the worker can start at the sink center with washing the foods, work to the mixing and range centers, and then to the dining room without frequent retracing of steps. Often the sink and mixing centers may be combined for a more satisfactory utilization of space and equipment. Although the planning and arranging of equipment into related work centers at first may seem difficult, it becomes surprisingly easy and interesting to plan for efficiency when the situation is studied.

Work Surface Heights and Storage Space

A comfortable working level contributes to efficiency. Cabinets may be custom built to any height, but commercially-built base cabinets are usually 36 inches high, a height which is probably acceptable to a majority of women. However, because different tasks frequently require work surfaces of different heights, at least three levels may be desirable. The counter adjacent to the range may be 36 inches and that on either side of the sink may be the same height or different. A lower height for the mix center might be more satisfactory; some workers prefer 32 inches here. Provision for a comfortable height for sitting while working is desirable. This may be accomplished by use of a sliding shelf or a lap board. Whether standing or sitting, the work surface height should permit the worker to carry out the tasks with back and shoulders straight and arms in a natural position.

Wall cabinets are usually 12 inches deep and contain three shelves. They may be hung 15 inches, 18 inches, or even more above the base cabinets, but here too height is important. The top cabinet shelf is often placed 72 inches above the floor on the premise that this is the maximum height the average person can reach without a stool; but even this may be too high for many workers. Since more energy is required to take a utensil from 72 inches or from 3 inches above the floor than from near elbow height, frequently used items should be stored on the lower shelves of the wall cabinets or in the upper part of the base cabinets.

Table 20–1. *Dimensions of Storage Spaces* *

	Width	Depth
Utensil storage at range	16 inches	14 and 16 inches
Utensil storage at sink	24 and 28 inches	16 and 18 inches
China and glassware storage	20, 24, and 36 inches	6, 8, and 12 inches (with 3-inch door storage)
Packaged supplies	24 and 31 inches	4 and 6 inches (with 2 and 4-inch door storage)

* Heiner, in *Journal of Home Economics*, 39: 70–72, 1947. Courtesy of the author and the American Home Economics Association.

Heiner has suggested that after allocation is made to the center of first use, items should be placed there within the work curve limits or the easy reach of the average woman (5 feet, 3 inches to 5 feet, 5 inches in height) in terms of frequency of use and by weight. Suggested widths and depths for storage are given in Table 20–1.

Selection of Equipment

With the stores full of equipment of all kinds and varieties, some of it attractive and useful, some merely attractive, and little of it labeled to show whether it meets specifications for durability or performance, it is small wonder that the homemaker sometimes is confused when making her selections. Frequently, she buys not only a poor quality but also more than she needs or uses.

To select kitchen utensils wisely it is necessary to consider the size of the family, the kind and amount of food cooked, the method of cooking, the amount and type of entertaining, the storage space available, and the relative importance placed on food and its use as compared with other items desired by the family. Having considered these points, one may also ask the following questions: Is the family permanently located? Is the size of the group relatively constant? Is the family just becoming established, or has it reached the stage where its members are leaving one by one so that the size is constantly being reduced? Is the family a temporary one made up of adults who are living together for a limited time?

In one situation, it may be wise to purchase a minimum of good equipment and gradually add to it; in another, a satisfactory plan may be to buy inexpensive and less durable equipment. If a group frequently entertains, it may be necessary to have more and larger pieces. The family that prepares all of the food in the home needs different equipment from the family that buys much of its food already prepared. In choosing equipment, the amount of money available will be an important factor.

The Range

The range is likely to be one of the most expensive items in the kitchen. Whether free-standing or built-in the range is a source of heat with surface units or top burners and one or more ovens and broilers. It may also have a rotisserie, automatic temperature and time controls for both oven and surface cooking, and such other special features as programmed ovens and/or top burners. Tri-level ranges as well as two-level and slip-in ranges have been developed, no doubt to satisfy the purchaser not content with a free-standing range with the ovens beneath the cooking surface. The tri-level range consists of a lower oven, cooking top, and eye-level oven. The two-level range has either an eye-level oven or a lower oven and cooking top. Built-in units provide greater flexibility in kitchen planning. They may incorporate all the features of a free-standing range, but the surface unit and oven unit may be installed in widely separated areas. The cooking surface or top may include both manually and thermostatically controlled heating units or burners and a griddle. The oven unit may be a separate oven; it may have a broiler below or in the oven. The broiler may also be a separate unit, or it may be combined with a rotisserie. Many other features such as a vertical broiler, cook-and-hold oven control, interval-timer, self-cleaning oven, or plug-in surface units may be found on modern ranges.

With few exceptions, ranges available today are gas or electric. The gas may be natural or LP. As indicated above, not only will the oven have automatic temperature control but many of the ranges are also equipped with a thermostatically controlled surface unit. The control operates to maintain the temperature for which the dial is set. It is located in the center of the burner or unit enabling a disc to make contact with the bottom of the utensil. Because the effectiveness of the heat control for surface cooking depends upon contact of the pan with the sensing unit, selecting pans and other utensils with flat bottoms is important. The utensils also should be of material that conducts heat well. The action of the thermostat is regulated by the temperature of the utensil in contact with the disc. Thus it is desirable for the food to cover the center of the pan; for example, when cooking chops one chop should be centered in the pan. Some electric ranges are so designed that the unit with the "thermal eye" may be adjusted to heat a 4-, 6-, or 8-inch area, thus increasing its flexibility.

Regardless of the type of range or of the kind of fuel used, the aim should be to obtain the best range possible for the money spent. Construction, materials used, durability, size of top and oven, insulation of the oven, and efficiency of the heating elements all affect the desirability of a given range. Cost of operating, convenience, and necessary care also should be considered. Each type of range has a wide price variation and since special features and accessories may add greatly to the cost, it is wise to choose only those extras which will be used fairly often.

Electronic ranges comprise only a fraction of a per cent of the electric ranges in homes today, but with increased use of prepared foods, with modifications to give increased flexibility in use, and with a decrease in the relative cost of electronic ranges or ovens, this may change. In electronic cooking, electromagnetic waves are produced which enter the food and cause the molecules of food to vibrate, a movement which produces heat. Another way of describing the action of the electronic range is that it cooks food by microwave energy. This is done at a greatly increased speed— from two to ten times faster than by conventional methods. Since microwaves are transmitted through glass, china, and paper, foods may be cooked in the serving container and transferred directly to the table. However, china with gold trim and pottery that contains metals cannot be used because metals will reflect the microwaves. The fact that ordinary electronic cooking does not brown the food may have delayed its general acceptance, but this is now being overcome by the addition of a browning element operated by a timing device which can provide the desired browning and perhaps also enhance the flavor.

According to some manufacturers, 90 per cent of conventional top-of-the-range cooking can be done in the electronic range at greatly increased speed. However, as quantity is increased, cooking time also increases; for example, if one potato bakes in four minutes, four will require eight minutes. Microwaves penetrate the food only about two inches. In roasts and other foods which are thicker, the center of the food is cooked by the transfer of heat inward.

The Sink and Food Waste Disposer

Sinks. Most often made of porcelain enamel on cast iron or steel, of stainless steel, or of Monel metal, sinks may have either double or single bowls installed in a counter or in a specially made cabinet. The sink-dishwasher is a sink and an under-counter dishwasher installed in a cabinet with a single top. A single spout which delivers either hot or cold water or a mixture is an advantage; there may be two faucet handles but more and more a single handle regulates the water temperature as well as the rate of flow. The faucet and handles should be located so that they are convenient to use and do not interfere with the cleaning of the sink.

Food Waste Disposers. These are installed so that the top of the disposer forms the opening from the sink. Disposers are of two types, the continuous-feed and the batch-feed or switch-top. The continuous-feed type, as the term implies, may have waste added either before or during operation. With either type, a generous flow of cold water during operation is essential to harden any fat present and to carry away the shredded or pulverized waste.

The Automatic Dishwasher

Unlike ranges, refrigerators, and sinks, automatic dishwashers are not considered essential for all kitchens, but their use is rapidly increasing. Dishwashers may be built-in, free-standing, or portable models. The built-in models are usually installed under a continuous counter top and adjacent to or near the sink. Free-standing or self-contained units also are most convenient when installed near the sink. Portable dishwashers are stored where space is available and then moved for use to the sink or other area where there is a source of hot water and drainage. Many special features are available in dishwashers, such as dial or pushbutton controls for cycles, "booster" heating elements, improved filtering systems, and dual detergent dispensers, which the prospective purchaser may wish to evaluate before making a final choice.

The Refrigerator and Freezer

The refrigerator should be purchased only after consideration of specifications covering its performance, durability, ease of cleaning, and permanence of finish. The manufacturer's guarantee of specified performance should be considered. When a separate freezer will not be available, the amount

Fig. 20–3. *Although not an essential item for the kitchen, an electric dishwasher is a labor-saving device.*

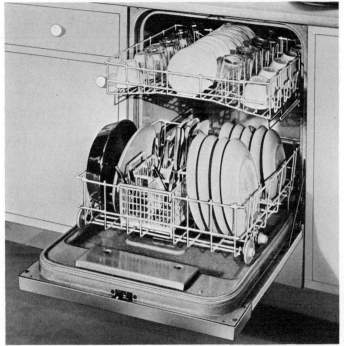

Courtesy of Hotpoint

of storage for frozen food and the temperature that can be maintained are important. A combination of refrigerator and freezer with two doors may be desirable. Automatic defrosting of the refrigerator compartment or of both the refrigerator and freezer areas is a feature worth considering. If a separate freezer is being selected, size or capacity, whether a chest or upright type, and special features should be investigated. In the choice of either a refrigerator or freezer, consideration should be given to initial investment, cost of operation, and character of service available locally, as well as to the care required and the ease of cleaning.

Small Equipment

Small equipment includes pots and pans, knives and spoons, and a great assortment of other items used in the three work centers. Many "minimum lists" or "lists of indispensable pieces" are published.[1] Although similar, they do not agree. They may be used as a guide, but each homemaker may develop her own list, keeping it at a minimum, and then adding to it as the need arises.

[1] *Tools for Food Preparation and Dishwashing.* Home and Garden Bulletin No. 3. United States Department of Agriculture, Washington, D.C., 1951. F. Ehrenkranz and L. Inman. *Equipment in the Home.* New York: Harper and Brothers, 1967, p. 74.

Fig. 20–4. *Utensils similar to these are considered basic kitchen equipment by many home-makers.*

Courtesy of The Aluminum Association

Utensils used for top-of-range or surface cookery include saucepans—fairly deep utensils with one handle which should be securely attached, well balanced, and easily held; saucepots—utensils resembling saucepans except they have two "ear" handles attached at opposite sides; kettles—usually large utensils with an overhead "bail" or handle; fry pans—also called frying pans, skillets and "spiders"; Dutch ovens; and pressure saucepans. The number of these utensils needed will vary with the activities carried on in the preparation of a meal. Oven cookery may require cake pans, pie pans, bread pans, baking sheets, muffin pans, roasting pans, casseroles, and custard cups. Equipment should be available for chopping, slicing, mashing, draining, grating, scraping, straining, sifting, cutting, stirring, beating, rolling, and mixing. Measuring utensils, mixing bowls, cutting boards, and can openers are other essentials. Measuring equipment should meet the standards set by the American Standards Association.

The number of small electric appliances to be purchased will depend, to some extent, upon the amount of money allotted to equipment and upon the wishes of the homemaker. Food mixers, portable mixers, blenders, a great variety of heating appliances, combinations of motor and heating

Fig. 20–5. *After the essentials have been selected, some of these useful extras might be added later.*

appliances, and knives are among the assortment of small electric equipment available. The least expensive articles are seldom good buys. All equipment should carry the Underwriter Laboratories Seal of Approval and a guarantee of at least one year. Some appliances are now guaranteed for five years.

Materials for Small Equipment

The durability, efficiency in heat conductivity, suitability to the purpose intended, and ease of cleaning and handling of any piece of equipment depends to a marked degree upon the materials of which it is made. No one material is suitable for all equipment, and so choice should be made upon the basis of the individual piece. Aluminum, porcelain enamelware, heat-resistant glass, glass ceramic, iron, steel, stainless steel, copper, tin, wood, and plastic are among the materials of which various pieces of small equipment are made. Some materials are better for certain uses than others, but frequently two or more materials are equally satisfactory for a particular piece.

Aluminum is widely used in the manufacture of utensils. Light in weight, attractive, and durable, it is second only to copper as a conductor of heat. Aluminum may be cast or pressed or stamped from sheets of aluminum.

It never rusts but it is darkened by alkalis. Acid foods remove this darkening, although foods are not harmed when cooked in darkened pans. Cast aluminum tends to be more porous than pressed or stamped aluminum, and may pit if food or hard water is allowed to stand in it for prolonged periods. Utensils made from the sheet metal are less affected. The weight of aluminum utensils varies widely. Very lightweight aluminum dents easily, transfers heat so quickly that foods tend to stick, and oftentimes the saucepans tip when empty. Some aluminum utensils are anodized, that is, an oxide is deposited on the surface which may or may not have color added. Anodized aluminum absorbs heat rapidly and gives a very brown bottom crust to such products as bread and pies. Cast aluminum may have a porcelain coating fused on the outside. This adds color and is attractive, but probably has little effect upon the efficiency of the utensil.

Aluminum should be washed after each use in hot, sudsy water, rinsed in clear hot water, and allowed to dry thoroughly. Slight discoloration or spots may be removed by rubbing with fine steel-wool pads and soap, followed by thorough rinsing and drying. Stubborn discoloration may be removed by boiling for twenty minutes in a solution of two tablespoons of cream of tartar to each quart of water, using enough of this solution to cover the discolored area. After standing until cold, the utensil may be rubbed with steel-wool pads and soap, washed, rinsed, and dried. The hammered finish on some makes of cast aluminum may be cleaned by rubbing with pumice and powdered soap, using a fine wire brush. Aluminum with a highly polished or an anodized finish, however, should not be rubbed with steel wool but should be polished with whiting or with silver polish. A plastic sponge or nylon net may be used to loosen food that cannot be soaked loose.

Porcelain enamelware, also referred to as enamelware, is a metal form with a vitreous or glassy material fused to its surface. Enamelware varies widely in quality. The more durable utensils have a relatively heavy base and may be dipped and heated to fusion temperature more than once to give a thick coating. Enamelware of good quality is nonporous, resists acids and alkalis, does not affect flavor or color of foods, and, as a rule, is easily cleaned. However, the lightweight ware is not a good conductor of heat, hot spots may develop and food tends to stick and scorch. Enamelware requires care in handling to prevent chipping or cracking; it should not be exposed to extremes in temperatures, nor allowed to boil dry. The heavy utensils with cast iron or aluminum forms permit uniform distribution of heat and excellent cooking.

Porcelain enamelware should be washed in warm or hot sudsy water, rinsed, and dried. Food which sticks to enamelware should be soaked loose and removed with a rubber plate scraper. Burned-on food may be loosened by boiling a solution of two tablespoons of baking soda to each quart of water in the utensil. Baking soda or a fine nonabrasive cleanser may be used to remove stains, or the utensils may be soaked for about fifteen minutes in a solution of three tablespoons of household bleach in a quart of water.

Glass absorbs and holds heat well. There are two types of glass utensils, flameware and oven glassware. The latter should never be used for top-of-range cooking. Glass utensils should be protected from direct exposure to heat and sudden changes of temperature. When glass is used for top-of-range cooking, hot spots are likely to develop and the food tends to stick and scorch. Before being placed over direct heat, glass utensils should be dry on the outside and have food already in them; they should never be allowed to boil dry. Medium heat is also recommended for this type of cooking.

Pyroceram, a glass ceramic developed first for use in guided missiles, is used for both oven and top-of-range cookery. Utensils from this material are attractive and have the same advantages as glass except for transparency. They are not damaged by extremes in temperature but may be broken if dropped on a hard surface.

Glassware and glass ceramic should be washed in warm or hot sudsy water, rinsed thoroughly, and dried. Scorched food may be removed by soaking with water and baking soda. A mild abrasive may be used to remove the white film sometimes left by some starchy foods. Mineral deposits from hard water may be removed by boiling vinegar and water in the utensil. Charred-on food and other fast-clinging stains should be removed with scouring powder or steel wool.

Cast iron is made from relatively impure iron which is not easily worked but which can be shaped by pouring into a sand mold while it is still molten. Heavy and porous, cast iron is durable and comparatively inexpensive but has a tendency to rust unless properly handled. It is used for fry pans or skillets, Dutch ovens, and for some types of bake pans. It distributes heat evenly and holds it well.

Before cast iron utensils are used for the first time, they should be "pre-seasoned" to prevent rusting, unless otherwise labeled. Any antirust lacquer which may have been used on the metal must be removed. When the utensil is clean and dry, it should be covered inside and out with unsalted fat and heated for at least an hour in an oven at about 121° C. (250° F.). After cooling, cast iron utensils should be washed in hot sudsy water, rinsed, and dried carefully. If not thoroughly dry, even seasoned utensils will rust. Manufacturers recommend that soap be used in washing cast iron utensils; synthetic detergents remove the fat from the pores of the iron and thus allow rusting of the metal. When stored for any length of time cast iron utensils should be well coated with wax or oil.

Some cast iron utensils are coated with porcelain enamel or with polyimide and lined with Teflon, making special handling as described above unnecessary.

Sheet iron or *steel* is more refined iron to which carbon has been added. It is harder and less porous than cast iron and can be rolled into sheets from which thin utensils may be shaped by stamping. Skillets, pie and cake pans, and knife blades are made from this material. It also rusts easily.

Stainless steel is the result of adding chromium and sometimes nickel to the molten steel. Although stainless steel cooking utensils and cutlery have been widely accepted as being just what the name implies, such may not always be true. There are wide variations in the composition and finish of so-called stainless steel products which affect their stain resistance. Many foods tend to spot stainless steel on prolonged exposure, depending on the composition of the metal. Heat may also stain or darken the metal, often permanently. Because stainless steel is a poor conductor of heat, many stainless steel pans have a copper or aluminum clad bottom. However, since both copper and aluminum stain, some manufacturers prefer to use a core of copper or aluminum protected by two layers of stainless steel.

Stainless steel tableware and utensils are easily cleaned in warm, soapy water. If food adheres to a pan, it may be loosened by soaking in soapy water prior to washing. After washing, stainless steel should be rinsed and dried.

Copper is the best heat conductor of all metals used in the manufacture of kitchen utensils. Copper cooking utensils are commonly lined with tin to prevent corrosion; if the lining wears thin, the utensil should be retinned because corroded copper utensils are undesirable for use. As already mentioned copper is also used in stainless steel utensils.

Copper utensils are expensive and attractive and require regular care. Copper discolors with exposure to air and from the heat of cooking. Special metal cleansers are available which keep it clean and bright with little or no rubbing.

Tin has a low melting temperature and is comparatively soft. It is used almost entirely for lining or coating other materials such as copper, iron, and steel. Pie pans and "tin cans" are familiar items using tin. Because tin is relatively soft, harsh abrasives should not be used; it should be washed in hot, sudsy water, rinsed, and dried. If the tin has been removed, the exposed iron or steel base will rust.

Wood is considered highly satisfactory for cutting boards, rolling pins, salad bowls, mixing spoons, and other items. Woodenware should be cleaned immediately after use so that no undesirable flavor and odors are absorbed. Wood should never be soaked or immersed in water. Salad bowls should be wiped out with a paper towel washed quickly in sudsy water, rinsed and dried. Other wooden pieces used at the table or in contact with prepared foods may be wiped off, washed with a small amount of soapy water, and rinsed. However, cutting boards and other woodenware in contact with such foods as fresh poultry, raw pork, and rabbit should be thoroughly washed in hot sudsy water and rinsed in hot water. All woodenware should be thoroughly dried. It should never be polished, rewaxed, or shellacked, and it should be stored in a dry, cool place.

Plastic refers to a product of synthetic origin which is capable of being shaped by flow at some stage of manufacture. The products may be formed from thermoplastics or thermosetting plastics. Thermoplastics used in the home include acrylics, nylon, polyethylene, polystyrenes, vinyl, and fluoroplastics. Each type varies in the way it reacts to heat; some become misshapen if washed in the dishwasher. Common articles made from plastics include salad bowls, mixing bowls, tumblers, kitchen funnels, ice cube trays, utility trays, and canister sets. Thermosetting plastic is used for tableware, mixing bowls, and counter tops. Melamine is the thermo-setting plastic most used for kitchen and tableware.

Plastic is easily cut and scratched. It should be washed in hot, sudsy water, rinsed, and dried. No harsh abrasives should be used; special stain removers are available should the plastic become discolored.

Teflon, a fluorocarbon resin, is applied as a coating on the inside sur-faces of a variety of cookware and bakeware made of aluminum, cast iron, glass, or steel. It is even being used as a coating on rolling pins and for oven linings. Teflon as first used was easily scratched by metal spoons, forks, and spatulas, as well as by metal sponges and harsh abrasives. For this reason emphasis was placed on the use of wooden spoons and special rubber, plastic, or Teflon spatulas. It is still a good practice to avoid use of sharp metal utensils even though the Teflon in wide use today (Teflon II) is somewhat harder and more resistant to scratching than the product first used. Teflon lined utensils may be washed in the dishwasher or with soap or detergents. They should be stored carefully so that the lining is not scratched.

Efficiency of Equipment

The efficiency of equipment may not always be easy to determine. Because research in this field is comparatively new, the standardization and labeling of articles to meet specifications of performance and durability have scarcely begun. When buying equipment, all the information possible should be obtained concerning its efficiency and wearing qualities. Rotary egg beaters that do not turn, waffle irons that stick, knives that do not stay sharpened, or toasters that are always out of repair demonstrate low efficiency. A pan should sit flat and cover the heating unit well. Utensils with straight sides are more efficient than those with flaring or bulging sides. Pans should be chosen to fit the dimensions of the oven and of the cooking surface.

The choice of the pan is important; the pan rather than the oven may be responsible when cakes, biscuits, or other baked products do not brown properly. Two cakes made from the same recipe, baked in the same oven for the same length of time and at the same temperature may brown quite differently if cooked in pans of different materials. In one type of pan the cake may come out an attractive even, medium brown; in another, the cake may be too pale; and in still another, too dark or unevenly browned. Usually enamelware baking pans give the deepest brown. Glass ranks next in rapid browning, especially in an electric oven, which has a high degree of radiant heat. Enamelware and glass both absorb radiant heat well. In enamelware, however, the browning often is mottled because this material does not distribute heat evenly. In aluminum and tinned baking pans, browning is less rapid and usually more even, unless the material is very dark or thin and warped so that the heat is uneven.

The shape of the pan also influences browning. Cake baked in a square pan, especially if the pan is of enamelware, is likely to become too brown at the corners. Browning is more even in round pans. Biscuits and cookies brown best on a flat sheet or on the bottom of an inverted pan. In a deep, high-sided pan these products often come out too pale because the high sides "shade" food from the radiant heat. Pan size also affects the browning. If the pan is too large for the recipe, a cake or bread mixture may be spread too thin and may become too brown.

The durability of a knife and the satisfaction derived from its use depend largely on the kind of steel employed in its construction, on whether the steel of the blade extends to the end of the handle (full length), on the grind of the blade, and on the details of handle construction. The material recommended for the blade is high-carbon, stain-resistant steel. Except for heavy-duty knives for which the sabre grind is desirable, a concave grind of the blade is generally preferred. The handle should be shaped to fit the hand, permitting a firm, slip-proof grip without undue pressure and tension. The handles should be made of durable material that will not chip or crack, warp or splinter. The number of rivets used to attach the handle to the blade is an indication of quality. Rivets of nickel, silver, or other rust-resistant material, flush with both sides of the handle, make a desirable "join" of handle and blade. A variety of knife shapes should be included in the kitchen equipment list to provide for efficient paring, chopping, dicing, slicing, trimming, and related work.

The purpose of a rotary egg beater is to facilitate the flow of air into the batter or other mixture being beaten. This action is accelerated as the number of cutting edges in the beater is increased from four to eight and as the beating proceeds in one direction only. The angle of the blades influences the ease with which the beater whips the batter and also the quantity of air enfolded. The turn of the blades should be in the same direction. Other details of the design should be considered carefully to determine how each will contribute to the efficiency of the tool. Details of construction may be equally revealing. A handle pinched into the metal frame without screw or stay or an egg-shaped wooden handle forced down over the metal may soon work loose, and when this happens, the beater will have to be discarded. The blades should be well fabricated and made of durable material;

all moving parts should be precision made and fitted to work well together.

The electric beater is of such great usefulness in food preparation that it merits special consideration. The principles used in its design are the same as those used for the rotary beater, except that the force employed is electricity. The choice of a stationary beater to which the food is brought, or of a lighter one that may be taken to the range and used there, seems an individual matter. As with other pieces of equipment, durable construction and ease of cleaning are desirable characteristics for an electric beater.

Pressure saucepans, although they may not be listed as essential equipment, have several advantages. Both time and fuel may be saved because the cooking time for many foods is greatly reduced. Succulent vegetables such as peas, for instance, are cooked in one minute or less. When a pressure saucepan is used, the suggested cooking periods, although they may seem short, must be followed exactly or overcooking will result.

Before the homemaker with an equipped kitchen buys additional equipment, she should consider what is already on hand. Sometimes a more intelligent use of available equipment is needed rather than new items.

Activities

1. What feature does a range you have used, either in the laboratory or elsewhere, have beyond the bare essentials? How much are these additional features used?

2. Draw to scale, on graph paper, the kitchen in which you prepare meals; mark the path traveled in preparing a single meal. To what extent do the lines cross and recross? How many work centers are there? Are any combined? What improvements in arrangement can you suggest?

3. Examine the small equipment in your laboratory. From what materials are these items made? Discuss desirable and undesirable features of four of these items.

4. Using either a graduated cylinder or gram balance, determine the accuracy of the measuring cups and spoons in the laboratory or some you may bring from home.

5. Make a list of small equipment you think essential for a given family. Compare your list with one given in a reference cited or in some other reference such as a U.S. Department of Agriculture or state extension bulletin. How does your list compare with those of other members of the class?

References

BEVERIDGE, E. *Choosing and Using Home Equipment,* 5th ed. Ames: Iowa State University Press. 1968.

Consumers All. Yearbook of Agriculture, 1965. U.S. Dept. Agr., Washington, D.C.: United States Government Printing Office.

EHRENKRANZ, F. and L. INMAN. *Equipment in the Home,* 2nd ed. New York: Harper and Brothers. 1967.

FITZSIMMONS, C. and N. WHITE. *Management for You.* New York: J. B. Lippincott Company. 1958.

PEET, L. J. *Young Homemakers Equipment Guide,* 3rd ed. Ames: Iowa State University Press. 1967.

PEET, L. J., M. S. PICKETT, M. H. ARNOLD, and I. H. WOLF. *Household Equipment,* 6th ed. New York: John Wiley & Sons, Inc. 1970.

VANZANTE, H. J. *Household Equipment Principles.* Englewood Cliffs, N.J.: Prentice-Hall, Inc. 1964.

WINGATE, I. B., K. R. GILLESPIE, and B. G. Addison. *Know Your Merchandise.* New York: McGraw-Hill Book Company. 1964.

21
sanitation in the kitchen

No matter how carefully the production and marketing processes have been handled before food reaches the kitchen, if high standards of cleanliness and sanitation are not practiced there, the food may become contaminated. Knowledge of how foods become infected helps one to understand the importance of strict sanitation. Refrigeration helps to retard the development of microorganisms in food and adequate heat will destroy them, but care should be exercised at all times in food preparation and handling to prevent food contamination and the spread of infection. Unless the knowledge and understanding of approved practices are channeled into habitual procedures by those in charge of meal preparation, there may be many opportunities for food contamination.

Controlled Sanitation Practices

Obvious measures to provide sanitation include those taken to assure that the food, the work space, and the storage space for food, dishes, and utensils are clean, rodent proof, and insect proof. Unless this is done, safe food brought into the home may be polluted, either by direct contact with the pests or by dirt and infected material carried or excreted by them. "Mouse traces," sometimes thoughtlessly brushed away from work surfaces, indicate that the health of the household is endangered, and that both thoroughgoing action to exterminate rodents as well as a cleanup that will make the kitchen sanitary is necessary. Insect infestations require similar action for their effective control, because they too create filth and spread disease. An extensive roach invasion may even require the services of a pest control agency. If such assistance is not at hand, instruction on measures to be taken are usually available from the state department of entomology or from the cooperative extension service.

Flies live and breed in filthy places. Attracted by food, they are drawn to the kitchen and enter through a break in the window screen or a door left ajar. Once in, they pollute food with disease-producing bacteria. Effective screening of homes and the use of effective insecticides on their breeding places are important means of lessening the health hazard they present.

Garbage or food waste which attracts flies may be collected by the city or by an operating firm designated as the agent of the city. Until it is collected, garbage should be stored temporarily in metal or plastic containers with tight-fitting lids. These containers should be scrubbed frequently, rinsed, and treated with a disinfectant such as a chlorine solution.

Mechanical food waste disposer units have replaced garbage cans in many kitchens. The food waste is ground fine by an electric grinder installed to empty into the drain. The pulverized waste is carried down the pipes by the force of a swirling stream of water, which prevents clogging and stoppage in the drain. In rural homes where modern or mechanical provisions for garbage disposal are lacking, a compost pit may provide a place where garbage can be buried with other organic waste for a period of decomposition, after which it may then be used as fertilizer.

Paper in which food has been wrapped and boxes which contained food should be put into a trash container with a tight fitting lid. Emptied cans and glass bottles and jars should be rinsed, the cans flattened, and placed in containers away from the kitchen until taken to centers for recycling. Food spilled on counter surfaces should be wiped up and the counter surface should then be washed and dried.

Kitchen Care

The kitchen should be kept clean so that the tasks of food preparation and service may be performed without hazards to the health and security of the family members. In kitchens where three meals a day are prepared, a regular cleaning schedule should be established. This should include such activities as cleaning the refrigerator and range; washing light fixtures, windows, sills, cupboard and other doors, counters, and work spaces; wiping down the walls; and thoroughly cleaning the floor. Some tasks may be done weekly, others monthly, and some only a few times a year. Periodically the dishes, kitchen utensils, and supplies may be taken from the cupboards and drawers so that these spaces may be cleaned.

Daily care includes attention to drains and sinks, wiping counter surfaces and the range, and sweeping the floor after the work centers have been cleaned.

Hygienic Practices

Even when effective sanitary practices are observed, it is possible that a family member may become infected with one of the many organisms causing disease and unknowingly or carelessly communicate it to other members of the household. If the infection is in the respiratory tract, like a cold, it can be spread directly by person-to-person contact or by spraying droplets of infective moisture into the air by coughing or sneezing; or it may be spread indirectly, as from person to handkerchief, from soiled and infected handkerchief to doorknob or book to person. Or it may be passed from person to spoon, fork, cup, or glass; these articles, washed but incompletely sterilized, may convey the organism to another person.

The organisms which cause such disorders as intestinal flu and typhoid fever are present in the excreta of an infected person and are sometimes passed on when the infected person fails to wash his hands thoroughly after using the toilet. Because of the hazard of transmitting an infection, only a person who is well and has no sores or skin infections should handle the food, dishes, glasses, and silverware used in the service of food to other persons. Sanitary procedures include the following:

1. Wash hands with soap and water before beginning work, especially after using a handkerchief, after each visit to the toilet, and after handling food packages, dustpans, and the like.
2. Keep work surfaces clean at all times, wiping up any spillage at once.
3. Use only clean utensils and dishes in the preparation and service of food.
4. Take hold of utensils by the handles, and of dishes and glasses in such a way that the serving surface is not touched.
5. Use a tasting spoon for any sampling of food and do not return the spoon to the food after it has been in your mouth.
6. Refrigerate unused foods.
7. Keep refrigerator and other food storage places scrupulously clean.

Dishwashing

Dishwashing procedure is a matter of major concern when the part it can play in transmitting communicable diseases is known. It is not enough that dishes look and feel clean, that is, are free from particles of food, grease, or stickiness. To truly be clean they must be free from the bacteria that cannot be seen. It is effective sanitary practice to provide for the addition of a sanitizer to the dish water and to maintain the dish water and the rinse water at the highest temperatures practicable for the method of dishwashing employed. For hand dishwashing, the highest temperature usually maintained is 49° C. (120° F.); for mechanical dishwashing, 60° C. (140° F.) or more may be reached.

A recommended procedure for hand washing of utensils, including glassware, tableware, and flatware, is to wash thoroughly in water at 49° C. (120° F.) to which soap or a suitable detergent has been added, then rinse in water of not less than 76° C. (170° F.) for two minutes or longer (or as suggested in Part 6 below, pour boiling water over the dishes in a drainer making sure that it reaches all surfaces), and finally place in racks to drain and dry. If these temperatures cannot be maintained the use of a sanitizer is highly desirable.

Washing Dishes by Hand. In many American homes hand washing is still the procedure used. Desirable equipment for dishwashing includes two dish pans (or one pan and a drain board), a wire drainer or rack, dishcloths, a plate scraper, a plastic sponge (or pieces of nylon net), steel wool, soap, polishes, scouring powder, and dish towels and cloths. Plenty of hot soapy water, clean towels and cloths, adequate facilities for rinsing with hot water, and a clean and protected place for storage are needed.

Some order for washing dishes should be decided upon and followed regularly. When dishes are washed by a right-handed person, it is convenient to work from right to left. The soiled dishes should be stacked at the right, the dishpan next at the left, and then the dish drainer. The first step may be to clean dishes with a rubber scraper or a brush immediately after use. They should be stacked according to kind in the order to be washed, and placed so as to be convenient for the one washing the dishes. Dishes and pans with food adhering to them should be put to soak. The following sequence is suggested: glass, silver, china, greasy dishes, kitchen utensils. The water should be changed as often as necessary for well-washed dishes. It is helpful to wash and put away many of the utensils while waiting for the various foods to cook.

Some recommended procedures based on a study of motion economy in dishwashing include the following: [1]

1. Wash the dish at water level to eliminate carrying water in the cloth to the dish.
2. Wash with a circular movement, using the left hand to pivot the dish instead of turning it with both hands.
3. Retain cloth in right hand (if right-handed) except when reaching for dishes. A common error is to grope for the dishcloth many times during the dishwashing period, wasting both time and effort.
4. After washing one item, move the hand with the cloth to the next item to be washed. This puts the cloth in position while the other hand disposes of the washed dish.
5. Place the washed dish in position to be scalded, using the hand nearest the drainer. Reaching across the body to dispose of a dish requires a longer time and more motion.
6. Rinse by placing the washed dishes in the drainer so that water can reach all surfaces, and pour boiling water over them and allow them to dry without wiping.
7. Some cooking utensils require thorough drying, and wiping with a towel is usually more effective for this purpose than drying over a flame or in the oven. Towels should be clean and dry.
8. After dishwashing, cloths and towels should be hung on a rack to dry, or if to be used again before laundering, they should be washed out in hot soapy suds, rinsed, and hung to dry. Dishes, utensils, and dishwashing equipment should be properly stored when dishwashing is completed.

A study made some years ago at Cornell University indicated that dishwashing for a family of four, which included clearing the table, putting the food away, stacking and washing the dishes, wiping and putting away the silver and glassware, setting the other dishes to drain, cleaning the sink,

[1] E. L. Goble. Work Simplification in Dishwashing. *Journal of Home Economics,* 40 (April, 1948).

caring for the garbage and garbage pail, washing the dish towels, and once a week washing the bread box—required for each meal an average of approximately 16 minutes, or about 4 minutes for each person served. The total daily time spent in dishwashing averaged around 48 minutes. If this time is compared with the longer time spent by many homemakers in this activity, the importance of adopting time-saving methods is at once recognized. The study also showed that two persons working together could wash the dishes in about half the time required by one person, but that a third helper lessened the time of the two only slightly.

Using an Automatic Dishwasher. Using an automatic dishwasher has several advantages: (1) The high temperature of the water used for washing improves the sanitation; (2) After preparing dishes for washing and putting them in the dishwasher the worker is relieved of the washing, rinsing, and drying; and (3) Soiled dishes may be stored in the dishwasher, releasing the sink for working space. One study showed that an automatic dishwasher saved 32 to 62 per cent of dishwashing time; some women who cooperated in the study washed 20 to 25 per cent of items by hand while others washed as few as one item a day.[2]

The process of dishwashing by automatic dishwasher differs somewhat from washing by hand both in the procedure followed and in the time required. A suggested procedure is:

1. Remove bones and food scraps from platters, plates, and other dishes with a rubber scraper or brush. Empty all liquids from cups, glasses, pitchers, bowls, and bottles. Soak and remove crusted or burned-on food from pots and pans.
2. Load the machine following the directions given by the manufacturer. A change in arrangement may later become desirable because of the size and kind of dishes and utensils to be washed. Cups, etc., should be inverted or tilted so that water will drain from them.
3. Add the detergent, close the door, and turn on the machine. The dishes will then be pre-rinsed, washed, rinsed (at least twice), drained, and dried automatically. The dishwasher automatically cleans itself. The temperature of the water should be 60° C. (140° F.) to 71° C. (160° F.), about 30 degrees Fahrenheit hotter than human hands can stand.

If spotting occurs in the automatic dishwasher, the specific detergent selected may not be well suited to the hardness of the local water supply. In addition to excessive hardness the water supply may have a high iron content. This condition may be remedied by using a rinsing agent or by installing water-conditioning equipment. When properly placed in the rack, chinaware and glassware are held steady, without motion, while being washed and therefore breakage or chipping is rare. Most plastic dinnerware and equipment used in the kitchen are not harmed by the action nor by the

[2] E. K. Weaver, C. E. Bloom, and I. Feldmiller. *A Study of Hand Versus Mechanical Dishwashing Methods.* Ohio Agricultural Experiment Station Bulletin 772 (May, 1956).

temperatures reached in the automatic dishwasher. Some of the lighter weight and less expensive plastics of polystyrene and polyethylene may be softened and lose shape at the temperatures reached in some dishwashers during the drying period.

Table Appointments Needing Special Care

Silverware needs special care to keep it attractive and in good condition, because it discolors or tarnishes readily due to the sulfur compounds in the air, in rubber and wood, in certain foods, and in some dyed and bleached materials. Methods of removing tarnish include the use of abrasive polishes, such as the conventional creams, liquids, and polishing cloths; electrolytic cleaners; and the dip-type cleaners. Of these, the last two are not advised for antique or oxidized articles. Whiting or chalk mixed with ammonia to form an abrasive polish and applied to the silver with a soft cloth or brush is a satisfactory method. The paste is allowed to dry and is then rubbed off with a soft cloth or brush. A number of commercially prepared abrasives for cleaning silver are also available.

The following is a widely used procedure for electrolytic cleaning of silver: Fill a porcelain kettle about three-fourths full of water, to which has been added one teaspoon of washing or baking soda and one teaspoon of salt for each quart of water. Place a piece of aluminum in the kettle and boil the silver for five minutes, taking care that the water completely covers the silver. Then rinse the silver and polish it with a soft cloth.

Stainless steel flatware is easily cared for and can be washed either by hand or in the dishwasher, but since it tends to spot readily it may be more attractive if towel dried.

Pewter can be cleaned with whiting or chalk and water. A special cleaner is available for pewter, but silver creams and pastes may also be used successfully when the discolorations are not too deep. When it is cleaned, pewter should be rubbed with the grain.

Brass and copper may be polished with special metal cleaners. Because they discolor readily, constant care is needed to keep them bright and shining.

Tarnish resistant finishes may be applied to silver and other metals by the manufacturer and are effective as long as the coating is not scratched. Sprays are available—in most instances a clear lacquer—which may be applied to metals not used for food. As long as the spray completely covers the metal, it protects against tarnish. However, when chipped it loses its effectiveness and the metal will tarnish unless relacquered.

Care of Small Equipment

The type of care required by small equipment depends upon the materials of which it is made. Except for cast iron and certain wooden utensils, practically all nonelectrical equipment can be washed in the automatic dishwasher. Before putting in the dishwasher, some equipment may need to be rinsed or soaked. In general dishes which have contained raw foods—eggs, milk, batters, doughs, etc.—should be soaked in cold water. Those in which foods have been cooked may be soaked in hot water. A nylon brush or piece of nylon net is effective in loosening food stuck to equipment. Small equipment made of wood and equipment with moving parts, such as a rotary egg beater, are best washed, rinsed, and dried immediately after use. Knives of various types used in food preparation may receive similar treatment. Recommendation for the care of equipment made of the various materials is given in Chapter 20.

Cleaning Kitchen Equipment

The range should be cleaned each time that it is used. All food, grease, or other substances should be carefully removed, and a method best suited to the particular range should be used for further cleaning. Enameled finishes can be washed with water and dried. Iron and steel can be washed and a stove polish of some type applied to retain the finish. Chromium trimmings require frequent polishing with a dry cloth.

Proper care of the refrigerator requires keeping it clean and dry. At regular intervals it should be thoroughly washed with cool water containing

Fig. 21–1. *The more range parts you remove for cleaning, the easier the job will be. Soak removable sections in very hot soap or detergent suds to loosen grease and burned on food. Then use clean suds to scrub them, rinse, and set to dry.*

Fig. 21–2. *With burner coils raised it is easy to wash every inch of the range top with warm suds.*

either washing or baking soda, then rinsed, and dried. Any food spilled on the refrigerator inside or out should be wiped up immediately. Only clean food and clean containers should be placed in the refrigerator. Instructions for special care required by each kind of refrigerator are given by the manufacturers. These include procedures for defrosting, placing and covering food, and cleaning.

The sink should be washed with hot, soapy water and thoroughly rinsed after each meal. If necessary, it should be scoured with a cleaning agent that will not roughen the surface. Grease or greasy water should not be poured into the sink. It not only makes the sink more difficult to clean, but may clog the drain pipes.

The method used in caring for table tops depends upon the material of which the top is made. They should be washed regularly and kept in good condition.

Electrical equipment should be carefully cleaned according to the directions provided by the manufacturer. Care should be taken not to allow the plugs and connection points to come in contact with water. Cords and plugs should be hung on hooks or stored in such a way that the wires are not broken.

Cleaning tools such as brooms and brushes should have the dirt removed from them and should be stored in a dry place and in a position that will not distort their shape or impair their usefulness.

Activities

1. Plan and test an efficient procedure for washing dishes. Note the condition of the articles washed.

2. Make a time and motion study of a kitchen cleaning task. Report the results in time saved, satisfaction in work, and the method of procedure followed.

3. Study the record of your state in the matter of food-borne diseases for the past two years. Report your findings to the class, giving the kind and scope of the disease, the causative factor if known, and the manner of its transmission.

4. The Jones family members have "gone from one cold to another" all winter. If you were asked to help them establish cold control what would be the points of kitchen sanitation you might check? List steps that could be taken to lessen the spread of infection.

References

BORGSTROM, G. *Principles of Food Science.* Vol. II. *Food Microbiology and Biochemistry.* New York: The Macmillan Company. 1968. Chapter 5.

Consumers All. The Yearbook of Agriculture, 1965. U.S. Dept. Agr., Washington, D.C.: United States Government Printing Office.

FITZSIMMONS, C. and N. WHITE. *Management for You.* New York: J. B. Lippincott Company. 1958.

GROSS, I. H. and E. W. CRANDALL. *Management for Modern Families.* New York: Appleton-Century-Crofts. 1963.

NICKELL, P., J. M. DORSEY, and M. BUDOLFSON. *Management in Family Living.* New York: John Wiley & Sons, Inc. 1963.

WOODBURN, M. Safe Food versus Food Borne Illness. *Journal of Home Economics,* 59: 448–451 (1967).

22

management in the preparation of meals

Successful management is usually the result of the wise utilization of available *means* or resources. The *means* are often listed as "the four M's": (1) *material;* (2) *money*—the funds which make possible the obtaining of needed commodities and provide operating expenses; (3) *man power*—the labor resources required to staff the organization, service, or project; and (4) *mind power*—the *managerial abilities* and *skills* which provide for the establishment of goals and direct the judicious use of the means to attain them.

To a large extent, managerial abilities are related to the *maturity* of the person attempting to manage. The indices of maturity are of concern to any who have or are preparing to assume managerial responsibilities in almost any field. These are:

1. The ability to make decisions and abide by them.
2. The acceptance of responsibilities and obligations.
3. The refusal to seek alibis or excuses for an awkward or unpleasant situation.
4. A reasonable detachment of one's self from one's work.
5. The ability to see issues clearly, and to take action without confusion or delay.
6. Perseverance.
7. Cheerfulness.

The overall managerial abilities and skills of the homemaker are important considerations both in establishing family goals and in determining whether or not these goals are reached. Although such goals may apply to all phases of family life, here we are especially concerned with those related to the selection, preparation, and service of the family's food. The homemaker or other family member who desires to be an effective food manager will formulate sound plans for proceeding toward the desired goals, realizing that time is required for the development of skill in carrying out these plans. Appreciation of competence and enjoyment of work, good health and nutrition, and acceptance of existing social usage are rarely achieved overnight but evolve in the slow growth of a personality.

The wise application of the four M's—*manpower, material, money,* and *mind power*—which is useful in industry is equally applicable in the management of the varied phases of work in the home. There is, however, this difference: in industry, the goal of an organization is to perform a needed service in an efficient and acceptable way which will assure the continuance of the business and the return to the owners or operators of suitable interest on their investment. The family usually has among its goals the happiness, day by day, of the family members; the healthy growth and maturing of each and all, physically, mentally, and emotionally; and the preparation of the children to become acceptable members of the social order of which they are a part. These are all long-time objectives; progress toward them is difficult to measure at any given time or by any one device. Money saved by frugal management of operating expenses or food costs can be counted with precision, but one cannot be as specific in evaluating human growth and development—or personal and social values—in relation to home conditions. Yet this fact in no way negates the importance of these values.

Controlling Food Costs

The mechanics of managing money and material in the home are much like those in industry. Successful home management calls for knowledge of standards for acceptable products and an understanding of the processes by which these are produced. Constant checks must be made on the money spent, on the kind and quantity of material obtained, and on possible alternates that might be used for one or another of the ingredients in a recipe.

In a commercial cafeteria, where food cost control is always important, the management requires a daily inventory of food bought and food sold, the establishment of standard portions (not too little and not too much), the calculation of the cost per serving for each food item served, and a counter check showing the acceptability of the various dishes made available to patrons. Thus, on the basis of known facts and collected data, meals for the next week are planned, recipes are indicated, the size of each portion is determined, and if the market price has changed, the cost per portion is recomputed. These same steps are important in controlling the cost of food prepared in the home. Computing the cost per portion does not mean that father's or Johnny's consumption of corn custard or rolls is to be limited. It does indicate that high consumption of a popular food may lessen the expected consumption of another, less appealing one. Similarly, knowledge of cost per serving of pecan pie does not necessarily lead to its exclusion from the diet; rather the cost of the meal may be kept in line by use of a cabbage slaw, or other inexpensive item.

An appreciation of food costs should lead to the acceptance by the homemaker or food manager of tested and approved recipes. These recipes are varied only after a product has been successfully made several times and the degree of acceptance by the family has been determined. Protests do not mean that a food should be eliminated from the diet or that efforts at cost control should be abandoned. Rather, it indicates that some experimentation with other ways of preparing or combining foods may be desirable. Careful storage or even freezing of leftover foods and the use of readily identified foods at meals spaced at least a day apart is a recommended practice. Vegetables may reappear in soup, in casseroles, in combination dishes such as succotash, or in salads. Rice may reappear in rice custard, in a meat or fish curry, in soup, in meat loaves, or served with fruit. Acceptable use in the family's meals of all the foods purchased is the only way to get one's "money's worth" out of the food allowance.

Resources of the Home

The homemaker—almost always the food manager in the home—wishes to achieve the desired goals using the available material, money, manpower, and mind power. The manpower of a high proportion of American homes is really the "womanpower" of the homemaker, supplemented to some extent by the services of children assigned to simple and usual tasks and those assumed by the husband in his afterwork hours. Some women receive help amounting to perhaps eight hours a week, but most do not. Some have important labor-saving devices but many homes are without them. Most, if not all, homemakers then must plan wisely and carefully if the human energy available is to prove adequate for the job of making a home.

In the home as in the factory, interest in and understanding of the job and its importance has much to do with the satisfaction and performance of the worker. The attitude the homemaker brings to her jobs of food planning, preparation, service, and cleaning up influences the other family members and can set a pattern of happiness or lack of it in undertaking and completing a given task in that home. Any task, assigned or assumed, should not be too difficult for the person taking it on, nor should it be too simple if there are others with less skill who are able and ready to undertake it. This calls for the successful matching of "man and job."

The use made of resources—money, time, energy, knowledge, skills, and abilities—by the intelligent homemaker will depend to a large extent upon the value she and her family place on food and the manner in which it is served. Food quickly prepared and simply served, may require a minimum amount of time and energy, be attractive and appealing, and satisfactory for many families. On the other hand, the woman who gets satisfaction out of decorating cakes and preparing attractively garnished foods may not consider the saving of a few minutes in food preparation important, especially if her family is appreciative of her efforts.

Organization

Mind power, that is, the composite of managerial abilities and skills of the homemaker or food manager, is expressed in the organization and dispatch of her job. Organization must precede production if there is to be efficiency and economy in operation, regardless of the scope of the operating unit or the diversity of its activities. The first steps in organizing are:

1. Careful consideration of the values and goals the group has accepted.
2. Formulation of a plan of action directed toward achieving these goals.
3. Frank appraisal of possible difficulties.
4. Careful analysis of resources.
5. Tentative choice of a line of action.
6. Testing of the tentative plan in action.
7. Evaluation of the results obtained in so far as these are measurable.
8. Revision of the plan.
9. Putting the revised plan into action.

The plan in operation is subject to continuous scrutiny and modification at each stage of its evolution. In this way, a plan may be developed that functions efficiently and effectively in a specific situation.

Abilities and Skills of the Food Manager

Skill in the various food preparation procedures enables the food manager to schedule the preparation of two or more foods simultaneously. For example, she may make effective use of oven heat and her own attention by preparing two or more foods in the oven at the same time. Her skill also enables her to check those recipes which require last-minute preparation and those which can be prepared earlier, possibly the day before. Thus, a meal plan can be devised that will leave the food manager relatively free from the stress of too many things requiring her attention at the same time and all at the last stage before serving. Work can be distributed over the entire time at her disposal. She can also extend her knowledge and skills by observation and practice. Recognition of the various aspects of her job might be presented under the following headings.

1. Responsibilities
    a. Is responsible for planning palatable and nourishing meals for the group.
    b. Is responsible for purchasing the foods needed for meals planned.
    c. Is responsible for food preparation.
    d. Is responsible for satisfactory meal service at the stated time.
    e. Is responsible for keeping work space and food preparation centers clean, sanitary, and in order during preparation and service.
    f. Is responsible for the clearing, washing, drying, and storage of glassware, flatware, and tableware.

    g. Is responsible for washing, drying, and storing utensils used in food preparation and for putting work area in order.

2. Job knowledge
    a. Should know principles of food selection and preparation.
    b. Should recognize characteristics of acceptable products of the major groups of foods as vegetables, fruits, meats, fish, beverages, batters, doughs, custards, and pastries.
    c. Should understand sound bases for menu planning.
    d. Should know rules for simple and attractive food service.
    e. Should know the principles involved in the use of equipment for food preparation.
    f. Should know the care needed to keep equipment in good order.

3. Skills
    a. Should possess the manipulative skills necessary in food preparation.
    b. Should be accurate in measurements of liquids, solids, and dry ingredients, in temperature, and in timing.
    c. Should appraise products honestly and fairly.

4. Rewards
    a. Should find satisfaction in the job at hand.

Planning the Work

The various time-consuming yet relatively unimportant activities in meal preparation and service should be charted, showing how long each is expected to take, how often each occurs, and the factors which may limit its usefulness. Then each activity should be scrutinized to see if the use of another recipe or a new product such as a "mix" would release significant amounts of time needed for other duties. In the dining area there are possible simplifications in service which, if adopted, might release ten or fifteen minutes for other tasks. Place mats of plastic may replace tablecloths, advantageously freeing the homemaker from laundry work. Likewise, time and energy required for serving an everyday meal in courses may be conserved for more meaningful activity by using a serving table or tea cart to hold foods and used dishes or by placing the entire meal on the table and serving it with a minimum of getting up and down.

A work sheet enabling her to take a quick look at a unit of work, such as the preparation and serving of a meal and the cleaning-up activities that follow is of special value to the inexperienced food manager. A work sheet of this type will list in chronological order all of the things to be done and the persons responsible for doing them.

Work simplification. This has been defined as "the conscious seeking of the simplest, easiest, and quickest method of doing a given job." The steps to follow in work simplification include the following:

1. Select the job to be done.
2. List in detail the activities comprising the job.

3. Question each detail asking "why, what, when, where, how, and who" (to quote Kipling's list of good servants).
4. Modify the plan for the job on the basis of your study, thus creating a new and better method of procedure.
5. Put the new method to work.
6. Note the saving of time and effort accomplished and check for further needed changes.
7. Check the product to see if it is of the desired quality.

Well-laid plans free the food manager from pressure so that she is able to carry these through and count chance out as a factor affecting the success of the meal.

Satisfactions attained. The smooth and efficient management of food planning, preparation, and service in a home requires numerous skills in these areas; it requires insight into the relationships of one process with another and of process with product. Its success or failure depends on the response that is given by the individual family. If the family members are well-nourished and healthy, satisfied and happy, well-mannered and friendly, there is proof enough that important goals of family life are being achieved by the effort.

Activities

1. Measure, without previous discussion, what you believe to be standard portions of five foods, such as corn, peas, string beans, apple sauce, and prunes. Determine the weight of the foods and record the data. Compare your results with those of at least four other class members. Determine the average portion of each food and the range of difference in the size of the portions. Is there close agreement in the size of the portions?

2. Compute the cost of each of the above portions of foods at current market prices. What increase in cost per portion may result from increase in size of serving? How would this cost be modified in the process of food preparation?

3. Four or five class members lead a class discussion on such subjects as:
a. Do families in your community have clear-cut goals toward which their efforts are directed?
b. How much does your family spend per person per day for food?
c. What amount of time is spent on food preparation in your family?

4. Divide into groups and each group select a food preparation job and plan for the possible simplification of it according to the steps given in this chapter.

5. Draft a plan of work for a food manager and one helper (both college age) for three dinners, each for four persons, one to be prepared ready to serve in one-half hour; one for which the time allowance per meal is one hour, and the third, for which the time allotment is two hours. Note the difference in the meal plans, including foods served, the extent to which they were to be partially or wholly prepared outside the home, the effect, if any, which this might have on the charm and palatability of the proposed meal.

References

Consumers All. The Yearbook of Agriculture, 1965. U.S. Dept. Agr., Washington, D.C.: United States Government Printing Office.

GILBRETH, L. M., O. M. THOMAS, and E. CLYMER. *Management in the Home.* New York: Dodd, Mead & Company. 1962.

GROSS, I. H. and E. W. CRANDALL. *Management for Modern Families.* New York: Appleton-Century-Crofts. 1963.

KINDER, F. *Meal Management,* 3rd ed. New York: The Macmillan Company. 1968.

WILMOT, J. S. and M. Q. BATJER. *Food for the Family,* 6th ed. New York: J. B. Lippincott Company. 1966.

23

preparation of meals

The final step before serving the meal is the preparation. If the planning has been carefully done and the necessary food purchased and properly stored, preparation may be relatively simple. A well-equipped kitchen conveniently arranged with respect to both major and small pieces of equipment may add still further to the ease of preparation.

Many steps have been taken before the preparation stage is reached. Meals for a family or group which eats three meals a day together may be evaluated by applying the following criteria:

The food is adequate to meet the nutritional needs of the group.

The meals for the day include the recommended number of servings from the four food groups.

There is provision for all members of the group regardless of size, age, sex, activity, and health.

The meal patterns are similar to those followed regularly by the group.

A "good" breakfast is included.

Each meal includes its fair share of the foods for the day.

The meals are physiologically satisfying.

The food can be readily prepared with the equipment at hand.

The food is not too difficult to prepare.

There is a minimum of "last minute" preparation necessary.

The food can be prepared in the time allotted to meal preparation.

The cost of the food has been kept within the limits set in the budget.

The cost is in keeping with the total available for living expenses.

Good use is made of seasonal food.

Partially prepared and prepared foods, when used, are considered from the standpoint of cost and quality as well as time.

Shopping has been done from a list made when the menus were planned.

Advantage has been taken of any sales or "specials" when they were really "good buys" even though it meant some change in the menu.

Foods are purchased in quantities which will be used while still of high quality, and in the grades best suited to the use intended.

The foods are liked by the group.

There is variety in the method of preparation.

The same food is not served twice in one meal and not twice in one day unless there is an abundance of that particular food in season.

Food mixtures (as casseroles and fruit cocktail) are used for only one or two dishes at a meal.

Foods that "go together" and food flavors that enhance each other are used in a meal.

A new or unusual food or a different method of preparation frequently is introduced.

The food is appropriate to the method of service being used.

The meal is attractive when the foods are served.

There are variations in shape, size of pieces, and texture as one looks at the prepared food.

The food is colorful and the color combinations are pleasing.

There is contrast in temperature—some foods are hot, some cold.

There is contrast in taste—perhaps sweet, sour, bitter, and salt.

There is contrast in texture—some foods tender, some crisp, others smooth, and some chewy.

The meal that satisfies most of these criteria should be a satisfaction to prepare. The homemaker who has planned with such care will undoubtedly be interested in following the best-known preparation practices.

The Preparation

Although even today many food preparation procedures are traditional, scientific methods are being developed through research and investigation. Common practices are examined and approved, or condemned and revised. Acceptable procedures are becoming standardized to create products of consistently high quality. Using such methods simplifies meal preparation. Often there are two or more satisfactory ways to prepare a food. However, once a method is chosen, it is wise to follow it with few deviations because the habit thus formed makes for ease and efficiency in performance and for assurance of a satisfactory product. These procedures are usually expressed as recipes, which are, in fact, formulas giving the proportions of ingredients to be used, the method of combining them, and the cooking processes involved.

Standard or basic recipes express for a whole group of dishes, such as batters, the general proportions and procedures to be followed, and also indicate possible variations. Familiarity with basic recipes and standard proportions, like an understanding of acceptable products, is fundamental to satisfactory meal preparation. Only as each separate dish measures up to the accepted standards for that product is the success of the meal assured. The problem in meal preparation, then, is to choose and follow tested procedures in such a way that the food will be ready and most palatable at the same time.

Time Required for Preparation

Quite as important as the money is the time spent in food preparation. Various studies indicate that the average time spent in activities related to food in different homes varies from two and four-tenths hours to four hours daily. These activities take approximately twice as much time as any other group of homemaking activities. A recent study shows an increase in the time spent on food preparation and dishwashing in 1968 as compared with 1952 for both fulltime and employed city homemakers.[1] Not all the time spent may be necessary. The efficiency of the worker and the carefulness in planning affect the time required for a given task. In most households there are limits to the amount of time that can be given to food preparation, hence the need for careful meal planning. If the homemaker has but thirty minutes to prepare a meal, she should plan her meal accordingly. If she hopes to be a serene hostess, she will not leave too many things to be done at the last minute. If she is to be at home most of the day, she can plan a menu that can be prepared at different periods in the day rather than during the hour just before meal-time. Obviously a meal that can be prepared in twenty minutes will differ in many respects from the one that requires two or three hours.

Below are listed some menus for meals to serve four to six persons, with the time required for their preparation. The use of partially prepared and prepared foods could greatly reduce the time required for some of these meals.

Menus

Breakfast

15 Minutes
Fresh Blueberries with Milk
Slice of Cheese
Toast   Butter
Milk

45 Minutes
Orange Juice
French Omelet
Muffins   Butter   Jam
Coffee

Luncheon

25 Minutes
Creamed Tuna on Toast
Head Lettuce Salad
Ambrosia
Vanilla Wafers
Cocoa

1 Hour and 30 Minutes
Fruit Cup
Egg Timbales with Cheese Sauce
Buttered Broccoli
Stuffed Tomato Salad
Hot Biscuits   Butter
Apple Tapioca
Milk

[1] F. T. Hall and M. P. Schroeder. Effects of Family and Housing Characteristics on Time Spent on Household Tasks. *Journal of Home Economics,* 62: 23–29 (1970).

Dinner

60 Minutes	*3 Hours*
Honeydew Melon with Lemon	Assorted Canapés
Broiled Club Steaks	Tomato Juice
Baked Potatoes Creamed Asparagus	Roast Chicken Dressing
Cabbage, Celery, Green Pepper Salad	Mashed Potatoes Gravy
Whole-Wheat Bread Butter	Fresh Green Beans with Almonds
Canned Plums Icebox Cookies	Pineapple Relish Salad
Coffee	Hot Rolls Butter
	Individual Cherry Pies
	Coffee

Plan of Work

Plans for food preparation are made in relation to the time set for serving the meal. Nothing that can be done earlier in the schedule should be left until the last minute, and no foods that are affected adversely by standing should be prepared earlier than necessary. Time sequences should be studied, and when once decided upon should be followed. If dinner is at 6:30, potatoes to be baked must be put into the oven for baking at 5:30, and Swiss steak started at 4:45. A frozen dessert should have been made several hours before. Recipes, table appointments, and the equipment needed should all be considered in planning the procedure.

A person unaccustomed to planning for meal preparation will find the following steps helpful in formulating a workable plan. First, determine all of the activities that are necessary in preparing the meal; second, determine the sequence in which these should be carried out, if possible doing similar tasks such as washing and preparing vegetables consecutively; third, list those activities in sequence as a plan of work and place this plan in the kitchen where it may be easily seen. A typical plan of this order follows.

Breakfast Served at 7:30 A.M.
Orange Juice
Bran Flakes   Milk
Scrambled Eggs
Muffins   Butter   Jelly
Coffee

Time	*Task to Be Done*
Day before	Check to make sure all supplies are on hand.
6:45	Turn on oven.
6:48	Prepare orange juice and set in refrigerator.
6:55	Prepare muffins.

7:05	Put muffins in oven to bake.
7:07	Set table and place bran flakes, milk, sugar, butter (or margarine), and jelly on the table.
7:15	Put coffee on to percolate. (Unless automatic, remove from heat when done.)
7:18	Prepare eggs and cook.
7:25	Place food in serving dishes.
7:30	Serve breakfast.

Dinner Served at 6:30 P.M.

Broiled Hamburger   Creamed Potatoes
Caraway-Buttered Cabbage
Tomato and Lettuce Salad
Bread   Butter
Rhubarb Sauce   Cookies
Coffee

Time	*Task to Be Done*
Some time before	Make and bake cookies.
5:30	Cook and chill rhubarb and prepare salad dressing.
5:38	Wash lettuce; peel and slice tomatoes. Chill.
5:45	Peel potatoes, and start to cook.
	Clean and shred cabbage. Keep cold.
5:55	Shape meat patties and set in refrigerator.
	Set table, warm plates and serving dishes.
6:05	Make white sauce.
	Prepare ice water.
6:13	Start coffee.
6:15	Put bread and butter (or margarine) on table and pour water.
6:18	Start meat to panbroil.
	Put cabbage on to cook.
6:20	Combine potatoes and white sauce.
6:23	Arrange salad on plates; add dressing.
	Place on table.
6:27	Arrange meat, potatoes, and cabbage in serving dishes and place on table.
	Place plates on table.
6:30	Serve dinner.

Dinner Served at 6:30 P.M.

Spanish Steak   Baked Potatoes
Buttered Snow Peas
Carrot and Apple Salad
Bread   Butter
Chocolate Blanc Mange
with
Whipped Cream

Time	*Task to Be Done*
Some time before	Check to see that all supplies are on hand.
	Make salad dressing.
4:45	Turn on oven.
	Pound steak and sear.
	Add vegetables, seasonings, and put steak in oven to cook.
	Make blanc mange, mold and set to chill.
5:20	Wash potatoes.
5:30	Put potatoes in oven.
5:32	Wash snow peas and set in cool place.
5:45	Wash ingredients for salad, and scrape carrots.
5:50	Set table.
	Warm plates and serving dishes.
6:00	Prepare ice water, and butter (or margarine)
6:05	Whip cream and set in refrigerator.
6:10	Finish preparing and combine salad ingredients, arrange on plates.
6:15	Put salad, butter, bread, and water on table.
6:18	Put snow peas on to cook.
6:23	Season snow peas.
6:25	Put steak, potatoes, and snow peas in serving dishes and place on table.
	Place plates on table.
6:30	Serve dinner.

A carefully detailed plan of work is more effective when certain practices are followed. Attention to the following suggestions may be of value to the beginner, helping her to be efficient in meal preparation and to establish good habits of work.

1. Keep recipes at hand. Follow carefully except when variations with known results are to be introduced. Evaluate new recipes in terms of known ratios of ingredients and food principles.
2. Assemble ingredients and equipment before beginning the preparation of a food. A tray is often useful in doing this.
3. Use as few utensils as possible.
4. Measure dry ingredients first, then fats and liquids, thus using the same utensils for all. Waxed paper may be used in place of a bowl to hold dry ingredients or solids before mixing.
5. When measuring, use the largest unit of measure for the amount needed. For example, if the recipe calls for 3 teaspoons, use a 1-tablespoon measure; if 4 tablespoons, use a $1/4$-cup measure; and for 2 cups, use a 1-pint measure.
6. Use short cuts whenever feasible; make drop biscuits, or if rolled biscuits are preferred, pat or roll out dough and cut into squares, thus saving rerolling; cook potatoes in jackets; when preparing a pot roast cook vegetables in same container with meat.

7. Do similar tasks consecutively whenever possible, as preparing all fresh fruits and vegetables in one block of time.
8. Combine related jobs whenever possible. If making a sauce at the range, prepare at the same time any other food that will require watching.
9. Whenever possible complete the jobs in one area before proceeding to another.

Sometimes the novice finds her sense of adequacy and assurance increased and time saved when recipes and methods are also included in the written meal plan. Such details will soon become unnecessary as procedures of meal preparation become routine. The experienced homemaker rarely formulates plans in writing except for a special meal or large company dinner.

If two or more persons are preparing the meal, the plan should be made in relation to the additional help at hand. Many homemakers find it helpful to outline the duties of each person in order that the work can proceed efficiently. Cooperation and teamwork are essential.

If by selecting recipes and planning the sequence of tasks the worker is able to complete the entire task of meal preparation so that it meets high standards in every detail, her personal satisfaction in the work is increased.

Activities

1. Plan a breakfast menu, compute cost, and decide on the methods of preparation and time procedure to be followed in its preparation.

2. Plan a luncheon menu, compute cost, and decide on the methods of preparation and time procedure to be followed in its preparation.

3. Plan a dinner menu, compute cost, and decide on the methods of preparation and time procedure to follow in its preparation.

4. Make a time and motion study of the preparation of a given meal under known conditions in a specific kitchen. What simplification would you suggest?

5. Make a job analysis of planning and preparing a specified meal.

6. Plan a menu for a breakfast, a luncheon, and a dinner at a given cost for each. Make substitutions whereby the cost will be increased 20 per cent but the food values will remain essentially unchanged. Make substitutions in the original menu whereby the cost will be decreased 20 per cent but the food values will remain similar.

7. Select two or three families whose members differ widely in number, age, and activities, and plan a day's meals for them from which each could meet his food needs.

8. Plan a day's meals on three different price levels for each of these families. How do the menus for corresponding meals differ?

9. Divide the class into groups of two to work as a team in planning, preparing, and serving meals. Each person should assume major responsibility for three meals—breakfast, lunch, and dinner. Use the suggested forms for organization of the various activities given in this chapter.

SUGGESTED GUIDES FOR PLANNING CLASS EXPERIENCES
IN MEAL PREPARATION

The following guides have been formulated in terms of a specific situation. Modifications may be necessary if used in other situations.

Days on which
Meals Will Be
Served

Meal	Date	Kitchen to be Used
Breakfast		
Lunch		
Dinner		

Group to be
Served

Four people are served at each meal. Each group consists of hostess and host (class members), guest, and evaluator. The hostess is responsible for the meal plans and the major part of the meal preparation; the host is her assistant. The hostess invites a friend to be her guest at the meal and the evaluator is a home economics faculty member or senior student. The hostess meets guest and evaluator in the lounge or other designated place prior to reporting to the dining room.

Money Allowance
for Meals

Breakfast	$1.60	.03 is deducted from each meal allowance
Lunch	$1.80	to cover costs of incidentals such as baking
Dinner	$3.20	powder, salt, soda, parsley for garnish, etc.

Steps in
Organizing
Meal Plans

1. Plan the menu for each meal in keeping with the requirements and limitations set up for the meal.

2. Submit the menu to the instructor for approval.

3. Write a recipe card for each food in the menu giving the amount of each ingredient required and the method to be followed in each recipe.

4. Determine the amount of food needed for 4 people using the suggested form for Organization of Market Order (p. 487).

5. Combine the amounts of the various foods required in all of the recipes. List the totals and also the equipment needed from the department storeroom on the market order form below in the following order:
a. Dairy products; milk, cream, cheese
b. Meats
c. Eggs
d. Fresh fruits and vegetables
e. Bread or bread crumbs
f. Canned foods
g. Cereals and cereal products
h. Fats
i. Sugars and sweets
j. Miscellaneous: vanilla, baking powder, soda, nuts, cocoa, etc.
k. Equipment from storeroom

6. Make a time and work schedule for both hostess and host (page 488).

7. Draw an "aerial" view of the table as it should appear when ready for the group to be seated (page 489).

8. Clip the menu, recipe cards, market order and table drawing together for final checking by the instructor.

9. Check the menus for all three meals to make sure all daily food requirements have been adequately met.

10. Check the planned expenditures to see that these do not exceed the amount allotted for the meals.

Requirements for Meal Plans and Procedures

1. The following should be included at least once in the meals planned: hot bread, made dessert, hot beverage, fresh fruit prepared in some way, and a cooked vegetable.

2. Canned vegetables and fruits may not be served unless used in a prepared dish. Fresh vegetable cookery is encouraged and preferred.

3. Canned fruit or vegetable juice may not be served in place of prepared fresh fruit.

4. All foods served in class meals are included in menu plans and costs. Food may not be brought from home or elsewhere and used in the meals.

5. One and one-half hours are allowed for preparation of the meal.

6. At the end of the three-hour class period, the meal must be over and the kitchen in order for leaving.

7. Trays and all leftover foods are returned to the storeroom immediately after meal is served. Extra utensils are returned when dishes are washed, before or after meal.

Organization of Market Order

Recipe	Foods needed	Amount	Unit Cost		Cost of Each Recipe
Fruit	Grapefruit			Totals	
	(sectioned)	3	.15	.45	
	MM cherries	2	.02	.04	.49
Main Dish	Eggs	6	.05	.30	
(scrambled	Bacon	2 sl.	.05	.10	
eggs)	Milk	1/3 c.	.08	.027	.427

Repeat for
all other
foods used.

Total cost of Meal _____

Market Order for Meal

Hostess
Host

Meal
Date and Time
Kitchen-dinette

Menu

Food List

Food	Amount	Unit Cost	Total Cost
Incidentals (storeroom charges)			.03
		Total	

Time and Work Schedule

Task to Be Done	Hostess Time	Host Time

*Table
Arrangement*

Table Diagram of _____ *Meal* _____

Host

Guest

Evaluator

Hostess

Menu

1. _____   12. _____
2. _____   13. _____
3. _____   14. _____
4. _____   15. _____
5. _____   16. _____
6. _____   17. _____
7. _____   18. _____
8. _____   19. _____
9. _____   20. _____
10. _____   21. _____
11. _____   22. _____

Write names of table appointments to be used and foods to be served by the above numbers and use these numbers on diagram to indicate placement.

**Score Sheet
for Meals** *

Hostess _____ Host _____
Meal _____ Date _____ Evaluator _____

1. Selection of food
a. Balance
Different foodstuffs represented _____

Comments:

b. Texture
Contrasting _____
c. Flavor
Contrasting _____
Palatable _____
d. Color
Colorful _____
Harmonizing _____
e. Adaptation
Foods in season _____
Foods suitable to meal _____

2. Preparation of food
a. Cooking
Suitable method _____
Neither overcooked nor undercooked _____
b. Seasoning
Pleasing _____
c. Organization
Work well planned (Instructor scores) _____
d. Economy
No waste of time (Instructor scores) _____
No waste of food _____

3. Service of food—Hostess
a. Punctual
Ready at time set _____
b. Appearance
Table neat, attractive, and correctly laid _____
Food inviting_____
c. Quietness
No rattling of silver and dishes _____
d. Correctness
According to standards set _____
e. Skill
Quickly and easily done _____

4. Service of food—Host
a. Correctness
According to standards set _____
b. Skill
Quickly and easily done _____

5. Handling of silver in serving and eating
a. Hostess handles silver correctly _____
b. Host handles silver correctly _____

6. Atmosphere
a. Hostess pleasing and at ease _____
b. Host pleasing and at ease _____

7. Conversation
a. Hostess guides talk pleasingly _____
b. Host participates _____
                Total score _____

Possible score—168
* Use key (put in number which corresponds to quality)
        1. Very poor   2. Poor   3. Fair   4. Satisfactory   5. Good   6. Superior

References

KINDER, F. *Meal Management,* 3rd ed. New York: The Macmillan Company. 1968.

McLEAN, B. B. *Meal Planning and Service,* rev. ed. Peoria, Illinois: Chas. A. Bennett Co., Inc. 1964.

WILMOT, J. S. and M. Q. BATJER. *Food for the Family,* 6th ed. New York: J. B. Lippincott Company. 1966.

24

table appointments

Every meal, no matter how simple or elaborate or what the style of service, requires some table appointments. These include table covering and napkins, often known as table linen; dinnerware, sometimes called chinaware; glassware; flatware and hollow ware; and some type of holders for table decorations. Because the enjoyment of a meal can be enhanced greatly by appropriate table appointments, their choice is important, and consideration should be given to them.

Table Linen

The term "table linen"—now a generic one—once referred to tablecloths and napkins made only from the linen fiber. The term still includes these articles but embraces as well place mats and runners which may be made of linen, cotton, rayon, acetate, nylon, dacron, or any combination of natural and synthetic fibers. Tablecloths were first called board cloths and were used only by the nobility and wealthy families; servants and commoners all ate from uncovered boards. Since the food was eaten with the hands until the introduction of forks in the seventeenth century, napkins were needed to wipe off the hands both during the meal and at its close. Under such conditions the value of having an ample supply of table linen was early appreciated.

Even though table linens are now made from many types of fibers, those made from linen still imply a note of elegance. The material for tablecloths may be plain in weave or figured, as in damask. The damask may be single or double, the latter usually being more lustrous and more expensive although often less durable than the single. Many of the traditional damask designs, such as poppy, rose, chrysanthemum, shamrock, and satin bands, which have been handed down through the centuries, are now copied in cloths made from other fibers. Despite its attractiveness, the white linen damask tablecloth is little used today, partly because it does not fit the modern setting well and partly because of the care required in its laundering.

More extensively used now are colorful solid or print materials which require comparatively little care. The designs may be bold or subtle, but the colors should be fast. Lace tablecloths made of cotton, linen, or synthetic threads in patterns of various sizes are still considered attractive on highly polished surfaces. They are used most often for such special occasions as teas and buffets.

Tablecloths may be purchased by the yard or by pattern, both hemmed and unhemmed, and in a variety of sizes and shapes to fit the many different tables used for meals. For teas, buffets, and dinners the tablecloth usually hangs over the sides from six to nine inches and over the ends from ten to sixteen inches. A silence cloth is often used under the tablecloth (unless lace) to deaden the noise from dishes, to protect the table, and to add to a generally smooth appearance. Silence cloths are made of cotton felt, double-faced cotton, quilted table padding, fiber glass, or plastic. Usually they have a slight drop on the sides and ends, thus providing a smooth edge around the table. Special asbestos table pads, sized to fit the table, are sometimes used instead of a silence cloth.

Tablecloths are being replaced to a considerable degree by luncheon and breakfast cloths, table runners, and place mats. Place mats are available in a variety of materials from linen and man-made fibers to reed, straw, plastic, or paper. They can add much color and charm to the table, are often inexpensive, and are also more easily laundered and cared for than tablecloths.

Napkins may match the table covering, or they may be of entirely different fabric and design. Sizes of napkins vary from 12 to 27 inches square. Napkins 12 to 18 inches square are the luncheon and breakfast size and

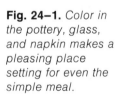

Fig. 24–1. *Color in the pottery, glass, and napkin makes a pleasing place setting for even the simple meal.*

are used with luncheon and breakfast cloths, place mats, and runners. Large napkins are used for dinner. Twenty-two inches is the most common size for dinner napkins though many people still prefer 24- and 27-inch sizes.

Paper table coverings and napkins are being used to an increasing extent for both family and informal company meals. Some of the paper place mats compete with plastic and even fabric mats in attractiveness, and a few may be wiped clean and used a number of times. Paper napkins vary widely in both quality and cost, but even an inexpensive paper napkin may be preferable to a soiled cloth one. Paper goods may be used effectively for special parties to carry out a theme and often to add a note of gaiety.

In selecting table linen, one should always consider the use and treatment that it will be given as well as the money available for its purchase and the time and effort involved in its care. Linen damask, although beautiful, is expensive and requires special care in ironing. However, linen washes easily and grease spots are simple to remove. Some cottons may not be satisfactory because grease spots and stains are difficult to remove. But many cottons are now treated for easy care. Good quality cotton damask, or gay printed cotton cloths or place mats may often be wise purchases. For some occasions plastic or paper place mats and paper napkins may be good choices.

Before the Use of Plates

In medieval England, trenchers,[1] formed from flat round loaves of bread made from a poor quality of flour, served as plates. These were baked at least four days before they were used. The loaf was then sliced through the center, separating the top from the bottom. The crusts were removed and the bread cut in smooth segments or trenchers. These were symmetrically piled in stacks of four upon the cloth at each place laid at the table. Food, such as meat stew, was taken from the dish with the thumb and two fingers of the right hand and placed on the trenchers, the knife being held with the left hand. The pieces of meat held on the trencher with the hand were cut and speared with the knife. The gravy then ran into the bread, which was afterwards eaten. Thus those who like bread and gravy are following a long and honorable tradition. Today a bit of toast served under creamed chicken or asparagus is an unconscious reflection of the practice of trencher days. The use of trenchers was, however, limited to those who had means sufficient to maintain a large household staff, including bakers to bake the loaves and trencher men, whose business it was to cut and shape the baked loaves properly. The lower and middle classes had not even trenchers as substitutes for plates. For them the problem was solved by carving in the table top a shallow bowl-shaped depression for each place.

[1] Sir D'Arcy Power. *The Foundations of Medical History*. Baltimore: The Williams and Wilkins Company, 1931, pp. 63–66.

In some cases the depressions so formed were connected with a draining trench, carefully carved along the side of the table to facilitate cleaning. In time, bowls or plates, carved from wood and used on a flat-topped table, replaced these trough-like facilities. The separate shaped bowl or plate of wood or "tree" marked the first step toward our present elaborate use of individual plates. During Queen Elizabeth I's reign wooden platters or plates were in common use, even for some state occasions. Only the very wealthy could afford silver or pewter dishes.

Dinnerware

Even in 1750, we are told, the possession of enough plates and cups of any material for each person to be served was a privilege of the upper middle classes and the nobility. It was about this time that Josiah Wedgwood turned from the making of butter crocks to the manufacture of dinner sets for the nobility, and plates and mugs for those whose limited means prohibited larger purchases. From his pottery at Burslem, queensware, so named because he was designated as potter to the Queen, was shipped to all parts of England and the English colonies in America. The interest in "queensware" by all people from the nobility to the laborer, first pronounced "a passing fancy" by Wedgwood's critics, proved to be permanent. Upon it has developed one of today's great industries which provides even the humblest homes of America with attractive and inexpensive dinnerware.

Most dinnerware available today is of chinaware, earthenware, or plastic. Many terms are used and it is not always clear as to just what is meant. Chinaware and earthenware are made of clay but differ due to the type and mixture of clay used in making them and the methods of firing. Chinaware is usually considered the best type of dinnerware but that of high quality is expensive. It is a hard, vitrified, translucent pottery, not easily chipped and resistant to blows. Dishes of this material were made in China about 1000 A.D. and were exported to other countries. Because of its origin it was referred to as chinaware. Today Americans generally refer to china while Europeans are more likely to speak of porcelain. In attempting to reproduce the chinaware of the Orient, bone china was developed in England. This is a beautiful translucent pottery made by adding pulverized bone ash to the kaolin. Well-known examples of chinaware include Dresden, Haviland, Minton, Spode, Royal Doulton, Wedgwood, Irish Belleek, Noritake, Lenox, and Castleton.

Earthenware products include semiporcelain, pottery, and stoneware. Semiporcelain may be considered as a separate class or type of clayware. Semiporcelain or fine earthenware is soft-bodied ware with porcelain covering or glaze. It is semivitreous, opaque, glazed, and fine in texture, and it usually has a white or ivory-colored body. It is less resistant to blows than porcelain or china. Much of the moderately priced dinnerware

Fig. 24–2.
Earthenware in attractive patterns and shapes is well-suited for today's informal settings.

Courtesy of Dansk Designs Ltd.

is of this type, and many lovely designs and patterns are available. Some of the English potteries that make porcelain and china also make fine earthenware. Thus such names as Wedgwood, Royal Doulton, and Spode appear on semiporcelain ware as well as porcelain. Some of the well-known semiporcelain wares carry the name of Homer Laughlin, Johnson Brothers, or Edwin K. Knowles. American manufacturers mark semiporcelain wares "semiporcelain" or "semivitreous"; the English mark theirs "fine earthenware."

The quality of semiporcelain varies widely, the finest closely resembling china, while the softer and more porous has many of the characteristics of pottery. Pottery and stoneware are also made from clay, which, however, differs in quality and kind from that used for china and semiporcelain. Pottery is fired or baked at a low temperature and is usually glazed both inside and out. It is vitreous, opaque, and heavy, but not brittle. It tends to chip easily, cracks, crazes, and absorbs grease. It stains when chipped and cracked. Pottery is available in a wide variety of colors and designs. Some earthenware is heat resistant and may be used for casseroles, platters, and other pieces for oven cooking and serving. The term stoneware may be applied to this type of earthenware.

Dinnerware, whether porcelain, semiporcelain, or earthenware, may be plain white, ivory, cream, tinted, or deeply colored. It may be decorated with a tiny gold line, with a delicate design, or with a heavy all-over pattern. Color decoration may be underglaze, that is, applied before the the glaze is applied, or it may be overglaze, that is, applied after the ware is glazed. Underglaze decorations are the more durable of the two. However, in the better qualities of overglaze, the ware being decorated has been fired sufficiently to make the decoration durable and permanent under normal use. Some dinnerware has a pattern molded in, thus giving a rough surface. A conventional design that is not too heavy and large is usually a preferred choice. The design should be one that goes well with the other table appointments and the furnishings of the dining area.

Pyroceram, a hard ceramic developed for use in the nose cones of guided missiles, is now used for tableware as well as for skillets, casseroles, saucepans, coffee makers, and other items which are used for both cooking and serving.

Plastic tableware on the market today is almost entirely of the thermo-setting plastic—melamine. Plastic tableware is available in a great variety of colors, patterns, and designs. Some is easily recognized as plastic, either because of color, shape, or design, while some closely resembles fine china in appearance. Plastic ware is resistant to chipping, cracking, and breaking. It is light in weight, easily handled, and is little affected by detergents, cleaning fluids, alcohol, oils, greases. It may be readily scratched by a metal sponge or by harsh abrasives, however, and most of it is stained by tea, coffee, and some other foods. It should not be placed in the oven to warm, but since it is a poor conductor of heat, preheating of plates and serving dishes is not of great importance. Since melamine withstands moderate heat it can be washed in a dishwasher.

Dinnerware is commonly sold in sets and is usually less expensive when purchased this way than when purchased in selected pieces. Sets may be made up in services for one, two, four, six, eight, or twelve people, and for any or all of the different meals. There are several qualities in each type of dinnerware. However, the grades have not been standardized, and generally adopted, so the purchaser needs to examine carefully the wares she is buying. One should decide on the amount she has to spend for dinnerware and then choose the type accordingly. Wearing qualities should also be considered. Dinnerware that chips and breaks easily, though low in initial cost, may prove to be expensive when replacement costs are counted. Attractive dinnerware is available in all types and price ranges. Before purchasing, the homemaker would do well to consider the possibilities of just one set of carefully selected dinnerware. It could be used with a variety of linens and table decorations and perhaps different serving dishes and thus suffice for all occasions. Such a selection could result in a saving of money and also of cupboard space and of time. Dinnerware

Fig. 24–3. For a more formal table fine china, crystal, sterling silver flatware, and a linen tablecloth might be used.

Courtesy of Royal Worcester Porcelain Co., Inc.

that would have cost a fortune and been the envy of the wealthy centuries ago, today is, like most other table appointments, within the reach of average-income families.

Glassware

The making of glass, like the making of pottery, is an old art. Table appointments made of glass have long been used and continue to be popular. Glass is made largely from sand with an alkali added to aid melting. Other ingredients added determine to a large extent the nature of the final product. The addition of lead oxide produces lead glass; lime gives lime glass and boric oxide results in borosilicate or heat-resistant glass. Lead glass is usually the most expensive, has the greatest sparkle, and because it is comparatively soft can be cut readily. Much of the inexpensive glassware for use on the table is lime glass. Colored glass results from adding mineral substances such as chromium, cobalt, copper, or gold. Opaque glass such as milk glass is made by adding fluorides, aluminum compounds, or other substances. Glassware is blown, molded, or pressed. Blown glassware is expensive and this method is seldom used except for high quality ware. Molding is widely used. Much of the glassware used in the household is molded. Pressing is used for such items as plates, large flat objects, and stems for sherbets and goblets. Lime glass and heat-resistant glass may also be pressed. Glassware adds greatly to the attractiveness of the table. Some foods appear to better advantage in glass than in dinnerware. Glass is more suitable for cold foods than hot unless it has been especially treated to withstand heat. Foods cooked in heat-resistant glass are usually served in the dish in which they are cooked. The plainer patterns of glassware are usually a better choice, and care should be taken to see that the glassware harmonizes with the other dishes in color, shape, size, and quality. As a rule, glass that is clear, smooth, transparent, and free from cracks or air bubbles should be selected.

Flatware and Hollow Ware

Knives, forks, spoons, and similar pieces used for serving or eating are termed "flatware"; teapots, creamers, sugar bowls, goblets, and other serving dishes are "hollow ware." The most used metals for flatware are silver and stainless steel; and for hollow ware, silver, aluminum, and pewter. Because silver was long the preferred metal used for flatware and hollow ware, the terms silverware and silver are often used to designate these table appointments.

Silverware is of two types: sterling, sometimes called solid, and plated. Sterling silver is an alloy made of 925 parts of silver combined with 75 parts of copper. Although expensive, its wearing qualities are high. Plated silver is made by depositing a silver coating on a metal base by means of electrolysis. There are different grades of plated silver, the quality depending upon the metal base and the number of ounces of silver in the plating. The terms single, double, and quadruple plate indicate the amount of silver used in plating. Of these, quadruple plate contains the most silver. The best metal base for plating is an alloy of copper, nickel, and zinc known as "silver nickel." It is durable and has the color of silver. To make spoons and forks more durable they are sometimes reinforced at the points of wear. This may be done by an inlay or overlay. If an inlay, a part of the base metal is replaced by sterling silver and if an overlay, added silver is applied at these points. Knife blades are usually of stainless steel.

Stainless steel flatware is made in a number of grades, the better ones being comparable in price to the best plated silverware. The handles, although usually of stainless steel, may be walnut grained plastic, black ebonite, or some other synthetic material. A flatware known as dirilyte, an alloy which looks like gold, is beautiful in appearance, but most people prefer silver-colored flatware for their tables. All types of flatware and hollow ware are made in attractive designs and patterns and even inexpensive types can enhance a table. The comparatively plain patterns may be wiser choices since they are more easily cared for; extremely plain and highly decorated patterns are the most difficult to care for. Silver tarnishes easily, and at best requires much care to keep it attractive and in good condition. Stainless steel, on the other hand, does not tarnish but does water-spot badly and must be hand dried immediately after washing if it is to retain

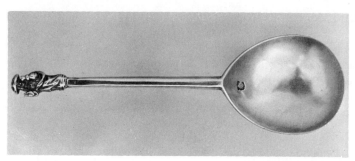

Fig. 24–4. Early spoons were shaped to accommodate the food and the way of eating.

A. An apostle spoon of the sixteenth century: hexagonal handle terminating in figure of St. John the Evangelist;

B. Several gold and silver Roman spoons of the Imperial period, said to have been found at Tivoli.

Courtesy of the Metropolitan Museum of Art, New York

its attractive appearance. Flatware, like dinnerware, may be purchased in sets or cases for one, two, four, six, eight, or twelve or by individual pieces. A common practice is to purchase a few pieces at a time, gradually acquiring a complete set. The type of flatware purchased will depend primarily upon the money available for the purpose. Although plated ware is the most commonly used, it is being increasingly replaced by stainless steel. Sterling silver is so expensive that families of moderate means may find the investment incurred in its purchase out of proportion to the values received. The family budget should be carefully considered before making such a purchase. The table linen, dinnerware, and glassware to be used with the flatware also should affect one's choice, as certain types and designs go better together than others. Table appointments as a general rule should all be of about the same quality.

Fig. 24–5. *Knives, forks and spoons like these were used in the sixteenth century.*

Courtesy of the Metropolitan Museum of Art, New York

Table Decorations

Decorations have come to have a significant place in table appointments. At even the simplest family meal, a small bowl of flowers or a potted plant as a table centerpiece will add to the pleasure of those present. Flowers, plants, fruits, vegetables, seeds, grasses, branches of trees and shrubbery, candles, and other decorative objects may all be attractively utilized.

Special holders or containers for table decorations are not necessary; cream pitchers, low dishes, or even bottles may be used. A single flower floating in a plate, a shallow bowl, or a snifter can be most effective. However, so many different containers for flowers are available that it is a temptation to keep a number on hand. They may be of any material desired but should be selected with care as they often become a part of the table decoration. Whether glass, pottery, silver, or other material, they should be appropriate for what they hold and in keeping with other tableware.

The table appointments often carry out a color scheme or the theme of certain ideas, seasons, and events, which may also be featured in the food served. For example, a Mexican luncheon is effective if the table linen and decorations as well as some of the dishes are of Mexican motif. The Christmas season suggests "snowy boughs," Christmas trees, holly branches, candles, Santa Clauses, and reindeer as decorations.

Table decorations should be appropriate for the meal, its service, and the size of the table. For family and small company meals they may be very simple. For more formal dinners the decorative arrangement may be more elaborate, but if placed in the center of the table, arrangements should be low enough not to obstruct the view. Candles, if used, should be either above or well below the eye level. However, candles are appropriate only if supplementary light is needed. If decorations are placed at the end or on one side of the table, height is not so important. Arrangements for formal buffets, teas, and receptions tend to be much more elaborate than for informal entertaining.

The money spent for table decorations should be in proportion to the cost of the meal. A suggested guide might be to keep the cost of the decorations within one-tenth to one-fifth of the total cost of the meal. However, this should not imply that it is necessary to buy table decorations. A little ingenuity in using materials at hand or collected from the roadside may produce interesting and attractive centerpieces.

The exact amount or number of table appointments desirable to have on hand cannot be stated, because people differ so much in their interests, needs, and customs. The type of table service used regularly, the frequency and number of guests, and the type of meals used for entertaining are determining factors. There should be sufficient table appointments to take care of the activities related to the serving of food satisfactorily. What this amount or number is can only be determined by first analyzing the situation, making estimates, and then checking against firsthand experience.

Activities

1. Visit a department store and examine the different types of dinnerware, glassware, and flatware. Note prices. How do you account for the difference in prices?

2. Make a list of table appointments needed for a young couple furnishing their first home. Justify the list in terms of the activities of the couple.

3. Using the list of appointments from the above activity, calculate the cost, if all prices are kept at the minimum. How much would these items cost for the quality you would select if you were not limited to minimum cost? A mail order catalogue may be helpful in working out this problem.

References

KINDER, F. *Meal Management,* 3rd ed. New York: The Macmillan Company. 1968.

McLEAN, B. *Meal Planning and Service,* rev. ed. Peoria, Illinois: Chas. A. Bennett Co., Inc. 1964.

POST, E. L. *Emily Post's Etiquette,* 12th ed. New York: Funk & Wagnalls Co., Inc. 1969.

SPRACKLING, H. *The New Setting Your Table.* New York: M. Barrows & Co., Inc. 1960.

WILMOT, J. S. and M. Q. BATJER. *Food for the Family,* 6th ed. New York: J. B. Lippincott Company. 1966.

WINGATE, I. B., K. R. GILLESPIE, and B. G. ADDISON. *Know Your Merchandise.* Chicago: McGraw-Hill Book Co., Inc. 1964.

25
etiquette—introductions, invitations, and table manners

From the beginning of "civilization" as we know it, the contact of one person with another and that of a person with the group—in fact, all the life of human beings in all stages of culture—has been primarily controlled by a vast mass of folkways handed down from the earliest existence of the race and developed to facilitate satisfactory human relationships. Probably they were at first merely ways of doing things to satisfy human needs and desires current in primitive society. From ways of doing, these procedures became habits, then customs accepted without reflection as important ceremonials, and so they have remained, perhaps in modified form, for thousands of years after their introduction.

It is easy to see how the service of food came under the rule of custom. Food and feasting have entered largely into the social life of human beings since earliest time. Joy over marriages, births, honors, and victories was expressed by feasting in which the presence of guests added to mirth and happiness. Grief over the death of loved ones was marked by the funeral feast, or wake, a ceremony less common today than in earlier times. The service of food, then, has ever been associated with intimate human contacts.

Customs

Customs, including those pertaining to food, are sustained through the satisfactions they afford. All groups, past or present, even those whose customs now seem queer, have found satisfaction in their conception and practice of correct social usages. The "goodness" or "badness" of such practices depends wholly upon their adjustment to the conditions of life and the interests of people living in a given time and place. It is a sign of satisfactory adjustment when the rules are not questioned and all members of the group conform to them seemingly by instinct. Conformity is exacted of a person through the fear of being ruled out of the group. He pays this price of agreement for "belonging" or for his sense of inclusion.

To the extent that ceremonials prescribed by custom are helps rather than hindrances in daily living, they are fostered and observed; they are "right." To the extent that they prove ill-adapted, they are liable to change. They have become "wrong," and when many people fail to observe them, they yield to change, and new social usages replace the old.

Etiquette

Now and again in the course of the centuries, social usage has become so complicated that numerous volumes have been published—classified under the general term "etiquette"—which set forth correct social procedure. Ponderous books of etiquette written by a wide variety of authors, including priests, laymen, Louis X of France, and even Napoleon, have all had as their purpose the direction of conduct for practically all events and human contacts common to persons in polite society.

Count D'Orsay, a Frenchman, whose famous book on etiquette was long held authoritative, stated that good manners come not from the heart but from the mind, and he defined etiquette as "the barrier which society draws around itself as a protection against offences the law cannot touch." [1]

The importance attached by the English to social usage is well typified by the admonitions given in Lord Chesterfield's "Letters to His Son." [2]

In one of these frequently quoted epistles appears the following statement: "Politeness and good-breeding are absolutely necessary to adorn any, or all other good qualities or talents. Without them, no knowledge, no perfection whatever, is seen in its best light. The scholar, without good-breeding, is a pedant; the philosopher, a cynic; the soldier, a brute; and every man disagreeable." [3]

Although Count D'Orsay may have stated that "good manners come not from the heart," most of us prefer the old saying "politeness is to do and say the kindest thing in the kindest way." This implies the importance of both word and deed in social relationships. In the service of food, one is often responsible for maintaining an established contact either as host or hostess or as guest. In the first instance a person is proffering hospitality and has the responsibility of determining the character of the hospitality extended and of securing the ease and satisfaction of his guests. In the second, a person as guest must receive the hospitality in a manner that assures the host of his pleasure and that adds to the shared enjoyment of the group.

[1] Quoted by R. L. Phillips in Etiquette, Old and New, *Bookman* 62: 259, November, 1925.
[2] *Letters to His Son,* Letter CXXVIII.
[3] *Letters to His Son,* Letter CXXVIII.

As the success of any occasion is a joint responsibility of host and guest, the direction of the efforts of both may be made easier by due consideration of the responsibilities that matter-of-course usage has allotted to each.

This is true in the simple matter of extending greetings and making introductions. Certain forms are accepted both by those who have given the matter "reasoned thought" and by those who unquestioningly follow common social usages.

Introductions

According to ancient custom, the right to speak first in extending greeting was regarded as a royal prerogative; in the absence of royalty it was accorded women; and within groups of one sex, it was usually given to the eldest. Custom, having established the rule, has gone further and given a formula by which the courtesy may be acceptably extended. On formal occasions the word "present" is more favored than the word "introduce," though both terms are used. The correct formal introduction is: "Mrs. Brooks, may I present Mr. Best?" or "Mrs. Brooks, may I introduce Mr. Best?" On informal occasions neither word need be expressed, though it is understood, as "Mrs. Brooks, Mr. Best," or "Mrs. Brooks, this is Mr. Best," or "Mrs. Brooks, I would like you to meet Mr. Best." It is often enough to say, "Mr. Best, do you know Mrs. Brooks?" or "Mrs. Jennings, do you know Mrs. Brooks?" Another form frequently used is: "Mrs. Jennings, have you met Mrs. Brooks?" or "Mr. Best, have you met Mrs. Brooks?"

The generally accepted way of acknowledging an introduction is to say in a friendly and pleasant manner, "How do you do?" or on many occasions only a friendly "Hello." If desired, the name of the person introduced may be added, but this is not necessary.

When introduced to her hostess or to a woman much older than herself, a woman always rises to acknowledge the introduction. However, a woman does not rise to receive an introduction from a man, unless she is the hostess. The hostess not only rises but also extends her hand to the guest. A man always rises when introduced to a woman or another man.

Custom and personal preference determine to a large extent whether there will be handshaking when introductions are made. With some groups, it is customary. Men generally shake hands when introduced. With women, the older woman has the prerogative in the matter of shaking hands; with a woman and man, the decision rests with the woman. However, one should never refuse an offered hand no matter who takes the initiative in extending it.

Often there are occasions when it is necessary to introduce oneself. One may say: "I am Helen Wilson," "I am Miss Wilson," or "I am Mrs. Harry Wilson." The hand may or may not be extended, as desired.

In leaving a person or group with whom introductions have been made, one may slip away inconspicuously after a brief period of conversation, or may end the conversation graciously with a remark such as: "I have enjoyed meeting you," "I hope we shall meet again in the near future," or "It has been so nice to meet you."

The wholesale introduction of a stranger to a large group has little of helpfulness or true kindliness in it. The person should make the acquaintance of two or three in a small group and should gradually meet the others as they come up. Unless very long, a conversation between two persons should not be interrupted to introduce a third.

Invitations

Extending and accepting invitations are steps in establishing social contacts that usage has reduced to routine. If rules were to be formulated to express this routine, they might run as follows:

1. The invitation should be in keeping with the nature of the event, for example, a formal invitation for a formal dinner or dance; an informal note or oral invitation for a picnic at the beach.
2. The response should be in keeping with the invitation, and should usually repeat date and time to prevent misunderstanding.
3. The response should be prompt.
4. When an invitation has been accepted, punctual appearance is obligatory.

A formal invitation, with due regard for spacing, is worded thus:

> Mr. and Mrs. Joel Rankin
> request the pleasure of
> Miss Sarah Louise Brown's
> company at dinner
> on Monday, the eighth of August
> at seven o'clock

A formal invitation calls for a formal response:

> Miss Sarah Louise Brown
> accepts with pleasure
> Mr. and Mrs. Joel Rankin's
> kind invitation for dinner
> on Monday, the eighth of August
> at seven o'clock

If it is necessary to send regrets to a formal dinner, the phrasing should be formal:

> Miss Sarah Louise Brown
> regrets that she is unable to accept
> Mr. and Mrs. Rankin's
> kind invitation for dinner
> on Monday, the eighth of August

An informal invitation is written in the first person. Response should be in similar form. A typical informal invitation follows:

Dear Mrs. Brown:

Will you and Mary have lunch with me on Wednesday, the fifth of August, at one o'clock?

I am eager to chat with both of you and hope you can come.

Most sincerely,
Sarah Black

An informal acceptance:

Dear Miss Black:

Mary and I will be happy to lunch with you on August fifth, at one o'clock. We both appreciate your thoughtfulness.

Cordially yours,
Anna Brown

An informal regret:

Dear Miss Black:

Mary and I are so sorry that it will be impossible for us to lunch with you August fifth. We are leaving on Monday for a holiday in the Scandinavian countries.

Thank you for thinking of us.

Sincerely,
Anna Brown

A form of invitation often used if there are two or more hostesses is shown in Figure 25–1. The R.S.V.P. in the lower left-hand corner, meaning *répondez s'il vous plaît,* requests an answer. If one likes, the phrase "please reply" or "a reply is requested" may be used instead. For hors d'oeuvres or cocktails the phrase "regrets only" may be preferred. The inclusion of the telephone number on an informal invitation implies that an answer is expected.

If the party is to be held in a club or other public place, the acceptance is customarily addressed to all the hostesses in the order in which their names appear on the invitation; the reply is mailed to the person whose name appears first on the list. It is permissible for a guest to send her acceptance to the hostess whom she knows best. If the party is to be given in the home of one of the hostesses, the acceptance or regret is addressed to her at her home address.

"Informals," small folding cards, and visiting cards may be used to issue invitations to picnics, bridge, buffets, and other informal affairs. They may also be used to confirm an invitation first issued by telephone. An abbreviated form may be used. For an example, see Figure 25–2.

Mrs. Allison   *Mrs. Edgar*
Mrs. Brown   *Mrs. Garson*

Dinner and Bridge
Country Club
Thursday, the seventh of May
Six-thirty o'clock

R. S. V. P.

Fig. 25–1. *When there is more than one hostess, a handwritten invitation such as this is acceptable.*

Invitations issued on informals, like an engraved invitation, with R.S.V.P. or "please reply" on it require an answer. It may be formally worded in the third person on personal stationery. However, it is quite acceptable to use the "informal" to convey acceptances or regrets. An example is shown in Figure 25–2.

When the invitation does not call for an acceptance, as for instance an invitation to a tea, the guest need not reply. However, many times, even in the case of a tea, it is helpful for the hostess to know that a guest is not coming. Therefore regrets, though not required, are most thoughtful and courteous.

A less formal invitation is that extended by telephone. This kind, too, should be well worded and given in a pleasing and courteous manner. The acceptance or regret usually comes immediately, which often is an advantage to the hostess.

Arrival of Guests

Guests for meals should be prompt. They are expected to arrive at approximately the hour set in the invitation, although customs differ with the communities and in some the guests may arrive five or ten minutes before the hour stated. This permits them to greet the host and hostess and one another. The hostess need not wait more than fifteen minutes for a belated guest. If one is prevented by circumstances beyond control from being on time, he should take his place at the table quietly, with a word of apology to the hostess. If the guest is a woman, both host and hostess rise to greet

Fig. 25–2. *Informals are often used for invitations and for replies to invitations.*

her, but if a man, the hostess remains seated. A tardy guest should ask to begin with the course then being served.

Table Manners

All people tend to establish rules governing the partaking of food and making of social contacts. Some of the rules of days past are honorable forebears of those accepted today.

The *Book of Curtesys,* published in 1447, admonishes:

> Bleve not in your drinks ne in youre potage
> Ne forsith not your disshe to full of brede
> Ne bere your knyfe toward your visage
> Fore theren is parell and maketh drede.

More than a hundred years later Hugh Rhodes in his *Boke of Nuture* advises:

> Suppe not loud thy pottage
> No tyme in all thy life
> Dip not thy meat in the salt cellar
> But take it with thy knife.

> Pick not thy teeth with thy knife,
> Nor with thy finger ends
> But take a stick or some clean thynge
> Then you do not offend.

The art of eating with propriety has evolved slowly, the emphasis shifting as plates, knives, spoons, and forks in turn became available.

In older times, places at the table were assigned by rank, the seats of honor being those nearest the host. This is perhaps the origin of the present seating arrangement and use of place cards. After the guests were seated, before they ate or drank, the food and drink were tasted at the table by persons of high rank, to show that they were free from poison. Doubtless from this custom is derived the rule that the hostess shall be served first and shall taste the food first. Modification of this rule of other centuries is now being made and the hostess is often served last. Food was served in courses then as now. The medieval host designated that the meal was at an end by rising. Today, the hostess assumes this responsibility and indicates when the meal is finished.

The observance of an established order in the meal service offered advantages as it does today. It reduced the service to a routine understood by guests and servants alike, and eliminated the confusion of numerous considerations and special instructions. The successful following of complicated accepted forms then gave a sense of satisfaction to the titled and rich. Even though the elaborate ritual of other days seems ponderous, the importance of some ceremony with the taking of food can scarcely be questioned. By its use, eating becomes not mere feeding, like that of an animal, but an act of social significance by which a person's enjoyment in life is increased. At the same time ceremony creates a condition in which the taking of food and its use are both bettered. In America there are relatively few families that have the number of servants necessary for a strictly formal way of living. The lack of servants may prevent an elaborate ritual of meal service, but there is no home in which some ceremony cannot bring its touch of nicety to the daily meals. The simplest ceremony will provide, as did the ritual of medieval times, for an orderly spread table and the prompt appearance of those who share the meal. It will limit the table conversation, as was done of old, to that which is pleasant and impersonal. The innovation lies in the fact that what once was the responsibility of servants often becomes the shared responsibility of the group, with an accompanying simplification of practices. The members of the group, however, should carry their duties with an ease that gives to the service something not to be brought by menials.

The tendency to informality in meal service and in other social affairs increases year by year. The proximity of our houses, the tiering of homes in apartments, the marketing practices of the homemaker, the daily employment of the husband and increasingly of the wife in an office, shop, or factory, and the trend for all members of the family to seek companionship and leisure activities outside the home are regarded as contributing to our state of informality. Formality and informality are relative terms. What may seem informal to one group is regarded as formal by another, whether it concerns mode of life, dress, or table service.

However, at even the most informal meal or party where food is served "good manners" are a means of expressing consideration for others. There is need for scrutiny of the old forms in terms of their usefulness today in expressing this consideration. In a number of areas of living certain manners are generally accepted and table manners are among them.

Commonly Accepted Table Manners

As a rule sit down and rise from the left side of the chair at the table. Do not move the chair unless it is necessary. Do not begin conversation until grace is said or until you see that it is not to be said. Carry on table conversation in a low, well-modulated voice. Make a special effort to include your neighbors at the table in conversation which will be of interest to all. Jonathan Swift admonishes host and guest alike to remember:

> Conversation is but carving!
> Give no more to every guest
> Than he's able to digest.
> Give him always of the prime,
> And but little at a time.
> Carve to all but just enough,
> Let them neither starve nor stuff,

And that you may have your due,
Let your neighbor carve for you.

Avoid loud talking or a tendency to monopolize the conversation, as these are indications of bad manners. Also, avoid arguments and unpleasant topics. If these are accidentally introduced, change the conversation to more pleasant topics as soon as possible.

Sit comfortably erect in your chair without resting your arms on the table, or crowding and inconveniencing your neighbor. Except when eating, the hands should remain in the lap.

Take your napkin from the table after the hostess has removed hers. Spread the napkin, if large, half unfolded upon the lap. With the smaller size, it is permissible to unfold it completely. Leave the napkin on the lap at the close of the meal until the hostess has placed hers on the table.

Touch the lips with the napkin as needed.

At the end of the meal place the napkin loosely beside the plate if you are a guest for only a single meal. If a guest for more than one meal, observe the hostess and follow her example. When called from the table, place the napkin loosely on the table at the left side of the plate, never on the chair.

If the number being served is small, wait until all at the table are served before beginning to eat. If the group is large or if seated at a long table, one should start to eat when the serving of those seated immediately adjacent is completed.

Observe the hostess and use the flatware she uses for each food. Pass foods, as a general rule, to the right. Offer food with the left hand and with the handle, if there is one, turned toward the person receiving it. It is received with the right hand or left as is most convenient. Pitchers are received and held in the right hand for serving. If there is any serving silver to be used, place it on the dish at a convenient angle before passing. Do not help yourself first unless the hostess suggests it. The passing is usually done at her request.

Eat slowly and quietly, never talking with food in the mouth. Take small bites.

When eating soup, the spoon is dipped away from the person, and the liquid is sipped from the side of the spoon. Usually a dish is not tipped to obtain the last of the food. Occasionally a nearly empty soup plate may be tipped slightly away from one. When eating soft foods, as desserts, the spoon is dipped toward the person and the food is eaten from the tip of the spoon.

When cutting food, hold the knife in the right hand and the fork in the left hand with the tines down. Hold the knife, blade down with the thumb extending along the knife handle and the forefinger resting near the juncture of the blade and the handle, the remaining fingers curled around the handle, the end of which presses into the center of the hand. Grasp the fork in a like manner in the left hand when used with the knife for cutting. Use

Fig. 25–3. When eating soup, the spoon should be dipped toward the far side of the soup dish.

Fig. 25–4. When cutting food the knife and fork are held as shown here.

Fig. 25–5. Bread is broken into small pieces before it is buttered.

the fork to hold the food firmly on the plate. Hold the knife and fork lightly. Cut only enough food for one or two bites at a time. The edge of the fork is often used to cut soft foods as fish, vegetables, and salads. A knife may be used to cut the salad.

As a rule cut meat from bones with the knife. At informal meals bones of chicken, spare ribs, and similar meats may be picked up after the first few easily-cut-off pieces have been eaten.

The American way of raising the food to the mouth is with the tines of the fork up. When meat has been cut, the fork is transferred to the right hand and the fork is placed under the food and then lifted to the mouth. The European or Continental method is to hold the fork as for cutting and carry food to the mouth with tines down, holding the fork in the left hand, if you are right-handed. Either method is correct. Use the fork rather than a spoon whenever possible. However, cereals with cream, desserts, fruits, and similar foods served in sauce dishes or sherbet glasses are usually eaten with a spoon.

When not in use the knife is left on the upper edge of the plate, with its cutting edge turned toward the center of the plate; the fork is left with its bowl centered on the plate. When the spoon is not in use, rest it on the saucer or dessert plate provided for this purpose. If there is no underliner plate, as when an ice is served with the main course, lay the spoon on the dinner plate, never on the tablecloth.

Hold a cup with the handle between the thumb and fingers keeping the fingers close together. Drink from the side of the cup at a right angle to the handle. Never "cuddle" the cup in both hands.

Break bread into small pieces before spreading. Lay it on the bread-and-butter plate, or if this is not provided, on the dinner plate. Place butter, jelly, celery, olives, and similar foods on the bread-and-butter plate if this is used.

The knife is used to butter bread and to put jam or jelly on bread. The fork is used to put butter on vegetables and jelly or relishes on meat.

Express some preference for a food when you are consulted. It may be a trivial matter to you, but it will aid the one who serves.

Accept a course even if you do not care for it. Eat whatever part of it you desire, trying to eat some. If necessary, leave it untouched, but do not give the impression of its being neglected. A little more attention to conversation on your part may prevent those about you from noticing that you do not eat some of the food.

Never remove food from a serving dish with personal flatware.

Take the last helping of any food which may be passed to you if you desire. It is quite proper to do so and to refrain looks as if you doubted the supply.

At an informal meal, accept a second helping of a food if it is offered and you want it, unless it would appear to delay the service. At a formal meal a second helping is never offered and one never asks for it.

Fig. 25–6. *The accepted way in America of conveying food to the mouth is shown at left; the accepted way in England and on the continent is shown below at left.*

Fig. 25–7. *At the end of the main course the flatware—knife, fork, butterknife and teaspoon— is placed in the proper position on the plates.*

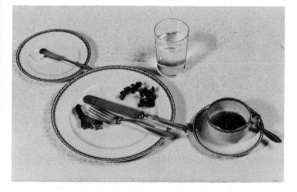

Fig. 25–8. *At the end of the meal the table appointments—flatware, napkin, and other articles —should be placed properly. The cover should present a more or less orderly appearance when the diner leaves the table.*

Do not reach in front of a person to obtain a desired article; ask to have it passed.

Speak quietly to the waitress when she is near if it is necessary to ask for anything during the meal.

Take care to finish a course at about the same time as the others at the table.

Ask to be excused if you leave the table before the others.

At all times avoid licking the fingers.

Dip only the finger tips, one hand at a time, in using the finger bowl. Dry the water gently from the finger tips with the napkin.

Express your regrets to the hostess if unfortunate enough to have an accident at the table. The hostess should courteously accept the apologies offered and promptly turn the conversation.

Avoid the use of a handkerchief at the table. When it must be used, do so as quietly as possible.

Do not touch the hair while at the table.

Criticizing or ridiculing local forms of etiquette is discourteous. Elderly people or people from different localities or countries are likely to use customs different from the established ways of the day or the place. Manners change several times even within a generation, and older persons may be merely following the customs of their day.

From the early custom of the use of the hand for food of all kinds from stew to dessert, we today have restricted its use to relatively few foods. Crackers, bread, corn on the cob, most raw fruits, pickles, potato chips, celery, radishes, and salted nuts are approved as foods to be eaten from the fingers. In some localities, asparagus and artichoke leaves are added to the list. The serving of certain of these foods may necessitate the use of the finger bowl between courses, as well as at the close of the meal. This seems an interesting refinement of ancient usage, which required the washing of the hands of all persons seated at the table during and at the end of the meal. In doing this, water was poured from a pitcher over their hands into a basin, after which a towel or napkin was supplied each person.

Activities

1. Show how certain of the factors pertaining to social usage are most powerful in *urban, rural, army,* and *college* life.

2. Explain how the economic level of a community affects its social usage.

3. Determine what tribal ritual pertaining to food still remains in the usual wedding festivities.

4. Choose one of the festive days of the year, such as Christmas or New Year, and describe the sources of some of the traditions pertaining to the usage of food.

5. Suggest possible points on which current social usage is changing.

6. Describe differing social usages in two or more localities, for example in a university community and your home community, and explain the reasons for the differences.

References

KINDER, F. *Meal Management,* 3rd ed. New York: The Macmillan Company. 1968.

MCLEAN, B. B. *Meal Planning and Table Service,* rev. ed. Peoria, Illinois: Chas. A. Bennett Co., Inc. 1964.

POST, E. L. *Emily Post's Etiquette,* 12th ed. New York: Funk & Wagnalls Co., Inc. 1969.

RAYMOND, L. with Good Housekeeping Institute, *Book of Today's Etiquette.* New York: Harper and Row, Publishers. 1965.

VANDERBILT, A. *Amy Vanderbilt's New Complete Book of Etiquette.* Garden City, New York: Doubleday & Company, Inc. 1969.

WILMOT, J. S. and M. Q. BATJER. *Food for the Family,* 6th ed. New York: J. B. Lippincott Company. 1966.

26

accepted procedures for meal service

The service for any meal should be as attractive, convenient, and efficient as possible under the existing conditions. The simplest meal may take on an air of glamour if it is beautifully served with a bit of fanfare.

The service should always be in keeping with the menu, the table appointments, and the equipment on hand. The available help, whether hired or contributed by members of the family, must be considered in deciding on the service to be used.

For a simple meal elaborate service is quite out of place and only serves to intensify the plainness of the fare. A breakfast of prunes, toast, and coffee scarcely requires that one member of the family be delegated to serve it, or that the food be separated into portions and served by the host at the table. On the other hand, a three-course luncheon for twelve or fifteen people cannot easily be served by the hostess alone, and requires careful planning.

There are many forms of table service and rules of etiquette to govern them. It is well to remember that rules have not been dictated by some all-powerful social arbitrator, but have evolved and been accepted because under certain circumstances and over a period of time they proved to be the most satisfactory. It is not a cardinal sin to break a rule but it is well to know the rules. Then if another method or a modification of the rule or order of service currently in use is considered more acceptable under existing conditions, there is no reason not to make an intelligent change. Usually one finds that the rules are sensible and came about because they exemplified the most gracious and efficient way of doing the job.

For most groups an informal service is convenient and desirable for regular use. The tendency in most families is to adopt some suitable form of service that through regular use becomes accepted as a family ritual in which all members share. Such service frequently strikes a characteristic and pleasing note that guests, as well as family, will enjoy.

The procedures in meal service and the details of service discussed in this and the following section are methods of serving which have proved satisfactory to many homemakers and hostesses. These procedures should be tried and then modified for personal use, if this seems desirable, keeping in mind that order, efficiency, and ease of service are important considerations if family and guests are to derive the greatest satisfaction from the meal.

In the discussion that follows, the terms homemaker and hostess have been used more or less interchangeably; mother might have been included also. Likewise, father might have been used in describing the duties of the host. The other members of the group could be guests or family members, but it is assumed that if they participate in the service of the meal they will, as a rule, be members of the family, although they may be close friends whom the hostess has asked to assist. Except for the meals served "with waitress," where the duties of a waitress are described, these usually refer to the homemaker, hostess, or some other member of the family.

Forms and Styles of Table Service

There are two general classes of table service, informal and formal. Informal service includes those occasions in which the host, hostess, and other members of the group, as well as the waitress or waiter, may participate. It should be friendly, gracious, and simple. In formal service the waitress or waiter alone participates; the host and hostess take no part other than watching to see that the procedure goes smoothly. It is dignified, elegant, and elaborate and has no place in the servantless home. Family (sometimes designated as American or country-style by some writers), English, compromise (referred to as family style by some writers), buffet, plate, and tray styles are all informal service; the Russian style is formal. The terms English and Russian here designate specific styles of service, although the styles may not necessarily be in general use in the country from which the name is derived.

Informal Service

Family style service is that used when the entire meal or the main part of it is placed on the table at one time and served by the persons at the table. The plates are placed at the individual covers and much or all of the food is on the table before the family is seated. Sometimes the dessert is brought from the kitchen by a member of the family at the time of its service, or it may be on the service table or tea cart. The hot food is placed on the table just before the meal is served. Family service is widely used in many homes. This is no doubt because it is simple in form and requires less time and effort than most other forms of service.

Fig. 26–1. *This springtime luncheon, arranged on the plates before the meal begins, consists of shrimp and orange slices on avocado halves and cream cheese-date nut sandwiches.*

Courtesy of Sterling Silversmiths Guild of America

English service is the style in which all food is served at the table by the host and hostess and other members of the family. It is a pleasing and hospitable form of service. The host carves the meat and serves the plates. He may also serve part or all of the vegetables, but frequently the plates are passed to the hostess or to some member of the family seated next to the host who may serve these. The hostess serves the beverage and the dessert. She also serves the salad or designates some other member of the group to do so. One course is served at a time and is removed before the next course is brought in. English service may be carried on with or without a waitress or waiter. If there is a waitress, she brings all plates and dishes to the guests after the food has been put on them. She also passes all accompaniments of the course and removes the plates and other dishes when the course is finished. If there is no waitress, the plates and other dishes and accompaniments are passed by those at the table. The dishes are then removed and the food for the next course is brought in by the hostess or other member of the group.

Courtesy of Fleischmann's Yeast

Fig. 26–2. *Snack trays hold an informal supper meal of barbecue beef, rolls and soft drinks.*

Compromise service is a combination of the English and Russian styles of service. It is convenient and well adapted for both family and guest meals. Some of the foods are served at the table, usually by the host, and others may be served in individual portions from the kitchen. Compromise service is suitable for any meal and may be used with or without a waitress. The choice in regard to food that will be served at the table or from the kitchen depends chiefly upon the menu and the facilities available. Usually the main dish and the accompaniments of the main dish are served at the table. Salad and dessert may be served at the table but often they are divided into portions and served from the kitchen. The service of the food is divided among the host, hostess, and others at the table and the placing, passing, and removal of dishes is done as in the English style according to whether or not there is a waitress.

Plate service is a quick and easy form of service. Food is placed on the plates in the kitchen and the filled plates are served the guests. If many plates are to be served there is a problem of keeping the food at the right temperature while serving. If more than four are to be served it is well to have more than one person working. This type of service offers opportunity to arrange the food attractively and in the size portions desired. Adequate space for setting out the plates greatly facilitates the serving. Another advantage of this type of service is that there are no serving dishes to wash. The plates may be served to the guests at the dining table or on lap trays or tray tables, or the plate may be held on the lap without a tray.

The use of trays is the outgrowth of informal living, and the trend toward the elimination of the dining room. The advent of television in almost every home has had its effect also. Tray service may mean lap trays or tray tables on legs. In either case, the trays may be set as for an individual cover with or without a place mat. Salt, pepper, butter, and any other item needed for each person may be provided on each tray. If the plates are served in the kitchen, not only the main course but also the beverage and dessert may be placed on the tray, which is then taken to the dining area. Trays also are frequently used for buffet service. The use of trays is an informal type of service, but at the same time is efficient and enjoyable.

Buffet service is a do-it-yourself service and is especially convenient for entertaining a number of guests when no maid is available. It is also a desirable form of service when there are more guests than can be seated conveniently at the dining table. The informality of the buffet service probably adds to its enjoyment. The food and table appointments are attractively arranged on a table, buffet, or chest and the guests serve themselves. The main dish and the salad may be served by friends of the hostess, although all of the food may be served by the guests themselves. The dessert may be served from the kitchen directly to each guest or it may be placed on the table after the main course is cleared and the guests again serve themselves. If the dessert is served from the kitchen, it is probable that the used dishes will be removed by a waitress or by friends of the hostess. If the dessert is served from the table, the guests will probably take their used dishes to a place indicated as they go for the dessert. Guests may stand while eating but it is best if there are chairs for all. Tables may be provided, either tables at which the guests sit or small tables on which plates and beverage or beverage only may be placed. Trays are often used if tables are not available.

Formal Service

Russian or continental style is the most formal and elaborate form of table service. It is seldom used in the home, but it is most attractive when well executed. Its principal use is for formal dinners and luncheons. However, any meal can be served Russian style. Hotels, restaurants, and tearooms use this type of service with various modifications and adaptations.

In Russian service, the food is all served from the kitchen, and requires adequate waiter or waitress service. The food may be arranged on the individual plates or dishes and placed before each guest by the waiter or waitress. In its most elaborate form, the food is attractively arranged in suitable serving dishes and passed by the waiter or waitress to the individual guests who may serve themselves but who are usually served by the waiter or waitress.

In a strictly formal meal, only Russian service is used. Goblets and service plates are always used, and place cards are almost a necessity. As a rule, no food appears on the table until the guests are seated. Butter is not served. Salt and pepper may or may not be on the table, as the hostess desires. Dessert silver is placed just before the dessert is served. Finger bowls are a part of the formal meal, and coffee in demitasse cups (without cream) is served as a separate and last course. A formal meal should not be undertaken without adequate and well-trained help. At least one waitress or waiter is needed for every six guests. Semiformal meals are more frequently served than strictly formal meals. In the service of such meals, the general pattern of Russian service is followed with modifications and variations made according to the situation.

Selecting the Style

Family meals are informal and any meal may be served by any of the informal styles described. Breakfast and luncheon are likely to be the most casual in most families. Frequently plate service is expedient and it may be very satisfactory. Other groups may prefer the family style for all three meals.

Breakfast and luncheon are often hurried meals; hence plans for the service of these meals should be adapted to the time available. This does not preclude observation of accepted table manners and common courtesy, but it does mean that active participation by each member of the group may be greater.

Dinner is usually the most formal meal of the day. Theoretically, the entire family is present, and the meal is eaten in a more leisurely fashion than are the other two. The service, no matter what type, is a little less casual than that for the other meals. There may be two or more courses and as a rule a greater variety of food is served. Because it is a time when the entire family may be together, its service should add to their pleasure and social life.

Company meals too may be served by any of the methods listed but there is a tendency for them to be less casual than family meals. More time is allowed for the eating of the meal and it is usually a social occasion. Company meals may be breakfast, luncheon or supper, dinner, or brunch— a combination of breakfast and luncheon. They may be as informal as the group desires but call for the observation of the niceties of meal service.

Picnics, barbecues, steak fries, and wiener roasts often include guests. These as well as brunches will be discussed briefly under "special meals and parties."

Meals at the Table
General Rules for Setting the Table

The following instructions will be found useful in preparing the table for meal service.

Dust the table; if a tablecloth is to be used lay the silence cloth or board, making it perfectly smooth and fastening it, if necessary, to hold it in position. Lay the tablecloth carefully with the middle lengthwise crease up and exactly centered. Smooth out any wrinkles in the cloth. The tablecloth should extend over the table an equal distance at each end, preferably ten to sixteen inches. When place mats and table runners are used no silence cloth is needed. They should be placed carefully in relation to the edge of the table, the number to be served and the size of the table. Place the decoration in the center of the table, at one end, or elsewhere as desired.

"Cover" is the term used to indicate the place set for each person at the table. This includes the flatware—often referred to as silverware or silver—dinnerware, napkins, and glasses for each person's use. Allow twenty to thirty inches for each cover in order to provide sufficient space for each person. When there is an even number of people at the table, the covers should be directly opposite each other.

If plates are placed at this time they should occupy the center of the cover and be one inch from the edge of the table. Place the flatware beside the plate, one inch from the table edge and perpendicular to it. Lay the flatware close to the plate but do not crowd.

Various methods are used for placing the flatware. Some prefer to place it in the order of its use during the meal. Others prefer to place the dinner knife and fork immediately to the right and left of the plate, thus marking its position. Some even like the flatware arranged in order of size. If the flatware is placed in order of use and only one knife is used, it is placed, sharp edge in, to the right of the plate; the forks, tines up, to the left of the plate, the dessert fork nearest the plate, then the salad fork (unless the salad is the first course), and the dinner fork to the far left; and spoons, bowl up, are placed to the right of the knife in order of use. If a cocktail or an oyster fork is used, it is placed to the right of the spoons or on the service plate. The fork or spoon for the dessert may be placed above the cover, horizontal to the edge of the table. If the knife is not needed, it may be omitted and the fork or forks may then be placed at the right where the knife customarily is placed. A salad fork is not necessarily used in the informal meal in which the salad is not served as a separate course. In the formal meal, and sometimes in the informal meal served in courses, some of the flatware is placed when a course is served. The flatware for dessert and for coffee, if it is not served with the main course, may be placed at each cover when these are served. Regardless of the method used, be consistent and be sure each piece is carefully spaced.

If food is to be passed, put each piece of serving flatware at a convenient place adjacent to the dish with which it is to be used, following the general line of the other flatware on the table—that is, parallel and perpendicular to the edge of the table. Provide service flatware for all serving dishes. Lay necessary pieces beside the dish. If but one piece is required, place it to the right of the dish; if two are needed—for instance, a knife and fork or a spoon and fork—place the knife or spoon to the right and the fork to the left of the dish. Do not put flatware intended for personal use into the serving dishes.

If the host is to serve the food, serving utensils to be used by the host may be placed by the serving dish if the dish is set above the host's cover, but with the host's flatware at the right if the dish is at the side of the host's cover. However, some hostesses prefer to put all serving flatware used by the host with his own service.

Place the napkin, neatly folded, at the left of the fork and in line with the silver with the loose corner at lower right and the open edges next to the edge of the table and the plate. If for some reason the appearance is better, the open corner may be at the lower left. The folded napkin may also be placed in the center of the cover. For a formal meal the folded napkin is placed in the center of the service plate unless the first course is to be placed before the guests are seated. At a family meal the napkin may be held by a ring or other device.

Place the water glass at the tip of the knife and slightly to the right of it. As coffee or tea cups are served and passed, place the cup at the right of the spoons with the handle parallel to the edge of the table and on a line that passes slightly below the center of the plate. If milk is served, place it at the right of the water glass.

Place salt and pepper shakers in convenient places, spacing them uniformly. One set for every two or three persons is desirable. If individual salt and pepper shakers are used, these should be placed directly in front of the cover. Place the sugar bowl and cream pitcher directly in front of the hostess, the sugar to the right of the cream, with the handles of both following the same line, preferably lengthwise of the table.

Place bread-and-butter plates, when used, at the tip of the fork slightly to the left. The butter spreader is placed across the top of the plate, cutting edge toward the center of the plate. If preferred, it may be placed on the right side of the bread-and-butter plate parallel to the other silver of the cover, or with the handle to the right and the blade in the center of the bread-and-butter plate.

A serving table or tea cart is often used to hold serving dishes, to save steps, and to facilitate service of the meal. It should be located near the dining table and convenient to the kitchen. It may have a cloth or doily on it, or it may be left bare, as preferred. Such articles may be placed on the serving table, as water and milk pitchers, coffee or tea service, extra flatware, and sometimes food for another course, such as salad or dessert. Space may also be left for the exchange of dishes between courses.

General Rules for Serving Informally

Provide warm dishes for hot foods and chilled dishes for cold foods. Serve hot foods hot and cold foods cold. Put ice in the water glasses, if desired, and fill them three-fourths full of cold water just before the meal begins. Refill the pitcher and place it conveniently near the member of the family who is responsible for refilling the glasses as needed.

If bread is served, cut in half-slices lengthwise, or in smaller slices if the loaf is large, and arrange them carefully on a plate. Place bread, butter, jelly, and other cold foods on the table shortly before the meal is served. Make sure that everything is assembled before announcing the meal.

Immediately before serving, either before or after the meal is announced, place foods conveniently near the person who is responsible for the serving or passing. If the beverage is served with the main part of the meal, its service accompanies that of the other hot foods. It may be served from the kitchen or at the table. Beverage cups should be filled three-fourths full. If the beverage is served at the table, place the pot near the one who is to serve it, with the handle of the pot parallel to the edge of the table at a distance convenient for grasping. It is preferable to place each cup in its own saucer with the handle slightly toward the right. When space does not permit this, two cups may be stacked together. Cream and sugar, if used, should be put in the cups before the beverage is poured. Each person should be asked whether he wishes cream, sugar, or both. After being filled, the cup on the saucer is passed with the handle to the right.

Arrange the food in a uniform manner on the plates, for example, the meat on the lower left side of plate with potatoes on upper left and other vegetable on right side of the plate. Plates should be passed or placed uniformly so that each cover appears the same.

If the food is to be passed at the table, a uniform plan should be followed. When starting to pass a food, place any necessary serving silver at a convenient angle on the dish.

Details of Service

The chief responsibility of the waitress, whether she is the hostess, other family member, or an employee, is to see that the service of the meal is as orderly, prompt, inconspicuous, and delightful as she can make it. Her movements should be quick, quiet, and skillful. She should meet any emergency that arises coolly, quickly, and quietly. Before the meal is served her responsibilities are as follows:

See that the dining room is comfortable in regard to ventilation and heat. Lay the cloth, arrange the decorations, set the table, and place the chairs.

See that suitable dishes and flatware are in readiness for each course.

See that food and dishes are of proper temperature, and that food is arranged properly upon the dishes. Have everything in readiness when the meal is announced. A meal is announced to or by the hostess thus: "Dinner is served."

In the service of the food, the following are generally accepted procedures:

When removing a dish and placing another at the same time, from left side, remove with the right hand and place with the left hand. In all other cases, place and remove from the left side with the left hand except dishes that are on the right side of the cover, such as water glasses, sherbets, and beverage cups. Place and remove these at the right side, with the right hand.

When a guest is to serve himself, offer food from the left side with the left hand. In presenting dishes of food, place a service napkin on the palm of the hand to protect it from heat. The service napkin is used only when placing the hot plates and when placing or passing dishes containing food. When the waitress offers the food, she holds it at a height, distance, and angle convenient for the person being served. Utensils for serving should be placed conveniently.

When refilling glasses, do not lift them from the table. If possible, fill without moving glasses from their place; otherwise move glasses to the edge of the table, grasping them near the bottom. Use a service napkin to catch the drip from the pitcher.

Repass bread or rolls and butter as needed.

In placing, passing, or removing several small articles and extra pieces of flatware, use a small tray which may or may not be covered with a doily or tray cloth.

Before the next course, clear the table in the following order: serving utensils and dishes, used plates and flatware, and any unused items provided for the course. If a separate salad course follows the main course, bread-and-butter plates may be left on the table until after the salad course. If an informal meal is being served, all dishes from a cover may be cleared at one time, as for example, remove luncheon or dinner plate and flatware, left hand, left side, transfer to right hand, then salad plate left hand, left side, place on plate in right hand and finally the bread-and-butter plate and spreader, left hand, left side.

Before placing dessert, remove all dishes, both serving and individual. Crumb the table with a small folded napkin and a plate or crumb tray. Crumb each cover with the open edges of the napkin left side, left hand, in the order in which the guests are served. If the meal is such that there are no crumbs on the table this step may be omitted. This may be especially desirable if the hostess or a member of the family is serving as waitress.

Buffet Service

Buffet service is a popular form of service and may be as elaborate or as simple as the occasion dictates. It is an efficient way of entertaining a number

Courtesy of Sterling Silversmiths Guild of America

Fig. 26–3. *Table set for buffet-style breakfast featuring asparagus-egg bake and apricot nut bread. Fruit juice, main dish, bread and butter, as well as napkin, fork, butter spreader and spoon are to be picked up by each person and carried to the eating area.*

of guests when the dining table seats few. It is also a way of serving a meal with the minimum of assistance from others. There is generally a feeling of informality and friendliness at the well-planned buffet. Perhaps the fact that all participate in the service adds to the enjoyment.

Buffet service is suitable for breakfasts, luncheons, dinners, brunches, after-the-theatre suppers and parties, coffees, teas, receptions, and in fact for any type of informal service of food. The setting may be as elegant as cut flowers, linen tablecloth, sterling silver, fine porcelain, and crystal can make it. It may, however, be made equally attractive and even more interesting through the use of garden flowers, peasant linens, and colorful pottery or plastic tableware with accents of wood, copper, or brass. The food should be in keeping with the occasion and the appointments used.

Seating arrangements are important in planning a buffet of any kind. Guests may stand to eat, although this is seldom if ever a satisfactory arrangement. Guests may return to the living room where enough seats are provided and hold their plates on their laps and set their beverage on the nearest table or even on the floor. If tables are not to be provided, lap trays are convenient and make it much easier to handle food and equipment. Tables at which the guests may sit make for the greatest ease in eating but because of space required may not be feasible. The dining table may be used or quartet tables. Then covers may be set as for meals at the table. Tray tables may be a compromise between trays and tables for eating. Tray tables and trays may be set with linen, flatware, and other accessories or they may be left bare and all items picked up by the guests as will be done if no table or tray is provided.

Food which is easily served and easily eaten is appropriate for the buffet. This is probably one reason casserole dishes are so popular for buffets, although the ease with which they can be kept hot is undoubtedly another reason. Bread or rolls already buttered and a salad of bite size pieces or easily cut foods are usually served. Meats which require a knife for cutting may be safely served if guests are to be seated at tables. Usually a fork and spoon are adequate for the main course at which a beverage is served. Food which can be prepared ahead of time and foods which do not deteriorate rapidly on standing are desirable.

The buffet table, whether for a complete meal or for light refreshments, is set so that the guests may move around it in an orderly fashion and may leave the dining room without passing through the line of guests waiting to be served. There are, of course, modifications for special functions and these will be considered later. But for most meals the food may be placed on one side, on one or both ends and one side, or on both sides and both ends. The size of the table, the number of guests and the number of foods to be served all help determine how much of the table is needed. If the number of guests is large, two lines of service may be needed. Then plates and food are divided so that a duplicate setting is possible. The plates and the main dish are usually first in the line of service and the flatware and napkins, if on the buffet, the last.

Many hostesses may ask a friend to serve the main dish or the main dish and the salad, although guests may serve themselves to all foods. When this is done, it is important to allow space so the plate may be set on the table near any foods that might require both hands for serving. As a rule, tumblers or iced-tea glasses are used in preference to goblets.

Beyond keeping in mind the need for ease and order in service, there is no one way of setting the buffet table. If decorations will make the table too crowded, they may be omitted and the food may add the color and interest. When decorations are used, they should be placed to make a pleasing balance with other table appointments and so they do not interfere with service. Color, texture, form, and interest are important in the foods chosen for buffet service, and for this reason, much time may be spent on the preparation of food and garnishes.

Special Meals and Parties
Brunch

Brunch, a meal that is a combination of breakfast and luncheon, is very popular in some localities. Served sometime between ten o'clock in the morning and one in the afternoon it is mostly a Sunday, holiday, or guest meal. The foods that make up a menu for brunch are among those often served at breakfast and luncheon. Included are such foods as eggs, bacon, corned beef hash, creamed chicken or sweetbreads, sliced tomatoes, hot breads, waffles, jelly, jam, honey, fruit, melon, and beverages. Being an informal meal, any type of service described under informal service is suitable for brunch.

Outdoor Meals

Eating outdoors is popular in America today, especially during the warm months of the year. Any meal may be eaten outdoors although the evening meal may be the most favored one for this purpose. Whether eaten at home on the porch or in a back yard, or in some lovely spot miles away, many people find outdoor meals a great source of enjoyment.

The food for these meals may be prepared in the home kitchen, or part of the food may be prepared inside and the remainder outside. Some people even like to prepare all of the food outdoors. A wide variety of equipment is available for outdoor cooking and a certain amount is necessary if this is done efficiently and appealingly. Because much emphasis is placed on cooking the meat out of doors, brick or stone fireplaces, portable barbecue grills and rotisseries, portable ice boxes or refrigerators, and wire racks are important pieces of equipment. Long-handled spoons, forks and tongs, shears, can and bottle openers, and sharp knives of different sizes and types are considered musts in small equipment. For many groups a coffee pot is essential. Paper and plastic table appointments are used and dish washing is kept to a minimum. Menu plans follow the same general pattern for indoor meals except that foods and recipes easily prepared and served outdoors are chosen. If the food is to be transported some distance, that which is easy to carry and keep in good condition is an important consideration.

The service of outdoor meals is informal and most always very casual. It is usually so closely related to the preparation of the food that the two cannot be separated. Some type of buffet service is often convenient although tray or plate service may be used. Guests may sit on chairs or benches, with or without tables, on cushions, or even on the ground. In any case the service should add to the friendliness, charm, and enjoyment of the meal.

Coffees, Teas, and Receptions

The hours popular for morning coffees are from nine to eleven o'clock, those for afternoon coffees and teas from three to five. These may vary widely in degree of informality or formality. There may be few or many guests. The menu and its service should be in keeping with the type of event

Courtesy of Kraft Foods Company

Fig. 26–4. *Food tastes so good when it's cooked on the outdoor grill, and clean-up time is cut to a minimum.*

and the character and size of the group being served. If only a few guests are present the hostess pours and a large tray, tea wagon, or small table may be set with coffee or tea service and the food.

For large groups the regular dining-room table or a special coffee or tea table is used, and one or two friends are asked to pour, the number depending largely on the size of the group invited.

Not even the buffet table is set with greater care. Table appointments should harmonize and they may be elaborate or simple. Except for a very small group the most usual form of coffee and tea service is really a buffet service with the beverage being placed at the end or ends of the table. If at one end only, the table may be placed against a wall and food, silver, and napkins placed on one side only, but if preferred both sides may be used. If two services are used, perhaps one coffee and one tea or punch, the setting of the two sides is usually duplicated except that cream may be provided for coffee and lemon for the tea. The decorations are then most often centered on the table.

The food served at a coffee or tea is light and dainty and of such nature that it can be easily eaten without soiling the fingers. The menu generally consists of coffee or tea, or other beverages, and its accompaniments, fancy sandwiches, cookies, nuts, and candies. Sometimes an ice and sandwiches, fancy crackers, or cake are served. In warm weather an iced beverage is often served instead of a hot one. Hot biscuits or rolls and jam are sometimes substituted for sandwiches, especially for a small, informal occasion. Fancy wafers or crackers, cinnamon toast, cheese straws, tiny eclairs, candied fruits, and similar foods are all popular for teas.

The hostess usually invites the guests to go to the table where they are served the beverage. They then help themselves to the other foods on the table, to napkins, and flatware, and stand or sit, depending upon the arrangements. After finishing their food, the guests place their used plates in some convenient place unless these are removed by the hostess and her assistants.

Receptions differ little from the large formal tea. They may be held in the evening whereas a tea is more often scheduled for the afternoon. However,

Fig. 26–5. *An informal setting is appropriate for morning coffee. This type of pot is used when instant beverages are desired.*

Courtesy of the Tea Council of the U.S.A., Inc.

Fig. 26–6. *The table has been carefully set for a formal reception, with the tea service at one end of the table.*

the "wedding reception" may follow the wedding either afternoon or evening. The reception today has come to be a gathering in honor of a prominent person or an important event. The refreshments, served at a carefully set table, may be as simple or as elaborate as desired.

Parties

The foods served at a party are usually called "refreshments." These may be served just before the party ends or soon after the guests arrive. When the latter is done the refreshments are usually called dessert and likewise are that type of food. Refreshments are generally simple, but there are occasions when elaborate ones are desired.

Daintiness and attractiveness are the keynotes in party menus, and the unusual in food and service is often sought. Sometimes color schemes are carried out, and food combinations are arranged that are delightful in both appearance and flavor. A menu can also be planned in relation to a special date or event, such as Halloween, Washington's Birthday, or Saint Patrick's Day.

The service for party refreshments may be of the plate, tray, buffet, or table type. The method selected depends upon the preference of the hostess as well as the kind of party and refreshments.

Menus for
Parties
Light

One Course

| Sandwiches or Cake | Frozen Dessert |
| Beverage | Cake or Wafers |

Medium

One Course

Salad	Frozen Dessert or equivalent
Sandwiches	Cake or other accompaniment
Beverage	Beverage
Nuts or Candies	Nuts or Candies

Heavy

Two Courses

First Course	*Second Course*
Salad	Dessert
Sandwiches or Wafers	Nuts or Candies
Relish	
Beverage	

Plate service is the simplest and the easiest of the four types of service. The guests may sit or stand, according to the nature of the party. The usual steps in service include the following:

Pass the napkins on a tray, or pass the napkin under the filled plate.

Pass a filled plate to each guest, serving first the guest of honor if there is one. The plates usually hold the beverage cup, without the saucer, and the flatware as well as the food. If preferred, the beverage may be served from a tray after the plates are passed. Pass the sugar and cream, if the beverage requires it, on a tray with the accompanying flatware. Take care that the handles are turned at a convenient angle that allows each guest to help himself easily.

When two courses are served, bring in the second course on a plate, and exchange it for the first course plate; or all first course plates may be removed, and the second course then served. After the guests have finished their food, the plates and napkins are removed.

Tray service is exactly the same as plate service except that the tray provides space for the napkin, a glass of water, and any other desired accompaniments. This makes less passing necessary. The tray, often made of metal, plastic, or fiber glass, may be covered before the plate is placed upon it; paper doilies may be used to advantage.

Buffet service for a party follows the same general plan as does buffet service for a meal. The details for this service have already been described in an earlier section.

Table service is the type used for serving refreshments at bridge or other card parties. It is especially convenient for the guests but requires more effort on the part of the hostess. The food may be served at the tables used for the games. These are usually of the folding quartet type. Frequently, the food is served when the guests first arrive, with games and other entertainment following. When the food is served after bridge or other games, the cards, score pads, and pencils are removed, and the hostess and her assistants spread luncheon cloths on the tables. A small vase with a bud or flower or other decoration may be placed in the center of each table. The napkins and flatware that will be required and a glass of water are properly located at each place. The filled plates are then placed on the tables. If the beverage is not served on the plate it should be placed as in a regular meal, depending upon whether it is hot or cold.

If two courses are served, the first course should be removed and the second one brought in and placed. The water glasses should be refilled. The plates may be removed after the guests have departed unless the refreshments have been served early in the evening and the party is to continue.

Activities

1. Observe and identify the types of meal service used in each of the following food services:
a. College residence hall
b. Small restaurant
c. Hotel dining room
d. Tea room

2. List the various ways in which dinner may be served. Under what conditions do you think each method might be chosen in preference to others? What are some of the advantages and disadvantages of each method?

3. Plan in detail the service for the meals that were planned for Activities 1, 2, and 3, listed in Chapter 23.

4. Plan and carry out the service of the meals planned as Activity 9 in Chapter 23. Evaluate in terms of the score sheet given at the end of Chapter 23.

5. Plan, prepare, and serve a buffet supper.

6. Plan and give a tea.

7. Plan and give a party.

References

KINDER, F. *Meal Management,* 3rd ed. New York: The Macmillan Company. 1968.

MCLEAN, B. B. *Meal Management and Table Service,* rev. ed. Peoria, Illinois: Chas. A. Bennett Co., Inc. 1964.

POST, E. L. *Emily Post's Etiquette,* 12th ed. New York: Funk & Wagnalls Co., Inc. 1969.

RAYMOND, L. with Good Housekeeping Institute. *Book of Today's Etiquette.* New York: Harper and Row, Publishers. 1965.

VANDERBILT, A. *Complete Book of Etiquette.* Garden City, New York: Doubleday & Company, Inc. 1967.

WILMOT, J. S. and M. Q. BATJER. *Food for the Family,* 6th ed. New York: J. B. Lippincott Company. 1966.

27

examples of various styles of meal service in detail

In order to outline the details of various types of meal service, selected styles of service are presented. Not every style of service is given for every meal because many of the details will be much the same. No descriptions for service of luncheons are given because the procedures are similar to those given for dinners except there are fewer foods.

In many instances alternate choices have been given under General Rules in the previous chapter, and for the most part, these are not repeated here. No matter what style of service is used, adaptations will nearly always be necessary, depending upon the menu served and available table appointments, equipment, and helpers.

The terms hostess, host, and guests have been used but directions may be equally appropriate if the terms mother, father, and children are substituted. Waitress (or waiter) refers to the person doing the serving whether a paid employee or a member of the family.

Informal Breakfast, Compromise Style
Menu

(Planned for a group of four)
Half Grapefruit
Wheat Flakes   Milk
Baked Eggs
Bacon Muffins
Butter   Jelly
Cocoa

Table Linens. Place mats, table runners, or a cloth are suitable for this meal. Napkins of small or medium size may be used.

Decoration. Garden flowers, or a small potted plant such as ivy may be used.

Laying the Cover. For this menu a fork, two spoons, and a butter spreader are needed. Place the fork at the right of the cover, as there is no need for a knife. Place the spoons at the right of the fork and in the order of their use, the one used first at the far right.

Place the plate, usually of dessert size, in the center of the cover. Place the bread-and-butter plate at the left and above the place for the plate. Place the butter spreader across the top of the plate parallel to the edge of the table, with the handle to the right.

Place the glass for water at the tip of the fork. Put the napkin at the left of the plate with the open edges next to the edge of the table and the plate.

Place the front edge of the chair even with and in line with the edge of the table and directly in front of the cover.

General Serving Dishes. Place the salt and pepper shakers so they can be easily reached by all, one set for each two persons is desirable. Place them in line with other objects on the table so as to give symmetry. The salt should be to the right of the pepper.

Directly above the hostess's cover place the milk and sugar, the sugar to the right of the milk, and to the right of the sugar bowl place the sugar spoon.

At the right of the hostess's cover place the cups and saucers for the cocoa and also the plate on which to set the cocoa pot.

Above the host's cover, place the silver to be used for serving the eggs. If only a spoon is required, put it at the right of the place where the dish of eggs will be set. If both a spoon and fork are used, place spoon at the right and fork at the left of the dish.

Place the jelly, in a suitable dish, in front of the person either on the right or left of the host. Place the jelly spoon to the right of the dish.

Serving Table. The serving table or tea cart is located within easy reach of the hostess. On it place a pitcher filled with ice water, the service napkin, and any extra flatware that may be needed. If the serving table is not used, place these articles on the dining table convenient to the hostess.

Last-Minute Details. Place the butter, ice cold, on the left side of the bread-and-butter plates. At each cover, place fruit on a smaller plate. Place cereal in the individual serving dishes directly in front of each cover. Pour the water.

The Service of the Meal

Duties of the Hostess. If guests are present, the hostess greets them and indicates distinctly their places at the table. The hostess sits next to the kitchen door as this saves steps.

She removes her napkin from the table, entirely unfolds it if a small one, and places it on her lap.

When all are finished with their fruit, the hostess places her own fruit dish on the lower shelf of the serving table. She then asks the person at the right of the host, then the host, and finally the person at the left of the host for their dishes. The host passes his dish to the person at his left, who passes it on to the hostess. The dessert size plate remains at each cover. The hostess picks up the cereal dish, sets it on the plate, places the spoon in the sugar bowl, and passes the milk and sugar to the person seated at her right, who serves himself and passes them on.

When all have finished with the cereal, the hostess places her plate and cereal dish on the lower shelf of the service table and asks for other dishes as before until all dishes are removed.

The hostess excuses herself, lays her napkin, loosely folded, at the left of her cover, and leaves the table. Before going to the kitchen she refills the water glasses if it is necessary, using the service napkin to catch the drip. If a tea cart is used she may wheel it to the kitchen and bring it back with the warm plates and hot food and beverage. If a tea cart is not used, she brings from the kitchen to the table warm plates, which should not be too hot, using a napkin as a protection for her hand but not as a holder. From the left side with her left hand, she places the plates directly in front of the host. She then brings in the main dish on a napkin, places it left side, left hand, in front of the host's cover. If the dish is covered, she removes the cover and places it upside down on the serving table. Finally she brings in the hot bread on a plate covered with a hot bread cloth, and the pot of cocoa; places the hot bread, left hand, left side in front of the person either at the right or left of host, where space is available; with her right hand she places the cocoa on the plate at right of cover and seats herself.

The hostess serves the beverage while the host is serving the main dish. Each indicates for whom the serving is intended.

The person at the right of the host is served first. Then the host serves the hostess, next the person at his left, and finally himself.

When all are served, the hostess starts to eat. She asks the person nearest the muffins to help himself and pass them. Later she asks the person nearest the jelly to help himself and pass it.

When hot muffins are needed, the hostess leaves the table (she need not excuse herself this time), goes to the kitchen, brings in hot muffins, and places the plate in its former position. After she is seated she again asks the person nearest to have a muffin and pass them. She never says "more" and on all occasions avoids implying that a second serving is being offered.

The hostess may offer a second serving of beverage; however, she need not prepare a second serving unless she cares to do so.

The service of the meal *without a serving table* differs in a few details. When all have finished with their fruit, the hostess excuses herself and removes the fruit dishes and spoons to the kitchen, left hand, left side, two services at a time, beginning with the person to the right of the host and proceeding to the left around the table. When all have finished with their cereal, the hostess removes the cereal dishes and spoons and dessert plates to the kitchen two services at a time, in the same order as before. Otherwise, the procedure is the same as that given for the service in which a serving table is used.

The hostess together with the host is responsible for directing the conversation. `

Duties of the Host. The host cooperates in every way possible with the hostess. He serves the main dish that is placed before him.

In serving he does not raise the plate from the table until it is filled and ready to pass to the person for whom it is prepared. If it is too difficult to serve the food in this way, an exception may be made.

The main dish should be placed close to the plates so that there is little danger of spilling the food in serving.

The host offers second servings of the main dish if the amount of food permits; otherwise he tries to divide the main dish into uniform servings.

Leaving the Table. Do not appear to rush the meal. Wait until all have finished and have placed their napkins on the table. The hostess places hers there first, and the host follows her lead. The others should be given a reasonable length of time to do likewise. Then hostess and host rise from the table at the same time.

Informal Supper, Buffet Style
Menu

(Planned for a group of sixteen or twenty)
Scalloped Chicken
Potato Chips   Stuffed Tomato Salad
Sandwiches   Pickles   Olives
Angel Berry Cake
Iced Tea

Two waitresses or assistants will be required for serving this meal.

Table Linens. A tablecloth made of linen, lace, embroidered fabric or other attractive material, or doilies, or runners are suitable for this meal. Luncheon napkins may be used.

Decoration. The decoration should be attractive and may be simple or elaborate depending on the remainder of the appointments. Garden flowers, flowers from the florist, fruit, or winter bouquets in season may be used.

Seating Plans. Before setting the table decide on the way the guests are to be seated. Although they may stand to eat, this is never comfortable. If they are to be seated at tables, necessary flatware, linens, and water may be on the tables so the guests pick up the food and perhaps another beverage,

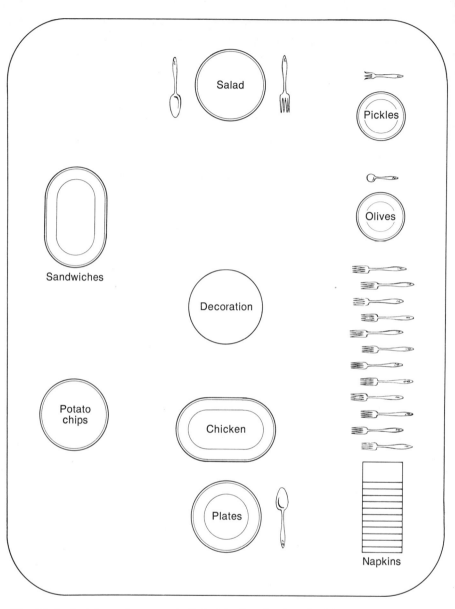

Fig. 27–1. *An informal supper, buffet style, has food and tableware so arranged that guests may serve themselves as they proceed left around the table.*

if one is served with the main course. If tray tables are used, they too may be set with flatware and linen although it may be more convenient to set up the tables while the guests are serving themselves, in which case it may be more expedient for the guests to pick up flatware, napkins, and beverage as they help themselves to food. If no tables are available, individual lap trays are quite satisfactory and may be picked up after the plates are served and just before the flatware, napkins, and beverage. The trays may be set with linen, flatware, and beverage if preferred. Lacking these facilities the plate may be held on the lap, but if at all possible some place to set the beverage is highly desirable. Unless the guests are to be seated at tables, it is important to select food which does not require a knife for cutting and to use no stemware which could be easily upset.

Arranging the Table. Two forks, one for the main course and one for dessert and one iced-drink spoon are needed for each person. One tablespoon, a salad serving fork and spoon, a pickle fork, an olive fork, a lemon fork, and a sugar spoon are needed for general serving.

Serve chicken at the end of the table nearest the living room. To the right of the plates, which are centered at this end of the table, lay the tablespoon for serving chicken. At the farther end, where the salad will be served, lay the serving fork and spoon for the salad. Allow room for the guest to set the plate on the table by any food that might require both hands for serving.

On the left side of the table place the dish of potato chips and the plate or plates of sandwiches covered with a sandwich cloth or napkin. On the right side of the table, place the pickles and olives and their accompanying flatware. To the left of these arrange forks for the main course in an attractive manner and finally the napkins if these are not already on the table.

If preferred, the table may be placed against the wall and only one side and the two ends used for serving. In this case the decoration may be placed at the back of the table near the wall.

Arranging the Buffet or Smaller Table. Place the iced tea service and glasses, spoons, sugar, and lemon with the accompanying flatware, in an attractive manner on the buffet or smaller table. Water may be placed there also.

Chairs. Place a chair at each end of the table for the two persons who are serving the chicken and the salad.

Last-Minute Details. Place plates, not more than six or eight at a time, in their position at the end of table nearest the living room.

Place the chicken above the plates. Place the salad at the far end of the table. Fill the iced-tea and water glasses. Also fill a pitcher with iced tea and another with water. Uncover the sandwiches.

The Service of the Meal

The meal is announced informally by the hostess, who invites the guest of honor or some other person to be served first. Others are asked to follow. Assisted by those serving at the table, the guests obtain food and a beverage and also a napkin and flatware. The chicken is served first. The served plate is handed to the guest, who stands at the left of the person serving. He proceeds down the left side of the table serving himself potato chips and sandwiches. He holds his plate so the salad may be placed upon it, then proceeds around the table helping himself to relishes and picking up a fork, and a napkin, and finally the beverage which is on the buffet. When served, the guests carry their plates into the living room and are seated. If small tables are provided for the guests, these may be located and arranged before the guests arrive.

Assistants or waitresses keep the serving dishes replenished with food during the service. After all are served, pass sandwiches, beverages, and other foods as desired. Remove plates and flatware to the kitchen when the course is finished. Bring dessert and fork on a dessert plate from the kitchen and serve each guest individually. Unless guests are seated at a table remove this course when finished, picking up the napkin with the plate.

The beverage glass may be retained through the second course. In this case refilling may be necessary.

Informal Dinner, Family Style
Menu

(Planned for a group of six)

Roast Leg of Lamb   Fresh Mint Sauce
Browned Potatoes   Buttered Chard
Avocado and Grapefruit Salad
Bread   Butter
Lemon Meringue Pie
Coffee and Milk

Table Linens. A tablecloth may be used for this meal but place mats are preferred and used by many. Dinner napkins may be used.

Decoration. Garden flowers or a small potted plant, fresh fruit, gourds, or vegetables may be used.

Laying the Cover. For this menu a knife, fork, spoon for the beverage, and fork for dessert are needed. Follow the general rules for setting the table, and place the appointments and food as space permits. In this style of service all of the food may be placed on the table at one time, although some prefer to place the dessert after the main course. A serving table placed near the hostess can hold some of the foods and thus prevent a crowded appearance on the table. Place chairs with the front edges even and in line with the edge of the table and directly in front of covers.

Placing the Food. Place the meat above the cover at the head of the table and the fork for serving it at the right of the dish. Place the potatoes at the right of the same cover and the chard at the left. Place the flatware for serving at the right of each dish. Place other foods convenient to persons who will be requested to pass them.

Place the salad according to the manner in which it is to be served. It may be placed on the table in individual servings, served in a salad bowl from which each person helps himself as it is passed, or it may be served on individual plates by someone at the table and passed. The dessert also may be served in either fashion or it may be on the serving table adjacent to the hostess.

Fill the milk and water glasses before the meal is announced, and then refill the pitchers and place them on the table or serving table.

The Service of the Meal

Meat should be passed to the right and followed by the potatoes, then the chard, bread, sauce, and butter. The hostess serves the coffee, with cream and sugar as each person desires. Cups and glasses are refilled by passing them to the person who serves the beverages.

The salad is eaten with the main part of the meal, using the dinner fork.

After the main course is eaten, the dinner plate is exchanged for the dessert service. However, the hostess may prefer to clear the table before placing the dessert.

Leaving the Table. All members of the group should leave the table together. The hostess indicates the time of leaving. If for any reason it becomes necessary for one person to leave earlier, he should ask the host or hostess for permission to be excused.

Informal Dinner, Compromise Style
Menu

(Planned for a group of four)
Braised Pork Chops
Baked Acorn Squash   Buttered Asparagus
Tomato and Grapefruit Salad
Toasty Garlic Bread
Prune Spice Cake
Coffee

Table Linens. A tablecloth may be used for this meal but the trend today is to use place mats even for dinners. Dinner napkins may be used.

Decoration. Garden flowers, fruit, or a small potted plant are suitable.

Laying the Cover. For this menu a dinner knife, dinner fork, dessert fork, and spoon for the beverage are needed. In current practice there seems to be a trend to eliminate the salad fork unless the salad is served as a separate course.

Place the front edges of the chairs even and in line with the edge of the table and directly in front of the cover.

General Serving Dishes. Place salt and pepper shakers so they can be reached easily by all. One set for each two persons is desirable. Place in line with other objects on the table so as to give symmetry. The salt should be at the right of the pepper.

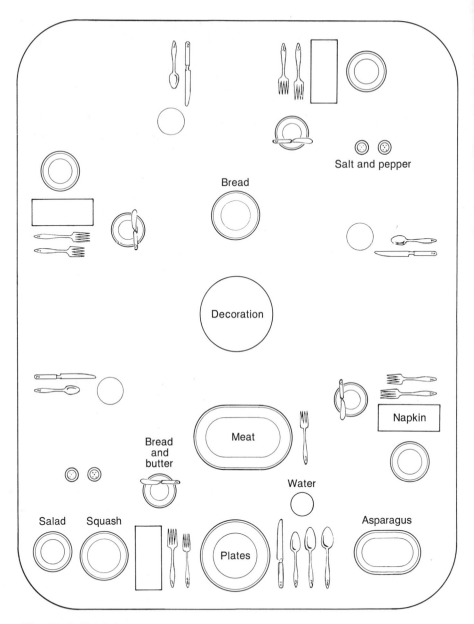

Fig. 27–2. *The informal dinner, compromise style, is ready for the host to serve the plates. After serving, he may exchange the position of the vegetable dish with his salad plate.*

In front of the host's cover place the flatware to be used for serving the meat. To the right of the host's cover place the flatware for serving the vegetables.

Serving Table. If coffee is to be served with the main course, the serving table or tea cart may be placed beside and within easy reach of the hostess, otherwise it is placed against the wall. The coffee cups and saucers, cream, sugar, and sugar spoon may be placed on the table along with the coffee pot. The pitcher of water on a plate with a service napkin beside it may also be on the serving table.

Last-Minute Details. Pour the water. Place the salads at the left of each cover. If preferred the warm dinner plates and all food for the main course may be placed before the meal is announced.

The Service of the Meal

Duties of the Hostess. The hostess announces the meal and directs her guests to the dining room, indicating distinctly their places at the table. The hostess's place is near the kitchen door. She asks guests to be seated, and if the food is not on the table, excuses herself, and goes directly to kitchen. She brings in the warm dinner plates on a service napkin and places them, left hand, left side, in front of the host. Then she brings in the platter of pork chops, using a service napkin, and with her left hand from left side places the meat in front of the host above his cover. Next she brings in the dish of squash on a napkin and places it right hand at right side of host's cover. After this she brings the dish of asparagus on a napkin and places it at left of the host, left hand. If preferred the two vegetables may be brought in at the same time without the use of the napkin. In order to save space it may be desirable to arrange the meat and one of the vegetables on the same platter. In this case the other vegetable would be placed at right of host's cover. She brings in the hot bread in left hand and coffee in right hand. She places the coffee at right of hostess's cover and then places the bread with the left hand, left side in front of the guest at the right of the hostess. The hostess seats herself, removes her napkin from the table and pours the coffee while the host serves the plates. After the plates are served and the coffee is poured, the hostess starts eating. She asks the person nearest the bread to help himself and pass it. Later she asks to have the bread repassed and offers second servings if the host fails to do so.

When all have finished with the main course, the hostess leaves her seat and removes the meat platter, left hand, left side, and the squash dish, right hand, right side, and carries them to the kitchen. She removes the asparagus dish, left hand, left side, and transfers it to right hand; she then removes the bread plate, left hand, left side, and carries them to the kitchen. She takes the coffee pot to the kitchen and brings in two desserts which she places on the serving table.

Beginning with the person at the right of host, the hostess removes to the kitchen the dishes and flatware of the first course from each cover. First she removes the dinner plate and flatware, left hand, left side and transfers it to her right hand, then she removes the salad plate, left hand, left side, and places it on the plate in her right hand. This service is then carried to the serving table. The hostess is careful to stack dishes back of the person. Next she clears host's cover in the same order. She then picks up the first service from the serving table with her left hand and carries both to the kitchen. On returning from the kitchen, the hostess brings the other two desserts and places them on the serving table. The covers of the other person and the hostess are next cleared as previously described and taken to the kitchen. The salts and peppers and any silver not needed for dessert, she removes on a tray. When she returns she brings in hot coffee and places it on the table.

The desserts are then placed, left hand, left side, in front of the guest at the right of the host, then the host, and other guest and the hostess. Many prefer to bring in and place the desserts as the covers are being cleared which is also an approved procedure.

When the desserts are served, the hostess seats herself and starts eating her dessert, pausing to offer second servings of coffee.

Duties of the Host. The host assists in directing guests to the dining room and seats the guest of honor if this form of courtesy is desired. He assumes responsibility for carrying on the conversation while the hostess places the food if it is not already on the table when the meal is announced. When the hostess is seated, he follows her lead in removing his napkin from the table and then serves the plates. When meat is not in individual servings, a sufficient quantity for all is carved by the host before serving any plate. He first puts the meat on the plate, then the squash to its right, and lastly the asparagus. He moves neither serving dishes nor plates from the table until ready to pass the first plate, which is served to the person at his right. Next he serves the hostess, passing the plate to his left, then he serves the person at his left, and finally himself. Later, the host may offer second servings.

Leaving the Table. The same rules that were given in serving the informal breakfast, compromise style, apply to this meal.

Informal Dinner, Compromise Style, with Waitress

This type of service is frequently used for an informal meal when the hostess wishes to remain seated at the table and to have assistance in serving the food. It is quite likely there will be more than four persons at the table so the order in which guests are served may be different from that described under "Informal Dinner, Compromise Style."

The serving table is used for the convenience of the waitress and is located near the door leading to the kitchen.

If a first course is served and it is a cold one, the waitress places it on the table before the guests enter the dining room; if a hot course, she usually serves it after the guests are seated, left hand, left side. The salad may be placed on the table either before the meal is announced or with the serving of the second course.

The waitress removes the preliminary course, left hand, left side; then, using a service napkin, she places, first, warmed plates, and then the main dish, in front of the host, left hand, left side. If the main dish is covered, she uses a service napkin to lift the cover, invert it, and carry it to the serving table; when the host has finished serving, she replaces the cover. Using a service napkin, she brings in the main vegetable and places it, with her right hand, at the right side of the host's cover. She then brings in the second vegetable and bread and may place these on the serving table.

The waitress stands at the left of the host with a napkin in her left hand; as the host serves each plate, she takes it from the pile in front of him, left hand, left side, and places it before a guest or the hostess. The hostess, the person to her right, or the person to the right of the host may receive the first plate. The service then proceeds in logical sequence around the table until all have been served. The hostess should have instructed the waitress, before the meal, the order she prefers. After all have been served, the waitress passes the second vegetable, left hand, left side, and then the bread, left hand, left side, using a service napkin.

She next brings in the coffee and places it to the right of the hostess, who pours. Standing at the left of the hostess, she receives each cup as it is filled, and places it at a cover, right hand, right side, with the handle to the right, serving in the order in which she served the plates. No napkin is needed in serving the coffee.

She repasses the bread and the second vegetable, as needed, in the same manner as before, and refills the glasses as necessary, right hand, right side, if possible without moving them. If a guest accepts a second helping of the main dishes, the waitress takes the plate from the cover, left hand, left side, carries it to the host (using a service napkin), and returns the filled plate to the guest.

When the course is finished, she removes the meat platter, with its serving flatware, then the vegetable dishes and their serving flatware, and the bread plate. Beginning with the person served first and progressing in the same order as for the service, she removes the dinner plate, left hand, left side, transfers it to her right hand, then removes the salad plate, left hand, left side, and carries them to the kitchen. She next removes the bread-and-butter plate, left hand, left side, and carries it to the serving table; from there she removes them to the kitchen by twos. She uses no napkin in removing the plates, and she should clear each cover completely before beginning to clear another.

The salts and peppers, and any silver not needed for the last course, she removes on a tray. She removes the coffee pot in order to reheat the coffee; after dessert is served she will replace it. As needed, she brushes crumbs from each cover, left hand, left side, with a folded napkin to a plate or crumb tray. The glasses are refilled if necessary.

The waitress then serves the dessert, left hand, left side. Flatware for the dessert course may have been placed at each cover when the table was set;

it may be placed from a tray, right hand, right side, before dessert is served; or it may be brought in on the dessert plate. At this time the waitress brings back the coffee, which has been reheating, and replaces it beside the hostess's cover, right hand, right side. She then brings each person's coffee cup to the hostess to be refilled and replaces it, right hand, right side.

Leaving the Table. For the manner of leaving the table, the same rules apply as were given for the informal breakfast, compromise style.

Formal Dinner, Russian Style
Menu

Shrimp Cocktail
Chicken Kiev
Saffron Rice   Zucchini Parmesan
Pineapple Ice
Hard Rolls
Hearts of Lettuce Salad
Cheese Wafers
Lemon Torte
Coffee
Nuts   Candy

Table Linens. For a formal dinner the hostess uses her best and most attractive linens. Only a tablecloth, preferably white, is suitable for this meal. Dinner napkins are essential.

Decoration. The table may be suitably decorated with flowers, fruit, winter greens, or other centerpiece, and candles may be used. The arrangement of the decoration should be formal and attractive. Place cards and favors, if used, may be placed on the napkin. Nut and candy cups may be placed at the top of each individual cover.

Laying the Cover. The general directions for setting the table, as already given, are followed, except that nothing is placed on the table except the decorations and the articles that belong to the individual cover. For this menu, a cocktail fork, a dinner knife, dinner fork, salad fork, dessert fork, and after-dinner coffee spoon are required.

Place a service plate at each cover. To the right of the service plate place the knife and the cocktail fork; to the left of the service plate, the salad fork; and to the left of the salad fork, the dinner fork. Dessert forks and coffee spoons are to be brought in with the course to which they belong. The goblet for water should be at the tip of the knife. The napkin is placed at the left of the forks if the first course is placed before the guests are seated; otherwise it is placed on the service plate.

Place individual salt and pepper dishes, salts to the right and peppers to the left, directly above each cover.

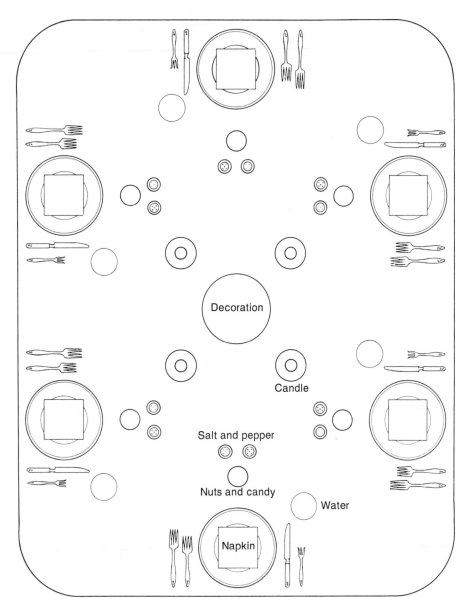

Fig. 27–3. *A formal dinner requires a formal setting of the table, as this diagram shows.*

Place the front edge of each chair even and in line with the edge of the table, directly in front of the cover.

Serving Table. The purpose of the serving table, if used, is to facilitate service by the waitress, and it should therefore be located near the door to

Fig. 27–4. *A table carefully set for company dinner.*

the kitchen. If a serving table is not used, all food will be brought directly from and removed directly to the kitchen.

Duties of the Hostess. The hostess receives the announcement of the meal by the waitress or waiter and so indicates by a nod or bow to the host. She and her escort are the last of the group to enter the dining room. She signals the guests to be seated, assists with conversation, indicates the time for serving and removing each course, and gives any needed directions to the waitress in a quiet and unobtrusive manner. When the dinner is over, she indicates the time for leaving the table.

Duties of the Host. The host, escorting one of the guests (usually the guest of honor), leads the group to the dining room. He receives the indication from the hostess for seating, and seats the guest of honor. The other men in the party do the same for the women they escort into the dining room. The host assumes the responsibility for directing the conversation.

Last-Minute Details. Just before announcing the meal, the waitress fills the goblets with water. She may place the chilled cocktail in a cocktail glass on a small plate on each service plate, or the cocktail may be placed after the guests are seated.

The Service of the Meal

Duties of the Waitress. A waitress or waiter is required for all of the service. A service plate is used for each cover and is left on the table until exchanged for the first hot plate. A guest is never left without a plate at his cover, except before the dessert course when the table is cleared and crumbed.

Plates are brought in and removed one at a time. All dishes of food are held on the left hand on a folded napkin when offered to the guests. When plates are being exchanged or dishes of food removed from the table the service napkin is not used.

The waitress serves first the guest of honor, then the other guests in an order previously indicated by the hostess, and last the host. She refills the goblets with water as needed; they should be kept well filled throughout the meal.

When the first course is finished, the waitress removes the cocktail fork, cocktail glass, small plate, and service plate together, right hand, left side, and places at the cover, left hand, left side, a warm plate with a serving of

Fig. 27–5. *The first course of a formal dinner is placed on the service plate at each cover.*

Courtesy of Lenox China and Crystal

chicken, rice, and zucchini. If a bread-and-butter plate is used, she places it (with a roll upon it but no butter), left hand, left side, slightly to the left above the fork. If bread-and-butter plates are not used, she passes a plate of rolls, left hand, left side, from which each person serves himself. The rolls may be placed directly on the tablecloth. If a second serving of rolls is offered, she removes the bread-and-butter plate, left hand, left side, and places the replenished plate in the same manner, or repasses the plate of rolls as in the first serving.

The ice is placed at the top of the cover and slightly to the right, or beside the cover and to the right, right hand, right side.

In Russian service, it is sometimes the practice for the waitress to place the plates for the main course at each cover and to offer the food in appropriate serving dishes, left hand, left side, so that each person may serve himself. The chicken, rice, and zucchini as well as the rolls may be served in this manner.

When the course is finished, the waitress removes from each cover the dinner plate and flatware used for this course, right hand, left side, and places the salad, arranged on a salad plate, left hand, left side. She next removes the bread-and-butter plate, if used, left hand, left side, and the dish in which the ice was served, right side, right hand. When the salad course is finished, she removes the salad plate, left hand, left side, and also removes onto a tray any unused silver, right or left hand.

The waitress then takes the salts and peppers from the table, one at a time, left hand, left side, and transfers them to a tray held in her right hand. She crumbs the table with a folded napkin and a small plate, left hand, left side, in the same order in which the guests were served.

She next places the fork for dessert, right hand, right side, or it may be placed on the upper side of the dessert plate with the dessert. She places dessert left hand, left side, following the same order as for other courses.

After-dinner coffee may be served at the table or in the living room. If coffee is served at the table when the dessert course is finished, the waitress removes the dessert plate, right hand, left side, and places an after-dinner coffee cup, left hand, left side, in front of each guest. The handle should be to the right, and an after-dinner coffee spoon, if used, lies on the saucer parallel with the handle of the cup. If sugar is offered, two lumps may be placed on the saucer, or it may be served with tongs on a tray presented by the waitress, left hand, left side. If coffee is served in the living room, it is usually poured by the hostess seated at a small table, and the cups are passed by the waitress. If candies and nuts are not served in individual portions at each cover, the waitress passes them at this time. If at the table, she offers them left hand, left side, using a tray.

When coffee served at the table is finished, the waitress removes the cup, right hand, left side, and places a finger bowl set on a doily on a small plate, left hand, left side. If coffee is served in the living room, the finger bowls are placed after the table has been cleared following the dessert course. Finger bowls are left on the table at the end of the meal.

Leaving the Table. The hostess indicates to the host the moment for leaving the table. The host then arises and assists the guest of honor, accompanying her to the living or reception room. Others do the same, with the hostess and her escort leaving the dining room last.

the preservation of foods

28

food spoilage

Food spoilage usually refers to undesirable changes taking place in food due to microorganisms, insects, enzymes in the food, purely chemical reactions, or physical changes due to freezing, burning, drying, pressure, etc. Food unfit to eat for sanitary reasons is, as a rule, not referred to as spoiled.

Although some methods of food preservation such as drying, salting, fermentation, and the making of cheese were used long before the agents of food spoilage were understood, great advances in food preservation have been made since these agents have been studied. Modern methods of preservation have made available a wide variety of food throughout the year. When only the most primitive methods of food preservation were known, it was necessary for people to live close to their source of food, and to struggle to keep an adequate food supply from one harvest to the next. These conditions exist even now in developing nations that lack knowledge of modern food technology and the capital necessary to put such knowledge into effect.

Foods vary greatly in the length of time they can be held in their natural form without spoilage. *Perishable* foods, such as milk, meat, seafoods, and many fruits and vegetables begin to deteriorate almost immediately unless they are preserved in some way. *Semi-perishable* foods, which include root vegetables, potatoes, celery, cabbage, and certain kinds of apples and pears, can be kept for several months in a cold place. *Non-perishable* foods such as nuts, cereals, dried beans, peas, and other legumes, can be stored for long periods of time, provided adequate storage facilities are available. The most obvious difference between foods in these three classes is their water content, which is high in the perishable foods and low in the non-perishable foods. It is also evident that certain fruits and immature vegetables are likely to be more juicy and more perishable than hard or firm fruits and mature vegetables. The firm covering of foods such as nuts, cereals, and legumes also offers protection.

It is not surprising that foods which nourish man are equally attractive to many other organisms. The rapid spoilage of most foods can be attributed to the growth of microorganisms and the action of enzymes that occur in the food itself or in the microorganism. These two agents of food spoilage, which must be controlled for successful food preservation, will be considered in this chapter. Other causes of food deterioration, such as infestation by insects, rats, or mice, will not be considered. It will be noticed that this chapter concerns safety in handling and preserving food. In this way it contrasts with most of the other chapters of the book, which discuss the preparation of attractive, palatable food.

Micro-organisms

As the name implies, microorganisms are visible only under the microscope, although in large numbers such as an abundant mold growth or a colony of bacteria they may be visible to the naked eye. The microorganisms that are most important in foods are molds, yeast, and bacteria, shown in Figure 28–1. Certain organisms in all three of these groups may be used to produce desirable changes in foods, but they are more often agents of food spoilage. Some of these microorganisms exist in both a spore form and a vegetative, or growing, form. The spores are usually more resistant to destruction by heat or other agents than the vegetative form.

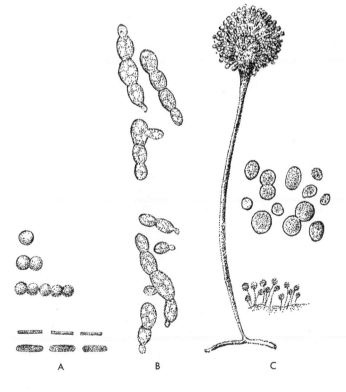

Fig. 28–1. *Common spoilage agents widely distributed and responsible for much of the spoilage of both fresh and processed foods are: A. bacteria, B. yeasts, and C. molds.*

A   B   C

Molds

Molds are used in curing cheeses such as Brie, Camembert, Blue, and Roquefort, and in making certain oriental foods such as soy sauce. They are microscopic plants made up of several cells. Many mold plants consist of a filament and a head that contains spores which can spread through the air and start new mold plants. Like other microorganisms, molds exist in a wide variety of forms. Under favorable conditions, spores germinate and produce a fluffy growth, often white or grey, but sometimes bluish-green, red, orange, or other color, depending on the variety. Molds grow on a wider variety of foods than do yeasts or bacteria. They grow on acid foods such as lemons and on neutral foods such as bread and meat, on sweet foods like jams and jellies, and even on organic substances other than food, such as leather, wood, and cotton. Molds are most likely to develop in warm, damp, dark places, although in general they require less moisture than yeasts or bacteria. Most molds grow well between 25° to 30° C. (77° to 86° F.) and a few grow well above 35° to 37° C. (95° to 99° F.). Some mold growth, however, can be expected even at refrigerator temperatures and a few molds grow slowly at freezing (0° C., 32° F.) temperatures. Molds can be destroyed by boiling for a few minutes and, with the exception of a few varieties, by heating to 60° C. (140° F.) for five to ten minutes.

A relatively small proportion of the molds found on foodstuffs are capable of producing toxic materials known as mycotoxins, the best known of which are probably the aflatoxins. These have been reported on peanuts and other agricultural products such as rye, wheat, and millet. Because molds do not usually produce harmful substances, a slight growth of mold on foods is often removed and the remainder of the food eaten. This is especially true of a surface growth of mold on jelly or jam. Of course if the growth of mold is heavy, all the food may be changed in flavor and in texture. Such foods should be discarded.

Yeasts

Yeasts are microscopic in size and usually have but one cell. Some of them reproduce by budding. For growth, yeasts require water and a source of energy, which is usually sugar but which may be other carbohydrates that can be changed into sugar, or even organic acids. Many yeasts grow best in an acid medium and in the presence of ample oxygen. Yeasts also require a source of nitrogen and certain other nutrients.

Yeasts convert sugar into carbon dioxide and ethyl alcohol. They are used in bread-making because of the carbon dioxide they produce. Yeasts are also used to make alcoholic beverages and alcohol for industrial uses. Yeast growth is most rapid between 25° to 30° C. (77° to 86° F.); it is retarded or stopped above 35° to 47° C. (95 to 116° F.). Yeasts are readily destroyed by boiling, and most yeasts are destroyed by temperatures of 50° to 58° C. (122° to 136° F.) in ten to fifteen minutes.

Foods are often contaminated with yeast for wild yeasts are always present in the atmosphere. Yeasts may cause spoilage of sauerkraut, fruit juices, syrups, molasses, honey, jellies, and other foods. Raw and cooked fruits that contain small amounts of sugar are likely to ferment.

Bacteria

A few common types of bacteria are shown in Figure 28–1. They are smaller than molds or yeasts and occur in great variety. Like other microorganisms they can play both beneficial and harmful roles in food preservation.

As indicated in Chapter 8, bacteria are used to produce cultured milks such as buttermilk, and the curds used to make cheese. A wide variety of cheese, including Cheddar or American, Swiss, Parmesan, Provolone, Brick, and Limburger, is ripened with bacteria. Butter and margarine also owe their characteristic flavor to the action of bacteria. Bacteria are responsible for the leavening of salt-rising bread, and the production of vinegar from a fermented sugar solution such as cider or grape juice. Sauerkraut is made from cabbage by the action of bacteria that produce acid.

Bacteria of different types vary greatly in size, shape, and growing conditions. Certain bacteria form spores that are much more resistant to heat than are the vegetative cells of the same bacteria. Bacteria also vary in their requirements for food, moisture, acidity, temperature, and oxygen. For this reason, specific types of bacteria are likely to flourish best on certain types of food. Foods high in protein may encourage the growth of certain types of bacteria, whereas those high in carbohydrate encourage other types. Bacteria require abundant moisture for growth. Water that is used to dissolve substances such as sugar or salt is not available for the growth of bacteria and such substances may even draw moisture from the bacterial cells. For this reason foods such as jelly, jam, and marmalade, or dried, salted fish are not likely to support bacterial growth. Most bacteria grow best on foods that are neutral or almost neutral in reaction, but others may be favored by a slightly acid reaction and a few types by a slightly alkaline medium. Bacteria also vary in the temperature at which they grow best. Although many bacteria are favored by temperatures between 20° to 45° C. (68° to 113° F.), a few bacteria grow at refrigerator temperatures or even as low as −5° to −7° C. (23° to 19° F.), and others, called thermophilic bacteria, grow best at temperatures of 45° C. (113° F.) and higher. Such bacteria sometimes cause difficulty in the heat preservation of foods. Although many bacteria are destroyed by the temperatures of pasteurization—63° C. (145° F.) for 30 minutes or 72° C. (161° F.) for 15 seconds—and most are destroyed at the temperature of boiling water, a few organisms, such as the spores of *Clostridium botulinum,* may require temperatures well above the boiling point for destruction. Meats and vegetables other than tomatoes must be processed in a pressure cooker to destroy these spores. Bacteria also differ in their requirements for oxygen. Aerobic bacteria require free oxygen for growth; anaerobic bacteria do not require free oxygen and grow better in the absence of air; whereas facultative bacteria can grow either with or without free oxygen. Anaerobic bacteria may grow in canned foods that have not been heated sufficiently to destroy the bacteria present in either vegetative or spore form.

Bacteria are often responsible for the spoilage of foods, especially those such as milk, eggs, meat, and fish that are moist and almost neutral in reaction. Because microorganisms are present in all foods except those that are sterilized by processing, or within healthy tissues such as fruit or meat, microbial growth occurs when conditions are appropriate. Canned foods that have not been processed adequately may swell because of gas formed by bacteria, or develop an acid taste called "flat sour" spoilage, or a much more serious type of spoilage that can cause illness (botulism); botulism will be discussed in the section on food poisoning. In general it can be said that bacterial spoilage may produce a wide variety of odors and flavors. For this reason, food that has an abnormal odor should be discarded without tasting because of its potential danger to the consumer. Although cloudy liquid in canned food sometimes indicates spoilage, it may also be caused by the starch of certain foods or the minerals of hard water. It is best to boil such food and to discard it if it has an abnormal odor or foams during heating.

Enzymes

Like microorganisms, enzymes are capable of producing both desirable and undesirable changes in foods. Even when they cause undesirable changes in color or flavor, however, they do not normally produce harmful substances. Enzymes are organic compounds produced by living cells, but unlike microorganisms they are incapable of reproduction. Some enzymes act within the cells in which they are made, whereas others act outside the cell. Like inorganic catalysts, they accelerate chemical reactions but retain their original form at the end of the reaction. Many changes are produced in foods by the enzymes they contain. Enzymes are, of course, active during the germination of seeds and during the development and maturing of the plant. They are equally important in the metabolism of animals, and therefore occur in animal foods. Changes in foods during storage can be produced both by the enzymes of the food itself and by enzymes formed by microorganisms that contaminate the food. For example, during the storage of fruit, the enzymes of the fruit continue to act and cause ripening. At the same time, however, the enzymes of contaminating yeasts might produce fermentation in a bruised spot. Enzymes in meat are probably responsible for some of the increased tenderness that occurs on storage. Enzymes from other sources can be added to meat to increase its tenderness.

Most enzymes act most rapidly at about body temperature and are rendered inactive by heating to the boiling point. Heat is used to inactivate the enzymes of foods in canning and of vegetables before freezing. If the enzymes in vegetables are not destroyed by scalding or blanching before freezing, they continue to act slowly in the freezer and cause undesirable changes in flavor. Enzymes may also cause fruits to darken during freezer storage and during canning if the temperature of the fruit rises so slowly that the enzymes have a chance to act before being inactivated by heat. Fruits are not usually heated to destroy their enzymes before freezing, but the syrup or sugar that is added to fruit slows down the action of enzymes and protects the fruit from oxygen in the air during freezer storage. As a rule enzyme action is not a problem in flesh foods during freezing; instead, they may have a tenderizing effect. Rancidity of fat, which occurs more rapidly in frozen pork, poultry, and fish than in beef, is probably due to the type of fat rather than to specific enzymes.

Food Illness

For the purpose of this discussion, "food poisoning" refers to an illness caused by a poison or toxin in the food when eaten. "Foodborne infection" refers to an illness caused by pathogenic organisms carried by the food and transmitted to man. This distinction is not always clear-cut for there are many borderline cases.

Poisoning

In a broad sense, food poisoning may be caused by a wide variety of harmful substances in the food, although this definition is not accepted by all workers. The food itself may be toxic as with inedible mushrooms. The food may be contaminated with poisonous chemicals such as lead, mercury, arsenic, a variety of pesticides, or any one of many other contaminants unintentionally introduced into the food. Fortunately, food poisoning caused by chemicals has been relatively rare in the past and the term has most often referred to illness caused by the toxin produced by bacteria that grow on the food. In the past the two chief sources of food poisoning were said to be *Staphylococcus aureus* and *Clostridium botulinum*. However, *Clostridium perfringens (welchii)* is receiving more attention now than in the past and appears to be an important source of food poisoning. Although it is generally agreed that foodborne illnesses are grossly under-reported, it is probable that the causes as reported by the Center for Disease Control[1] are fairly representative. For 1970 the three major bacterial causes of foodborne illness were listed as follows:

Staphylococcus	27.5 per cent of all outbreaks
	19.8 per cent of all patients
Clostridium perfringens	14.7 per cent of all outbreaks
	29.7 per cent of all patients
Salmonella	13.1 per cent of all outbreaks
	20.4 per cent of all patients

Staphylococcal Poisoning. Poisoning by the toxin formed by *Staphylococcus aureus* is so common that most people have suffered from it, often several times. This is a pus-forming bacterium that occurs in infected sores,

[1] *Foodborne Outbreaks—Annual Summary 1970.* Center for Disease Control. United States Department of Health, Education and Welfare, Atlanta, Georgia.

Fig. 28–2. *Food and Drug Administration scientists are searching for ways to identify and differentiate staphylococcus enterotoxins which are responsible for illness in food poisoning cases.*

and in the nose and throat of most people. It may enter the food during handling or by contact with a contaminated surface. The bacteria grow best on food held at 21° to 36° C. (70° to 97°F.), although it is said that the toxin is produced at an appreciable rate at temperatures between 18° and 46° C. (64° and 115° F.). Most of the illnesses due to staphylococci reported in 1968 were due to foods eaten in public eating places.[2] Cooked meats, including fish and poultry, custards, and cream fillings support growth of the organism and are often held responsible for staphylococcal food poisoning.

Danger of food poisoning of this type can be minimized by strict rules of personal hygiene. Hands should be thoroughly washed before preparing food. Persons who have infections, especially of the nose, throat, or skin

[2] M. P. deFigueiredo. Staphylococci Control and the Food Processor. *Journal of The American Dietetic Association,* 58: 109–114 (1971).

should avoid handling food. Because the organisms grow at room temperature, food not to be consumed at once should be cooled to 4° C. (40° F.) or less, immediately after it is cooked, unless it is kept hot (60° C., 140° F.). Unfortunately the toxin is heat-resistant, retaining its potency in some systems even after one hour of boiling. It is therefore not destroyed when food is heated for serving.

Botulism. Although poisoning by a toxin produced by *Clostridium botulinum* is rare compared with that produced by *Staphylococcus aureus,* it is much more deadly. *Clostridium botulinum* is a spore-forming organism that is unusually resistant to heat. It occurs in the soil of many areas, and therefore contaminates food. Ingestion of the organism causes no harm because it does not multiply or produce its toxin in the digestive tract. However, the organism can multiply and produce toxin in anaerobic areas such as the undersurface of foods and sealed containers. Even small doses of this toxin cause serious illness, resulting in paralysis of the respiratory muscles and, at one time, death in over 65 per cent of the cases. (During the last ten-year period this has been reduced to 25 per cent.) Underprocessed smoked fish and meat pie stored in a warm oven overnight have both caused cases of botulism, and most near-neutral foods are potential problems. Although emphasis is often placed on the use of proper methods in the canning of foods to prevent botulism—and this is important—all processed foods should be handled with care.

Because the spores of *Clostridium botulinum* are more easily destroyed in an acid medium than in a more nearly neutral medium, acid foods such as fruits and tomatoes can safely be processed in a water bath. More nearly neutral foods, such as meats and vegetables other than tomatoes, must be processed in a pressure cooker so that a temperature above the boiling point will be attained and will destroy any organisms that may be present. If food has been improperly canned, boiling it in enough water to cover for twenty minutes will destroy any toxin formed by *Clostridium botulinum* if it is present. However, this is not a substitute for safe canning methods.

It is important to realize that although staphylococcal organisms are more easily destroyed by heat than *C. botulinum,* the toxin of staphylococci is more resistant to heat than that of *C. botulinum.*

Perfringens Poisoning. The bacteria causing this type of food poisoning are the spore-forming *Clostridium perfringens (welchii).* The spores differ considerably in their resistance to heat, some requiring from one to four hours at 100° C. (212° F.) for their destruction while others are destroyed within a few minutes. Thus organisms causing perfringens poisoning frequently survive the cooking of foods. Surviving bacteria grow when conditions are favorable. These occur when the food is cooled slowly. To avoid this type of food poisoning, cooked foods, especially meats and gravies, should be held at 60° C. (140° F.) or above, or rapidly cooled and stored at 4° C. (40° F.) or below.

Infections

Sometimes the food acts as a carrier of bacteria or viruses rather than as a growth medium for the bacterial production of toxins. These organisms may result in foodborne infections and there may be a comparatively long incubation period within the body. Diphtheria, streptococcal infections, typhoid, or dysentery may result from food contaminated directly or indirectly by a diseased human being. Some organisms such as those of tuberculosis and brucellosis or undulant fever may occur in either humans or animals. Cows infected with these diseases produce infected milk. Organisms of the genus *Salmonella* are found all too frequently and can multiply in many foods. They also produce illness by infecting the host.

Salmonellosis. Although about 20,000 cases of salmonellosis are reported each year, it is thought the actual number of cases may exceed two million.[3] Salmonellae constitute a large group of organisms widespread in nature. The source of salmonellae found in food may be a human being who has the disease or who is a carrier. A carrier has the organisms in his body, although he does not show symptoms of the disease. The organisms may also come from a wide variety of animals, including poultry and their eggs. Salmonellae grow best on low-acid foods such as meat, poultry, dressing, fish, eggs, and dairy products, and may be spread to other foods by means of the hands, poorly washed utensils, or contaminated work surfaces. These bacteria grow readily at room or body temperatures, but not in the refrigerator. They are destroyed by the temperatures used in pasteurization, but sometimes products such as cream or custard fillings or soft meringues are not heated sufficiently to destroy organisms that may be present. The frequent occurrence of salmonellae in cracked and dirty eggs explains why The Egg Products Inspection Act requires that eggs be pasteurized before freezing or drying.

Salmonellae infections are characterized by headache, nausea, vomiting, diarrhea, abdominal pains, and fever. The incubation period is from twelve to thirty-six hours, and the infection is likely to last two or three days or even longer.

Summary

Food spoilage resulting in foodborne illness is responsible for loss of productive time and for a significant dollar loss. Many factors contribute to the transmission or perpetuation of organisms responsible for foodborne illness.[4] Among these are failure to refrigerate potentially hazardous foods; failure to thoroughly cook or heat process contaminated foods; allowing foods to remain warm (at bacterial incubating temperatures); bringing con-

[3] E. M. Foster. The Problem of Salmonellae in Foods. *Food Technology,* 23: 1178–1182 (1969).

[4] F. L. Bryan, New Concepts in Foodborne Illness. *The Journal of Environmental Health,* 31: 327–337 (1969).

taminated foods into kitchens and cross contaminating other foods by equipment and workers; obtaining foods from unsafe sources; employing infected persons (they may or may not be diseased); failure to practice good personal hygiene; and failure to clean and disinfect kitchen equipment.

References

BORGSTROM, G. *Principles of Food Science.* Vol. II. *Food Microbiology and Biochemistry.* New York: The Macmillan Company. 1968. Pp. 83–103, 145–148.

DEFIGUEIREDO, M. P. Staphylococci Control and the Food Processor. *J. Am. Diet. Assoc.* 58: 109–114 (1971).

FRAZIER, W. C. *Food Microbiology,* 2nd ed. New York: McGraw-Hill Book Company, Inc. 1967.

JAY, J. M. *Modern Food Microbiology.* New York: Van Nostrand Reinhold Co. 1970.

Keeping Food Safe to Eat. U.S. Dept. Agr., Home and Garden Bull. No. 162 (1969).

Toward the New. U.S. Dept. Agr., Agr. Info. Bull. No. 341 (1970). Pp. 17–22.

RIEMANN, H., Ed. *Food-borne Infections and Intoxications.* New York: Academic Press Inc., 1969.

VESTER, K. G. *Food-Borne Illness. Cause and Prevention.* Rocky Mount, N.C.: Food Service Guides. 1967.

29

food preservation

Food can be kept for extended periods only if the microorganisms and enzymes it contains are destroyed or prevented from acting. Because microorganisms need warmth, moisture, and food to grow and reproduce, growth may be retarded or even prevented by the use of high or low temperatures, by drying the food, or by the use of certain chemicals. Some chemicals such as acid and alcohol can be produced by the action of certain microorganisms in the food during fermentation, whereas others may be added. Both microorganisms and enzymes can be destroyed by heat and ionizing radiation, although enzymes are more resistant than microorganisms to radiation. In all methods of food preservation it is important to reduce the amount of microbial contamination by prompt, careful handling of the food and by the use of clean working surfaces and containers. In this chapter the principles of preservation methods, some of which can be used only commercially, will be discussed. In the following chapters methods of food preservation commonly used at home will be described.

Common Storage and Chilling

Undoubtedly cold places have been used for storing food ever since man discovered that just a few feet below the earth's surface evenly cool temperatures prevail throughout the year. In temperate climates this is about 10° to 15° C. (50° to 60° F.). Natural caves and springs of cold water served as the first storerooms, but later cellars were provided in which food could be protected from freezing in winter and remain cool during the summer. This method of preservation is sometimes called common storage. Even today, cellars, either under a house or dug as a "root cellar," are sometimes used for the storage of root vegetables and fruits such as apples. These foods keep well throughout the winter if care is taken to keep the temperature low, to store only foods of the proper maturity, and to remove spoiled items periodically. In countries where refrigeration is limited, common storage may be used for all foods.

Fig. 29–1.
Underground food storage offers protection from the heat of summer and the cold of winter.

Food can be chilled by ice or by refrigeration. In 1805 insulated ice houses were built for the storage of natural ice cut from the surfaces of lakes or ponds, and by the middle of the last century this practice had become common. Ice was made by mechanical means during the latter part of the nineteenth century when a shortage of natural ice made it urgent. During the 1930's, mechanical refrigerators began to find their place in the home as well as in industry and replaced ice in the chilling of food.

The temperature of home refrigerators should be maintained below 6° C. (42° F.). For some foods as meat, milk, eggs, and leftovers a temperature just above freezing is desirable; hence these foods are stored in the coldest part of the refrigerator. Other foods such as sweet potatoes and some varieties of apples may be injured by low temperatures. It is well known that bananas stored in the refrigerator turn dark. Commercial refrigeration takes into account the nature of the food being stored, and temperature, humidity, and the proportions of carbon dioxide and oxygen in the atmosphere are all carefully controlled to give the conditions which best retain quality in a particular food. In the home refrigerator, humidity control is achieved, to an extent, by means of covered compartments or plastic bags or wraps.

Freezing

The low temperatures used in freezing foods make possible the preservation of many of the qualities of the fresh product for extended periods of time. Nutritive value as well as other chemical and physical characteristics of the food are well preserved during storage in the freezer. Freezing decreases the microbial population but does not destroy all the microorganisms present in the food. The growth of microorganisms is retarded or prevented not only by the cold temperature but also by a lack of water, which is not available to them when it freezes. Enzymes act very slowly at the temperatures of freezer storage, but their action is noticeable over a period of time.

Although a few foods were frozen commercially as early as 1925, they did not become important commercially until about 1940. Vegetables, fruits, fish, and poultry were among the first foods widely and successfully distributed in frozen form. More recently, fruit juice concentrates and prepared and precooked foods including frozen prepared meals have become popular. Frozen red meats are widely used by those who have home freezers, but they have not gained wide acceptance in the retail market.

Although terminology is not uniform, quick freezing is sometimes considered to require thirty minutes or less, whereas sharp or slow freezing may require three to seventy-two hours. Commercially, foods are usually quick frozen. This can be accomplished by placing the food in flat rectangular packages on metal plates through which a refrigerant flows. After the packages have been arranged, the plates are brought close together by means of hydraulic pressure. The close contact of the packages with the plates causes the food to freeze rapidly. Food can also be quick frozen by placing it in a blast of cold air. One of the most rapid methods of freezing is by direct immersion of the food in a refrigerant. Unpackaged foods such as berries can be frozen in a refrigerated syrup, or fish in brine. Either packaged or loose food can be frozen very rapidly by direct contact with liquid nitrogen.[1] Tomato slices, which become mushy when frozen by ordinary methods, are said to be frozen successfully in liquid nitrogen.[2]

Quick freezing has certain advantages over the slow or sharp freezing that occurs in the home freezer, for the action of enzymes is quickly retarded by quick freezing. Quick freezing results in the formation of small ice crystals in the food in contrast to large ice crystals that form during slow freezing. The microscopic appearance of quick frozen foods is better than that of slow frozen foods, in which there appears to be considerable mechanical destruction of cells because of the large ice crystals. On thawing, however, the microscopic appearance of most quick and slow frozen foods is similar, and there is little difference between their palatability and nutritive value except with a few foods such as asparagus.[3]

[1] Liquid-Nitrogen Freezing—Promise and Problems. *Food Engineering,* 34: 70–71 (September, 1962).

[2] Exciting Breakthrough: Freezing Sliced Tomatoes. *Food Engineering,* 36: 56–57 (January, 1964).

[3] F. A. Lee, et al. *Industrial and Engineering Chemistry,* 38: 341–346 (1946); *Food Technology,* 3: 164–169 (1949); *Food Research,* 15: 8–15 (1950); *Journal of The American Dietetic Association,* 30: 351–354 (1954).

Early in the development of commercial freezing, manufacturers learned that moisture-vapor-resistant materials were necessary, that moisture-vapor-proof materials were highly desirable for packaging, and that vegetables must be scalded or blanched before they were frozen in order to inactivate the enzymes that would otherwise cause unpleasant flavors to develop during freezer storage. Some softening of the tissues occurs during freezing and thawing, which causes vegetables to lose the crisp texture that is desired in most vegetables served raw. Similar softening of the tissues of fruits makes it desirable to have a few ice crystals in raw fruit at the time it is eaten.

Dehydro-freezing

Dehydrofreezing is a combination of dehydration and freezing in which fruits and vegetables are dried to about 50 per cent of their original weight and volume and then frozen. This smaller weight and bulk of the product makes it easier to package, freeze, store, and ship than regular frozen foods. The product must be kept frozen until it is to be rehydrated and cooked. Dehydrofrozen fruits and vegetables are used in institutional food service and by manufacturers in the processing of foods such as soups and pastries.

Drying

Dried foods keep well because their water content is so low that microorganisms do not grow on them. The enzymes of vegetables are usually inactivated by blanching before drying, whereas those of light-colored fruits may be inhibited by sulfur dioxide or a sulfite. Dried foods, because of their small bulk and weight, are easy to package, ship, and store. Although the term "dehydration" usually refers to drying by artificial means, as contrasted with "sun drying," the terms dehydration and drying are often used interchangeably. For example, it is customary to speak of dried milk although milk is dehydrated under carefully controlled conditions.

One of the oldest methods of food preservation still widely used is to spread out the food and dry it in the sun. Dates, figs, raisins, apricots, and even fish dried in the sun have probably been used since prehistoric times. Early settlers in the United States dried corn, apple slices, meat, and other foods. Long before the action of enzymes was understood, it was learned that light-colored fruits were protected from browning during drying if they were exposed to the fumes of burning sulfur before drying. Later, sulfites were found to be an effective substitute for sulfur dioxide in preventing browning.

Forced hot air is widely used at present to dry foods because it is more rapid and more reliable in many climates than sun drying. Pieces of fruits and vegetables may be dried on trays; mashed potatoes or pumpkin on drums or rollers; and liquid foods such as milk, eggs, and coffee extract are often sprayed into a heated cylinder. Spray drying is widely used in the production of nonfat dry milk, dried eggs, and instant coffee.

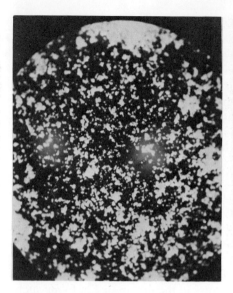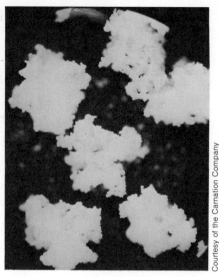

Courtesy of the Carnation Company

Fig. 29–2. *At the left is a photo of conventional spray-dried nonfat dry milk; at right, agglomerated instantized nonfat dry milk. Both photos were taken at the same magnification.*

Powdered dry foods disperse in water more readily if their particles are clustered or agglomerated after drying. This process is sometimes called "instantizing" and is used with nonfat dried milk, wheat flour, and other foods. The dried powder is moistened enough to agglomerate the particles and the material is dried again to produce a light material that wets easily.

Concentrated liquids can be made into a foam before they are dried by adding a foaming agent and forcing a gas into the liquid. In the process called foam-mat drying, the foam is dried on a perforated tray or a continuous belt. This method has been used for milk and for tomato and fruit juices. The foam, made by injecting a gas such as nitrogen into concentrated milk, dries quickly when sprayed into a heated cylinder. The dry powder reconstitutes rapidly without requiring the further process of "instantizing."

Explosion-puffing, which resembles the puffing used for cereals, is sometimes used in drying foods. The pieces are partially dehydrated, put into a pressure vessel, and heated by superheated steam under pressure. When the vessel is opened suddenly, the return to atmosphere pressure causes the food to "explode" because of sudden vaporization of water within the pieces. Drying can be completed rapidly because the material has been made porous. Fruits and vegetables dried in this way reconstitute in water more rapidly than those dried in the conventional way.

A process known as reverse osmosis (R.O.) offers promise as an economical method of removing water from liquids, as whey, and semiliquids, as fruit purees. To achieve reverse osmosis the material to be concentrated is separated from a more dilute liquid by a semipermeable membrane. Pressure is applied to the liquid to be concentrated thus setting up conditions that cause the water to move from the concentrated to the dilute solution rather than in the usual direction. The resulting product may be further treated in evaporators, centrifuges, or spray dryers.[4]

Freeze Drying

Freeze-dried foods, which first became available about 1961, are still not widely distributed in retail stores, although freeze-dried meat, chicken, and mushrooms are used in some dry soup mixes. Freeze-dried foods are used by the armed forces, in space explorations, and on camping trips because they are light in weight and are stored without refrigeration. The high cost of the process has tended to limit it to relatively costly foods. Freeze-dried coffee is widely available.

In this process, food is first frozen and then water is evaporated from the ice crystals without melting them (a process called sublimation) by means of reduced pressure and small amounts of heat. Because little heat is used, the foods retain much of their original structure and quality. The freeze-dried food may be almost as large in volume as the raw food, but very light and porous. It is usually packed in nitrogen or in a vacuum to prevent deterioration. The porous structure of these foods makes them easy to rehydrate.

The palatability of freeze-dried foods is usually superior and their structure and quality better than that of foods dried by the usual process. The freeze-dried foods are likely to be inferior in palatability to frozen or fresh foods, however, which is not surprising because freeze-dried foods must first be frozen and then dried. Some freeze-dried meats are less tender than their frozen or fresh counterparts.

Canning

By coagulating protein, heat is capable of destroying both microorganisms and enzymes. This ability to inactivate the agents of food spoilage makes heat a valuable means of food processing. Foods such as milk are sometimes pasteurized to destroy disease-producing microorganisms which, fortunately, are usually more sensitive to heat than other microorganisms. Pasteurization may be supplemented by other methods of food preservation, such as refrigeration for milk or ice cream mix, dehydration for dried fruits, and the presence of acid for vinegar. Pasteurization prolongs the storage life

[4] K. Bird. The Food Processing Front of the Seventies. *Journal of The American Dietetics Association,* 58: 103–108 (1971).

Fig. 29–3. *The three freeze-dried pork chops on the right weigh as much as the single fresh pork chop on the left. After preparation, the freeze-dried meat resumes normal weight (only moisture has been removed) and has a similar flavor and texture as fresh.*

of a food, but more thorough heating, as occurs in the canning process, is usually required if food is to be kept for long periods of time.

Modern canning methods originated with Nicolas Appert, who won a prize offered by the French government in 1809, and published a book on canning methods a year later. At the time it was thought that the foods kept because they were sealed in air-tight containers. It was another fifty years before the discovery of bacteria led to the recognition that microorganisms were the real cause of food spoilage, and that they were destroyed by heat during the canning process.

The containers used by Appert were wide-mouthed glass bottles sealed with corks. Earthenware containers were later tried unsuccessfully. Soon tin containers were made by hand and filled through small openings in the tops. Modern machinery has made possible the production of open-topped cans that may be sealed efficiently. Such cans are now made of steel plate coated with tin. The inside of cans used for foods that might corrode the tin plate, such as red fruits and certain vegetables, are coated with enamel. Glass containers with tight seals are also used for canning.

Although the canner attempts to sterilize food by heat, it is not always possible to kill every organism present. Canning is successful if the food keeps without spoilage, and the canned food is then termed "commercially sterile." It is assumed that enzymes have been inactivated in any canning process because of the temperatures used.

The conventional commercial canning method resembles home canning because the food is sealed in containers and processed, usually with pressure, for the required length of time. The time and temperature depend on the nature of the food and the size and type of container in which it is packed. After processing, tin cans are usually cooled rapidly with water. Foods such as meats and vegetables are likely to be overcooked when the conventional canning method is used. The amount of heat required to destroy harmful bacteria such as spores of *Clostridium botulinum* causes undesirable palatability changes, and the food near the outside becomes overcooked in the time necessary to sufficiently heat food in the center of the can.

In order to reduce quality deterioration, canning processes have been developed recently which use higher temperatures and shorter times than do conventional methods, and most importantly, provide rapid distribution of heat throughout the food. In one method the cans are violently agitated during cooking by moving them either on their axis or end over end. The rapid distribution of heat by this means is less likely to result in overprocessed food near the outside of the container as occurs in the conventional method when attempting to sterilize food in the center of the can.

Another technique, the so called high-temperature-short-time (HTST) process, has been especially beneficial in canning heat-sensitive foods such as yogurt, sour cream, whipping cream, salads, puddings, sauces, and baby foods. When this process is used in combination with aseptic canning,[5] temperatures can be even higher and times shorter than in processing with agitation. In this method the food is heated and then packed aseptically into containers that have been sterilized separately. A mild heat treatment may follow the sealing of the cans. Currently this method holds greatest promise for foods that are extremely heat sensitive; foods that are now sold only in frozen, refrigerated, or dehydrated form; foods for which there is need to upgrade the nutritional, palatability, or appearance level; low-acid foods difficult to preserve by the usual canning methods; and pumpable foods.[6]

Radiation

Radiation is a comparatively new method of preserving food by means of ionizing radiations. It is sometimes called "cold sterilization" because, although large amounts of energy are involved, the temperature of the food does not rise appreciably during radiation. Either beta or gamma rays are used. Beta or cathode rays are produced by an electron accelerator,

[5] Aseptic means free of harmful microorganisms. For example, surgery is done under aseptic conditions. The inner tissues of plants and animals are normally aseptic, and therefore do not spoil unless they are contaminated.
[6] K. Bird.

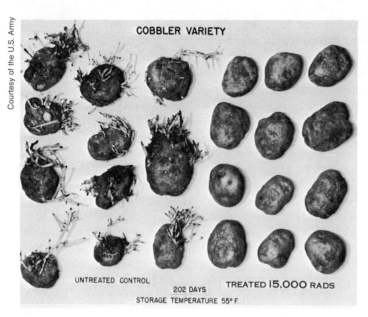

COBBLER VARIETY

UNTREATED CONTROL   TREATED 15,000 RADS

202 DAYS

STORAGE TEMPERATURE 55° F.

Courtesy of the U.S. Army

Fig. 29–4. *Radiation inhibits the sprouting of potatoes as shown in this photograph taken approximately seven months after treatment.*

whereas gamma rays come from radioisotopes such as cobalt 60. Of the two, gamma rays penetrate better than beta rays. Foods can be irradiated and stored in packages of many types, including light, flexible materials as well as cans and glass. The radiations are able to pass through the packaging materials as well as through the food.

Intensive research on radiation preservation, which started in 1946, is being done in many countries. In the United States much of the research on this subject is being carried out for the armed forces because of their interest in preserving foods without refrigeration. Irradiated foods may find future use in developing countries where there is often a lack of refrigeration.

Relatively small doses of radiation are required to prevent the sprouting of root vegetables and to destroy any insects that may be present. The United States Food and Drug Administration now permits the radiation of potatoes to inhibit sprouting and of wheat and wheat products to destroy insects.

Microorganisms can also be destroyed by ionizing radiations which, by hitting cells, cause them to die. As with heat sterilization, the spores of *Clostridium botulinum* are more resistant to destruction than are the vegetative cells of bacteria. Another similarity between these two methods of food preservation is that a less strenuous treatment is required for pasteurization than for sterilization. It is possible to use radiation to reduce the number of organisms in a food, such as *Salmonella* in eggs and poultry or *Trichinella spiralis* in pork. These applications of radiation have not yet been approved for commercial use.

Additives

Additives have been included in this chapter even though food preservation is only one of their functions. The use of additives has made possible a more abundant supply of better quality foods than would be possible without them. Food additives have been defined[7] as "a substance or a mixture of substances, other than a basic foodstuff, which is present in a food as a result of any aspect of production, processing, storage, or packaging." As already mentioned in Chapter 2, a food additives amendment passed in 1958 requires that the producer or manufacturer pretest any additives that are to be used in food. Evidence concerning the tests is presented to the Food and Drug Administration. If the evidence is satisfactory, use of the additive is permitted. This regulation is intended to insure that no harmful additives are used.

The label of a food often reveals information about additives as well as other ingredients. If no standard of identity has been adopted for the food, the label must give the name of each ingredient in the order of their predominance by weight. Spices, flavorings, and colorings can be so designated without naming each. As shown in Table 2–1, standards of identity have been adopted for many products including several types of bread and rolls, flours, macaroni products, chocolate and chocolate products, margarine, most types of cheese, tomato catsup, and many canned fruits and vegetables. Ingredients of such foods need not be declared on the label except that the standards may require declaration of optional ingredients.

It is perhaps unfortunate that the names of some of the additives sound frightening and are difficult to pronounce. Many people would not recognize the following as names of essential vitamins: ascorbic acid, biotin, calcium pantothenate, niacinamide, pyridoxine hydrochloride, sodium pantothenate, and α-tocopherol acetate. It is important not to fear blindly the use of "chemicals" in foods, but to realize that foods are entirely made up of chemicals, such as carbohydrates, proteins, fats, minerals, and vitamins.

At the time of the passage of the food additives amendment in 1958 the decision was reached that (1) substances that FDA had previously considered favorably and (2) substances that had an unmarred history of use in foods could be safely exempted from the need for premarketing clearance. In other words these substances were "generally recognized as safe," thus the GRAS list was developed. Common food ingredients, such as salt, pepper, sugar, vinegar, and baking powder are not included in this list, be-

[7] Food and Nutrition Board. *The Use of Chemicals in Food Production, Processing, Storage, and Distribution.* Research Council Publication No. 887. National Academy of Science, Washington, D.C., 1961.

cause it is impractical to list all substances that are generally recognized as safe. For some additives, a tolerance and limitations or restrictions on use are included.

In 1971 it was estimated that a total of 1,810 GRAS additives were added either directly or indirectly to foods with an additional 2,940 regulated additives in use. Considering 860 duplications in the two lists there remained a grand total of 3,890 substances added to food for specific technical effects.[8] Twenty-six food categories for additive use and 30 specific technical effects of additives used are recognized.[9] The following brief discussion, based on a United States Food and Drug Administration publication[10] and on current listings,[11] gives the principal classifications.

Anticaking Agents. Anticaking agents are added to such foods as table salt and baking powder. These agents include aluminum calcium silicate, calcium silicate, and other silicates with levels of use usually definitely specified.

Chemical Preservatives. There are many different types of preservatives, each type being best suited to a particular type of product or more effective against a particular spoilage organism or chemical change. Preservatives for fatty products, for example, are called antioxidants. Examples of antioxidants are butylated hydroxyanisole (BHA), butylated hydroxytoluene (BHT), propyl gallate, and tocopherols.

The preservatives used in bread are called mold and rope inhibitors, or antimycotic agents. Those permitted in bread include sodium and calcium propionate and acetic acid. Sorbic acid and sodium and potassium sorbates are antimycotic agents for cheeses. Still other antimycotics prevent molding of citrus fruits. These are called fungicides because they stop the growth of the mold or fungus spores. Other common preservatives are benzoic acid, sodium benzoate, sulfur dioxide, and of course vinegar (acetic acid). Sugar and salt, when present in sufficient concentration, also exert a preservative action.

Sequestrants. Another group of additives are the sequestrants, which aid in processing foods by setting apart in inactive form, or separating, traces of substances that otherwise interfere with the processing. Common sequestrants used in dairy products include sodium salts of citric, tartaric, metaphosphoric, and pyrophosphoric acids, and calcium and potassium salts of

[8] R. L. Hall, GRAS Review and Food Additive Legislation. *Food Technology* 25: 466–470 (1971).

[9] R. L. Hall.

[10] *What Consumers Should Know About Food Additives.* Food and Drug Administration Publication No. 10. United States Department of Health, Education, and Welfare, Washington, D.C., 1962.

[11] *Code of Federal Regulations,* Title 21, Part 121.101. 1971.

certain acids. A different type of sequestrant is used in the manufacture of soft drinks to remove traces of metals, which cause clouding or other undesirable effects.

Emulsifying Agents. Emulsifiers are used in such foods as bakery products, cake mixes, ice cream and frozen desserts, and confectionery products. They affect characteristics such as volume, uniformity and fineness of grain (bakery goods), ease of emulsification and smoothness (dairy products), and homogeneity and keeping quality (confectionery). Some common emulsifiers are the mono- and diglycerides of edible fats and oils and propylene glycol. Chemists sometimes call the emulsifiers "surfactants"—short for "surface active agents."

Nonnutritive Sweeteners. These are the sugar substitutes permitted in foods for people who must restrict their intake of ordinary sweets. These include ammonium saccharin, calcium saccharin, saccharin, and sodium saccharin.

Nutrients and/or Dietary Supplements. These are the vitamins and minerals added to foods to improve nutritive value and sometimes to replace those removed in processing. For example, thiamine (vitamin B_1), riboflavin (vitamin B_2), niacin (another B vitamin), and iron must be added to bread if the bread is to be called "enriched." Other foods to which these same nutrients are commonly added are flour, farina, corn meal, corn grits, macaroni, and noodle products. Vitamin A is added to margarine and certain cheeses and vitamin D to milk. Iodized salt contains added potassium iodide to furnish the iodine necessary to prevent simple goiter. There are of course other nutrients that may be added to certain products as dietary supplements.

Stabilizers. Smoothness of texture of confectionery, ice cream, and other frozen desserts; uniformity of color, flavor, and viscosity of chocolate milk; "body" of artificially sweetened beverages; homogeneity of certain fruit juices: these are typical of the purposes for which stabilizers are used. Stabilizing agents include vegetable gums (carob bean, carrageenan, guar), gelatin, and agar-agar.

Miscellaneous and/or General Purpose Food Additives. In this category may be listed acids, alkalies, buffers, and neutralizing agents. The degree of acidity or alkalinity is important in many classes of processed foods. The acid ingredient reacts with the alkali in chemical leavening agents in baked goods, and releases the gas that causes the rising. The taste of many soft drinks is due largely to an organic acid. Acidity of churning cream must be controlled for flavor and keeping quality of the butter. Acids contribute flavor to confectionery, and help to prevent a "grainy" texture.

Buffers and neutralizing agents are chemicals added to control acidity or alkalinity, just as acids and alkalis may be added directly. Some common chemicals in this class are ammonium bicarbonate, calcium carbonate, potassium acid tartrate, sodium aluminum phosphate, and tartaric acid.

A great variety of flavoring agents, bleaching agents, and bread improvers may also be included in this group as well as propellants for products packed under pressure in dispensing cans and many, many other substances.

Activities

1. Purchase some foods fresh and in as many processed forms as possible. Record the weight, price, time required for preparation, and number of servings. The servings should be the same weight, if possible. Prepare the food for serving, mark with a code, and score its palatability. Calculate the cost per serving.

2. Discuss the changes that would be necessary in your diet if no frozen, dried, or canned foods were available. Choose one month, preferably during the winter, for the discussion.

3. List the ingredients of a processed food and identify the purpose of each additive.

References

BIRD, K. The Food Processing Front of the Seventies. *Journal of The American Dietetic Association.* 58: 103–108 (1971).

BORGSTROM, G., *Principles of Food Science.* Vol. II. *Food Microbiology and Biochemistry.* New York: The Macmillan Company. 1968. Pp. 171–207.

Current Status and Commercial Prospects for Radiation Preservation of Food. U.S. Dept. of Commerce, Business and Defense Services Administration, TID-21431 (1965).

FRAZIER, W. C. *Food Microbiology,* 2nd ed. New York: McGraw-Hill Book Company, Inc. 1967.

POTTER, N. N. *Food Science.* Westport, Conn.: The Avi Publishing Company, Inc., 1968. Chapter 23.

TRESSLER, K., W. B. VAN ARSDEL, and M. J. COPLEY (Eds). *The Freezing Preservation of Foods,* 4th ed. Vol. II, *Factors Affecting Quality of Frozen Foods;* Vol. IV, *Freezing of Precooked and Prepared Foods.* Westport, Conn.: The Avi Publishing Company, Inc. 1968.

VAN ARSDEL, W. B. and M. J. COPLEY (Eds.). *Food Dehydration.* Vol. 1, *Principles;* Vol. 2, *Products and Technology.* Westport, Conn.: Avi Publishing Company. 1963; 1964.

WIERBICKI, E. and F. HEILIGMAN. *Present Status and Future Outlook of Radiation Sterilization Processing of Meats.* Proc. Conf. on Research, Council on Research Am. Meat Inst., Univ. Chicago, 16th Conf. 1964. Pp. 57–72.

30

home preservation by canning

Canning is the preservation of foods in sealed containers and usually involves the application of heat. The heat cooks the food, changes the physical nature, the flavor, and often the appearance. During canning part or all of the microorganisms are destroyed and the rest are rendered inactive. Heat also destroys the activity of the enzymes. A hermetic seal prevents the entrance of organisms from outside sources.

Although the aim of successful canning is to sterilize the foods, the ease with which this may be accomplished is determined largely by the nature of the food. Heavily contaminated food is, as a rule, more difficult to render "practically sterile." The physical nature of the food affects the speed of heat penetration in the container and hence the time required for the center of the container to reach the desired temperature. For example, cream style corn permits little or no circulation of liquid and the recommended processing time for commercial canning of a No. 2 tin can at 115° C. (240° F.) is 105 minutes, whereas whole grain corn in brine permits more rapid transfer of heat and only 50 minutes processing time is recommended.[1]

The acidity of the food is also a factor in the sterilization process. As explained in Chapter 28, spores of *Clostridium botulinum,* as well as of many other bacteria, are more readily destroyed by heat in an acid medium such as that of fruits and tomatoes than in a more nearly neutral medium. This difference is reflected in the recommended times and temperatures given in Table 30–1 for processing fruits and vegetables.

Selecting and Preparing the Food

Quality is important in the selection of foods for canning, particularly of the low-acid foods. The spoilage of non-acid foods is largely responsible for botulism, the most serious illness that results from eating canned foods. Other forms of illness are also attributed to the eating of canned low-acid foods which have spoiled. Stale food or food which has started to decay is difficult to sterilize, and the chances of spoilage are greater than when high

[1] Processes for low-acid canned foods in metal containers. Bulletin 26–L, 9th ed. National Canners Association, Washington, D.C., 1962.

Table 30–1. *Time for Processing Various Foods in Quart Jars* *

Product	Processing Period in Boiling Water		Processing Period in Pressure Canner at 10 Pounds Pressure (240° F.) †	
	Minutes		Minutes	
	Raw Pack	Hot Pack	Raw Pack	Hot Pack
Apples	—	20		
Apricots	30	25		
Blackberries	15	15		
Cherries	25	15		
Peaches	30	25		
Pickled beets	—	30		
Tomatoes	45	10		
Tomato juice	—	10		
Asparagus			30	30
Beans, snap			25	25
Baby beets			—	35
Corn, whole grain ‡			85	85
Greens			—	90
Okra			—	40
Peas, green			40	40
Pumpkin, cubed			—	90
Sweet potatoes, wet pack			—	90
Meat, depends on kind			75–90	75–90

* For exact methods of canning see state extension or USDA publications.

† If a pressure saucepan is to be used, follow directions for processing given in government publications.

‡ Corn, cream style, should be canned in pint jars and processed for 95 minutes at 10 pounds pressure if raw pack and for 85 minutes if hot pack.

quality fresh food is used. Canning is not a means of using food unfit for other purposes.

Fruits have the best flavor when mature and ripe; vegetables are best when young and tender. "Two hours from field to can," although desirable for all foods, is most important for vegetables. After harvesting, changes occur more rapidly in the flavor and texture of fresh vegetables than of fresh fruits. This makes it important to select strictly fresh foods for canning and to can them as soon as possible. If a few hours must elapse between harvesting and canning, the food should be chilled and kept cold.

To obtain an attractive product, the food should be sorted according to maturity, size, color, or other characteristics, and then prepared as for cooking. First, the food is thoroughly cleaned. Small vegetables or fruits can be held in a sieve or colander under running water. Cleaning of large vegetables and fruits is hastened by scrubbing with a brush. Meats may be carefully wiped with a clean damp cloth or paper towel. Some foods may need to be peeled or scraped. Tomatoes and peaches are often blanched, that is, dipped in boiling water, then in cold water, to facilitate the removal of the skin. Cores or seeds are removed when necessary. Large pieces are usually halved, quartered, or sliced.

Proportions

As a rule sugar and salt are the ingredients added to foods being canned. The degree of sweetness desired, the use for which the fruit is intended, and the acidity of the fruit influence the proportion of sugar to be used. In home canning, the syrup is often classed as heavy, medium, or thin. In laboratory work and in commercial canning, a sugar hydrometer, which measures the percentage of sugar in the syrup, may be used. The percentage of sugar by weight is then indicated as degrees Brix. A thick or heavy syrup contains about equal parts of sugar and water and tests from 50° to 55° Brix. A thin syrup may contain one-fourth as much sugar as water and tests 25° Brix. Very thin syrups contain even less sugar. When salt is used, the proportion is generally one teaspoon to a quart of vegetable or meat.

Selecting the Equipment

Although there are essential pieces of equipment which may be used only at the canning season, most of the equipment will already be on hand in the home kitchen. It is, of course, good management to assemble all the equipment in order of its use.

Needed first is an assortment of brushes with stiff, medium, and flexible bristles for cleaning the food, and also brushes for cleaning the jars. A colander or sieve is useful for holding the food under running water. Knives of various shapes are necessary, including a knife with stainless steel blade for peeling fruit, one for cutting and slicing, and one for removing pits or cores. Cherry pitters, rotary peelers, and cutting and dicing equipment are also available. A kitchen scissors is very helpful.

Measuring cups, measuring spoons, and a pint or quart measure are necessary, and a scales is especially valuable when making preserves, jams, and similar products for which weights are used instead of measures. A jelmeter is an aid in determining the pectin content of juices, and a thermometer in determining when jellies, jams, and marmalades have reached the right concentration.

A large utensil is needed for scalding or blanching foods, and a wire basket or a sack to hold the foods as they are dipped into the water. A wide-mouthed funnel and a cup-like ladle are convenient for pouring liquids and for filling the containers. Jar tongs which grip the container firmly and do not slip are very useful for handling the hot jars. If zinc top closures are used, a wrench for tightening the lids will facilitate sealing the jars.

A steam-pressure cooker or canner is essential for processing meats and low-acid vegetables. To make it easier to maintain the necessary uniform

Fig. 30–1. *The equipment shown here makes for ease and efficiency in food preservation.*

temperature throughout the processing period, the cooker should be fairly large. However, a pressure saucepan equipped with an accurate gage may be used for pint jars and No. 2 cans. Acid foods may be processed at the temperature of boiling water; hence a regular hot water bath, a good-sized bucket, a large kettle, or a boiler with a rack to hold the jars off the bottom of the utensil may be used. The utensil should be deep enough so that the jars are covered by one to two inches of water during processing.

Utensils used should be of materials which are not affected by the foods. Aluminum, stainless steel, glass, enamelware, plastic, and wood are all suitable. Plenty of towels and dishcloths, a chair or stool on which to sit, and adequate table space will also be needed for rapid and efficient work.

Containers

The choice of the container is important. Either glass or tin may be used, but glass jars are more widely used in home canning. Although of greater initial expense than tin containers, glass jars may be used for many seasons. Only the sealing device need be replaced. Glass jars are breakable, but with care the loss is usually small. Glass displays the food, thus setting a premium on attractive packs.

Tin cans are less expensive to purchase than glass jars, and with care may also be used for more than one season. A mechanical sealer is required, but the seal is fairly sure. The tin cans in use today have the entire top open so that packing is easier than in some types of glass jars. When processing low-acid foods in tin cans there is no danger of breakage or loss of liquid should the pressure in the canner fluctuate greatly. The cans may be cooled rapidly in a cold water bath, thus decreasing danger of spoilage caused by thermophilic bacteria and minimizing problems of over-cooking. From the standpoint of storage, tin containers have the advantages of requiring less space than glass jars and of protecting the food from light so that storage in dark places is not required.

Containers have three major parts: the container proper, the cover, and the sealing medium. Glass jars may have either small or wide mouths. Tin cans are tall or flat and available either plain or enameled. The choice of tin cans should be on the basis of the food to be canned. A "C" enamel finish is adapted to such foods as corn and hominy, and the "R" enamel finish is particularly suited to the red fruits, rhubarb, and such vegetables as beets or pumpkin.

Glass jars usually have metal covers. The two types most frequently used are a zinc porcelain-lined cover with shoulder rubber ring and a flat metal lid edged with sealing compound held in place by a metal screw band. When rubber rings are used to effect a seal, they should be live rubber— that is, pliable and elastic as contrasted to brittle and inelastic. A live rubber ring when creased firmly between the thumb and finger will show no mark when released. Rubber rings should not be stretched. Tin containers have tin covers with a continuous ring of sealing compound around the edge of the covers. This melts when heated and flows into any open spaces, effecting a seal. Containers with a simple sealing device are desirable because any delay in sealing the sterilized food increases proportionately the chances for spoilage.

Can-cooked Canning

The can-cooked method of preserving foods has wide application and is recommended for fruits as well as vegetables and meats. The foods are packed in the container, either tin or glass, and then processed or cooked.

After being packed with the prepared food, the container is sealed partially or entirely, heated for a given period, then completely sealed if this has not been done previously. If properly carried out, this method gives no opportunity for contamination between cooking and sealing. Can-cooked products retain quite well their natural flavor and shape, although the color is not always good.

Raw-pack Canning. Can-cooked foods may be packed into containers either cold or hot.[2] The processes are designated accordingly as raw-pack

---

[2] Directions for "raw-pack" canning are given in *Home Canning Fruits and Vegetables,* and *Home Canning of Meat and Poultry.* Home and Garden Bulletins No. 8 (1969) and No. 106 (1970), United States Department of Agriculture, Washington, D.C. According to W. C. Frazier, however, "The cold-pack method is not recommended for vegetables and meats." *Food Microbiology,* 2nd ed. New York: McGraw-Hill Book Company, Inc., 1967, p. 107.

(or cold-pack) and hot-pack canning. Raw-pack canning consists of packing raw prepared food into cans or jars and adding hot water, syrup, or juice as needed to cover the food. Tin cans are sealed before processing, which means that food packed raw must be heated in the cans (exhausted) before sealing. This is said to drive out the air so there will be a good vacuum in the can after processing and cooling. Food in the can should register at least 77° C. (170° F.) when the can is sealed. If glass jars are used, the jars are filled and the covers are placed on them as described under "Preparing and Packing the Containers."

Hot-pack Canning. The hot-pack is probably more generally recommended and used than the raw-pack method because it is suitable for practically all foods. With hot-pack canning, a precooking period precedes packing the hot food into the container. Precooking consists in heating the material for a short time in steam or in boiling liquid in order to shrink or wilt it. The precooked food is then packed boiling hot into hot containers and processed immediately. This method reduces air in containers to a minimum.

To prepare fruit for hot-pack canning, sugar, syrup, or water is added as desired and the fruit heated thoroughly, but not cooked until soft. Vegetables should be precooked in steam or in water. Steaming eliminates, to a large extent, the loss of soluble elements into the water. It may, however, increase the loss of natural color of foods, just as cooking certain vegetables, especially green ones, in a covered utensil tends to destroy the color. Steaming a vegetable may result in a greater change in the flavor than occurs when it is boiled in an uncovered kettle. There are various ways of precooking meat, but a recommended method is to place the meat in a large shallow pan with just enough water to prevent sticking, and cook slowly with occasional stirring until medium done. It is usually advisable to avoid adding flour, which soon becomes stale in flavor. Precooked foods are packed hot, a valuable aid in processing.

Preparing and Packing the Containers

Containers and closures should be inspected and any with cracks, chips, dents, or rust discarded. They should be washed in hot, soapy water and rinsed well. If a porcelain-lined cap is used, the wet rubber ring should be fitted on the jar shoulder before filling. Some lids may require special treatment before use, such as holding in boiling water. The manufacturer's directions should be followed. Hot food should be packed into the hot containers quickly and, as a rule, not too tightly. With too loose a pack, however, the excessive shrinkage of certain foods may result in partially filled containers. Foods such as peas and shell beans, which tend to swell during cooking, should be packed loosely, otherwise incomplete sterilization may result. Corn, sweet potatoes, and other foods that pack tightly into the container should be weighed to avoid over-packing. Care is required to obtain a pack of just the right consistency since these foods are poor conductors of heat and, unless free liquid is present, may be incompletely processed.

After the containers are filled, the covers are placed on them. When foods are packed boiling hot in tin cans, they are sealed immediately. If the raw-pack method is used, the food must be heated in the can to at least 77° C. (170° F.) before sealing.

If a glass jar with a porcelain-lined cap is used, the rim of the jar and the rubber ring are wiped clean. The cap is then screwed down firmly and turned back one quarter inch. If a glass jar with a metal screwband and flat metal lid with sealing compound is used, the lid, with sealing compound down, is placed on the jar rim, which has been wiped clean after the jar has been filled. The metal band is screwed tight by hand. There is enough give in the lid to allow steam to escape during processing. The sealing of this type of closure does not take place until the compound is melted by heat and later solidified by cooling.

Processing and Sealing

The filled containers may be processed in the water-bath canner or the pressure canner. The water-bath, which is the simplest and least costly type of canner, consists of a kettle, a rack, and a tight cover. The kettle should be deep enough to permit one to two inches of water over the jars and a one- to two-inch space for brisk boiling. It should be fitted with a perforated false bottom or rack on which to place jars. This permits water to circulate freely about jars.

The steam-pressure cooker or canner is essential for canning low-acid foods such as meats and vegetables. Steam under a pressure of ten pounds reaches a temperature of 115° C. (240° F.) at sea level, which is the temperature recommended by the United States Department of Agriculture specialists for all low-acid foods.[3] It is important that the gage on the canner be checked periodically to make sure that it is working properly and that the indicated pressure is actually maintained. A uniform pressure is also necessary if the results are to be satisfactory.

Processing consists of heating food in cans or jars, with lids in place, to the temperature where the food will keep. Processing kills certain organisms and sterilizes as nearly as possible the contents of the container. Complete sterilization is often not effected, and certain heat-resistant aerobes may survive the processing period. However, due to unfavorable conditions for growth they usually remain dormant in the processed container and cause no difficulty.

Processing should be sufficiently prolonged to insure that the food will keep, but should not be continued longer than is necessary or an over-cooked product results. There is an interplay between temperature and time in processing. The characteristics of the food to be canned must be considered in determining the processing period, since as has been mentioned the freedom of the food from gross contamination and the composition of the food are important. Only foods of high quality, free of molds and decay, should be canned. Pasty or semi-solid foods such as cream-style corn, pump-

[3] *Home Canning of Fruits and Vegetables* and *Home Canning of Meat and Poultry.*

Fig. 30–2. To can tomatoes by the raw (cold) pack method:
Use fresh, firm, red-ripe tomatoes, free of spoilage and cracks. Wash and drain. Scald in boiling water to loosen skins, then dip in cold water.

Cut out cores and green spots. Remove skins and cut tomatoes in quarters or leave whole.

Pack tomatoes into hot jars. Cover with hot tomato juice or press tomatoes until spaces fill with juice. Leave $\frac{1}{2}$ inch head space. Add 1 teaspoon of salt per quart. Run a rubber bottle scraper or similar non-metal utensil between tomatoes and jar to release air bubbles.

Wipe jar tops and cover with lids and bands. Stand each jar on the rack in canner of hot, not boiling, water. Water should cover the jars 1 to 2 inches. Boil for recommended time.

Courtesy of Ball Brothers Company

kin, and sweet potatoes are poor conductors of heat, hence the center of the can becomes hot much more slowly with these foods than with those in a brine or syrup such as snap beans, peaches, and similar foods. A very heavy sugar syrup, on the other hand, may retard heat penetration. Large containers generally require a longer processing period than small ones. The acidity of the food is perhaps the chief factor influencing the time required for destruction of spoilage organisms. The common fruits and tomatoes contain enough acid so they may be safely processed at 100° C. (212° F.). Vegetables and meats low in acid are difficult to sterilize, hence it is recommended they be canned only when a processing temperature considerably in excess of that obtained in boiling water is available. If a pressure canner is not available for processing, it is unwise to attempt to preserve such low-acid foods by canning.

Exact directions have been developed for the preparation, packing, and processing of each food and these should be followed in detail. Each food has a specific processing time as indicated in Table 30–1. Immediately after processing, zinc tops should be tightened and checked to make sure there is a seal. Jars sealed by a sealing compound should not have the screw bands tightened, for the melted compound may be "squeezed" out of place and thus no seal will be formed.

Cooling, Testing, and Storing

The sealed containers should be cooled as rapidly as expedient. Glass jars should be placed top side up on a rack or folded cloth, never on a cold surface. They should be set far enough apart so that air can circulate around each jar, but kept away from drafts, and of course left uncovered as this will speed cooling. Tin cans may be cooled in cold water changed as needed to cool the cans quickly. The cans should be removed from water while still warm so that they will dry.

The day after canning, each container should be examined to be sure it is sealed. Jars with zinc top closures can be turned on their sides to check for leaks. Jars with two-piece closures are checked by pressing the centers of the flat metal lid; if the lid is down and will not move, it is probably sealed. A clear, ringing sound when the lid is tapped with a metal spoon means a good seal; however, a dull sound does not always mean a poor seal. Tin cans should be examined for any leaks. After checking, the containers should be wiped clean and bands removed if that type of closure is used. Containers may then be labeled and stored in a dry, cool place above freezing temperature. When glass containers are used, storage in the dark may retard loss of color.

When a leaky container is found, the unspoiled food should be used at once, or it may be canned again by the same process as used originally. The container should be examined before using again to make sure it is not defective. Recanned foods are likely to be over-cooked.

Fig. 30–3. To can green beans by the hot pack method:

Thoroughly wash fresh beans which are young, tender, and crisp. Drain.

Trim ends; remove any strings; cut or break into pieces. Prepare only enough for one canner load.

Cover the beans with boiling water and boil for 5 minutes.

Stand hot jar on wood or cloth to fill. Add 1 teaspoon salt per quart; cover beans with boiling water, leaving 1 inch head space.

Wipe top and threads of jar. Put lid on jar with the red rubber sealing compound next to the glass. Screw band down evenly and tightly.

Put jars into a steam-pressure canner containing 2 to 3 inches of hot water, or the amount recommended by the manufacturer. Place canner over heat. Lock the cover according to instructions. Leave the vent open until steam escapes steadily for 10 minutes, then close the vent.

After processing for the recommended time, remove canner from heat. Let pressure fall to zero. Wait 2 minutes, then slowly open the vent. Unfasten the cover, tilting the far side up first so steam escapes away from you.

Remove the jars. Do not tighten the bands. Stand jars apart, out of drafts, to cool. When cool, remove bands. Test the seal by pressing the center of the lid. If the dome is down, or stays down when pressed, the jar is sealed.

Courtesy of Ball Brothers Company

Quantity of Canned Product from Fresh Food

The ratio of uncooked to canned products varies with the type of food. It is often helpful to know approximately the quantity of canned food which may be obtained from a given amount of the uncooked product. Table 30–2 indicates approximate quantities.

Causes of Inferior Products

Certain foods such as peaches discolor in the presence of oxygen if the enzymes are not destroyed during canning. Ascorbic acid may be added to prevent discoloration of peaches, apples, and other fruits, but if properly processed, canned fruits should not need it.

Often fruits float in the liquid. The character of the fruit is largely responsible; for example, this condition is likely to occur with strawberries and other extremely soft juicy fruits. Too much liquid in proportion to the fruit, over-cooking so that the fruit is soft and mushy, or a too-heavy syrup with a density much greater than that of the fruit are also frequent causes of floating fruits.

Fading of fruits is usually due to exposure to light, although some fruits such as strawberries always lose their attractive color when canned. Foods

Table 30–2. *Approximate Yield of Home-Canned Product from Raw Fruit and Vegetables* *

Product	Amount of fresh product needed to can 1 quart	No. pints or quarts of canned foods to one bushel or crate	Approximate weight or measure of 1 bushel † or crate
Apples	2½–3 pounds	16–20 quarts	48 pounds
Apricots	2½–3 pounds	16–22 quarts	50 pounds
Berries (except strawberries)	1–2 quart boxes	12–18 quarts	24 quart crate
Cherries, as picked	2–2½ pounds	22–32 quarts	56 pounds
Grapes	2½–3 pounds	16–20 quarts	48 pounds
Peaches	2–3 pounds	18–24 quarts	48 pounds
Pears	2–3 pounds	20–25 quarts	50 pounds
Plums	1½–2½ pounds	24–30 quarts	56 pounds
Tomatoes	2½–3½ pounds	15–20 quarts	53 pounds
Asparagus	2½–4½ pounds	8–12 quarts	45 pounds
Beans, lima, in pods	3–5 pounds	6–8 quarts	32 pounds
Beans, snap	1½–2½ pounds	15–20 quarts	30 pounds
Beets, without tops	2–3½ pounds	17–20 quarts	52 pounds
Carrots, without tops	2–3 pounds	16–20 quarts	50 pounds
Corn, sweet in husks	3–6 ears	8–9 quarts	35 pounds
Greens	2–6 pounds	6–9 quarts	18 pounds
Peas, green in pods	3–6 pounds	12–15 pints	30 pounds
Pumpkin or winter squash	1½–3 pounds	15–20 quarts	50 pounds
Sweet potatoes, fresh	2–3 pounds	18–22 quarts	55 pounds

* Compiled from *Home Canning of Fruits and Vegetables*. Home and Garden Bulletin No. 8, Agricultural Research Service, United States Department of Agriculture, 1965, and from *Home Canning of Fruits and Vegetables*, Agricultural Information Series Bulletin No. 64, United States Department of Agriculture, 1947.

† Legal weight varies in different states; average weights are given here.

canned in glass jars should be stored in a dark place, particularly the red foods.

Failure to obtain jars completely filled may be due to a pack too loose for the type of food. Often it is practically impossible to have a full container if the foods are packed raw. Precooking permits the shrinkage to take place before the container is filled.

Lack of liquid in the jar may be due to a tight pack that leaves no room for added liquid. A tight seal may sometimes be the cause, for as steam forms, considerable pressure is developed before it can escape and then a part of the liquid will escape with it. When a pressure canner is used, fluctuating pressure or rapid lowering of the pressure is likely to cause the liquid to escape.

Spoilage of Canned Food

Spoiled canned foods may differ in odor, flavor, and appearance from canned foods of good quality, and the container also may be affected. Tin cans may exhibit some swelling due to the formation of gas. A "swell" or a "hydrogen swell" is a can with bulging ends due to the formation of considerable gas, in the first instance by microorganisms and in the second by chemical reaction. A "springer" is a mild swell or hydrogen swell, and a "flipper" is a can in which only a small amount of gas has formed. "Flat sour" is a type of spoilage caused by growth of microorganisms without the formation of gas. The food usually tastes sour and may have a sour odor. "Leakers" are cans in which the seal is broken for any one of several reasons, for example, improper sealing at the time of processing, perforation from the inside, or rusting of the outside of the can.

Botulism is the term applied to a type of food poisoning caused by the toxin of *Clostridium botulinum*, a term dating from a particular outbreak of food poisoning early in the nineteenth century. In its early history botulism was associated with the eating of spoiled meats, but more recently vegetables seem to have been the chief bearers of the toxin. Home-canned foods are now more frequently responsible for the outbreaks of botulism than commercially canned foods. Green beans, corn, pork products, spinach, asparagus, beets, peppers, beef products, seafoods, pears, apricots, figs, okra, chicken, and beans are among the foods which have been responsible for botulism. The spores of the organism have been known to withstand heating at 100° C. (212° F.) for as long as five hours.

It is never wise to taste home-canned meats and vegetables before heating. Boiling destroys the toxin produced by *Clostridium botulinum*, the most serious of the poisonings encountered in canned foods. Hence if the food is boiled for some time before tasting (meat, corn, and spinach for twenty minutes; other low-acid vegetables for ten minutes), there is little danger of botulism. Without preliminary heating the use of the home-canned foods listed above in the preparation of salads may prove disastrous.

Causes of
Spoilage or
Deterioration

Most of the spoilage in canning is due to inadequate processing. Despite the use of approved methods the food may not be sterilized during canning because of any of the following: the food is packed too tightly in the container; the food is allowed to stand too long before canning and is high in bacterial content; the length of the processing period is counted incorrectly; or the canner is not at the proper temperature. Excess contamination may require longer heating. Improper manipulation of the packed food outside of the processor is sometimes responsible for spoilage. Allowing packed hot food to stand for some time before processing encourages the development of thermophilic bacteria[4] and souring frequently occurs. The same type of spoilage sometimes occurs in certain foods after canning if the containers are not cooled in a reasonable length of time. Delay in sealing the containers after the food is processed and containers which do not give a tight seal may result in food spoilage. Storage of food in warm places also greatly increases the chances of spoilage.

Deterioration of canned foods may be due to chemical action. Food in the top of the container may darken if not covered with liquid. Darkening of corn or the developing of dark deposits in corn or peas may be due to the formation of iron sulfide or copper sulfide. The iron or copper may come from the cooking utensils, from the water, or from the container. When canning in tin cans, such discoloration is largely controlled by the use of enamel-lined cans, previously mentioned, which tend to prevent the formation of these sulfides. Corrosion and even perforation of the can, which occurs in some instances, is especially evident with acid fruits such as apples, plums, and berries, and is not unknown with low- or medium-acid foods such as pumpkin. Although many conditions affect the rate of corrosion, one of the most important means of controlling it is the removal of oxygen prior to sealing by effectively exhausting the can.

Activities

1. Can fruits, vegetables, and meats by the can-cooked method.

2. Compare the cost and quality of the food thus canned with that of the commercially canned product.

References

AYRES, J. C., A. A. KRAFT, H. E. SNYDER, and H. W. WALKER (Eds.). *Chemical and Biological Hazards in Foods.* Ames: Iowa State University Press. 1962.

FRAZIER, W. C. *Food Microbiology,* 2nd ed. New York: McGraw-Hill Book Company, Inc. 1967.

GRISWOLD, R. M. *The Experimental Study of Foods.* Boston: Houghton Mifflin Company. 1962. Pp. 211–217.

[4] Thermophilic bacteria live and develop at a temperature much higher than that suitable for other bacteria. These bacteria grow best at a range of 45° to 71° C. (113° to 160° F.).

Home Canning of Fruits and Vegetables. U.S. Dept. Agr., Home and Garden Bull. No. 8 (1969).

Home Canning of Meat and Poultry. U.S. Dept. Agr., Home and Garden Bull. No. 106 (1970).

Pressure Canners, Use and Care. U.S. Dept. Agr., Home and Garden Bull. No. 30 (1953).

The Almanac of Canning, Freezing and Preserving Industries. Westminster, Md.: Edward E. Judge and Sons. 1971.

31

home preservation by freezing

The ease with which foods may be prepared for freezing and the high quality of properly handled frozen foods have helped make them popular with the homemaker and her family. Home freezers, freezing compartments in refrigerators, and locker plants have all contributed to the wide use of frozen products. Today about the only foods not available in frozen form are the crisp, succulent foods which are served raw as relishes or salads. The freezing of prepared and precooked foods has expanded rapidly in recent years, probably due in part to the convenience of the home freezer. Many foods that require a large number of ingredients and considerable time to prepare may be made in quantities, part to be served immediately and the remainder, properly packaged, to be frozen for later use.

Selecting and Preparing the Food

Much the same guides can be observed in selecting fresh food for preservation by freezing as for canning. Only food of high quality should be frozen. Fruits and vegetables free from all signs of spoilage, bruises, and decay, and at the stage of maturity or ripeness most desirable for eating or cooking give best results.

Not all kinds and varieties of fruits and vegetables are equally desirable for preservation by freezing. Probably the best way to find out what varieties are suitable in a particular locale is to write to the nearest state experiment station or Cooperative Extension Service. Varieties adapted to one locality and suitable for freezing may not do well in another part of the country.

Meat should be of high quality, but it is probably not necessary, and in some instances not even desirable, to freeze it within a few hours after slaughter. Beef and lamb may be hung in the cooler for a period of from five to seven days to allow enzymatic changes (ripening) to take place. Pork and veal should be thoroughly chilled for one or two days after slaughter. Poultry should be thoroughly chilled, and some research indicates that holding for twelve hours in the refrigerator before freezing helps to assure tenderness. Fish are best frozen as soon as possible after they are caught.

Because freezing does not sterilize food, everything possible should be done to reduce bacterial contamination. Fruits and vegetables should be carefully and thoroughly washed, and made ready to cook or serve before freezing. Small fruits such as berries may be left whole, or they may be crushed or sliced. Fruits like peaches are peeled and pitted, and then left in halves, sliced, or crushed. Fruit purees keep well and have a number of uses. Vegetables such as cauliflower and broccoli should be divided into portions suitable for serving, beans should be snipped and may be broken, and asparagus may be broken into lengths as desired. Vegetables must be scalded or blanched before freezing in order to inactivate the enzymes in the plant tissue. This is not necessary for other types of food, although some studies indicate that certain fruits such as apples and blueberries may keep better if scalded. Heating must be long enough so that every part of the food reaches the desired temperature. If this is not done, small amounts of enzymes will be left which will soon cause deterioration of all the food in the container. On the other hand, if heating is too prolonged, the loss of vitamins increases, the fresh flavor is lost, and the quality decreases.

The scalding period recommended for different vegetables varies depending upon the vegetable and the size of the pieces. The range in time recommended for individual vegetables in Table 31–1 is due to the difference in size of pieces. Sufficient water should be used so there is little drop in temperature when the vegetables are added. At least one gallon of water to

Table 31–1. *Recommended Time for Scalding Vegetables in Boiling Water* *

Product	Time Required for Scalding	
Asparagus	2–4 minutes	(variation is due to size of stalks)
Lima beans	2–4 minutes	
Snap beans	3 minutes	
Broccoli	3 minutes	(flowerets not more than 1½ inches across)
Cauliflower	3 minutes	(broken or cut into pieces 1 inch across)
Peas	1½ minutes	
Spinach	1½–2 minutes	(variation due to size and tenderness of leaves)
Corn on cob	7–11 minutes	(some of the variation is due to size of ears) †
Cut corn	4 minutes	(blanch before cutting)

* *Home Freezing of Fruits and Vegetables.* Home and Garden Bulletin No. 10, Agricultural Research Service, United States Department of Agriculture, 1970.

† Not recommended for general practice as the results are often disappointing and valuable space is wasted.

a pound of vegetables is recommended. Immediately after scalding, the vegetables should be plunged into fresh, cold water and thoroughly chilled.

Meat should be cut into portions of a suitable size for cooking. These may be steaks, roasts, cubes for stews, or other shapes as desired. For economical use of space the bone may be removed from the meat prior to wrapping. The bones may be used for making soup or broth, which may be concentrated and frozen for later use. Ready-to-cook poultry may be frozen whole, in halves, or in serving-size pieces. Fish may be frozen whole as they come from the water, or drawn, or dressed. They may also be frozen as steaks or fillets.

In many homes prepared and precooked foods, both home and commercially prepared, probably occupy a greater portion of the freezer space than do fresh frozen foods. Popular precooked and prepared foods include: soups, a number of vegetables, certain fruits, meat dishes of various types (preferably covered with a sauce), combination dishes such as chicken à la king and meat stews, sandwiches, quick breads, yeast breads, cakes of all types, puddings, cookies, and pies.

The same principles observed in the freezing of fruits, vegetables, and meats should be used for ready-to-eat foods. A good quality raw product must be used. Special ingredients are sometimes recommended: for example, in making sauces waxy rice flour may be substituted for wheat flour as a thickening agent to prevent texture changes due to freezing. Precautions should be taken not to over-cook ready-to-eat foods. Slight under-cooking of those which will be reheated for serving is probably a good practice. Flour mixtures may be baked before freezing or immediately before serving, although more often recommendations are given for baking before freezing, with the possible exception of pies. Since either method seems to give acceptable results with pies, homemakers may need to experiment in order to determine which one suits their needs.

Selecting the Container

A great variety of materials are suitable for packaging foods for freezing. Although a hermetic seal is not essential, it is important that loss of moisture from the package be prevented and that as much air as possible be excluded to reduce the possibility of oxidation. Hence a container or packaging material that is moisture-vapor-proof is desirable for retaining high quality in frozen food. Many packaging materials available for frozen foods are not moisture-vapor-proof but many are sufficiently moisture-vapor-resistant to give satisfactory results. Rigid containers of aluminum, glass, tin, plastic, or heavily waxed cardboard are suitable for many foods but are especially desirable for semi-liquid, precooked foods such as soups, stews, and combination dishes, and for fruits covered with a syrup. Wrapping materials and bags recommended for freezer storage may be of heavy aluminum foil, pliofilm, polyethylene, laminated papers, or other materials or combinations of materials. They should be durable and not crack at low temperatures.

Almost every type of container and packaging material has certain points to recommend it. The choice then depends upon availability, cost, nature of food to be frozen, and ease of handling by individual user. For example, vegetables, which are usually emptied from the container while hard-frozen, should be frozen in a container with no constriction or inset at the top. In the case of fruits that are often thawed in the package in which they are frozen, it is especially important that the container be designed so that the syrup will not leak. Visibility of the product may often be desirable but is not essential. Flexibility and ease of shaping to the product are important factors in selecting material for wrapping. Ease of sealing is also to be considered, whether the sealing is done by means of tape, heat, or rubber band. Containers that stack well in the freezer make for economical use of freezer space.

Packaging Food

Liquid foods or those covered with a liquid such as fruits packed in a syrup will expand when frozen. Allowance is made for this by leaving a head space of one-half to one and one-half inches in rigid containers. Large containers with narrow top openings require the greater head space. Foods packed dry may not require head space but in some instances a one-half-inch head space may be recommended.

Sealing the container or the package should be carefully done to prevent loss of moisture and exposure to air. The sealed container or package should be clearly labeled. It is well to keep a record of foods frozen and of those used.

Fruits. Fruits for freezing may be divided into two classes. One class contains those fruits which may be cleaned and prepared whole and which are not subject to discoloration when exposed to oxygen. These include a number of the small fruits. Some, such as blueberries and cranberries, are suitable for dry pack freezing but most are packed in sugar or syrup.

The other group includes fruits which must be pitted or peeled, or both, before freezing. These tend to discolor when exposed to the air. Fruits of this class, excepting cherries which may be packed in sugar, are usually packed in a syrup. The syrup tends to retard discoloration by covering the fruit and excluding the air. The use of ascorbic acid is effective in retarding color changes of certain fruits, both before freezing and during the process of thawing. The ascorbic acid may be added with sugar directly to the fruit, but it may be more effective when added with a syrup. Although the amount of ascorbic acid required will vary, the most usual recommendation is for one-half teaspoon (1,500 mg.) of ascorbic acid to each quart of syrup. More may be used for apricots or pears. When a syrup is used the ascorbic acid should be added to the cold syrup immediately before pouring over the fruit. This prevents unnecessary oxidation of the ascorbic acid. Various commercial preparations also are available that may be added to the syrup to prevent fruit discoloration. When these are used, the directions for the product should be followed. The sugar concentration of syrups may vary from 30 to 60 per cent. However, for most fruits a 40 per cent syrup made of three cups of sugar to four cups of water is recommended. The fruit is placed in the container, the syrup is poured over it, and the mixture allowed to stand in a cold place long enough for the syrup to penetrate into the fruit. Because the added water in the syrup tends to dilute flavor, fruits packed in this way may be less desirable for use in pies, jellies, and preserves than those packed with sugar only. For this reason many persons prefer to use sugar even with such fruits as peaches which discolor easily.

Freezing with sugar is said to be the oldest and most commonly used method of freezing small fruits. Fruits frozen with sugar may be whole, sliced, or crushed. Although the proportions will vary with the fruit and the type of product desired, it is important to remember that the higher the sugar content, the lower the freezing point. The fruit and sugar should be mixed thoroughly and allowed to stand until all sugar is dissolved and enough syrup is formed to cover the fruit when packed. This will require a longer time for whole fruit than for sliced or crushed.

Although fruits may be packed dry, with sugar, or with syrup, as a rule fruits have better texture if sweetened before freezing. Some small fruits may be satisfactorily packed dry, and others desired for use in pies, jellies, jams, preserves, or for special diets may also be packed dry. Because fruit packed dry is easily dehydrated, the packs should be tightly sealed and kept at a constant low temperature. An advantage of the dry-pack method is that it does not necessitate the freezing and storage of sugar or syrup. It is particularly suitable for short storage periods.

Meat and Fish. Meat and fish may be wrapped in suitable moisture-vapor-resistant packaging material. Place two layers of waxed paper between chops, steaks, and fillets so that individual frozen pieces can be separated easily, then package. Pull wrapping material tightly around meat to drive out air; make package smooth and seal seam by folding edges together. Fold ends and tape.

Poultry. Poultry may be packaged in wrapping materials as described for meat and fish, in bags, or in rigid containers. The choice of package will depend in part on whether whole or cut-up poultry is being frozen.

Vegetables. Vegetables are packed dry. Improved packaging materials as well as improved storage conditions make the added protection of a brine no longer necessary. Vegetables are much easier to handle both before and after freezing when packed dry.

Prepared and Precooked Foods. The method of packaging prepared and precooked foods will depend upon the food. Baked cookies, breads of all types, sandwiches, and unfrosted cakes may be carefully wrapped and frozen. Frosted cakes, unbaked pies, and some other foods may be frozen and then wrapped. Both fruit and meat pies, and many types of casserole dishes may be packaged in the containers in which they will be heated for serving. Many other prepared foods are satisfactorily packed in regular freezer-storage containers.

Freezing and Storing

The necessity for prompt freezing of fruits and vegetables cannot be over-emphasized. If the delay between harvesting and freezing is prolonged, freshness is impaired, sugars in such vegetables as peas and corn change to starch, vitamins are lost, and bacteria and other microorganisms multiply. For short periods of unavoidable delay the food should be kept as cold as possible.

Vegetables should be frozen immediately after scalding and chilling. If for any reason this process is interrupted, the food should be kept cold, that is, just above the freezing point. Fruits when packed with sugar or syrup should be allowed to stand just long enough to allow the sugar to dissolve and the syrup to penetrate the fruit. They should be kept cold. Meat should be kept cold and, after being cut and packaged, should then be frozen as soon as expedient.

Because of the number of factors involved, definite recommendations for the best freezing temperature cannot be given. However, as discussed in Chapter 29, rapid freezing of most products is important. It is wise to put no more unfrozen food in the home freezer than will freeze in 24 hours. More rapid freezing is desirable. The storage temperature should be $-18°$ C. ($0°$ F.) or below and should not fluctuate. Frozen foods deteriorate with storage even when all conditions are favorable. Probably few foods should be held for as long as twelve months and for most of them shorter periods are advisable.[1]

Preparing Frozen Foods for Serving

Except that thawing is required, frozen foods are prepared for serving much as fresh foods. The best practice for cooking most frozen vegetables is to drop the hard frozen vegetables into a very small amount of rapidly boiling water. Experimental work indicates that the color and food value of frozen vegetables are not affected by covering the utensil while cooking, and thawing and cooking are probably more rapid in a covered utensil. It is usually

[1] *Home Care of Purchased Frozen Foods.* Home and Garden Bulletin No. 69. United States Department of Agriculture, Washington, D.C., 1967. Although recommendations are for commercially frozen foods, the home storage periods recommended may also serve as a guide for home processed foods.

Fig. 31–1. To home-freeze strawberries in dry sugar:
Select fruit that is fresh, without bruises or decay, and of the right degree of ripeness.

Wash the fruit in cold water, handling them gently. Lift from the water and drain. Fruit should not be allowed to stand in the water. Remove leaves and stems.

Unless freezing whole fruit, slice the strawberries and spread them in a shallow dish.

Add the sugar and gently turn the fruit over and over until the sugar dissolves and juice is formed.

Put the fruit and the syrup which forms into airtight containers. Shake the container to pack the fruit as closely as possible without crushing. A $1/_2$ inch head space should be left because food expands as it freezes.

Wipe the tops of the containers with a clean, damp cloth. Cover tightly and label, indicating the type of pack and the date of freezing. Freeze as quickly as possible after packing.

Courtesy of the U.S. Department of Agriculture

better not to thaw vegetables prior to cooking to prevent possible loss of vitamin content and spoilage. There are a few exceptions: corn-on-the-cob if not thawed before cooking will be either over-cooked or icy in the center. Also cooking of leafy vegetables such as spinach will be more uniform if thawed just enough to separate the leaves. Care should be taken to see that frozen vegetables are not over-cooked. The blanching and freezing of food affect the fiber and therefore frozen vegetables cook in much less time than fresh ones. Because blanching and freezing do not render food sterile, frozen vegetables must always be cooked before they are eaten or even tasted, and they should be cooked promptly when taken from storage.

Many frozen fruits are served without cooking. They should be thawed just before time to serve them. Fruits such as strawberries and raspberries may even be served while still in the partially frozen or "mushy" stage. Peaches tend to darken rapidly after thawing. Frozen fruits which are to be used in cooked food such as pies, jams, or preserves are more easily handled if at least partially thawed.

Fig. 31–2. *Food for the lunchbox can be frozen in quantity ahead of time, and individual packages removed from the freezer as needed. The date indicates when the package was frozen.*

Courtesy of Saran Wrap

Meat, including fish and poultry, may or may not be thawed before cooking is begun. As was mentioned in Chapter 10, the length of the cooking period must be increased when the meat is not thawed before cooking. Research on the cooking of frozen meat indicates that the method of thawing— whether at room temperature, or in the refrigerator, warming oven, or oven —has little effect upon the quality of the cooked meat.

The handling of prepared and precooked foods will depend upon the product. Although some ready-to-eat foods may be thawed at room temperature and served, most main dishes, soups, and many other foods to be served hot may be heated in the oven, in the top of a double boiler, or over low heat. Care should be taken not to over-cook these foods. Fruit pies if frozen unbaked of course must be baked; but if baked before frozen they may be thawed at room temperature or they may be reheated in the oven. Many persons believe that with the latter procedure the product more nearly resembles the freshly baked one.

Quantity of Frozen Produce from Fresh Food

The yield of frozen vegetables from the fresh produce is approximately that given for canned foods in Table 30–2. The yield of frozen fruits may vary for fruits for freezing are usually not heated and therefore there is less shrinkage than in canning. Meats, poultry, and fish change little in quantity unless excess fat and bones are discarded. Table 31–2 shows the approximate yield of cuts from a side of beef of Yield Grade 3.

Causes of Inferior Product

Some of the factors which affect the quality of frozen foods are the quality of the food selected, the way the food is handled prior to packaging, the method of packaging, the speed with which the food freezes, and the temperature and length of time of storage.

As previously mentioned, some varieties of fruits and vegetables are better adapted to preservation by freezing than others. Also, foods that are held too long before freezing may be inferior in quality because of changes that occur on standing. Corn that is too mature, asparagus that is woody, strawberries that are soft and watery, and blackberries that are dry and seedy will not yield a high quality frozen product. Peas and other green vegetables blanched for too short a time tend to develop a "strawy" odor and flavor and to lose color during frozen storage.

Packaging materials should give proper protection to foods so that they will not dry out or be exposed to air, as this causes undesirable changes in almost all types of frozen foods. Freezing foods too slowly may give poor results, but slow freezing is not as likely to occur in a properly operated locker plant as in the home freezer where the addition of a large quantity of unfrozen food may result in some packages remaining unfrozen for many hours. Too large a package size may also result in slow freezing.

Table 31–2. *Approximate Yields of Cuts from Beef Quarters * (300 lb. Side, Yield Grade 3)*

	% of Quarter	Pounds
Hindquarter (144 lbs.)		
Round Steak	18.8	27.0
Rump Roast (Boneless)	6.9	9.9
Porterhouse, T-Bone, Club Steaks	10.6	15.3
Sirloin Steak	17.3	24.9
Flank Steak	1.0	1.5
Lean Trim	14.6	21.0
Kidney	.6	.9
Waste (fat, bone, and shrinkage)	30.2	43.5
Total hindquarter	100.0	144.0
Forequarter (156 lbs.)		
Rib Roast (7″ cut)	11.7	18.3
Blade Chuck Roast	17.1	26.7
Arm Chuck Roast (Boneless)	11.2	17.4
Brisket (Boneless)	4.0	6.3
Lean Trim	31.6	49.2
Waste (fat, bone, and shrinkage)	24.4	38.1
Total forequarter	100.0	156.0

* *How to Buy Meat for Your Freezer.* Home and Garden Bulletin No. 166, Consumer and Marketing Service, United States Department of Agriculture, 1969.

A high storage temperature as well as a fluctuating temperature may result in food of inferior quality. If a uniformly low storage temperature of at least −18° C. (0° F.) cannot be maintained, frozen foods should be held for relatively short periods. Even at −18° C. (0° F.) prolonged storage will result in loss of quality.

Activities

1. Prepare and freeze typical fruits, vegetables, and meats.

2. Prepare and freeze suitable fruits with and without the addition of ascorbic acid.

3. Use and compare different kinds of packaging materials.

4. Compare home and commercially prepared products of the same kind. Note the form, color, firmness or mushiness, and flavor of the products.

5. Prepare two packages of a green vegetable for freezing. Freeze one in the freezing compartment of a one-door refrigerator, the other in a home freezer. After one month of storage in the same area where frozen, cook and compare quality.

References

FRAZIER, W. C. *Food Microbiology,* 2nd ed. New York: McGraw-Hill Book Company, Inc. 1967.

Freezing Combination Main Dishes. U.S. Dept. Agr., Home and Garden Bull. No. 40 (1965).

Freezing Meat and Fish in the Home. U.S. Dept. Agr., Home and Garden Bull. No. 93 (1970).

GRISWOLD, R. M. *The Experimental Study of Foods.* Boston: Houghton Mifflin and Company. 1962. Pp. 217–228.

HESELTINE, M. and U. M. Dow. *The New Basic Cookbook,* rev. ed. Boston: Houghton Mifflin Company. 1967.

Home Freezers, Their Selection and Use. U.S. Dept. Agr., Home and Garden Bull. No. 48 (1970).

Home Freezing of Fruits and Vegetables. U.S. Dept. Agr., Home and Garden Bull. No. 10 (1970).

Home Freezing of Poultry. U.S. Dept. Agr., Home and Garden Bull. No. 70 (1970).

How to Buy Meat for Your Freezer. U.S. Dept. Agr., Home and Garden Bull. No. 166 (1969).

32

jelly

Jelly is a fruit product familiar to everyone, yet because different products are termed "jelly," a description of good fruit jelly may be useful. Goldthwaite gives the following description: "Ideal fruit jelly is a beautifully colored, transparent, palatable product obtained by so treating fruit juice that the resulting mass will quiver, not flow, when removed from its mold; a product with texture so tender that it cuts easily with a spoon, and yet so firm that the angles thus produced retain their shape; a clear product that is neither syrupy, gummy, sticky, nor tough; neither is it brittle and yet it will break, and does this with a distinct, beautiful cleavage which leaves sparkling characteristic faces. This is that delicious, appetizing substance, a good fruit jelly." [1]

Essentials for Jelly-making

Good jelly contains pectin, sugar, and acid dissolved in water, each bearing a definite relationship to all of the other ingredients. To obtain such a product requires considerable skill in determining the jellying qualities of the fruit, the proportion of sugar to use, and the degree of cooking necessary. As mentioned previously, fruits contain a number of substances including sugar, organic acids, various minerals, cellulose, pectin, volatile oils responsible for the flavors, some color pigments, and vitamins. Found in the juice are flavoring substances, acids, some minerals, natural fruit sugars, pigments, and pectic substances. Only the juice is used in jelly-making and therefore it is the soluble substances of the fruit that determine its jellying power. The presence or absence of pectin is an important factor in determining the suitability of a fruit for jelly-making. An attempt to make fruit jelly without pectin is comparable to an attempt to make a gelatin dessert without gelatin.

Pectin is a carbohydrate-like substance found in fruits. Protopectin is found in underripe fruit, and as the fruit ripens the protopectin changes to pectin. If ripening continues, the pectin is changed possibly to pectic acid and alcohol. It is believed that the largest amount of pectin is present in

[1] N. E. Goldthwaite. *The Principles of Jelly-Making*. University of Illinois Bulletin 31, 1914.

fruit when it is slightly underripe. Neither protopectin nor pectic acid has jellying properties; hence it is best to use the fruit when either slightly underripe or just ripe. However, underripe fruits lack the natural fruit flavor of ripe fruits.

Not all fruits, even when slightly underripe, contain pectin in appreciable amounts. Pectin is precipitated by alcohol, and use is made of this fact in testing fruit juices for pectin. A given amount of the juice, about one tablespoon, is added to an equal amount of alcohol (90 to 95 per cent) and mixed. The amount of precipitate formed indicates the amount of pectin present in the juice. With little or no precipitate there is insufficient pectin for making jelly, but when a heavy precipitate is formed there is sufficient pectin. If the juice to be used is deficient in pectin, either a commercial or homemade pectin concentrate or another fruit juice which is rich in pectin, such as apple juice, is added.

A fruit juice ideal for jelly-making contains acid. No simple home test for determining the acidity of fruit juice has been developed. Fruit juice as tart as the juice of sour apples is said to be of the correct acidity, but obviously this standard is indefinite. Juices lacking in acid may need additions in the form of lemon juice or commercial citric or tartaric acid. Fruits which contain sufficient pectin and acid for jelly-making include certain varieties of grapes, crab apples, cranberries, currants, gooseberries, grapefruit, lemons, limes, loganberries, sour apples, sour blackberries, sour guavas, sour oranges, and sour plums. Fruits rich in pectin but lacking in acid include sweet guavas, quinces, and sweet apples. Among those high in acid but low in pectin are apricots, pineapples, rhubarb, sour peaches, and strawberries. Bananas, elderberries, and pears are low in both pectin and acid.

Effects of Ingredients

There are many theories as to the physical-chemical structure of jelly, but perhaps the most generally accepted is that as the jelly is formed, the pectin is precipitated to give an intricate network within which the syrup is held. The strength of the network depends upon the concentration of the pectin, hence in a dilute solution the network may be so weak that the syrup is not held firmly enough to form a true gel. The presence of acid results in a firmer gel. Acid may toughen the network and thus make the jelly firmer. On the other hand, jellies which are high in acid tend to "weep," or show syneresis. Sugar may act as the precipitating agent, causing the pectin to form the network of the jelly.

Jelly may be deep red, purple, pale pink or some other color, depending upon the color of the fruit juice. Occasionally artificial coloring is added, but this is seldom done when jelly is made in the home. The flavor varies with the kind of fruit used as well as with the degree of ripeness. The clearness or transparency of the jelly is largely determined by the care taken in extracting and straining the juice, though the ripeness of the fruit is also a factor. Green fruit contains considerable starch, some of which may remain in the juice giving a cloudy appearance. Jellies made from fruit juice are more likely to be clear and sparkling than are artificial jellies made of pectin concentrate, acid, sugar, and flavoring material, because salts, such as are present in fruits, are a valuable aid in obtaining these qualities. The consistency of jelly is largely dependent upon the proportions of pectin, acid, sugar, and water, but certain salts also play an important role.

Certain proportions give what is known as a good jelly. Studies to determine what effect variations in the proportions may have upon the jelly show that when all other factors remain unchanged, increasing the pectin or the acid[2] increases the stiffness or strength of the jelly, whereas increasing the sugar decreases it. Yet each of these findings is true only within certain limits. The flavor and color as well as the strength of the jelly are affected by the method of extracting the pectin. Boiling longer than thirty minutes is undesirable. Boiling pectin in the presence of acid is more injurious before the sugar is added than afterward. Long boiling is harmful to flavor, strength, and color. Therefore, several short extractions are preferable to one long one.

The percentage of sugar in the finished jelly is practically constant regardless of the amount added within the limits used for jelly-making. Therefore, to a large extent the amount of sugar added determines the yield of jelly. However, the acidity of the juice definitely affects the amount of sugar that can be safely added. All jellies are practically saturated sugar solutions; consequently the boiling point of the finished product varies only within a limited range, 103° to 105° C. (217° to 221° F.) being the accepted temperature range. Because the boiling point is affected by atmospheric pressure, perhaps a more accurate test is 4.5° C. (8° F.) above the boiling point of water—as determined just prior to making the jelly. Even with the recommended concentration of soluble solids, excellent jelly results only when the ratio of pectin to acid to sugar is within certain limits.

Effect of Quantity

As a rule, better results are obtained when the quantity cooked at one time is not too large. One or two quarts are a satisfactory amount to use. However, Carlsson says that "when fruit juice from the same source was used, fully as good results were secured with a large recipe as with a smaller one."[3] She does not state the quantity used.

Extracting the Juice

In some raw fruit juices pectin may not be found at all or only in small quantities, yet juices from these fruits when cooked may contain it in abundance. With all fruits containing pectin, the juice obtained by cooking is richer in pectin than that obtained by cold extraction.

[2] The hydrogen ion concentration, not the total acidity.

[3] Victoria Carlsson. A Comparative Study of Jellies and Jams Made With and Without an Extracted Pectin. *Teachers College Record*, Vol. 28, Part II: 784–794 (April, 1927).

If the fruit to be used for jelly is soft and juicy, as with raspberries and grapes, only enough water to prevent burning need be added. The fruit may be crushed to aid the extraction of the juice. It is helpful to cut more solid fruits like quinces and apples into one-eighth-inch slices across the fruit; from one-half to equal parts of water is then added. Citrus fruits, after being cut in thin slices, may have two or three times their volume of water added. Fruit low in acid should have acid added before the juice is extracted. The acid is apparently of value in freeing the pectin from the tissues.

The time of cooking varies. With soft fruits, such as berries, 2 or 3 minutes of boiling may be adequate. Firm fruits, such as apples and quinces, may yield the best quality juice when cooked 15 to 20 minutes; oranges and other citrus fruits may require from 30 to 60 minutes. After cooking, the mass is transferred to a cheesecloth wrung out of hot water or to a fine-meshed sieve and allowed to drain. This makes the first extraction. A second extraction may often be made of fruits rich in pectin, such as currants, loganberries, cranberries, and lemons. In this case, fruit is returned to the kettle in which it was previously cooked, covered with water, and mixed thoroughly. Again it should be heated slowly to boiling, and again drained. This may result in much or little pectin. If the second extraction is high in pectin, a third extraction may be made in the same way as the second. Usually not more than three extractions are made. The juice from the first extraction is highest in flavor and pectin, and it is recommended that it be used alone in making jelly. The second and third extractions will yield juices progressively lower in both flavor and pectin. These may be used separately or combined, depending upon the quantity of the juice and the time available. After the juice has been drained through the cheesecloth or sieve, it may be strained again, this time through a bag made of linen, cotton flannel, or cheesecloth. Each time the juice should be allowed to drain through freely; the pulp should never be pressed or squeezed.

Using Added Pectin

Extracted pectin or pectin concentrate is frequently added to fruit juices in the making of jelly. This is undoubtedly a desirable practice if juices low in pectin are to be used. Although directions were once readily available for the homemade pectin concentrate, today the commercial preparation is used almost entirely. It is a consistent product that produces jellies of high quality and actually adds little to the cost. A comparative study of jellies made with and without added pectin showed that, even when the cost of pectin was included, jellies made with extracted pectin cost less per glass than jellies from the same fruits made without the extracted pectin.[4] In most cases, at least twice as much jelly was made from the same quantity of juice when pectin was added. Although the extracted pectin may be prepared from both apples and citrus fruits, today the commercial pectins are obtained almost

[4] Carlsson.

entirely from citrus peel. Both liquid and powdered forms are available. Because directions for their use varies, package directions for the order of combining the ingredients and the timing should be accurately followed. Only a one-minute boiling period may be recommended. The prepared pectin in the liquid form has limited keeping qualities, and once exposed to the air it must be used shortly or it will deteriorate. Pectin in the powdered form keeps longer and the entire package need not be used as soon as opened. However, since it too has limited keeping qualities, it should not be held from one year to the next.

The use of extracted pectin not only makes it possible to prepare jelly from fruits low in pectin, but also greatly shortens the preparation time. This results in more jelly because as the time of boiling is materially lessened, the amount of evaporation is less. Jelly made with extracted pectin is usually bright in color and transparent. Added pectin practically ensures a jelly which jells, but because the fruit varies in pectin content, sometimes too stiff a jelly may be formed.

Directions have been developed for making uncooked jellies using frozen juice concentrates, such as orange, grape, or tangerine, with extracted pectin. The result is a delicate gel with the fresh fruit flavor well retained. However, due to the fact that it is not sterilized, uncooked jelly has limited keeping qualities and must be stored in the refrigerator or the freezer.

Proportions

It is not possible to formulate satisfactory recipes for making jelly without added pectin. Because even the same kind of fruit varies in pectin content in different sections of the country and in different seasons, the same results cannot be obtained with exactly the same proportions from year to year. However, it helps to understand the reasons for success or failure in jelly-making and to know the methods which most frequently give good results. As Goldthwaite wrote years ago, "Good jellies cannot be made from all juices by rule o' thumb. Jelly-making as practiced in the home is an art—an art founded on scientific principles. It consists in so controlling results by means of sugar and acid, and by boiling, as to cause the pectin to 'set' in a continuous mass throughout the volume allotted to it."[5] This uncertainty regarding the quality of jelly made only from fruit juice and sugar is undoubtedly an important reason for the wide use of commercial pectin today.

Adding the Sugar

The use of the jelmeter, an instrument which measures the viscosity of the extracted juice, frequently is of value in determining the correct proportion of sugar to juice. Juice with a high pectin content is more viscous and therefore runs through the capillary tube in the jelmeter more slowly than juice low in pectin. The point on the jelmeter that the juice reaches in a given time will indicate the appropriate proportion of sugar to be added to the juice. If the juice is at the highest mark after running from the jelmeter for one

[5] Goldthwaite.

Fig. 32–1. *The jelmeter aids in determining the amount of sugar desirable for making jelly from a specific juice.*

Courtesy of Jelmeter, Inc.

minute, one and one-fourth parts of sugar should be added to one part of juice. If the juice has run to the mark designated as one-half, then one-half as much sugar should be used as juice. If the juice is so thin that it runs below the one-half mark, it will undoubtedly require the addition of pectin concentrate to make good jelly.

Applying the alcohol test to the juice to determine the amount of pectin present is also helpful in determining the amount of sugar to be added. Making samples of jelly with different proportions of sugar and juice is another method. Jelly of the juice from the first extraction, if obtained from a fruit high in pectin and acid, may be made with the sugar and juice in the ratio of 3/4:1 or 1:1. The juice from the second and third extractions will require much less sugar. Often the ratio of 1/8:1 or 1/4:1 is satisfactory. Unless too much sugar is used, the jelly from the later extractions should be of about the same quality as that from the first extraction.

The time of adding the sugar to the juice requires consideration. Since research indicates that boiling the fruit after the sugar has been added has much less effect on the pectin than if the juice alone is boiled, recipes frequently call for adding the sugar at the beginning of the cooking period.

When sugar is added at the beginning of the cooking period, however, much inversion may occur from boiling the sugar with the fruit acid. Such inversion affects the texture of the jelly and causes a syrupy consistency. This problem may be offset by cooking the jelly in small quantities so that an unduly long cooking period is not required. When the sugar is added near the end of the cooking period, little inversion of the sugar will occur and the sucrose will remain much in its original form; therefore crystallization is more likely to result. If the right proportion of sugar has been used, the syrup will jell when cool if cooked to the proper degree. But if incorrect proportions are used, the syrup will probably not jell at any concentration.

Testing for Sufficient Cooking

Cooking the syrup just the right amount is important. Many tests are given for determining the exact degree, and each requires some practice. A traditional test is to place a sample on a cold dish and allow it to cool. With this test there is little danger of undercooking but great danger of overcooking, for while the sample is cooling the cooking continues. The spoon or sheet test is perhaps the most used test for sufficient cooking; when a cool metal spoon is dipped into the boiling jelly and the syrup runs off the spoon as two drops which flow together to form a sheet, the sugar is concentrated enough to form jelly. Some homemakers test by dipping a silver fork into the syrup. When the syrup forms a sheet between the tines it is cooked sufficiently. The appearance of the bubbles as the jelly boils is another fair indication. A few large bubbles that tend to jump out of the kettle, rather than uniformly small ones, indicate relatively higher concentration of the syrup. But the most accurate measure for telling when jelly is done is to use a thermometer. The temperature is an indication of the concentration of the sugar. When the syrup boils at 4.5° C. (8° F.) above the boiling point of water, jelly will form if the right proportions have been used.

Fig. 32–2. *Sheet Test for testing jellying point. Dip a cool metal spoon into the boiling jelly mixture. When jelly leaves the spoon two drops at a time or in a sheet, the sugar is concentrated enough to form jelly. (Ball Blue Book, Ball Brothers Company, Muncie, Indiana, 1969, p. 67.)*

 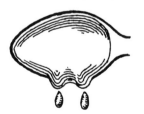 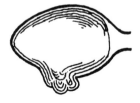

Jelly drops first are light and sirupy.

Then they become heavier and show signs of sheeting.

When jelly point is reached, the jelly breaks from spoon in a sheet or flake.

Selecting,
Filling, and
Sealing the
Containers

Clean, hot glasses or jars should be used for the jelly. Glasses which are fairly low with a wide base are an excellent choice because they form attractive molds of jelly that will stand upright when turned out of the glass. The jelly should be poured into the containers while hot and covered immediately with a thin layer of hot paraffin or jar lids to make a seal. This protects the jelly from microorganisms, which otherwise will settle on the surface. The jelly should be stored in a cool, dry, dark place and for best flavor used within a few months.

**Causes of
Difficulties**

The greatest cause of failure in jelly-making is the use of too much sugar. An excess causes a soft jelly; a great excess results in a syrup. Soft jelly may also be the result of insufficient cooking, too much or too little acid, lack of pectin, or prolonged boiling with accompanying loss of the pectin.

Tough jelly may be due to too little sugar, too much pectin, or overcooking.

Cloudy jelly is usually due to improper extraction. Straining the juice through a coarse cloth or pressing while straining allows some of the pulp to pass through with the juice. Sometimes green fruit gives a cloudy jelly because of the starch present in the juice.

True jelly does not ferment and seldom molds. However, jelly that does not set or jelly that once sets and later liquefies may ferment.

Syneresis or "weeping" of jelly is frequently the result of using a juice high in acid content.

Crystallization in jelly is most frequently the result of too great a concentration of sugar. Usually it occurs in jelly made from fruits low in acid, thus resulting in little or no inversion taking place. It may also occur when sugar is added near the end of the cooking period. Goldthwaite states that such crystallization is not likely to occur "if the sugar has been originally properly proportioned to the pectin in the juice and if the resulting jelly has been properly sealed up."[6]

Cream of tartar crystals frequently occur in grape jelly. Allowing the juice to stand for twelve to fourteen hours and decanting or straining the cold juice before making the jelly often removes enough of the cream of tartar to prevent the formation of these crystals in the jelly.

Strong flavor and dark color are usually the result of too long a cooking period.

Activities

1. Test fruit juice for pectin, using the jelmeter and the alcohol tests.
2. Prepare jelly using natural fruit juice.
3. Prepare jelly using commercial pectin concentrate.
4. Prepare uncooked jelly using a frozen juice concentrate.

[6] Goldthwaite.

References

BORGSTROM, G. *Principles of Food Science*. Vol. I. *Food Technology*. New York: The Macmillan Company. 1968. Pp. 326–332.

Food. The Yearbook of Agriculture, 1959. U.S. Dept. Agr., Washington, D.C.: United States Government Printing Office.

GRISWOLD, R. M. *The Experimental Study of Foods*. Boston: Houghton Mifflin Company. 1962. Pp. 229–236.

How to Make Jellies, Jams, and Preserves at Home. U.S. Dept. Agr., Home and Garden Bull. No. 56 (1970).

HUGHES, O. and M. BENNION. *Introductory Foods*, 5th ed. New York: The Macmillan Company. 1970.

KERTESZ, Z. I. *The Pectic Substances*. New York: Interscience Publishers, Inc. 1951.

PECKHAM, G. C. *Foundations of Food Preparation*. New York: The Macmillan Company. 1969.

YEATMAN, F. W. and M. C. STEINBARGER. *Home-made Jellies, Jams, and Preserves*. U.S. Dept. Agr., Farmers' Bull. No. 1800 (1967).

preserves, marmalades, conserves, jams, and butters

Preserves, marmalades, conserves, jams, and butters are among the most popular of the food products preserved in the home. Delicious as the commercially manufactured product may be, to many persons it lacks the quality of the "homemade." Because of the high sugar content in most of these products, their keeping qualities are excellent. Acid fruits are most often used; even when low acid fruits are chosen, they are usually combined with the more acid fruits. Besides contributing flavor to the product, the acid aids in preservation. These products or "spreads," with the exception of certain butters, contain added sugar in varying amounts.

Types of Products

Preserves. Preserves contain small whole fruits or larger fruits cut into pieces of uniform size held in a syrup varying from the thickness of honey to a soft jelly. The fruit is preserved with sugar, but the fruit flavor should not be masked by an excess of sugar. The preserves should be plump, glistening, mellow, and clear, and attention given to retaining the original shape of the fruit.

Marmalades. Marmalades have small pieces or thin slices of fruit suspended throughout a smooth, clear, jelly-like mixture. They are made of pulpy fruits, with citrus fruits being the favorites.

Conserves. Although generally a combination of several fruits to which raisins and nuts are often added, the name is sometimes applied to the products more commonly known as marmalades or jams. A conserve of the latter type contains pieces of the fruit which may be in a thick syrup or in a jelly. Conserves are soft and easily spread.

Jams. Jams are often made from small fruits such as berries, although larger fruits either crushed or chopped may also be used. The fruit is cooked with sugar until soft and jelly-like. No attempt is made to preserve the shape of the fruit, and the finished product may be quite smooth and uniform, or it may contain pieces of the fruit.

Butters. Butters tend to be less sweet than the other products of this group. They are usually made of large fruits, which are cooked until soft; the pulp is then run through a sieve. The water is evaporated by cooking. Sugar and spices may or may not be added, but a large quantity of sugar is seldom used. Butters are fine and smooth in texture and those of low sugar content mold readily. Fruit pastes are prepared much as fruit butters and then are dried to an almost solid consistency.

Factors Affecting the Quality

All products are influenced by the quality of the fruit used, and the ripeness of the fruit determines its quality. Underripe fruit lacks natural fruit flavor and aroma and is usually high in acid and low in sugar. Green fruit is firm or even hard and in some cases may be difficult to cook. Hard-ripe fruits retain their shape best during cooking, but the soft or mellow-ripe fruit, as a rule, possesses maximum flavor and may be used advantageously when retention of shape is of no importance. Irregular and imperfect fruit may be used for many of the jam-like products, but stale fruit should not be used because spoilage may result and the product is sure to be of poor flavor.

The predominating flavor of the product is chiefly determined by the fruit or the combination of fruits, but it is also affected by the amount of sugar used. The proportion of sugar used depends upon the product being made and somewhat upon the purpose for which it is intended. For example, fruit butter to be served as a spread or a sweet would require a higher ratio of sugar than a butter to be served as an accompaniment for meat. For a given product, the ratio of sugar to fruit varies with the type of fruit and its acidity and with individual taste. The proportions are sometimes varied in adjusting to the increased cost of either sugar or fruit.

The proportion of sugar affects both the quantity and the consistency of these products, just as it does that of jellies. The texture of the fruit in the finished product is largely determined by the time of the addition of the sugar. Fruit cooked in a sugar syrup, or that to which the sugar is added at the beginning of the cooking period, tends to retain its shape, whereas fruit cooked in water breaks up more readily. The sugar syrup draws a portion of the water from the fruit and toughens somewhat the tissues of the fruit. Commercial pectin may be added in making marmalades, conserves, and jams. This may affect both the quality and the yield.

Cooking makes the fruit tender and changes the flavor and sometimes the color. It breaks down the fibrous structure, dissolves the pectin, facilitates the absorption of the sugar by the fruit, and also reduces the volume by evaporation of moisture. Cooking for too long a time, however, may darken the color and tends to produce a caramel flavor, especially if much of the cooking occurs after the sugar is added. Prolonged cooking also breaks down the pectin to pectic acid and destroys its jellying power, thus affecting the consistency of the product. Large batches should not be made at one time. It is best not to double the recipe but to repeat if greater quantities are desired.

The equipment available for use may affect the character of the finished product. A large flat-bottomed kettle is desirable. Too small a kettle may necessitate a slower rate of cooking, which may retard the rate of concentration and result in a darker color and a strong flavor. Metal kettles and metal spoons may also cause a darkening of the product. The material of the cooking utensil as well as the character of the heat will affect how easily the product may scorch.

The judgment and skill of the worker influence the quality of the finished product. To make a superior product, the worker needs to know the time to

Fig. 33–1. *Boil fruit and sugar in a large, flat-bottomed kettle, stirring the mixture to prevent sticking and scorching as it thickens.*

Courtesy of Certo Fruit Pectin

add the sugar, the intensity of heat desirable, and the degree of cooking which is satisfactory. Tests are given for sufficient cooking of each product, but even then experience is necessary for their effective application. A temperature of 5° C. (9° F.) above that of boiling water is given as a satisfactory end-point for preserves, marmalades, conserves, and jams made without added pectin. When made with added pectin, directions differ and should be followed carefully.

The sugar content largely determines the method of protecting the finished product. Mixtures low in sugar and those which do not gel should be sealed in hot containers as quickly as possible after cooking is completed. Processing the filled containers for a short time in a hot water bath is desirable. Products high in sugar may be sealed with a layer of paraffin or they may be sealed in a jar as are other canned foods. These products, like most canned foods, tend to lose quality with long storage.

Preserves

A general rule for making preserves is to allow three-fourths of a pound of sugar to each pound of fruit, but there are many exceptions to this, as the ratio depends upon the acidity of the fruit. Hard fruits, such as quinces, should be cooked in water until tender. The aim in making preserves is to introduce the syrup into the fruit. The syrup is of a different density from the liquid in the fruit. This difference tends to be equalized as the fruit is cooked in the syrup. If the syrup is of medium density, it enters the fruit only a little more slowly than the juice is drawn out. Then the fruit, although somewhat shrunken and flabby, does not become tough. If the syrup is heavy, the juice is drawn out far more rapidly than the syrup enters, and the preserves shrink excessively. Recipes for preserves of various fruits generally indicate the type of syrup to use or the ratio of water to sugar desirable for a particular fruit.

Fruit for preserves should be cooked as rapidly as possible. When the fruit is tender, clear, bright, and of a good color, it should be removed from the heat. Preserves may be canned immediately, but it is generally considered better to allow the fruit to remain weighted down in the syrup in the kettle overnight. This allows for a greater exchange of liquids, the fruit becomes plumper and higher in sugar content, and the syrup becomes thinner. After standing overnight the fruit may be packed into the containers and the syrup concentrated to the desired density, then poured over the fruit in the containers. This method insures a rich, sweet product without the danger of scorching and overcooking which may result from a one-period cooking.

To prevent molding, the preserves may be processed in a hot-water canner after packing in the container. A simmering temperature, 82° C. (180° F.), is best for delicate products. This temperature is sufficient to destroy molds, and it least affects the quality of the preserve. Twenty minutes at 82° C. (180° F.) is sufficient for pint jars of preserves. Ten minutes at 100° C. (212°F.) is an acceptable alternative, if preferred.

Some preserves, such as those made from strawberries and cherries, do not necessarily have to be boiled. The fruit may be covered with a hot syrup and allowed to absorb the syrup in a slow heat such as that from the oven or the sun.

Marmalade

Marmalades sometimes contain equal parts of sugar and fruit, but frequently the proportion of sugar exceeds that of the fruit. Citrus fruits are most often used for marmalades. Pectin, essential to produce a jelly-like consistency, is present in the skin of these fruits. A greater volume of marmalade is obtained when as much of the pectin as possible is extracted. This is accomplished by allowing the thinly sliced fruit to stand in water for a day, heating it, and then allowing it to stand for another day. The greater the surface of peel exposed, the more readily the pectin is brought into solution. After the pectin is in solution, part of the water should be evaporated, the sugar added, and the cooking completed in a short time. Marmalade is cooked sufficiently when the jellying point is reached, as determined by any one of the tests previously given. If the marmalade is stirred for five minutes after being removed from the heat, the fruit will be better distributed throughout. It is then packed in hot containers and sealed at once. Paraffin may be used for this purpose.

Conserves

Conserves contain, as a rule, from one-half to three-quarters of a pound of sugar to each pound of fruit. Any combination of fruits desired may be used. Many conserves contain raisins and most of them nuts. If conserves are made of hard fruits or vegetables, these ingredients are cooked before the sugar is added. Soft fruits may have the sugar added at the beginning of the cooking period. Conserves should be cooked rapidly. The nuts should be dipped in boiling water a few seconds before they are added to the fruit. They should be added not more than five minutes before the cooking is completed because long cooking destroys their flavor. When done, conserves are thick and may give a jelly test. They are packed in hot jars and may or may not be processed, depending upon the proportion of sugar used.

Jams

Jams contain from three-quarters to one and one-quarter pounds of sugar to each pound of fruit. The fruit is cooked until tender and the water is well evaporated before the sugar is added. Then, bringing the mixture to a full boil is often the only cooking necessary. Care should be taken to see that the fruit is not too concentrated before the sugar is added, otherwise a jelly may form before the sugar is thoroughly mixed with the fruit. This will be broken by the stirring and an even jelly will not form again. If the sugar is not thoroughly dissolved, crystals may form as the mixture stands. Jam, when sufficiently cooked, gives a test similar to that for jelly, and the mixture "heaps up" on the spoon. A more uniform distribution of fruit may result if the jam is stirred for five minutes after being removed from the heat. It is then poured into hot containers and sealed immediately.

Uncooked jams made from frozen or fresh fruits, a pectin concentrate, and sugar are delicate in flavor and texture. They retain the fresh fruit characteristics well but must be stored at low temperatures if they are to be kept for any length of time. The ease of preparation as well as the quality of the product has led to rather wide use of these uncooked products.

Butters

Fruit butters may contain either no sugar or as much as one-half pound of sugar to one pound of fruit pulp. Imperfect and irregular fruit is often used for butters. However, any spoiled or bruised portions should be carefully removed and only the sound, firm fruit used. The washed fruit is cooked in water or steam until tender. The cooked fruit is pressed through a sieve or food mill and the cores, peelings, and other similar substances are removed. The sieved pulp should be evaporated until thick enough to round up on a spoon before the sugar is added. After it is added the cooking should be completed rapidly with constant stirring. Spices, if used, should be added after the fruit pulp is concentrated, since they lose their volatile oils and their fragrance with long cooking. The butter is cooked sufficiently when it is thick and more or less transparent. It will heap up on the spoon and will drop from the spoon in sheets. Butters should be packed in hot containers, the lids adjusted, and processed for ten minutes in a hot water canner at 100° C. (212° F.).

Causes of Difficulties

Shriveled preserves may result from starting the cooking in too heavy a syrup. The cooking should be started with a thin or medium syrup.

Preserves that break up badly may have been cooked in too thin a syrup, or they may have been made from overripe fruit. Stirring during the cooking period and over-cooking also break up the fruit.

A hard or tough preserve sometimes results from the use of an unusually hard fruit, such as quinces and some varieties of apples and pears. If such a fruit is started to cook in a heavy syrup, it never becomes tender. To prevent such hardness the fruit should be partially cooked in clear water and then added to the syrup. Sometimes starting the cooking in a thin syrup is sufficient.

A dark color in any of these products may be the result of overlong cooking. This often occurs when too large a quantity is cooked at one time. A strong flavor also results from cooking for too long a time, especially if the sugar has been added at the beginning of the process.

Fermentation of the finished product usually indicates a low concentration of sugar and a lack of processing after sealing in a container. A low sugar concentration may result from insufficient evaporation because of too short a cooking period.

Mold may occur on the products that contain a small proportion of sugar if they are not sealed immediately after being cooked. However, mold growth may occur when the sugar concentration is as high as 70 per cent. Conserves frequently mold when the nuts have not been sterilized.

Crystallization of sugar in marmalades and in jams usually results from too high a proportion of that ingredient, either because incorrect amounts of sugar have been used or because the product has been over-cooked. Occasionally adding sugar too late in the cooking process causes crystallization.

Activities

1. Prepare preserves, marmalades, conserves, jams, and butters, making use of available fruits in season; of canned fruits; of dried fruits.

2. Compare the costs of products made in class from these different sources with those of commercially made products of similar quality.

References

DEPARTMENT OF FOODS AND NUTRITION, KANSAS STATE UNIVERSITY. *Practical Cookery*. New York: John Wiley & Sons, Inc., 1966. Pp. 238–240.

Food. The Yearbook of Agriculture, 1959. U.S. Dept. Agr., Washington, D.C.: United States Government Printing Office.

How to Make Jellies, Jams, and Preserves at Home. U.S. Dept. Agr., Home and Garden Bull. No. 56 (1970).

34

pickles

Pickles, aromatic and spicy, stimulate the sense of taste and act as appetizers. Because of this stimulating effect, pickles are frequently called relishes. They have a place in the meal occupied by no other food. If unqualified, the term "pickles" often connotes cucumber pickles, but these are by no means the only variety. Included are many vegetables, pickled alone or in combination, and a number of fruits.

Types of Pickles

Pickling is the preservation of vegetables, fruits, or meat with acid; hence all pickles contain acid, either produced during the fermentation process or added, usually as vinegar. Because of the difference in the products produced by these two methods, pickles are often classified as brined or fermented and fresh-pack or quick-process.

Brined Pickles. Such products as sauerkraut and dill pickles are brined pickles. The appropriate vegetable is covered with a dilute brine made from salt and the juice from the vegetable or added water and allowed to ferment for a period of three weeks or longer. During this time the color and texture of the vegetable changes and, if conditions are right, a desirable flavor develops. Added flavoring substances such as dill, garlic, onion, turmeric, and spices give variety and character to the product.

Fresh-pack Pickles. As the term implies, these pickles do not undergo a fermentation process; instead fresh vegetables such as cucumbers, green beans, and green tomatoes may be brined for several hours or overnight to remove a portion of the water in the vegetables and, thus, prevent excessive dilution of the pickling solution. After brining, the foods are drained and combined with vinegar containing spices, sugar, onion, and other seasonings depending upon the type of pickle being made.

Varieties of Pickles. Many kinds of pickles are made by the fresh-pack method. These are described according to the food being processed or the kinds of seasonings added. For example, there are "cucumber pickles," "beet pickles," "mustard pickles," "spiced pickles," "sour pickles," or "sweet pickles." Fruit pickles are fruits covered with a vinegar-spice-sugar mixture and include pickled peaches, spiced crabapples, and other fleshy fruits. Mixed pickles are a mixture of vegetables. Any combination that is desired may be made. Cauliflower, cucumbers, onions, green and red peppers, tomatoes, small ears of corn, tiny melons, and string beans are often used. The vegetables are usually left in fair-sized pieces, although the term "pickle" is sometimes applied to finely chopped mixtures such as chow-chow. More often these are referred to as relishes.

The term relish, although sometimes applied to all forms of pickles, most often refers to mixtures of fruits and/or vegetables which are cut or chopped, seasoned, and cooked to the desired consistency. Popular relishes include piccalilli, chutney, catsup, and chili sauce.

Piccalilli or Indian pickle was made originally in the East Indies. It contains a large variety of finely chopped vegetables and is pungent with spices.

Chutney, a hot, spicy, sweet pickle, was first made in India, and from that country still come some of the best grades. Mangoes were the basis of the original chutney. Gradually other foods were added. Today a variety of sweet or acid fruits are used with suitable seasoning, such as ginger, chilies, garlic, mustard seed, and vinegar. Chutney may be served with meats of various kinds but it is considered especially suitable as an accompaniment for curries.

The term "ketchup" or "catsup" is derived from an East Indian name of a pickle. Catsup was originally the spiced juice from salted mushrooms, but now the term is applied to a highly seasoned sauce made of the strained pulp of tomatoes, grapes, green walnuts, or other fruits.

Chili sauce is a sauce made of chilies, tomatoes, and spices cooked in vinegar. It is not strained.

Effect of Ingredients

Pickling is accomplished by the use of salt or vinegar or both. Often sugar and spices are added. Each of these substances has specific uses as a pickling agent.

Salt. Salt affects the flavor of pickles, just as it does that of all other foods to which it is added. When present in sufficient quantity, salt acts as a preservative. The proportion of salt added to the food depends upon the type of preservation desired. A weak brine, three tablespoons to one-half cup of salt in a quart of water as used in the making of dill pickles, allows rapid fermentation and formation of the maximum amount of lactic acid in a comparatively short time. A medium brine, about three-fourths cup of salt in a quart of water, is used to "cure" cucumbers for later processing. The medium brine prevents growth of spoilage bacteria but permits growth of bacteria responsible for the production of lactic acid. From six to twelve months may be allowed for the "curing." A strong brine, one cup of salt in a quart of water prevents both bacterial action and the formation of lactic acid.

Salt may be added to the food either dry or in the form of a brine. If added dry, juices from the food are drawn out and the salt dissolves in these to form a brine. Whether the salt is added dry or in the form of a brine, the juices and the soluble substances in the food to be pickled are drawn out by the process of osmosis. The fermentable sugars dissolved in these juices are also extracted. These serve as food for the lactic-acid-forming bacteria. When the conditions are favorable and there is sufficient sugar present, considerable lactic acid is formed. This may progress to the point where all bacterial action is practically stopped. As the acid acts upon the food, the color, flavor, and texture are changed to produce the pickled state. The drawing out of the liquid from the vegetable by the salt hardens the tissues or makes them firm.

Vinegar. The flavor of the pickles is affected by vinegar; it adds an acid flavor which differs somewhat from that caused by lactic acid fermentation. It also acts as a preservative. Bacteria are almost if not entirely inactive in acid solution. However, molds and yeasts develop even in rather strong acids, and pickles of a high acidity may mold when exposed to air.

Sugar and Spices. Sugar acts as a preservative mainly by increasing the density of the pickle solution, thus making the food less accessible to the organisms. Spices are valuable chiefly because of their volatile oils which add to the flavor and interest of the product. Ground spices may be added, but they impart a dark color to the product. Whole spices may be steeped in the vinegar, or they may be tied in a bag and placed directly in the pickle mixture while cooking. Essential oils of spices, such as cinnamon and cloves, may be added if preferred. Allspice, cinnamon, and cloves are thought to show some antiseptic action on yeasts and molds. Other common spices apparently have little if any effect.

Selecting the Method for Pickling

The choice of method to be used is influenced by the product desired, the facilities and equipment available, and the type of food to be processed.

Product. Whether cucumber pickles are made by fermentation or by use of a vinegar mixture depends somewhat on the preference for the flavor of one type or another. Sweet cucumber pickles may or may not be fermented, but in either case the final treatment is to cover them with vinegar seasoned in some manner. Dill pickles undergo fermentation. Cabbage may be allowed to ferment, in which case sauerkraut is produced, or it may be treated with a vinegar mixture and a pickled cabbage results. Fermented pickles may differ in color, flavor, and texture from pickles prepared with vinegar.

Facilities. Unless facilities allow the recommended temperature to be maintained, it is seldom wise to attempt fermented pickles. For example, when making sauerkraut a temperature of 21° to 24° C. (70° to 75° F.) encourages lactic acid fermentation and, if other conditions are right, results in a high quality product. A temperature of 15° C. (60° F.) will result in slow and incomplete fermentation, whereas above 26° to 29° C. (80° to 85° F.) abnormal fermentations will result.

Equipment and Storage. Pickling may be done with the simple equipment ordinarily used for meal preparation, although some special equipment is usually desirable. Scales are important in determining the proportions of preservatives to add to the food. The correct proportion of salt to water may be obtained by accurate weights or measurements, but a salinometer facilitates the determination. Because many materials react with acid, the material of which utensils are made is an important consideration in selecting equipment. Copper utensils are not recommended for pickle-making. Copper reacts with vinegar to form a salt, copper acetate, which may affect the taste and which in certain quantities is harmful. Iron, too, reacts readily with vinegar and tends to discolor pickles. Enamel pans which are chipped, thus exposing the iron base, are undesirable for pickle-making. Aluminum, unmarred enamelware, and stainless steel are suitable materials for heating pickles. Stoneware, earthenware, and glass utensils are much used for the fermenting process. Wooden, Teflon, or plastic spoons and paddles are good, although those of aluminum or stainless steel may be preferred. Glass jars and lids and a water-bath canner or a kettle deep enough to allow for one or two inches of water over the jars are essential equipment since it is recommended that pickles sealed in suitable containers be heat processed.

Brined pickles, including sauerkraut, should be packed in clean, hot glass jars at the end of the fermentation period, and processed in a boiling water bath. Fresh-pack pickles, too, should be processed in a boiling water bath to assure destruction of organisms that may cause spoilage and, for those not previously heated, to inactivate enzymes that may affect color, flavor, and texture. As when processing other canned foods, it is important to follow directions carefully to make sure the pickles will keep but to avoid overcooking. Storage in a cool, dark, dry place aids in retaining quality.

Preliminary Treatment of Food. Vegetables are first treated with either dry salt or brine. Dry salt is used for vegetables with an exceedingly high water content, such as green tomatoes. This removes a large proportion of the liquid and results in a firmer product. Firm fruits, such as certain kinds of apples and pears, are first cooked in water or in a dilute pickle syrup. Soft fruits, such as some peaches, may be placed directly in a heavy syrup, which draws out a portion of the liquid. The fruit, though more or less shriveled, becomes firmer as a result of this treatment. As the fruit stands in the syrup,

Fig. 34–1. *To make cross-cut pickle slices:*
Wash cucumbers thoroughly. Slice unpeeled cucumbers into ⅛- to ¼-inch crosswise slices. Wash and remove the skins from onions. Slice into ⅛-inch slices.

Combine cucumber and onion slices with peeled garlic cloves. Add salt and mix thoroughly. Cover with crushed ice or ice cubes. Allow to stand 3 hours. Drain thoroughly; remove garlic cloves.

Combine sugar, spices, and vinegar; heat to boiling. Add drained cucumber and onion slices and heat 5 minutes.

Pack loosely into clean, hot pint jars to ½ inch of top; adjust lids. Process in boiling water for 5 minutes. Start to count processing time as soon as the water in the canner returns to boiling.

Remove jars and complete seals if necessary. Set the jars upright, several inches apart, on a wire rack or a folded towel to cool.

Courtesy of the U.S. Department of Agriculture

some of the syrup is absorbed and the fruit becomes plumper. Thus the prepared, drained food may be added to the pickling solution, heated, packed in jars, and processed; or it may be covered with the hot pickling solution and allowed to stand overnight. When this is done the solution may be drained off, reheated, and again poured over the food. If a sweet pickle is being made, sugar and vinegar may be added each time the solution is reheated.

Selecting the Ingredients

Cider vinegar is generally considered to have a better flavor and odor than distilled vinegar. Cider vinegar may be dark in color; for some types of pickles this may be objectionable, and in such cases it is better to use distilled vinegar. Commercial vinegar varies from 4 to 6 per cent acidity. Only vinegar of known strength should be used. Salt and sugar are highly purified substances. Iodized salt is not recommended for it may cause darkening of the pickles. Spices are best when fresh because their flavor is dependent upon their volatile oils, which gradually escape on exposure to the air. Only high quality vegetables or fruits should be used. Tender, crisp, freshly harvested vegetables are necessary to assure a good quality product. Fruits should be firm and such fruits as peaches and pears may be slightly underripe. Foods to be pickled whole should be uniform in shape and size if an attractive pack is to result. If foods must be held before processing, refrigeration delays deterioration.

High quality food and up-to-date methods should give satisfactory pickles. However, calcium chloride may be used to give added crispness to such foods as watermelon rind, cantaloupe, and green tomatoes. The calcium chloride apparently combines with the pectic acid to form an insoluble substance that binds the cells together and helps to prevent breakdown of the structure during cooking.

Causes of Difficulties in Pickling

Difficulties are frequently encountered in making pickles, especially fermented ones. Soft or slippery pickles are not uncommon. Once a pickle becomes soft, it cannot be made firm. Slippery pickles may be pickles in the first stage of softening and often result from too weak a brine, which permits the development of undesirable organisms. Soft pickles also may result from exposure of the pickles to the air. They should be completely covered with brine.

Sometimes in the early stages of fermentation bacteria develop which secrete pectolytic enzymes and cause softening by hydrolysis of the protopectin. Blossoms not removed from the cucumbers during washing may contain fungi and yeasts responsible for enzymatic softening. Young, immature cucumbers are most susceptible to the action of these enzymes.

Spoilage of pickles occurs when scum forms on the surface of the brine in which vegetables are fermented. This scum is composed of wild yeasts, molds, and bacteria, which destroy the lactic acid of the brine and permit action of putrefactive organisms. This action may result in softening of the pickles and the development of an undesirable flavor.

Failure of the pickles to cure properly may be due to the use of hard water, which may interfere with the formation of acid. The wrong temperature also may prevent proper curing. Lactic acid bacteria develop rapidly at 21° to 24° C. (70° to 75° F.). Above 26° to 29° C. (80° to 85° F.) or below 15° C. (60° F.) activity of the organisms may be retarded and an abnormal flavor or other undesirable characteristics may develop.

Hollow pickles probably are most often due to improper development of the cucumbers. However, the hollowness sometimes is said to result from the lapse of too long a period between picking and brining, from too rapid fermentation, or from too strong or too weak a brine during fermentation.

Shriveling occurs sometimes in brine and sometimes in the vinegar mixture. This is often caused by too strong a salt, vinegar, or sugar solution at the beginning of the pickling process. If a highly flavored product is desired, the pickles should first be treated with a weaker solution, and the stronger solution should be applied later. Although within limits the pickling solution may be made to suit the taste, for the most part, proportions used in making pickles are carefully worked out and should be followed closely. Shriveling also may result from over-cooking or over-processing.

Dark pickles may be caused by use of ground spices; too much spice; iodized salt; overcooking; minerals in the water, especially iron; or use of iron utensils.

Activities

1. Prepare vegetable pickles of various kinds.
2. Prepare fruit pickles.
3. Prepare relishes, catsups, and mixed pickles.

References

BORGSTROM, G. *Principles of Food Science.* New York: The Macmillan Company. 1968. Vol. I. Pp. 191, 275, 313–316; Vol. II. Pp. 64, 71, 107–109.

Effect of Household Processing and Storage on Quality of Pickled Vegetables and Fruits. U.S. Dept. Agr., Home Econ. Research Rept. No. 28 (1965).

Food for Us All. Yearbook of Agriculture, 1969. U.S. Dept. Agr., Washington, D.C.: United States Government Printing Office. Pp. 244–248.

FRAZIER, W. C. *Food Microbiology,* 2nd ed. New York: McGraw-Hill Book Company, Inc. 1967.

Making Pickles and Relishes at Home. U.S. Dept. Agr., Home and Garden Bull. No. 92 (1970).

suggested readings

Books

Borgstrom, G. *Principles of Food Science:* Vol. I. *Food Technology.* 397 pp., Vol. II. *Food Microbiology and Biochemistry.* New York: The Macmillan Company, 1968. 493 pp.

Charley, H. *Food Science.* New York: The Roland Press Co., 1970. 520 pp.

Consumers All. The Yearbook of Agriculture, 1965. U.S. Dept. Agr., Washington, D.C.: United States Government Printing Office. 496 pp.

Department of Foods and Nutrition, Kansas State University. *Practical Cookery: A Compilation of Principles of Cooking and Recipes,* 23rd ed. John Wiley & Sons, Inc., 1966. 279 pp.

Farmer's World. The Yearbook of Agriculture, 1964. U.S. Dept. Agr., Washington, D.C.: United States Government Printing Office. 592 pp.

Food. The Yearbook of Agriculture, 1959. U.S. Dept. Agr., Washington, D.C.: United States Government Printing Office. 736 pp.

Food for Us All. The Yearbook of Agriculture, 1969. U.S. Dept. Agr., Washington, D.C.: United States Government Printing Office, 360 pp.

Griswold, R. M. *The Experimental Study of Foods.* Boston: Houghton Mifflin Company, 1962. 577 pp.

Halliday, E. G. and I. T. Noble. *Hows and Whys of Cooking,* 3rd ed. Chicago: University of Chicago Press, 1946. 328 pp.

Handbook of Food Preparation.[1] American Home Economics Association, Washington, D.C., 1971. 116 pp.

Heseltine, M. and U. M. Dow. *The New Basic Cook Book,* rev. ed. Boston: Houghton Mifflin Company, 1967. 718 pp.

Hughes, O. and M. Bennion. *Introductory Foods,* 5th ed. New York: The Macmillan Company, 1970. 576 pp.

Kinder, F. *Meal Management,* 3rd ed. New York: The Macmillan Company, 1968. 552 pp.

Longree, K. and G. G. Blaker. *Sanitary Techniques in Food Service.* New York: John Wiley & Sons, Inc., 1971. 225 pp.

Lowe, B. *Experimental Cookery,* 4th ed. New York: John Wiley & Sons, Inc., 1955. 573 pp.

Meyer, L. H. *Food Chemistry.* New York: Reinhold Publishing Corporation, 1960. 385 pp.

Peckham, G. C. *Foundations of Food Preparation,* 2nd ed. New York: The Macmillan Company, 1969. 497 pp.

Potter, N. N. *Food Science.* Westport, Conn.: Avi Publishing Company, Inc., 1968. 653 pp.

---

[1] Purchase by all students is recommended.

Sweetman, M. D. and I. MacKellar. *Food Selection and Preparation,* 4th ed. New York: John Wiley & Sons, Inc., 1954. 645 pp.

Terrell, M. E. *Professional Food Preparation.* John Wiley & Sons, Inc., 1971. 596 pp.

Wilmot, J. S. and M. Q. Batjer. *Food for the Family,* 6th ed. New York: J. B. Lippincott Company, 1966. 729 pp.

Wright, C. E. *Food Buying. Marketing Information for Consumers.* New York: The Macmillan Company, 1962. 410 pp.

Periodicals

Food Engineering. Chestnut & 56th Sts., Philadelphia, Pa. 19139.

Food Technology. 221 North LaSalle Street, Chicago, Ill. 60601.

Journal of Food Science. 221 North LaSalle Street, Chicago, Ill. 60601.

Journal of The American Dietetics Association. 620 North Michigan Ave., Chicago, Ill. 60611

Journal of Home Economics. 2010 Massachusetts Ave., Washington, D.C. 20036.

What's New in Home Economics. 466 Lexington Ave., New York, N.Y. 10017.

index

Acetic acid, 370

Additives to food, 575–579: color, 26–27; defined, 577; FDA regulation of, 25–27; types of, 577–579

Adulteration of food, 26–27

Agencies protecting food supply, 22–33: Department of Agriculture (USDA), 22–25, 31–32, 174, 232–236, 426, 428; federal, 22–30; Food and Drug Administration (FDA), 25–30, 263, 426; Public Health Service (PHS), 29–30, 32; state and local, 30–33

Agricultural Marketing Service, 23$_n$

Agriculture, Department of. *See* U.S. Department of Agriculture

Air, as leavening agent, 284

Albumin, 163

Aleurone layer, 262

Allium family, 116. *See also* Onions

All-purpose flour, 261; in shortened cakes, 324; weight per cup, 279

Allspice, 376

Aluminum, 455–456

Amino acids, 5–6, 115–117

AMS (Agricultural Marketing Service), 23$_n$

Amylase, 261

Anemia, 11

Angel food cakes, 332

Anise, 380

Anthocyanins, 115

Anthoxanthins, 115

Anticaking agents, 578

Appert, Nicholas, 574

Apples, 42–43: nutritive value of, 54; seasons for, 43; selection of, 42; use of, 43; varieties of, 42–43

Appliances, kitchen, 453–461

Appointments for the table. *See* Table appointments

Apricots: nutritive value of, 54; selection of, 42

Arrowroot starch, 264

Artichokes: characteristics and cooking of, 124; selection of, 104

Ascorbic acid (Vitamin C): added to fruits before freezing, 347; effect of canning on, 55; effect of storage on, 53; functions of, 9, 14; sources of, 9, 14; in vegetables, 117–118

Asparagus: characteristics and cooking of, 124; cost of, 120–121; nutritive value of, 118; selection of, 104; washing of, 121

Aspics, 140

Association of Food and Drug Officials of U.S., 31

Automatic dishwashers, 452, 467–468

Availability of foods: of fresh fruit, 41; and planning meals, 400–403; of vegetables, 103

Avocados: nutritive value of, 54; selection of, 42, 56

Bacteria: in custard and cream pies, 344; in food spoilage, 561–562; in milk, 148

Baking powder, 286–288: acid constituents in, 287; double-action, 287; as a leavening agent, 286–288.

Baking soda, 285–286

Bananas: nutritive value of, 54; selection of, 42

Barley: characteristics of, 69–70; nutrients in, 72

Basal metabolic rate, 7

Basic Four, 15–19, 396–398

Basic Seven, 18

Basil, 378

Bay leaves, 378

B-complex vitamins, 9–11: biotin, 11; folic acid, 11; niacin, 10; pantothenic acid, 11; riboflavin, 10, 118, 163; sources of, 18–19; thiamine, 9–10, 118; Vitamin B$_6$, 10; Vitamin B$_{12}$, 11

Beans: canning of, 590–591; characteristics and cooking of, 124; costs of, 120–121; nutritive value of, 118; selection of, 104; vitamin content of, 122

Beef: cuts of, 195–202; grades of, 209–213; home freezing of, 606; steaks, 198–199; yields of cuts from quarters of, 606. *See also* Meat

Beets: characteristics and cooking of, 124; costs of, 120; nutrients in, 118; selection of, 104

Beltsville turkeys, 232, 236

Beriberi, 10

Berries, 44

Beverages, 82–99: cocoa, 95–98; coffee, 82–91; milk, 147–167; tea, 91–95

Bibb lettuce, 134–135

Biotin, 11

Biscuits, 305–308, 310, 318

Blanc mange, 270–272

Bonbons, 358

Boston lettuce, 134–135

Botanical classification of plants, 36–37

Botulism, 561, 563, 565, 593

Brains, 227, 229

Bran, 262

Brands as food purchasing aid, 429–430

Brassica family, 116

Bread flour, 261

Breads, 298–320; biscuits, 305–308, 310; convenience forms of, 317–319; costs of, 318; daily food guide for, 397; frozen, 319; griddle cakes, 301–303, 309; muffins, 298–310, 308; nutrients contributed by, 19; popovers, 304–305, 309; proportions used in, 299; quick, 298–310; waffles, 303, 309; yeast, 310–317

Breakfasts: of differing costs, 413–414; meal patterns for, 405–407; menus for, 436–438, 538; service of, 538–541

Brine cure, 205

Broccoli: characteristics and cooking of, 124; cost of, 121; nutritive value of, 118; selection of, 104

Broiling of meat, 218–221

Bromelin, 388

Brown sugar, 351

Brunch, 531

Brussels sprouts: characteristics and cooking of, 124; cost of, 121; nutritive value of, 118; selection of, 104

Buckwheat, 71, 72

Buffet table service, 523, 528–530; example of use, 541–544

Bulgur, 66, 72

Bureau of Commercial Fisheries, 29, 250

Butter: compared with margarine, 291; ingredients in, 275

Buttermilk, 152–153

Butters, fruit: defined, 619; making of, 623

C & MS (Consumer and Marketing Service), 23–25, 233, 426, 428

Cabbage: characteristics and cooking of, 124; nutritive value of, 118; selection of, 104–105; vitamin content of, 122

Cabbage family (Brassica), 116

Café au lait, 91

Café noir, 91

Caffeine, 86–87

Cake flour, 262: in shortened cakes, 324; weight per cup, 279

Cake frostings, 355–356

Cake mixes, 346–347

Cakes, 322–334: angel food, 332; baking of, 328–329; convenience forms of, 345–347; foam, 322, 331–334; freezing of, 347; icings for, 355–356; mixing methods for, 325–328; proportions for, 323

Cakes, shortened, 322–331: causes for deviations in, 330–331; characteristics of, 330–331; cookies, 331; defined, 322; freezing of, 347; ingredients in, 322–324

Calcium: in fish, 250–251; function of, 6, 13; in milk, 163; sources of, 6–7, 13; in vegetables, 118

Calcium chloride, 630

Calf, 210

Calories: excess intake of in U.S., 3; sources of, 3

Candling of eggs, 175

Candy, 354–361: crystalline, 356–360; noncrystalline, 360–361; stages of, 360; uncooked, 360

Cane syrup, 353

Canning: commercial, 573–575; history of, 573–574; home, 581–594

Canning at home, 581–594: of beans, 590–591; cancooked, 585–593; containers for, 584–585; equipment for, 583–584; preparation of food for, 581–583; proportions for, 583; selection of food, 581–583; spoilage, 593–594; of tomatoes, 588

Cantaloupes, 54

Caraway, 380

Carbohydrates, 3–4: in cereals, 73; composition of, 3–4; foods high in, 4; function of, 13; as source of energy, 3; sources of, 13; storage as starch by plant, 4; in vegetables, 116–117

Carbon dioxide: in baking powders, 286–287; in baking soda, 285–286; in egg storage, 172; in fermentation of bread, 282; as a leavening agent, 284; produced by yeast, 560

Cardamon, 380

Carotenoids: in egg yolk, 170; in flour, 261; in vegetables, 114

Carrots: characteristics and cooking of, 124; cost

of, 121; nutritive value of, 118; selection of, 105

Casein, 163

Cassava, 264

Cast iron, 457

Catsup, 625

Cauliflower: characteristics and cooking of, 124; selection of, 105

Cayenne, 376

Celeriac, 124

Celery: characteristics and cooking of, 124; nutritive value of, 118; parsley seed variety, 381; selection of, 105

Cellulose: foods high in, 4; purpose in diet, 4

Cereals, 62–81: breakfast, 64–65; daily food guide for, 397; enriched, 74; history of, 62–63; hot, 64–65; kernels of grain, 64; monthly cost of, 75; nutritive value of, 19, 71–74; preparation of, 76–80; processing of, 64–71; ready-to-eat, 65; selection of, 74–76; structure of, 63–64; whole-grain, 73

Cerelose, 354

Cheese, 154–162: cold pack, 159; cured, 155–159; legends of origin, 154; manufacture of, 155; nutrients in, 165; processed, 159; ripening of, 155–159; selection of, 161–162; storage of, 161–162; uncured, 155; varieties of, 158; whey, 159–160

Cherries: comparative costs of, 47; selection of, 44

Chervil, 378

Chicken: cost of, 236–237; grading of, 234–235. *See also* Poultry

Chicory, 133

Chiffon cakes, 334

Chili sauce, 625

Chili seasoning, 381

Chinaware, 495

Chinese cabbage, 124

Chlorophyll, 113, 114

Chocolate, 96–98: baking, 96–97; bitter, 96–97; caffeine in, 86–87; fat content of, 97; hot, 97–98; preparation of, 97–98

Chocolate creams, 358

Chocolate fudge, 359

Cholesterol, 5

Choline, 11

Chutney, 625

Cinammon, 376

Citrus fruits: costs of, 48; cutting of, 57; nutritive value of, 54; preparation of, 56–58; selection of, 44; varieties of, 44

Class experiences in meal preparation, 486–491

Cleaning of kitchen equipment, 469–471

Clear flour, 261

Clostridium botulinum, 561, 563, 565, 593

Cloves, 377

Coagulation: of eggs, 190; function of, 180; of milk, 164

Cocoa, 95–98: alkali-treated, 97; breakfast, 97–98; caffeine content of, 86; fat content of, 97; origin of, 95; preparation of, 97–98; processing of, 96–97; tannin content of, 97; theobromine content of, 86–87

Cocoa beans, 95–96

Cocoa butter, 97

Coconuts: costs of, 48; as drupes, 382

Coffee, 82–91: caffeine content of, 86–87; composition of, 86–87; demitasse, 91; espresso, 91; fro-

zen, 84; history of, 82; iced, 91; instant, 85; niacin content of, 87; preparation of, 87–91; production of, 82–84; selection of, 84–86; tannin content of, 87; theobromine content of, 86–87
Coffee cake, 316–317
Coffee makers, 88–90
Coffees, teas, and receptions, 531–534
Cold sterilization, 575–577
Cold-pack canning, 585–586
Collagen: in connective tissue, 203; formation of gelatin from, 384
Collards: characteristics and cooking of, 124; nutritive value of, 118; vitamin content, 122
Color Additives Amendment of 1960, 27
Combinations of foods, 401–402
Compromise table service, 522: of breakfast, 538–541; of dinner, 545–550
Confectioner's sugar, 351
Connective tissue, 203
Conserves: defined, 617; making of, 621
Consumer and Marketing Service of USDA, 23–25, 233, 426, 428
Consumer protection. *See* Protection of food supply
Consumption of: crop products, 101; fats and oils, 289; livestock products, 233; sugar, 350
Convenience foods' costs, 425–427
Cookies, 331
Cooking of: breads, 298–320; cakes and pies, 322–348; cereals, 76–80; cocoa, 97–98; coffee, 87–91; desserts, 270–272; eggs, 180–191; fish, 251–255; fruit, 58–60; flour and starch, 265–295; meat, 216–230; milk, 164; poultry, 239–244; tea, 94–95; vegetables, 113, 119–129
Cooking methods: baking, 127, 184–185, 253–254, 274–348; boiling, 123, 126; braising, 225–226; broiling, 218–222, 239–241, 251–252; electronic, 128, 227; frying, 183–184, 221, 241, 252–253; at high altitudes, 129, 295; moist-heat, 255; poaching, 183; pressure, 124–127; scrambling, 185; steaming, 126; stir-frying, 127–128
Copper, 7, 458
Coriander, 381
Corn: as a cereal, 68–69; characteristics and cooking of, 124; costs of, 120, 121; nutrients in, 72, 118; selection of, 105–106
Corn meal, 272
Corn oil, 69
Corn syrup, 69, 354
Cornstarch: described, 264; how obtained, 69; use in puddings, 270–272
Cost of food: of commercially vs. home prepared items, 427; at different expenditure levels, 432–433; factors affecting food prices, 423–427, 435; of fruits, 47–48; management of, 473–474; and meal planning, 409–414; and purchasing wisely, 418–419; reducing, 411–412
Cover (table setting), 526
Cream, 153–154: fat content of, 153; light, 153; nutrients in, 165; sour, 153; substitutes for, 153; whipped, 164
Cream pie, 343–344
Cream puffs, 304
Cream soups, 267–270
Cream of tartar, 286
Crêpes, 302

Crop products consumption, 101
Crystalline candies, 356–360
Crystallization: of candy, 356–358; of jelly, 615; in marmalades, 623
Cucumbers: characteristics and cooking of, 124; selection of, 107
Cumin, 380
Curd, 155
Curry powder, 381
Custard pie, 344
Custards, 188–191
Customs in eating, 398–400
Customs in food, 504–505
Cyclamates, 26

Daily food guide, 396–398, 405
Dairy products. *See* Milk; Milk products
Dandelion greens, 124
Decorations, table, 501–502; examples of various styles, 539–553
Dehydrofreezing, 571
Department of Agriculture. *See* U.S. Department of Agriculture
Department of Health, Education and Welfare, 29, 30
Desserts: cakes, 322–334; frozen, 361–367; pies, 334–344; sauces, 270–272
Dextrins, 265
Dextrose (glucose), 3–4: chemical formula for, 3_n; comparative sweetness of, 352; in starch, 263; in vanilla, 371
Diet, need for variety in, 2
Dietary allowances, 15
Dietary supplements, 579
Dill, 380
Dinners: compromise style service of, 545–550; of differing food level costs, 413–414; family style service of, 544–545; formal service of, 550–555; meal patterns for, 408; menus for, 408, 436–438, 544–545, 550
Dinnerware, 495–498
Disaccharide, 3
Disease. *See* Illnesses from food
Dishwashing, 465–468: by automatic dishwasher, 467–468; by hand, 465–467
Divinity fudge, 359
Donated Foods Program, 174
Dough: proportions of ingredients in, 275; rolling of, 337–339
Doughnuts, 295
Dressings, salad, 141–145
Drupes, 36–37, 382
Dry cure of meat, 204–205
Drying for food preservation, 571–573
Dunham, D. F., 238, 345, 347

Earthenware, 495–496
Eclairs, 304
Economic considerations in meal planning, 400–401. *See also* Cost of food
Edie, L. D., 423
Egg Products Inspection Act of 1970, 23, 175, 566
Egg whites: effect of overbeating on, 192; foams, 191–193; number per cup, 179; structure of, 170

Egg yolks: as emulsifying agent, 181; number per cup, 179

Eggplant: characteristics and cooking of, 125; selection of, 106

Eggs, 169–193: baked, 184; in cakes, 324; candling of, 175; classification by size, 179; coagulation function of, 180–181; composition of edible part, 171; cooked in the shell, 182; deviled, 182; drying of, 174; as emulsifying agent, 181; in flour mixtures, 283; freezing of, 173–174; fried, 183; functions in cookery, 180–181; grading of, 31–32, 175–179; as leavening agent, 181; number per cup, 179; nutritive value of, 170–171; poached, 183; preparation of, 181–193; preservation of, 171–174; price of, 180; scrambled, 185; selection of, 175–180; standards for, 31–32, 176–178; storage of, 172–173; structure of, 169–170; vitamin content of, 171; weight classes of, 179; in yeast breads, 312

Elastin, 203

Electronic cooking, 128, 227

Emulsifiers in shortening, 291

Emulsifying agents, 181, 579

Emulsions, 142

Endive, 133

Endosperm, 202, 257

Energy units, 3

English muffins, 317

English table service, 521

Enrichment of food, 7

Enzymes: amylolytic, 285; control in home preservation, 631; and food spoilage, 561–562; meat treated with, 228; in yeast, 285

Equipment for the kitchen, 445–471: arrangement of, 446–449; care of, 464–471; efficiency of, 459–461; selection of, 450–453; small, 453–459, 468–469; storage space for, 449

Escarole, 133

Espresso coffee, 91

Essential oils, 373

Ethyl alcohol, 371

Ethylene gas, 39

Etiquette, 504–518: arrival of guests, 509, 511; introductions, 506–507; invitations, 507–510; table manners, 511–517

Expenditures for food. See Cost of food

Explosion-puffing, 572

Extracts, 371

Facilities for meal preparation. See Equipment for the kitchen

Fair Packaging and Labeling Act of 1966, 27, 430

Family Food Plan, 18

Family style meal service, 520, 544–545

Farina, 72

Fats and oils, 288–295: caloric content, 5, 292; chemical formulas for, 288; clarification of, 294; composition of, 5; cookery functions, 292–295; foods high in, 5; function in diet, 5; keeping quality of, 292; nutritive value of, 13, 292; origin of, 5; processing of, 289–292; smoke point of, 294; sources of, 13; types of, 289, 291; in yeast breads, 312

Fatty acids, 5, 289

Federal agencies. See Agencies protecting food supply

Federal Wholesome Meat Act of 1967, 208

Fennel, 380

Fermentation: of breads, 313–314; in pickling, 630; of preserves, 622

Finfish, 245–249

Fish, 244–255: amount per serving, 250; buying guide for, 246–247; canned, 248–249; composition of, 240; convenience forms of, 249; cost per serving, 250; cured, 249; frozen, 249; home freezing of, 600; inspection and grading of, 33, 249–250; nutritive value of, 250–251; preparation of, 251–255; selection of, 245–250; sources of, 244–245; storage of, 250; varieties of, 245–249

Fish and Wildlife Service of USDI, 250

Flatware, 499–500

Flavonoids, 114, 115

Flavor potentiators, 375, 382

Flour, 257–263: air classification of, 258–260; all-purpose, 261, 279, 324; enrichment standards for, 263; grinding of, 258; hydration capacity of, 281; instant blending, 262; milling of, 258–261; mixtures, 274–297; nutrients in, 263; nutritive value of, 262–263; preparation of, 266–272; self-rising, 262; separation, 258–260; as a thickening agent, 264, 271; types of, 261–262; in yeast breads, 310–311

Flour mixtures, 274–297: ingredients of, 281–295; mixing methods, 280–281; proportions in, 274–275. See also Breads; Cakes; Pies

Fluorine, 7

Foam cakes, 322

Folic acid, 11

Fondant, 356–358

Fondues, 188

Food: additives, 575–579; adulteration, 26–27; Basic Four of, 15–19, 396–398; brands, 429–430; canning, 573–575, 581–594; combinations, 401–402; convenience, 425–427; costs, 409–411, 473–474; daily guide for, 396–398; expenditures, 419, 432–433; freezing, 569–571, 596–606; grading, 209–213, 426–429; groups, 15–19; guides, 15–19, 396–398; illness, 563–566; individual preferences in, 401; keeping quality of, 435–436; labels, 430–431; manager, 475–476; measuring, 275–280, 426; mixing, 280–281; non-perishable, 558; nutrients, 2–15; perishable, 558; pigments, 113–115; poisoning, 563–565; preparation, 472–491; preservation, 568–580; prices, 423–426; purchasing, 417–443; quality as price factor, 421–422; requirements, 409; seasonability, 41, 400–403; seasonings, 369–382; semi-perishable, 558; service, 519–555; spoilage, 558–567; 593–594; standards, 23, 28–29; staying quality of, 404–405; storage, 433–435, 568–569; supply for one week, 439–440; supply protection, 22–33

Food Additives Amendment of 1958, 26

Food and Drug Administration, 25–30, 263, 426

Food and Drug Officials of the U.S., Association of, 31

Food, Drug, and Cosmetic Act, 25, 26, 429–430

Food for Fitness—A Daily Food Guide, 15–19

Food and Nutrition Board of the National Academy of Sciences, 2

Foods: beverages, 82–99; candy, 354–361; cereals, 62–81; cheese, 154–162; eggs, 169–193; fish, 244–255; fruits, 35–61; meat, 195–230; milk and milk products, 147–167; poultry, 232–244; salads, 132–146; starches, 257–349; sugars, 350–367; vegetables, 100–131

Formal table service, 523–524, 550–555

Four basic food groups, 15–19, 396–398

Frankfurters, 217

Freeze drying, 573

Freezer, selection of, 452–453

Freezing, 569–571, 596–606: containers for, 598–599; dehydrofreezing, 571; for food preservation, 569–571; at home, 596–606; preparation of food for, 596–598; quick, 570; selection of food for, 596–598; of strawberries, 602–603; of vegetables, 597

French dressing, 141–143

Frosting, cake, 355–356

Frozen desserts, 361–368

Frozen foods: causes of inferior product, 605–606; preparation for serving, 601–605. *See also* Freezing

Fructose, 3, 352

Fruits, 35–61: availability of, 40–41; botanical classification of, 36–37; canned, 49–50; care of, 39; comparative costs of, 47–48; container sizes for, 51; cooked, 58–60; daily food guide for, 396; defects in, 40; defined, 35–36; dried, 50–52, 60; frozen, 50, 60, 231–232, 599–600; home freezing of, 599–600; inspection of, 32; in jelly making, 234–237; nutritive value of, 19, 52–55; as pie filling, 342; prepackaging of, 39; preparation of, 55–56; in preserves, 618–621; processed, 47–52; raw, 55–58; in religious literature, 35; ripening of, 38–40; selection of, 40–47; shipping of, 39; storage of, 38–40; vitamin retention by, 53–55

Frying, deep-fat, 293–295

Fudge, 359

Galactose, 3, 352

Gel, 266, 385

Gelatin, 384–388: convenience forms of, 388; factors affecting, 388; manufacture of, 384; nutritive value of, 384–385; preparation of, 385–387; uses of, 385

Gelatinization, 265, 266, 272

"Generally Recognized As Safe" list, 26, 577

Ginger, 377

Glassware: kitchen utensils, 457; for the table, 498–499

Globulin, 163

Glucose. *See* Dextrose

Glutamic acid, 115–116, 375

Gluten, 281, 282

Glycerin, 371

Glycerol, 5, 288

Glycogen, 4

Government agencies. *See* Agencies protecting food supply.

Grade A Pasteurized Milk Ordinance, 30–33, 148

Grading of food: of eggs, 31–32, 175–179; as purchasing aid, 426–429; of meat, 209–213. *See also* Protection of food supply

Grains. *See* Cereals

Grapefruit: cost of, 48; cutting of, 57; nutritive value of, 54; preparation of, 56–58; selection of, 44

Grapes: nutritive value of, 54; selection of, 44–45

GRAS ("Generally Recognized As Safe") list, 26, 577

Gravies, 270

Green beans: characteristics and cooking of, 124; nutritive value of, 118; selection of, 104; vitamin content of, 122

Greens: salad, 132–135; selection of, 106–107

Griddle cakes, 301–303, 309, 318

Grits, 69

Guests, arrival of, 509–511

Guides, food: Basic Four, 15–18, 396–398; Basic Seven, 18; daily, 396–398, 405; Family Food Plan, 18

Half-and-half, 153

Ham, curing of, 205

Hand washing of dishes, 467–468

Handbook of Food Preparation, 220

Harp, H. H., 238, 345, 347

Heart, 227, 229

Hearth breads, 310

Hemoglobin, 7

Herbs, 371–375: defined, 372–373; dried and fresh equivalents, 374; listed, 378–379; preservation of, 373; suggestions for use, 376–381

HEW (Department of Health, Education and Welfare), 29, 30

High-altitude: baking, 295; boiling, 129

High-temperature-short-time canning, 575

Holloware, 499–500

Home canning. *See* Canning at home

Home freezing, 596–606. *See also* Freezing

Homemaker as manager, 472–474

Hominy, 69

Homogenization, 149

Honey, 353–354

Host, duties of, 541–555

Hostess, duties of, 539–555

Hot dogs, 217

Hot-pack canning, 586

HTST (high-temperature-short-time) canning process, 575

Hydrogenated fats, 324

Hydrogenated shortening, 291

Hygienic practices in the kitchen, 464–465

Ice cream, 362–367: commercial, 362–363; home-made, 364–367; nutrients in, 165, 364; refrigerator made, 366–367; stirred, 364–366

Ice milk, 363–364

Icings for cake, 355–356

Identity, standards of, 28

Illnesses from food, 563–566: botulism, 565; infections, 566; perfringens, 565; poisoning, 563–565; staphylococcal, 563–565

Indian pudding, 272

Individual food preferences, 401

Informal table service: of breakfast, compromise style, 538–541; of dinner, compromise style, 545–548; of dinner, compromise style with waitress, 548–550; of dinner, family style, 544–545; rules for, 520–523, 527–528; of supper, buffet style, 541–544

Inositol, 11

Inspection of food: by Consumer and Marketing Service of USDA, 23; of eggs, 22, 31–32, 175–178; of fish, 29, 33, 249–250; by Food and Drug Administration, 25–30; of meat, 23–24, 208–209; of milk, 23–33; of poultry, 233; as a purchasing aid, 426–429. *See also* Protection of food supply
Instant blending flour, 262
Instantizing process, 572
Interstate commerce in food, regulation of, 22–25
Introductions, 506–507
Invert sugar, 352
Invitations, 507–510
Iodine: function of, 13; in sea food, 250; sources of, 7, 13; in thyroxin, 7
Iodized salt, 370
Iron: function of, 7, 13; sources of, 7, 13; in vegetables, 118

J (joule) unit, 3
Jams: defined, 618; making of, 621–622
Jelly, 608–615: causes of failure in making, 615; containers for, 615; effect of quantity on making, 610; extracting juice for, 610–611; ingredients in, 608–609; tests for, 614
Jelmeter, 612–613
Jerusalem artichokes, 124
Joule unit, 3

Kale, 118
Keeping quality of food, 435–436
Kernels of grain, 64
Ketchup, 625
Kidneys, 227–229
Kitchen, 446–449: arrangement of equipment in, 446–449; care of, 464–471; efficiency of equipment, 459–461; plans for, 446–449; sanitation in, 463–471; selection of equipment for, 450–453; storage space in, 449
Kneading of bread, 312–313
Kneading of flour mixes, 281
Kohlrabi, 125
Kumquats, 44

Labels: as consumer protection, 32; federal requirements for, 27; as a food purchasing aid, 430–431
Lactose, 3, 351
Lamb: cuts of, 202; grades of, 211–213; methods of cooking, 219. *See also* Meat
Lard, 289
Lasagna, 80
Lattice-top pie, 342
Leavening agents: eggs as, 181; in flour mixtures, 282–284; measuring of, 280; types of, 283–284; yeast as a, 284
Lecithin, 5
Legumes, 382
Lemon extract, 371
Lemon juice, 47
Lemon pie, 343
Lemons: nutritive value, 54; selection of, 44
Lettuce, 133–139: how to open iceberg, 137; nutritive value of, 118; varieties of, 133–135
Levulose, 352
Likes and dislikes, individual, 401
Lima beans: characteristics and cooking of, 124;

cost of, 120; nutritive value of, 118
Linens, table, 492–494, 538–555
Lipids, 5
Liquids: in flour mixtures, 282–283: in shortened cakes, 324; in yeast breads, 311
Liver: cooking of, 227, 229; nutritive value of, 216–217
Livestock products, consumption of, 233
Lobsters, 245–249
Luncheons: of differing food level costs, 413–414; meal patterns for, 407–408; menus for, 434–438

Macaroni products: cooking of, 79–80; described, 66; lasagna, 80; nutrients in, 72; varieties of, 67
Mace, 377
Maltose, 352
Management in meal preparation, 472–479: controlling food costs, 473–474; food manager's skills, 475–476; maturity of homemaker, 472; organization of work, 475; work plan for, 476–478
Manioc, 264
Manners, table, 511–517
Maple sugar, 353
Margarine, 291
Marinade, 141
Marjoram, 379
Market order organization, 487–488
Marmalade, 617, 621
Mayonnaise, 143–145
Meal evaluation, 479–480
Meal patterns, 405–408. *See also* Menus
Meal planning, 392–416: adequacy of foods, 392; availability of foods, 395–398; combination of foods, 401–402; daily food guide, 396–398, 405; ease of food preparation, 405; economic considerations, 400–401, 411–414; effect of seasons on, 402–403; guides for, 414; meal patterns, 405–408; and staying quality of foods, 404–405; tradition and customs in, 398–400. *See also* Menus
Meal preparation, 472–491: facilities for, 445–461; guides for class experiences in, 486–491; management in, 472–478; time required for, 481–482; work plan for, 482–485
Meal service, 519–555: breakfast, compromise style, 538–541; buffet, 523, 528–530, 541–544; compromise style, 522; English style, 521; examples of, 538–555; family style, 544–545; formal, 523–524; informal, 520–523; outdoors, 531; parties, 534–536; plate service, 523; Russian, 523–524; selecting the style of, 524–525
Measuring of foods, 275–280, 420
Meat, 195–231: aging of, 203–204; amount per serving, 213–215; buying guide for, 214; composition of, 217; cooking methods, 216–227; cost per serving, 213–215; curing of, 204–208; daily food guide for, 396; frozen, 229–230, 608; grading of, 209–213; home freezing of, 608; inspection of, 23–24, 208–209; muscle and connective tissue in, 202–203; nutritive value of, 19, 215–216; prepackaging of, 204; preparation of, 216–230; selection of, 208–215; servings per pound, 215; structure, 195–203; temperatures for cooking, 223; tenderizing methods, 228; treated with enzymes, 228; variety meats, 227–229; wholesale and retail cuts, 195–202

Meat Inspection Act of 1906, 23
Melamine, 497
Mellorine, 364
Melons, 45–46
Menus: breakfast, 407, 436–438, 538; buffet sup-
  per, 541; for different food cost levels, 413–414;
  dinner, 408, 436–38, 544, 545, 550; for a family
  of four, 436–438; forms of, 414–415; luncheon,
  408, 436–438; for parties, 535; and preparation
  time for meals, 481–484; for summer, 403; for a
  week of meals, 436–438; for winter, 403. *See also*
  Meal planning
Meringues, 192–193, 343
Metabolic rate, 7
Metzelthin, Pearl V., 398–399
Microorganisms, 559–562, 568
Microwave cooking, 227
Milk, 147–167: chocolate, 150; concentrated, 151–
  152; condensed, 151; cultured, 152–153; daily
  food guide for, 397; defined by ordinance, 148;
  disease organisms in, 148; dried, 151–152; evaporated, 151; fat content of, 163; filled, 150; fluid,
  148–151; fortified vitamin, 150; homogenized,
  149; lowfat, 150; mineral, 150; nonfat dry
  (NFDM), 66, 152, 166, 572; nutritive value of,
  19, 162–165; pasteurized, 148–149; preparation
  of, 164–166; processing of, 14, 147–160; protection of public supply of, 29–30, 32–33; protein in, 163; selection of, 160–161; skim, 150;
  storage of, 160–161; two per cent, 150; vitamin
  content of, 163; vitamin D, 150
Milk products, 153–160: cheese, 154–160; cream,
  153–154
Minerals, 6–7, 13
Mint, 379
Mints, 358
Misbranding of food, 27–28
Mixing methods, 280–281: creaming, 280; for flour
  mixtures, 280–281; folding, 281; kneading, 281;
  "one-bowl," 328
Moist-heat cookery, 255
Molasses, 351, 353
Molded dishes: desserts, 387–388; salads, 140–141
Molds: destruction of, 560; growth on preserves,
  622–623; use in curing cheese, 560
Monosaccharides, 3
Monosodium glutamate, 115–116, 375, 382
Monounsaturated fatty acids, 289
MSG, 115–116, 375, 382
Muffins, 298–301, 308, 318
Muscle and connective tissue, 202–203
Mushrooms, 107
Mustard, 376
Mustard greens, 125

National Research Council allowances, 2–3, 15
NFDM (nonfat dry milk), 66, 152, 166, 572
Niacin: functions of, 10, 14; sources of, 10, 14, 19;
  in vegetables, 118
Nonfat dry milk, 66, 152, 166, 572
NRC allowances, 2–3, 15
Nucleic acid, 382
Nucleotides, 382
Nut pies, 344
Nutmeg, 376

Nutrients, 2–15: carbohydrates, 3–4; as essential
  to life, 2; fats, 5; functions and sources of, 13–14;
  interrelationships of, 12; minerals, 6–7; possible
  imbalances of, 15; proteins, 5–6; vitamins, 7–11;
  water, 11
Nutrition, 2–20: defined, 2; food guides, 15–19;
  nutrients, 2–15
Nuts, 382–384

Oatmeal: nutrients in, 71–72; use, 71
Oats, 70–71
Oils. *See* Fats and oils
Okra: characteristics and cooking of, 125; nutritive
  value of, 118; selection of, 107
Oleo stock, 289
Oleomargarine, 291
Omelets, 185–187
Onions: green, 107; mature, 108; nutritive value of,
  118; varieties in family, 116
Orange juice: cost of, 47; nutritive value of, 54
Oranges: ascorbic acid in, 53; cutting of, 57; nutri-
  tive value of, 54; preparation of, 56–58; selection
  of, 44
Oregano, 379
Organization by homemaker, 475
Outdoor meals, 531

Pancakes, 301–303, 309, 318
Pans, selection of, 328
Pantothenic acid, 11
Papain, 228
Paprika, 376
Para-aminobenzoic acid, 11
Parsley, 135, 378
Parsnips: characteristics and cooking of, 125; selec-
  tion of, 107
Parties: menus for, 535; service at, 534–536
Pastas, 66–67. *See also* Macaroni products
Pasteurization: for food preservation, 573–574;
  methods of, 148–149
Pastry, 335–348: baking of, 339; causes for devia-
  tion in, 339–342; defined, 335; fat for, 335; in-
  gredients in, 335–337; mixing of, 337; plain,
  335–342; rolling of, 337–339; shells, freezing of,
  348. *See also* Pies
Pastry flour, 262
Patent flour, 261
Peaches: comparative costs of, 48; nutritive value
  of, 54; selection of, 46
Peanuts, 382
Pears: nutritive value of, 54; selection of, 46
Peas: characteristics and cooking of, 125; cost of,
  120; nutritive value of, 118; selection of, 107
Pectin: alcohol test for, 613; commercial, 611–612;
  gel formed by, 385; function in jelly, 608–609;
  fruits rich in, 609
Peg board for kitchen, 448
Pellagra, 10
Penuche, 359
Pepper, 377
Peppers, green: characteristics and cooking of, 125;
  selection of, 107–108
Peppers, red, 107–108
Per capita consumption of: crops, 101; fats and oils,
  289; livestock products, 233

Perfringens, 565

Pesticide residue in food, 27

Pesticides Chemical Act of 1954, 27

Phosphorus, 7

PHS (Public Health Service), 29–30; Grade A Pasteurized Milk Ordinance, 30, 32–33, 148$_n$

Piccalilli, 625

Pickles and pickling, 624–631: causes of difficulties, 630–631; choice of methods, 626–630; defined, 624; effect of ingredients in, 625–626; making cross-cut pickle slices, 628–629; types of, 624–625

Pies, 334–344: convenience forms of, 344–348; fillings for, 342–344; freezing of, 347; shell for, 338, 339; varieties of, 334

Pigments of foods, 113–115

Pineapples: cost of, 48; nutritive value of, 54; selection of, 46

Pizza, 317

Plan of work, 476–477, 482–485

Planning of meals. See Meal planning

Plastic, 459

Plate table service, 523

Plums, 46, 54

Poaching, 183

Poisoning, food, 563–565: botulism, 565, 593; defined, 563; perfringens, 565; staphylococcal, 563–565

Polysaccharides, 4

Polyunsaturated fatty acids, 289

Popovers, 304–305, 309

Poppy, 381

Porcelain enamelware, 456–457

Pork: cuts of, 202; grades of, 213, 216; methods of cooking, 219; and trichinosis, 206. See also Meat

Potassium iodide, 370

Potato chips, 118

Potato starch, 265

Potatoes: characteristics and cooking of, 125; grades of, 108; nutritive value of, 118; selection of, 108–109; vitamin content of, 122

Poultry, 232–244: amount per serving, 236–238; classes of, 234–236; color changes of, 244; composition of cooked, 240; cost per serving, 236–238; frozen, 244; grading of, 233–234; home freezing of, 600; inspection of, 233; as a meat substitute, 232; nutritive value of, 239; preparation of, 239–244; selection of, 233–239; storage of, 238–239; terms used to identify, 235

Poultry Products Inspection Act of 1957, 24–25

Powdered sugar, 351

Preparation of food. See Cooking; Meal preparation

Prepared foods, 425–426

Preservation of food, 568–580: by additives, 577–580; canning, 573–575, 581–594; by drying, 571–573; by freezing, 569–571; by radiation, 575–577; by storage and chilling, 568–569

Preservatives, chemical, 578

Preserves, 617–623: causes of difficulties in making, 622; defined, 617; making of, 620–622

Pressure cooking, 124–127

Prices of food: factors affecting, 423–427; trends in, 435. See also Cost of food

Protection of food supply, 22–34: by Department of Agriculture (USDA), 22–25; egg inspection,

31–32, 175–179; by federal agencies, 23–30; by Food and Drug Administration (FDA), 25–30; grading of food, 426–429; GRAS list, 26; interrelationship among agencies, 30; meat inspection, 23–24, 209–213; misbranding, 27–28; poultry inspection, 24–25; by Public Health Service (PHS), standards of identity, 28–29; by state and local agencies, 30–33

Proteins, 5–6: in cereals, 71–72; complete or adequate, 6; composition of, 5; cost of recommended dietary allowance for a day, 440; in flour, 281; foods high in, 5–6, 13; functions of, 13; incomplete and inadequate, 6; in meat, 215–217; in milk, 163, in poultry, 239, 240; sources of, 13

ProTen, 228

Prothrombin, 9

Protopectin, 609

Provitamins, 8

Public Health Service (PHS), 29–30, 32

Puddings, 270–272

Pumpkin pie, 344

Pumpkins, 125

Purchasing of food, 417–443: convenience foods as price factor, 425–426; determining factors in, 418–423; determining food to be purchased, 431–443; grades and brands as aids to, 426–431; guide for, 441–442; packaging as price factor, 422; quality as price factor, 421–422; source and season as price factor, 421; suggestions for, 441; supply and demand as price factor, 423–424; supply for a week, 439–440; weights and measures in, 419–420

Pyroceran, 457, 497

Quality of food: grading of, 210–212; as price factor, 421–422

Quick breads, 298–310: biscuits, 305–318; causes for deviations in making, 308–310; griddle cakes, 301–303; muffins, 298–301; popovers, 304–305; proportions in, 298; waffles, 303

Radiation, 575–577

Radishes, 109–110

Rancidity of fats, 292

Range: cleaning of, 469–470; electronic, 451–452; selection of, 450–452

Raw-pack canning, 585–586

Receptions, 531–534

Refrigerator selection, 452–453

Relish, 625

Rennin, 155

Reverse osmosis, 573

Rhubarb, 110

Riboflavin (Vitamin B$_2$): functions of, 10, 14; in milk, 163; sources of, 14, 18–19; in vegetables, 118

Rice: characteristics of, 67–68; nutrients in, 72; preparation of, 78–79; varieties of, 68

Rice starch, 264

Rigor mortis, effect on meat, 203

R.O. (reverse osmosis) process, 573

Roasting: of meat, 221–225; of poultry, 241–243

Roller milling, 258

Rolls, 316–317, 318

Rosemary, 378

Russian style table service, 523–524, 550–555
Rutabagas, 125
Rye, 71

Saccharin, 354, 579
Saffron, 377
Sage, 378
Salad dressings, 141–144
Salads, 132–146: defined, 132; frozen, 140–141; fruit, 139; greens for, 132–135; main-dish, 141; molded, 141; service of, 144–146; vegetable, 134
Salmonella, 173, 566
Salsify, 125
Salt, 369: iodized, 370; use in meat curing, 204–205; use in pickling, 625–626; in yeast breads, 312
Sanitation of kitchen, 463–471
Sauces, 266–272: dessert, 270–272; white, 267–270
Sausages, 206–208
Savory, 379
Savory jellies, 140
Scurvy, 7
Scutellum, 262
Seafood. *See* Fish
Sealing of home-canned foods, 587–589
Seasonal availability: of fresh fruit, 41; and planning of meals, 400–403; of vegetables, 103
Seasonings, 369–382: extracts, 371; flavor potentiators, 375, 382; herbs, 371–375, 378–379; seeds, 380–381; spices, 371–376
Seating plans, 541–543
Seeds, 380–381
Self-rising flour, 262
Sequestrants, 578–579
Service of meals. *See* Meal service
Sesame, 381
Setting, table. *See* Table Setting
Sheet iron, 458
Shellfish, 245–249: buying guide for, 247; cooking of, 255; standards for, 29–30. *See also* Fish
Sherbet, 363–364
Short cakes. *See* Cakes, shortened
Silver sulfide, 182
Silverware, 468, 499
Sink, selection of, 452
Small equipment, care of, 468–469
Smith, M. F., 102
Smoking of meat, 205
Snap beans: characteristics and cooking of, 124; nutritive value of, 118; selection of, 104, vitamin content of, 122
Sodium bicarbonate, 285–286
Sodium citrate, 388
Sodium chloride. *See* Salt
Soft-serve frozen desserts, 363
Sorghum syrup, 353
Soufflés, 187–188
Soups, cream, 267–270
Sour milk, 286
Special meals and parties, 531–537
Spices, 371–377: defined, 372–373; listed, 376–377; for pickling, 626; suggestions for use, 376–381
Spinach: characteristics and cooking of, 125; cost of, 120; nutritive value of, 118
Spoilage of food, 558–567: agents of, 559–563; by

bacteria, 559, 561–562; of canned foods, 593–594; by enzymes, 562–563; infections caused by, 566; by microorganisms, 559–562; poisoning from, 563–565
Sponge cakes, 333–334
Sponge method of bread making, 315
Squash: characteristics and cooking of, 125; nutritive value of, 118; selection of, 110
Stabilizers, 579
Stainless steel, 458, 499–500
Standards of fill, 28, 29
Standards of quality, 23, 28, 29. *See also* Protection of food supply
Staphylococcus, 563–565
Starch, 263–272: changes during cooking of, 265–266; elements of, 3; foods high in, 4; in plants, 4; preparation of, 266–272; as thickening agent, 270–271; types of, 264–265
Steaks, beef, 198–202
Steam as a leavening agent, 283
Steel, 458
Stir-frying, 127–128
Storage of food: "common storage," 568–569; by chilling, 568–569; of home-canned foods, 589–590; for preservation, 568–569; as purchasing factor, 433–435
Storage of kitchen equipment, 446–450
Stove: cleaning of, 469–470; electronic, 451–452; selection of a, 450–452
Strawberries: home freezing of, 602–603; nutritive value of, 54
Sublimation process, 573
Sucrose, 3, 371; in sugar, 350–352
Sugar, 350–354: beet, 351; brown, 351; in cakes, 324; cane, 351; chemical elements of, 3; comparative sweetness of various types, 352; confectioner's, 351; in cornstarch pudding, 271, 272; crystals, 357; in flour mixtures, 283; granulated, 351; invert, 352; in jelly, 612–614; maple, 353; powdered, 351; for preserves, 618, 620; produced by plant, 4; U.S. consumption of, 350; in yeast breads, 311–312
Sugar beets, 350, 351
Sugar cane, 350–351
Summer menus, 403
Supper, buffet service of, 541–544
Supply of food for a week, 439–440
Supply protection. *See* Protection of food supply
Sweet potatoes: characteristics and cooking of, 124; nutritive value of, 118; selection of, 109
Sweetbreads, 229
Sweeteners: nonnutritive, 579; synthetic, 354
Syneresis of jelly, 615
Synthesis of starch, 4
Synthetic sweeteners, 354
Syrups, 353–354

Table appointments, 495–502: decorations, 501–502; dinnerware, 495–498; examples of, 538–555; flatware, 499–501; glassware, 489–499; linens, 492–494; special care of, 468
Table decorations, 539–553
Table linens, 492–494; for various styles of meal service, 538–555

Table manners, 511–517: commonly accepted, 512–517; history of, 511–512

Table service. *See* Meal service

Table setting: for buffet supper, 542; for formal dinner, 551; for informal dinner, 546; rules for, 525–527

Tableware, 497–501: metal, 499–501; plastic, 497

Tangelos, 44

Tangerines: nutritive value of, 54; selection of, 44

Tannins: in cocoa, 97; in coffee, 87; in fruit, 38; in tea, 94

Tapioca: in pudding, 272; varieties of, 264

Tarragon, 379

Tartar, cream of, 332

Tea, 91–95: black, 92; caffeine content of, 86–87, 93; composition of, 93–94; green, 92; history of, 91; iced, 94; oolong, 92; "pekoe," 92; preparation of, 94–95; production of, 92–93; selection of, 92–93; tannin content of, 94; theobromine content of, 86–87

Teas, service of, 531–534

Teflon, 459

Testing of home-canned foods, 589–591

Theobromine, 86–87

Thermostabilization, 173

Thiamine: functions of, 9–10, 14; sources of, 10, 14; in vegetables, 118

Thyme, 379

Thyroxine, 7, 13

Tin, 458

Tomatoes: canning of, 588; characteristics and cooking of, 125; nutritive value of, 118

Tongue, 227, 229

"Trace elements," 6

Trenchers, 494–495

Trichinosis, 206

Triglycerides: composition of, 288; fats, 5

Tripe, 227, 229

Tumeric, 377

Turkey, 232, 236, 242–244. *See also* Poultry

Turnip greens: characteristics and cooking of, 125; nutritive value, 118; vitamin content of, 122

Turnips: characteristics and cooking of, 125; nutritive value, 118; selection of, 111

U.S. Department of Agriculture (USDA), 22–25: Beltsville turkeys, 232, 236; Consumer and Marketing Service (C & MS), 23–25, 233, 426, 428; Donated Foods Program, 174; egg regulation by, 31–32, 175; meat grading by, 209–213; poultry grading by, 233–234; protection of food supply, 23–25, 31–32

U.S. Department of Health, Education and Welfare, 29, 30

U.S. Department of the Interior: Bureau of Commercial Fisheries, 29, 250; Fish and Wildlife Service, 256

U.S. Food and Drug Administration (FDA), 25–30, 263, 426

U.S. Public Health Service (PHS), 29–30, 32

Utensils for the kitchen, 453–459

Vanilla, 371

Variety meats, 227–229

Veal: cooking methods, 219; cuts of, 202; grades of, 210, 211. *See also* Meat

Vegetable oil, 291

Vegetables, 100–131; canned, 128; classification of, 101; color of, 113–115; cooked amount obtained from standard containers, 113; cooking methods for, 123–129; daily, food guide for, 396; dried, 128; effects of cooking on, 120–122; effect of high altitudes on, 129; flavor of, 115–116; fresh, 101–111; fresh compared with processed, 111–112; frozen, 112, 128; grading of, 101–102; green, 113–114; history of, 100; home freezing of, 597; inspection of, 32; nutritive value of, 19, 116–119; part of plant to be eaten, 102; pickling of, 626–630; preparation of, 119–129; processed, 111–112; red, 115; scalding times for, 597; seasonal availability of, 103; selection of, 101–113; serving of, 129–130; storage of, 101–113; vitamin content of, 117, 122; white, 115; yellow, 114–115

Vinegar, 370–371; for pickling, 626

Vitamin A, 13, 117–118

Vitamin B_1, 9–10, 14, 118

Vitamin B_2. *See* Riboflavin

Vitamin B_6, 10

Vitamin B_{12}, 11

Vitamin C. *See* Ascorbic acid

Vitamin D, 8, 14

Vitamin E, 9, 14

Vitamin K, 9

Vitamins, 7–11: in diets of primitive peoples, 7; function of, 7–8, 13–14; listed, 7–11; sources of, 13–14; synthetic, 8; in vegetables, 118, 122

Vitelline membrane, 170

Volume equivalents, 276

Waffles, 303, 309, 318

Waitress' duties: compromise style, 548–550; Russian style, 553–555

Washing dishes, 465–468

Waste disposers, 452

Water in body, 11

Water ices, 363–364

Watercress, 135

Watermelon, 54

Waxy starch, 264–265

Week's food supply, 439–440

Week's menus, 436–438

Weights and measures, checking of, 420

Wheat, 65–67: bulgur, 66; flour, 257–263; hard, 257; kernels of, 64; macaroni products, 66–67; milling of, 258–261; nutrients in, 72; soft, 257; spring, 257; winter, 257

Wheat starch, 264

Whey, 159

Whips, 154

White of egg. *See* Egg whites

White flour, 261

White sauce, 266–270

Whole wheat flour, 261

Whole-grain cereals, 73

Wholesome Meat Act of 1967, 23, 24

Wholesome Poultry Products Act of 1968, 22, 23, 25, 31, 233

Winter menus, 403

Wood, use in kitchen, 458–459
Woodenware, care of, 459
Work plan for meal preparation, 482–485
Work simplification, 476–477

Yeast: in breads, 311; and food spoilage, 216; as a leavening agent, 284–285
Yeast breads, 310–317: baking of, 314–315; causes of deviations in, 315–316; hearth breads, 310; ingredients for, 310–312; kneading of, 312–313; mixing of, 312–313
Yeast products, 316
Yield from fresh food: of frozen product, 606; of home-canned product, 592
Yogurt, 153
Yolk of egg. *See* Egg yolks
Yorkshire pudding, 304